THE COMMUNAL EXPERIENCE

THE
COMMUNAL
EXPERIENCE

ANARCHIST AND MYSTICAL COMMUNITIES

IN TWENTIETH-CENTURY AMERICA

Laurence Veysey

THE UNIVERSITY OF CHICAGO PRESS

Chicago and London

FOR JOHN
as a help in deciding what role to follow

Published by arrangement with Harper & Row, Publishers, Inc.
Originally published as *The Communal Experience: Anarchist
and Mystical Counter-Cultures in America*

The University of Chicago Press, Chicago 60637
The University of Chicago Press, Ltd., London

84 83 82 81 80 79 78   54321

ISBN: 0-226-85458-2
LCN: 78-55045

Contents

PART II
COMMUNITIES OF DISCIPLINE

Preface to the Phoenix Edition

Small bands of people have often attempted to set themselves apart from the everyday society of their time and place, hoping to create more intense and closely knit communities. This impulse originally was religious, flowering, for example, in the German and English Reformations, where it produced Anabaptists, Mennonites, Diggers and Levellers. The religious side of this drive toward separation has remained strong, now frequently shifting away from Christianity to an embrace of Eastern traditions, as with Hare Krishna and the followers of the Reverend Sun Myung Moon. Meanwhile, during the last two centuries, secular communitarian experiments have appeared, representing analogous aspirations often tied to a socialist or anarchist philosophy. Groups of both sorts have flourished (relatively speaking) in the somewhat tolerant climate of the United States.

The brief but spectacular resurgence of alternative communities in this country from about 1967 to 1973 furnished a superb opportunity to study them at firsthand. This book offers the fruits of such direct investigation, set against accounts of strikingly similar undertakings which existed several decades earlier.

Most of the book consists of comprehensive studies of four little-known communities, two of them highly structured and religious in the Eastern vein, two of them inspired by anarchism (the belief that voluntary relationships should be substituted for all coercive institutions). Two of the groups were founded in the late 1960s and visited by the author in New Mexico during the summer of 1971. The others were founded early in this century, in one case quietly surviving today.

This format allows observation of continuities and changes in the style of such groups in America over the course of the twentieth century, as well as the exploration of such themes as the role of specific belief patterns, organizational structures, and charismatic leaders in sustaining communities of this kind. Comparative study of several groups thus has major advantages over the chronicling of one group in isolation.

The present book was written as the flurry of excitement over secessionist communities had already begun to slacken, allowing an assessment based on their perennial interest as a strikingly intense kind of social movement rather than on the more faddish concern over them that lasted only for a short time. On their religious side, such movements have continued to make headlines (for instance, regarding the Reverend Moon's following). But the persistently recurrent character of such communal undertakings gives them their claim to attention by serious students of society, especially those who possess a sensitive anthropological interest in the inner workings of the unusual.

Just as many groups had flourished long before the season of their wide publicity at the end of the 1960s, so a number go on operating even now, ignoring fashion. One such is the community in northern New Mexico described at great length in Chapter 5 of this book, where it is identified only as "the ranch." Founded in 1967, it very much remains in existence in 1978 (and continues to prefer anonymity).

On March 18, 1978, I returned to "the ranch" for two days so that I could see how it had evolved since my stay there in 1971 and my brief visit in 1972, recorded in that chapter. The impression I gained was, above all, one of steadfast continuity in style of operation, though within this frame there were suggestions of some highly interesting changes. I had predicted that this was a rugged group, probably destined for long survival, but I was nonetheless surprised to find how many oldtime members remained attached in 1978. Of those described (pseudonymously) as individuals in the text, Ezra, Eva, Al, Clovis, Herb, Jacob, Gene, Champ, Stan, Isaac Hull, Malcolm, John, David, and Lennie are still in the group, or fourteen out of thirty-two people, and three others remain who were also there in 1971 but whom I did not describe because they were away or mere children. Almost no desertions occurred after my visit in 1972, except that Jackeen left early in 1978, and two returned who had been gone. The new members, who push the total to something like twenty-five, appear for the most part to have joined in the last two years and include several non-Americans, gained through the group's activities overseas.

Externally, the group has undertaken larger ventures. In 1974 some members built a boat of ferrous concrete and began sailing over the world's oceans on a continuous basis, bringing back such items as rugs from Nepal for resale in New Mexico and fulfilling the theme of "planetary" adventure which had been so strong in the group's consciousness. The boat continues as a separate operation, and in addition, some members spend most of their time touring the United States and Europe as an acting company, while a "home guard" remains on the ranch. The home group recently launched a project of building thirty adobe condominiums on prime land it had purchased in the nearby town, hiring much outside labor. This well-executed activity brought needed financial returns, though the style of living on the ranch remains conspicuously Spartan. Further additions have been made to the ranch buildings (the dining area is much more spacious and attractive). The property, however, still seems mostly run-down. Ecologically, it is much closer to self-sufficiency. The gardens have flourished; home-grown pigs and chickens furnish much of their meat. Wind-generation provides a share of their electricity.

In part the group slips more into being a diverse business venture. The personalities of several old-time members have become noticeably mellower, more relaxed. Alcohol is served at "feasts" in quantities unknown in 1971. New members are now free to ignore the philosophic texts of J. G. Bennett and Gurdjieff. But it would be wrong to conclude from these signs that the group has simply moved closer to the mainstream. Its adherence to its own rituals and code-formulas for living remains extremely strong (still hampering, for instance, the adequate projection of character in the theater production I saw). The group retains a proud sense of its separation from the ordinary life of the surrounding world, and the town still regards its ways of doing business as strange. The energies and loyalties of its hard-core members go on feeding exclusively into the group.

Ezra and Eva now live on the ranch less than half the time. They were not there when I returned. From intimations, I gather that Ezra's personality has not basically changed; there are still "confrontations" (see p. 293), though less often now. But Ezra is less of a constant or ultimate leader, more to one side of the group's activities. I think, after talking openly with several newer members, that this is genuinely true and not a "front." It leaves me wondering why he is content to stay there in a reduced role. Only another long visit would permit me to reach firmer conclusions, but my distinct impression is that group rituals and loyalties maintain themselves on a warmer collective basis nowadays, seemingly at considerable expense to Ezra's charisma and to the harsher thrust of Gurdjieff's philosophy, although people on the ranch still do work extremely hard.

The contrasting anarchistic community in New Mexico, the subject of

Chapter 3, disintegrated within a year after my 1971 visit. Its real name was Stone Mountain, and it was located at Lindrith, about fifty miles due north of Cuba, New Mexico, in the far northwest part of the state. Where and how its members now live, I do not know.

A correction: Elizabeth Paw Tun (pp. 254, 256) was an American woman who later married an Asian.

As this new edition appears, I would like to add my very deep thanks to David Riesman and to Robert Wiebe, as well as to the Research Committee of the Academic Senate, University of California, Santa Cruz, for enabling me to revisit New Mexico in 1978, and to the University of Chicago Press for generous favors.

LAURENCE VEYSEY

Acknowledgments

Personal contacts, even more than archives, made this book possible. I am deeply in debt to a large number of people who freely gave me information, candid interpretation, and encouragement. Located in many parts of the United States, ranging in age from centenarians to college dropouts, they willingly shared their lives with me, often far beyond the limits of mere courtesy. I very much regret that promises of anonymity prevent me from acknowledging by name most of those associated with the two present-day communities in New Mexico.

It sobers me to realize that some people who have helped me greatly with various parts of the book will energetically disagree with certain of the things I have written. There can often be a frustrating barrier between inside and outside points of view; what pleased me was to discover the gulf beginning to disappear on a number of occasions. To those who, from within, are unhappy with my portrayal of what they intimately know, I can only plead that I had to stay faithful to my own sense of history. But for this reason it is especially important to absolve each of my informants from the final result. Full responsibility for the account rests with me alone.

My heaviest debt is to several persons who, at the early stages of research, gave me entry into the particular environments I decided to explore. Richard Drinnon, Paul Avrich, Hugh Van Dusen, Eugene Exman, Minor Van Arsdale, Richard Rubenstein, and Dilip Basu often had no direct connection with the movements I was studying, but if they had not actively helped me to establish crucial contacts, this book could never have been written.

For granting interviews with me about Stelton, I must thank Nathan Marer, Sally Axelrod, James Dick, Jr., Nellie Dick, Rina Garst, Carl Zigrosser, William Morris Abbott, Max and Grace Granich, Donald Sinclair, and a number of Modern School graduates who gathered one evening at Paul Avrich's apartment in New York. In addition, Alexis C. Ferm, Clarence C. Abbott, Mrs. Joseph Ishill, Marion Booth Trask, Roger Baldwin, and Harry M. Laidler corresponded with me. For reviewing an earlier draft of the Stelton chapter, often with important criticisms, I am grateful to Terry Perlin, Stan Liptzin, Arthur Mark, the late Alexis Ferm, Carl Zigrosser, and Jo Ann Burbank.

For consenting to interviews with me about Vedanta, I thank Kali Le Page, B. K. Bagchi, Christopher Isherwood, Swami Prabhavananda, Srimata Gayatri Devi, and a number of residents of the Ananda Ashrama, La Crescenta, California, and Cohasset, Massachusetts, and at the Trabuco Canyon monastery in California. John Farquhar, Sister Daya's nephew, spoke with me about her and the Jones family several times on the telephone. But especially in regard to these informants, it should be emphatically understood that their names are to be in no way linked with my own interpretations of the movement and of some individuals within it. Dilip Basu read this chapter in draft. As an academic historian who is a Bengali and whose mother is a devotee of Ramakrishna, he was able to give me many valuable insights.

My brief account of Gerald Heard and Trabuco College depends very heavily upon interviews with Mrs. F. Douglas Grundy (Ena Curry), Margaret M. Gage, William Forthman, Michael Barrie, Allan A. Hunter, Eugene Exman, Ray Magee, Emilia Rathbun, Francis Hall, and Christopher Isherwood. To these people I apologize for the way in which I reluctantly condensed the account to a small fraction of its originally intended scope.

The opening chapter greatly benefited from the sharp criticisms of a group of Santa Cruz colleagues, organized by Carolyn Elliott, who regularly gather to discuss faculty work in progress in the social sciences in a frank and open spirit. In particular, I thank Jonathan Beecher. Barry McLaughlin offered many helpful suggestions from his wide knowledge of social psychology.

Students in my undergraduate seminars at the University of California, Santa Cruz, on the search for a new life style have helped me by sharing freely a broad range of interests, attitudes, and personal experiences connected with the recent movement toward "liberation." The same may be said for many of our friends and neighbors when we lived in Boston and New Mexico.

Libraries and archives were nonetheless important sources for all but the contemporary movements. Edward Weber, curator of the Labadie Collection at the University of Michigan, helped greatly on two occasions in making its resources available to me; it was there that I first learned of the existence of Stelton and the Modern School. For long periods I worked in the Harvard College Library, both on Stelton and Vedanta, and in the library of the University of California, Santa Cruz, where special thanks must go to Joan Hodgson. Donald Sinclair, head of Special Collections at the Rutgers University Library, gave me indispensable assistance with the extensive papers of the Modern School Association of North America. Other libraries which yielded important materials included those at the University of Pennsylvania, the University of California at Los Angeles (Department of Special Collections), the University of Iowa (Social Documents Collection), the University of California at Berkeley, the University of Chicago, and the University of Florida; also the Huntington Library; the Bund Archive, New York; the Harvard University Archive; the Houghton Library at Harvard; the Radcliffe College Archive; the Tamiment Society Library, New York; the library of the Vedanta Society of Northern California, San Francisco; and the library of the Philosophical Research Society, Los Angeles.

Some years ago Jane Levington Comfort lent me certain of her father's rarer publications. More than that, she and her husband, Paul Annixter, gave me the sustained awareness of the mystical state of mind which, along with my father's journals of the 1930's, made the book in its present form conceivable.

A fellowship grant from the American Council of Learned Societies in 1969–1970 enabled me to get my first major start on this book. Grants from the Research Committee of the Academic Senate, University of California, Santa Cruz, permitted me to travel to the Labadie Collection in Michigan and to do research in Southern California. The final text was measurably improved by Margaret Cheney's copy-editing.

My wife, Sheila, has been a truly indispensable help, not least through the variety of her responses to all the experiences we went through together.

L.V.

THE COMMUNAL EXPERIENCE

But then how does anybody form a decision to be against and persist against? When does he choose and when is he chosen instead? This one hears voices; that one is a saint, a chieftain, an orator, a Horatius, a Kamikaze; one says *Ich kann nicht anders— so help me God!* And why is it *I* who cannot do otherwise? Is there a secret assignment from mankind to some unfortunate person who can't refuse? As if the great majority turned away from a thing it couldn't permanently forsake and so named some one person to remain faithful to it?

—SAUL BELLOW, *The Adventures of Augie March*

Introduction

Intentional communities have long fascinated me, but I wrote this book primarily to explore three broader questions: how much and in what ways is America really changing, how great is the distance between the familiar and the "far-out" in our society, and how closely do the secular and religious forms of cultural radicalism resemble each other? Perhaps these three questions boil down to one: has there been a distinctive tradition of cultural radicalism in America, sustaining itself over time?

When the counter-culture began to astonish us in the 1960's, two sharply contrasting ways of making sense of it entered our minds. The first emphasized its apparent novelty. Here was a challenge to accepted institutions and thought processes which seemed to be without parallel in the American past. Not only the ingrained patterns of adult living but fundamental standards of reason were seen as newly threatened. Moderates and conservatives talked somberly of a new race of barbarians, and when they reached for historical precedents, their minds fastened not upon the native or home-grown but upon the frighteningly alien eruption of Nazi youth. For their part, those within the counter-culture often liked to stress the novelty of their vision. What they were saying and doing seemed all the bolder if it announced the arrival of an entirely new form of consciousness, sometimes heralded as the Age of Aquarius.

But these images did not go unchallenged. Many who viewed the scene, especially if they had an acquaintance with American history, began to note a number of interesting parallels between the current youth revolt and such hallowed episodes as the transcendentalism and abolitionism of pre–

Civil War decades. Or their thoughts turned to the broader history of bohemian movements in the past century and a half, to the founding of utopian communities and to the appeal of Asian mysticism among certain Americans over an equally long span of time.[1] Thus a second, quite different way of looking at the recent youth culture began to take shape. It was tempting to define the entire phenomenon (aside only from drugs) as little more than a cyclical recurrence of aims, attitudes, and life styles which first blossomed in the generation of Thoreau and Walt Whitman. The deeply romantic quality of much of the new culture was often remarked, and romanticism after all had been a very specific transplant from early nineteenth-century Europe. The dream of small-scale communities to replace existing governments had first emerged in those years. When it was discovered, in the pages of Louisa May Alcott's description of Fruitlands, that a garment called the poncho had actually been worn by colonists in that Massachusetts utopia of 1844, the case for continuity seemed to be symbolically sealed. Moreover, the recent celebrators of a "new" way of life likewise glanced backward, not only at Thoreau and the whole memory of pre-industrial America, but at Emma Goldman and the I.W.W., and in another direction at such earlier religious prophets as Sri Ramakrishna, a saintly figure of nineteenth-century India.

Comparisons over time can help pinpoint continuities and changes within American cultural radicalism. In themselves, they do not answer another equally central question about the nature of these recent happenings. How successfully have the rebels achieved an identity which distinguishes them from the larger society against which they are revolting? To what extent, and in what ways, has the counter-culture offered something more than a prismatic distortion of widely accepted values? It is a question which may be asked with equal relevance of the rebels of 1840, 1915, and today.

Much in my own past had made me assume the existence of a profound division between an American mainstream and an intellectual underground. My father and mother were both intensely committed to mystical and occult ideas, pursued not with the aim of achieving success in this world, but in the opposite sense of a consuming inward quest. Trying to become a writer and poet, my father increasingly spent his time in spiritual contemplation, recording his dreams, visions, and ordeals in twenty-seven volumes of journal notebooks before his premature death in 1937. For several years

1. In this vein see M. Peckham, "On Romanticism," *Studies in Romanticism*, IX (1970), 217–24; Bennett Berger, "Hippie Morality—More Old Than New," *Trans-Action*, V (1967), 19–20.

of my childhood, we lived in virtual retreat in the Ojai Valley, near Los Angeles, holding ourselves apart even from the Theosophists and followers of Krishnamurti who gave the entire community there a set-apart flavor. The separation between us and the outside world was simply an inbuilt fact of life.

In graduate school in the 1950's I learned that the consensus theory of American history, as powerfully presented by Daniel J. Boorstin, was tacitly based upon a similarly sharp distinction between radicals and other Americans. Communists, anarchists, and others who stood outside the dominant drift were dismissed as a numerically unimportant fringe, though paradoxically such "extremists" were also to be feared as a dangerous influence. (It is true that it takes only one man to steal state secrets.) Behind the manifest injunction to ignore such people in viewing the national past, I sensed an awareness that they were indeed very real but that a barrier was being erected to prevent an open discussion of their role. Unknowingly, I had stumbled into a battle then raging within the historical profession for ethnic acceptance and justice, in which every argument for the pervasive assimilation of minorities by the pragmatic mainstream was a highly charged counter in an emotional game. Later, I came to see the many difficulties in an unmodified consensus view. But it still impressed me that the sense of a firm division between radicals and other Americans was just as deeply implanted in Arthur Schlesinger, Jr.'s, mind as in Boorstin's. The social science of Edward Shils and Seymour Martin Lipset, indeed of nearly the entire sociology profession until the mid-1960's, further reinforced the assumption which, in a different way, I had inherited from childhood.

And yet there were others, particularly in the field of American studies, who liked to argue, with a certain degree of smugness, that no man can truly escape his culture, as if meaningful rebellion were simply impossible. "The Americanness," not only of Whitman and Thoreau, but of all nativeborn socialists and anarchists, was labored in a score of works by literary critics and cultural historians. Kenneth Lynn showed how maverick novelists, like it or not, had been caught up in success worship. Conservative admirers of Burke pictured all of early nineteenth-century America as anarchic, and Thoreau as the most representative man of his age. In essence, of course, this kind of argument became the most extreme version of the consensus viewpoint, since it lent further fuel to the effort to downplay the reality and vigor of any American radical tradition. Meanwhile, radicals themselves were torn on the question of their "Americanness." If they were believers in world revolution, they nonetheless liked to insist that they were patriotic in the mold of Tom Paine. Or, if their radicalism was of an inward, other-worldly kind (which often produced a bent toward pacifism in the political sphere), they measured American materialism against the "eternal" standard of India, China, or Judea, while at the same time invoking the largely home-grown tradition of free thought and tolerance for individual dissent.

So there are few firm guideposts in the search for boundaries between American radicalism and the larger culture. Like the question of the novelty of radical ideas, this one is answered in a clear-cut way neither by academic scholars nor by the men and women who have lived this kind of life. When the counter-culture mushroomed in 1967, I was as well equipped to understand it by my unusual childhood memories as by the rather self-contradicting shelf of books I had acquired since.

The present study probes these questions of novelty, distinctiveness, and internal cohesion within certain phases of what we call "radicalism." It is necessary, first of all, to show the extent to which there has actually been a tradition, or a series of parallel traditions, of cultural radicalism in the United States over the past century. This is the concern of the opening chapter. During the course of this argument, I found it helpful to construct a definition of American cultural radicalism so that concrete movements and tendencies might be measured against it. But the definition should be regarded as less important than the more general effort to establish historical points of reference.

In the final chapter I have again moved broadly into various phases of cultural radicalism in order to compare past with present. But in this book I have not tried to deal with the entire scope of radical activity in the United States. First of all, I have bypassed some of the most familiar left-wing and right-wing organizations in favor of groups geared to the discovery and practice of a new way of living. And, even within the "cultural" realm, I have chosen to place the weight upon several intensive case histories, which seem more revealing than an amorphous survey.

As an avenue into the subject, the study of intentional communities immediately suggests itself. Community founding has had a long tradition in America, as well as a conspicuous revival in recent years. Thus it seems ideally accessible as a topic for comparisons between the radicalism of different generations. Beyond this, communitarian movements have an in-built definiteness of form. The step of creating an intentional community brings forth an immediate commitment to geographical and psychic separation from the larger society. It implies an effort to construct an alternative social order from the ground up. Every aspect of life and thought tends to become self-consciously re-examined in such a venture. Community building is no less than an act of internal secession. All forms of this act take on a peculiar interest in a society which has so often captured the loyalties of its members merely by offering them a vision of individual economic reward.

For such a gain in clarity of sample there is indeed a price. The history of intentional communities in America is deeply intertwined with the history of rural nostalgia, a theme which comprises a much broader undercurrent in our culture. Both in the period around 1915 and in the 1960's, as we shall see, many urban radicals accused their brethren who were fleeing to the countryside of abandoning their commitment to the cause of revolutionary change. It is undoubtedly somewhat less militant to grow crops and raise children (however collectively) in remote corners of Vermont or New Mexico than it is to seek a martyr's death on the streets of Chicago.

Yet, for this very reason, intentional communities retain a further advantage for serious study. Located away from the stimuli of political battle, and forced to cope with all the everyday tasks of sustaining human existence, their members are confronted by some of the severest temptations from the larger culture. These reflect themselves in decisions to desert or to disband once the crowd is no longer watching. More than this, the entire tone of ongoing community life is at stake every moment of the day. A steady diet of beans and goat's milk can produce a powerful urge to sneak in a can or two of Coca-Cola. Sexual jealousies induced by deliberate experiment can bring about hasty retreats into monogamy. In communities the test of fidelity to an aim of genuine separation from the mainstream is peculiarly severe. Every victory, however temporary, takes on great meaning, for these are efforts at cultural birth.

Highly politicized radicalism deserves its own historical treatment, but I believe that more interesting questions are raised by attempts to carry into practice unusual beliefs, attitudes, and styles of living. The effort to live communally engages all levels of the personality, and not just during moments of extraordinary confrontation.

I have narrowed the scope of the central portion of this book still further, to concentrate upon a few communities in twentieth-century America which have been influenced by either of two highly specific philosophies —anarchism or religious mysticism. In so doing, I have acted on the belief that careful comparison lies close to the heart of historical explanation. But what does precision in comparison mean? I was not persuaded that a quantitative approach would yield as much reward as the close study of a handful of environments, both past and present. Accounts of "utopian" communities which are mere catalogs unfortunately abound. So do isolated narratives in the innocent vein of local history. I wanted to avoid these twin pitfalls, much as I did in my earlier book about universities. More than this, I have a strong sympathy for the traditional historian's (and anthropologist's) conviction that getting to know a few social settings as intimately as possible—to be sure, always with larger questions in mind—is the necessary prelude to generalization.

The time period has been limited to the twentieth century, and this decision also calls for comment. Another book, which would compare recent communities with some of the famous early-nineteenth-century utopias, could easily be written. But, if one starts with the question of the novelty of the counter-culture in the 1960's, then the most relevant comparison is with the immediate past rather than with the events of a more remote time. By placing communities which flourished only a few decades ago against those of the present, the issue of a sudden cultural break is posed in a much sharper form. The parents of the 1960's radicals might well have lived at Stelton (though none except Joan Baez's mother seem to have done so); the parents of the highly disciplined youth on the New Mexico desert in 1971 might well have been in Vedanta or at Gerald Heard's Trabuco. In a single generation, has the meaning of what it is to be "far out" in American society basically altered?

It would be less than candid not to admit that I have another motive for presenting accounts of these twentieth-century communal groups at such length. It is one of the historian's oldest, most natural desires to make his audience aware of some intrinsically fascinating, but previously unknown, things that have happened. The terrain of Brook Farm, Oneida, and the Shakers is relatively familiar. By contrast, none of the groups, movements, or personalities in this volume has been treated before (at any length, in print) by historians or sociologists.[2] To a very large extent, American his-

2. I soon learned that the Stelton anarchist colony had also just been discovered by at least two other scholars, Terry Perlin and Stan Liptzin, who are writing about it in the contexts of the transition of European anarchist thought to America and of American educational progressivism, respectively. See Terry Perlin, "Anarchism in New Jersey: The Ferrer Colony at Stelton," *New Jersey History*, LXXXIX (1971), 133–48. Henry F. May, *The End of American Innocence* (New York: Knopf, 1959), p. 307, contains a paragraph on the Ferrer Center. A voluminous and often very helpful Ph.D. dissertation on the history of the Vedanta movement in America was completed in 1964 at UCLA by Carl Thomas Jackson. A modestly descriptive account of Vedanta appeared in Hal Bridges, *American Mysticism: From William James to Zen* (New York: Harper & Row, 1970). J. P. Rao Rayapati, *Early American Interest in Vedanta* (New York: Asia Publishing House, 1972), appeared too late to be

torians have tended repeatedly to go over familiar ground, sticking to the best-known streams of tradition even within radicalism. Not until the sudden jolt of the counter-culture did we begin to wonder very much, for example, whether such philosophies as anarchism and Eastern mysticism had earlier antecedents in American culture. A few years ago, a stimulating book by Christopher Lasch, called *The New Radicalism in America* (*1889– 1963*), made its appearance. Yet the figures whose minds Lasch explored were often liberals, not radicals. We knew most of their names already and were glad to learn more about them. Similarly, Kenneth Keniston wrote about activist liberals in his important study entitled *Young Radicals*.

Many of the real radicals in twentieth-century America have remained unknown, even by those who followed in their footsteps several decades later, much less by a broader public. The stories of people like J. William Lloyd, Leonard Abbott, Harry Kelly, Elizabeth and Alexis Ferm, Sister Daya, Sister Shivani, Gerald Heard, and the still less well-known leaders of present-day movements, all deserve attention, if only because they are representative of whatever genuine counter-cultural tradition may be said to have existed in America in the last three-quarters of a century. Only when biographies of more people of this kind, and accounts of the movements they were active in, become familiar to us, can we begin to assess the impact of radicalism on the American mind.

Anarchism and mysticism seem to have been the two most striking intellectual tendencies in the counter-culture of the 1960's. To explore their past roots, in the context of communitarian living, is to grapple with the problem of cultural novelty at its very center.[3]

Anarchism comprises a distinct intellectual tradition, often traced to the writings of the Englishman William Godwin.[4] In the early nineteenth century its ideas sprang up independently both in Europe and America. Its most famous advocates were the Frenchman Pierre-Joseph Proudhon and the Westernized Russians Michael Bakunin and Peter Kropotkin.[5] Mean-

consulted. By far the best comparison between the classic nineteenth-century communities and those of today is made by Rosabeth Moss Kanter, *Commitment and Community* (Cambridge, Massachusetts: Harvard University Press, 1972).

3. By 1970 another major ideological strand had appeared in the counter-culture, the resurgence of Christian Fundamentalism. I avoided this, just as I avoided the militant urban socialists, in the belief that the most interesting case for elements of cultural novelty and distinctiveness lay elsewhere.

4. William Godwin, *An Enquiry Concerning Political Justice and Its Influence on General Virtue and Happiness* (London: G. G. J. and J. Robinson, 1793). Anarchistic ideas have, however, been found even in the ancient world. See Kingsley Widmer, *The Literary Rebel* (Carbondale, Illinois: Southern Illinois University Press, 1965); George Woodcock, *Anarchism* (Cleveland: Meridian Books, 1962), pp. 37–59.

5. Woodcock, *ibid.*, provides the best history of the entire movement to 1939.

while, the minds of such New Englanders as Josiah Warren were moving in much the same direction. At three intentional communities, named Equity, Utopia, and Modern Times (all founded by Warren between 1834 and 1850), anarchist ideas were first put into practice in the United States.[6] The flow of German and Russian immigrants, many of them Jewish, suddenly Europeanized the flavor of the American anarchist movement after 1880, giving it more of a social revolutionary orientation. Nerving themselves, Emma Goldman, Alexander Berkman, and others sought for a while to practice the "terror of the deed," the assassination of political and industrial leaders. However, during the twentieth century, American anarchists generally moved in a pacifist direction, so that communitarian experiments again could seem appropriate. The movement, however, was decimated by the Russian Revolution of 1917, which persuaded many immigrant radicals to support the needs of the new socialist society overseas. Not until the 1940's, in the context of pacifism, did anarchism more than barely cling to life. Then, briefly in Dwight Macdonald and more sustainedly in Paul Goodman, it acquired eloquent new spokesmen. In this period it sometimes collaborated with promoters of economic decentralism, whose ideas had led to the forming of several intentional communities. Handfuls of pacifists, anarchists, and believers in going "back to the land" again held precariously to existence until they were suddenly overwhelmed by a new generation of youth saying many of the same things in the mid-1960's.

The essence of the anarchist creed is opposition to all forms of coercive authority, especially that of the state. Holding to an extreme form of Enlightenment optimism about human nature, anarchists claim that once these external bonds are broken true fellow feeling will be released, and the voluntary commitments which spring into existence will permit a society to flourish in which there is nothing but genuine human relationship. Anarchists have long disagreed about the economic form of the new society.

Leonard I. Krimerman and Lewis Perry, eds., *Patterns of Anarchy* (Garden City, New York: Anchor Books, 1966), offers a diverse selection of first-hand anarchist writings.

6. Warren's anarchism developed as a direct response to the experience of living in Robert Owen's community at New Harmony, Indiana, in 1825. The Equity community in Ohio soon failed as a result of malaria, but Utopia (in Ohio) and Modern Times (on Long Island) both lasted effectively for about two decades. By far the best book on the early phase of the anarchist movement in America is James J. Martin, *Men Against the State: The Expositors of Individualist Anarchism in America, 1827–1908* (De Kalb, Illinois: Adrian Allen Associates, 1953), which contains histories of these communities. See also Richmond Laurin Hawkins, *Positivism in the United States (1853–1861)* (Cambridge, Massachusetts: Harvard University Press, 1938), pp. 110–24.

"Individualist" anarchists, often native-born Americans, would retain private property and emphasize absolute freedom of self-expression in all areas of life. Communal anarchists, who have dominated the movement in the twentieth century, look forward to the spread of voluntary, small-scale, self-sufficient communes, trading with their neighbors for the few necessities which cannot be internally produced. American anarchists agree in demanding total racial and sexual equality; on these subjects their writings of nearly a hundred years ago still seem contemporary in their ring. In contrast to the Puritanism of many socialists, anarchists urge expression of all deeply felt human desires, confident that only good can ultimately result. "I am in favor of absolute freedom," declared an extreme anarchist named J. L. Jones in 1900. "I am in favor of free love and free lust, free land and free whisky and free everything else."[7]

Religious mysticism, of course, has a much longer history than anarchism. It too is often a collective endeavor, as in medieval monasteries and their less formal equivalents in ancient India. However, its spokesmen have always insisted that community is only a secondary goal in comparison with individual realization of the Divine. The mystic is distinguishable from religious believers of other persuasions (including orthodox Christians) by his insistence that the ideal life does not consist in mere obedience to God, as if man were an eternally separated creature, but in a process of self-development which leads to actual union with the Infinite. Mystics tend strongly toward pantheism; the Divine is already present in each human being and needs only to be progressively awakened. Put another way, the duality between God and the world is located entirely within the mind; there the struggle for realization is to be played out, rather than in battles with heathen or in efforts to abide by the edicts of "heaven-sent" scriptures or ecclesiastics.[8]

In the United States, mysticism was present in the thinking of a few exceptional Puritans, such as Jonathan Edwards, and more notably among Quakers, although the concept of the "inner light" did not appear in its full dimension until the beginning of the nineteenth century. The leading transcendentalists of New England, especially Thoreau, were greatly affected by the fresh arrival of mystical literature from India.[9] In the late

7. *Discontent* (Home, Washington), May 9, 1900, p. 1; July 4, 1900, p. 3.

8. The best anthology of worldwide writings in this tradition is Aldous Huxley, ed., *The Perennial Philosophy* (New York: Harper & Brothers, 1944). Also very helpful is Swami Prabhavananda, *The Spiritual Heritage of India* (Garden City, New York: Doubleday, 1963). Bridges, *op. cit.*, is the only scholarly attempt at a history of the movement in twentieth-century America.

9. See Arthur Christy, *The Orient in American Transcendentalism: A Study of Emerson, Thoreau, and Alcott* (New York: Columbia University Press, 1932).

nineteenth century several major religious movements, distinctly un-Christian from an orthodox point of view, sprang up in America, vaguely or specifically influenced by these ideas. Among them were Christian Science, New Thought, Theosophy, and Vedanta. The latter two produced a series of semi-intentional communities (Krotona, first in Hollywood, later at Ojai; Point Loma, near San Diego; and several Vedanta ashrams).

Intellectually, the movement became clouded by the issue of the occult. Occultism, as distinct from mysticism, is the pursuit of contact, not directly with the Divine, but with intermediary beings, alleged to have been "sent" to mankind as teachers and spiritual guides (avatars, or world saviors; on a lesser plane, Mahatmas or members of the Great White Brotherhood, whom Theosophists believe reside in the Himalayas). Indian thought had always been partially submerged in this realm, and in America also the tendency was to lose sight of God realization as a personal goal in a welter of gossip over psychic phenomena—travel outside one's own body, revelations about previous incarnations, messages from the dead, private lines of communication to the spiritually great, and, eventually in the 1950's, similar encounters with intelligent beings on flying saucers.[10] Vedantists, unlike Theosophists, made a bold effort to counter this trend.

The placing of American anarchists and religious mystics side by side establishes a broad comparison of the outward- and inward-turning forms of radical belief.[11] In addition, I soon realized that these two traditions conveniently illustrate an important sociological distinction between communities. In terms of group organization, anarchism always promotes a loose, voluntaristic, unstructured pattern of living. Mysticism, on the other hand, usually implies the presence of a guru, and therefore a much more leader-oriented and well-defined plan of everyday existence. Upon the comparisons between past and present and between the inner and external could then be superimposed another one, frequently emphasized by observers of the recent communal scene—that between deliberately formless experiments and those with a standardized discipline.

The central chapters, which provide studies of particular communities, have been arranged to focus upon this intellectual and structural contrast. In each case, I have tried to look closely at the interplay between the group's world view, its style of leadership, and its internal structure, whether

10. A convenient source for these ideas is Theosophical Society, American Section, *A Primer of Theosophy* (Chicago: by the Society, 1909), especially pp. 6–7, 13–42.

11. However, it will become clear that anarchist experiments have sometimes themselves included both an internal (mind-oriented) and an external (society-oriented) approach.

minimal or highly developed. The result of this investigation is to reopen the meaning of Max Weber's central contrast between bureaucratic and charismatic forms of authority. In the movements to be examined in this book, it happens that elaborate internal subdivisions, seemingly rational in their impersonality, go hand in hand with the most extreme versions of charismatic authoritarianism, while, on the other hand, the anarchistic movements which have been relatively formless have avoided a stifling degree of forced leadership as well. It is a conclusion which lends some support to the critics of intricately fashioned modern organizations rather than to the academic social scientists of the previous generation, who tended to assume that there was an intrinsic connection between rationality and democratic moderation of outlook.

The discovery of intensely authoritarian patterns of human relationship in certain of these communities means that this book, especially its second part, is also a study of the circumstances in which some people willingly allow themselves to be dominated by a guru or leader. Here I have tried to weigh biographical and situational evidence as closely as possible in determining the role of upbringing, conversion experience, and the subsequent communitarian pattern in producing such an outcome. Though these problems have been dealt with by social psychologists examining social movements, they deserve to be linked with the broader study of cultural innovation.

An element of chance, and another, stronger element of deliberate intent went into the final selection of communities to study. I wanted to choose groups which in each case would represent a given alternative (past and present, this-worldly and other-worldly, structured and unstructured) at its "best." The selection of groups of each kind at their "best" seemed appropriate if the aim was to give the communitarian tradition the maximum opportunity to display its importance and potential. But what does "best" mean? It implies first of all a reasonably "pure" case of its kind. Beyond that, it involves a judgment as to the highest degree of vigor, idealistic dedication, "genuineness," stability, and prospect of longevity. Of course choices made according to such criteria are highly subjective, based upon an awareness of the alternatives.[12]

12. The only other major anarchist community in the early twentieth century besides Stelton was Home, near Tacoma, Washington. I have read three detailed manuscript histories of Home (at least one of which, by Charles Pierce LeWarne, will soon be published). Wherever relevant, I have compared Stelton with Home in the course of my account. The most conspicuous alternative to the Vedanta Society is the Self-Realization Fellowship of All Religions, which also has some communitarian elements. Its relative unsuitability on qualitative grounds is made clear later on. In addition, there are numerous other older religious communities in Southern

The structure of this study suggested the use of an unusual method of approach. The comparison between past and present fascinated me because it offered a rare means of joining the usual archival research with participant observation as a technique for investigation. I would study the older movements in libraries and then try to live in two contemporary equivalents to get their "feel." And that is in the main what happened. (Interviews with survivors proved to be a further indispensable source for the earlier movements.) History merged for a time with personal experience during a summer spent in New Mexico in 1971. Perhaps it doesn't need to be added that five weeks, or even a single week, of living contact with a group of people gives one a far better sense of its inner quality than do many months of work in the stacks, even when the sources are unusually rich, as they are for both Stelton and Vedanta. Thus I feel most confident of what I have said about the present-day communities, least sure of my judgments in writing about the Ferrer Colony. One learns from this mixture of methods how much is irretrievably lost in the transition between life and history. In one sense, my account of Stelton is a pale substitute for

California. But I am convinced that Vedanta presents an unusually austere case for study. In dealing with the contemporary picture, it was less easy to be sure that I had made properly informed choices. A reading of Robert Houriet, *Getting Back Together* (New York: Coward, McCann, and Geoghegan, 1971), which surveys the national communal scene, reassures me that Rockridge, discovered through chance contact with one of its members, was not a bad selection, although a number of larger communes in northern California and Oregon might seem to have greater prospects for stability, and Libre (*ibid.*, pp. 221–31) sounds impressive. The selection of the structured New Mexico group in Chapter Five came after a conversation with Minor Van Arsdale, formerly liaison officer for the state in dealing with all the communities there. Aware of my criteria, Van Arsdale suggested the group I studied as probably the best for my purposes. Nationally, its closest equivalent in economic or external terms might have been Twin Oaks (*ibid.*, pp. 282–325). Twin Oaks is less authoritarian, nonmystical and rather less able in practical business terms (*ibid.*, pp. 288–89); thus, though equally structured, it seems altogether less striking. Ideologically, both the Hare Krishna movement and the Brotherhood of the Spirit might have offered interesting present-day parallels to Vedanta (*ibid.*, pp. 331–43, 346–61). But I could not have studied either of these at any length without pretending to be a convert, and the Gurdjieff-Sufi philosophy of Ezra's group in Chapter Five is at least equally relevant as a counterpoint to Sri Ramakrishna's. Hare Krishna is clearly more authoritarian than the group I studied, and it recruits largely from ex–heroin addicts, in contrast to the more diverse people on Ezra's ranch. The authoritarian leader of the Brotherhood of the Spirit (*ibid.*, pp. 355, 359–60) resembles Ezra to an uncanny degree. The Lama Foundation is atypically noncommunal in its living arrangements. The two contemporary groups that I shall describe in depth generally bear out the central tendencies noted in a much larger sampling of communes by the Berkeley sociologist Benjamin Zablocki, "The Genesis of Normative Systems in Rural Hippie Communes" (unpublished paper, 1971), except that Zablocki claims there are genuinely leaderless communes. Similarly, my distinction between anarchistic and discipline-oriented communities roughly corresponds to that between retreat and service communes in the recent excellent study by Rosabeth Moss Kanter, *op. cit.*

the narration of the community written by four of its leaders, published in 1925, and today in dead storage in the Harvard library.

The experience of living in and around New Age communities for a summer changed me, however, less than I was hoping. In both the groups I spent time with—anarchistic and highly structured—I felt a distinct loss of personal freedom as compared with my ordinary rhythm on the outside. I sensed fewer options, more tacit surveillance. The life inside these communities confirmed me in my previous bent toward privacy, diversity of daily experience, and monogamous parenthood, as bequeathed in part also from a childhood in Southern California. I returned to Santa Cruz glad to be leading the kind of existence I normally do. However, I would claim no general significance for this reaction. I am often made aware that a professor clings to one of the most unusual and privileged roles now available in our society. It is a role which also permits a milder form of deviance of its own distinct kind. My personal contentment may therefore be only the result of an atypical twist of fate.

Quite aside from these reactions, I have written this book as a partisan of the general movement in the past two hundred years toward an expanded definition and practice of human freedom. I do not believe that the standard patterns of living which have emerged in industrial societies offer an adequate scope for human potential. Experimental communities can make us aware of new opportunities as well as of some very old hazards. It will become apparent that I am severely skeptical of the power of the American radical tradition, at least in this version, to widely influence the quality of American life. But this skepticism, partly the product of a historian's commitment to assess all situations in cool, hard-headed terms, should not be confused with a moral identification with the status quo. If mankind is divided into factions of those who are content merely to relish existing comforts and those who seek rapid change in humane directions, then I certainly must record an allegiance to the party of humanity.

Such a statement, of course, scarcely disposes of the problem of an author's point of view. In this connection, John Lofland has fruitfully suggested that at least three self-contained world views, each with its own vocabulary and internal logic, mutually compete in our society for the allegiance of seeking individuals. These are the political, the religious, and the psychiatric.[13] According to the first, man is forever an actor on a public

13. John Lofland, *Doomsday Cult* (Englewood Cliffs, New Jersey: Prentice-Hall, 1966), p. 42. A fourth world view, that of family-centered privatism, also needs to be recognized. It is no doubt the most powerful of all in the mainstream of American society, though, unlike the other three, it has no particular relevance to radical movements. Of course there are still other world views that survive among small

stage, a citizen, a member of a body politic or a social order. The second defines man as a being whose truly important relations are with the unseen cosmos, as someone always in the process of purposeful evolution toward an eternal destiny. The third view, which has become increasingly fashionable of late, regards man primarily as a personality with deep inner problems, needs, and desires, whose goal is the elimination of mental conflicts and the realization of his potential for insight and effective expression. The last two outlooks frequently, though somewhat deceptively, appear to merge; both of them focus upon states of mind rather than society.

These competing world views actually lie at the heart of the problem of bias. Becoming increasingly aware of their implications, I have tried as an intellectual and social historian to stand outside them all. This is precisely how someone in my field differs from a political scientist, a religious philosopher, or a psychologist. But at the same time all our thinking is powerfully molded by these several perspectives, and it will become plain where I have lapsed into the vocabulary and critical stance of one or more of them. Especially as regards the political and psychiatric frames of reference, I find myself, like many others, wholly pleased with neither of them, yet unable to function without them. In particular, if a reader wonders why I have not always shrunk from psychological probes while studying these individual lives and group relationships, I can only answer that there is no other way to begin to capture the poignancy and inward depth of these experiences and situations. But I have tried to explore this dimension, where it seemed justified, only in close conjunction with a sociological awareness.

Behind the clash of these several world views lies the fundamental dualism of inner, or mind-oriented, and external, or socially oriented, approaches to the improvement of the human condition. Historically, in Western culture, these have long been bitter rivals. The question of balancing or integrating them is, of course, the great unresolved problem of our age. My effort to stand apart from both these predispositions and to weigh their consequences within concrete living groups will not be wholly satisfying to the intense partisans of either route toward liberation. But this mode of attack at least offers some promise of getting beyond the clichés of these two timeworn attitudes. Perhaps there is already a growing body of opinion seeking clues outside the framework of Marxism, Freudianism,

---

minorities, e.g., the scientific and the aesthetic. For an interesting discussion of this entire subject, see Clifford Geertz, "Religion as a Cultural System," in Michael Banton, ed., *Anthropological Approaches to the Study of Religion* (London: Tavistock Publications, 1966), pp. 26–39.

or religious mysticism—not content with any of these traditional molds for discussion, yet not willing to drop back into the still more familiar categories of the conservative-liberal mainstream. There must be many of us who find all the customary world views and their vocabularies to be inadequate and confining, yet who retain a sense of urgency in beholding the American and the human condition. This book has been written primarily for such an audience.

CHAPTER ONE

In Search of a Counter-Cultural Tradition

In two remarkable, almost entirely unknown utopian novels which appeared in 1902 and 1904, the anarchist J. William Lloyd portrayed a small group of Americans who had deliberately left the city in order to lead a collective life that was extremely primitive and close to nature, with only minimal need for possessions or technology. Lloyd's fiction provides a convenient bench mark for the historian, revealing the furthest limits of the American imagination, both sexual and socio-economic, at the turn of the twentieth century.

Though Lloyd's dropouts called themselves the Simplicists, their informal name in the neighborhood was "the Tribe." When they arrived on horseback at a nearby village one afternoon, their appearance made everyone turn and stare:

> What were they? Indians, Gypsies, masqueraders, or a circus company?
> They were certainly mostly white people, and their faces intellectual and refined, tho sunburned like sailors.
> But all of them, men, women and children, wore on their faces the same expression—something so vividly untamed, free and care-free, frank and glad, that it affected the traveller like a breath from another world. He had never seen that expression on a grown-up person before.

The members of the Tribe dressed to please themselves. Many appeared in "brilliant colors, artistically blended, and [with] strange, barbaric ornamentation, consisting mainly of profuse but exquisite embroidery & fringework." No one in the group looked at all conventional. Instead,

> a wild, half-savage freedom expressed itself in all. Bare heads, arms and feet

were common, . . . bare chests and bare legs were there. The full beard was almost invariable, with the men, many wore long hair, & many of the women had their locks loose and streaming or in long braids down the back. . . .

A strong suggestion of Indian taste, freely adapted, was discernible in all their dress and trappings.

The women rode astride, like the men, and seemed equally at home on horseback.

It was evidently a holiday pageant; a singularly childlike, un-American abandon moving them all, and there was much fluting and luting and singing of gay songs.

"Them's them," said a local villager who peered out at the astonishing scene. "Them's the Tribe."[1]

In this description one is soon aware of having stumbled into the presence of the very first "hippie" band in the history of the American imagination. Perhaps, just as the 1960's saw a real trip to the moon after decades of fantasizing on the subject, the desire to secede from civilization and "live like the Indians" had also been lurking for a long time in the minds of a people who were supposed to be industrialized, success-oriented, and matter-of-fact. Of course, in both cases it can be questioned whether the eventual reality satisfyingly fulfilled the prophecy. Throngs of youth would one day emerge answering to Lloyd's physical description in just about every detail, but when the time came all too few of them wore facial expressions that could honestly be called "care-free, frank and glad." Clearly there are both similarities and subtle but profound differences between the primitivism of J. William Lloyd's generation and that of our own.

The leading personage in the Tribe, a man whose example inspired everyone else, was a highly idealized figure, Forrest Westwood. The name itself suggests the peculiar blending of the natural and the "refined" which lingered in Lloyd's fantasy. Westwood is presented as a pagan, yet a highly cultivated one. He reads Greek and Latin. His way of living is adapted from the Epicureans as well as the Indians. Although Westwood means to push further than someone like Thoreau in a primitivist direction, his aim is still one of compromise—to become a "gentle savage, or refined barbarian."[2] In part he seems to be a product of the distinct turn-of-the-century epoch which could send Isadora Duncan onto the dance stage and build Greek temples on a Berkeley hillside.

1. J. William Lloyd, *The Dwellers in Vale Sunrise: How They Got Together and Lived Heppy Ever After* (Westwood, Massachusetts: The Ariel Press, 1904), pp. 7–10. This book was a sequel to Lloyd's earlier utopia, *The Natural Man: A Romance of the Golden Age* (Newark, New Jersey: Benedict Prieth, 1902).

2. *Ibid.*, pp. 14. 24–25, 27, 29, 62–63.

Yet he is also a more unusual creation. He is, first of all, clearly an attractive form in the author's bisexual imagination.[3] Westwood often wears no clothes except for knee-length corduroy trunks. Outdoor life has made him "brown as a nut with sun-tan." His muscles stand out "sculpturesquely" as he lies on his back, "one knee drawn up, one hand under his head, the other thrust into a great pouch at his girdle." His voice is soft, and he has a "happy dreaming face."[4] Like many American youth of the 1960's, he sees no reason why the narcissistic pleasures of childhood should be abandoned as one grows older. Why not dangle your feet in a running stream? Why not lie on your back, looking up into the sky, hearing the bees murmur in the distance? "You would enjoy it just as much now as you did then [as a child]," he encourages a young woman who has come upon him in the fields.[5] Like Tarzan, who emerged into print twelve years later, Westwood swings joyously from tree branches, holding on to vines.

Westwood defines happiness as the main aim in life. Still, there is compromise. Even the most Eden-like utopia of 1902 retains a certain intellectuality in its flavor. What a man needs altogether, Lloyd declares, is "buoyant health, leisure, intimacy with Nature, time to read, to think, to realize your own happiness, to work out your own artistic longings, room to grow and be yourself, creature comforts, & untrammeled liberty."[6] The recipe is one of bohemian self-expression; in it the sensuous narcissism which links it to the recent counter-culture is, after all, only one striking ingredient.

Exploring further, in these novels we discover Westwood at first living alone, in an Arcadian natural setting, much of which he has cultivated into a park. (Thus he thrives in the pleasantly pastoral landscape, less wild than a real wilderness, which had appealed to a great many nineteenth-century Americans.)[7] Though he "rather despises property," Westwood has received this land through inheritance. He is explained as having grown up

3. Lloyd, commenting in his own magazine. *The Free Comrade* (N.S., III [October, 1902]. 6–7), on Edward Carpenter's open embrace of "homogenic love," said that when a "True Mate" or "Central Love" of the opposite sex arrives, "the homogenic passion takes a secondary place. but this argues no condemnation of the love itself." He pleaded that all forms of love be accepted in an enlarged, purified context. Such an attitude in itself resembles the prevalent view in the 1960's counter-culture.

4. Lloyd. *The Natural Man,* pp. 12–13. 57.

5. *Ibid.,* pp. 17–18.

6. *Ibid.,* pp. 65–66.

7. See Leo Marx. *The Machine in the Garden* (New York: Oxford University Press. 1964).

half wild after the early death of his father. With his mother he had an unusually close relationship, but when she died, during his young manhood, he withdrew from the world onto this terrain. One year he lived with the Indians on a reservation in upstate New York. Now, in his maturity, he has become largely self-sufficient, though he writes poems to augment his income.

In a number of the details of his life he might indeed pass as a time traveler in the Haight-Ashbury. He eats "natural foods," plays a flute, has a special fondness for dogs, and hands flowers to people he meets.[8] But in other respects he is quite different. Most noticeably, Westwood refuses stimulants of nearly every kind, for they are "unnatural."[9] He also goes further toward renunciation than members of the recent counter-culture by spurning china and glassware for hand-carved tools and dishes. On the other hand, he maintains a gun collection and does not hesitate to kill animals for his food. He defends this practice by invoking the concept of the "natural" in a Darwinian manner. Human life is what he absolutely respects, though he always tries to kill animals painlessly, and various creatures are described as having a special affinity for him, bounding toward him in response to his whistle.[10]

Westwood imitates the Indians somewhat more convincingly than the youth of the 1960's:

> Thoreau bought shoes, I make my own moccasins or sandals and wear those only on rough journeys or in winter. He bought clothes. I make mine of leather or corduroy, for I can tan as well as an Indian, and can cut and sew as well as any tailor. . . . I make my own bows and arrows, boomerangs, raw-hide lassoos, sometimes even bone fish hooks. . . . My arrows are tipped with real Indian-made flints, picked up here and there in many states. . . . The bow strings are made of sinew. I sleep in skins. You see how simple my agriculture is: my grapes and berries grow wild, my apples need little care. my garden is but small and the work in it a delight.

8. Lloyd. *The Natural Man*, pp. 37–38. 46, 58–59, 61, 128. However, the details of his "natural food" diet were quite unlike those of the 1960's. For an unexplained reason Westwood has an aversion to grains. preferring fruit and nuts. milk. eggs, herbs and roots.

9. *Ibid.*, pp. 56–57. 78.

10. At one point Westwood consciously tries to refute the argument that the urban and artificial is no less "natural" than the wild and untamed. since it too developed inside the laws of nature. "If charms are equal," says the objector. "the city is as good as the forest, the artificial life as the natural—aha! I have you, Sir Savage!" "Not yet." Westwood replies. "I repeat, charms are abstractly equal but race history and individual constitution justify our preferences—the city charms, artificiality has joys. luxury delights. vice and crime and all evil have attending pleasures—yet man was wilderness-born and wilderness-reared. The few generations of artificiality have not aborted the instincts inherited through long ages of nature." *Ibid.*, pp. 87–88.

In this vein another character says awesomely: "To see Forrest sitting on that Buffalo head, dressed like an Indian, the collies, mastiffs & beagles sprawled about . . . while the flame-light danced around the room and lit up the carvings and those drawings on the buckskin tapestries, made a savage picture I shall never forget."[11]

And yet there is something more generalized about this portrait. Westwood is partly a pagan king, a demigod, or someone with magic powers. He does not merge himself in nature in a passive sense. Instead he exercises singular control over the animals in his domain. One of his pets in the cave-house where he sleeps during the colder months is a six-foot boa constrictor. Calling out to his ravens and fearlessly petting his snake, Westwood merges briefly into the painting by Henri Rousseau which hangs at the Jeu de Paums, entitled "The Charmer of Serpents." On one level, this aspect of his personality may reveal enough lingering traces of the Christian tradition in his creator's mind (as in Rousseau's) to infuse the idea of paganism with a sense of the Satanic. On another level, Westwood's tone of kingly authority makes him the inevitable teacher and leader of the others who eventually decide to join with him in forming a community. Besides being the "natural man," the one who "lives like the Indians," Forrest Westwood is also an archetypical guru figure, a source of profound wisdom. His physical beauty joins with his inner qualities to produce the kind of being near whom a dedicated band of followers would willingly stay indefinitely.

It is not entirely startling when Westwood calmly announces, "I am an egoist." Amplifying his meaning, he says: "I am not willing to sacrifice myself to things. *I* am more than clothes, houses, money, business, reputation, etiquette, religion, fashion, codes, & institutions." The "evolution and fruition" of the self are what lead to happiness.[12]

> Why they [in the mass] no sooner begin to start in life than they begin to think about other things & other people more than themselves. They have what they call "ambitions." Clothes like other people, houses like other people, food like other people, business like other people, opinions like other people, customs, manners, religion, politics all like other people. That's the way the race runs, & every man in the race is trying so hard to catch up with the one before him that he has no time to think of himself. . . . Not

11. *Ibid.,* pp. 63–64, 77. Another character is elsewhere made to say: "We claim that the Indians, and indeed most savages, by the simplicity, communism and brotherhood character of their tribal arrangements secured a beauty, health and sanity of social life infinitely superior to that which most white men know." Lloyd, *The Dwellers in Vale Sunrise,* p. 40.

12. *Ibid.,* pp. 22–23; Lloyd, *The Natural Man,* pp. 67–68.

one is contented, or can give any sane reason for his "ambitions." Now that is a true picture of civilization. Bah! I would rather be a savage.[13]

Yet Westwood does have an alternative social vision, and it often connects directly with the later counter-culture. Making a claim remarkably like one heard in many recent rural communes, Westwood says that the entire population of the planet could support itself just as he is already doing, especially since the soil on his own estate is stony and of poor quality. Like the commune dwellers, Westwood has to decide where to draw the line in accepting the fruits of the existing civilization. He would reject everything "except books, Art, and a few of its simplest inventions." In this spirit he has built his own dwelling high up in the rocks, designing it to merge into the surrounding landscape. A man's house should be the expression of his character; each person should be his own architect, and preferably builder as well. Further, "every thing in my home should be home-made, or at least, hand-made," and thus "full of associations."[14] Cave-Gables, Westwood's home, sounds considerably more finished and elaborate than the very modest houses I saw being built at communes in New Mexico during 1971. But the underlying intent in such construction remains the same. Also unchanged is the attitude toward the existing legal and governmental system. Neither Westwood nor the present-day communalists really believe in government. But in both cases their argument is that taxes should be paid and open civil disobedience avoided, in order to keep out of unnecessary trouble. Along with this practical compromise goes the hope that, as the new way of life spreads, the old order will peacefully crumble.[15]

Westwood terms his ideal society a "Federation of the Free."

> In my dream the people seemed to be gathered together over the world in hamlets and village-groups, drawn more by similarity of taste and feeling than by necessity. Not exactly or totally communistic, but co-operating in so many ways as in some things to approach that. The land possessed only by those who used it and while using it.
>
> In my dream everybody took a share in the necessary work, & thus a few hours apiece was enough all day, and all were employed and all compensated. The rest of the time, everybody took pleasure, read, studied, did artistic work, what they pleased. . . . And I seemed to see all habits, customs, behavior, much freer and simpler than now. No social law except that of non-interference; no fashions, no restraints, no inquisitions in morals

13. *Ibid.,* pp. 66–67.
14. *Ibid.,* pp. 64–65, 69, 73; cf. Lloyd, *The Dwellers in Vale Sunrise,* pp. 90–91.
15. Lloyd, *The Natural Man,* p. 90.

or religion, individual tastes followed everywhere, and every human flower after its own kind.[16]

Ultimately all coercive agencies were to disappear, even if it would be foolish to force the issue just now. "Free contributions will support whatever institutions the people desire, just as churches are supported now in these States."[17]

Forrest Westwood emerges not only as an anarchist, but also as something of a mystic. In his adulthood, he says, he became a pantheist.

> As a youth I rejected all creeds, revelations, gods. I was atheist, or, better, agnostic, for I said I did not know. But neither did I believe. But gradually a strange feeling of kinship between myself and nature grew in me. I gave myself up more and more to these strange invisible currents of life, as the sea obeys the moon and the sap the seasons. . . . Suddenly the whole thing crystallized . . . and I saw that the whole universe was One Great Life.

This life is in constant evolution—man is part of a vital, eternally changing cosmos.[18] Quoting Emerson, Thoreau, and Whitman as authorities, Westwood enunciates a creed which is both spiritualistic and libertarian. "Tell me the secret of happiness," a female admirer breathlessly begs of him toward the end of the first novel. His reply once again anticipates the vocabulary of the counter-culture in the 1960's: " 'Feel your identity and agreement with the universe and appreciate the joy of the moment.' "[19]

By this time he has become the full-fledged guru. His audience only half jokingly calls itself his "disciples." The grove where he sits is like a temple.[20] Soon his growing band of followers decides to purchase land next to his, and the properties become merged in an intentional community. Of the group, Westwood is the leader "in a mental sense," while his new "high-bred" female companion, Mabel Earle, is the leader "in a business sense."[21] But, Lloyd hastily adds (as if all at once recalling good anarchist principles), "nobody is bound to stay, acquiesce or obey."

When we next meet Forrest Westwood, the Sunrise community has been established for some time. Despite Westwood's belief in unrestricted individual self-expression, social patterning has already become noticeable.

16. *Ibid.*, pp. 126–27.
17. *Ibid.*, p. 91.
18. *Ibid.*, pp. 93–94, 97. However, p. 104, he admits that he is not sure whether he believes in reincarnation.
19. *Ibid.*, p. 107.
20. *Ibid.*, pp. 89, 91–92.
21. *Ibid.*, p. 137. Compare the very similar husband-wife roles of Ezra and Eva, described in Chapter Five.

Indeed, a newcomer reports that "their eyes were singularly alike, deep, mystical, penetrative, but childlike and unworldly. I felt they were judging me by new standards & felt very strangely. I told them my needs. They seemed hardly listening, only looking *into* me." There is a strong sense of barrier between their way of life and the world outside. " 'Brother,' Westwood tells the new arrival, 'you were never at home out there, and that is why it sickened you. You will find your own among us.' "[22]

Land ownership is legally collective, and some of the colonists prefer to farm and share all their goods in common. But a majority are informally assigned acre plots on which they can spread themselves with a sense of privacy. Despite the hints of solidarity, the population is described as extremely diverse. It includes some writers and artists (here the memory of Brook Farm is explicitly invoked), but also quite a number of unintellectual, old-fashioned country people who enjoy a plain manner of living. Moreover, the community is interracial, including Chinese, Japanese, and, specifically, at least one ex-slave. This touch reminds us of the almost unique spirit of social brotherhood advocated by turn-of-the-century anarchists.

Among all these colonists "the utmost childlike *camaraderie*" prevailed. And yet it was claimed that one might live there like a hermit if one wished. The motto of the Sunrise community was "This is the Land of Equal Do-As-You-Please."[23] Thus did anarchists, no less than such mainstream thinkers as Frederick Jackson Turner, like to reconcile the ideals of individualism and democracy. The anarchists differed only in widening both definitions. They greatly increased the scope of practical cooperation while also refusing, so they said, to indulge in any form of coercion.

Nonetheless, many central details of the life in Vale Sunrise were strikingly unlike those in American society at large. Possessions of all kinds were reduced to a minimum. Human relations, including those between the sexes, were pointedly described in terms of "a wonderful freedom and affectionateness." There was no gossip, no jealousy, no obscenity, or "low" talk. All questions of love, marriage, parentage, and separation were decided on a voluntary basis, though to satisfy the outside world legal marriage was encouraged, and Lloyd seems to have assumed that everyone would live either in couples or in solitary fashion.[24] At the age of twelve,

22. Lloyd, *The Dwellers in Vale Sunrise*, pp. 14–15.
23. *Ibid.*, pp. 19–21, 25.
24. *Ibid.*, pp. 47–48, 96–97.

children would choose their own names ("self-names"), though meanwhile they had been given "tribe names." Children were especially honored. Education was voluntary at all levels; a number of teachers operated small schools, giving children and parents a choice among approaches.[25]

Unpleasant kinds of work were divided equally among the whole population (with the implication that here might be an unstated exception to the general rule of voluntarism).[26] Mornings were spent working in common, and the rest of the day was free for whatever one wanted.[27] A strong artistic life flourished, and nearly everyone excelled in the performance of a craft. Pride in workmanship, soon to be urged upon all Americans by writers like Herbert Croly, was notably strong. Meanwhile, sewage was recycled in a sand pit for eventual use as compost; the colonists were pleased not to be polluting nearby streams.[28] Waste was avoided in every way. Clothes were patched until entirely worn out (but, unlike in the recent counter-culture, they were never allowed to get dirty or torn). A public bathhouse existed, with attendants always on duty, perhaps a counterpart to the sauna. In summer infants usually went naked, and older children stripped down to loin cloths. Adults could undress as they pleased, but Karl, the nudist, willingly donned a fig leaf when in public.[29] Many people slept and ate outdoors in warm weather. A large portion of the land, called the Sanctuary, was deliberately left as a wild reserve into which individuals could retreat whenever they felt the need.

In this utopia, there was considerably more structure and organization than might at first appear. New arrivals had to pass through a probationary period before they were permanently accepted. However, their past histories were never inquired into.[30] Troublemakers, it was briefly admitted,

25. *Ibid.*, pp. 111, 115–16, 125. Lloyd's educational ideas were far less unconventional than those of the anarchist-influenced Stelton educators, Elizabeth and Alexis Ferm, described in Chapter Two.

26. "For we hold that each should do his fair share of the dirty and disagreeable work that must be done." *Ibid.*, p. 28. By contrast, at the actual anarchist colony at Home, Washington, it was boasted: "Here one can work or play, live on a raft, in a hollow stump, or with others, and if he wishes to visit elsewhere he does not have to ask permission of anyone nor can he be fined for not returning within a specific time." James W. Adams, "Things As I See Them," *Discontent,* November 24, 1900, p. 1.

27. Some use of positive incentives was made in getting people to work at the less pleasant tasks; e.g., giving them more leisure in return, or giving them special badges of honor. This whole side of the community's existence takes its tone quite directly from Edward Bellamy's *Looking Backward.*

28. Lloyd, *The Dwellers in Vale Sunrise,* pp. 37–38.

29. *Ibid.*, pp. 96–97, 129, 142.

30. This last practice recurs in Vedanta monasteries and in Ezra's New Mexico group, Chapters Four and Five.

could be thrown out. Foremen, elected by unanimous vote, supervised the morning work periods. A Council Lodge was housed in its own building, and a simplified form of parliamentary rules prevailed during its debates. Informal public opinion was also a potent force. As in Indian tribes, the wisest elders (most notably Forrest Westwood) were expected to advise the others and to set a personal example.[31] Finally, rituals were concocted to formalize communal bonds. An initiation for new members was devised as an explicit parallel to individual marriage. During a lengthy interchange of speeches, the newcomer was asked to declare: "In joy and in pain, in health and in sickness, in strength and in weakness, in life and in death, I hold you my brothers, my sisters." The ceremony was followed by a tribal "feast."[32]

No doubt in all these arrangements there was much contradiction. On the one hand, work was held to be "the joy of life"; on the other, free time was openly treasured.[33] The anarchism ("a man's life should be from *himself* outward") clashed with the socialism casually introduced into many of the provisions. Technology crept into the account more and more. A brick works, a sawmill, a wood yard, a tannery were all eventually said to exist. Stockbreeding was pursued on a businesslike scale.

Toward the end of his second novel, aware perhaps of these incongruities and of a shift in his thinking away from the primitive, Lloyd introduced a three-sided debate which reveals a range of choices present in the early twentieth-century communitarian imagination.

In one corner stood Karl, who represented the most undiluted nature worship and also, it seems likely, the author's least censored sexual fantasies. A German immigrant, Karl was said to be "shy and reserved," an enthusiast who "lives in the deepest woods and is not often seen." Consistently vegetarian, he spurns eggs and milk and worries because "even the roots, fruit, vegetables he eats are alive and likely suffer pain & shrink from death." He is also a spiritualist, in touch with the departed. Alone in the forest, he abandons clothing entirely.

> His body is bronzed and hairy and rugged as a tree-trunk, his beard reaches to his waist and his hair to his knees. . . . He says animals have the same rights as men and so he never tames any, for tame animals, he says, are slaves. . . . When birds, squirrels, etc., are babes in the nest he vies with the mother in bringing them food, and they grow up with the feeling that he is a foster-parent. . . . Birds flutter down on him as a

31. *Ibid.*, pp. 13, 41–43, 45, 55, 57.
32. *Ibid.*, pp. 181–83. Again, such "feasts" recur in Chapter Five.
33. *Ibid.*, pp. 105, 174.

perch, squirrels run down the trees at his approach, rabbits are as tame as house-cats to his touch. . . . He lives mostly on nuts in the winter, basks in the sun on warm days, and sleeps like a woodchuck on cold, dark ones. . . . He tells me he eats nothing for a week, sometimes, sleeping nearly all the time. Tho strange, fanatical & eccentric he seems perfectly sane.

Like Dr. Dolittle, Karl even talks to the animals in a vocabulary of squeaks and grunts, afterward writing down what he has learned in notebooks.

He has made him a flint axe and a flint knife and these are his only tools, except wooden tappa-mallets, sticks, thorns, and the bags and baskets he weaves to carry his provisions.

I saw him yesterday in the woods, asleep in the sun, curled up at the foot of a tree, naked as a snake.[34]

The character of Karl illustrates one recurring strain in the American radical imagination. It is the side which, ever since Whitman, has led toward nudism, vegetarianism, and the desire for an almost literal merger with nature. The goal is to live more like the animals than like the Indians. This strain has reappeared in the recent counter-culture, perhaps especially on the West Coast. Believable reports were heard, in the late 1960's, of bands of young Californians who had moved to the outer Hawaiian Islands and were living, in roving groups, the extreme form of the possessionless life. By then the followers of this ideal had grown much more open in their celebration of sensuality, and they were willing to enjoy the ecstasy of the psychedelic drug experience in a way foreign to earlier generations.[35] But the striking continuities in this vision of "total" primitivism suggest that a consistent inner pattern may be at work. To go all the way toward *ahimsa,* or harmlessness with respect to one's fellow creatures, and toward giving up possessions (clothes as well as tools), is to achieve a complete shedding of armament.[36] The self has become unshielded, as if it were a body politic renouncing all protective weapons. When there is nothing of one's own to reach for, a wholly new manner of relating to the external environment is ushered in. Such an unconscious logic may link much that is seemingly arbitrary in the life of the far-out "nature freak."

But in the novel Karl hardly represents Lloyd's final answer. As the

34. *Ibid.,* pp. 140–47.

35. The 1970 version was also captured by an undergraduate in a Santa Cruz course on the subject of life style, who as his project made a film in which he ate a mushroom, took off his clothes, and then wandered through open fields and woods, mingling himself with flowers. water, trees, and sky.

36. Conceivably therefore it may be masochistic in origin. It is interesting that independently in India some monks go entirely naked when in retreat, from a similar desire to renounce possessions without compromise. John Yale, *A Yankee and the Swamis* (Hollywood: Vedanta Press, 1961), pp. 159, 167.

debate continues, Westwood accuses Karl of ignoring the equally "natural" facts of human evolution. "The use of tools & materials goes with the evolution of the brain, increasing with its growth. Therefore much of what we call 'artificial' in man's life is really most natural." Westwood's perspective is middle-of-the-road, closer to a rationalistic individualism, though it allows great scope for physical pleasure. He wants to exclude "both conventionality & crudity & attain the truly poetic mean." Is a certain amount of inconsistency in one's life really so bad, he wonders? The externals of tool use are relatively unimportant. The real test of the quality of one's existence is a psychological one, which Westwood puts into language we now think of as Freudian, though in 1904 it is only barely conceivable that his creator had heard of Freud: "The natural life is the *expressed* life, the artificial life is the *repressed* life."[37]

And then a third speaker, the urban socialist James Harvard, rises. "What a contrast he was, clean-shaven, dressed in the height of fashion, elegant and polished, to the two splendid demi-savages who had preceded him." Carrying Westwood's evolutionary point further, Harvard declares:

> There is nothing abnormal about machinery. Kropotkin is right when he says our present killing servitude to the machine "is a matter of bad organization, purely, and has nothing to do with the machine itself"; and Oscar Wilde is right when he claims that the machine is the helot on which our future civilization shall rise. The steam engine is as natural a product as a bird's nest and as normal a tool as Karl's flint.

Machinery may seem complex, but in evolution simplicity and complexity come in alternating cycles. Inventions create a period of disagreeable confusion, but eventually "the new arrangements of materials and forces are all smoothly adopted and coordinated and then a new stage of simplicity is reached. When a house is finished it looks as simple as a rock." Moreover, few inventions can compare with the intricacy of the human body.

"It isn't the machine or the organization, remember that, but the spirit behind these that grinds men," concludes the socialist speaker. He con-

---

37. Lloyd, *The Dwellers in Vale Sunrise*, pp. 151–56. Lloyd's italics. Nor is it possible to be certain whether the anarchist writer Hulda Potter-Loomis had heard of Freud when she wrote, around the same date, that "many physicians and scientists . . . declare that restrained or restricted sexual desire has been the cause of insanity in thousands of cases." Yet "none of these authorities have the courage to advocate freedom of sexual intercourse as a remedy for the cases now in hand or as a preventive of future possible cases. . . . To be happy is the chief end and aim of human existence." Hulda Potter-Loomis, *Social Freedom: The Most Important Factor in Human Evolution* (Chicago: M. Harman, n.d.), pp. 6–7. The important point is that as soon as Freudian ideas appeared radical libertarians were already on hand to appropriate them to their own established point of view.

fesses that he looks forward to the perfection of "a social organization so complete, united & perfectly integrated that it will seem almost as simple as a single man and no unit will feel it abnormal or himself restrained." Individuality will not be "repressed" in such a society, if only because all men will enjoy so much more leisure.[38]

On this note congenial to Edward Bellamy the debate ends. And then comes an astonishing development. Suddenly, in a way that leaves the reader entirely unprepared, it is announced that the socialist, James Harvard, has not only joined the community (taking the tribal name of Freeman Worth), but has become its "leading spirit and admitted chieftain." Forrest Westwood inexplicably retreats to the background. (His sexual problems, involving an admitted lack of self-confidence with women, were solved through union with a highly masculine girl who put him fully at his ease. By this time the pair had produced three boys and a girl.)[39] Perhaps Westwood is no longer a very necessary figure in the author's imagination; perhaps, on a more rational plane, Lloyd has been temporarily converted from anarchism to socialism. In any event, the book concludes with an embrace of the virtues of organization. The colonists still supposedly have it both ways, but the claim is perfunctory and unconvincing. Vale Sunrise is physically transformed until little would seem left of its Edenlike qualites:

> First all the arable lands were ditched and drained by machinery, swamps drained, impeding rocks blasted out, terraces built, roads made perfect. Then great machine-plows and earth-mixers went over all the fields, subsoiling them, turning-up, mixing & blending the soils, and sifting out every stick and stone impediment. . . . Then wind-mills went up, with pumps to irrigate fields and gardens when needed. Great fertilizer-sheds were built.[40]

A final touch is even more ominous. The colonists, under Freeman Worth's direction, discover the collectively useful task of automobile manufacture. A building for this purpose is erected, and the "tribal" population turn cheerfully to the production of motor cars and trucks![41] The dream of mystical union with nature is all but forgotten, as the author's imagination swerves back toward the American mainstream with a vengeance.

J. William Lloyd's fiction may seem to show the full extent of the trend in American life out of the parlor and into the sunshine, which John Hig-

---

38. Lloyd, *The Dwellers in Vale Sunrise,* pp. 165–75.
39. *Ibid.,* pp. 18–19, 65, 68, 85–87.
40. *Ibid.,* p. 191.
41. *Ibid.,* p. 188. The idea of total economic self-sufficiency remains dominant, however, even in the new and far more elaborate economy here being projected.

ham has pointed to as a notable phenomenon of the 1890's.[42] However, it actually has little in common with the growing widespread interest in the out-of-doors. This appeal centered on strenuousness, linked with the American cultural ideal of masculinity.[43] Lloyd, perhaps aided by a bisexual imagination, could view nature through different eyes. The real importance of Lloyd's fiction is that it significantly bridges the chronological gap between Thoreau and Whitman and the recent youth culture. It suggests a recurrent "underground" intellectual tradition in America, with its own characteristic themes and images, among them the avoidance of callous masculine aggressiveness.

We know that Lloyd was not entirely alone when he dreamed of a direct rapport with nature. In 1904 Mrs. Maude Johnson was running a "Nature Colony" on the outskirts of Pasadena, California, in which sick people indulged in a rare form of therapy known as "the *sun-bath*" while simultaneously listening to talk about industrial problems. Meanwhile, at the anarchist colony called Home, near Tacoma, Washington, the septuagenarian Mrs. Lois Waisbrooker was publishing a magazine called *Clothed with the Sun,* in which she wrote articles on themes of sex, marriage, and the emancipation of women.[44] Controversy over nude bathing would be a major cause of the breakup of that colony a few years later. And in Ojai, California, during the mid-teens the future Vedantist nun Georgina Jones Walton was glorying in the open life, sleeping outdoors and taking nude sunbaths, to help cure her kidney trouble. These scenes reflect more than just a health fad. Belief in the restorative power of nature formed a distinct element in the thinking of many American radicals during the Progressive Era. The autobiographies of Harry Kemp and Upton Sinclair, for instance, are filled with these preoccupations.[45]

As for John William Lloyd himself, we know all too little of his life. But what we know is highly revealing. A native of New Jersey, he was living in

42. John Higham, "The Reorientation of American Culture in the 1890's," in John Weiss, ed., *The Origins of Modern Consciousness* (Detroit: Wayne State University Press, 1965), pp. 25–48.

43. See George M. Fredrickson, *The Inner Civil War* (New York: Harper & Row, 1965), pp. 217–25.

44. Mrs. Johnson's colony was favorably reported by the aged Kansas anarchist Moses Harman in his magazine *Lucifer,* June 9, 1904, pp. 105–106. See also her advertisement, p. 111, where she states: "No users of liquor, tobacco, meat or corsets need apply." Mrs. Waisbrooker was seventy-eight years old in 1904; on her see the forthcoming study of Home by Charles Pierce LeWarne.

45. Harry Kemp, *Tramping on Life: An Autobiographical Narrative* (New York: Boni and Liveright, 1922), especially p. 168; Upton Sinclair, *Autobiography* (New York: Harcourt, Brace and World, 1962).

Florida when, as a young man in 1885, he began joining the circle of contributors to Benjamin R. Tucker's individualist anarchist magazine, *Liberty*. Around 1900 he took over the editorship of *The Free Comrade*, a journal which already had a leaning toward sexual radicalism. Within the anarchist movement of the day, Lloyd and two others (E. C. Walker and M. E. Lazarus) occupied an unusual position. During the 1890's, almost alone they argued for rural decentralization and colonization, themes which had then gone out of fashion among radicals though they would take on new luster a half century later. Lloyd was not a typical anarchist of his own generation, and so it is no accident that his writings often seem to bridge a gap in time.[46]

Lloyd was probably in his late thirties when he published the two novels. He was then living in semi-rural retreat at Westfield, New Jersey. Above his study desk he displayed the portraits of Darwin, Thoreau, Whitman, and William Morris. These names suggest a radical tradition which joins what are now regarded as opposites: scientific rationalism and romantic belief in a cosmic oversoul; sexual freedom and (in Thoreau's case) stern sexual repression. An adequate definition of an American free-thought tradition, surviving from the nineteenth century, must pay heed to these incongruities, these seeming contradictions.

It is most interesting that during the course of his life Lloyd came to be highly regarded in both anarchist and Vedantist circles. In New Jersey he was a warm friend of Leonard Abbott, who played a leading role in the Francisco Ferrer Association.[47] Later Lloyd moved to Roscoe, California, where he reigned over an estate known as Freedom Hill, on the edge of the San Fernando Valley. There, in a long series of pamphlets, he promulgated a self-concocted "religion of beauty," advocated *karezza* (sexual stimulation short of climax), and wrote romantic prose poems about nature and society.

One of his poem-essays, which appeared in print in 1939, wrestled

46. James J. Martin, *Men Against the State* (De Kalb, Illinois: Adrian Allen Associates, 1953), pp. 238, 241, 248–49.

47. See Chapter Two. For an appreciation of Lloyd in the anarchist context, see Leonard D. Abbott, "J. William Lloyd and His Message," *Mother Earth*, III (December, 1908), 360–68. Describing some of Lloyd's unpublished writings on sex, Abbott gingerly warns his audience: "These are extremist documents. They are bound to be misunderstood. From my own individual point of view they are too ready to assume that the human instinct is 'varietist,' and too ready to ignore the age-long, deep-rooted instinct favoring loyal and faithful union between one man and one woman. But they represent an earnest and fearless effort to enunciate a logical and liberating sex-philosophy."

with the same issues that had engaged him at the turn of the century. A "terrible mistake, lie and delusion," he now wrote,

> fills life with jealousy in love, hypocrisy in religion, perversion in morals, injustice in law, treachery in business, defectiveness in products, tyranny and corruption in government. . . .
>
> We live then in a state of Barbarism, not Civilization, and the world has always hitherto been barbaric, except for small seed-spots and nuclei, here and there, of good men, living sweetly and faithfully together, as far as they could make that possible.

The vulgarity of the mass sickens these few, who go off into the wilderness or into retirement, to live as "hermits, recluse scholars, yogis, monks, or champions of 'The Simple Life.' " But, Lloyd cautions, "such fleeing from the world is no curing of its evils." Nor are cities intrinsically wrong, nor such institutions as private property. He ends on the same curiously ambivalent note that he had struck in the closing pages of *The Dwellers of Vale Sunrise.*[48] But this inconclusiveness did not disturb the Vedantist nun Georgina Jones Walton, by this time long known as Sister Daya. In a rare gesture she stepped outside the confines of her own movement to honor Lloyd in the pages of the magazine she edited for the Ananda Ashrama of nearby La Crescenta, terming Lloyd "this wise man of the west, who lived simply and profoundly in the hills of California and who, in dying, left a legacy of mystic philosophy too little known."[49] It was an epitaph for one of the many troubled American radicals who had dreamed of community but failed to find one.

What, then, is the case for a counter-cultural tradition, inherited from the mid-nineteenth century, burgeoning somewhat after 1900, remaining alive on the fringes, and then leaping into a new prominence after 1965? The argument seems well worth exploring, if only because it can help test what is genuinely new about the recent youth culture.

Confining ourselves primarily to the themes of anarchism and mysticism, what is the evidence concerning the continuity of interest in these directions over roughly the past century? As an initial groundwork, a brief factual survey of the extent to which Americans have turned toward these

48. J. William Lloyd, "The Scripture of Civilization," *From Hill-Terrace Outlooking: Poems of Intuition, Perception, and Prophecy* (Los Angeles: Samuel Stebb, 1939), pp. 17–24.

49. *Message of the East*, XXXIV (January, 1945), 43. She reprinted some of his philosophical writings. Lloyd is the only person to be conspicuously saluted both here and in the pages of *Mother Earth*.

beliefs, and of the generational changes within both traditions, is indispensable.

We might begin by reminding ourselves that radicalism in life style was indeed a conspicuous element in the outburst of reform activity which swept over the northern United States prior to the Civil War. This involved not only the well-known names of Thoreau, Alcott, and Margaret Fuller, but also a host of more obscure individuals who were tempted to pursue a pattern of living along strikingly rational (which is to say eccentric) lines. For instance, the anarchist community of Modern Times on Long Island in the 1850's is recalled to have attracted a definite "fringe" of such people into its rank-and-file. A number of unmarried couples boldly lived together there, causing the issue of "free love" to rear itself in much the same form as it would among the anarchists who gathered at Home or Stelton in the early twentieth century.[50]

After the Civil War, the anarchist movement (still almost entirely native-born) retreated from the realm of communitarian demonstration to that of journalistic propaganda. But in this form, unlike many other phases of prewar radicalism, it did not die out, and if anything for a time gained steam. The New England Labor Reform League, founded in 1869 and lasting until 1893, was increasingly dominated by the anarchist Ezra Heywood; its annual conventions gave focus to radicalism of this stripe. Some of Heywood's pamphlets reportedly sold 80,000 to 100,000 copies.[51] One-man crusaders such as William B. Greene and Lysander Spooner wrote prolifically. After 1877, Benjamin R. Tucker promoted individualist anarchism from New Bedford and New York; his magazines, *The Radical Review* and *Liberty,* which survived until 1908, directly carried on the New England radical tradition of the mid-nineteenth century, offering the most important forum for far-out opinions in this area. Over the years Tucker attracted a stable of about thirty native-born anarchist contributors, many of whom wrote pamphlets and lectured on their own as well. These people, and indeed the entire base of support for the indigenous American anarchist movement, came from a wide spread of geographical backgrounds, though as might be expected New England and the Midwestern and Far Western states earlier settled by New Englanders were disproportionately represented. One leading figure, Victor Yarros, was a Ukrainian who had settled in New Haven. Another, Henry Bool, was a merchant in Ithaca, New York, who established a radical lending library there. Small-town backgrounds (such as those of C. L. James, from Eau Claire, Wis-

50. Martin, *op. cit.,* pp. 74–77.
51. *Ibid.,* pp. 112–13, 116–17.

consin, and Moses Harman, the sexual radical from Valley Falls, Kansas)
seem notably to recur. Many of Tucker's contributors were journalists who
kept their social opinions to themselves during working hours (E. C.
Walker was the chief editorial writer for the Galveston *Daily News*). In
social terms, they tended to come from two distinct strata—the level of
craftsmen, especially the printing trade, and (far more often) that of college graduates. Tucker's magazine generally had a circulation below one
thousand, though it included many radical opinion leaders at home and
abroad.[52]

The anarchist movement was drastically changed almost overnight,
starting in 1880, when a substantial number of immigrants from Germany
and eastern Europe, espousing their own version of these beliefs, began to
pour into major American cities. In the years immediately before the
famous Haymarket affair of 1886, anarchism reached its widest extent in
America, thanks to this sudden new infusion. At first the native-born
individualist anarchists tried to cooperate with the new immigrant contingent, but by 1883 the two wings were already drawing apart, as a result
of the communal orientation and far more activist tone of the newcomers.[53]
In this period about six thousand Americans, mainly recent immigrants,
belonged to the International Anarchist Congress, which had been formed
in London in 1881; half of them lived in Chicago. Five anarchist papers
were now being produced in that city (a German daily, two German week-
lies, a Bohemian weekly, and an English fortnightly, *The Alarm*). Their
combined circulation was over thirty thousand. Moreover, anarchists had
achieved wide influence in the Chicago labor movement.[54] Meanwhile, in
New York a Yiddish anarchist daily newspaper, the *Freie Arbeiter Zeitung,*
began its long existence.

The Haymarket affair, during which anarchists were circumstantially
linked with the throwing of a bomb that killed several policemen at a Chicago labor demonstration, stigmatized the movement during a season of
rising anti-radical hysteria. From then on, and especially after the assassination of McKinley in 1901 by a man who had attended anarchist meetings, the movement began to decline. Most of the native-born individualist
anarchists were now frightened away from it, though their wing survived

52. *Ibid.*, pp. 232–73. The ideas of many of the figures mentioned in this brief
factual summary will be discussed in Chapter Six. On Tucker see also Charles A.
Madison, "Benjamin R. Tucker: Individualist and Anarchist," *New England Quarterly*, XVI (Fall, 1943), 444–67.
53. On the distinction between individualist and communal anarchism, see above,
p. 11.
54. George Woodcock, *Anarchism* (Cleveland: Meridian Books, 1962), p. 462.

long into the twentieth century in small circles to be found in Los Angeles, Detroit, Phoenix, Minneapolis, and elsewhere. At least twenty-four English-language anarchist periodicals still reflecting the older individualist viewpoint were published in various parts of the United States between 1880 and 1917; some of them lasted for a number of years.[55]

After 1886, most of the numerical strength of American anarchism was immigrant-based and reflected the more nearly Marxist orientation of European left-wing thought. Down to the First World War, major centers of this new and more militant version of anarchism existed in New York, Chicago, and Paterson, New Jersey, among other locations, though even here the numbers were slowly declining, except perhaps during the upsurge of labor militance in the years 1910–1914. A number of journals were published, though only a minority were in English. Some, such as *Free Society* (San Francisco, 1897–1904) and the several emanating from the Home, Washington, anarchist colony, 1898–1913 (*Discontent, The Demonstrator, The Agitator*), were neither clearly communal nor individualist in their orientation. As the magnetic figure of Emma Goldman rose to increasing dominance over the movement, her monthly vehicle, *Mother Earth* (1906–1917), came to eclipse the rest. In 1904 the circulation of *The Demonstrator,* for instance, was well below 1,000, while *Mother Earth*'s widely distributed subscribers appear to have totaled more than 40,000 as of March, 1911, even if many were doubtless more interested in her than in the movement. A typical Emma Goldman lecture in a medium-sized city might draw 250 people.

The Russian Revolution seduced much of the remaining anarchist strength. Anarchists who self-consciously identified themselves with the older generation were barely able to survive and publish magazines during the 1920's and 1930's. *Free Society* was briefly revived around 1921, and Harry Kelly published *Road to Freedom,* first from the Stelton colony and then from New York, 1923–1930. Aloof from everyone else, the aristocratic Albert Jay Nock edited *The Freeman* from 1920 to 1924. Literary, individualistic, and later on a near-Fascist, Nock in this period quoted Kropotkin and called for a general strike.[56]

Minor anarchist revivals, closely tied to immigrants and to depression labor militance, occurred in the 1930's. The *Clarion* appeared monthly in

55. Martin, *op. cit.,* pp. 260, 291–92. Martin claims that at least nine propagandists of this persuasion continued actively into the 1920's and 1930's. A few short-lived new periodicals continued to be founded.

56. For an excellent brief study of Nock, see Michael Wreszin, "Albert Jay Nock and the Anarchist Elitist Tradition in America," *American Quarterly,* XXI (Summer, 1969), 165–89.

New York from 1932 until at least 1934; though clearly anarchist, it showed a new sympathy for the Soviet Union, as well as publishing J. William Lloyd on sex and health. *Challenge,* an anarcho-syndicalist weekly in newspaper format, was able to survive in New York from May, 1938, until September, 1939; its links were with Kelly and the Ferrer Association. In Chicago, a Free Society Group had been formed by 1932; it published a pamphlet as late as 1951. The International Anarchist Relation Committee of America, tied to the Chicago group in 1932, revealed attempts at national federation. Doubtless there were sporadic organizing efforts by anarchists in other American cities during this period; one such group, called Man!, was active in Los Angeles in 1940. The last magazine of the older, continuous anarchist left was *Views and Comments,* published between 1955 and 1965 in New York. It was the mimeographed organ of the Libertarian League, an organization which admitted it had very few members. Bravely trying to come to terms with the universe of B. F. Skinner and Erich Fromm, this journal reached practically no members of the younger generation. Still, the older anarchist movement in New York carries on to the present moment, a fact which a listing of publications could never reveal. The League for Mutual Aid prides itself on making loans to high-risk borrowers, and the Libertarian Book Club annually fills the upper floor of a large West Side restaurant at a luncheon where reminiscence is keen despite the pointed effort to include a few college students at the table.

Meanwhile, in the early 1940's a new group of pacifist intellectuals who had little contact with the survivors of the orthodox movement independently rediscovered anarchism. Far more aware of the need to wrestle with the contemporary scene on a respectable, freshly thought-out plane of encounter, these figures included the young Paul Goodman, Dwight Macdonald, and such poets as Kenneth Rexroth, Kenneth Patchen and Michael Grieg.[57] Opposing American and Soviet militarism (to the point that they were unable to support Henry Wallace in 1948), this circle produced left-wing dialogue of a high order, in Macdonald's magazine *Politics* (1944–1949), in *Why? An Anarchist Bulletin* and its successor *Resistance* (1942–1952), and in the somewhat related *Retort* (1942–1947). New York was of course the main center of this group's operations, though some active supporters lived in the San Francisco Bay area and Holley

57. On Goodman and Macdonald, see Richard King, *The Party of Eros: Radical Social Thought and the Realm of Freedom* (Chapel Hill: University of North Carolina Press, 1972), pp. 30–43, the first serious study of this intellectual circle. Rexroth had far more contact with the older anarchist tradition than did most of the others. I once asked Macdonald whether he had heard of Voltairine de Cleyre, and he had not.

Cantine edited and hand-printed *Retort* at upstate Bearsville. To the extent of occasionally reprinting such authors as Voltairine de Cleyre and troubling to review (even if hostilely) Elizabeth Byrne Ferm's Stelton-based book on education, *Resistance* kept older traditions alive. But its mood was really up-to-date. It anticipated the civil rights movement by dramatizing the plight of a black who deliberately invaded a white barber shop in 1949. Staughton Lynd reported on his experiences living at the Macedonia intentional community at Clarksville, Georgia, in 1947, and the ideas of Wilhelm Reich were enthusiastically discussed. The act of saying no to all three sides in the Second World War had effectively recreated an independent American left, however small-scale, which would increasingly gain vigor as Communism proved its irrelevance. In a much-changed climate, *The New York Review of Books* could emerge as its fairly direct and far more influential descendant.

Also especially active in the 1940's were Dorothy Day and her sometime collaborator, Ammon Hennacy. Definitely anarchistic, they nonetheless insisted on retaining a tenuous tie to the Catholic Church. (Hennacy renounced Catholicism shortly before his death in 1970.) The Catholic Worker movement, like the literary anarchism of this period, was Tolstoyan and Gandhian in tone. It engaged in civil disobedience against American militarism alongside other organizations, such as the War Resisters League, which had sprung into existence in this period on the issue of pacifism alone.[58]

There are still other distinct strands of somewhat related beliefs. Southern agrarianism, which partly belongs in this context because of its celebration of rural decentralization, was a major literary event of the 1930's. More clearly tied to anarchism was the rural decentralist Ralph Borsodi, who in 1938 founded a community at Suffern, New York, called The School of Living. From this headquarters, and then from Brookville, Ohio, where it moved in 1944, a long string of publications poured forth: *Homestead Bulletin, The Decentralist, The Interpreter, The Green Revolution,* and finally *A Way Out.*[59] Mildred J. Loomis, its aging guiding spirit in recent years, strove valiantly to come to terms with the new generation in the mid-1960's, even beginning a new community at Heathcote, Mary-

58. See Dorothy Day, *The Long Loneliness* (New York: Harper & Brothers, 1952); Ammon Hennacy, *Autobiography of a Catholic Anarchist* (New York: Catholic Worker Books, 1954); William D. Miller, *Dorothy Day and the Catholic Worker Movement* (New York: Liveright, 1972).

59. See William H. Issel, "Ralph Borsodi and the Agrarian Response to Modern America," *Agricultural History,* XLI (April, 1967), 155–66. Borsodi's major book was *Flight from the City* (New York: Harper & Brothers, 1933).

land. But her perspective, like Borsodi's, remained wedded to the formalistic land-trust concept of the Henry George school of economics. Clearly here was a small radical upthrust of the 1930's which remained too ingrown to affect the larger scene.

The same may be said of the separate flurry of near-anarchist publications, emerging in the 1930's and 1940's, which far more than Borsodi's carried right-wing political tones. Frank Chodorov (whose handsomely printed magazine *Analysis* was established in New York in 1944) and the novelist Louis Bromfield were rural individualists who might refer to Thoreau but only in the context of a defense of private property which could not appeal to many youth of the 1960's.[60] The still different decentralist movement of Ralph Courtney (former chief European correspondent for the *Herald Tribune*), located at Spring Valley, New York, and dedicated to the ideas of Rudolf Steiner, also reached a dead end despite its political liberalism and receptiveness to the occult.

Far more relevant to the new counter-culture was the distinct movement of persons interested in forming intentional communities in America during the 1950's. The last of the communitarian ventures of the early twentieth century (except for Stelton), the socialist colony of Llano, had expired around 1934, a decade after moving from Pearblossom, California, to Leesville, Louisiana. There had been a few attempts to live communally in the 1930's, notably Joseph J. Cohen's Sunrise Community in rural Michigan (he may have taken the name from J. William Lloyd's novels), which fell to pieces in two years. Some twenty-five rural communities were founded by the Catholic Worker Movement in the late 1930's; one of them survives. Student communes also existed in the New York area around 1940. The late 1940's saw a definite revival of interest in this direction, partially sparked by the appearance of B. F. Skinner's *Walden Two* in 1948. As of May, 1953, there were known to be at least eleven intentional communities functioning in the United States, one of which was named after the Skinner novel. Moreover, despite their extreme diversity (some were religious, some not), these eleven banded together into a nationwide Fellowship of Intentional Communities, which began holding annual conferences in 1954 at such locations as Yellow Springs, Ohio, and Pendle Hill, Pennsylvania. By 1959 some seventeen communities, including the standoffish Bruderhof, were represented in the year's review of progress. A multilithed yearbook was published, and an *Autonomous Groups Bulletin* (1948–1960) kept local members informed of what was happening elsewhere. For a shorter time (1949–1956) a more ambitious magazine,

60. Chodorov did publish a magazine, *Fragments*, from 1963 to 1965.

Cooperative Living, served a similar function; it was produced by the independent but congenial Group Farming Research Institute, headed by the wealthy Harvard graduate and Zionist Edward A. Norman. Both the FIC and the GFRI had emerged tardily from the inspiration of Arthur E. Morgan and the hopes for the Resettlement Administration under the New Deal.[61] The GFRI, in particular, kept one foot in the respectable world of academic social science, quoting friendly words from David Riesman and talking in the language of planned experiment, though it remained cool toward Skinner. *Cooperative Living* kept in touch with the Israeli kibbutzim as well as Staughton Lynd's further experiences at Macedonia.

Still, the links between all this and the greatly enlarged commune world of the late 1960's are evident only in a few cases. The FIC put forth a new mimeographed publication, *Intentional Community,* in 1965; its second issue in January, 1966, circulated to 220 persons. At that time there were four new communities to report, founded during the early 1960's, as well as a revival of Llano and a desperate attempt to survive at Kerista, a long-established community of Americans in British Honduras. A man in Madison, Wisconsin, was proposing to found a new anarchist-pacifist community there. The journal thus revealed no inkling that a "commune revolution" was just around the corner. Instead, the tone is one of growing hope that this tiny movement might at least hold its own.[62] By contrast, the San Francisco bi-monthly called *The Modern Utopian* was completely in the orbit of the new counter-culture; it was founded in 1967 and lasted until at least 1971, attempting to serve the same clearing-house function for the communes which these other journals had provided for the older intentional communities.

Other antecedent strands suggest, however, a more continuous underground tradition relevant to the recent counter-culture. In the late 1950's, *Newspaper,* mimeographed in New York by Jack Green, promoted Reichian sexual liberation in a manner as far-out as anything more recent. Pos-

61. See Arthur E. Morgan, *The Small Community* (New York: Harper & Brothers, 1942).

62. A Skinnerian regional magazine, *The Southeastern Walden Pool,* reported that only five students and a bystander professor attended an organizational meeting at Emory University on March 13, 1966, to found yet another Walden Two community. But this tiny group was even then thinking of going to New Mexico. A national convention of Skinner admirers in Michigan during August, 1966, produced eighty-three people, some of whom purchased land in Virginia for the Twin Oaks community, still functioning in 1973 and described in Robert Houriet, *Getting Back Together* (New York: Coward, McCann and Geoghegan, 1971), pp. 282–325. Another link between older and younger radicals, at Bryn Athyn, Vermont, is recounted in Chapter Three below. Lack of continuity is emphasized by Richard Fairfield, editor of *The Modern Utopian,* in his personal account of the mid-1960's in *Communes, U.S.A.: A Personal Tour* (Baltimore: Penguin Books, 1972), pp. 20–38.

sibly more intriguing was the Church of Thelema, active in South Pasadena, California, around 1938, which took its name from Rabelais and preached the commandment "Do as thou wilt."

Outside the narrower realm of intentional communities, the Old and New Left can sometimes blur as one reaches the mid-1960's. A conscious attempt to fuse the generations appeared in Seattle, where high-school students in 1965 began editing *Appeal to Reason* under the apparent inspiration of older radicals who brought forth their own *Seattle Group Bulletin*. The latter expressed the hope that the new generation would embrace anarchism, but blessed them in their broader sense of rebellion, which included extreme hostility to religion, advocacy of full sexual freedom (with definite awareness of the earlier free-thought tradition in America), astrology, and vegetarianism. Though Martin Duberman complained that the New Left generally had no awareness of the history of anarchism, and Paul Goodman appeared more standoffish than sympathetic toward hippies, there were at least a few concrete cases that pointed to a bridging of the two worlds. Murray Bookchin, a New York anarchist theorist of the 1960's, had exerted some kind of influence upon several of the new communal groups.[63] Paul Goodman had an important following for a time on some campuses. A few individuals with a youth orientation publicly referred to their reading of Bakunin and Kropotkin, and it is no accident that in the late 1960's publishers quickly put forth anthologies of classical anarchist thought.[64] What, if anything, all these visible links add up to is, of course, a different and far more complicated question.[65]

A brief résumé of the historical evidence involving religious mysticism can only record the tip of a much larger iceberg. Certain mystical or occult movements have long attracted relatively big audiences. Whereas active anarchist sympathizers in the interwar period may have been only a few thousand, the I Am movement alone received an income of $1,000 a day in 1938 and numbered its followers above 100,000 for a brief period. Still, this contrast is only partially meaningful, for it is a noteworthy fact that

63. Bookchin is discussed at more length in Chapter Three.

64. See Martin B. Duberman, "Anarchism Left and Right," *Partisan Review*, XXXIII (Fall, 1966), 615; Paul Goodman, "The Black Flag of Anarchism," *New York Times Magazine*, July 14, 1968, pp. 10–22; Paul Cowan, letter to the editor, *The New Republic*, CLII (May 1, 1965), 34–37; David Rosenthal, book review in *The Nation*, CCXVII (November 1, 1971), 439–40. On a rather isolated academic level, the anarchist revival registered in such books as Robert Paul Wolff, *In Defense of Anarchism* (New York: Harper & Row, 1970) and April Carter, *Political Theory of Anarchism* (New York: Harper & Row, 1971).

65. But there is surely more continuity here than allowed for by David E. Apter, "The Old Anarchism and the New—Some Comments," *Government and Opposition*, V (Autumn, 1970), 403.

the occult movements with the largest popular appeal were frauds or near-frauds. Mankind United may have had 14,000 followers in California around 1940.[66] Some 27,352 Spiritualists were listed in the religious census of 1936.

By contrast, after its major period of initial growth (1890–1892), Theosophy had only 6,000 followers in 1896, declining to 4,000 in 1900. Several organizational splits occurred in the movement between 1895 and 1909, affecting the total, but in 1925 the Americans loyal to the international organization at Adyar, India, totaled only 7,333.[67] The splinter groups, such as Katherine Tingley's community at Point Loma, usually numbered only in the hundreds. One faction of this kind, the branch of Rosicrucians whom Max Heindel led to Oceanside, California, in 1913, could muster only 62 persons at their 1935 summer school.[68] The well-known Los Angeles mystic Will Levington Comfort mailed his literature regularly to about 1,500 persons at the time of his death in 1932. Another ex-Theosophist, Alice A. Bailey, who began operating the Arcane School of Wisdom in New York, Geneva, and London in the 1920's, had sent out 35,000 pieces of literature by 1958.[69] Biosophy, founded in 1932 by Frederick Kettner, was undoubtedly somewhat larger; like Theosophy, it held weekly lectures in many cities. Meanwhile, Vedantists numbered only 340 in 1906 and had less than doubled by 1936. Buddhist groups, which have continuously existed in America since the late nineteenth century, were far larger, but mainly peopled by Asian immigrants. Zen centers were founded in New York in 1930 and in Los Angeles the next year; by 1969 there were eight of them, and a semi-communal retreat at Tassajara, California, was established in 1967. Sufism, dating from 1910, had established eight American centers by 1930.

The depression and world political situation of the 1930's and 1940's affected movements of this kind, though less directly than on the secular

66. The leader of Mankind United was exposed as having led a luxurious double life outside the movement. The I Am movement was prosecuted for mail fraud. Also much larger are various New Thought groups, Religious Science, and Christian Science, which do not so clearly belong in this accounting.

67. Emmet A. Greenwalt, *The Point Loma Community in California, 1897–1942: A Theosophical Experiment* (Berkeley: University of California Press, 1955), pp. 47, 171; Charles Braden, *These Also Believe* (New York: Macmillan, 1949), p. 241.

68. *Rosicrucian Magazine* (Oceanside, California), XXVII (September, 1935), 386. These Rosicrucians are not to be confused with the group of the same name more recently active in San Jose, whose mail-order policy makes it impossible to guess the number of actual adherents.

69. Will Levington Comfort, *The Yucca Story* ([Los Angeles: by his family], 1934), Foreword, unpaginated; n.a., *Lucis Trust* (New York: by the Trust. 1958), p. [3].

left. A revival of communitarian interest occurred when Mankind United, whose followers believed that wars and earthquakes were controlled by an underground race of Hidden Rulers, established a network of cooperative communities, sealed off from outside contact, in California at the end of the 1930's.[70] This interest continued after the war. Among the intentional communities of the 1950's was the Essenes of Kosmon, a group basing itself upon the occultist philosophy of J. B. Newbrough, first revealed in 1881.[71] Another prominent example, the Krishna Venta movement (or W.K.F.L.), attracted a large resident population outside Los Angeles in the early 1950's, until the leader was exposed as a fraud. Those who know the Southern California area well are aware of a score of ventures of this kind.

While the experience of the Second World War was stimulating anarchists and pacifists into renewed life, it was having a parallel effect on at least one very small group of blacks in Chicago, where Marie Harlowe Pulley decorated her magazine *World Philosophy* with the swastika as an ancient occult symbol, argued eloquently against the dominant drift of American society, and urged her readers to explore the Buddhist and Mohammedan traditions as alternatives. At Tecate, California, near the Mexican border, "Professor" Edmond Bordeaux Szekely issued the *Essene Quarterly* in 1949, inviting groups to come for a season of natural living punctuated by grape-juice fasts. The sudden surge of interest in flying saucers found believers in the occult well prepared. Gabriel Green published *Thy Kingdom Come* in an engagingly frank vein for the Los Angeles Interplanetary Study Groups around 1957.

But if the mystical tradition without doubt claimed a much larger following during these decades than the anarchist, its own overall limits should be kept clearly in mind. A door-to-door religious survey taken in 1959 indicated that even in Southern California only about 10 percent of the population adhered to an interest in the mystical or occult.[72]

Like the anarchists, the long-established mystical movements eventually had to try to come to terms with a new generation of potential believers.

70. Its ideology was derived from Theosophy, but far more Manichaean in tone. See H. T. Dohrman, *California Cult: The Story of Mankind United* (Boston: Beacon Press, 1958).

71. *Cooperative Living*, VII (Winter, 1955–1956), 14. The Essenes were a mystical community in Judea slightly before the time of Christ. For a description of much other literature in the mystical vein in twentieth-century America, see Hal Bridges, *American Mysticism: From William James to Zen* (New York: Harper & Row, 1970), pp. 143–50.

72. Richard R. Mathison, *Faiths, Cults and Sects of America* (Indianapolis: Bobbs-Merrill, 1960), p. 130.

The Self-Realization Fellowship was probably the most successful in bridging the gap; today it is flourishing and some of its congregations are made up almost entirely of the hip, who apparently respond to its emphasis upon practical yoga exercises and glamorous psychic miracles. Theosophy, on the other hand, has steadily withered away, until it may now be not much bigger than the Libertarian Book Club; it is equally caught up in its own past. Vedanta falls somewhere between. It has grown slightly, and at its services long-haired youth are always conspicuously present, though a minority. A much larger share of the young, however, have entered entirely new movements such as the Hare Krishna, founded in 1965 by an ex-businessman who came directly from India, or the Maharishi's Student International Meditation Society, estimated to have 12,000 followers in 1968.

The question of continuity needs to be approached on a much deeper level than is possible in an initial factual probe. But the evidence here presented suggests a series of wavelike rises and falls. During the course of these ups and downs, a basic philosophy or point of view remains recognizably constant, though the members of new generations attracted to the same ideas often have rather little personal contact with the survivors of similar movements in the past. Continuity exists, but it is of a tantalizingly loose kind. The entire last chapter of this book will seek to define the elements of continuity and change more closely.

One other major factual question begs for discussion at this preliminary stage. How are anarchism and mysticism related to each other? Is it a mere fluke that in Lloyd's novels Forrest Westwood is identified with both? In the counter-culture of the 1960's the two tendencies appeared in close proximity, almost as if they were alternative directions in the new life style: the outer versus the inner, the left wing versus the apolitical, the unstructured versus the structured. One wonders whether they have really shared this degree of parallelism over a long period of time.

The first question to ask is how their spokesmen have perceived their own mutual relationship. Anarchists and communitarian socialists of the turn of the century reveal a surprising, though uneven, amount of concern for the spiritual and the occult. One would expect, naturally, to find them all militant atheists, and indeed a great number were. But at Home, the anarchist colony in Washington state, Theosophy and spiritualism gained widespread, persistent attention. Classes in Asian philosophy and hatha-yoga were even conducted there.[73] James G. Morton, a leading figure in the

73. David Fisher, "Home Colony: An American Experiment in Anarchism"

colony, lectured in Tacoma on the unity of purpose between Theosophy and anarchism. If one widens the net to include socialist communities of the 1890's, the result is the same. A prominent figure in the Equality colony near Seattle was a spiritualist who even then talked of space travel. Cyrus Willard, who played a leading role in the Brotherhood colony, became and remained a Theosophist. Max Wardall, also at Brotherhood, spent much of his later life at Katherine Tingley's Point Loma Theosophical community near San Diego. A leading member of Freeland, still another socialist community in the state of Washington, finally departed for Halcyon Colony, a Theosophical settlement at Oceano, California. At Freeland it is also reported that around 1902–1903 a definite faction of the membership turned to spiritualism, receiving derision from the others for having done so. A few people lived in both worlds. The single-taxer Bolton Hall turns out to have been a friend of both Emma Goldman and Ralph Waldo Trine, dedicating a book to him in which he quoted from the Bhagavad Gita. In Los Angeles a "liberal" figure of the Progressive Era, the Reverend Benjamin Fay Mills, casually divided his time between the social gospel and New Thought.[74]

Surveying the radical literature of the day, one encounters surprisingly frequent references to New Thought, Theosophy, and similar topics in such anarchist periodicals as *Firebrand, Free Society,* and *Lucifer.* Though often hostile or contemptuous, their mere presence arouses interest, for they seem to confirm the mystical or occult as somehow a "natural" rival for the attention of their audiences.[75] Emma Goldman thought it was worth devoting

---

(M. Litt. thesis, University of Edinburgh, 1971), p. 75; *The Demonstrator,* October 12, 1904, p. 4. Fisher remarks that there had been traces of spiritualism at Modern Times, the anarchist colony of the 1850's. In his forthcoming book on intentional communities in western Washington, Charles Pierce LeWarne provides still more abundant evidence of this kind.

74. Bolton Hall, *Life, Love and Peace* (New York: The Arcadia Press, 1909), pp. 5, 167, 169; Carey McWilliams, *Southern California Country* (New York: Duell, Sloan, and Pearce, 1947), p. 257. Similar connections between Theosophy and the Bellamy socialist movement of 1890–1892 were emphasized by Arthur E. Morgan, *Edward Bellamy* (New York: Columbia University Press, 1944), pp. 29–33, though a more meticulous analysis of local Bellamy clubs by Everett W. MacNair, *Edward Bellamy and the Nationalist Movement, 1889 to 1894* (Milwaukee: The Fitzgerald Co., 1957), pp. 329–30, concluded that Morgan had exaggerated the overlap.

75. The anarchist C. L. James said: "In a very different, and, I admit, highly questionable manner, the followers of Swedenborg have brought transcendental individualism to the masses. However ill we may think of their dogmas, their influence is not to be despised. They have insured, for one thing, a wide diffusion of tendencies ripe for Anarchistic use. Scratch a Spiritualist, and you will find an Anarchist." *Origin of Anarchism* (Chicago: A. Isaak, 1902), p. 15. Several decades later a New York anarchist magazine found it necessary to confront the same issue, though less optimistically: "That this personal mystical experience can co-exist with non-authoritarian concepts we recognize. But this mystical idea is too far removed

half a page of *Mother Earth* to a scornful account of Krishnamurti's first arrival in America as the announced Theosophical avatar.[76]

At the Stelton anarchist colony, interest in the mystical or occult was much less noticeable than at Home, perhaps because the Russian Revolution had intervened. But Nathan Marer, son-in-law of the leading figure Harry Kelly, had been both a Theosophist and a Rosicrucian before moving there, and Alexis Ferm, who figures prominently in the next chapter, had also once been a Theosophist and was invited to go to Point Loma, although he later went out of his way to denounce occultism.[77] Carl Zigrosser, likewise active in the anarchist Ferrer movement, became engrossed in Hindu thought after meeting Ananda Coomaraswamy at the Sunwise Turn Bookshop in New York, later going on to develop a pronounced interest in Gurdjieff and Ouspensky.[78] More recently, the prominent anarchist spokesman Ammon Hennacy was married to a woman in the I Am movement.

When one pushes in the other direction, from mysticism toward anarchism or socialism, the results are less impressive. Yet Annie Besant, the leading English Theosophist, had been an atheistic free thinker before her conversion to the occult, and she always retained a strong commitment to the ideal of social brotherhood. Theosophical pronouncements of the 1890's often have a definite utopian ring to them. The idea of service to

---

from the common conception of God for the vast majority of us to understand. The confusion that results is very harmful." *Resistance,* VII (July-August, 1948), 15.

76. *Mother Earth,* VIII (September, 1913), 196–97. It is likely that interest in the occult declined at such places as Home as a result of an upsurge of political involvement after 1910. E.g., see *The Agitator,* August 15, 1912, p. 1. Another suggestion, highly interesting in view of the evidence to be presented in Chapter Four, is that at Home women were much more prone than men to reveal these interests. "I have for years observed that when the subject of a meeting was either Spiritualism or mysticism, or some other chimerical illusion the hall was always crammed to the doors by women." Jay Fox in *The Demonstrator,* September 5, 1906, p. 6.

77. Alexis C. Ferm, *The Problem of Education* (Stelton, New Jersey: Modern School Association, ca. 1935), p. 17; Ferm to Leonard Abbott, September 1, 1949, Abbott papers, in possession of William Morris Abbott, New York; Ferm to the author, September 11, 1970.

78. Carl Zigrosser, *My Own Shall Come to Me* ([Philadelphia: by the author], 1971), pp. 158–70, 298, 304, 332. Leonard Abbott, J. William Lloyd's friend and another founder of the Ferrer movement, said "I . . . have only known two or three theosophists in my entire life." Yet eventually two people tried to convert him to Theosophy within a single year. Abbott to Nell T. Craig, April 17, 1951, March 13, 1952, and to Stella Smith, October 8, 1951, Abbott Papers. To Mrs. Smith he wrote: "I am really *not* a mystic; I do not pray; but the mystical sense is so universal that I suppose there must be something in it. My nearest approach to mysticism is a sense of harmony with nature—at times ecstatic—in some experience of great beauty. I say 'harmony with nature,' but I realize that nature can be very cruel and absolutely indifferent to our aspirations. . . . I have always liked Ralph Waldo Emerson, but I think that he is much too optimistic."

mankind becomes translated into the concept of the advanced spiritual leader who "may guide the civilizations and races of men in their evolution, enabling them to attain far higher ground than would otherwise be the case."[79] Even more significantly, the Marxist anticipation of a millennium after the overthrow of capitalism is paralleled by the idea of a New Age to arrive for all mankind, brought about by a mixture of willful effort and inbuilt astrological determinism.[80] "The call from the Cosmic Heart is vibrating throughout the earth," announced a Los Angeles teacher of these beliefs in 1918; "the New Age is here, and the Spiritual vibrations are refreshing the earth and all living things."[81] The founder of the more austere Vedanta movement, Swami Vivekananda, was passionately dedicated to social amelioration in the context of rising Indian nationalism, though later swamis struck a more consistently otherworldly note. Later on, the Los Angeles mystic Will Levington Comfort spoke of the Great Depression in the same tones as would befit a militant secular radical—seeing it as a welcome

79. Theosophical Society, American Section, *A Primer of Theosophy* (Chicago: by the Society, 1909), p. 8. The Hindu belief in the cosmic evolution of souls could mesh easily with the evolutionary "stage" theory present in much nineteenth-century European social thought. E.g., see William Q. Judge, *The Ocean of Theosophy* (2nd ed.; New York and London: The Aryan Press, 1893), p. 84.

80. On the other hand, William Dudley Pelley joined occult belief with fascism in the 1930's, and there were fascist undertones in the I Am movement. See William Dudley Pelley, "Seven Minutes in Eternity: The Amazing Experience That Made Me Over," *American Magazine,* CVII (March, 1929), 7–9, 139–44; Gerald B. Bryan, *Psychic Dictatorship in America* (Burbank, California: The New Era Press, 1940), especially pp. 26–27. Rosicrucians of the same decade apparently did not believe that a black person could be reincarnated as a white. *Rosicrucian Magazine,* XXVI (November, 1934), 517, and XXVII (August, 1935), 371. However, perusal of much literature of this kind, and years of contact with such people in Southern California when I was a child, persuade me that these are exceptions even in the context of the 1930's. Most followers of the mystical and occult have been politically liberal, sometimes even radical in a left-wing sense, to the extent that they have paid attention to politics at all. Often they would vote in turn for Roosevelt and for Eisenhower, while claiming all the while to be privy to "hidden" knowledge which made all such politicians superficial by comparison. As illustrations of a distinctly liberal trend in these circles, see Horatio W. Dresser, *A History of the New Thought Movement* (New York: T. Y. Crowell, 1919), pp. 309–11; *Democracy's Guarantee Is America's Liberty* (Rosicrucian pamphlet, n.p., n.d.); *Thy Kingdom Come* (Los Angeles), June, 1957, pp. 3, 6; Will Levington Comfort, *Letters: The Mystic Road* (Los Angeles: Comfort Book Room, 1921), II, 119; Dane Rudhyar, *Modern Man's Conflicts* ([New York:] Philosophical Library, 1948), p. 48; and note this trend in Sister Daya's thinking, Chapter Four. A Texas occultist group of the 1950's went out of its way to counter anti-Communist hysteria, urged that even one's apparent enemies be loved, and pleaded against racial discrimination. *The Return of Christ to Earth* (Corpus Christi, Texas: The Essene Press, n.d.), pp. [1–3]. A clear distinction must be made between mystical and occult groups and Christian Fundamentalist groups from this important point of view.

81. Elizabeth Delvine King, *The Higher Metaphysics* (Los Angeles: J. F. Rowny Press, 1918), p. 56.

and necessary step toward the dissolution of the old order and the arrival of the New Age.[82] In the 1940's the Vedantist Christopher Isherwood lavished praise upon "those daring and dissatisfied spirits who strike out, no matter why, into the dangerous no-man's-land beyond the laws and the social conventions, to find the inner truth of our human relationships and to restate it in action." With the pacifists of the Second World War in mind, he termed such an ideal personality type "the anarchist-objector."[83] Moreover, ever since 1947 the unofficially Theosophist weekly *MANAS* (Los Angeles) has achieved a wide underground reputation for its thoughtful coverage of world affairs and social issues, even though its position emphasizes the need for thought transformation.

Anarchism, communitarian socialism, and Asian mysticism had all appeared more or less simultaneously in early nineteenth-century Europe and America. All of them comprised varieties of a backward-looking (or "timeless," rather than progressive) response to the spectacle of industrialism.[84] While the mainstream of socialism and Communism would eventually join the mainstream of capitalism in accepting the fruits of large-scale organization, the followers of these other philosophies remained on the outside, rejecting the world they found around them. Bakunin and Fourier promoted drastic alternatives to the centralized state; in her own way, Madame Blavatsky offered a beguiling form of withdrawal from the practical claims of the here and now. In the America of the 1840's, phrenology and spiritualism vied with utopian socialist experiment as expressions of the impulse toward the "far-out." And at Concord lived Thoreau, mystic and near-anarchist, in both these twin roles the most highly respected prophet of the recent counter-culture.

82. "Do you realize that there would be no power to levitate a new social order if it were not for the intolerable drag and settle of the old? Do you not see that a return to prosperity on the old terms is a return to coma, our most serious threatened distraction, the instant thinner of ranks?" Comfort, *The Yucca Story,* unpaginated.

83. Introduction to Holley Cantine and Dachine Rainer, eds., *Prison Etiquette: The Convict's Compendium of Useful Information* (Bearsville, New York: Retort Press, 1950). Isherwood impulsively confirmed this sympathy for anarchism when I spoke with him in 1971, though immediately recalling how apparently inconsistent it was with his belief in obedience to a Vedanta guru.

84. In *The Unfinished Revolution* (New York: Vintage Books, 1960), Adam B. Ulam has emphasized the ambivalent pull of early Marxist thought in this same direction. Judith Shklar, *After Utopia: The Decline of Political Faith* (Princeton, New Jersey: Princeton University Press, 1957), pp. 145–46, links anarchism and mysticism in this context. Eunice Minette Schuster, *Native American Anarchism* (Northampton, Massachusetts: Smith College, 1931), pp. 13–39, far too glibly assumes that the two traditions are really the same.

Perhaps especially in the late nineteenth century, anarchism, socialism, and Asian mysticism shared a sense of revolt against "orthodoxy," social and political in the first case, Christian in the second, yet to an important degree interfused. Thus Horatio W. Dresser, the prominent New Thought leader, could declare in two adjacent sentences: "The old theology held men in bondage. Conventional society was in many respects an obstacle."[85] Anarchists and mystics both made use of the term "liberation." They did not give it entirely the same meaning. Yet at least one secular anarchist magazine could later quote Krishnamurti at length on the idea of individual freedom with no evident embarrassment.[86] Again, anarchists might quarrel only with the words "divine" and "spiritual" in Dresser's formulation: "Man is by divine purpose, by birth, and his true human inheritance, free. He must come forth and 'claim his freedom,' the true freedom of his inner or spiritual nature."[87]

Against this evidence of a parallelism between them, the fact remains that most anarchists and nearly all religious mystics would today hotly deny that they share anything significant in common with their opposite numbers. The very fact that I have joined the two traditions in this book will seem rather unnatural and distasteful to adherents of both persuasions. These sentiments, which I detected in the course of my interviews with older people, naturally cannot be ignored. Horatio Dresser also captured this sense of their dissonance when he said that New Thought and socialism had rather little in common because socialists wished to change the environment, while New Thoughtists wanted instead to change the constitution of man.[88]

The tone of debate on this issue which could sometimes occur in radical circles several decades ago is revealed in an editorial J. William Lloyd wrote for his magazine *The Free Comrade:*

> I am sorry when I see colonies founded on "spirit direction." Not denying the existence of spirits, mind you, nor the reality of their sometime communication with mortals. Only intimating that . . . such vaporish, fantastic folk are rather poor company for practical, work-a-day, muscle-and-bone mortals. Be proud of your bodies while you have them, brother, and get the good out of them, and don't contemplate your navels over-much while weeds grow in the garden.

85. Dresser, *op. cit.,* p. 161; cf. also p. 312.
86. *Road to Freedom* (New York), VI (September, 1930), 3.
87. Dresser, *op. cit.,* p. 161.
88. *Ibid.,* pp. 308–09.

Found your colonies on Nature, hard work and common sense and bid
the next world bide its time.[89]

Many youthful radicals of the 1960's still would warm to plain-sounding
words like these, but others in the counter-culture would just as emphatically deny their validity, as they sought for a synthesis.

Views of the relationship between anarchism and mysticism will partly
depend upon the width of one's vision in time and space. In medieval
Europe and in tribal society the categories of sacred and secular, "internal"
and "external" tended to merge. Within our own civilization, they are
sharply separate. In America it is assumed to make all the difference
whether one spends one's energy affecting outer existence through social
action or affecting the inner through meditation and self-mastery. The recent counter-culture has often tried, with only halting success, to return to
something more like the pre-modern merger of these sensibilities.

The concrete evidence has so far shown that the two traditions have
more connection than one might initially think. Along with several other
major perspectives, among them socialism, Communism, Freudianism, and
Christian Fundamentalism, they have long competed against each other for
the allegiance of "seeking" men and women. More strongly than most of
these others, they have operated to turn people aside from the main flow
of modern life. This makes them especially interesting in the context of the
study of cultural innovation, and suggests that they jointly possess a
peculiar relevance to the impulse toward community formation.

But it will become clear during the course of this study that anarchism
and mysticism lead to vastly different results when they become sociologically visible in a communitarian setting. Whatever their relationship on the
plane of ideas, they impel those who come under their influence into
markedly dissimilar patterns of living. After this contrast has been developed in the next four chapters, we shall return to the broader dimensions
of this subject in the final one, when it will be easier to see the kind of
more ultimate comment the two traditions furnish on each other.

But, meanwhile, what more generally are mysticism and anarchism examples of? Up to this point, many large issues of historical conceptualiza-
tion have been left hanging. What is it to be a "radical" in more than an
immediately political sense? Can one identify a broad tradition of cultural
radicalism which embraces these two subtraditions among others? If so,

89. *The Free Comrade*, N.S., III (February, 1902), 34. Yet *ibid.*, III (June, 1902),
8, he urged mixing skepticism and faith in equal parts in one's life.

how does it relate both to political radicalism and to the pressures and strains of life in modern industrial society?

Previous definitions of radicalism have suffered for one of two reasons. Either they have dwelt exclusively upon a psychological syndrome alleged to characterize the radical mind, entirely avoiding the specific content of radical beliefs, or they have gone to the opposite extreme of dealing solely with radical manifestoes, platforms, and ideologies in a literal fashion. Both these styles of definition serve polemical purposes. From Joel Rinaldo to Eric Hoffer and Nathan Adler, amateur and professional psychologists have self-confidently described the mentality of the "true believer," primarily in such a way as to lend comfort to a conservative point of view.[90] On the other hand, writers friendly to a radical persuasion have carefully adopted the most narrowly rationalistic model of the human mind, as a way of insisting that the ideas be treated with serious respect. Both these approaches avoid the many points of contact between feeling and reason.

Very early on, the anarchist Victor Yarros combatted the already prevalent psychological attack on radicalism by asserting that "radicalism is not a matter of temper or even of method. There are Conservatives, or Reactionaries, whose temper and methods are offensive and dangerous. On the other hand, there are Radicals who personify sweet reasonableness itself in disposition and temper. Radicalism is a matter of opinion, of doctrine, of outlook, philosophy, Weltanschauung."[91]

However salutary this rebuttal may be, it too leaves something out. If "temper" is defined as mere quarrelsomeness of daily disposition, then Yarros is certainly right. But at another level "temper" merges with "outlook," a word Yarros uses approvingly. And an "outlook" is something deeper and broader than can be contained in formal rhetorical platforms. An adequate definition of radicalism must find a place both for the content of specific ideas and for a more general state of mind that underlies their expression. I am convinced that there is a radical "outlook" in which certain key substantive areas of thought, often brought into play by the concrete problems facing the larger society at a given moment, are magnified by the mind in accord with rather special psychological rules. Radicalism is the abandonment of "common sense," the accepted wisdom of the established social order, but only in relation to a series of major issues

90. Joel Rinaldo, *Psychoanalysis of the Reformer* (New York: Lee Publishing Co., 1923); Eric Hoffer, *The True Believer* (New York: Harper & Brothers, 1951); Nathan Adler, "The Antinomian Personality: The Hippie Character Type," *Psychiatry*, XXXI (November, 1968), 325–38.

91. Victor S. Yarros, "Contemporary American Radicalism," *International Journal of Ethics*, XXXI (1921), 353–54.

which are likely to press hard upon individuals who take great pains to "think for themselves."

This conjunction of feeling and content may be illustrated in an attempt to define cultural radicalism, the focus of the present book. But first cultural radicalism must be distinguished from political radicalism and something said about how each relates to American history. The hallmark of political radicalism is that it engages directly in the immediate struggle for power, relegating all other considerations to a distinctly secondary role, or, at its most extreme, insisting they be abandoned entirely. In particular, it shuns any call to form secessionist communities, seeing in them an unwelcome diversion of energy. Cultural radicalism, on the other hand, is usually related to a communitarian impulse. True, one can easily think of lonely exceptions like Thoreau, and the history of bohemian movements reveals strong tendencies toward a goal of individual privacy. (I shall take account of this seeming paradox at a later point.) But from the days of the Anabaptists down to the present, cultural radicals have recurrently been moved to break off from the ordinary flow of life around them and collectively share in a new existence arranged according to a deliberate ("intentional") pattern. The self-directed living of life rather than the contest for power is the primary aim of cultural radicals. It is true that they dislike orthodox authority and that they have often been caught up in a practical struggle for survival when faced with the hostility of their neighbors or the state. But their main intention has been to go off, sometimes as individuals but more commonly in groups, to practice a pattern of existence which is their own creation.

Until the 1960's, cultural radicalism had generally been paid little serious attention by American historians, even those who were most interested in dealing with the radical tradition.[92] Radical history was believed to center in socialism, Communism, and the labor movement. Thus, for many academics and older radicals, as well as for the great mass of Americans, the recent "counter-culture" came as an alien shock. Now that it has occurred, one can see that important dimensions of radical consciousness had been bypassed in the former approach to the subject. To be sure, some enthusiasts of the new cultural wave, such as Charles Reich, muddied the waters with their own exaggerated claims. But the events of the past decade genuinely reminded us of aspects of the radical experience which have lacked an adequate accounting.

In the first place, cultural radicalism, as it is here being defined, has

92. Arthur Eugene Bestor, Jr., *Backwoods Utopias* (Philadelphia: University of Pennsylvania Press, 1950), is one of the few outstanding works of an older vintage.

a history which stretches back over a very long period of time. The link between Thoreau and recent anarchists and mystics, between the founders of intentional communities in the nineteenth century and our own, dwarfs the entire Communist movement in America. This is true even though the counter-cultural tradition has many ambiguities of its own, which this book is attempting to explore. In chronological terms, one realizes that the Communist party had an effective life span of only thirty-seven years (1919–1956); it seems centrally important only if one focuses on the 1930's and 1940's rather than upon 1840, 1915, or 1970. Probably it is best regarded as an aberrant deflection, feeding divisively upon the call to support the Soviet Union as an established power. Nor does the history of the socialist movement offer such great continuity, when it is looked at closely. In 1915, socialism formally dominated the radical stage. But in effective terms, several years before that date it had already begun to compromise its previously somewhat radical impulse, turning decisively in the direction of moderation. (Freeman Worth, in Lloyd's novel, embodied this tendency.) Losing its distinctiveness, socialism no longer remained an important carrier of radical ideas.

The locus of American radicalism has often alternatively been placed within certain large "home-grown" labor organizations and "share-the-wealth" movements. But the Industrial Workers of the World, the Townsend and Coughlin and Huey Long crusades, despite their militance and their great numerical strength for brief periods, even more clearly lacked the ultimate staying power of such themes as anarchism, decentralization, the search for an ideal community, and contemplative withdrawal from the world.

Genuine proletarian radicalism, such as the I.W.W. represented, may have been possible only during a brief, transitory phase in the history of industrialization. Though created by men who felt themselves to be "outsiders," the I.W.W. was not unlike orthodox socialism in the way that it dreamed of a fairer distribution of the existing economic pie. The Wobbly leader Bill Haywood pictured the future society as containing "a wonderful dining room where you will enjoy the best food that can be purchased; your digestion will be aided by sweet music which will be wafted to your ears by an unexcelled orchestra. There will be a gymnasium and a great swimming pool and private bathrooms of marble. . . . The workrooms will be superior to any conceived. Your work chairs will be morris chairs, so that when you become fatigued you may relax in comfort."[93] The working-

93. "Haywood's Battle in Paterson," *Literary Digest,* XLVI (May 10, 1913), 1043–44.

class imagination, even at its most extreme, could prove disappointingly commonplace, both in its pursuit of affluent symbols of status and in its acceptance of "fatigue" as a normal fact of life. Huey Long's slogan, "Every Man a King," conveys the same oddly conventional flavor. It can indeed be radical to work politically for a redistribution of wealth, for such a campaign directly challenges the centers of social and economic power in the society, but this kind of radicalism offers no sense of a profound alternative to existing styles of living or patterns of human relationship. Perhaps for this very reason the radical movements of the 1930's could become co-opted with so much ease by the political center. Like the very different Ku Klux Klan, these movements were tied to segments of the society which have gradually been moving upward into the mainstream.[94]

By contrast, another radical tradition which is defined as centering in such impulses as anarchism, mysticism, and the founding of intentional communities shows every sign of greater staying power, despite a much smaller initial numerical base. Far more than its own followers would like to admit, this kind of radicalism has always been middle-class, indeed elitist. But, in an increasingly affluent society, this is actually the most dependable social basis for any long-term radical movement. (Blue-collar workers, by comparison, are a declining force.) Equally important, such cultural radicalism has always offered a more sharp-edged alternative to majoritarian assumptions about the nature of the good life. Radicals who grow up with certain worldly or intellectual advantages at least do not construct utopias that look like the men's room of the Palace Hotel, whatever their own blinders may sometimes be.

Of course there is a point beyond which it becomes absurd to argue about who is "really" more radical than someone else.[95] My attempt in

94. This may be the real significance of the high vote for George Wallace in the 1972 primaries. Radicalism that is populistic in its appeal to out-groups may flourish all the more intensely, even gaining semi-respectability, as affluence conveys increasing numbers from the out-groups closer to the social center, while events rekindle their prejudices.

95. Yet it is necessary to go this far in defending the importance of cultural radicalism, if only because so many liberals, who are deeply committed to a life of constant political engagement, scorn all forms of privatism as "escapism." (Thus, in Merton's terminology, the Stelton anarchists moved from rebellion to retreatism, while Vedanta illustrates both retreatism and ritualism. Robert Merton, "Social Structure and Anomie," *American Sociological Review*, III [October, 1938], 676.) Politicization naturally affects the liberal's perception of the various forms of radicalism. Cultural radicalism, when blatantly visible on the streets, may even seem so threatening to one's own norms that the impulse is rapidly to avert one's eyes from it, instead paying conscious heed to the reassuringly rational universe of political activity (which oddly enough can include violent demonstrations). For these reasons, despite the spectacular quality of the recent counter-culture, there remains a

this book is to do nothing more than rectify a major imbalance. Other definitions of American radicalism could easily be constructed which would have the rural poor, urban socialists, or right-wing racists as their central focus. But the recent counter-culture, with its many echoes from the mid-nineteenth-century radical style, suggests that it may be fitting to reassess what were once firm assumptions about the relative importance of various kinds of radical groups in the United States. With a new emphasis, a somewhat unusual cast of characters comes into view. To be sure, their ideas are not as unfamiliar as they might have seemed a few years ago, but that is very much to the point.

In America over the long run, what I am calling cultural radicalism has involved itself with a wide range of themes, some of them often assumed to be mutually incompatible: opposition to established agencies of social authority, such as governments and churches; the ideal of uncompromising social brotherhood; economic decentralization and self-sufficiency; inner self-development and the search for mental clarity; the pursuit of a guru or other enlightened leader; religious free thought; mysticism and spiritualism; the quest for individual or collective states of ecstasy; pacifism; racial and sexual equality; abolition or modification of the nuclear family; belief in a simpler, more natural way of life, for instance in matters of clothing and diet; and extreme progressivism in education.[96]

Must we be left with nothing more than this bewildering variety of substantive concerns in our attempt to define cultural radicalism? One is struck by a number of apparent internal contradictions in this list of themes, just as one had puzzled over the incongruity of the portraits hanging in J. William Lloyd's study. What can one make of a list that comprehends both anarchism and communitarian socialism, atheism and mysticism, pacifism and theoretical willingness to engage in violence, the search for clarity and for ecstasy?

Thinking further, one realizes that these are not just incongruous opposites. Rather, they represent extreme stands of one kind or another taken

---

powerful tendency among liberal academics to refuse to take cultural radicalism seriously.

96. To be sure, the term "cultural radicalism" can also conjure up quite a different image, of those people interested in living at the cutting edge of advanced technological innovation, turning themselves into futuristic characters from science fiction. The thinking of Buckminster Fuller has some of these implications, so it is not entirely alien to the spirit of the recent counter-culture. But as a rule this kind of interest is hard to distinguish from the American cultural mainstream, with its pursuit of gadgetry and speed; it is a kind of extended fantasy of these dominant drives. By contrast, the cultural radicalism which is the subject of this book concerns itself with patterns of belief and social arrangements which go against the generally accepted grain; in this sense it more truly deserves to be called radical.

upon certain fundamental issues or areas of human life and thought: individualism and community, coherence in the universe, the sanctity of living persons, the fullest realization of individual consciousness. Psychoanalytic theory has prepared us to look behind such seeming opposites for unitary forms of emotional engagement which lie underneath. And here, to a greater degree perhaps than in other respects, the teaching of Freud coincides with what men have generally learned about themselves during the course of the twentieth century.

Examining my initial list of recurrent themes in American cultural radicalism, I see no fewer than nine important areas of intellectual and emotional engagement within which radicals may take strong substantive stands of varying kinds, some of them indeed glaringly opposite:

God (universal coherence)
authority
violence (sanctity of life)
the individual and the community (intensification and loss of self)
sex
maximization of consciousness (clarity/ecstasy)
possessions and fixity of abode
bodily and intellectual intake of substances and ideas
optimism/desperation

This revised formulation certainly claims to possess no finality; it is meant to be exploratory. My aim in constructing it has been to go beyond particular radical programs and platforms, but without losing sight of them completely, so as to reduce these themes to a logical core. In addition, I have taken the liberty of adding two categories, those at the end, which are suggested not so much by the recurrent issues themselves as by a more general apprehension of the style of radical thought.

Some of these areas of radical engagement are very nearly self-explanatory. Others may seem less obvious. Not all of them have formed the basis for openly proclaimed intellectual positions, either of indulgence or denial, but all, I would argue, have figured prominently in the world view of radicals seeking a new way of life.[97] In some cases, programs included

97. Some may wonder why attitudes toward legality or "staying within the law" are not included in this list. But, except as radicals view law as an instance of coercive authority, this is not a matter in which their own feelings have usually been strongly engaged. Rather, it is the moderate or liberal, viewing radical actions from the outside, who tends to become highly involved with the issue in this form. To be sure, the cause of civil liberties, essentially liberal rather than radical, has often been invoked by radicals, but I think that its use has mainly been strategic.

in my first informal tally of the issues may be seen to relate to more than one area of concern in this restatement of them. Thus the plea for economic decentralization appears to combine elements of resistance to authority, desire for intimate community, and the wish to be rid of excessive possessions. The concept of a "natural" or primitive way of life similarly links strong views about sex, possessions, and bodily intake. Educational progressivism may be seen as a tool for raising the consciousness of the new generation in every one of these respects.

One of these areas of radical engagement, which I have termed "bodily and intellectual intake of substances and ideas," is unusual enough to demand immediate explanation. The bafflingly intense manner in which questions of diet have been argued for many decades among anarchists, mystics, and many socialists begs for illumination in some larger context. At the same time, radical statements reveal the continual tone of high seriousness which surrounds the act of personally accepting or rejecting intellectual systems and philosophies. The parallelism here seems quite suggestive. In an important sense, ideas are "imbided" (or vehemently rejected) like foods. In both realms, the radical may be the one who pauses self-consciously before choosing either to embrace or to stand apart from a specific body of thought or of nutriment. The act of acceptance is made into a major occasion. In each of these forms of nourishment, "impurity" is a constantly feared enemy.[98] Moreover, from such a perspective the drug culture of the last decade may finally be seen as something more than just an inexplicable contemporary oddity.

"Free expression" generally means freedom to spread definite ideas, or else it is idealized in connection with the temporary period in one's life when one is defined as a "seeker," preliminary to a conversion experience. E.g., see Martin, *op. cit.,* p. 205. Again, the realm of work presents an instance where mainstream attitudes have been extreme and those of radicals rather moderate by contrast; Ezra's community in Chapter Five is exceptional in this respect.

98. "Where a Personality takes in alien experience which it cannot assimilate into its own spiritual substance, such experience becomes an impurity to it; 'purity' in reference to Personality meaning the absence of all elements alien, heterogeneous and disharmonious to the Personality." Unidentified clipping from Dane Rudhyar's magazine *Hamsa* (Los Angeles), ca. 1933. Questions of medicine and physical health form a closely connected area of concern, for a similar reason. "No monopoly in theology, no monopoly in medicine," wrote the anarchist Benjamin Tucker. "The individual may decide for himself not only what to do to get well, but what to do to keep well. No external power must dictate to him what he must and must not eat, drink, wear, or do." Benjamin Tucker, *State Socialism and Anarchism: How Far They Agree, and Wherein They Differ* (Alpine, Michigan: Charles W. Berman, n.d.), pp. [9–10]. This sentiment, directed more exclusively at the area of medicine, of course played a major role in the Christian Science movement. On this general parallelism, see also Herman Melville, *Pierre* (New York: New American Library, 1964), pp. 338–40.

The meaning and relevance of each of the areas of radical engagement which I have identified should become clear if we pause briefly to measure each of our chosen movements, anarchism and mysticism, against them. Mystics and anarchists commit themselves strongly in nearly all of these areas, though often with the degree of internal vacillation between opposites that one might expect.

Anarchists either fervently deny God or, more rarely, embrace mystical philosophy themselves; in either event, they join with Theosophists and Vedantists in taking an extreme position which lies far outside the casual American mainstream.

The second area, authority, is central to anarchist teaching. It is rejected absolutely whenever coercive. But anarchists do not warn against the voluntary embrace of authority, such as Forrest Westwood's in Lloyd's novel, and indeed are likely to emphasize the near-saintly role of such figures as Bakunin and Kropotkin.[99] Meanwhile, Vedantists and other mystical groups pointedly deny the institutionalized authority of all the established churches, while allowing themselves to be swept up into the charismatic authority of the guru, in a style equally strange to most Americans.

As regards violence and its opposite, belief in the sanctity of life, anarchists have taken conflicting positions while seeing this as one of the most urgent questions for internal debate and personal resolution. They have been both assassinators and pacifists, but never routine in their response to the subject. Religious mystics have generally shared the pacifism of many anarchists, sometimes going beyond it to practice *ahimsa* (harmlessness) toward all forms of animal life.

Both groups have again taken pronounced and unusual positions about sex. Anarchists have defended what used to be called "free love" as part of their refusal to admit to any form of state authority. Though hampered by an undertow of monogamous backsliders in their own midst, they have stood officially against the repression or externally enforced channeling of physical impulses. The followers of an intensely spiritual life, on the other hand, have ever considered sex their peculiar enemy. The history of American communal experiments is dotted with sexual practices which veer eccentrically in the directions both of free indulgence and abstinence. The Vedantist monasteries in twentieth-century America are a prominent case of the latter kind.

99. Closer to home, admiration within the movement for the magnetic figure of Emma Goldman knew few bounds, and the obituaries for the saintly, self-sacrificing Voltairine de Cleyre are the same in tone as those for the Vedantist Sister Daya.

The attempt to maximize consciousness, which can involve either an intense desire to achieve clarity in one's thinking or, on the other hand, the cultivation of states of ecstasy, obviously involves mystics more than it does anarchists. But members of both groups may be observed to regard intellectual "confusion" as a distinct enemy to be overcome; the very act of accepting an ideology marks a desire to reduce reality to a series of simple, clear-cut, all-sufficient propositions. Again, the mystic's traditional hunger for the ecstasy of God contact has at least recently been matched by the quest for it in drugs or sex, often by those who regard themselves as anarchistic in spirit.

The theme of individualism and community appears at first glance to lie closer to the accepted concerns of the American mainstream. Much confusion about radicalism in relation to this issue can be avoided if the idea is retranslated into a concept whose poles are intensification and loss of self. Radicals frequently display an uncommon self-concern in some form. (This is not to deny that all kinds of people in our society are "wrapped up" in themselves. But cultural radicals tend to be highly concerned with the self as an entity detached from customary occupational roles and family relationships, and this gives their self-attention its distinctive quality.) A marked degree of self-involvement, whether in the form of self-love or self-hatred, is common to the effort to "express" oneself, to "purify" the self, or to "lose" it, either in organic community or in the Divine. Variations on this theme recur repeatedly in the context of specific communal environments. It needs to be recognized as a single theme with these seemingly opposite manifestations.[100] (Thus, in Lloyd's utopia, hermits were an accepted element in what was supposed to be a close-knit community; monastic communities embody this same paradox.) The long-standing split between "individual" and "communal" anarchists gains new meaning when seen in these terms, as does the pronounced Vedantist hostility to "the ego" while also encouraging lifelong self-development into sainthood.

Rejection of the clutter of material possessions, and endorsement of the simple life, are shared by anarchists and religious mystics.[101] Renuncia-

100. "From isolation we take refuge in solidarity, from too much society we seek relief in isolation; both solidarity and isolation are, each at the right moment, freedom and help to us. All human life vibrates between these two poles in endless varieties of oscillations." Max Nettlau, "Anarchism: Communist or Individualist? —Both," *Mother Earth*, IX (July, 1914), 172.

101. It is interesting that, so far as I know, no radical movement has ever based itself on the opposite desire—to hoard possessions. The only equivalents are various collectors' societies, sometimes mildly eccentric but never carrying socially radical

tion of attachment to physical things has always been a major concept in mysticism, even if well-to-do Vedantists interpret this in no more than a "spiritual" sense. The related question of fixity of abode may seem to count for less in both traditions, until one reflects upon the meaning of the monastery in the one case and of the "permanent" intentional community in the other. The ambivalences in both traditions on this point (for the one endorses wandering among hoboes and hippies and, vicariously at least, the other accepts a strikingly similar pattern among young *sannyasin* in India)[102] merely heighten the impression that it too is no trivial matter.[103]

As already mentioned, questions of diet recur noticeably in both settings. Partly these are linked to respect for the sanctity of life, but there is also evidence of a restless experimentation going beyond simple vegetarianism. Swami Paramananda's daily choices of food were somehow always finding their way into the pages of the *Message of the East,* and extreme fads of this kind were conspicuous at Stelton. Concerning ideas in this same sense, the pattern in both circles is one of great pride in initial discrimination, a highly serious process of internal wrestling before any are deliberately incorporated, and resolute fidelity to the choice once initially made.[104]

Finally, twentieth-century anarchists and mystics often share a sense of great urgency in viewing the present and future. On the optimistic side, they have looked forward to the imminent arrival of a New Age, whether produced by political revolution or by a drastic change in human consciousness. Meanwhile, the existing state of mankind can easily fill them with dismay.

Substantively, this brief review can do no more than introduce these centrally important themes in the study of cultural radicalism; all of them will be discussed more extensively in the closing chapter of this book. But it should be clear by now both that radical thought contains a diversity of

---

overtones. Perhaps in this case something close to the polar opposite of renunciation has simply been incorporated into the mainstream.

102. The tradition is for the young monk to wander for several years, begging daily for his sustenance as he goes, wearing almost nothing, and spending no more than three nights in any town or village, in order to develop nonattachment to places as well as to possessions. After going through this experience, he settles down near a guru.

103. Is it an accident that Jack Kerouac, author of *On the Road,* ended his life an extreme stationary recluse?

104. Lifelong fidelity to an early commitment was overwhelmingly usual among the anarchists and Vedantists I spoke with or read about, though it had often been preceded by a single earlier commitment to socialism, New Thought, or Theosophy. Of course my sample was doubtless biased in this direction.

focal points and that there are nonetheless recurrent issues in it of a sur-prisingly definite nature.[105]

In these terms, cultural radicalism might then be defined as the display of a strongly held attitude or position concerning any of these concrete areas of engagement. More usually attention fastens upon several of them in combination. One-issue radicals, it is worth briefly noting, constitute a special case. In such realms as food, possessions, extreme desire either to keep moving physically or to stay put, and indeed regarding sex, radicalism sometimes shades over into private monomania or mere "crankishness." Thus the diet or nudist fanatic is an almost standard character in American intentional communities, but he or she is usually remembered as having lived on the margin of the genuine group life. Such persons have lost any interest in a broader conception of liberation for mankind because they have withdrawn so very far into themselves, perhaps as a kind of radical equivalent to severe cases of bureaucratic dehumanization in the main-stream. But this is a side issue.

It is natural to wonder how this definition of cultural radicalism con-nects with the broad phenomenon of cultural change and also with the life histories of individuals who become committed to some form of radicalism. As William James was perhaps the first to observe, such a commitment appears nearly always to result from a definite experience of conversion, in adulthood or adolescence. (An exception must be made for the children of radicals who retain their parents' beliefs.) Radicals are "twice-born" people, in contrast to the great majority, ever since the 1650's in Massa-chusetts, who go through life maintaining the values imbibed during a gradual, more or less routine process of socialization. This sudden jump onto another groove of thinking is what makes radicalism so important from the point of view of cultural innovation. Every extreme social move-ment may be regarded as a mutation, harboring the potential for the sud-den spread of a new culture or subculture.[106] The fact that only one in a thousand such nascent cultures survives in more than atrophied form hardly detracts from their interest, because Christianity and Marxism fur-

105. This approach exposes the flippancy of such statements as James Joll's that anarchist ideas merely "offer something for everybody." "Anarchism—A Living Tradition," *Government and Opposition,* V (Autumn, 1970), 542, 553.

106. Throughout this book I have used such terms as "social movement," "cul-ture," "subculture," "community," and "group" wherever each seemed most appro-priate, without laboring fine distinctions. It may be that the main point of difference among these words, apart from "culture," has only to do with physical size. In the context in which I employ them, they all share the common characteristic of attempted secession from the larger society and existing culture, and therefore this quality of incipient cultural mutation. See also below, p. 373, n. 58.

nish examples of movements which have begun in precisely this way and have gone on to envelop millions of people. Though cultural change may indeed far more often proceed through gradual shifts of focus in existing mainstreams (invoking the fanciful image of a Lamarckian pattern long discredited in biology), the very suddenness of these rarer leaps and jumps in the cultural realm deservedly attracts attention, so that one wants to know about how they occur. Even American historians, long conditioned to expect gradualism and continuity in what they observe, might well profit from a sharper awareness of both sides of this contrast.[107]

Of course there is a curious paradox here. If cultural radicalism—for instance, the founding of intentional communities—has had a long tradition in the United States, from this other perspective it is its continuing promise of novelty which seems so very striking. But both things about it are simply true. The matter seems confusing because the word "new" tends to be used in two different senses. Secession from society may be a perennial tendency, and various forms of the desire for it may jell into historical traditions, linking the early nineteenth century to our own times. But each social movement or would-be culture, as it comes into being, is "new" in the sense that it aspires to differ sharply from the existing culture of the moment. A continuing store of potential anthropological and sociological novelties may thus be harbored in what amount to long-standing intellectual traditions.[108]

On the level of biography, one comes back to the primacy of the conversion experience. The question of an underlying tendency toward such conversion in certain individuals (as against a more purely circumstantial explanation of it as an event in their lives) must be firmly separated from the matter of the convert's state of mind from that time forward. Previously, perhaps, one has been a "seeker," paying unusual heed to the quest for a satisfyingly coherent world view, shopping among various authors and platform speakers for a definite answer.[109] On the other hand,

107. Still another possible major form of cultural change does sometimes happen: widespread sudden change in the mainstream without the catalytic presence of a social movement. England after 1660 and postwar Germany and Japan would seem to be examples.

108. For further discussion of this point in the context of Ezra's New Age community in New Mexico, see below, p. 372, n. 56.

109. E.g., see the discussion of the "seeker" mentality in William R. Catton, Jr., "What Kind of People Does a Religious Cult Attract?" *American Sociological Review*, XXII (October, 1957), 561–66; John Lofland and Rodney Stark, "Becoming a World-Saver: A Theory of Conversion to a Deviant Perspective," *ibid.*, XXX (1965), 862–75; John Lofland, *Doomsday Cult* (Englewood Cliffs, New Jersey: Prentice-Hall, 1966), pp. 31–62. Much more study of "seeking" and of "conversion" is needed, however, and in a greater variety of intellectual settings. For

as will be illustrated by some of the members of Ezra's New Mexico community to be described later, one may be drifting quite unself-consciously, without any prior sense of being possessed by an unusual psychic hunger. But if, for whatever reasons, one becomes strongly convinced of certain "truths," a new logic, a new mode of apprehending the world begins at once to take over one's life. It is at that point that we can begin confidently to talk of a radical "temper" or "outlook" in conjunction with any of these areas of intellectual and emotional engagement.

All this may still seem to harbor the danger of an excessive psychologizing of history. But I would point out that the definition of cultural radicalism which I have presented is deliberately dual in character. It links the phenomenon of "strong" commitment to certain specific, substantive themes, each of which is perfectly amenable to orthodox historical treatment. Indeed, the several areas of engagement which I have listed make firm connections with the subject matter of such academic disciplines as philosophy, political science, sociology, and psychology, as well as history. By joining each of them with the locus of "strong" commitment, my aim is to recognize the extent to which emotion and intellect characteristically merge in creating a total result.

This definition of cultural radicalism does indeed make an important distinction between "strong" and "weak" forms of belief in any of these areas of engagement. More precise equivalents for these terms would admittedly be desirable. Yet the distinction they suggest is real. In the later stage of one's life, after a conversion experience, one is indeed "possessed by" or "obsessed with" certain ideas; these phrases have their equivalents in radical circles, such as "selflessly idealistic," "unswervingly faithful," and "right on!" What must be developed is a more neutral vocabulary for describing these distinct states of consciousness, which again are of little interest apart from the substantive themes to which the mind has become joined in this fashion.

The hallmark of "strong" belief is the attempt to put one's ideas into daily practice. This urge toward demonstration is continually being countered by the force of existing habit patterns in the larger society, leading

---

instance, it would be profitable to explore the ways in which academics sometimes become "converted" to a Freudian, neo-Marxist, or neo-positivist perspective, in order to locate the common elements in all such forms of experience, regardless of the respectability of the views adopted. For a ground-breaking discussion of commitment, focusing not on its origins in the conversion experience but on the requirements for maintaining it over time, see Rosabeth Moss Kanter, *Commitment and Community* (Cambridge, Massachusetts: Harvard University Press, 1972), pp. 61–138. Also highly relevant is Michael Walzer, *The Revolution of the Saints* (New York: Atheneum, 1968), especially pp. 317–20.

to the failure, for instance, of intentional communities and to the general sense of discouragement and compromise evident in the case of J. William Lloyd. Here, in other words, lies the continually shifting battle line between cultural radicalism and the established social order. But the initial impulse actually to lead a new kind of life, rather than simply talk about one, appears again and again.[110] Both affirmatively and defensively, the cultural radical is someone who is greatly tempted to vote with his body. Interestingly, this is true even of a pacifist contemplative who chooses to sit out a war in a monastery. The liberal, by contrast, as the term is being used in this book, always works within the system and in practice tends to focus on a somewhat different range of concerns.

To take a pronounced stand on any of the concrete issues that have been listed (so pronounced that one may actually vote with one's body in several different ways at once) is to set oneself apart from the majority of Americans, who have often convincingly been described either as pragmatic and utilitarian, or else as vague and evasive, in viewing each of these same areas of concern. It is usually granted, for instance, that most Americans affirm a token belief in God without letting it seriously affect their everyday conduct, and that they like to grumble about the authority of politicians while (even to a degree in 1972) marching dutifully to the polls on election day. Again, if most Americans kill, it is unthinkingly in a domestic dispute or when ordered to do so in time of war. Mainstream Americans also no doubt believe in the casual mixture of individualism and neighborliness which prevails in Middletown or on Sesame Street. Though it has become harder to discover what Americans think about sex (there being a notable breakdown of consensus in this area), general attitudes still hold aloof from the extremes of free participation and deliberate continence which radicals have so often idealized. The concept of ecstasy is alien to the mainstream rhythm of workaday routine punctuated by the pursuit, often vicariously in the mass media, of an occasional titillating orgy. Relentless pursuit of mental clarity is on the other hand left to a small number of intellectuals, whose dislike of logical inconsistency renders them faintly suspect. Again, mobile as Americans undoubtedly are, the sight of backpacking freeway hitchhikers strangely attracts their unsympathetic attention. And, though the mainstream may be less indiscriminately attached to possessions than radicals would have us believe, a

110. To some this urge toward practical demonstration will doubtless seem very similar to the pragmatism of the American mainstream. But the latter centers in applied technological inventiveness, not in the steadfast display of fidelity to unusual beliefs. For more discussion of the relations between anarchism and pragmatism, however, see pp. 464–65.

barefoot, shirtless, empty-handed wanderer seen thumbing rides in the eight-thousand-foot wilderness of Tioga Pass creates the sense of a dividing line, even in California. Nor do most Americans squirm over matters of meat eating or the swallowing of definite philosophical systems, unless, like Roman Catholics, they have inconveniently been born into one. Finally, most Americans act neither as if they were about to be "liberated" or as if the world were ending soon.

These lines of division running between accepted and radical forms of behavior and belief do not, of course, by any means settle the matter of the relations between radical movements and the society into which they are born. The paradox must be fully confronted that radicalism is "strange," "alien," "different," while at the same time almost any radical undertaking may be shown to reflect the values of the larger culture in some important respect. Further, an assortment of halfway radical groups immediately leaps to mind, clouding the sense of a precise border.[111] The existence of all the barriers of attitude which have just been described makes pronounced cultural innovation possible, but the impulse toward it may easily be drowned out or subverted at any point along the way. Here it is enough to argue that a boundary between radicalism and the social mainstream does surely exist, though in places it may seem obscured from view. But its water-tightness is an empirical question, to be kept in mind throughout the detailed discussions of secessionist communities in the next several chapters, and then to be examined in its broad dimensions, as it has

111. Two of these, Christian Fundamentalists and academic intellectuals, occupy especially fascinating intermediate positions. The strong affirmation of God among Fundamentalists and other conservative Christians certainly entitles them to be called radicals in terms of this definition. If they are one-issue people, they cannot be accused of self-absorption in the manner of diet faddists; rather their intense single focus reminds one somehow of gay or women's liberation, though it is universalistic in its avowed content. Moreover, Fundamentalist groups often place great emphasis on the practice of a sanctified life, thus "voting" with their behavior, though in the twentieth century they have seldom shown interest in intentional communities (at least until the Children of God). Beyond doubt any comprehensive study of American cultural radicalism would have to include them. Academic intellectuals occupy another very special landing place. Even when, as is usual, their substantive positions are "liberal" rather than radical, they commonly display symptoms of the radical's characteristic desire to take great pains in thinking one's way through to clear convictions, and often with respect to these several areas of engagement. But this activity largely takes the place of a more practical activism; it becomes its own end. The result is apt to be a series of intensely held beliefs, the product of unusually protracted inner debate, which turns out finally to prove compatible with support of the Democratic party or the Episcopal church of the American mainstream. For an interesting discussion of commitment in this context, all the more because its focus is on scientific intellectuals, see Egon Bittner, "Radicalism and Radical Movements," *American Sociological Review,* XXVIII (December, 1963), 928–40.

involved cultural radicalism in America since the late nineteenth century, in the concluding one.

In quite an opposite direction, to posit such a boundary between radicalism and everything else is to raise the issue of whether it does not deserve to be traced on a scale far wider than that of American society. How important are the seemingly perennial elements in the radical approach to life? Is "moderation" as readily identifiable in ancient Rome as it is in the Middle West? Nothing is so irritating in the writing of older scholars as unexamined assumptions about American uniqueness.

Some years ago the anthropologist Anthony Wallace presented the intriguingly universal concept of the "revitalization movement." He described such movements, in ideal-typical terms, as passing through a series of stages from birth (usually marked by a major seer or prophet), to the recruitment of a small band of followers, to the attempt to convince the entire culture of the truth of the new message, and then, rarely, to success (as among the early Christians and modern Russians), or, more usually, collapse and ossification.[112] The virtue of Wallace's approach is that it tried to account for phenomena appearing in many dissimilar parts of the world under a single rubric. In this direction it proceeded far more boldly than Crane Brinton's earlier effort to find a common pattern in several major political revolutions.[113] Millennial movements, cargo cults, all ancient and modern revolutions (so long as they promised a New Age in ideological terms) were seen as diverse manifestations of a single, recurring response in human life, perhaps appearing notably at moments of profound cultural strain. Since Wallace offered this suggestion, scholars in a number of disciplines have sought to follow such a lead further. The contents of Sylvia Thrupp's anthology, *Millennial Dreams in Action,* reveal the range of this comparative effort, moving to Brazil, the South Pacific, and again to the Florence of Savonarola. Meanwhile, working entirely within medieval and Renaissance Europe, Norman Cohn has scanned the centuries with a similar lens. Certainly as portrayed by him the northwest German town of Münster, when taken over by Anabaptists in 1534, displayed an interlocking series of responses to the areas of radical engagement which I have set forth that is extreme enough to claim the kinship of modern anarchists. Few who have read it can forget it.[114] The cumulative impact

112. Anthony F. C. Wallace, "Revitalization Movements," *American Anthropologist,* LVIII (April, 1956), 264–81.
113. *The Anatomy of Revolution* (New York: W. W. Norton, 1938).
114. Sylvia Thrupp, ed., *Millennial Dreams in Action: Essays in Comparative*

of this recent literature makes any American historian wary of viewing local forms of radicalism in isolation.

If the specific themes which I have identified with an American tradition of cultural radicalism are now placed in this much broader perspective, one may conceive of beginning to sort out the distinctively modern and local from the relatively universal. This is not to claim that certain whole areas of engagement may easily be set apart in this respect. It is to suggest, rather, that elements which are more universal and others which are more parochial and time-bound may usually be found to be joined within each area. Thus, for instance, the quest for coherence in the universe, usually religious in its implications, may well be, as Clifford Geertz argues, one of the most central and recurrent concerns of man, encouraging radicals (or the followers of "revitalization" efforts) to take extreme positions about it at widely differing times and places.[115] But atheism and mysticism, the most important forms of radical response to such questions in the American context, are also patterns of belief with highly specific histories attached to them, in the one case deriving from Humean skepticism and the Darwinian controversy, in the other from the gradual communication of Indian thought to the West.

Similarly, one may choose to consider authority as another of the ultimate human problems, or one may dwell instead upon the particular intellectual and political traditions expressing this theme which have run their course in Europe and the United States during the industrial epoch. Here an interesting suggestion presents itself. Can it be that the entire left-wing political tradition of the last two centuries in the West amounts to a very specific historical deflection from other, more perennial, apolitical forms of radical withdrawal from existing society? The rise of the left in the modern sense (including anarchism) covers just about the same span of time, and, initially, much the same geographic territory, as does economic industrialism.

From this point of view, the secular and socially oriented forms of American radicalism in the twentieth century are the product of "history" in its fully concrete and circumstantial meaning. The radical of this kind

---

Study (Supplement II, Comparative Studies in Society and History; The Hague: Mouton & Co., 1962); Norman Cohn, *The Pursuit of the Millennium* (2nd ed.; New York: Harper Torchbooks, 1961), pp. 283–306.

115. Clifford Geertz, "Religion as a Cultural System," in Michael Banton, ed., *Anthropological Approaches to the Study of Religion* (London: Tavistock Publications, 1966), pp. 13–24.

rejects the usual version of modern life, industrial civilization, either by withdrawing from it psychically and physically or else by seeking violently to bring it down. But he has been profoundly affected by its science and in particular by its view of causality. After Darwin he cannot believe in God. Nor can he help believing that the effective path to change, even of states of mind, lies through ordinary external techniques—the printing press, the soapbox or lecture platform, the visible interaction of men in groups, indeed sometimes even bullets. In this the secular radical, like the moderate, is an empiricist, someone who accepts the reality of the world revealed by the senses. And so, though anarchists express an eternally recurring hostility to the injustice of coercive authority, they are also children of the Enlightenment.

From this same point of view, the inward-turning forms of American radicalism might seem to offer themselves as the less historically mediated representatives of a truly perennial philosophy or psychological response. This is certainly how the followers of Vedanta and similar movements would like to view their own role. But unfortunately it is not quite so simple.

One of the most interesting aspects of the Vedanta movement, as will eventually be seen, is that it arose among a highly Westernized elite in late-nineteenth-century Bengal. Though mysticism can indeed be traced back for thousands of years in a number of cultures, it too, like anarchism or socialism, has acquired a specific character of a more immediate kind in what we roughly call the industrial age.[116] In twentieth-century America, as we have already noted, the idea of inner withdrawal from the materialism of the society competes, more or less as an equal, with the idea of a left-wing withdrawal from that same materialism. Some historians, indeed, have gone to an opposite extreme, interpreting "mind-cure" religions (such as Vedanta may be in part) as symptoms of the psychic toll of industrialization in a peculiar sense.[117]

116. To be sure, not always as crudely adaptive as in Swami Yogananda's formulation, in a Self-Realization Fellowship publication, of the external world as "nothing but a vast dream-vitaphone presentation. . . . O Divine Operator, through Thy Cosmic-Vibratory-Current, Thou are showing us a new, infinite series of all-talking and all-sensing cosmic motion-pictures, every day, just to keep us amused and entertained." *Whispers from Eternity: Universal Scientific Prayers and Poems* (Los Angeles: Yogoda and Sat-Sanga, Mount Washington Center, 1929), pp. 95–97.

117. E.g., Donald Meyer, *The Positive Thinkers* (Garden City, New York: Doubleday, 1965) and Richard Weiss, *The American Dream of Success* (New York: Basic Books, 1969). However, both Meyer and Weiss make the major error of ignoring the other-worldly component in the more dedicated movements of this kind, equating the entire tradition with mainstream utilitarianism and success worship. See Chapter Four below.

What, then, about the relation between cultural radicalism and man's social condition in the specifically modern context? During the 1950's a number of social scientists linked what they called "extremism" with the concept of "mass society."[118] Alerted to the possibilities of an alarming social breakdown, both by the Nazi experience and by anti-Fascist writers like Erich Fromm, they pointed to a growing absence of genuine community in modern industrial societies in a way that interestingly parallels the more recent statements of American radicals. In "mass society," the individual increasingly drifts without attachment to firm social roles, such as might automatically have been his in medieval Europe or in tribal cultures. He is isolated, detached, "anomic," lacking clear norms. He floats through life without knowing why. In such a state he becomes prey to radical ideologies, strange religions, groups which promise to restore meaning to his existence. Coming from the rural Midwest to a city like Los Angeles, he feels deeply uprooted. After a while he finds himself singing hymns in Aimee Semple McPherson's Foursquare Gospel church, or passing out leaflets on Technocracy.

To the radical critic of industrialism, this description of the pitiful isolation of modern man says enough by itself. It amounts to a withering indictment of the quality of contemporary life, a justification for the call to a genuine social or cultural revolution. But here of course the critic parts company with the social scientist. The sociologist, for better or worse, cannot resist asking the further question: why do some people, more than others, become detached from conventional norms? No matter that to the critic it is an irrelevant, even an annoying question. An academic remains uneasy until it has been explored.

The social scientists of the 1950's responded to this challenge by attempting to reduce mental states of anomie or alienation to attitude scales with which they could peg samples of unsuspecting Americans. The questionnaire thus handed to 401 bus riders in Springfield, Massachusetts, in 1950, probing their deepest feelings about their relations with their fellow men, sent a ripple through the scholarly journals that lasted for years.[119] From this research emerged the conclusion that anomie was definitely correlated with social class in an inverse fashion. That is, meaningless drift was far more likely to affect people at the bottom of the socio-economic

118. E.g., William Kornhauser, *The Politics of Mass Society* (New York: The Free Press, 1959). Joseph Gusfield, "Mass Society and Extremist Politics," *American Sociological Review*, XXVII (1962), 19–30, offers a useful summary and critique of these views.

119. For the basic description of the project, see Leo Srole, "Social Integration and Certain Corollaries; An Exploratory Study," *ibid.*, XXI (1956), 709–16.

scale or among the geographically marginal people in small towns.[120] Such findings fit in well with a theory of relative deprivation. Men and women who are aware of the affluence and success easily available to others in the society, yet who for economic, geographical, or ethnic reasons are unable to experience such a life, become frustrated at their inability to share the rewards of the majority. The contrast between expectations and reality breeds apathy and detachment—in short, the "cool" response to life.[121] Some may turn to drugs, if they are readily available, while others take the more time-honored routes of escape into violence or into dramatic forms of religion.

Events in the black ghettoes during the 1960's seemed to confirm the validity of this earlier research. And clearly these findings are not entirely wrong. Yet a historian might have told the social scientists that such an explanation for radical behavior was not comprehensive enough. Detailed probes of local environments which have been seed beds of political and religious radicalism in recent centuries have ended with an anguished awareness of how hard it is to account for decisions to bend one way or another.[122] Then came the counter-culture, which turned out to be dominated by white middle-class youth, the kind with good educations who perform well on aptitude tests and who might easily have succeeded in conventional terms had they chosen to do so. When this fact became known, it brought other prominent episodes in twentieth-century American radicalism back to mind: the upper-class alienation of some New Englanders, the wealth that trickled into Vedanta, the tendency of many people who were moneyed and famous to flirt with Communism in the 1930's (while the masses willingly voted for Roosevelt), and the support of Texas oil millionaires for the John Birch Society. If there is a radicalism of the dispossessed, there is also a radicalism of the affluent. There is also the peculiar radicalism of the sons and daughters of former radicals, which I am told by their friends was responsible for some of the most dramatic scenes of confrontation in America during the 1960's. Finally, the hip movement also made us aware that there *can* be a radicalism of the inconspicuous middle, as with the many Massachusetts flower children from

120. Wendell Bell, "Anomie, Social Isolation, and the Class Structure," *Sociometry,* XX (1957), 105–16; Ephraim Harold Mizruchi, "Social Structure and Anomia in a Small City," *American Sociological Review,* XXV (1960), 645–54.
121. Dorothy L. Meier and Wendell Bell, "Anomia and Differential Access to the Achievement of Life Goals," *ibid.,* XXIV (1959), 189–202.
122. Whitney Cross, *The Burned-Over District* (New York: Harper Torchbooks, 1965); Charles Tilly, *The Vendée* (Cambridge, Massachusetts: Harvard University Press, 1964).

Irish or Italian homes. When one stops to ponder the cases of brothers and sisters from the same middle-class family going in opposite directions, just as in the American Revolution or Civil War, the analyzing mind may begin to falter.

At this point the social critic seeks triumphantly to confront the sociologist. Everyone turns out to be a potential radical; the question of origins wasn't worth asking. (At the same time, however, many radicals inconsistently call attention to the social origins of groups who are their enemies, such as the corporate elite.) Here the social scientist may stand his ground by insisting that most radicals do come either from unusually privileged or unusually deprived backgrounds, with the sons of radicals and the Irish hippies as highly special instances.

One result of this apparent impasse, and of a growing effort to find rapport with the radicals, has been for social scientists to turn away altogether from the frustrating question of origins and instead explore in great depth the immediate circumstances and process of recruitment into either a radical movement or a form of behavior commonly defined as deviant. A study showed, for instance, that Detroit blacks were far more liable to toy with violence during a season of high joblessness than they were two years later when comparatively good times had returned.[123] Howard Becker pointed out that the rate of induction into marijuana smoking depended in part upon the availability of a supply.[124] Recent studies of prison life emphasize the impact of that environment after the inmates have lived in it, rather than the reasons for their initial confinement. More broadly it has become fashionable to say, *"I could have been a Nazi, had I been placed in that situation."* In this reasoning, sociology increasingly yields ground to existential philosophy.

One problem with this mode of retreat is that it neglects both the fact of radical traditions, operating historically over time, and the deeper hints, found in cross-cultural studies, of phenomena such as mysticism and millennial movements which appear to have recurrent forms. Exclusively to stress the immediate is to run the risk of ignoring the continuities which furnish the well-defined "places" to which people at any given moment may conveniently attach themselves.

123. David Street and John C. Leggett, "Economic Deprivation and Extremism: A Study of Unemployed Negroes," *American Journal of Sociology*, LXVII (1961), 53–57. See also Albert K. Cohen, "The Sociology of the Deviant Act: Anomie Theory and Beyond," *American Sociological Review*, XXX (1965), 5–14, which emphasized that deviant social roles were in fact social roles like any other.

124. Howard S. Becker, *Outsiders: Studies in the Sociology of Deviance* (New York: The Free Press, 1963).

Earlier I made a distinction between the conversion experience which most radicals undergo and the separate and far more complicated question of the direction these individuals' lives had taken up to that point. But of course there is a third major element in this situation, the intellectual traditions which operate in the minds of those who are seeking to convert others to their way of thinking. The accounts of the conversions undergone by many individuals described in later parts of this book often do reveal the importance of seemingly chance encounters—a lecture hall in Boston in the 1890's, into which Harry Kelly happened to wander, a next-door neighbor in San Francisco who happened to be named Ezra. But it is surely of equal importance that the Boston lecturer presented the case for anarchism, a viewpoint with decades of intellectual history already behind it, and that Ezra was deeply influenced by Gurdjieff, a man who had died nearly twenty years before.

It is also likely that many social scientists gave up rather too easily in the effort to locate the historical antecedents of those who were prone to be converted. Though the complexities of fact and interpretation are enormous, radical movements do often recruit members from conspicuously patterned sources. The I.W.W. was genuinely proletarian; Vedantists have been preponderantly upper middle class and female; and there is also good evidence that hippie dropouts did come disproportionately from middle-class and professional families, as well as representing a particular age group.[125] Social position and intellectual tradition, as well as immediate situation, must inform any adequate account of what it is to become a radical.[126]

Within each communitarian venture one may sense a constant interplay between immediate circumstance, social background, long-lived ideals, and deep psychological commitment, in shaping the outcome. All these elements, except in some respects the last, are linked to the concrete flow of history and are probably best understood in its terms. But to what extent can history help us? The fundamental fact of history is the unevenness of rates of change. History, like the landscape of Mars, is composed of broad plateaus which give way to sudden jagged ruptures. Patterns emerge,

125. James R. Allen and Louis J. West, "Flight from Violence: Hippies and the Green Rebellion," *American Journal of Psychiatry*, CXXV (1968), 366, concerning the Haight-Ashbury; David Whittaker and William A Watts, "Personality Characteristics of a Nonconformist Youth Subculture: A Study of the Berkeley Non-Student," *Journal of Social Issues*, XXV (April, 1969), 72–73.

126. The most impressive treatment of this analytical problem which I have seen, balancing an awareness of both kinds of factors in the explanation of social movements, is Neil J. Smelser, *Theory of Collective Behavior* (New York: Free Press, 1963).

but they seldom enable prediction. Thus, for instance, it is impossible to know whether we are indeed living in a "sick" society, as the theorists of mass society like to argue, for the really persuasive judgments about "sickness" occur only after some cataclysmic event. The sociologists divide into eloquent moral critics, who frequently misuse history, and gatherers of fascinating bits of data. The historian can try in a more careful way to use past time as a yardstick, but he is nearly as helpless in discovering the edge of a future precipice. In the main, the historian understandably retreats to the task of seeking patterns in past outcomes, hoping at best to reveal a measure of coherence *ex post facto*.

The construction of a definition of cultural radicalism, with implications both for the study of American history and for cross-cultural research, has produced its predictable share of uncertainties. For some, an effort of this kind will merely confirm the futility of attempting large-scale generalizations over time and space, or of trying to confine human beings in sharp-edged categorical cages. For others, it may spark a desire for further reflection and research. To continue working in this direction is, at the very least, to counter the parochialism which focuses our attention too exclusively on individual nations, decades, and areas of life. The very fact that radical behavior is so often spectacular, "unusual," "deviant," may suggest that in important respects it is indeed set apart from the rhythms of ordinary conduct in most times and places. One way of trying to get beyond the admitted tautology in such a formulation is to continue seeking out the precise points of encounter between history and the recurring efforts of some men to transcend it.

Each of the communitarian ventures next to be studied may provide a partial answer to the supremely fascinating question of whether Western civilization will ever transcend itself because a few determined people choose experimentally to reorder some of its most basic categories of thought. Though concrete attempts to do this can often seem marginal and local, behind them lies this compelling interest. Doubtless for this very reason, the ordinary American neighbors of such groups as the Stelton anarchists, the La Crescenta monastics, and the youthful population at Ezra's desert ranch have often regarded these secessionist pioneers with incredulity and suspicion. But, to know what these closely gathered bands of people have truly been about, it is necessary to enter as fully as possible into their miniature worlds.

PART I / ANARCHISTIC COMMUNITIES

Our faith is in the forces of life itself and in the perfectibility of human nature. We believe that humanity is rapidly outgrowing government and militarism and coercion. All about us we see the germs of a future that shall be very different from the present. . . . The new movement toward industrial unionism, the movement toward free thought in religion, the increasing disposition to face the problems of sex and to try to understand them—are all carrying us forward in the right direction.

    —LEONARD D. ABBOTT, President of the Ferrer Association,
      in *Modern School*, No. III (Winter 1912–1913), p. 11

the old culture is dying—while a new way of life struggles to be born . . . u can see it if u trust yr senses: in the suffocating ugliness of cities, buried up to their ears in cement / & in the tentative beauty on the faces of those we see & hope will become our lovers.

    —ALAN HOFFMAN, undated broadside
      (San Francisco, ca. 1968)

CHAPTER TWO

The Ferrer Colony and Modern School
of Stelton, New Jersey

One of the most notable—though unremembered—attempts to create a counter-culture in America was launched on June 12, 1910, in New York City, when twenty-two anarchists and anarchist sympathizers founded the Francisco Ferrer Association. Their group was named in honor of a radical freethinker, probably a one-time anarchist, who had built up a large network of anticlerical private schools throughout Spain. After a week of violent revolt which occurred in Barcelona in 1909, Ferrer was suddenly arrested and executed.[1]

The American movement in Ferrer's memory created a cultural center and evening school, then an experimental day school, and finally, in 1915, a colony on 140 acres of land near New Brunswick, New Jersey. In the context of American society, this movement—which lasted for over four decades—was striking in several respects. Ethnically, it brought a remarkable series of talented dropouts from the college-educated Anglo-Saxon world into close contact with recent eastern European Jewish immigrants, at a time when such mingling was still rare.[2] It also marked a determined—

---

1. It was believed at the time that the charges against Ferrer were false, but recently it has been shown that in 1906 he was indeed at the center of a plot to assassinate the king. J. Romero Maura, "Terrorism in Barcelona and Its Impact on Spanish Politics, 1904–1909," *Past and Present,* No. 41 (December, 1968), 141–43, 146, 183. Ferrer's martyrdom on October 13, 1909, which became a special cause in anarchist circles, was a major event, dominating the headlines of the *New York Times* and producing a spate of books and articles in the general press. A statue of Ferrer was erected in Brussels, pulled down by the Germans in 1915, and restored after 1918. There was no direct link between the Ferrer movement in America and similar organizations abroad.

2. By contrast, in these terms Mabel Dodge's famous salon carried the tone of a

if not wholly successful—effort to join intellectuals with workingmen in the common cause of building a new society. In educational terms, the Ferrer Modern School became, by the 1920's, one of the handful of truly advanced progressive schools in the United States, comparable in some respects with Summerhill in England. (Ferrer children often did not learn to read until they were ten or twelve.)

Though not doctrinaire, the ethos of the Ferrer Association tended toward extreme radicalism. The membership was generally in sympathy with the syndicalist movement and strongly supported the well-known strikes and radical protest activities of the years 1911–1914. This was almost the only American milieu in that day where views on racial and sexual equality and on the nature of authority were already strikingly similar to those of socially conscious young Americans in the 1970's.

Most interestingly of all, the Ferrer movement tried to link cultural and educational radicalism with a spirit of militant class consciousness. For a long time it ran the only progressive school in America which deliberately sought a working-class clientele.[3] Bound into this effort were two distinct goals—that of initiating men, women, and children into lives of free self-expression, and that of nurturing a collective social commitment. In this sense the anarchist movement could itself sometimes promote both an "internal" and an "external" approach to liberation. But the pairing of these aims raised some hard questions. Could individuals be released one by one from the constricting bonds of the existing social system? If so, would this strategy foster the growth of a strong radical movement in the United States? Did personal liberation really have anything intrinsic to do with human solidarity, or might it not lead in a hundred directions irrelevant to the social struggle? Already the thinking of a John Dewey posed most of the same dilemmas. But the minds of the anarchist educators who wrestled with them were not constantly held in check by conventional notions of social responsibility, and this lends an unusual fascination to their effort.

The Ferrer Center and the Immigrant Life of New York

In the Ferrer movement as in any other, broad issues like these mingled with a share of local accident and personal complication. It came into

---

special occasion rather than an everyday experience; see the description of it in Margaret Sanger, *An Autobiography* (New York: W. W. Norton, 1938), pp. 73–74.

3. The Manumit School, founded in 1924 near New York with some assistance from the American Federation of Labor, appears to have been the only other school which meets all these qualifications.

existence within the cultural ferment of New York City, then in one of its liveliest periods. And its leading figures had strikingly vivid personalities.

By 1914 the Ferrer Association claimed several hundred adult members. The Ferrer Center, the group's headquarters, was a place where workers could come to hear lectures on social or literary topics, to debate the issues of the day in unrestrained fashion, watch bold new plays, listen to music (perhaps performed by the "Modern School Trio"), or view the paintings of Man Ray. For many, the Center was a place to polish one's newly acquired English. It was also a place where women could sit long hours drinking tea, where men and women could meet and dance (without the oppressive paternalism of the settlement house), and finally where revolutionaries could plot counter-attacks against capitalists. Its political role was, of course, considerable. Some of the children who were evacuated from Lawrence, Massachusetts, during the textile strike of 1911 ended up at the Ferrer Center. Frank Tannenbaum's effort to mobilize the unemployed in the spring of 1914 was in part superintended by the Center's members. And, after a demonstration in Union Square, several hundred factory workers might be given a welcome and a meal.[4]

The evening courses for adults were described by Carl Zigrosser, who taught English in the program, as containing "the germ, as it were, of a genuine people's university, one deeply rooted in the masses." Their appeal was not mainly to "cranks and intellectuals," but rather to "a humanity struggling to know."[5] Most of the teachers were unfriendly toward academic formalism, though their offerings tended toward subjects which now seem relatively respectable despite the iconoclastic interpretations they were given. Sometimes these classes were taught on a high level by well-known people. For some years the art class, which featured drawing from a live model, was conducted by the painters Robert Henri and George Bellows.[6] Bayard Boyesen, the son of a distinguished Columbia professor,

4. Vivid descriptions of the atmosphere at the Center are in Will Durant, *Transition* (New York: Simon and Schuster, 1927), pp. 188–96; Sanger, *op. cit.,* pp. 74–75; Carl Zigrosser, *My Own Shall Come to Me* ([Philadelphia: by the author], 1971), pp. 69–78; and in Abe Grosner *et al.,* eds., *Twenty-Fifth Anniversary of the Modern School of Stelton* (New York: by the alumni, 1940), p. 29, hereafter cited as *25th Anniv.*

5. Carl Zigrosser, "The English Class," *Modern School,* I (July 1, 1914), 4.

6. Robert Henri became a devoted admirer of Emma Goldman early in 1911, after having been influenced in an anarchistic direction by reading of Whitman and Emerson; he remained a philosophical anarchist until his death in 1929. Through Emma Goldman he learned of the Ferrer school. He decided to teach in it after breaking with another art school where an assistant was more enthusiastic about the avant-garde. He taught at the Ferrer Center in New York, usually two evenings a week, from 1911 to 1918; among his pupils were several artists who later became

taught comparative literature during the Center's first session; Gilbert E. Roe, once Robert La Follette's law partner, taught principles of government. In 1914 it was announced that Margaret Sanger would organize "Mothers' Meetings" to discuss birth control.[7] Earlier there had been lecture series on sex and hygiene. The English classes often included discussion of current and historical topics from a proletarian point of view. Courses on great radical thinkers of the past, on the history of philosophy (sometimes conducted by the young Will Durant), and on free thought and comparative religion were further mainstays of the program. A sizable group set about busily learning Esperanto. Perhaps the most famous student at any of these classes was Leon Trotsky, who attended Henri's art instruction during his brief stay in New York early in 1917.

Single lectures were also held, usually on Friday evenings and Sunday afternoons. Clarence Darrow, Hutchins Hapgood, Edwin Markham, Lincoln Steffens, and Frank Tannenbaum drew large audiences, in Darrow's case several hundred people, who taxed the capacity of the small auditorium. Earnest group discussions would always follow. "As a rule," recalled the ever-present Harry Kelly, these heated sessions were "worth while," although he confessed, "inevitably there was a certain amount of loose talk by persons obsessed with ideas which they thought would revolutionize society overnight and solve all problems, social and personal. . . . The place seethed with animation and debate of vital issues, and no cause was too poor nor too radical or delicate to be denied a hearing." Ethnically, though Jews predominated, a great variety of nationalities made the atmosphere at the Center cosmopolitan. The "loose thinkers" and the "down-right ignorant" were balanced, according to Kelly, by "many who were serious and intelligent."[8]

A "Free Theatre" was established at the Center during the winter of 1914–1915 by Moritz Jagendorf, later a well-known folklorist. It antedated the much more famous Washington Square Players, though it had drastically limited resources and used actors sometimes barely able to pronounce their lines in English. On occasion the group presented original plays on social themes, or new plays sent to them in manuscript; in this fashion at least one of Lord Dunsany's dramas received its world première.

well known, including Man Ray. William Innes Homer, *Robert Henri and His Circle* (Ithaca, New York: Cornell University Press, 1969), pp. 172–74, 180–81.

7. Margaret Sanger enrolled her own children in the Ferrer school for a time in 1915.

8. Harry Kelly's manuscript autobiography, pp. 220–21, 234–35, in the possession of Nathan Marer, Croton-on-Hudson, New York.

At other times Greenwich Village troupes such as Floyd Dell's would come to perform before the Ferrer audience.

Experimentalism at the Ferrer Center retained a refreshingly unself-conscious quality. For instance, when the young musician Hyman Rovinski improvised by the hour on the piano to accompany the art class while it drew from the nude model, no one thought of pretentiously calling the result a "multimedia production." Instead, those present were given a nameless but powerful form of experience which was likely to stay with them for a long time.

The Ferrer Center had obviously not come into being for the fearful or the fastidious. But for those who were not put off by a tone of motley comradeship, or by free-for-all discussions about such topics as sex and violence, it may well have been the most stimulating small-scale environment then to exist in the United States. It was certainly the least inhibited.

Meanwhile, another central purpose of the Ferrer Association was to found a day school for young children along radically libertarian lines. The Ferrer Modern School, destined to last through many changes until 1953, was first established on October 13, 1911. The founders believed in part that they were imitating the example of the martyred Francisco Ferrer in Spain. But Ferrer's principles were never literally copied by his American admirers, and his death was no more than an occasion for the creation of the school in New York.[9] Far more relevant in explaining their impulse was the general contemporary upsurge of interest in progressive education. Some American anarchists had begun to believe that here was a cause deeply congenial to their own faith in human liberation.

Immigrant radicals no doubt also turned toward education in part because of its high value in Jewish culture. Moreover, European anarchists (unlike strict Marxian socialists) had emphasized the role of ideas and values in shaping the future. In practical terms, parents were anxious to see their children educated away from the deradicalizing influence of the American public schools. So there was a natural market for the undertaking.

9. This was largely admitted as early as 1913, when one of the most active founders recalled: "No definite program was mapped out. . . . Even the principles were undefined—as, in fact, they remain to this day. A deep, underlying protest against the shooting of Ferrer, and a broad, general understanding as to the desirability of a school such as he had started in Spain, was what brought and held us together." Harry Kelly, "A Short History of the Francisco Ferrer Association," *Modern School*, No. 5 (Autumn, 1913), 7. Ferrer's own educational thinking had been vague and amateurish; it sprang basically from French anticlerical rationalism. See Francisco Ferrer, *The Origin and Ideals of the Modern School* (New York and London: G. P. Putnam's Sons, 1913), especially pp. 17–22, 26, 29, 69–72, 75–76, 116–17. One oddity was that Ferrer explicitly sought to appeal to all social classes in Spain (*ibid.*, p. 46), whereas his American imitators were strongly class-oriented.

In these first years the leaders of the Ferrer Association—by their own later confession—knew almost nothing about education.[10] Few of them were parents themselves. They only knew that they wanted to found a school which somehow would allow children to develop in freedom—but which at the same time would help spread a basic awareness of social injustice. In short-range terms, such a school would enable the recently arrived to defend their cultural "island" against all the pressures of middle-class American life; in the longer range, it might become an offensive bastion, an active agency of ever-widening cultural (and possibly political) revolution.

Because the leaders of the movement knew so little about educational philosophy or previous experiments in teaching methods, and because their resources were so limited, much about the early history of the school was accidental indeed. Yet their plans, as compared for instance with the Progressive Walter Rauschenbusch's vague talk at this time about establishing the kingdom of God on earth, may well seem refreshingly concrete.

In part, the unplanned, undogmatic character of the school was deliberately intended. Though a "libertarian impulse" was described by Harry Kelly as being "at the base of all our work," no effort was made

> to pledge the members to any specific thing. . . . The predominating spirit is anarchistic; yet it cannot be too strongly insisted on that the association as such is not committed to any special economic theory or political ideal. . . . The association . . . has for its aim the reconstruction of society upon the basis of freedom and justice. The interpretation of freedom and justice and how to attain them differ, but free expression of opinion and interchange of ideas is the working method. To hold robust opinions without being dogmatic is a good war cry. The teacher of the day school is neither asked nor expected to teach specific social or religious theories. He or she is but expected to have the libertarian spirit and answer the child truthfully on any question presented.[11]

Meanwhile, another of the guiding spirits in the association, Joseph J. Cohen, was candidly admitting how hard it was for "amateurs" such as

10. Several of them, including Kelly, had taught in radical Sunday schools run by the Workmen's Circle (a Jewish labor organization) a few years earlier, and this experience seems to have whetted their appetites for the idea of teaching children along unorthodox lines. However, on the basis of his earlier attempt, Kelly formed a low opinion of his own teaching ability. Kelly's manuscript autobiography, pp. 217–18.

11. Kelly, "A Short History," p. 11. It should be understood, however, that the word "libertarian" has much the same pointedly self-descriptive meaning in anarchist circles that the word "friend" has among Quakers. A teacher who had "the libertarian spirit" could be neither an orthodox Marxist nor an unthinkingly traditional American.

themselves to agree upon matters of policy. He could, to be sure, cite consensus "on the basic principle that education means the drawing out and development of the potential powers of the child instead of forcing knowledge on the child as it is being done in the public school today." But, he confessed, as soon as discussion shifts to the level of detail "our opinions differ very widely and being all laymen and radicals, who do not believe in authority, each one insists on his theory [and] the debates are heated and passionate but without any results."[12] A still more extreme tendency existed on the part of ordinary members "to interfere in the classrooms, though doubtless with a desire to be helpful, and many wordy battles over this practice took place at the Association's meetings."

The shortcomings of this style of participatory democracy in developing a continuous educational policy were very real. Another cause of drift and uncertainty was the group's dependence upon a rapidly changing series of teachers. Though they were usually paid, salaries were never sufficient to attract them on that basis. Sometimes there were desperate searches for a new teacher or principal to keep the school going. The staff included many remarkable people. But as individuals its members rapidly came and went. Between 1911 and 1916, no principal remained in charge of the school for much longer than a single year, and some resigned in midyear.

The physical surroundings were also severely limiting. A day school had been altogether impossible at the first hastily established location of the Ferrer Center, 6 St. Mark's Place, because there was no outdoor yard and no access to a park. Better quarters were found at 104 East Twelfth Street, just in time for the opening of the school in the fall of 1911. Here, though there was little equipment and the accommodations were admittedly "far inferior to those provided by the public and parochial schools of the city," an enclosed outdoor area did at least exist, which made life pleasant both for the children and adults at the Center during the warm months. A grave disadvantage, however, was that East Twelfth Street by this time was no longer a heavily residential neighborhood and few radical families seemed to be living within walking distance. Under these conditions it was difficult to obtain pupils, especially from the poor but well-disposed parents who were likeliest to respond, so another move was made a year later, on October 1, 1912, into a house at 63 East 107th Street.

This part of Harlem was then crowded with recently arrived immigrants, and although the surroundings were described as providing "actually rather a sordid atmosphere for our juvenile charges," Central Park was

12. Joseph J. Cohen, "The Difficulties of the Modern School," *Modern School,* I (September 1, 1914), 3–4.

only three blocks away. The building (for which a monthly rent of $50 was charged) was about a hundred years old and lacked the more modern conveniences. Though it was three stories high, the ground floor was apparently an unusable basement, leaving only three rooms which could be occupied—a large hall on the whole of the second floor, where during daytime hours two teachers might try to hold different classes simultaneously, and a small, dark office and kitchen on the floor above it. Adult anarchists, loudly discussing the state of the world, often filled the upstairs office and casually wandered through the rest of the building. No wonder, then, that in good weather the teachers and children would often trek to Central Park, preferring to face the hazards of traffic, passersby, and unsympathetic policemen.

Soon, however, despite the rapid turnover in staff and the discouragingly inadequate facilities, the school, like the adult activities at the same location, began to show every sign of flourishing. By mid-1914, enrollment had risen to thirty pupils, and more than half of those who applied had to be turned away.

Two equally legitimate explanations may be given for this success. On one level there is the simple fact of the eager, good-spirited receptiveness of the children, and the answering affection of nearly all their teachers. The environment that came into being at the Ferrer Modern School was one of expressiveness and love. Will Durant recalled the scene in vivid terms:

> They [the children] gathered about me hungrily; some sat on chairs, some on the table; some stood beside me, competing for the privilege of putting their arms around my neck. . . . They never had enough of my stories . . . when one was finished they clamored for another. "Tell us more, Jack, more," they pleaded. Astounded passersby [in the park] wondered what manner of man this was who, hatless and coatless, tumbled about with a dozen children a-top of him, and then suddenly subsided into science or history. . . . When we parted at three they clung to my coat-tails till I had to shake them off and take to my heels. Many of them gave me their affection with a trustful abandon which made their parents jealous.[13]

Clearly the teachers of these New York working-class children faced none of their successors' difficulties two generations later.

But these scenes suggest that the success of the Ferrer school in its first years may also be credited to certain broader circumstances. It was

---

13. Durant, *op. cit.*, pp. 196–97, 199; Will Durant, "Problems en Route," *Modern School*, No. 4 (Spring, 1913), 6. For a similar reaction see the recollections of Henry T. Schnittkind quoted in Joseph J. Cohen and Alexis C. Ferm, *The Modern School of Stelton: A Sketch* (Stelton, New Jersey: Modern School Association of North America, 1925), pp. 15–16, hereafter cited as *Sketch*.

peculiarly fortunate that at this time such a movement could hope to join recently arrived Jewish immigrants, bringing with them a warmly affectionate family pattern and a deep hunger for education, with older-stock Americans who thought it a privilege to be their teachers. This union of enthusiasms needs to be explored from both sides, because here lay the social basis of the Ferrer movement as a whole.

Most of the students in the Ferrer school were recruited from the families of politically radical workers in the garment industry. Such families, especially those with anarchist leanings, were by 1911 already a declining element within the huge immigrant community in New York. The first large-scale influx from eastern Europe had occurred in 1882. A process of assimilation had thus been under way for nearly thirty years by the time the Ferrer movement began. Assimilation meant an abandonment of the ideological intensity which the more Westernized and secularized of the immigrants had picked up from the cultural influences of Germany and France. The main trend among these newcomers to America was exemplified by the powerful newspaper editor Abraham Cahan, whose commitment to socialism lessened with each passing year, while he encouraged his readers to become lovers of baseball and apple pie, and at the same time (not inconsistently) began relaxing his guard against symptoms of Jewish nationalism.[14] Anarchism, which had once fought a fairly even battle with socialism (and Judaism) for the loyalty of immigrant minds, fell far behind in the race.

But around the year 1910 extreme radicalism began to experience something of a second wind throughout the Western world. Syndicalism breathed new hope into the movement. Recent revolutions in Russia, Mexico, and China seemed most encouraging. The tempo of strikes and violence again increased. Anarchism, long burdened by the memory of the McKinley assassination, now gained a certain degree of fresh credibility.[15]

Immigrant anarchists were enormously proud of their working-class identity, defined in terms of the international proletariat. Yet at the same time these particular radicals often displayed symptoms of a tacit elitism.[16] Hungering after intellectuality, they secretly disdained the dull tasks of organizing the working masses. Cultural and educational activities could easily lure them. Indeed, from a later standpoint, their intense admiration

14. Ronald Sanders, *The Downtown Jews* (New York: Harper & Row, 1969), gives an excellent intellectual history of the Lower East Side, and a well-balanced portrayal of Cahan. On anarchism see pp. 125, 159–60.

15. This mood of returning optimism is very well captured in Harry Kelly, "An Anarchist in Reflection," *Mother Earth*, VIII (August, 1913), 183–84.

16. For a discussion of anarchist elitism, see pp. 422–23.

of the outward signs of intellectual proficiency, their open-mouthed regard for whoever in their midst might be able to get up on his feet and speak, could seem naïve. But at the time these enthusiasms marked them as among the most emancipated, secularized, and well educated of the Jewish immigrants. Frequently they were skilled workmen, and thus something of an economic elite as well.

These particular immigrants thought of themselves as members of a worldwide proletariat; they also aspired to enter a universal intelligentsia. What they strikingly minimized was their identity as Jews.[17] All this meant that immigrant anarchists (and revolutionary socialists) were enormously receptive to assimilating themselves speedily into the American environment. They were eager to learn English. They were anxious to join forces with native-born Americans of a similar viewpoint. They would even have little hesitation about marrying Gentiles, providing their politics were similar. They did all these things because they wished to devote themselves in the most efficient way to the work of the proletarian struggle, whether they happened to be living in Russia or in the United States. But theirs, of course, was hardly the bourgeois assimilationism of a David Levinsky, the kind that would look at first tolerantly, and then enthusiastically, upon the nationalism of America and eventually that of Israel. These Jewish radicals sought unhesitatingly to assimilate, not because their perspective was that of the nation-state, but because it had already become that of the world as a whole. There was a final irony in this, for a global, class-conscious perspective was essentially Western European, whereas to begin to think of oneself once more as a Jew was the very American middle-class form of self-identification.

From an ethnic point of view, these were the reasons why the school and the movement could initially succeed. But it is just as important to try to account for the other side of the equation. Why did such a striking group of native Americans, many of them from rather well-off backgrounds, turn toward anarchism, and the Ferrer Center in particular, in these years?

Why Native Americans Joined the Ferrer Movement

For it is a notable fact that the early leadership, both in the Ferrer Association and the Ferrer Modern School, was overwhelmingly native

17. Sanders, *op. cit.,* pp. 53–54. At its most extreme, this kind of radical viewpoint could even endorse anti-Semitism in the context of hostility to Wall Street. In this vein see Leon Samson, *The American Mind: A Study in Socio-Analysis* (New York: Jonathan Cape & Harrison Smith, 1932), p. 47.

American in background. Of the several men who played a major role in building the association, only one, Joseph J. Cohen, was an immigrant (and he entered the movement three years after it began). Leonard D. Abbott, who effectively headed the association and spoke for it on public occasions during its first several years, was from an old, well-to-do New England family. The untiringly faithful Harry Kelly, despite his Irish-sounding name, was born in Missouri of a Cornish immigrant father and a mother who was descended from the Calverts of colonial Maryland. The largest financial donor to the Ferrer school in its earliest years was Alden Freeman of East Orange, New Jersey, a man who participated in pompous ceremonials to honor his early New England ancestors.

The native-born, well-situated pattern is even more pronounced among the first several principals of the Ferrer Modern School. Though they rapidly came and went as individuals, collectively they comprised an unusual group. For instance, of the seven principals between 1911 and 1920, four came to the school with B.A. degrees from Columbia, Harvard, or Yale (in one case, with a Harvard Ph.D. as well), and a fifth, Will Durant, soon went on to complete a Columbia Ph.D. Commonly, that is, they were dropouts from the Ivy League. Only one of them was Jewish.

Why did these people choose to identify themselves with an anarchist educational movement? One may point to several tendencies within the "advanced" segment of the urban upper-middle class in this period: a certain restless impatience with the conventional, for instance in the area of educational theory and practice; an altruistic interest in the poor and the downtrodden, which more often expressed itself in the social-settlement movement; finally, among a smaller number, a growing curiosity about the exotically foreign, especially the so-called "ghetto," a taste for which had begun to show itself during the bohemian craze of the mid-1890's.[18] Among the adventurous group of well-off Americans who began to identify with the emerging literary and artistic avant-garde, the life that flowed in New York's "ghetto" seemed exhilarating, especially when set against the predictable sobriety and commercialism of their own family circles.

In this appreciative spirit Hutchins Hapgood, a one-time Illinois farm boy and later an occasional lecturer at the Ferrer Center, "discovered" and wrote about the Yiddish cultural scene in New York during this period.[19]

18. See Albert Parry, *Garrets and Pretenders* (New York: Covici, Friede, 1933), pp. 76–109; Sanders, *op. cit.,* pp. 192, 220–21.

19. Hutchins Hapgood, *The Spirit of the Ghetto: Studies of the Jewish Quarter in New York* (New York: Funk & Wagnalls, 1902). However, a reader of Hapgood's autobiography, *A Victorian in the Modern World* (New York: Harcourt & Brace, 1939), is bound to conclude that Hapgood was partially impelled by an obsessive need to debase himself.

Similarly, Carl Zigrosser, the native-born offspring of a non-Jewish Austrian-Swiss family in Newark, thus described his own decision to spend so much time in the slums of the East Side:

> One impulse was altruistic, a desire to help those who were more unfortunate than myself. . . . My identification with the Ferrer Center, however, was based not only on my sympathy for the underdog but also on my quest for new experience. I had lived a relatively solitary life in the pursuit of knowledge, mostly from books. Now I wanted to know people, all kinds of people in every walk of life. I was meeting affluent people . . . but I felt that there was more to society than its upper segment. I wanted to discover "how the other half lives." I was also fascinated by the idea of New York as a world in miniature. . . . I wandered about by day, but mostly by night, and explored all sections from the Battery to Harlem, from the East Side to the West Side. . . . Most picturesque of all was the teeming East Side, the abode of the hopes and despairs of many who had emigrated to seek the Promised Land of Freedom. The area was tingling with life. . . .[20]

Though the advanced culture of urban America was then beginning to define sophistication in these new and more exotic terms (terms which would ultimately give men like Henry James and T. S. Eliot their oddly parochial quality), the steady trickle of these well-off Americans into a movement such as the Ferrer Association was after all a far more special phenomenon. What drew them, not just to the Yiddish scene but to Emma Goldman's particular circle? Anarchists were among the most generally feared and despised people in the nation. To show sympathy for them was by no means just a casual alternative to working in a social settlement house.

It is often frustrating to inquire, with such questions in mind, into individual biographies, in this case of the dozen or so native-born Americans who became prominent in the Ferrer movement. Not only are there many lacunae but there is also a sometimes equally embarrassing wealth of ambiguous detail.

Leonard D. Abbott, the first president of the Association, has left much evidence about his state of mind. He was the only member of his conservative New England family to move away from conventional paths. Growing up in England, where his well-to-do father spent twenty years representing American firms in Liverpool, the young Abbott attended Uppingham, a rather fashionable public school. One wonders—here, alas, with no shred of confirmation—whether contact with upper-class English boys in this snobbish environment may not have induced in him an in-

20. Zigrosser, *My Own Shall Come to Me,* pp. 76–78.

tensely democratic reaction. In any event, either while there or very shortly afterward, Abbott first read Tom Paine's *The Age of Reason*. He was to claim that this single book pried him loose from religious orthodoxy and launched him toward his eventual radical beliefs.[21] By the time he returned to the United States in 1898 at the age of twenty, Abbott wished to immerse himself in social causes and would not consider attending a university, even though his family could easily have afforded it. Indeed, thereafter he often begrudged the time spent working in his conventional career, which was as a respectable magazine editor (for *Literary Digest,* then for *Current Opinion*), although this dual life was also to make him, by his own confession, a uniquely valuable "front man" for the Ferrer movement.

Throughout its early years in New York, Abbott was always the spokesman for the Ferrer Association who was quoted publicly, for instance in the pages of the *New York Times*. The gentlemanly, high-minded, yet tireless Abbott possessed just the traits that made him a superb head for such a group as this one. To the Ferrer rank-and-file, indeed to the young Will Durant, Abbott seemed awesomely aristocratic; his diction, for instance, though not quite English, was yet too formal to be really American. With "his tall figure, his dark brooding eyes, his handsome and sensitive face," and above all his ready, booming voice, Abbott was the ideal chairman at lively meetings; it was he, if anyone, who could keep emotions from getting out of hand. He is recalled as having shown a unique capacity to rise above factional quarreling, along with an unfailing willingness to say yes to time-consuming requests for help. His dignity was enhanced by his steadfastly conservative external manner. He avoided alcohol, disliked profanity, and always dressed in formal clothes even though one of his closest friends was J. William Lloyd, the author of an open-air utopia.[22] A man who could combine such impeccable personal propriety with such broad intellectual sympathies was a fortunate find indeed for the group.

Abbott had the incidental honor of first converting Upton Sinclair to socialism, and he long wavered between socialist and anarchist convictions. He had met Emma Goldman almost as soon as he came to live in New York, but he did not ever wholly commit himself to her philosophy. Like many sensitive Americans in the twentieth century, he found himself pulled

21. Leonard D. Abbott to M. Scheer, March 11, 1952, Abbott Papers, in the possession of his son, William Morris Abbott, New York; interview with his son, March 21, 1970. On Abbott see also Durant, *Transition,* pp. 190–91; Hapgood, *A Victorian in the Modern World,* pp. 282–83; Zigrosser, *My Own Shall Come to Me,* pp. 69–70; *25th Anniv.,* p. 23. A letter from Clarence C. Abbott to the author, March 30, 1970, shows only bafflement at his older brother's course in life.

22. Above, pp. 18–33. Abbott once had a homoerotic relationship with George Sylvester Viereck.

in an increasingly radical direction by a first involvement in the issue of free speech. Since anarchists, far more than socialists, were being denied their civil liberties during the Progressive Era, the very fact of their greater repression may have impelled him in their direction. The execution of Ferrer by the Spanish government genuinely stirred Abbott at the time, before anyone dreamed of a Ferrer Association. He wrote to a close friend: "I tell you, that made my blood BOIL!" When Italian anarchists approached him, asking him to chair a large meeting in Carnegie Hall to protest the killing, Abbott felt they did him a great honor. "I shall never forget the night. . . . I tell you the cry of that Ferrer meeting, those Latins—a cry of *rage*—was like music in my ears!"[23]

But Abbott's mind was complex. However deep his emotions ran, he was often torn by introspective doubts. Somewhat later, writing to the same friend with great relish about all his work for the Ferrer school, he suddenly confided: "I am becoming more Anarchistic, but my enthusiasm is in my mind rather than in my life. Radical ideas go to my head, like wine. They intoxicate me!" And soon after this, in an astonishing confessional outpouring, Abbott revealed a truly Hamlet-like mentality:

> I am both more radical and more conservative, I think, than I have ever been before. I understand *both* points of view almost equally well, feel the strength and limitations of both almost equally. Of course my sympathies are overwhelmingly with the radical point of view. Yet whereas in past years I took the radical attitude impulsively and almost spontaneously, now I am almost painfully conscious of the *two* points of view. I want to feel the radical point of view more ardently than I do.[24]

Urgently hoping for what he called "a kind of 'second wind'" in his radicalism, he accepted the relativistic caveat that "every partisan" must inescapably "deal in half-truths as though they were whole truths," and further admitted being torn by an odd desire to defend the classical tradition, notably in literature. He, the head of an organization dedicated to spreading the ideal of self-expression in education, privately admitted that although he fought with one hand for such literary principles as "'self-development,' 'individualism,' etc.," he also believed with equal force in the classical ideal of "self-sacrifice"—which, significantly, he linked with socialism, in contrast to anarchism. Rousseau, Victor Hugo, and the like "all got drunk on Romanticism," Abbott went on, "and they all had to sober

23. Abbott to Albert Mordell, November 20, 1909, Mordell Papers, University of Pennsylvania. His italics.
24. Abbott to Mordell, April 14, 1912. The image he uses is especially revealing in view of his known antipathy toward alcohol.

up on the very principles that we radicals are so apt to attack, and that yet are so necessary if we are to keep out of the mad-house!"[25] Two years after revealing all this internal tension, Abbott was to name his baby daughter after Voltairine de Cleyre, among the most stirring of anarchist propagandists. Only after 1917, when it became increasingly clear that anarchism had no future as a movement, did he decisively swing over to socialism.[26]

Abbott's mind lacked the original vigor of, say, John Jay Chapman's. Though he held to high critical standards in his literary judgments, he was a born summarizer and popularizer. Yet he furnishes a striking case of the conversion to pronounced radicalism of a talented, old-stock American at the turn of the century. Already in private he wrestled with the central dilemma of the Ferrer Association, the conflict between ideals of unhampered self-expression and disciplined self-sacrifice.

The native-born anarchist Harry Kelly played a dominant role in the Ferrer movement for a much longer period than Abbott, who dropped out of it after its transfer to New Jersey in 1915.[27] Kelly's radicalism was of a different kind. He had the temperament which tries forever to convince people, rather than the one which secretly muses about the problem of being convinced. Yet, within the terms of an unyielding commitment to anarchism, Kelly displayed qualities of mind which deserve to be called flexibly resourceful, perhaps even pragmatic.

Kelly's Missouri boyhood was beset by the problems of downward social mobility. His father had been a one-time partner of Tom Scott, the magnate who built the Pennsylvania Railroad. Eventually he lost his stake, retreated to the job of mine inspector, and died in poverty when his son was less than five years old. The boy, born in a thirteen-room house in St. Charles and christened in the local Episcopal church, which his father had staunchly supported, found himself leaving school after the fifth grade to help his family.[28]

Kelly's later radicalism was almost certainly not the result of a revolt against his mother or father. Indeed one senses that the deceased father,

25. Abbott to Mordell, July 25, 1912.
26. In another characteristically divided comment in 1912, Abbott called Wilson "tame, conventional, bourgeois. Roosevelt interests me infinitely more. But I shall vote for Debs." Abbott to Mordell, August 28, 1912. In 1948 Abbott was still voting for Norman Thomas.
27. It is clear that Abbott lost his basic interest—and probably his confidence—in the Ferrer school by the early 1920's. However, down to the 1950's he continued occasionally to see and write to his old friends in the movement, taking great pains never openly to reveal disenchantment.
28. The major source for Kelly's early life is his manuscript autobiography, pp. 1–66.

as often happens in such situations, became a powerful affirmative influence in the boy's life. Father and son shared at least two major traits—a migratory restlessness, and a certain interest in books and ideas. His much younger mother Kelly recalled as "a simple good woman without much schooling" (she had been the father's second wife, married when he was a widower with children), and "a person of character," one who had "a great deal of natural intelligence." Kelly said that his mother hated only two things: alcohol and the Roman Catholic Church. Because both his parents had been opposed to liquor, the young Kelly long refused to drink beer with the boys his own age. And in anarchism he would find a philosophy squarely at odds with the *bête noire* of his mother's religious imagination.

There are hints of temperamental Puritanism in the young Kelly's makeup, as might befit someone struggling dutifully to keep a declining family afloat.[29] By contrast, when Kelly grew older he came consciously to relish the camaraderie of social occasions, and he praised the anarchist movement for its avoidance of the strait-laced tone that had infused German socialism. Also, like many other anarchists, he indulged (in a highly principled fashion) in a long-term free-love relationship. But this broadening of himself in several directions appears to have been gradual and in no way a bitter reaction against home training.

From the record of Kelly's youth emerges a pattern of enormous hardworking diligence, yet a growing desire to be constantly on the move, seeing more of the world. "By the time I was fourteen," Kelly remembered, "I felt like an adult and went around with boys much older than myself." He learned the printing trade, which intermittently gave him his living for the next thirty-five years. When he was about twenty, he began to be overwhelmed with wanderlust, riding the rods and living with hoboes. Until quite some time after his conversion to anarchism, he seldom remained in one city for longer than a year or two. He journeyed to England in the mid-1890's, partly to become acquainted with his father's relatives but also to meet the circle of well-known social revolutionaries then encamped in London. Thereafter he visited Europe many times, thinking of it as a definite spiritual home.

Meanwhile, at nineteen Kelly had already become an organizer for the International Typographical Union. The depression of 1893, which found

---

29. E.g., he spoke scornfully of the atmosphere in a small Missouri mining town he visited: "Nothing but work, drink, and the usual sexual diversions to occupy its inhabitants." *Ibid.*, p. 16. His mother, he complains, could never learn to be economy-minded.

him in Chicago on the eve of the great Pullman strike, radicalized him further, just as it did Eugene Debs. In 1894, while living in Boston, Kelly permanently embraced the anarchist cause. He claimed this conversion was accidental. It came on a Sunday when he was wandering aimlessly along Washington Street, intending to go to South Station for no other reason than to lose himself in a crowd where he would "feel less lonely."[30] His eyes rested on a handbill advertising an anarchist speaker from England, Charles W. Mowbray. Kelly was curious about anarchism, after all the publicity it had received since the Haymarket bombing. "Others were drifting into the hall, and I went in with them." Greatly stimulated by the lecture, he joined the study group which was formed at its close. He was the only native-born American in that particular audience to have done so.

Kelly said that he became an anarchist in order to work for an ideal society in which "there would be food and shelter and cultural opportunities for all. That society would be beautiful in itself, and harmonious in all its human relations." He noted that up until then he had never exactly thought of himself as one of the "oppressed," despite his family's poverty.

In all this evidence there is room for more than one interpretation. From the standpoint of his social circumstances, Kelly was just the sort of idealistic, self-reliant, highly skilled craftsman whom Kropotkin hoped would form the basis of the anarchist movement; and Mowbray, the speaker who converted Kelly in Boston, emphasized the thinking of both Kropotkin and William Morris in his presentation. But a less rationalistic account of Kelly's Boston experience would see him instead as a classic victim of urban anomie, a lonely nocturnal wanderer in an endless succession of cities, self-educated and therefore perhaps a bit naïve, in short ripe for conversion to an extreme world view that would give him the sense of fixity missing in his fatherless home from boyhood.

It is only certain that, from this point forward, Kelly gave unflagging service to a highly unpopular cause. If such an adherence for the next sixty-three years on the part of a lively young Missourian makes a psychological explanation of his motives seem appropriate, then some of these hints, gleaned from a rather reticent autobiography, may be suggestive. But much that was central in Kelly's upbringing was if anything characteristically American. Both his capacity for hard work and his physical restlessness were highly typical of his time and place.[31] Moreover, the young Kelly

30. *Ibid.*, p. 2. The same occasion is described, without such striking details, in Harry Kelly, "An Anarchist in the Making," *Mother Earth*, VIII (April, 1913), 50–51.
31. Kelly himself noted this in a letter to Carl Nold, September 27, 1930, Labadie Collection, University of Michigan.

loved both baseball and the popular theater of his day. Biographical detail which merely emphasizes individual peculiarities can furnish a one-sided picture.

And yet Kelly was willing very frankly to admit the important psychological functions of commitment, once it had been made. "Striving for such a cause as Anarchism creates a bond of friendship that makes conventional relationships pale in comparison. Earning a living was a painful necessity, but the real life was in the movement and intercourse with one's comrades. The latter compensated me for the drudgery of my daily life . . . and prevented me from going into melancholia."[32] In turn, his daily life may well have seemed like drudgery in contrast to the distinctly upper-middle-class expectations of his earliest childhood.

Kelly had tirelessly labored for anarchism for some sixteen years before the Ferrer Association was created. He had been a regular contributor to Emma Goldman's magazine *Mother Earth* since its founding in 1906, and it was she who first acquainted him with the Ferrer movement. Kelly was at this time about forty, or seven years older than Abbott. His warm personality, varied experience, and strong enthusiasm for pushing practical projects elevated him into a central role. He became the group's first "organizer," a term borrowed from labor unions. Paid a salary of twelve dollars a week by the association, he was supposed to devote half his time to bringing word of the movement to outsiders. From then until 1923, when his interests began to change, Kelly more than anyone else held the whole group—eventually the colony—together and made sure, as much as anyone could, that day-to-day things really got done.

He was a frail, short, mustached man who could talk tirelessly whenever he wanted to be persuasive, yet could impress people as somehow gentle underneath. Though naïvely incorruptible, he had many of the instincts of a shrewd promoter. Blessed with a sense of humor and radiating knowledgeable enthusiasm wherever he went, Kelly could always restore the confidence of the rank-and-file, suggest ways out of difficulties and settle minor disputes almost like a one-man government. Kelly was undeniably headstrong and sure of himself, and in the eyes of some could be long-winded. But his buoyant spirits and tireless labors gained him general admiration.

No one would call Kelly original as a thinker. Neither an economic determinist nor a real believer in the masses, Kelly placed his faith in the practical power of an intelligent minority of the workers—the anarchist

32. Harry Kelly, "An Anarchist in Evolution," *Mother Earth*, VIII (May, 1913), 93.

revolutionary elite, a conception which has odd parallels to Gompers' trade-union elite.[33] Kelly's candor and openness must have added to his appeal. It was usual for him to begin his speeches on a realistic note, eschewing all far-reaching claims. Then, perhaps having attracted attention by his matter-of-fact concessions to reality, he would move forward in a cheerful but determined way to outline future goals. Since anything might be possible, he seemed to be telling the Ferrer audience, their own humble activities were quite likely to succeed, despite obvious difficulties that needn't be denied. Far more modest in his rhetorical style than such a mainstream politician as Woodrow Wilson, the Missouri anarchist became the Moses who would one day lead the group of immigrants out into the wilderness of central New Jersey. There is much to ponder in the contrast between the grandiloquent rhetoric of so many Americans in the moderately liberal tradition and the jaunty, down-to-earth manner of this avowed enemy of the system.

Carl Zigrosser, who attained a different kind of prominence in the Ferrer movement, was the very soul of the sensitive literary rebel. His parents, who had moved from Indianapolis to Newark when he was nine, were outwardly serene in temperament, but with hints of explosive possibilities. They were highly moralistic but not deeply religious. His mother was a Lutheran and his father a lapsed Catholic; after one vain attempt, they allowed the boy to desert churches altogether. As a Columbia undergraduate, Zigrosser was both apolitical and unsocial, holding aloof from most of his classmates.[34] Within this shell, he was becoming passionately, lyrically utopian in his thinking. The three definite intellectual influences upon him as a young man, he volunteered when I talked with him in 1971, were Whitman, Nietzsche, and Blake. Something of a hero worshiper, he wrote to Kropotkin in the summer of 1912 when he was twenty-one, asking advice on what career he should follow as a socially conscious young man of his time. (Kropotkin's reply was rather abstract and noncommittal.) Zigrosser had also been encouraged to identify himself with the role of social rebel by the lectures of James Harvey Robinson.

A more important direct influence upon him was an instructor of literature, Bayard Boyesen, who was to be the first principal of the Ferrer Modern School. The son of an eminent Norwegian professor who had moved to the United States, Boyesen combined aristocratic snobbishness

33. Harry Kelly, "Socialism and the Concentration of Capital," *Mother Earth,* II (1907), 98–99.

34. Zigrosser, *My Own Shall Come to Me,* pp. 38, 95, 330, 341. His papers are at the University of Pennsylvania.

with anarchistic radicalism, pushing the latter until it verged on solipsism. Boyesen had introduced Zigrosser to Kropotkin's writings; and it was Boyesen's example that Zigrosser followed in suddenly dropping out of Columbia after half a year of graduate study, protesting against the pedantry of academic life. Boyesen, meanwhile, had been discharged by Nicholas Murray Butler for appearing with Emma Goldman at a public meeting. Through Boyesen Zigrosser first heard of the Ferrer Center, although it was not until 1913 that he began to frequent it. After a year spent on a farm in order to "experience something real," Zigrosser obtained employment in 1912 with Frederick Keppel and Co., a prominent dealer in prints and etchings. There he embarked on a five-year apprenticeship in the art world, engrossed in it as well as the Ferrer movement. From 1914 to 1916 he roomed with Randolph Bourne, whom he had originally known on the literary magazine at Columbia. They eventually quarreled, and Zigrosser does not think that he greatly influenced Bourne's thinking, although Bourne abruptly turned in an anarchist direction during the crisis of the First World War.

Anarchism, as Zigrosser approached it, was more a mode of awareness than a concrete political movement. Politics in the ordinary sense he always abhorred. His tendency remained one of detachment, of remaining on the fringe of whatever circle he moved into.[35] Though he enjoyed giving evening classes at the Ferrer Center, his principal service to the association was as editor of the *Modern School* magazine, which he transformed during his tenure (1917 to 1920) from a routine monthly newsletter into what both Hart Crane and Wallace Stevens praised as the most beautifully printed magazine to exist anywhere in the United States.[36] Throughout this period the Ferrer movement, which by then had physically removed to New Jersey, remained in the consciousness of avant-garde New York primarily as a result of the untiring efforts of Zigrosser, who, however, stayed behind in the city.

As a "little magazine," the *Modern School* under Zigrosser blossomed both in typography and in substance. Its cover and many of its inside pages featured woodcut decorations in an ecstatically primitivistic mood, carved by his friend Rockwell Kent. The entire appearance was rich, yet simple and tasteful. Zigrosser said at the time, "I have tried to make it a beautiful thing, a medium of expression for creative thinkers and artists. It deals with

35. *Ibid.*, pp. 75–76, 319–20. As he grew older, his radical utopianism faded away. *Ibid.*, pp. 322–23.
36. Hart Crane to Zigrosser, December 30, 1918, February 12, 1919; Wallace Stevens to Zigrosser, August 20, 1917, Zigrosser Papers.

radical ideas in education, and by education I mean every activity that broadens and enhances life."[37] As an editor, Zigrosser was extremely resourceful in soliciting poems and articles from lively corners of the intellectual landscape even though no payment could be made. *Modern School* published poems by Crane and Stevens, and also by Maxwell Bodenheim, Mike Gold, and Rabindranath Tagore. With great relish Zigrosser and his contributors surveyed the whole range of literary and educational ferment from an advanced point of view.[38] The tone of the magazine, while ebullient, was never giddy.

But there was eventually little connection between Zigrosser's magazine and the rest of the Ferrer movement. As Joseph J. Cohen told him, "you have made the magazine the most beautiful and worthwhile publication in the radical movement the world over," and yet at the same time "a person can read the magazine every month from cover to cover and not suspect even that we are running a school and having a hard time to make ends meet."[39] In a similar vein, William Thurston Brown (principal of the school after 1916) reported that the magazine was not appealing to the rank-and-file whom he met on his national speaking tours. By 1919 the colony leaders openly complained that it was "rather too much devoted to theory and the discussion of literary and aesthetic questions and not enough to a concrete statement of the work . . . at the Modern School."[40] The world of Greenwich Village thus did not always mesh smoothly with the world of immigrant radicalism. Yet, when Zigrosser finally did step down, it was in an atmosphere of good feeling. Dropping all radical involvement, Zigrosser went on to a long career as curator of prints for the Philadelphia Museum of Art.

The several early principals of the Ferrer Modern School moved in and out of the movement more rapidly. Bayard Boyesen remained head of it only for a few months before retiring to live for the rest of his life on a remote Massachusetts farm. Next briefly came the sixty-year-old John Russell Coryell, originator of the Nick Carter detective stories and later a founder of the Macfadden publishing empire. After one week the suicide attempt of a student so unnerved him that he turned the school over to his

37. Zigrosser to John Cotton Dana, n.d. (ca. September 1, 1918).

38. Some of Zigrosser's writing had been turned down by Floyd Dell of *The Masses* back in 1915; *Modern School* doubtless gave him an alternative vehicle.

39. Cohen to Zigrosser, January 25, 1918, Zigrosser Papers.

40. Brown to Zigrosser, March 10, 1918 (from Columbus, Ohio); John W. Edelman, "Report on the School at Stelton," *Modern School*, VI (1919), 328. Financial data are available for the magazine in the period between January 1, 1917, and June 14, 1917. During that time the total deficit incurred was $36.95. Typical monthly subscription income was between $30 and $40. This surely was not a bad record.

wife, Abby, who ran it for several months. The Coryells had long been active anarchist speakers and writers; Emma Goldman described them as among her dearest American friends.

Will Durant, who lasted as principal for well over a year in 1912 and 1913, was then twenty-six years old and from a very different background. His Irish mother had once pushed him toward the priesthood, but he read Darwin and Spencer and grew skeptical. With much soul searching he departed from the church. This brought about a temporary break with his family, entirely against his own wishes. A crucial moment came when he heard Emma Goldman speak at a small meeting near his home in New Jersey. Though Durant was never greatly attracted by her as a person, her talk whetted his appetite for new ideas, and he began spending his weekends in New York. Trying to earn extra money by lecturing, he was put in contact with the Ferrer Association and invited by them to give a Sunday-afternoon talk on "The Origins of Religion." His heavily sexual interpretation of this topic, rather novel in 1911, pleased his hearers. This same lecture caused his excommunication.

Apart from his success with the young children, one senses that Durant was never fully at home in Ferrer circles. He had apparently been offered the principalship despite Emma Goldman's own preference for George Brown, a rather theatrical anarchist from Philadelphia.[41] Always hostile to violence, Durant broke with his anarchist acquaintances after the Lexington Avenue bomb explosion in 1914, and by 1916 he was voting for Woodrow Wilson. With considerable insight Durant once said, through the mouth of an autobiographical character: "My skepticism and rationalism have always been matters of the head, that never crossed the medulla into the deeper roots of my behavior and my being. At bottom I am as romantic and sentimental as a high-school girl or an old maid."[42]

The parade of principals continued. Cora Bennett Stephenson, who came from Marion, Indiana, to take charge of the school during 1913–1914, must have been hired partly out of desperation. Primly conventional in her bearing and a slavish disciple of the well-known psychologist G. Stanley Hall, she was a most unlikely libertarian. Yet she had been discharged from teaching in an Illinois public school after making a public declaration of some kind over Ferrer's death, and she had begun corresponding with Emma Goldman.

41. Durant, *Transition*, p. 186. On George Brown, who might have been disastrous, see Voltairine de Cleyre to Joseph J. Cohen, February 7, 1911, March 8, 1911, Cohen Papers, Bund Archive, New York.
42. Durant, *Transition*, p. 296.

Her far more sophisticated successor in 1914–1915 was Robert H. Hutchinson. It is not known how he first came into contact with the Ferrer Association, but his commitment to unorthodox educational methods went far beyond that of the school's other early principals. He may have developed this interest while teaching at a private school in the Berkshires immediately after graduation from Harvard. But his political education appears to have advanced most greatly in New Zealand. Taking his bride there on a nine-month honeymoon visit, he began to see flaws in the state socialism in which he had previously believed, and his mind veered in a decidedly libertarian direction. Immediately after this trip he took over the classrooms at the Ferrer Center; he was then twenty-seven, almost as young as Durant. Serving without salary because of an adequate private income, he boasted that he had given up a well-paying job elsewhere in Manhattan to take the Ferrer position.[43]

Hutchinson's wife was the former Delia Dana, a granddaughter of Henry Wadsworth Longfellow. The Dana family, at 113 Brattle Street in Cambridge, betrayed a strong tendency toward individualism. One of Delia's brothers was a rather eccentric vegetarian; another was discharged from Columbia by Nicholas Murray Butler for opposing American entry into the First World War. Delia herself had dropped out of Radcliffe and done the bold thing, for a girl in her social position, of training at Johns Hopkins to be a nurse.[44]

A young upper-class couple such as the Hutchinsons could rebel from convention with very little sense of an open break. Though it is not clear exactly how Hutchinson's Episcopalian family of Philadelphia lawyers regarded his flirtation with the anarchists, we do know that Delia's aunt had liked Robert Hutchinson ever since he was a freshman and that the girl's parents both thoroughly approved of the engagement.

Their assured social position also enabled the couple to be expressively far-out in their thinking and behavior. Delia Hutchinson, who wrote booklets about a new "natural" approach to motherhood and child care, practiced it openly on her own infants. Wearing a short tunic which left her pregnancies boldly undisguised, she was at once "an incarnation of a pagan goddess" and the epitome of the liberated mother.

43. On him see *Modern School*, I (October 1, 1914), 8; *Sketch*, pp. 24, 25, 63–64; *New York Times*, May 18, 1915; Zigrosser, *My Own Shall Come to Me*, pp. 82–83; *25th Anniv.*, pp. 23–24, 27; and his class books in the Harvard College Archive.
44. On Delia Dana, see the *Boston Herald*, May 8, 1913; Zigrosser, *My Own Shall Come to Me*, p. 83; *25th Anniv.*, pp. 25, 27; and the letterbooks of her aunt, Elizabeth Ellery Dana, extending from 1913 to 1919, in the Dana Papers, Radcliffe College Archive.

The Hutchinsons suddenly decided to leave the Ferrer school and found a still more radically libertarian one of their own (which, incidentally, soon collapsed).[45] They were at least able to recommend a successor: Henry T. Schnittkind, a classmate of Hutchinson's who had gone on to receive a Ph.D. Though a Russian-born Jew, Schnittkind had come to America when he was three, and he was almost wholly assimilated in comparison with the rank-and-file of the Ferrer group. It is noteworthy that he found his experience at the Ferrer school to be profoundly joyous and meaningful, though his wife's complaints soon forced him reluctantly to depart. Schnittkind was still telling the world twenty years later that his brief time at the school in the fall of 1915 had been the most exciting event of his entire life. Perhaps this was because his background had enabled him to relish it doubly, as partial insider and outsider.[46]

With William Thurston Brown in 1916, the Ferrer school again had a native-born radical as its head, and one who remained at the post for more than three years. The son of a clergyman in upstate New York, Brown was descended from the seventeenth-century founders of Rhode Island. He graduated from Yale in 1890 and from the Divinity School there five years later. Becoming pastor of a prestigious Congregational church in Madison, Connecticut, Brown preached an advanced form of the social gospel which badly divided his audience. He was a handsome young man with penetrating eyes and a magnetic appeal to the youthful members of his flock. An elderly, more conservative minority greatly resented his ideas and accused him of heresy and irreverence. He was tried on these charges before a statewide ecclesiastical council of the Congregational church, but with the sympathies of leading figures clearly on his side he was easily acquitted.[47]

45. On it see Delia D. Hutchinson, "Ethics and the Infant," *Modern School,* IV (November, 1917), 130–35; *Sketch,* pp. 63–64. Their idea was that the children should be "thrown entirely upon their resources and responsibility, without any interference from the adults. The preparation of meals and the other work around the place should all be done by the children in turn, and if neglected they should go without meals or stay in uncleaned quarters." Thus did radical educational progressivism come full circle to the Puritan notion of the child as a miniature adult. Hutchinson divorced his wife in 1920 and thereafter retreated into a more innocuous pattern of upper-class life, living in England for many years and managing a Red Cross canteen in the London blitz.
46. On him, see *Sketch,* p. 65; *Modern School,* II (July-August, 1915), 87; and Class of 1910 reports, Harvard College Archive, especially the Twenty-Fifth Anniversary Report. He had grown up in Boston, attending the Latin School, and had become actively interested in socialism.
47. The trial is thoroughly covered in the *New York Times,* March 13, 15, 23, 25, and 26, 1896. The Yale Class of 1890 reunion books, in the Yale Archive, are the best source on Brown's life. See also *Sketch,* pp. 30–31, 34, 36–41, 66, 67; *25th Anniv.,* p. 27; and his letters in the Zigrosser Papers.

In 1899 Brown became a socialist and began to write militant tracts for the party. Then he became friendly with Emma Goldman. He lost another ministerial post at Rochester in 1902 because in the wake of McKinley's assassination he had ventured publicly to "give reasons for Czolgosz's act." That same year he ran for Lieutenant-Governor of New York on the Socialist ticket. Thereafter he moved often from place to place, especially in the Rocky Mountain states, lecturing and preaching. (By this time, perhaps inevitably, he had become a Unitarian.)

Soon after Francisco Ferrer's martyrdom, Brown attempted to open a Ferrer Modern School, first in Salt Lake City and then in Portland, Oregon, and for this activity he was rewarded by expulsion from the increasingly moderate Socialist party of America. He had lectured at the Ferrer Center in New York in 1913 and had also tried to found a Ferrer school in Chicago in 1915. In many respects, therefore, he was a highly logical choice for the position at Stelton (where the school had now moved from New York). But, though the children did not dislike him, Brown was a rather remote figure. His intellectual outlook, derived from the evolutionary social science of Lester F. Ward, was becoming rather old-fashioned. He lacked both the avant-garde sophistication of the Hutchinsons and the youthful energy of Will Durant. His ponderous rhetoric, unimaginative pedagogy, and, even more, his temporary wartime support of Woodrow Wilson made him a discordant and disappointing figure.[48]

The native Americans who thus converted to anarchism or more briefly espoused anarchist sympathies in this period comprised a rather distinct group.[49] They were disproportionately from old families and advantaged backgrounds. But one must point out how various were their temperaments. Though they seem nearly all to have undergone pronounced intellectual conversion experiences of one kind or another, suggesting a "twice-born" characteristic, the conversions took place in such a variety of contexts that it would appear forced to reduce them all to a single formula. And, although they did take certain ideas with unusual seriousness, their subsequent lives and thoughts often revealed much reasonable common sense and flexible drift. Only William Thurston Brown strikes one as an archetypical

48. For a time in 1918 his views were far to the right of the other leaders' in the Ferrer movement; he drew Carl Zigrosser's wrath for trying to ram an advertisement for Liberty Bonds into the pages of *Modern School!* But in 1919 he became and remained a dedicated Communist. He later taught in a boy's school in Menlo Park, California.

49. Other native Americans figured in the Ferrer movement (e.g., the aging single-taxer Bolton Hall, Princeton '77, and the artist and novelist Manuel Komroff), but played a much less important role. Elizabeth and Alexis Ferm are described at length later.

"true believer." It would seem ludicrous to regard all these diverse, active, and often very independent-minded people as psychic casualties, either of their family situations or of the process of industrialization.

These native-born anarchist sympathizers did share one further characteristic. This was literary ambition. At some point in their lives nearly every one of them wrote fiction, poetry, biography, or social criticism. Moreover, several of them eventually became prolific writers in a popular vein.[50] Desire for book sales often proved stronger than commitment to political or social causes. For such people involvement in the Ferrer Center may be viewed as a stage in the process of groping toward a mass audience. It was a mere episode in their lives. Except for Harry Kelly and perhaps initially Leonard Abbott, the native Americans simply did not enter the Ferrer movement in the spirit of someone who stays with a single cause for a lifetime. (In this respect, the contrast with the American followers of Vedanta, in the next chapter, is very striking.) Nor were they the type of person who drifts perennially from one similar cult-like cause to another. Instead, most of them were artistically inclined persons of middling (but not inconsiderable) talent who were also daring enough at this time to express their concern for social justice in an unusually far-out fashion. And anarchism, as we have seen, was the left-wing perspective most congenial to the idea of creative self-expression.

Even if in the long run these people tended to live more for their self-development than for the sustenance of the movement, it would be wrong to minimize the importance of a commitment to radicalism in their lives. Its power to affect their down-to-earth behavior is especially revealing in the area of ethnic attitudes and relations. Radical intellectual commitment did not entirely dissolve ethnic tensions within the Ferrer movement. However, in comparison with the rest of the United States in that period, such problems were incontestably reduced to a very low level.[51] Marriage (or free-love relations, which anarchists on principle preferred) became fairly common between Jews and non-Jews in the group.[52] Here was impressive

---

50. This is revealed in any major library catalog when one looks up the names John Russell Coryell (or "Nick Carter," pseudonym), Leonard D. Abbott, Henry Thomas (the later name of Henry T. Schnittkind), Will Durant, and Manuel Komroff. Only Harry Kelly confined his writings within the anarchist movement. Even Cora Bennett Stephenson wrote a novel.

51. Occasionally one finds explicit evidence of such tension in these circles. See the honestly troubled letter on this theme by Voltairine de Cleyre to Joseph J. Cohen, n.d. (ca. February, 1908, "Midnight Friday"), Cohen Papers; also Hutchins Hapgood, *An Anarchist Woman* (New York: Duffield & Co., 1909), pp. 192–94.

52. Leonard Abbott, who married a Rumanian immigrant, is believed to have felt quite keenly, with the passing years, the effects of partial isolation from both

testimony to the power of radical ideas in overcoming mainstream prejudices. For this reason alone the Ferrer Center was highly remarkable for its day.[53] Its human relationships almost entirely lacked the poisoning quality of condescension found so often in American society during those decades.

Flight from the City

It must not be thought that the Ferrer Association led a serene existence in New York City. It came into being in a turbulent period. Political events increasingly threatened its survival. So storm-ridden did it become that at the end of 1914 the fateful decision was made to shift the Ferrer Modern School away from New York altogether.

The original moving force behind the Ferrer movement was the militant anarchist spokesman Emma Goldman. She had kept its impetus going during the earliest months, when otherwise it might have quietly died.

Most of its leading figures during the early years were her own friends or acquaintances, and some of them had been specially recommended by her. It is true that, once the movement was firmly under way, she took little direct part in its affairs, seldom appearing at the Center. And so far as the school was concerned, although she had a rather abstract interest in the idea of libertarian education, she did not appear to feel at ease in the presence of young children. (In this respect her long-time associate Alexander Berkman proved a far more willing emissary.) But the offices of her publication *Mother Earth* were only about eight blocks away from the Ferrer Center after it moved to Harlem, and to many outsiders the movement appeared to be entirely her creature. No doubt the Ferrer Association was widely believed to have a more sectarian flavor than it actually possessed, and this image must have greatly reduced its broader impact. (The *New York Times* almost invariably referred to the Center in direct connection with the anarchist movement, and at moments when there were events such as strike rallies or bomb scares). The Ferrer movement seems to have been misunderstood by all those who could not allow that a generally

---

families. His own relatives were anti-Semitic in the fashion then usual among the established population of New England.

53. The anarchist movement was just about the only radical group in this period unequivocally calling for the liberation both of blacks and women from an inferior social and legal position. However, because anarchists disliked all forms of cultural nationalism, they disapproved of black spokesmen who emphasized ethnic advance at the expense of proletarian solidarity. This of course directly paralleled their negative attitude toward Zionism and Jewishness. See "Association and School Notes," *Modern School,* undated issue (ca. January, 1914), p. 4.

radical perspective might combine with a large degree of internal freedom and open-endedness.

Still, one would like to know more about the relations between Emma Goldman and Alexander Berkman on the one hand and the Ferrer membership on the other. The evidence that does exist points toward a gradually increasing sense of separation, the outcome of which was the decision to move at least some of the Ferrer activities outside New York.[54] If true, this certainly did not mean an open break. Emma Goldman subsequently came once to speak at the Ferrer colony at Stelton, New Jersey, during the summer of 1916. Starting the next year, her own prosecution and deportation by the American government placed her on a pedestal of martyrdom, making it natural for all who remained anarchists to forget earlier difficulties within the movement. Thereafter, living abroad, far removed from local conflicts, she became an unquestioningly revered figure among the small band of the faithful.

Yet back in 1914 the issue of violence was proving enormously divisive within the ranks of New York anarchists.[55] With the Ludlow massacre in Colorado following not long after the Paterson silk workers' strike, the tempo of industrial conflict in the United States was quickening. Still more electric in their local effects were a series of explosions, beginning with one on the morning of July 4, 1914, which tore apart a residential building on Lexington Avenue, taking the lives of three anarchists. Exactly like the Eleventh Street blast of 1970, this one was caused by the premature ignition of home-made bombs, rumored to have been intended for John D. Rockefeller.[56] Throughout the fall of 1914 bombings and rumors of bombings kept New Yorkers (and, incidentally, anarchists themselves) constantly on edge.

Within the movement, opinions had long differed as to the desirability and the effectiveness of violent revolutionary tactics. But a major taboo existed against publicly revealing these internal disagreements and most especially against seeming to join in the public clamor against violence, regardless of one's own private feelings on the issue. The reason for such a taboo is plain. If this small, beleaguered band ever allowed itself to become openly fractured by such a divisive question—one which involved the most determined feelings of the hostile American population—then the

54. According to Carl Zigrosser, Emma Goldman once told someone that the only good thing to come out of the Ferrer Modern School was its magazine.
55. E.g., see Durant, *Transition,* pp. 188–96, describing a long debate over the issue at a Ferrer Center meeting.
56. The Lexington Avenue bombing may, however, have been a deliberate suicide. For a fictional description of it, see *ibid.,* pp. 207–13.

anarchist movement, already torn internally in many other ways, might just as well give up all hope for survival as a coherent social force.

It was a symptom of the depth of debate within anarchistic circles during 1914, however, that hints of just such infighting did reach the light of day, frequently involving the Ferrer Center. Special lecture topics at the Center during August, 1914, for example, included "A Searchlight on Our Enemies: Fighting Fire with Fire," by one L. A. Fehr; and a week later, "Why I Am Opposed to Violence," by Will Durant.[57] Meanwhile, Leonard Abbott had already denied to the *New York Times* that the Ferrer Association was responsible for the Lexington Avenue bombing, and an editorial statement in *Modern School* magazine, addressed to the outside public in the wake of the incident, tried its best to remind everyone that the principal work of the Ferrer Association had always been strictly educational.[58]

Yet the Ferrer leaders, like it or not, found themselves in the midst of a heated public controversy during the weeks that followed. At a mass meeting in Union Square on July 11, presided over by Alexander Berkman and attended by an estimated five to twelve thousand people, Leonard Abbott spoke on the subject of the three anarchists who had just died, trying to set a tone of discussion which would preserve the usual taboo intact. Their deaths, he said, must be understood as a minor incident in the worldwide social struggle. After recalling their bravery in other recent episodes, Abbott went on to ask whether they were to be blamed if they had resorted to violence after having exhausted all peaceful methods. A hostile society, and police brutality in particular, had pushed them inevitably in this direction. "If men of generous and ardent minds are driven to the manufacture of dynamite bombs as a remedy for the wrongs under which they suffer, there must be something fundamentally wrong with our social system."[59]

This was the bold public façade. But inside the Ferrer Association an atmosphere of turmoil and discord now threatened to cripple the movement. Leonard Abbott, Harry Kelly, and a few others had always managed skillfully to keep affairs at the Center on an even keel. Carl Zigrosser recalled with admiration their wise manner in handling what he termed "the lunatic fringe." "In dealing with silly or unbalanced opinions," he said, "they were patient and tactful, their appeal was always to reason and

57. *Modern School*, I (August, 1914), 8.

58. *New York Times*, July 7, 1914; "To the Public," *Modern School*, I (August, 1914), 1–3; *Mother Earth*, IX (July, 1914), 131–32. A survivor of the blast was also suspected of fleeing to Abbott's home near Westfield, New Jersey.

59. Leonard D. Abbott, "The Lexington Avenue Explosion," *Modern School*, I (August, 1914), 3–5; *New York Times*, July 12, 1914.

common sense. Their organization was for education, not direct action. They were not wild-eyed revolutionaries, but were honest, decent, and cooperative in their dealings."[60] Zigrosser's description also offers an interesting hint of what the Ferrer leadership wanted the whole movement to be like. Their tone seems to lack the fieriness of an Emma Goldman or an Alexander Berkman—though it was true that Emma herself, more grudgingly, was moving toward a renunciation of violence during these same years.

It would be easy to oversimplify this sense of internal disagreement. Abbott, for instance, remained bold enough to serve as chairman of a large draft-resistance rally held in the Bronx on June 4, 1917, and in December of that year he presided at a victory celebration honoring the success of the Russian Bolsheviks, which the *Times* said was attended by the most extreme radicals of all persuasions.[61] Similarly, Harry Kelly did not wish to think that his radical zeal was becoming muted by the stormy events of these years. And, if one may detect a distinct shift toward nonviolence in his writings during the period preceding 1913, this after all was only to move in the same direction Emma Goldman herself was taking.[62]

All these nuances must be kept in mind if one is to grasp the import of the decision made by the Ferrer leaders (afterward endorsed democratically by the membership) to relocate the main center of effort outside New York City. There was no open split. And some entirely practical considerations entered into the decision, as will be seen. But the fact remains that a fairly distinct parting of the ways seems to have occurred. A lively session at the Ferrer Center in mid-October 1914, just after a new bomb explosion in New York, was thus recorded by a reporter:

> At the Ferrer Centre in East 107th Street the ranks of the anarchist students were split over the bombs. Leonard D. Abbott, at the head of one

60. Zigrosser, *My Own Shall Come to Me*, p. 73.
61. By then Abbott was an official of the No-Conscription League. Regarding the Bolshevik victory party, the *Times* said Abbott was "the mildest of the lot" who attended but was nonetheless "proud to acknowledge his kinship and sympathy for the Bolsheviki in Russia." *New York Times*, June 5, July 7, and December 3, 1917.
62. In 1907 Kelly had attacked the older American anarchist Benjamin R. Tucker for opposing revolutionary violence; see "Three Quotations and a Comment," *Mother Earth*, II (1907), 167–68. This accords with Emma Goldman's praise of Kelly as a real believer in revolution, *ibid.*, II (1907), 387. But in 1913 Kelly wrote: "If 'being yourself' means the extinction of another, eternal war must ever be the result. . . . Expression that thrives on the liberty and at the expense of others must be combatted." Harry Kelly, "Voltairine de Cleyre," *Mother Earth*, VIII (1913), 120. As an old man, confronted by the spectacle of Hitler, Kelly maintained: "I never was . . . and am not now a pacifist. . . . My anarchism has always been based upon self-defence and as I see it to preach pacifism is to make more assured a Nazi victory." Kelly to Abbott, October 9, 1941, Abbott Papers.

group, was for repudiating the act of setting off the bombs and denouncing it,[63] while Alexander Berkman was in favor of complimenting the police on their theory that a church raider probably was responsible [for the latest dynamiting].

Abbott announced that no more meetings of the Anti-Militarist League, of which Berkman was President, would be held at the Ferrer School, and that no more meetings of any kind of agitators would be held at the Ferrer Centre.

According to the same *Times* story, Berkman agreed to these conditions as laid down by Abbott and confirmed that henceforth his group of anarchists would remain away from the Center altogether.[64]

Abbott's apparent decision finally to speak up in this manner certainly led to no break with Emma Goldman.[65] But a move of this kind on his part is wholly understandable. The basic atmosphere of the Center was at stake. An extreme degree of politicization had occurred. Emma Goldman characteristically boasted that several of the young students in the Ferrer school had been arrested in connection with anti-militarist demonstrations then going on.[66] To others, such a heady mixture of children's education with radical activism seemed less desirable. "It was felt to be unfair to the children and harmful to their development as free spirits," Harry Kelly recalled in 1920, "to grow up in an atmosphere of violent partisanship and fierce revolutionary ardor inevitable with men and women engaged in a daily struggle with the powers of darkness. We were not then and are not now neutral where liberty is violated and economic injustice prevails, but where children are concerned, less passion and calmer judgment should prevail, if we would have them grow into rational and liberty loving men and women."[67] At the time Abbott and Kelly also openly declared in the pages of *Mother Earth:* "The agitation which is carried on by the Association is both necessary and desirable. But it is possible such activity may have a harmful effect on the children and warp their minds; children require brightness and joy and they can best receive that far, and yet not too far, from the 'madding crowd.' "[68]

63. If so, one may see how greatly he had moderated his position since the preceding July; now he was apparently willing to break the usual taboo against joining the public clamor against violence.

64. *New York Times,* October 15, 1914.

65. In 1916 he shared the platform with her at a birth control meeting; in 1917 he was a major witness in her behalf at her trial.

66. Emma Goldman, *Living My Life* (2 vols.; New York: Alfred A. Knopf, 1931), II, 535.

67. Harry Kelly, *The Ferrer Modern School* (Stelton, New Jersey: Modern School Association of North America, 1920), p. 4.

68. Harry Kelly, Fred Hirsch, and Leonard D. Abbott, "A Ferrer Colony," *Mother Earth,* IX (December, 1914), 333.

The most scathing condemnation of the daily mood at the Ferrer Center during this turbulent period came not from one of the native Americans but from the Yiddish-speaking Joseph J. Cohen, who may with every reason be regarded as a trustworthy witness. Cohen looked upon the scene with fresh eyes; he had arrived from Philadelphia on December 1, 1913, to begin serving as "organizer" for the association after a long period of faithful work in the anarchist cause. In New York, he quickly became one of the leading figures in the Ferrer movement. Cohen was a dogged, strong-minded man, active in many phases of the labor struggle. Like Harry Kelly, Cohen combined down-to-earth qualities with high-mindedly idealistic ones. His opinions always drew great respect.[69]

This was the man who, reminiscing about the Ferrer Center a decade later, commented that radical circles had always attracted both "the very best and purest types of humanity" (among whom he carefully named Emma Goldman) and also what he termed "the light-hearted and vacant-headed butterflies and moths of short-lived duration. This has been and is the curse of the radical movement. . . . The doors of radical circles are . . . always wide open to all the charlatans and quacks of social and medical propensities." The Ferrer Center, though it attracted some of the most idealistic people in the metropolis, also lured a number "who exploited everything and everybody for their own selfish ends. Quite naturally the latter were the most vociferous, the most revolutionary in the lot. . . . It required a great effort to rid the place of the undesirable element in order to make room for those who were more or less particular about their associates."[70]

As time went on, said Cohen, the "whole atmosphere" of the Ferrer Center became "permeated with decadence and negligence." What Cohen called "a group of 'spittoon revolutionists' " began holding forth in the basement of their building. To be sure, the lectures and evening classes were still well attended, and "the place teemed with life and action." But the fervent involvement of many people at the Center in demonstrations against unemployment, against militarism, and against the Ludlow massacre created a constant mood of tension, heightened further by the bomb explosions of the summer and autumn of 1914. An increasing number of

69. Cohen's autobiography unfortunately covers only his youth in Russian Poland, where he was raised in an ill-educated but increasingly prosperous family. Joseph J. Cohen, *The House Stood Forlorn* (n.p.; privately published, 1954). On his personality see Harry Kelly to Elsie Kelly, n.d. ("March 12"), in possession of Nathan Marer, and Manuel Komroff to Abbott, April 3, 1940, Abbott Papers.
70. *Sketch*, pp. 50–51.

government spies and provocateurs were becoming plainly visible at their meetings.[71] On one earlier occasion, after a large nearby rally, a wave of police had swept through the Center building briefly. The temptation to seek quieter surroundings was a natural one in view of so much internal turmoil and external harassment. Indeed, the very survival of the movement seemed to be at issue. Alden Freeman, who had hitherto underwritten much of the expense of the school, now became fearful of a possible grand jury investigation directed against him, and in a state of panic he dropped all ties with it.[72]

At this point an option was open to a small group such as the Ferrer Association, which lacked an expensive physical plant. It could pull up stakes. Yet such a strategy carried grave risks. A marginal group relies upon a high degree of visibility. Away from Manhattan, the Ferrer movement might purchase safety at the price of growing obscurity.

Finding itself in this dilemma, the Ferrer membership decided to move the school outside New York, though only after a long and sometimes heated debate, in which a minority argued that to abandon the city would be to remove "the vital spark" from the whole undertaking. It is interesting that Harry Kelly, a prime force behind the relocation in 1914–1915, years later confessed he thought the minority had after all been correct.[73]

Though circumstances pushed the group toward a fast decision, the argument reawakened one of the most ancient issues to concern all those who reflect upon their environment: whether the quality of life is better in the city or in the country. This question has affected nearly every communitarian or secessionist movement in America. The radicals of these earlier decades often had decided opinions on the respective merits of urban and rural life, views which correlate in no precise way with political philosophy. Emma Goldman wrote, for instance, in 1911: "Those who decry the evils of the city should go through the small towns of America. They would soon realize that the city, with all its misery, represents life, motion, change, and interest, as against the lethargy, stagnation and self-sufficiency of the average American town. America as a whole is still very much in the provincial stage, but the mind of her sons of the soil, and even

71. *Ibid.,* pp. 23–24.
72. See above, p. 87. Freeman anonymously gave the Ferrer school $2,500 in 1911 and paid all the teachers' salaries until 1914. During the First World War he became slavishly Wilsonian.
73. Kelly's manuscript autobiography, pp. 278–79. Leonard Abbott also came to think the departure from New York had been a mistake; see his letter to Kelly, September 7, 1949, Abbott Papers.

the average townsman, is so dull that it surpasses every conception."[74] Most of the Ferrer leaders in 1914 disagreed with such a judgment. This did not mean that they denied her assertions about the small-town mentality, and it certainly did not mean that they identified themselves with the American farmer (or even knew much about farming in practical terms). For as Joseph Cohen later recalled, "We selected a homesite [in New Jersey] without knowing anything about the requirements of soil, drainage, shade, bathing facilities and all the other things that make life in the country attractive and pleasant."[75] But it did mean that the majority of the Ferrer membership had by then come abstractly to idealize rural living, believing that it offered benefits intrinsically missing in the modern industrial city.

Though Harry Kelly, for instance, had initially resisted the idea of a rural move "because by nature I was an agitator and felt that the city was the place for me," for a time he now revealed great enthusiasm for the rural way of life. The "breakdown of cities," he went so far as to say, "seems to me inevitable if Anarchism is ever to be realized." It was a mystery, he went on, that some comrades thought anarchism was compatible with urban centers of several million people—for any community existing on such a scale would require a complicated organization out of keeping with the anarchist spirit. And perhaps more than a promotional zeal caused Kelly to state categorically in 1915: "Most radicals would like to live in the country and many of them dream of the time when they can settle there permanently."[76]

But if Kelly's conversion to rural values was rather sudden—it may have been partly occasioned by the fact that the woman he loved had just moved out to a rural colony—the same could not be said of Joseph Cohen, whose role in founding the community at Stelton was nearly as great. At the opening of the new venture, Cohen confessed with obvious sincerity:

74. *Mother Earth,* VI (1911), 152–53. Still more pointedly, another anarchist affirmed: "In many respects it [the city] is hell, but the fires of this hell drive the motors of intellectual and moral revolt. Men cannot stagnate here as in the country. . . . Always there is more surveillance, more interference, more despotism in the country than in the city." E. C. Walker, "Should Radicals Colonize?" *Free Society,* May 15, 1904, p. 2. In the 1890's Walker had advocated colonization.

75. *25th Anniv.,* p. 10. He remembered being approached at this time by a professor of agriculture at nearby Rutgers, who asked him why they had bought a farm whose soil had no humus in it, and being too embarrassed to ask the helpful man the meaning of the totally unfamiliar word "humus."

76. Kelly's manuscript autobiography, p. 273; Kelly to Abe Grossman, April 23, 1924, in possession of Nathan Marer; Harry Kelly, "The Ferrer Colony," *Modern School,* II (April, 1915), 33.

"For many a year, since my older child was born, have I been dreaming about a libertarian school in the country, where the children would be perfectly safe from the dangers surrounding childhood in our large cities and removed from the evil influences and temptations of our artificial life."[77] Long afterward, in the midst of the great depression of the 1930's, Cohen was to found a far more ambitious (but short-lived) agricultural commune in the swampy wilds of western Michigan.[78] His deepest urge, at least from 1915 onward, appears to have been to lead a group of people back into a wholly natural, mutually self-sufficient relationship with one another. Cohen was by no means an extreme primitivist; in Michigan he was quite willing to make use of heavy machinery. But his boyhood spent in the Polish forests had deeply shaped his view of the good life.

Kelly and Cohen both seem to have overestimated the appeal of rural living in the minds of radicals. In 1920, commenting on the difficulty of attracting good teachers to the Ferrer Modern School, Acting Principal John W. Edelman said "the main and principal reason is that there is but the smallest handful of genuine libertarians who will leave the so-called amenities of city life for the parochial life of a place like Stelton." In a similar vein the next year, Harry Kelly agreed sadly that "most revolutionists are city-bred people and think in terms of factories and tenement houses." These comments are all the more striking inasmuch as the Stelton site of the Ferrer colony was located within a reasonable distance of the main line of the Pennsylvania Railroad, and most of the colonists still commuted to work daily in the garment district. That the shift to a rural locale of this essentially suburban type should occasion so much idealized satisfaction on the one hand and so much aversion on the other surely testifies to the importance of this issue in the minds of turn-of-the-century radicals, regardless of which side they took.

After the move away from New York, the leaders of the Ferrer movement would always find it necessary to defend themselves against the charge that they were retreatists who had opted out of the class struggle. The move could easily seem a betrayal of one's basic activism, an initial fateful step toward suburban laziness and acquiescence. Only the building and maintaining of an effective counter-culture, over a long period of time,

77. Joseph J. Cohen, "The Realization of a Life-Long Dream," *Modern School,* II (June, 1915), 65. See also *Sketch,* pp. 44–45.

78. A full account of this later communal effort is contained in Joseph J. Cohen, *In Quest of Heaven: The Story of the Sunrise Co-operative Farm Community* (New York: Sunrise History Publishing Committee, 1957).

could justify such a seeming act of withdrawal. In 1914 the fate of scores of earlier communal ventures in America was well known. The Ferrer leadership was perfectly aware of the advice that history seemed to give in these matters, ever since so many Fourierist phalanxes had failed in the 1840's and 1850's.[79] Though a few colonies had been founded more recently, none had made a great dent in the established civilization of the Western world. Against all these arguments, there is only the blunt fact that the urge to establish communities along radical lines has shown an astonishingly high degree of persistence ever since the early nineteenth century.

Moreover, at least some of the immigrants from Russia brought with them a specifically communal ideal, hoping to found collective settlements after coming to the United States. Several thousand Jews had actually banded together in farming communities in southern New Jersey during the two decades after 1882. Though many who went there were primarily lured by a dream of individual economic advancement, some were consciously idealistic, influenced by the thinking of Tolstoy and the *narodniki*. A few Jewish radicals had even been inspired by the earlier American utopian colonies which they had read about in Russia.[80] In 1908 Abe Isaak proposed a communal scheme in the pages of *Mother Earth* which anticipated the Stelton plan in almost every detail, including the existence of a school.[81]

Colonization was a question about which men might honestly change their minds over the course of time. In 1908 Harry Kelly had rejected the Isaak colony scheme in these ringing words:

> To live one's life in one's own way is a fascinating thing; propaganda by example is often more effective than the written or spoken words; but if there are any who believe that to bury ourself on a farm or in a colony is to spread libertarian or humanitarian ventures, a study of such ventures will soon undeceive them. . . . Philosophic speculations as to freedom

79. At a banquet held in New York for the benefit of the Ferrer Colony early in 1915, Harry Kelly "gave his reasons for believing that it was going to avoid the snags on which such previous Utopian experiments as Brook Farm and the Oneida Community had foundered." *Modern School*, II (April, 1915), 33. Voltairine de Cleyre had earnestly warned Joseph Cohen of the probable failure of all colony ventures, February 1, 1912, Cohen Papers. William Thurston Brown also publicly warned that most earlier colonies had failed.

80. Joseph Brandes, *Immigrants to Freedom: Jewish Communities in Rural New Jersey Since 1882* (Philadelphia: University of Pennsylvania Press, 1971), especially pp. 5–9, 19–20; Sanders, *op. cit.*, pp. 39, 68. Though thousands of Jews had indeed farmed in Russia, the immigrants who chose to adopt this life were nearly all from urban backgrounds, without previous farming experience.

81. A. Isaak, "Attention," *Mother Earth*, III (1908), 239. The Krimont family, who included Kelly's lover and who were prominent in the Ferrer colony, had already lived in a socialist colony near Portland, Oregon, for a time around 1900.

do not make for vitality in a movement; activity is wanted, and the one place for activity is among the people.[82]

In 1914 Kelly was ready—for several reasons, both personal and intellectual—to shift over to an enthusiastic promotion of such a community.[83] A certain loss of revolutionary ardor cannot be ruled out as a cause of this change in his thinking, especially in view of the fact that he appears to have altered his views on violence during the same period of time. But if, in accord with his words of 1908, "propaganda by example" was an entirely legitimate form of revolutionary activity, as it has remained in the minds of many committed idealists, then the significant change that Kelly and others were undergoing was merely one of tactics. A libertarian school and colony, only thirty miles from New York City, could perhaps even hope to be a more effective force for basic social change in America than a decrepit rented building in Harlem through which trooped bands of highly politicized adults, children, spies, and policemen, at all hours of the day and night. To sidestep the established order may be a shrewder strategy than to court a sure martyrdom by meeting it head on.[84]

The move of the Ferrer group from New York to Stelton would raise all these very large questions. But, when viewed as a practical gambit during a moment of great need, the idea had a highly attractive logic. The school and colony, it was explained, would be entirely separate, neither one having a voice in the affairs of the other. Yet the presence of each would help sustain the other. Communal ventures had often failed because educational and cultural stimulation were lacking in rural surroundings. The school would attract such an intellectual life. On the other hand, the colony would help to shelter the school. The children would not be confronted by a hostile, alien world as soon as they stepped outside the classroom. Instead, all their experiences would take place within a single enveloping milieu. Meanwhile, the school would be enabled to survive for a

82. Harry Kelly, "Anarchism: A Plea for the Impersonal," *Mother Earth,* II (January, 1908), 561.
83. The personal influences of Joseph Cohen and the Krimonts may have been important in changing his mind. Also, the change seems to have gone along with a deeper level of disillusionment on Kelly's part with the existing working class. In 1908 he had said on this subject: "Mock and insult the masses because of their seeming supineness in allowing themselves to be exploited; but remember it is death to one's enthusiasm and an end to activity to separate from them." *Ibid.*
84. Against this interpretation of Kelly's motives, there is the fact that by 1921 Kelly was capable of remarking (no doubt half in jest, but in the context of enthusiastically describing the colony's social activities) that "if questions of state were settled after a good dinner there would be much less friction in the world." Harry Kelly, "The Ferrer Colony," *Modern School,* VIII (October, 1921), 15.

time, in economic terms, by the "profit" made on the resale of land to the individual colonists.

"We did one big thing which will one day have greater significance than it has at present," boasted Kelly a few years later. *"We built a community around a school,* something which has never been done before so far as we know. Communities always come first and schools after but we reversed the order and today the school dominates the community instead of being an incidental part of it. We dramatized education and every serious visitor is struck with the fact that here is a community where children rule."[85] In other words, this was to be a very special kind of colony, one whose main purpose was to prepare a new generation to move toward a much freer kind of life, not necessarily to "save" the existing generation.

For a time it was hoped that the Ferrer Center in New York could be maintained simultaneously with the colony at Stelton. But the two undertakings drifted ever further apart, and the old Ferrer Center gradually became a casualty of wartime events. In the summer of 1916 the Stelton leadership—prominently including Kelly, Abbott, and Cohen—moved to break its formal tie with the Francisco Ferrer Association in New York and instead to make Stelton the center of a new nationwide movement for libertarian education. Toward this end, links with radical groups in Philadelphia, Newark, and Paterson were rather pointedly stressed, and a new organization, the Modern School Association of North America, was created to run the school at Stelton and to foster similar educational experiments in other cities.[86] Shortly after this, the Russian Revolution and American entry into the First World War caused the Ferrer Center in New York to lose much of its existing audience. Many comrades were returning to Russia to take part in events there, or else going to Mexico to flee the draft. These emigrations, more than direct governmental harassment, seem to have been responsible for the Center's decline, though the Lusk Committee later tried to take credit for it. Its headquarters on East 107th Street were closed early in 1918. For one more year, until June, 1919, the

85. Harry Kelly, manuscript speech, "25th Anniversary F.A.S.," p. 3, in the possession of Nathan Marer; his italics. In 1924 Kelly also wrote privately: "The Ferrer Colony was created primarily because Joseph Cohen, Leonard Abbott and myself felt the school should be moved to the country and needed people living around it and secondarily because a number of people of radical thought wanted to live in the country." Kelly to Abe Grossman, April 23, 1924, in possession of Nathan Marer. Yet Kelly afterward became deeply involved in the promotion of two other communitarian ventures.

86. There had been a number of efforts to found Ferrer schools in other American cities during 1910–1911, none of them very successful. The new spurt of energy in this direction during 1916–1917 likewise produced only a few abortive results.

Association continued to offer lecture series in another rented hall. Then it entirely suspended its activities. Thus ended a distinct phase in the history of the Ferrer movement.

The Building of the Colony

But meanwhile a new phase had long since begun. In the summer of 1914, shortly after the Lexington Avenue bombing, Harry Kelly happened to pay a visit to the woman he loved, Mary Krimont, who had just moved into a socialist colony at Stelton, New Jersey, two miles north of New Brunswick. This colony, called Fellowship Farm, had been founded a year or two earlier and would remain the next-door neighbor of the Ferrer colony, even though the two communities (rather like rival book dealers on the same block) were to have little mutual contact.[87] In the preceding years a number of socialist or "single tax" colonies had sprung up, especially in the New Jersey and Delaware areas.[88] Of them all, the largely German-speaking Fellowship Farm seems to have been unusually strait-laced and moralistic. For this reason, the few freer spirits who had wandered there, including Mary Krimont and a Scotsman named Robert Graham, were already being made to feel unwelcome and were looking about restlessly for another home. Kelly recalled that, on his visit to see Mary, "Graham said to me half-jokingly, 'Harry, there's a fine farm across the road for sale cheap. Why don't you get some of your friends to buy it and start a colony?' " This suggestion quickly took root, though it might still have withered in the months that followed had not Joseph Cohen kept aggressively pushing it forward.[89]

In this part of New Jersey the land is almost entirely flat, with only a slight suggestion of rises and falls. The soil in this spot, the colonists later found out, was of unusually poor quality. Many who visited the site during succeeding years came away with a strong sense of its bleakness, although today the presence of numerous trees, planted by the colonists and now grown large, creates a gentler and more enjoyable impression. On a clear

87. In later years a cooperative store was maintained jointly by the two colonies, and there are scattered reports of Fellowship Farm colonists attending evening events at the Ferrer colony, but on the whole the pattern was one of mutual avoidance. As of 1919 the two colonies were about the same size, but by 1922 the Ferrer colony had become slightly larger.

88. Their flavor is captured in such books as Harry Kemp, *Tramping on Life* (New York: Boni and Liveright, 1922), and Konrad Bercovici, *It's the Gypsy in Me* (New York: Prentice-Hall, 1941).

89. Kelly's manuscript autobiography, pp. 273–75; *Sketch,* pp. 44–45. Some effort was at first made to canvass the whole area within thirty miles of New York for alternative sites, but attention kept magnetically returning to Stelton.

day a range of high hills is barely visible on the far northern horizon. No rivers or lakes are nearby, but an all-year brook—in places tree-shaded—wound its way through the colony, giving fun to several decades of Ferrer schoolchildren. Despite the stream (and its inevitable mosquitoes), a general lack of shade produced a dry, dusty atmosphere in the summer. A fruit orchard occupied some of the ground. The plot also contained what William Thurston Brown described as "an unusually ugly farmhouse" of six or seven rooms, along with "an uglier barn." There was no adequate water supply or source of heat for the winter, and of course no roadways existed.

Yet it was not true that the colonists had made a transparently foolish purchase. The location at Stelton combined ready access to New York with rural privacy and peace. A walk from the colony of about a mile and a half to the south brought one to the railroad, where local trains required an hour and ten minutes for the journey into Manhattan. This made daily commuting (for instance, to the garment district) tedious but by no means impossible. A more isolated location would have forced many colonists to choose between active participation in the life of the colony and the need for personal self-support; at Stelton, all sorts of practical compromises in this respect, including seasonal ones, became readily possible. Like other suburbanites, the Stelton colonists were to enjoy many of the advantages of both urban and rural living. As Harry Kelly was later to discover, if the group had instead gone north up the Hudson River a similar distance, its members would have had all the same advantages and much pleasanter scenery in addition. But oases so close to New York City and within reach of good transportation were hard to find even then, and the colony leaders should probably not be chided over their choice except as to the poor quality of the local soil. (And, even so, it was never made clear just how seriously agriculture was regarded as a means of sustenance.)

In financial terms, the entire basis for the Ferrer colony lay in the well-known fact that land costs more per unit when it is purchased in small quantities than in large. Thus 143 acres which cost the Ferrer organization about $100 an acre in bulk could be resold at fair market value to the individual colonists (in lots of one or two acres each) at the price of $150 per acre. This income enabled nine acres of land to be set aside for the exclusive use of the school, along with other land to be shared by the colonists in common for roadways and the like. Some of the profit was also spent on a water-supply system, which served part of the colony. Ready buyers for the acre plots were found, and although some later defaulted, enough paid up to make the venture solidly successful. The mortgage on the land was entirely paid off late in 1918.[90] Indeed, so much greater was the demand for plots than had initially been expected that the size of the colony was twice increased during its first year, and it ended up occupying more than double the amount of land originally contemplated.[91]

The individual ownership of plots of land was entirely in keeping with the anarchist belief in voluntarism. No one was to be compelled to remain in the colony any longer than he wished; he could always sell out his holdings and leave. Anarchists, unlike orthodox Marxists, had no single attitude toward the holding of private property; some approved of it while others wanted ultimately to abolish it.[92] Joseph Cohen's experience at Stelton, in fact, whetted his appetite for a more thoroughgoing form of communism, and at his later Sunrise colony in Michigan there was completely common ownership and sharing of goods. But it is tempting to see the individual ownership of land at Stelton as one source of the stability which enabled the colony to survive for more than thirty years. Of course it is incontestably true that the turnover of individual plots was great; in 1925 apparently only a single family had lived continuously in Stelton over the whole preceding ten years. But such a turnover is endemic in many communitarian ventures and has no necessary relation to landholding arrangements. Individual changes of plan were apt to be especially frequent in a decade of world-shattering events.

Not believing in formal government, the anarchists of Stelton at first organized their colony only for external legal purposes.[93] No declaration

90. Kelly said that land in the adjoining Fellowship Farm colony was being sold to individuals for $250 an acre. Cohen was proud that in the Ferrer colony persons who wished to withdraw were always fully reimbursed, even if they failed to live up to their side of the purchase agreement. All land was sold at an identical price and distributed to individuals by the drawing of lots. Colony members were allowed to purchase acres with payments of $10 per month for the first four months and $5 per month thereafter. The colony charged 6 percent interest and a $1 handling fee. *Modern School*, VIII (October, 1921), 13–14, and V (November, 1918), 342; *Sketch*, pp. 48–49; Kelly's manuscript autobiography, p. 275.

91. Three distinct tracts of land thus comprised the colony, and Cohen noted that important differences sprang up among them; for instance, there was a greater tendency toward cooperation on the first tract because it was the only one with a common water supply rather than individual wells. *Sketch*, p. 47. A fourth tract was about to be purchased for still further expansion when the exodus of radicals from this country began at the time of the Russian Revolution.

92. The anarchist colony at Home, Washington, retained much of the land legally under common ownership. Its colonists were mainly native-born, middle-aged Americans, but with the same contrast between "literary" and "plain workingman" types as at Stelton. The Home colony occupied 213 acres of logged timberland.

93. After the mid-1920's more formal organization appears to have crept in. Other anarchist groups were sometimes less consistent than the Ferrer movement on this point. The Boston Anarchist Club had a three-page formal constitution, which

of principles was imposed upon new arrivals, and anyone was welcome to visit the colony who wished to do so. Indeed, it would remain a "colony" only for as long as those who happened to be there still chose to breathe life into the conception. But this absence of coercion, this utter dependence upon freely given personal assent, was the essence of the anarchist philosophy.

The financial crisis was extremely severe, despite proceeds from the resale of the land, and only minimal improvements could at first be made. A new dormitory building was hastily pushed toward near-completion. So very poor was everybody that the parents had to supply beds and bedding for the children. But all was made ready, and on May 16, 1915, the thirty-two young students were taken from New York to Stelton by train, along with a crowd of two or three hundred well-wishers. Alas, it poured rain during much of the day. Joseph Cohen vividly recalled the scene as they gathered that morning at Pennsylvania Station:

> Everything was gloomy and unpromising. Still, we were scheduled to go . . . so go we did. All our efforts to secure a special train were in vain. Among the ordinary crowd of suburban travelers we made our debut as commuters. . . .
>
> At the station there was no one to meet us. Over . . . in the old farm house, the vanguard was busy clearing away the debris of the ceiling that came down with a crash just on the eve of our arrival. A group of volunteer-painters . . . were putting the last touches on the renovated sitting-room, now turned into an office and reception-hall combined. The few caretakers were preparing the noon-day meal for the coming hungry crowd. None could be spared to meet the new arrivals. . . .
>
> The previously planned triumphal march from the station to the farm had been abandoned. Everyone was anxious to get under cover. Few were fortunate enough to be carried in the overcrowded tin-lizzies of the neighboring farmers at so much per head. . . .
>
> The small old farmhouse and the one wing of the open front dormitory, that we had succeeded in erecting before the School was moved, couldn't shelter all the people. . . .
>
> Still, within our hearts and souls there was sufficient light and warmth to keep our spirits high. The two-score city children filled the air with their bright ringing voices, and between the onslaughts of the rain we managed to gather the people in front of the unfinished dormitory, in order to formally dedicate ourselves and the place to the great service of libertarian education.[94]

There at three in the afternoon Carl Zigrosser planted two lilacs which

---

established voting procedure along normal lines of majority rule. Since the entire club was voluntary, it was explained, nothing was wrong with this.

94. *Sketch*, pp. 9–10.

had been donated, and a number of brief speeches were made against a colorful background of posters from Francisco Ferrer's original Escuela Moderna in Barcelona, sent for the occasion by Margaret Sanger. Abbott, Will Durant, Kelly, Cohen, and Robert Hutchinson (who was at this time the principal) all addressed the audience. Abbott explained that the Ferrer Modern School taught no "ism" or dogma, though at the same time its background was one of free thought, anarchism, syndicalism, and socialism. "There is need of the Ferrer schools in New Jersey," Abbott was reported as saying, "when ten thousand people are traveling daily to hear Billy Sunday in Paterson." Harry Kelly was heard to affirm: "When so-called civilized nations are slaying human beings in murderous delight . . . the children of coming generations should be brought up in a spirit of anti-militarism and anti-nationalism." And he praised the group for already showing a tenacity far beyond that of the average man or woman.[95]

The hardships of the weeks and months that followed were akin to those experienced by the most severely disadvantaged groups in American society. Some days that spring they found themselves literally with scarcely a penny. (Small wonder they made it a point to boast, a bit later, about how remarkably free from illness the children had always been. A strong tendency toward vegetarianism in the group helped stretch their money further.) Seventeen shacks or tents were put up by the colonists in short order. Vegetable gardens were planted. As the summer advanced, the empty fields became filled with activity, especially on weekends.

In the first rush of construction, a mood of generous solidarity appears to have developed. "We have no greedy employers, no submissive workers, no wages, no hours,—we have artists expressing themselves joyfully under conditions of cheer and encouragement. . . . Members here do not discuss questions of solidarity, brotherhood and mutual aid—they go right ahead and practice them. A spirit of friendship, of deep, genuine love has so quickly sprung up amongst us that we feel as members of a great family of workers."[96] This claim was supported by the rapid near-completion of the dormitory building on a voluntary basis, although there was less cooperation in road- and house-building than at the anarchist colony of Home in Washington state. Interest in the school and colony mounted. A new tract of acre plots was rapidly sold, and over two hundred applications for places in the school were received.

95. *Modern School,* II (June, 1915), 70–71; the *New York Times,* May 18, 1915; and the *Daily Home News* (New Brunswick, New Jersey), May 17, 1915, whose account is strongly tinged with hostility.

96. Anonymous, "Life in Stelton," *Modern School,* II (June, 1915), 75.

Cohen remarked, "People are telling us that we have accomplished wonders in this short while. Little do they know at what a horrible price these things were brought about." Funds were lacking even to enclose the walls of the dormitory; in places its sides were left open to the elements. The barn was allowed to remain half reconstructed for want of fifty dollars. The place for a woodworking shop was found, but not the tools or materials. Running water was brought in (though so primitively that the pipes remained a constant problem), but they could not afford to install modern plumbing. "We are getting mountains of praise," Cohen noted, "but very little substantial support. And, meanwhile, the summer is passing. Soon all the buildings will have to be made habitable for the cold weather. Some heating apparatus will have to be installed and fuel provided. Teachers must be found and cared for. But where we shall get the means none but the Unknowable knows." The resignation of Robert Hutchinson only a few weeks after the school had made its transfer from New York City and the uncertainty of a replacement soon removed much of the incentive from the work of school building.

The winter of 1915–1916 brought so much severe hardship, and such low spirits, that the undertaking came close to utter collapse. The new principal, Henry Schnittkind, again stayed only a few weeks, because his young wife could not stand the primitive conditions. As cold weather drew near, still no money was on hand for enclosing and heating the thinly constructed dormitory building. Since most of the shacks and tents hastily thrown up by the colonists were also unheated, all but five families (and the brave boardinghouse staff at the school) returned to New York for the winter. For those who stayed, the sense of isolation amid great physical discomfort grew almost unbearable. The few people were scattered over the acreage so that "no more than one or two lights were visible from any one point." Mud and snow inhibited travel. "Seldom would anyone venture to visit a neighbor after nightfall even with a lantern."

Finally in desperation Mary Krimont suggested holding a communal dinner every Saturday evening in the boardinghouse. A Victrola and a few records gave incalculable comfort; the shivering colonists danced until the small hours of the morning. When a rare visitor from New York brought more discs for the small group to listen to, it was a major event. Meanwhile, the three dozen children in the school were being less consciously heroic. "For weeks and days there were no stoves either in the house or in the dormitory. Water for bathing and washing had to be heated on slow-burning kerosene stoves, and the children kept warm by exercise or with the aid of bonfires lighted in some sheltered nook of the woodland. . . .

Many a meal was eaten by the children and teachers huddled up in their overcoats."[97] With none of the customary comforts, New Jersey could readily transform itself into another Siberia.

Loans finally did allow minimal heating facilities to be installed in the kitchen and dormitory of the school at the end of November; no longer did the children have to wash in ice-cold water from the pump. But for several months no new principal could be lured to Stelton, and the mood of gloom did not dispel until the first anniversary celebration in May, 1916, which brought hundreds of members, parents, and friends out to visit the colony and inaugurated a new summer season in which, all over again, everything seemed possible.

The worst was now over. The venture had survived the fury of the elements and the greatest conceivable poverty of resources. A seasonal pattern thereafter became fixed. Each summer would bring life, crowds, and festivities—and best of all, renewed income and support. Every year it would be easier to get through the following winter. The war and the Russian Revolution never crucially interfered with the steady operation of this annual cycle. The year-round residents would eventually develop airs of superiority over the summer-only people, but the dependable seasonal influx made the whole undertaking possible.

Cleverly seizing upon these facts, Kelly and Cohen arranged to hold two major "weekends" at Stelton each year—one in May or early June, to celebrate the aniversary of their arrival in 1915, and the annual convention of the Modern School Association of North America, held at Labor Day and devoted to a wide-open conference on educational policies. In this way, bonds of solidarity could regularly be reforged between the city and country radicals, and Stelton might remain somewhat in the public eye despite its loss of a New York location. In an age when most American families traveled on summer weekends by train or trolley to outdoor picnics, these semiannual celebrations could be counted upon to be highly popular.

The colony was still to know extremely hard times; during early February, 1918, for instance, its bank balance temporarily stood at five dollars. But, from 1916 forward until the mid-1920's, both school and colony grew almost continuously. By September, 1918, fifty-one dwellings existed in the colony, and about twenty families lived there year-round. The summer population was then estimated at two hundred. The old farmhouse had been refurbished with new floors and ceilings, redecorated walls and im-

97. *Sketch*, pp. 27–28, 57.

proved furniture. It now had running water. The barn was transformed to include a library, a stage, and an area where classes could be held in the warmer months; the lower part eventually became the woodworking shop. The dormitory was completely closed in, a second wing was built (raising its capacity to twenty-four children), and plumbing and bathing facilities were added. The most splendid achievement of all came soon after this: the construction of a completely new building to house most of the classes at the school. It was constructed in large part by the voluntary labor of colonists and weekend helpers from the city. Some $6,000 was raised to help pay for it, but, as construction costs were doubling in the inflation of 1919, a large deficit also accrued. During the summer of 1920 it was finished. The building contained four classrooms and a large auditorium, all heated; as can be imagined, it made life for the children and their teachers incomparably more pleasant from then on.

The winter of 1919–1920 brought a marked rise in the number of year-round residents in the colony, not only because radicals in New York were fleeing persecution during the Palmer raids, but also because of an unusually mild season and a major housing shortage in the city. By 1922, some eighty or ninety houses had been built in the colony; this was to be about the peak number.[98] Probably more than three-quarters of the colonists continued to be of Russian Jewish background. Other sizable minorities were of English, Spanish, and Italian nationality. Native Americans tended more often to visit the colony for brief periods than to settle in it.[99] The school also greatly increased its size during these years. It doubled to about 60 children by the fall of 1919 and doubled again to 120 within the next two years. In terms of sheer numbers of people, Stelton was an assured success within six or seven years from its founding.

The first flush of arrival in the countryside, during the summer of 1915, brought with it a mood of realized liberation, a sense of scarcely interrupted idyll. Many of the children ran naked in the hot sunshine and began living in trees. Afternoons were spent digging a swimming pool in the mud of the brook—a project which kept spirits high, even though it was ultimately left unfinished. Joseph Cohen boasted:

> One by one, we are discarding our old habits and superstitions. We are

98. As of 1940 the colony was said to contain about 100 families in the winter months and double that number in summer. Thus Stelton was slightly larger than the Home colony, which at its peak had 213 residents, of whom 75 were children.

99. The Spanish and Italian anarchists who lived at Stelton are recalled as having been a numerically sizable group who stuck to themselves and went almost wholly unmentioned in any of the colony's printed publications. The English contingent, headed by James and Nellie Dick, arrived in 1917, seeking to escape the war.

beginning to *live,* naturally and fully. We wake up early in the morning and are done with our breakfast before eight o'clock. The breakfast, like all the rest of the meals, is prepared by one of the care-takers with the assistance of two children. Till noon we spend our time around the house, working, writing and gardening. Then we gather again at the common table . . . and in the afternoon the brook is our shop and playground until the evening meal. In the twilight we play games and sing until it gets dark and the kids begin to retire to their beds.[100]

Stelton always remained something of a children's paradise. They were able to roam freely anywhere in the colony, forever assured of a welcome.

As facilities improved and numbers grew, more activities could take place in the evenings. At first these were held on the grass outside the old farmhouse; later, when the barn was in better condition, they could be moved indoors in bad weather. Talks and discussions retained much of the seriousness, iconoclasm, and informality of gatherings at the Ferrer Center in New York. However, Kelly noted a declining interest in economic questions, a trend which he said showed the effects of country air and of down-to-earth colony building upon minds previously more attuned to the class struggle. Instead, the Steltonites came to prefer what Kelly called "philosophical or speculative subjects," especially questions of educational theory and policy. "Year in and year out this last area was dealt with, both with great logic and with intense emotion. Though the same arguments were voiced again and again, the participants seemed never to tire of them."[101] In keeping with the basic philosophy of the movement, children were given full equality with adults in these group conversations, including equal voting rights when the meetings became more formal.

One of the most interesting discussions came about spontaneously one night during the first summer at Stelton. About forty people were present. It occurred to them to ask what each person thought the function of the Ferrer colony should be, and also to describe as frankly as possible the motives which had prompted him or her to join it. Quickly the talk moved into the sensitive question of how much freedom should be allowed in the colony, especially freedom to go against (and possibly even undermine) the dominant spirit of the place. For instance, should the aged father of one of the comrades be permitted to utter loud prayers every day in public? "The discussion was earnest, even intense at times, but all in good spirit, and the general opinion seemed to prevail at the conclusion that while the Colony was not a colony of Anarchists, it was an Anarchist Colony—that

100. Joseph J. Cohen, "The Realization of a Life-Long Dream," *Modern School,* II (June, 1915), 69.
101. Kelly's manuscript autobiography, p. 297.

a freedom prevailed here even to the extent that men could say their prayers, if they so desired." Such questions of personal freedom, like those of educational policy, were always talked out openly. A week later, by way of contrast, Dr. Cecile L. Greil came to the colony from New York to speak on "The Girl and Her Mother," from the point of view of the person's expanding sexual consciousness during adolescence. "The discussion brought out sharply divergent views, on some matters. . . . It was pleasant to note that for the first time at one of these meetings a woman was the opening speaker and there were as many women—or more—who participated in the discussion as there were men."[102]

By the summer of 1918 lectures were being held every Saturday evening on some phase of politics, history, or the arts, often combined with violin and piano recitals, and always followed by free-for-all discussions. On Sunday evenings there was music or dancing. Smaller specialized groups within the colony or the school met nearly every weekday night. The annual celebration and convention weekends became ever more strenuous affairs; some fifteen hundred people came to the colony at Memorial Day in 1920. Regular evening classes for adults were also begun around the same time. Plays were now put on at all seasons of the year, thanks to the new heated auditorium. "The social life of the colony has become so interesting," Harry Kelly boasted, "that we venture the assertion that the Ferrer Colony is one of the most vital communities in the country." Meanwhile, the large summer influx greatly improved the school's income, as admission fees charged for the entertainments were set aside for that purpose. In 1921 the general financial picture looked more encouraging than ever before.

Even the winter months now saw far more social activity. Communal dinners, prepared by groups of two or three women acting in turns, were again held every Saturday night. Singing and folk dancing were introduced on Sunday evenings, always continuing until long past midnight. Special dinners were held to honor arriving or departing colonists or unusual guests. Fund-raising dinners benefited such causes as children's relief in the Russian civil war. Sometimes these occasions attracted so many people from New York that they overtaxed the women and had to be temporarily discontinued for that reason. In 1921 two hundred people attended Harry Kelly's fiftieth birthday party, even though they braved a January storm to do so. Saturday-night discussion topics now included "poetry, literature, the drama, the revolutionary labor movement, the organization of industry,

102. "Lectures and Discussions at Stelton," *Modern School*, II (July-August, 1915), 89.

the story of the conscientious objectors of Leavenworth, Kansas, and other subjects by such speakers as Bernard Sexton, Howard Scott, Roger Baldwin, Earl Humphries, Albert de Silver, Elizabeth Gurley Flynn and our own local talent. Questions of a communal nature such as roads, water, lighting the colony, a co-operative store and the maintenance of the school are all discussed and decisions arrived at, not always in the most satisfactory manner but as best we could under the circumstances."[103]

The children might enjoy running wild, and the adult colonists might revel in their evening entertainments, but for Joseph Cohen and many of the other dedicated members of the colony these years were a period of immensely hard labor, a time of attempting to construct a physically satisfactory basis for living with practically no resources. Considering how little they began with, they accomplished a great deal. Though there was indeed something unworldly about the colonists, which oddly reflected itself in their ability to relish the joys of the moment, it would be wrong to make too much of their impracticality. Cohen in particular, though inexperienced, had much common sense; he could learn rapidly from mistakes, and he was capable of driving a shrewd financial bargain.[104] On the whole, the colonists were less hindered by their naïveté than by the sheer limit of their capital.

Meanwhile, seemingly they fulfilled a variant of the tantalizing Marxian formula, reading or working hard in the morning, going swimming in the afternoon, and dancing or hearing a lecture after dinner, all without an oppressive sense of schedule. Willing to work, they were by no means puritanical about pleasure. Such a casually mixed attitude toward work and play might prove difficult for other radical groups to recapture a half century later, when the issue of work had become far more self-conscious. Though in some respects the atmosphere of the community began to erode even as the colony grew to its full proportions, for a brief time the Stelton venture revealed the promise of an alternative society in which men, women, and especially children could lead a more natural, joyful, and integrated kind of life.

Beyond this, there was long a powerful spirit of mutual helpfulness among the colonists at Stelton, one which was intensified in the early years by the poor physical circumstances in which everyone lived. Mothers could

103. Harry Kelly in *Modern School*, VIII (Spring, 1921), 30. The atmosphere of intellectual discussion and entertainment appears to have been very similar at the Home anarchist colony.
104. See especially his vivid description of experiences while building the water system, finding out about the soil, and having the land surveyed, in *25th Anniv.*, pp. 10–11.

leave their children at any time, knowing they would be adequately cared for wherever they might choose to wander.[105] Doors were seldom closed and never locked. Even comparative strangers would help look after each other and run errands when someone was sick. And these practices continued for a long time after factionalism had begun to appear. Of course such traits are hardly peculiar to utopian colonies; in this respect, the Stelton life style was actually quite similar to that of a large sector of the English working class and, to a lesser degree, that of the traditional American small town. But it is important to note how strongly these virtues happened to be present at Stelton.

Many who visited the colony or stayed in it for a time found themselves unwillingly repelled by it, however, despite an almost universal admiration for the idealism of its leaders. They were repelled because, to middle-class eyes, Stelton became a scene of physical ugliness and squalor. The colony, with its shacks and home-built cottages, never could claim to be an aesthetician's delight, and some who were unkind termed it a rural slum, unpleasanter even than the tenement buildings which had just been forsaken. Roads were left unpaved (and, worse, ungraded) because the colonists could never unanimously agree to assess themselves for improving them. Much litter was scattered about in broad view, and the children often played freely in it; this was mentioned as a flagrant problem year after year. (Perhaps it derived partly from the sudden influx of irresponsible summer visitors.)[106]

Opinions differed as to how badly off Stelton was in these terms. Hans Koch said that as of 1920 the school grounds and buildings "were awfully neglected. It seemed as if it never entered the mind of anybody there, that the higher a cultural state a human being attains, the more important his environment becomes to him."[107] When Agnes Inglis visited from Michigan the next year, Stelton did not strike her "as a place [in which] anyone could stay for any length of time"; it was "a very dreary place—all but

<hr/>

105. Jo Ann Burbank cautions against any emphasis on "women's liberation" at Stelton (to the author, September 23, 1970). To her, the typical scene was of the husband lying on the couch reading the *Freie Arbeiter Stimme* while the wife slaved at firing up the furnace and getting the children to bed.

106. On the litter problem, see for instance Alexis Ferm's reports of June 4, 1922, p. 1, May 6, 1923, p. 1, and April 12, 1936, p. 3, and Anna Schwartz's report of 1940, p. 1, all in Modern School Association of North America Papers, Rutgers University. The Home anarchist colony does not appear to have had these problems; it is recalled as having been neat in appearance.

107. Hans Koch, "Elizabeth Byrne Ferm," *The Roman Forum* (Los Angeles), XIII (November, 1944), 3; cf. the complaint of William Thurston Brown in *Modern School,* V (September, 1918), 272, that "an aesthetic conscience has been conspicuous by its absence."

the school house."[108] Manuel Komroff, visiting the colony in the 1930's long after he had deserted the Ferrer movement, reacted with the extreme horror of someone who has a high emotional investment in escaping from the slums. "Such sordid squalor I have never believed possible. The shanty towns built on the river's edge in the very low of our [Jewish] existence presented a better appearance and some were even neat and trim. If Stelton is the result of 20 years of building by idealists then I say: Gessus No! I doubt if the look of the thing can be matched anywhere in America. . . . I call tin-cans, no trees, no shrubs, no paint or shades, a sweat shop left with 20 sewing machines in the center of the colony, no sign on the road, no road worth calling a road . . . I call this all hugger-mugger."[109] But in fact there were trees, and Jo Ann Burbank said that those along the brook "were grand. Near our hut a spreading oak tree, as least five centuries old, made a perfect spot for the children to play. . . . To walk down the street after the end of a Saturday night affair, some thirty or so of us, singing in harmony, was an experience to treasure."[110]

Alexis Ferm, co-principal of the school after 1920, attacked the dirt and clutter in terms that may betray a hidden middle-class bias of his own. When he arrived "it was a dump . . . most of the houses were bare and unattractive." Moreover,

> there was no creative activity or initiative, excepting in the way of marauding peach and apple orchards. And civic consciousness had not been awakened. The whole atmosphere of the country was so new to these city bred people, workers who had had no vacation in the country before, that they had not yet been able to understand what the country required of them. Yet they were at heart good-natured, anxious to make the world a better place for everybody, only they did not know how to go about it. In the city they did not have to clean their own door-step.

He cited, as an example of the extreme ignorance of a few of the colonists, one couple who built a small two-story house with their own labor and completely forgot (until it was finished) to provide any staircase leading to the upper floor. Privately, Ferm became bitter about the continuing lack of energy for civic improvements at Stelton. Why, he complained, should one "expect these people to be of the ability of the managing class? If they were they would not be here. They are workers who have very little ability, excepting to talk."[111]

108. Agnes Inglis to Leonard D. Abbott, March 7, 1943, Abbott Papers.
109. Manuel Komroff to Leonard D. Abbott, March 25, April 3, 1940, Abbott Papers.
110. Jo Ann Burbank to the author, September 23, 1970. She arrived at Stelton in 1929.
111. Alexis C. Ferm, "A Sketch of the Life of the Modern School" (manuscript),

In at least one major respect, the Stelton colonists soon began deviating from conventional working-class patterns, whether European or American. This was in their pronounced tendency toward faddism especially in matters of diet and health. "There is hardly another community elsewhere in this world where the immature panaceas of the quack doctor, the osteopath, the chiropractor and the naturopath are so willingly accepted and followed as in the Ferrer Colony," Joseph Cohen observed in 1925. "The poor children and some of the adults have paid the price."[112] The price in physical terms, as has been noted, was surprisingly small. Despite extreme experimentation in matters of diet (especially in the direction of serving only one item of food in large quantities at a given meal), there was remarkably little illness among the children, perhaps because they also obtained food from the various homes in the colony. Even the influenza epidemic of 1918 bypassed Stelton almost completely.

Psychologically, it was sometimes a different story. "There is a boy in Philadelphia," Cohen recounted,

who even now shudders at the memory of his dietetic experiences at Stelton nine years ago, when he was a child of five or six. There were . . . times when . . . vegetables were, on principle, cooked in their jackets—and quite often with part of the dirt to boot—in order to preserve the iron contained in the skin. Still other times there were when the children were instructed to chew their food thirty-two times and count the number of raisins eaten at one meal. The last and most astonishing fad . . . is the serving of mud to be taken for the internal purification of the body. The Stelton children talk more about elements, starches, acids and body-poisons than about games.[113]

It is well remembered that over the years Stelton attracted quite a few people who wished to practice eccentric patterns of living. Some of them did not even share much interest in radical political ideas. (The same was true at the Home anarchist colony.) For such persons, the main attraction of the place must have been its atmosphere of tolerant individualism.

To sustain themselves, most of the colonists either commuted to jobs in New York or else tried to raise poultry and grow vegetables on their acre plots. At least in some seasons, chicken farming became profitable, thanks to a steady market for eggs in the vicinity. It was reported that "quite a

p. 19, M.S.A.N.A. Papers; Ferm to Leonard D. Abbott, April 27, 1940, Abbott Papers.

112. *Sketch*, p. 52.

113. *Ibid.*, pp. 52–53. Apparently the Ferrer children had often been vegetarian even in New York around 1912. See Rion Bercovici, "A Radical Childhood," *Scribner's Magazine*, XCII (August, 1932), 103. However, an extreme "back to nature" life style was not always regarded with respect by others; see *25th Anniv.*, pp. 23, 32.

number do very well at this work with only a couple of acres to do it on, and the will to work and see it thru."[114] Some gained further income by boarding children who were attending the school. Since the garment trade was seasonal, a varied alternation among these activities often became possible. The local cooperative store helped the colonists satisfy many of their needs at fair prices, although, as often happens in such ventures, it lost money and after fifteen years had to be abandoned.

Survival was easily possible for Steltonites all through the 1920's. Times became very hard during the depression of the 1930's (bringing about a desperate experiment with a "production-for-use" cooperative), but Stelton people were at least glad to live where they could grow much of their own food. The economic viability of life in the colony showed itself in the fact that so many families remained there long after the original community spirit had begun to evaporate, or else returned there after trying to live in other locations.[115] Such viability was purchased, of course, at the price of genuine self-sufficiency. In economic terms, the colony was not a self-sustaining counter-culture at all, thanks to its partial dependence on the New York job market. But, if the members had seriously tried to exist on the basis of agriculture alone, it is not hard to predict a far speedier end to their efforts.

The colony was supposed to help sustain the school, but after the initial sale of land its support became rather minimal and indirect.[116] The school was thus forced to reach outward for aid in a great variety of directions. These efforts were especially needed because tuition and board fees were kept extremely low in order to enable ordinary workingmen to send their children. During the earliest years at Stelton, such was the mood of desperation that the children would occasionally go forth on walking tours to nearby towns, where they sang and danced in the streets for coins.[117] The children often performed plays or skits for New York audiences in rented halls. During the year ending in September, 1918, only a quarter of the school's $4,000 income came from tuition charges. The rest was made up

114. James H. Dick to Mrs. Anna Throop Craig, December 3, 1930, Dick Papers, in possession of Nellie Dick, Miami, Florida. One man worked in a printing shop, and another did carpentry for the New Brunswick Woolworth's.

115. At various times large numbers of colonists drifted away—to Russia around 1917, to a colony begun somewhere in Pennsylvania, and to Joseph Cohen's Sunrise Colony in Michigan in 1933. Yet a surprising number of these emigrants would return to Stelton later on. Stelton was a secure refuge for many who also recognized, especially in later years, its limitations as an environment.

116. Partly this was due to political factionalism in the colony, as will eventually be seen.

117. Ray Porter Miller, "My Teachers at Stelton," *25th Anniv.*, p. 27.

by benefit balls and entertainments, personal contributions and dues. Salaries paid to the staff were still far below average.[118]

For several years after 1919, trade unions became a significant source of support for the school. Though the Ferrer movement had been friendly toward the idea of syndicalism, its members also believed in working for greater militance within the AF of L, rather than trying to splinter, for instance, the promising and successful ILGWU. This tactical moderatism was rewarded when ILGWU Local 20 donated $200 to the school in the summer of 1919. During 1920 a number of union officials visited Stelton for the first time, and such gifts greatly increased. Several unions made annual contributions over a rather long period. However, most trade-union support for the Ferrer school came from individual locals where pockets of militant radicalism existed, and not from the higher echelons of the labor movement, which were naturally much less friendly toward a school with an anarchistic reputation. Though a desperate appeal made directly to David Dubinsky in 1937 did produce a small sum after much delay, even this degree of response from on high was exceptional.

Yet it is surprising how few symptoms there were of extreme hostility between the Ferrer colony and the outside world, either in the New Brunswick area or more generally. By and large Abbott, Cohen, and Kelly had gambled correctly that a move to the country would give them peace and seclusion. The closest neighboring farmer was always friendly, though another neighbor became a member of the Ku Klux Klan. During the turmoil of the First World War and the Red scare that followed it, those who lived at Stelton managed to avoid much of the highly political atmosphere which prevailed in New York. To be sure, there were a few close escapes. When the colonists grew so bold as to hang a red flag from the top of their sixty-foot water tank, in celebration of the German revolution of 1918, armed vigilantes soon appeared—reportedly led by a prominent New Brunswick businessman—and demanded that it be lowered. The colony was practically deserted at the time, but Joseph Cohen sturdily refused to comply with their orders. Thereupon they mounted the tower themselves, took down the flag, and carried it off as a memento. Apparently they were satisfied with the gesture, for they never returned.

Far more serious was the arrival, about a year later, of several agents sent directly from the office of Attorney-General A. Mitchell Palmer. After prowling around the colony and engaging Cohen in blunt dialogue about

118. By 1921 some 40 percent of the school's income was coming from tuition and board charges. Large private gifts were few, though Pryns Hopkins, wealthy director of a progressive boys' school in Santa Barbara, once gave them $1,000.

bomb throwing and free love, these men left. But they were soon followed by the federal district attorney, who spent four hours interrogating Cohen and arguing heatedly with him.[119] In a report whose contents were soon smuggled to the comrades, the district attorney confidentially urged that every inhabitant of the colony be removed to Ellis Island and deported from the United States. This recommendation was quietly put aside, apparently for reasons intrinsic to the colony's rural location. "What saved us," Cohen later recalled, "was the fact that we were all property owners, tied up with all kinds of obligations and entanglements. Even Mitchell Palmer did not have the nerve to uproot a whole community of people against whom there was nothing but their belief that could be objected to."[120]

Thus the Stelton colony remained unmolested, while many New York anarchists were being herded aboard the *Buford* and forced to leave the country. Other, more minor instances of harassment occurred during the Red scare period, but they likewise led to no important result.[121] The peaceful, educational emphasis of the anarchists' activities at Stelton operated strongly in their favor. Hostile reports on the colony almost invariably conceded an important degree of difference between anarchists such as these and real bomb throwers. To this extent, the colonists had gained freedom from persecution at the price of diluting their radicalism (despite the bold way in which they sometimes talked back to visiting government agents).

Yet the Ferrer movement often faced intense hostility which stopped short of outright vigilantism. The Cooper Union refused its facilities to the Ferrer group (and to all other anarchist meetings) in 1910. When the school was located on East Twelfth Street, it was visited one day by a Tammany agent after a complaint from the local Catholic priest. Harry

119. From Cohen's account, the district attorney appears to have been under some inner compulsion to try to convince Cohen through argument of the righteousness of the Palmer deportation policy. Cohen answered the man boldly, putting him on the defensive and making him increasingly furious. *Ibid.,* p. 12.

120. *Ibid.* Postal authorities were quite clearly tampering with the school's mail in July, 1919. See Elsie Pratt to Carl Zigrosser, July 26, 1919, Zigrosser Papers. One person from the Home colony was sent to Ellis Island for deportation.

121. The New York *Tribune* tried to stir up hostility against the colony in its Sunday edition of September 14, 1919, with a banner headline, "An Anarchist Colony 70 Minutes from Broadway," and a long story about conditions in Stelton written in a blatantly provocative spirit. The Lusk Committee of the New York State Senate attacked the Ferrer Center in New York City (then in its death throes anyway), but nothing came of this. "The Lusk Report on the Modern School," *Modern School,* IX (Midwinter, 1922), 18–23; Kelly's manuscript autobiography, p. 354. A free-lance anti-Communist named Archibald Stevenson also tried to inflame feeling against the Ferrer movement; see the *New York Times,* January 24, 1919.

Kelly outtalked the intruder, partly by pretending he was Irish. On the other hand, during the season of 1913–1914 the day school was visited by no fewer than forty-two interested strangers, most of whom seem to have been sympathetically curious. These included teachers, settlement workers, and three professors from German universities, as well as reporters and private detectives. But the press long remained largely hostile. Editorials attacked the movement by name in Brooklyn and Philadelphia, and the New York *Tribune* printed an apparently spurious interview with Harry Kelly in 1915, designed to do the group harm.[122] When the colony at Stelton was first dedicated, the New Brunswick newspaper reprinted (without comment) a strongly hostile editorial about the movement which had just been published in Newark. Town Hall in New York wanted to deny the school its facilities for a benefit concert in 1921, after learning of the group's background. The children at Stelton further recalled having to endure insulting questions from outsiders when they boarded the local train to ride into New Brunswick, and some of the girls received physical advances from farmers when they were offered lifts in automobiles while walking toward town. (This was of course because of the "free love" reputation of the colony.) New Jersey education officials interrogated the staff of the school in an edgily political fashion, probably more than once. In the late 1920's the local superintendent of schools testified hostilely when the Modern School sought tax exemption from the state. Only much later was the Modern School given accreditation by New Jersey. Of course many Stelton children went on to attend New Brunswick high school; though they sometimes were valedictorians, performing outstandingly well as students, they were also conspicuous for their poor clothing, extreme earnestness, and generally unconventional views.

Yet, despite all such evidences of friction between the members of the Stelton community and the larger society, it is clear that outright conflict gradually diminished. Increasingly the two worlds glided past each other without making contact. Colonists were no longer scorned as anarchists; now they were faintly stared at as eccentrics, on the basis of a crudely stereotyped notion of their pattern of living. Thus the commonest image of the Stelton radicals in the New Brunswick area as time went on seems to have been "that free-love colony," or "that nudist colony." And such an image was only a casual one, faintly held. Most often the people in the surrounding area simply did not think about the colony at all.[123]

122. The tone of these editorials was not always hysterical; the movement was often simply attacked in the straightforward language of rational argument.
123. Interview with Donald Sinclair, archivist at Rutgers University Library,

The colony was greatly protected by its geographical isolation. During most of its history it had few neighbors closer than a mile away. Occasionally, however, opposition could be felt even in later years. In 1948 a Catholic veterans' group threatened a Communist speaker at the colony with bodily harm, and some local public school teachers were noticeably prejudiced against children from the Modern School even in 1952. Yet such evidence could be more than balanced by gradual symptoms of integration and acceptance: Stelton colonists were actually elected to the local Board of Education; teen-age boys from the colony played a basketball game in 1933 against a local outside team; a weekly newspaper in nearby Dunellen was consistently friendly toward the colony, partly because of a personal connection; a few colony people eventually founded local businesses; many local businessmen cheerfully advertised in the school benefit programs.

Beyond these isolated bits of testimony, one senses that indifference and simple incomprehension prevailed most of the time. Such indifference was no doubt crueler and more deadening to self-esteem than overt hostility would have been. The surrounding society casually smothered Stelton in the single label "crackpot." It was an ugly label, one that could deeply wound the person who did not keep his defenses against it carefully raised.[124] The younger children, from all indications, do not seem to have absorbed this conception of themselves; to them, the colony way of life was simply life itself, and only as they grew up did they come to realize how very different the rest of the world could be. But the adult members no doubt shared a highly poignant awareness of what it meant to have chosen to exist for a lifetime outside the American mainstream.

Such an awareness made Harry Kelly's rhetoric momentarily bitter when he boasted, in 1921, that "Stelton has ceased to be considered, by radicals at least, as a place for freaks where people expect to escape the laws of economic determinism and inaugurate a Utopia by raising children

---

March 18, 1970. Sinclair is a trained historian, highly knowledgeable in local history, who also grew up in a neighborhood near the Stelton colony during the 1930's; he reported this as his firm impression. Sinclair was also certain that the colonists did not become widely stereotyped as Jews. The built-up portion of the New Brunswick area closest to the colony was ethnically diverse; it included some Rutgers professors as well as clusters of Italian immigrants. On the whole, Sinclair describes the New Brunswick area as relatively cosmopolitan and tolerant in its attitudes.

124. "It does not answer anything to call ideas 'crackpot ideas.' A man does that when he has no answer. It is merely a sign of weakness. Mental weakness." Alexis C. Ferm to Leonard D. Abbott, September 18, 1942, Abbott Papers. The last two words show his depth of feeling.

and chickens."[125] He meant, of course, to be funny. But the phrases must have stuck uncomfortably in the minds of his hearers.

The Educational Radicalism of Elizabeth and Alexis Ferm

As conceived by its original leaders, the colony above all meant the school. "The liberation of the human race through libertarian education" was their boldly stated aim as they moved to Stelton.[126] It was in the school that a basic clash between "inner" and external, educational and politicized forms of radicalism began to take on clear outlines. At the same time, the Ferrer Modern School acquired an important life of its own after the arrival of Elizabeth and Alexis Ferm as co-principals in 1920.

For the most part, the five years that preceded the Ferms were a time of genuine chaos in the school—of anarchy with a very small "a." Children were given practically no discipline, in part because certain members of the staff really believed in such an extreme policy, but also as a result of the simple state of confusion that prevailed. The frequent shifts from one teacher to another, and the intervals between teachers, had a highly unsettling effect. Conditions in the boardinghouse grew so wildly uncontrolled that caretakers would usually resign after a few weeks.

Some of the staff then sincerely thought "that the function of the Modern School was just to let the child do as it pleased whether that happened to be to smash the piano, windows, victrola, your face, or some other child's head. If he insisted on doing these things, he must get his lesson from experience." As a result it became "quite the usual thing to find . . . the victrola out of commission, books, pencils, clothing scattered about and the children walking over them, presenting a chaotic condition of dirt and disorder." Certain staff members for a time resorted to a harsh method of punishment: deprivation of meals. This produced a "smoldering . . . feeling of hostility among the children, directed against all grown persons who came to care for them; a general sullen disregard of any but themselves, and an organized system of petty thieving to get what they believed belonged to them." Fortunately, still others would appear on the staff—like Nellie Dick in 1917—who "had no particular theories, but a kindly disposition toward the youngsters, who worked with harmony amongst themselves and made the kiddies comfortable." Thus "there were times when

125. Harry Kelly, "Report of the Organizer for 1920–21," *Modern School,* VIII (September, 1921), 24.
126. *Modern School,* I (September 1, 1914), 4.

hope burned strong, and looking upon our work we thought it good. At other times it seemed as though any kind of a home would be an improvement on this."[127]

By the end of 1919 the school was on the verge of collapse. Early in 1920 it was both saved and transformed. The turnabout was produced by the two most commanding personalities ever to ally themselves with the Ferrer movement: Elizabeth and Alexis Ferm. The Ferms were to make the school for a short time one of the most remarkable educational experiments in the United States.

Elizabeth Byrne Ferm, known to everyone at Stelton as "Aunty," was the dominant of the newcomers; she had the more powerful and controversial personality. Aunty was a tall, slender woman, "beautiful, with large green eyes." When she smiled, it was a "complete" smile. Her voice had a "lilting note . . . like the voice of one who sang much in her youth," yet it was also "firm and positive." Sometimes her eyes twinkled with good humor; they might also seem to burn like a fanatic's. Always they drew everyone toward her. A critical ex-member of the colony long afterward termed her "one of those rare beings you see but once and they stay with you." About her movements, "from the play of her knitting needles to the swaying of her chair," there hung a certain distinctive quality of "self assertive calmness." Yet she was also aggressively outgoing, easily breaking forth into demonstrative enthusiasm over whatever was immediately happening. Irresistibly her enthusiasm would spread. " 'It is a wonderful day,' she says. . . . There is so much emphasis placed on the word 'wonderful' that I also begin to see the day as wonderful." The children remembered her lively quickness, her ability to be everywhere at once, forever in the center of what was going on. Especially they recalled how she played the piano at the morning assemblies she had established, proudly seated at the keyboard like a queen.[128]

She had been born in Galva, Illinois, in 1857, of relatively well-off Irish parents.[129] Her father was a pioneer farmer of great determination. Her grandfather, who stayed in Ireland, left the family a two-thousand-

127. Mary Hansen, "Facts and Theories at the Living House," *Modern School,* VIII (September, 1921), 3.

128. Konrad Bercovici, *op. cit.,* p. 65; Jacob Robbins, "Two Persons and an Ideal," *Modern School,* VIII (October–December, 1921), 6–10; Koch, *op. cit.,* p. 3; Nancy Adams to Alexis C. Ferm, April 18, 1944, Ferm Papers, University of Florida; and interviews with a number of her students and fellow staff members.

129. It may or may not be significant that Galva, Illinois, was the seat of the Bishop Hill colony, a communal experiment of Swedish immigrants, which broke up in 1859 when she was two years old. Charles Nordhoff, *The Communistic Societies of the United States* (New York: Hillary House, 1960), p. 347.

dollar legacy, and with it they later moved to Montreal. By this time, like Harry Kelly, Elizabeth Byrne had been left fatherless, at the young age of six. In Montreal the girl was placed in small private schools and then in a convent at nearby Lachine. She studied the piano seriously. Later she recalled this period as one in which "piano playing, painting, drawing and fancy work [were] extolled, and manual work classed as low and menial. I accepted these conventional ideas and lived the life of a formalist and conformist by suppressing my natural inclination to be one 'who did things.' "[130] At twenty she married an older man, Martin Battle, and moved to New York, where they established a bookstore. Battle had firm ideals of wifely submission in everyday life, but Elizabeth refused to accept his authority. When he kept her locked at home all day one Sunday, she threatened him with a hatchet until he opened the door to let her out. Soon after this she left him and resumed studying the piano, graduating from the New York Conservatory of Music in 1885. Meanwhile, she had become an active follower both of Henry George and of the woman's suffrage movement. Her mother now came down from Montreal, bought a house in Brooklyn, and lived there with Elizabeth, who supported herself by giving piano lessons.

When her sister died, leaving two small children, Elizabeth Battle conceived the idea of mothering them herself. (She never had any children of her own—a fact that definitely spurred her interest in working with other youngsters.)[131] She decided to embark on a program of formal child study. In 1889 she graduated from the Training School for Kindergartners associated with All Souls' Episcopal Church in New York, having received instruction in Froebel's methods, which remained her formal pedagogical tool.

At once she began attracting attention for her unusual ability with children. A year later she was persuaded to take charge of the kindergarten run by the Brooklyn Guild. At this time she also appears to have become interested in Theosophy.[132]

At a Theosophy meeting in the early 1890's, Elizabeth Battle met her second husband, Alexis C. Ferm, who was speaking to the group on the

130. Elizabeth Byrne Ferm, "The Democracy of Whitman," *Mother Earth,* I (January, 1907), 29.
131. Alexis Ferm (to the author, September 11, 1970) said that if Elizabeth had had a child of her own she would not have started her first "free school" in 1901.
132. Alexis C. Ferm, "Elizabeth Byrne Ferm—A Biographical Note," in Elizabeth Byrne Ferm, *Freedom in Education* (New York: Lear, 1949), pp. 189–91; Alexis Ferm to Leonard D. Abbott, September 1, 1949, Abbott Papers; *New York Times,* June 18, 1971.

subject of education. Ferm, born in 1870, had endured a much harder early life. His father was a beer-loving Swedish shoemaker who brought him to America when he was two and settled on Nevins Street in Brooklyn, a mixed neighborhood of tenements and private houses. The boy began working full time in a dry-goods store when he was eleven. On the side he began turning himself into a self-taught intellectual, devouring Emerson, Thoreau, and Longfellow, and gleefully discarding his religious faith when he first noticed contradictions in the Bible. He also appears to have been a physically rather timid boy, afraid of all forms of fighting and injury, and greatly devoted to his mother and sister. As a young man, he began moving upward into middle-class occupations, as bookkeeper and store manager, then as secretarial clerk in a series of newspaper offices and manufacturing firms. In maturity he could be described as "a tough-minded, resilient Swede," "a man of reason and good-will," who might sometimes become indignant but would never lose control of himself in anger. He was always a "doer," a man who loved to be active with his hands.[133]

As soon as he married Elizabeth Battle in 1898 (after the death of her estranged first husband), Alexis Ferm subordinated his own ambitions to those of his wife. He was thirteen years younger than she. Apparently recognizing her extraordinary gifts, he began taking only those jobs which would leave much of his time free to assist her in her educational work. Of course, since he had long been interested in the field of education, he managed in this way to fulfill his own desires. Though never in danger of losing his own dignity, he nonetheless became his wife's willing disciple.

In 1901 the Ferms opened their first "free school," deliberately designed for workers' children. Called the Children's Playhouse, it was located in a tenement district in New Rochelle. A year later the couple moved to the Dyker Heights neighborhood of Brooklyn, where a philanthropist gave them an entire new building in which to carry on their work. In making this change, they uncharacteristically accepted middle-class surroundings and, with them, an undoubted sense of dependence upon their benefactor. Here also, however, their fresh outlook and methods first began to attract attention in libertarian circles. At this time they became acquainted with such figures as Emma Goldman and Leonard Abbott.

By now Elizabeth Ferm's thinking had become lyrically egalitarian in the tradition of Whitman. She extolled "the democratic consciousness" which she believed would someday "force man to throw off all the extraneous matter with which he has adorned and thereby disguised himself,"

133. Jo Ann Burbank to the author, September 23, 1970.

leaving his soul stripped bare "until not one thing shall stand between him and another soul." As a primitive romantic rather than a pragmatist, she attacked "formalism," by which she meant adherence to the artificial, the conventional, the affected. Though in her own way intensely idealistic, she rebelled against the hypocritical "idealism" of the genteel.[134] Hostile to all organized institutions of the orthodox type, she attacked their effects upon the human mind in terms which anticipate the radical critique of sixty years later, though she had never heard of the concept of social role: "Man has divided himself into three segments. The home has charge of his body, the school of his mind, and the church of his soul. Is it any wonder that man has so many conflicting ideas of himself? How can he work out from his own centre when he has no opportunity for self-activity? How can he realize himself as a whole, so long as he is treated in fragments?"

Children, especially very little ones, she exalted above adults, precisely because they had not yet been induced into conventional grooves of thinking. Children cared nothing about luxury, because it only interfered with their freedom of action. Children had no respect for property except on the basis of immediate use. Moreover, "The child has no idea of cleanliness, so he does not divide people into clean and dirty. . . . He has no moral, no ethical ideas, so he does not over-rate certain things or qualities at the expense of his fellow man." Children, by their naïve directness, were often able to break down formal barriers between adult human beings. This, for instance, was the effect of their "smile, touch, and chatter" when they traveled on crowded streetcars. Best of all, children had no intellectual pretensions.

> The child is attracted to any form of action, so the work of the laborer and mechanic interests him more than the occupations which we have become accustomed to look upon as more intelligent and refined. The child has no respect for words, so the closet life of the professional man seems unprofitable to him. The child wants to see you act, but does not care to hear you talk. He has no contempt for the jumper of the mechanic and neither has he any respect for the dress suit of the man of fashion. The child, like Whitman, is not curious about God, but very curious about himself and the life about him.[135]

134. Elizabeth Ferm, "The Democracy of Whitman," *Mother Earth,* I (January, 1907), 23–24, 29; II (February, 1907), 17–18; Elizabeth Byrne Ferm, *The Spirit of Freedom in Education* (Stelton, New Jersey: The Modern School, 1919), p. 9.

135. Elizabeth Ferm, "The Democracy of Whitman," *Mother Earth,* I (January, 1907), 25, 28–29. She also praised life in the outdoors because it had the same effect of breaking down social barriers and conventions. Camping trips in particular were wonderful devices for getting rid of "formalism." Women will don bathing

Children represented the great promise of the future. Elizabeth Ferm confessed that she believed in a spiritual evolution which was gradually expanding the consciousness of the entire human race. (Here could be detected an important vestige of her flirtation with Theosophy.) It was our duty to help speed up this development, especially by permitting our own children to unfold and to express themselves without trammels. Perhaps already replying to the verbal abstractions of a John Dewey, she declared: "If we adults were in full earnest about the democratic life, we would recognize the signs in childhood and devote our lives to its preservation. Not by teaching the child about democracy, not by training him to be . . . a democrat, but by recognizing that he *is* one, and not attempting to instill into his life the artificiality and conventionality with which we were inoculated." For, she concluded, even if we cannot hope to leap free of "the conventional rut into which we have fallen," we can, she was sure, "if we are even half earnest, stop driving our children along the same road."[136] Elizabeth Ferm believed that true education was entirely alien to the concept of "teaching." In education, one stood back and simply let the child be and develop, with complete trust and love. The cardinal item in her faith, and in her husband's, was that all genuinely worthwhile activity was entirely voluntary, self-generated and self-sustaining.

After four years in Brooklyn, relations began to grow tense between Elizabeth Ferm and a number of the parents. So the couple decided to abandon their splendid physical plant and move into a working-class neighborhood of Manhattan on their own.

In an area near the East River on Madison Street, from 1906 until 1913, the Ferms conducted a "free school" along extremely unusual lines, with only the meagerest of resources. Konrad Bercovici has given us one of the very few surviving descriptions of it:

> An empty store with a few chairs and a piano, the Free School was open to the children of the neighborhood from eight in the morning to seven in the evening. Mrs. Ferm was always there, to pose questions, to answer them truthfully, and to listen to complaints. . . . Mrs. Ferm, patient as a angel, directed the lives of hundreds of youngsters without seeming to do anything of the kind. Somehow she managed to feed the children when there was nothing at home, and managed to see that at least some of the parents were not always hungry.

suits and "well-off young men will roll their sleeves up while repairing a gasoline engine on a boat dock and become indistinguishable from the mechanics. . . . Watching these people when they felt they were off guard, convinced me that there is nothing innate in man which separates him into a class or caste." *Ibid.,* pp. 29–31.
136. *Ibid.,* II (February, 1907), 20–21.

Her husband . . . came to the school every afternoon. In a corner of
the room he had placed a lathe and a workbench, and he gathered the older
boys about him to teach them to work and to instill in them the joy and
pride of work.

By themselves and with no fanfare or outside help, these two people
. . . did more for the morale of the neighborhood than all the settlement
institutions put together.[137]

Thus the Ferms, not the settlement houses, were doing the kinds of
things which look directly ahead to some of the recent urban antipoverty
programs. Operating alone and in obscurity, the Ferms were half a century
ahead of their time. This assertion by no means disposes of the problem of
unconscious paternalism and authoritarianism in their work, as will later be
seen, for these qualities are so subtle and insidious that they are liable to appear in some form whenever any outsider seeks to "help" another group. But
the Ferms had clearly seen through—and gone far beyond—the usual pattern of charity and cultural education for the poor as it existed in the
Progressive Era. Among New Yorkers of that day, their achievement was
probably unique.

During this period the Ferms had once visited the Ferrer Center and
were even invited to take charge of its school while it was located on East
Twelfth Street. But the attitude of the Ferrer membership toward education
struck them as too amateurish and in important respects too conservative;
they were also afraid that such a vociferous group might give them constant interference. Instead, soon after this Alexis Ferm, who had briefly
fallen ill, persuaded his wife to retire with him to the country, where they
could recuperate and practice an even simpler style of living. They bought
a farm in Hampton, Connecticut, on which they stayed until persuaded to
come to Stelton in 1920.

Early that year Harry Kelly traveled to their farm and begged them to
take charge of the children's dormitory—perhaps hoping that, once at Stelton, they might be induced to head the entire school. Alexis was most reluctant. He was greatly attached to the farm, where he relished the natural
beauty and treated the animals as pets. Only when Elizabeth revealed her
determination to go to Stelton did he agree to accompany her.

The Ferms arrived in May of 1920, traveling in homely fashion by
horse and buggy. She was then sixty-two, he forty-nine. Immediately their
presence began to work a large effect on their new surroundings. They
pointedly renamed the boardinghouse the Living House and soon trans-

137. Konrad Bercovici, *op. cit.*, p. 65. Alexis Ferm (to the author, September 11,
1970), modestly denied that the school was much different from "the usual kindergarten" and recalled that it was open from 9 A.M. to noon only.

formed its atmosphere from chaos to harmony and order. Elizabeth could not resist establishing a kindergarten. Before long, when Joseph Cohen approached them about taking over the entire school, they were willing to accept. After they had explained their ideas on education to the throng during an inevitable evening of open debate at the annual Labor Day convention, their selection as principals was overwhelmingly ratified.

At that convention the Ferms were given complete freedom to alter the curriculum. Hitherto the principals of the school had talked much about libertarian education, but they had continued for the most part to offer a conventional academic training, aiming to prepare the students to enter high school (and very likely college as well). The Ferms made no secret of their utter contempt for such orthodoxy of goal and method. Alexis Ferm told the Board of Management that he was frankly "very little interested in the academic side of the school." And at the September convention he was heard to say: "The workers will one day have concretely all that which the intellectuals now think they possess. But the workers will lay out plans based on concrete experience, not paper knowledge as is now the case."[138] What good was it, he asked, to study such subjects as arithmetic, English, history, or chemistry, simply because we think they are "needful in this industrial or commercial age"?

The Ferms arrived at Stelton just as the new classroom building was being finished. They insisted on completely changing the way in which its interior space would be utilized. Instead of the four conventional classrooms which had been planned, each room was to be given over to a different craft or manual-training activity, and the large assembly hall was to become a kindergarten area. Only one room, the library, would remain devoted to academic work, and it was to be available only for those children who specially requested it. Though the other members of the teaching staff were not entirely happy about these drastic changes, they responded to the powerful impact of the Ferms' personalities (and the obvious good effect they were having on the fortunes of the school) by cooperating fully in executing them.

It is clear that in many subtle ways the Ferms discouraged the children from spending their time with books. One of the younger teachers, James Dick, was supposed to sit regularly in the library waiting for children who might seek instruction in reading or arithmetic. "At first there were a great many who went in," Alexis Ferm recalled, "since many had had nothing else but abstract work and did not know what else to do. But gradually

138. *Modern School*, VII (April, 1920), 132; VII (October, 1920), 173.

as they became interested in other activities they forgot to go to Jim's class and after a while Jim was left very much to himself, so that he finally took up the [teaching of] basketry, though he remained ready to take up their abstract needs."[139] Ferm's description of this change reveals much of the style of their takeover at Stelton. When Dick tried at one point to combine a reading session with basket weaving, the Ferms apparently called a halt to it, claiming "that it would have a disastrous effect because of the diversion of interests," so Dick's whole attention was thereafter given "solely to chair-caning, basketry, & outdoor games."[140] On the other hand, when children did wish to learn to read, they often plunged directly into books that were seriously adult.

The Ferms' aversion to intellectual abstraction, even of the simplest kind, ran very deep. "The greatest bugaboo in our midst," said Alexis, "is the fear that our children may not learn to read and to count their money. But our parents do not seem to notice when our children lack co-ordination or ability to use their hands, have poor control of their bodies and become knocked-kneed and flabby."[141] (The Ferms, like Samuel Butler's Erewhonians, seem to have regarded physical illness as a shameful sign of inner weakness.) Once Alexis even went so far as to call mathematics "something foreign to the human being's growth." Such "metaphysical thinking" placed an alien pressure upon youthful minds. "Why," he wondered, "will the adult always impose his stereotyped thought on the young?"[142] Yet he resented being called "anti-intellectual."[143] When, in later years, some of his former students told him that he should have pushed them a bit more toward academic work, he reacted with genuine hurt and puzzlement. The Ferms always hoped that, if children were raised in a completely natural fashion, they might choose simply not to care about the categories, honors, and rewards of the existing society. "Each time I see a brood of small children come along," Alexis Ferm wrote, "I think that the hope may lie in them. Maybe they will be the ones to rejuvenate the world. Maybe they will not be affected by the artificial glamore [sic] of the commercial part of the world. Maybe. Some day some youngsters will grow up who will be

139. *Sketch*, p. 87.
140. James H. Dick's report of September, 1922, pp. 2–3, M.S.A.N.A. Papers.
141. Alexis C. Ferm, "Education Through Self-Dependence," in *The Modern School: An Experiment in Libertarian Education: Thirty-Third Year* (Stelton, New Jersey: by the school, [1948]), p. 11.
142. Alexis Ferm's report, September 1, 1946, p. 2, M.S.A.N.A. Papers.
143. "What a wrong impression! . . . It is in the intellectual atmosphere that we usually lived. Where else could we explain our educational ideas?" Alexis Ferm to the author, September 11, 1970, criticizing my earlier draft.

stronger than their surroundings."[144] At a time when anthropologists were showing how powerfully man is held prisoner by his cultural circumstances, the Ferms continued to display an unyielding faith in the ability of individuals to break through these limits. To an extreme effort at realizing such an ideal they devoted their lives.

In order to achieve these goals, the Ferms really wanted nothing less than complete control over the children's environment. How could children be raised effectively in freedom if half their waking hours were spent imbibing the dim, conventional prejudices of their parents? Though Elizabeth Ferm carefully reassured inquiring mothers at the convention of 1920 that she did not theoretically believe in separating children from their homes, one senses that this reply was an expedient. In fact, during the same discussion it was proposed (with the Ferms' obvious approval) that the school and the Living House should become "interchangeable terms." No barrier was to exist between school and life. Thus a prominent memory in the minds of many Stelton alumni was the extent to which Aunty discriminated in practice between the Living House children and those who came to the school only during the day from homes elsewhere in the colony. This created much antagonism and helped lead to the Ferms' temporary resignation in 1925. Yet, from their point of view, the older generation constituted an enormous obstacle to the liberation of children, one which must be circumvented as much as possible. (Theirs was an emotion which, after all, many public school teachers have shared in a milder form.) To compromise with the parents would be to surrender the central core of their radical commitment. Meanwhile, the Living House sheltered "one large happy family . . . the happiest one I ever saw, and 'Aunty' . . . was the happiest member of it."[145] By the fall of 1921 there were a hundred names on the waiting list for vacancies in its three dozen places.

The Modern School curriculum now became entirely centered in manual activities: printing, weaving, basket making, art, music, and carpentry, all the arts and crafts for which materials could easily be found. Nature study and out-of-door experiences became more important than before. Uncle Ferm sometimes took groups on week-long hiking expeditions through central and northern New Jersey, during which they slept on the ground in whatever open fields they could find. In his view such tramps offered a valuable lesson in hardihood and endurance. In none of the school's activities was there compulsion. Children could roam the country-

144. Alexis Ferm's report, September 2, 1939, p. 6, M.S.A.N.A. Papers.
145. Koch, *op. cit.,* p. 3.

side rather than coming to classes, and in good weather many of them did so.[146]

The only occasion at which everyone had to appear was the daily morning assembly. This had something of the quality of a communal ritual. According to James Dick, "Aunty Ferm often re-iterated that the assembly was the spirit of the school." It took place at the hour "when all the children are fresh and bubbling over with life." Holding hands and forming a circle, adults and children intermingled freely. "Aunty Ferm, in spite of her years, kept the spirit of songs & dances very much alive with her astounding vitality."[147] In a regime which greatly encouraged individual independence, such a daily hour spent in rhythmic motion as a group must have been an important counterweight. Decades later, mention of the morning assemblies brought a special look of joy to the faces of aging Stelton alumni.

After the assembly, the auditorium was turned over to the younger children, the age group with which the Ferms always felt a special kinship.[148] Benches were pulled out, and everyone was encouraged to become busily absorbed in making things. The children's art work attracted unusual attention when it was exhibited, alongside similar work from other progressive schools, on one occasion in New York. The productions from Stelton, as compared with those from the Walden or the Lincoln schools, were notable for their colorful individuality and the absence of any obviously academic qualities or telltale evidence of a teacher's guiding hand.[149] From time to time the children also put together their own magazine, using numerous attractive examples of their art and poetry. They boasted that it was the only magazine produced mainly by those who could neither read nor write!

The effectiveness of the Ferms' regime could not be questioned in terms of its immediate impact. Greatly devoted to their daily routine, the children hated ever to be away from it or to have it interrupted. Nor can the initiative shown by them be exaggerated. On one occasion they actually

146. The atmosphere of the school in the early 1920's is best conveyed in *Sketch*, pp. 73–99; in several descriptive articles by members of the teaching staff published in *Modern School* during 1921–1922, and in the manuscript reports of Alexis Ferm during these years in M.S.A.N.A. Papers. A number of students' recollections are in *25th Anniv.*, pp. 24–28.

147. James H. Dick's report, September, 1922, pp. 1–2, M.S.A.N.A. Papers.

148. The Ferms had no interest in high-school education. Though there had been much desire earlier to establish a high school (and even a workers' college) at Stelton, after the Ferms' arrival such talk died out.

149. Koch, *op. cit.*, p. 4; Agnes de Lima, *Our Enemy the Child* (New York: New Republic, 1926), p. 239.

took charge of the entire functioning of the school for two or three weeks. The Modern School ordinarily stayed in session the year round, with no fixed terms or vacations, and in a certain December the whole teaching staff decided to take a long holiday rest. The children loved the school activities so much that they first tried to prevent the staff from leaving, and when that proved impossible they assumed all the responsibilities, from heating and cleaning the building to conducting the classes by themselves.

Alexis Ferm noted with pleasure that a regime of freedom often tended to produce unselfish and highly responsible impulses. Children would sometimes voluntarily pick up the trash, or they might insist upon running out with raincoats to a returning group who lacked them in a storm. But these were merely indirect results of the Ferms' approach, which always began by emphasizing the individual in isolation. Alexis Ferm said (with little real justification) that "it was too much to expect that children who did not yet know how to work singly should know how to work in groups. It takes developed people to work in groups, to co-operate."[150] The Ferms were therefore most elated when they could report that a particular boy or girl, with no external prompting, had spent the day completely self-absorbed in a constant flow of purposeful activity—of what precise kind it did not really matter.

What the Ferms did not like openly to admit was the extent to which their own presence—and often, indeed, their direct suggestions—were influencing all these results. Thus, when the children in the Living House proved undependable in their efforts to keep the place clean, Aunty called them together and gave them a detailed report on the current financial situation, making clear how costly it would be to hire custodial help.

> She then asked them if they were willing to cooperate by doing some of the work. They all indicated their willingness to cooperate and thus fell into the work again without compulsion. Two boys sweep the dormitory, another tends the fire, another carries up the coal, another burns the papers, another sweeps the dining room, others clean the windows, sweep the porch, etc. and both boys and girls take part in washing the children and putting them to bed. Some feed the chickens, and one boy looks after the cow.[151]

Though Uncle proudly used the phrase "without compulsion" to describe these regular contributions to the welfare of the whole, it is clear that a reasoned (and therefore all the more powerful) form of persuasion was being used by the adults to bring about a desired end.[152]

150. "Living House Report," August 27, 1922, p. 1, M.S.A.N.A. Papers.
151. *Ibid.*, pp. 1–2.
152. "Keeping them up to their work [in constructing a new shop building] with-

On the other hand, the Ferms failed to interfere with the children in many situations when other educators would have done so. Even very small children were allowed to use dangerous tools. Nor did Aunty stop them when they tied up one of their number with rope. Equally interesting is the tolerant detachment of Alexis Ferm when he witnessed another variant of spontaneously cruel punishment:

> One morning sometime ago I wondered what it was that took them [all] off so mysteriously after doing a very little work, when one said to the other in an understanding sort of way, "are you coming?" To me they merely said that they did not feel like doing any work that morning. Later I happened into the Kindergarten Room, when I beheld them all, excepting the oldest boy, playing at a game that they had created or concocted. . . . It was some kind of "captive" play where they could capture some one and put him in limbo, but whatever it was, they were so alive to it, so active, so interested, that I could not help seeing that my work was dead in comparison.
>
> It might be said that they were not learning anything useful or that they were learning to be gangsters or policemen or something of that sort, but that complaint, if it is legitimate, will have to be taken to the home or the conditions surrounding us for they have learned about such things either from the cinima [sic] or the radio or both. At the school they try the thing that they see or hear about as if they would understand what it is all about by putting themselves in the place of characters that they either admire or abhor. . . .
>
> At all events, I thought how much more fruitful was their creative play than the work they were trying to do so laboriously out of books.[153]

Uncle Ferm's passivity as he watched these children isolating and ostracizing one of their number probably stemmed from his intense belief in the virtue of stoic self-reliance. He wanted them to be able to endure just about anything, rejoicing for instance when they had to plough through deep snowdrifts to get to the school building during a winter storm.[154]

---

out seeming to be harsh was quite a problem sometimes so after they had been called together a number of times regarding their work I decided that it would have to be up to them whether they should go on with their work or not. I therefore asked them to elect their own president and secretary and call the meetings on Mondays themselves. On Nov. 8 they called a meeting, discussed the work and decided the penalties for the boys that did not appear for work. One penalty was that any body who did not appear in his regular time for work should not be permitted to play in the games with the other boys for three days. And so they got along in their meeting much better without our help than with it." Alexis Ferm's report, December 2, 1923, p. 1, M.S.A.N.A. Papers. A careful reading of A. S. Neill's *Summerhill* (New York: Hart Publishing Co., 1960) reveals many similar instances of pronounced guidance from above.

153. Alexis Ferm's report, September 2, 1939, pp. 3–4, M.S.A.N.A. Papers.

154. "And every day thru the storm they came. Even little Socrates, a mere baby, coming up all alone at times. Nothing seems to give a finer atmosphere for sturdiness

Elizabeth Ferm, for her part, was feared as well as worshiped.[155] She was remembered not only for her vitality and radiance, but also for her demanding insistence that things be performed a certain way without fail. There are hints that she had the instincts of a meddler—someone who cannot resist being her brother's keeper.[156] And it is recalled that she played favorites among the children in a rather shameless fashion. One of her staff described her as "fierce, imperious, imaginative, playful, willful, courageous, and a man's woman, to boot." In a colony where many were stubborn individualists, she stood out as "a love-hate person, both in giving and receiving. Who was not with her was against her." Yet she did not hold grudges and may simply have relished a good open fight.[157] But it was only to be expected that quite a few of the parents, themselves people of decided convictions, would grow to dislike and resent her.

It would be much too facile, of course, to say that the Ferms turned anarchy into some simple form of tyranny at Stelton. The subsequent lives of the Stelton children were far too varied to reveal a single dominating influence upon their minds. A large minority—greater than the contemporary proportion among the American population—went on to college. In this they were being loyal to the aims of their immigrant parents, who often hoped their children would become professionals, and not to the thinking of the Ferms. A still larger number drifted into routine white-collar positions, or became labor-union organizers. Few seem to have spent their lives working with their hands, despite the Ferms' high esteem for manual activity. None of the students, incidentally, appears to have become really famous later on.[158]

The Modern School of Stelton deserves recognition as one of the most

---

than the storm. When mothers can appreciate this they will not try to keep their children in when the storm is raging outside." Alexis Ferm's report, February 1, 1925, p. 1, M.S.A.N.A. Papers.

155. That she was worshiped, at least by some staff members, there can be no doubt. One young woman teacher began imitating Aunty's manner in every detail, talking and dressing like her.

156. "I used to be a very fussy housekeeper and took great pride in having everything spic and span. Auntie came to the shack once and looked around and then tactfully told me a little story about a friend of hers who was also very fussy. She was so fussy that she dusted the keyholes. That cured me." Marucci to Alexis C. Ferm, April 17, 1944, Ferm Papers.

157. Jo Ann Burbank to the author, September 23, 1970.

158. Three alumni do deserve mention in this respect: Edgar Tafel, who became an assistant to Frank Lloyd Wright; Ethel Butler, who danced in Martha Graham's troupe; and Joan Bridges, who was the mother of Joan Baez. The school could occasionally produce hard-hitting, success-oriented persons, such as James Dick, Jr., son of its principal from 1928 to 1933, now a pediatrician living in a fifteen-room mansion at Oyster Bay, L.I. Another alumnus was a vice-president of General Telephone Co.

radical experiments to occur in the history of American education. By comparison, the better-known progressive schools of the 1920's, such as the Lincoln, Walden, and City and Country schools in New York, and the Organic School at Fairhope, Alabama, tended more toward compromise in their programs, usually retaining age-graded classes and a tacit or open commitment to academic excellence in the long run, even if they employed daringly permissive means for the younger children.[159] Most important, their tone and clientele were pervasively middle class. For his part, John Dewey increasingly dissociated himself from all the more drastic trends in progressive education, attacking the "anarchy," "license," and bad manners in the more extreme schools, where, he said, "the fear of adult imposition has become a veritable phobia. When the fear is analyzed, it means simply a preference for an immature and undeveloped experience over a ripened and thoughtful one."[160] Dewey and other mainstream progressives clearly sided with science and civilization rather than with an idea of natural self-expression.

Still, the Ferrer Modern School was in some important respects far from up-to-date. Radicalism is too often confounded with novelty in all its senses. Radical humanism has its own distinct tradition stretching back into the eighteenth and nineteenth centuries. It therefore should not seem surprising that the Ferms took their intellectual sustenance from Froebel and Tolstoy, rather than from John Dewey or Sigmund Freud. Their lack of enthusiasm for Dewey is quite understandable in view of Dewey's far less venturesome mentality. But their neglect of Freud was more serious.

159. On the Lincoln School, see Agnes de Lima, "The New Education," *The New Republic*, X (1924), 11; Otis W. Caldwell, "An Experimental School," *Education*, XXXVIII (1918), 698; *School and Society*, IX (1919), 229. On the City and Country School, founded in 1914, see Caroline Pratt, "The New Education Ten Years After," *The New Republic*, LXIII (1930), 172–76. The Walden School and the Organic School were closest to Stelton in practice. See Lawrence A. Cremin, *The Transformation of the School* (New York: Alfred A. Knopf, 1961), pp. 147–53, 211–14. All these schools postponed learning to read past the usual age, but then tended to push the children toward academic goals with a vengeance in their upper-level classes.

160. John Dewey, "The New Education Ten Years After," *The New Republic*, LXIII (1930), 204–206. For other typical mainstream progressive statements, see Boyd H. Bode, *ibid.*, LXIII (1930), 61–64, and Harold Rugg and Ann Shumaker, *The Child-Centered School* (Yonkers, New York: World Book Co., 1928), pp. 105–107, 244. Dewey once visited Stelton, according to the memory of the staff, but was unimpressed. The Ferms were by no means ostracized from the progressive-education movement—only from the historical memory of it. Alexis Ferm regularly attended the meetings of the Progressive Education Association, uttering sharply critical words from the floor. In 1926 Elizabeth published an article in *Progressive Education*, and its news notes regularly mentioned the school. In another direction, Jacob L. Moreno, founder of the psychodrama movement, took much interest in the school around 1930.

During these same years Summerhill in England and the Walden School in New York were becoming deeply steeped in Freudian ideas. This led to an undeniable faddism, in which oedipal complexes were constantly being unearthed and parents were routinely psychoanalyzed.[161] But it is hard to deny that its effect was to deepen the understanding of human personality, both in children and adults.

And the Ferms simply were not part of this world.[162] They were by no means blind to the existence of emotional conflicts in the minds of children. But they believed in developing the human will as the best tool for overcoming them, in contrast to the Freudian view that liberation comes through self-understanding. In this important respect, the Ferms' thinking betrayed lingering prejudices of the nineteenth century. Alexis Ferm believed that children had to learn to control their emotions in order to live amicably with their fellow men, a thoroughly old-fashioned sentiment.[163] Moreover, he sometimes spoke of personal "power" as the aim of education, in a sense not very different from that of mid-nineteenth-century college presidents when they used the same phrase.[164] Still more revealingly, he disliked idleness and believed in the intrinsic value of work. "We are what we do," he liked to emphasize.[165] His perspective did not allow him to endorse a merely passive aestheticism. The side of Thoreau to which he strongly responded was that of practical self-sufficiency and plain living, not the side of contemplation. He especially hated waste.[166]

Initiative, tenacity, and the ability to endure hardship were the qualities which the Ferms most wanted to instill in the children's minds. They despised all forms of softness and luxury. They could use with approval such phrases as "physical and moral backbone." They judged the children's progress with their handicrafts according to "how they handle their ma-

161. For a knowing description of this particular educational scene, see Stella Crossley Ward, "Children of Freedom," *Harper's Magazine*, CLXII (1931), 296–305.

162. Alexis Ferm appeared explicitly to reject Freud; see *Modern School*, IX (Midwinter, 1922), 31.

163. Alexis Ferm's report, September 3, 1944, p. 6, M.S.A.N.A. Papers.

164. He was reported as telling a convention crowd that he wanted the child "to have the use of everything, books included but only if it gives him power, and not if it sets him day-dreaming of what some other person does." *Modern School*, VIII (October, 1921), 34–35. Again, he once wrote about "developing the running powers" of an animal or a child, using a muscle-building analogy that was a favorite of nineteenth-century educators. *Sketch*, p. 102.

165. However, when he saw children idle, he by no means immediately interfered with them. Such behavior made him feel uneasy, but he believed he must respect the natural rhythms of the child even though they sometimes produced these periods of quiet gestation.

166. E.g., see *Inklings of Activities at the Modern School, by the Principals and Staff* (Stelton, New Jersey: The Modern School, 1937), p. 3.

terial, how self-reliant they are, how they make their own designs, how they control themselves in trying to accomplish something, how or if they make their designs without expecting help from the staff and how much they have observed of the shortcomings in their own work."[167] "Initiative" was a highly regarded word in their vocabulary, though Alexis Ferm defined it in a sense that made it sound like incipient rebelliousness, giving it a tinge of meaning it lacked on the lips of American conservatives.[168]

All these central tendencies in their thinking make it entirely under-standable that the Ferms remained pre-Freudian in their outlook. "Mate-rialistic" they unthinkingly employed as a bad word, "spiritual" as a good one. Toward sex and the body their views were quite strait-laced. This amounted to a backward step. From its beginning the Ferrer movement had promoted such causes as birth control and enlightened sex education. Around 1915, the Stelton colonists had briefly embraced the mood of bodily liberation suggested by Isadora Duncan.[169] But, in the 1920's, the Ferms' prejudices inhibited the school from moving in a more radically sensuous direction. Alexis Ferm was strongly opposed to jazz music (and this is quite revealing, because he was not markedly hostile to such other novelties as radio itself). His opposition came to the surface when mem-bers of the colony wanted to begin holding large evening parties in the school auditorium, with dancing. Though this might seem to be a harmless request, Ferm fought it vigorously. He demanded that nothing like a "dance hall" atmosphere ever be allowed in the school area.[170]

In the Living House the two sexes slept in different rooms and bathed separately (except in the brook during the summer months); even on long-distance hikes they did not sleep together. "Never at any time was particular stress laid upon the sex functions, in the classrooms or out of them," Harry Kelly once stated. Elizabeth Ferm disapproved of masturbation in a com-pletely traditional spirit, a point which later anarchists held against her in assessing her contribution to libertarian education.[171] In her final years, she

167. Alexis Ferm's report, September 1, 1941, p. 4, M.S.A.N.A. Papers.
168. For children "to have . . . initiative" was the same as to have "opinions of their own in regard to their daily activities" and to "prove a bother to their parents when the parents want them to behave in a certain dignified manner. . . . Are they just docile or do they rebel against authority?" Alexis Ferm's report, 1945, pp. 2–3, M.S.A.N.A. Papers.
169. Examples of this are described below, p. 432.
170. Alexis Ferm's report, July 9, 1922, pp. 2, 4, M.S.A.N.A. Papers.
171. E.g., see the standoffish reviews of her book *Freedom in Education* in *Re-sistance,* VIII (August-September, 1949), 12, and in *Freedom* (London), XI (August 19, 1950), 2. After a one-day visit to Stelton in 1930, Eunice Schuster claimed the two sexes did sleep together; *Native American Anarchism* (Northampton, Massa-chusetts: Smith College, 1931), p. 172.

grew slightly prudish, refusing to allow girls to wear slacks or short-sleeved blouses and even reprimanding one small girl for appearing topless on a hot day. The students remembered her intense dislike of anything that could be considered "vulgarity."[172] From this point of view, the Modern School of Stelton does not bear comparison with Summerhill, where A. S. Neill in these same years was coming under the influence of Wilhelm Reich.[173]

The Ferms' Spartan radicalism, less sexually realistic than the novels of J. William Lloyd, resembles that of back-to-the-land communal decentralizers such as Ralph Borsodi.[174] This viewpoint was perhaps backward-looking in the sense that it reaffirmed a critique of industrialism which had been steadily put forth by a small minority of artists and social critics ever since the end of the eighteenth century. But the American version of this critique, as embodied for instance by Thoreau, Whitman, and the Ferms, was never as reactionary as the British or European version. The Americans who thought in this vein did not invoke the memory of the Middle Ages; that would be left to latter-day Aristotelians, who generally wished to return to a medieval conception of human freedom as well. The Ferms, unlike orthodox Marxists as well as most other Americans, deeply questioned the whole idea of material progress.[175] But they did this from an essentially timeless perspective of transcendental "self-realization," not from a desire to restore some specific earlier state of society.

Though the Ferms valued willful effort, initiative, and self-reliance, they did not praise competition. Alexis Ferm believed strongly in the virtue of hard work, but for the sense of "accomplishment" rather than for any extrinsic prizes. "Success" meant completing a project resourcefully, independently, imaginatively, with an expressive personal flair. It did not mean elbowing someone else in a scramble for wealth and prestige. Again, freedom was to be gained "rather by freeing ourselves from the need of many things than by immeshing ourselves in a net work of manufactured

172. When Alexis Ferm read this sentence in draft he hotly replied: "This [is] *positively untrue.* . . . I ought to know." However, these stories of Elizabeth came independently from more than one source. Her style of living and thinking remained neo-transcendental; she liked sometimes to wear a long white robe in almost nunlike manner and loved to see the children march with candles, no doubt in memory of her girlhood in the convent.

173. Neill forbade the Summerhill students to have sexual intercourse, but only on the ground that otherwise the state would order the school closed. It is not often realized, incidentally, that Wilhelm Reich himself became something of a sexual prude in the closing years of his life. See Paul A. Robinson, *The Freudian Left* (New York: Harper & Row, 1969), p. 72. The connection between libertarian beliefs and odd lapses into prudery is a subtle one which needs more exploration.

174. See above, p. 38.

175. *Sketch*, pp. 100–102.

articles."[176] Whereas John Dewey closely linked the idea of democracy with vocational training, thereby revealing the extent of his commitment to social orthodoxy, the Ferms preached a general aloofness from all occupational roles, though they reserved special scorn for business and the professions. Moreover, up to a point they tried to instill in the children's minds a communal rather than a rigidly individual conception of property.[177]

One can sense Alexis Ferm's notion of the ideal Stelton alumnus in the following proud description, written in 1939:

> We had a visit the other day from a boy who had spent his early days at the school and in the colony. He is now about to be graduated from college where he has majored in education, but has been working on a farm between times. He seems to know just where he is going and does not seem to be affected by either of his parents as to his thinking but has learned to think for himself. He expects to teach . . . out where he lives in the country but if he does not succeed in getting what he wants he has the farm and feels just as sure of himself there as in teaching. He asks for no help from the government and feels that he can take care of himself.

In pencil after this recounting, Ferm added the satisfied sentence: "He didn't know how to read at nine or ten."[178]

Conflict Over Ideals

Because they held to a more inward and individualistic conception of radicalism, and because of Elizabeth's personality, the Ferms remained profoundly suspect in the eyes of many parents. Sensing this, the couple offered to resign in 1921, only a year after coming to Stelton; instead they received a renewed vote of confidence at the convention. After a seven-month leave of absence to recuperate from a severe illness, in April, 1922, Elizabeth again announced her resignation, saying she felt "she had finished her work there," although Alexis pointedly did not join her in this gesture and instead demanded still greater freedom in running the school. Hostile attacks continued to be made on Elizabeth, and finally in 1925 such criticism became unbearably strong. They decided to resign together and leave the colony. A decade later, as a very elderly couple under quite different circumstances, they were induced to return and take charge of the school once more.

The parents of the Ferrer children had always tended to call for definiteness in the instruction, both morally and intellectually. In effect they de-

176. *Ibid.,* pp. 107–108.
177. Alexis Ferm's report, September 3, 1944, p. 2, M.S.A.N.A. Papers.
178. Alexis Ferm's report, September 2, 1939, p. 6, M.S.A.N.A. Papers.

manded that the children be given the basic tools to enable them to rise in society at the same time that they be indoctrinated with the social consciences of militant revolutionaries. These attitudes had caused some trouble even before the Ferms' arrival. Harry Kelly noted in 1917 that the issue involved whether the school should teach "adaptation to one's environment, its ideals and moral codes" in a thoroughly "practical" spirit, or whether it should encourage "trying to raise oneself above them. The parents," he added, "have with the exception of two or three laid most stress on the practical even when they proclaimed idealism to the heavens."[179] Even parents who were politically radical could well feel torn on such an issue, legitimately fearing that their children might grow up too innocent and ill-equipped to be able to cope with life as it really was.

Under the Ferms the sense of these dangers greatly increased. Radical educational policies (for instance, not encouraging children to learn to read) may detach the new generation from the present corrupt industrial civilization, but in such a way as also to unfit its members for anything else. Indeed, if there has been a miscalculation, such policies might conceivably handicap a person for life. Norman O. Brown would eventually affirm in *Life Against Death* that children remain more human when they are kept apart from what usually passes for "civilization." But only a very brave or indifferent parent will chance the immediate application of this theory.[180]

With good reason, the Ferms became bitter over the lack of idealism among the fathers and mothers. All private boarding schools are grimly familiar with the problem known as "dumping"—the placing of one's children in a school away from home as a mere matter of personal convenience. The reasons for doing this can often be compelling: separation or divorce of the parents, emotional problems which the school may be able to help, and the like. And, from the point of view of the Ferms' desire to build a new social environment, such children might often furnish unusually receptive material. The main objection to "dumping" lay not in the existence of these practical motives, but in the casual abruptness with which the children were withdrawn from the school as soon as circumstances in the home had changed. A new society could never be built if, whenever a child's psychological problems abated and he began to thrive as a person, his parents pulled him out of the group and returned him to his former environ-

179. Harry Kelly, "Specialization and the Modern School," *Modern School,* IV (1917), 105.
180. The consensus among the Stelton graduates whom I interviewed was that most of the children there were not greatly handicapped afterward by the late age at which they had learned to read, but that there were a few exceptions.

ment. In 1920 and 1921, while numbers at the Modern School greatly increased, the transiency of the population became very marked. Of the ninety who were attending the school in the fall of 1920, only fifty remained there a year later, to be joined by an influx of seventy newcomers. More pointedly, of the thirty-three children in the Living House in September, 1921, only twenty had been there for more than a year and only six for more than two years. Not surprisingly, at the convention that year it was urged that the staff "look into the cause of our floating school population and bar those whose parents are making only a convenience of us." The very low tuition fees and the fact that the Modern School operated year-round without the usual vacations must have made it highly attractive to parents in these terms.

Still, the sources of the conflict ran much deeper. "Usually the children take on the attitude of the home," Alexis Ferm complained many years later. "If we have not had a large list of children [lately] it is because there are not many people who want this kind of thing. Even our own parents [i.e., those in radical circles] want their children to compete with the children of the conservative class."[181] Or, to put this more concretely: the Ferms' curriculum in effect idealized the simple, sturdy way of life of the craftsman; the immigrants, on the other hand, were all too familiar with that life under unfavorable conditions and admired the intellectual skills that would enable their children to enter into far more interesting careers. Political radicalism was after all compatible with many forms of cultural assimilationism, for which a conventional education could be of great help. In this respect, the immigrant and the native-born versions of libertarianism ultimately failed to connect.

An unacknowledged social class barrier remained in existence at Stelton. The Ferms remained middle-class persons who had chosen to identify themselves with the cause of the workers. Though they had rid themselves of the flagrant forms of condescension, a certain subtle line of contrast still marked their relationships with rank-and-file parents or colonists.[182] "The Ferms were up on a pedestal; but it was entirely different with us—it was easy for everyone to get along with us because we were of the workers," recalled Nellie Dick, who became co-principal of the school in 1928.[183]

181. Alexis Ferm's report, September 1, 1946, p. 4, M.S.A.N.A. Papers; Ferm to Leonard D. Abbott, April 27, 1940, Abbott Papers.
182. Thus Alexis Ferm once said (ibid.) that "we are trying to give to the children of workers the opportunity to develop themselves in freedom, in a way that only the well to do have been able to do heretofore."
183. Interviews with Nellie Dick, May 3, July 13, 1970. She had been born in Russia, though she spent her girlhood in anarchist circles in London.

For his part, Alexis Ferm somewhat pointedly characterized the parents as "working people" who "considered themselves intellectuals."[184]

Within the colony, as within the entire anarchist movement, one could also find tension over the issue of how intellectual or artistical the good life should be. The question ultimately carried political echoes, for those who became caught up in art and self-expression were apt to devote less of their energy to the proletarian struggle, even if their opinions remained radical in a formal sense. Variant views on the subject sometimes came out in the open. When the monthly magazine *Road to Freedom* was founded at Stelton in 1925, "many of the comrades mentioned that it should be a live workingman's paper. Other comrades thought it should be a literary paper." And, while Harry Kelly was rather grandly declaring that "we have no desire to divorce ourselves from those close to the soil and loom," one colonist was naming his bungalow "Little Nirvana."

In this context, curiously enough, it was anti-intellectualism which could seem abstract and impractical as a philosophy of life, while a certain crude version of intellectual formalism—at least involving the three R's and Charles Darwin—meshed more easily with a proletarian and activist view of the world. The naming by his parents, around the year 1909, of one of the future children at the school "Herbert Spencer Goldberg" well captures the simple intellectualism which underlay the working-class side of this contrast.

The middle-class leadership of the Ferrer movement had always been wedded, however, to the concept of "self-expression." Carl Zigrosser boasted how greatly the Modern School emphasized individuality. All children, he believed, should adopt the "artist's attitude toward life," and would do so naturally if they were allowed to grow up without interference. Even William Thurston Brown, whose conception of individualism was more old-fashioned, identified educational goals with the "appreciation and love of the beautiful . . . life as Art." And Will Durant had gone so far as to affirm that the liberation of the unrepressed instincts was the key to libertarian education.[185] Harry Kelly, it is true, had initially wavered, sensing in the idea of "self-expression" a potential conflict with revolutionary

184. Alexis Ferm to the author, April 10, 1970; and see above, p. 127. Leonard Abbott seems privately to have had much the same attitude, and Carl Zigrosser once spoke of "the tragic futility of teaching the children of the working classes." *Modern School,* IV (1917), 91.
185. *Modern School,* No. 5 (Autumn, 1913), 22; V (January, 1918), 29; V (September, 1918), 269; William J. Durant, *The Ferrer Modern School* (New York: Francisco Ferrer Association, 1912), pp. 1–3.

ardor. But, especially after the move to Stelton, he too began readily to adopt the rhetoric of self-development.[186]

According to this ideal, nothing should be imposed upon the mind of the child. Therefore "dogma" and "propaganda" should never be inculcated in the classroom. From almost its beginning, the Ferrer school claimed that it avoided everything of the kind.[187] Many supporters of the school were quite earnest in emphasizing this aim, even deploring, for instance, the prominence in the children's voluntary compositions of "thoughts on Anarchism, Free Speech, Death, Boycotting, and so forth," all of which were "only abstract ideas that would not come into a child's head, unless introduced by an artificial environment."[188]

Later on, Elizabeth Ferm must have rankled many of the historical materialists at Stelton with her talk of "the inner life, the spiritual life of the individual," and with her insistence that, since every person was unique, teaching should never make use of examples taken from the past, presumably not even from the history of class struggle.[189] By 1921 it was becoming far more difficult to reconcile proletarianism with an ideal of "inner" liberation than it had been in the expansive years just before the war.

Politically, the Ferms were more moderate than most of the rank-and-file colonists. Both of them were lifelong Single Taxers. In 1925 Alexis did identify himself with those "who are not satisfied with things as they are, who are rebels against the present order, not for the sake of being rebels, but because we do not like to see suffering that is unnecessary or unearned, because we want to see justice play a larger part in the scheme of things." (Even here, why did he limit himself to opposing only the suffering which the individual had not "earned" or deserved?) During the depression of the 1930's he grew more openly mild in his political stance, eventually renouncing revolution in favor of gradual change and even expressing contempt for the sitdown strikes being led by the CIO. The real revolution must be "in ways of living, in attitudes towards others." Cultural radicalism, I am convinced, can often be more devastatingly extreme than political radicalism. But, in the case of the Ferms, it might easily seem that they lacked true zeal.

186. Cf. Harry Kelly's remarks in *Mother Earth*, II (1908), 558–59, with those *ibid.*, VIII (1913), 120, 182; Kelly's manuscript autobiography, pp. 319–20; Kelly, *The Ferrer Modern School*, p. 7; and *Modern School*, VIII (October, 1921), 19.
187. *Modern School*, No. 5 (Autumn, 1913), 6; I (May 1, 1914), 3.
188. "J. D." (not otherwise identified), "Our Children and Philosophy," *Modern School*, II (May, 1915), 53.
189. *Ibid.*, V (June, 1918), 182; VII (April, 1920), 131; VIII (October, 1921), 25.

Down through the years Alexis Ferm unceasingly attacked what he called "propaganda in education." Debating Scott Nearing on this subject at the Rand School in 1925, Ferm used Froebel's analogy of the child as a plant which must grow and develop unhindered, according to the laws of its own nature. Children, he implied, must be shielded as much as possible from the ordinary, rough-and-tumble world, so that their talents might develop without interference. In rebuttal, Nearing noted that any fruitful garden must receive adequate cultivation from outside agents. Whenever a simple warning of impending danger is given by someone (who, for instance, sees an avalanche on its way and yells, "Look out!" to those in its path), a "coercive signalling" has occurred of a kind which "must continue in every society, in every type of struggle . . . between social groups." Wouldn't Ferm warn a small child that a stove was hot? Wouldn't he go out of his way to suggest that brushing one's teeth is a good idea? Then why not warn children about the evils of capitalism as well?

Some of Ferm's replies to these counter-thrusts were a bit lame: Luther Burbank "did not put it over on plants; he simply gave them their freedom." Children should learn to dodge dangers in a self-reliant fashion and not be artificially protected from anything—whether hot stoves or automobile traffic in the city. For "if you permit the child's mind to develop thru experience he will know how to act under all conditions." But Ferm concluded on a stronger note. Pacifist propaganda has never prevented men from going to war—"cultured men, radicals, men who had talked against it all their lives." Therefore, strong individuals are needed, who will be able to resist the pressure of the surrounding environment when it really counts.[190] Such strength came from self-development. It was a position which Ferm kept putting forward, time and again, over the years that followed, and it remained the standard creed of the Modern School of Stelton.

If one looks at both sides of the argument, the contrast between Ferm and a political radical like Nearing was hardly as clear-cut as both men seem to have imagined. Ferm advocated artificially protecting children against social propaganda, while Nearing sought to warn them about avalanches and automobiles. Nearing might have asked why Ferm was not willing to allow children to toughen themselves in the world "as it is" in the realm of politics too. The Ferms, in fact, wished to shield young minds

190. *Has Propaganda Any Value in Education? Debate Between Dr. Scott Nearing and Alexis C. Ferm at the Rand School, January 23, 1925* (Stelton, New Jersey: The Modern School Press, 1925), pp. 7–9, 20, 26–28. For other extended arguments of the same kind, see Alexis C. Ferm, *The Problem of Education* (Stelton, New Jersey: Modern School Association, ca. 1935), especially pp. 7–23, and *Road to Freedom*, VI (January, 1930), 5.

from ideology and abstraction, just as the political radicals wished to shield them from all the widely accepted middle-class myths.

The entire issue of "freedom" versus "manipulation," as posed by the Ferms (and in a milder way by other educational progressives), was probably a false one.[191] For these educators were also manipulating the environment, creating a special atmosphere for children. Reverting to the plant analogy on another occasion, Alexis Ferm admitted: "I sometimes carry water to them myself." And he said, "We [the teachers] must supply conditions and materials suitable to their growth and development."[192] By this he meant fostering a deliberate absence of organization in the classroom— but was not this as definite a design, in its own way, as any other? When spontaneity is strenuously insisted upon, and all distracting influences are rigorously excluded, is there not something forced about such an environment? The Communist artist Hugo Gellert, who lived in the Stelton colony, thought so when he accused the Ferms' libertarian education of producing "hot-house flowers."[193]

All these questions arise quite apart from the incontestably great charismatic force of Elizabeth and Alexis Ferm. From all these angles it becomes fair to ask: Is education without manipulation either possible or conceivable? Educational radicalism can probably never bring about "freedom" in the sense of a complete lack of influence over children's thoughts and actions. For any degree of attention will infallibly signal to the children a hint of what is expected of them, and thus influence them. Only an inhuman degree of indifference would allow adults to be physically present on the scene without offering the children at least some attention.[194] Elizabeth Ferm liked boldly to declare: "Outside suggestion or direction only serves to interrupt and retard the work of the self-active child." Again she

191. This same point has recently been made in more general terms by John Holt in *Summerhill: For and Against* (New York: Hart Publishing Co., 1970), pp. 85–97.
192. Alexis Ferm, *The Problem of Education*, pp. 9, 11.
193. Hugo Gellert, "Teachers Who Flunked," *New Masses*, V (March, 1930), 12.
194. Alexis Ferm replied to my draft version here by saying: "When we talk of freedom in education we are not talking about the children being alone. The adult who is with the children . . . does not interfere with their expression or try to correct their work. . . . If the child . . . is puzzled about his expression, about his ability, he will turn to the educator for encouragement, not for adverse criticism." But Ferm's reply does not really answer the central point about the effects of *any* attention in shaping the responses of children. Naturally Ferm objected most strongly to my use of the word "manipulation" in this context. "Why make a word cover a multitude of sins? . . . Leaving an environment free or open is not manipulating it. . . . Is the English language so short of words that we must use large words to cover opposing ideas?" Ferm to the author, September 11, 1970. Dictionary definitions of manipulation include "artful management." Another definition might be to induce anyone to do anything which he might likely not have done in the absence of the inducement.

maintained: "We hear . . . of 'freedom restricted,' 'freedom under the law.' The first word precludes the last and the last contradicts the first. No one can give freedom to another; each one must earn it for himself."[195] When statements of this kind are set against the record of what the Modern School was actually like, it is only possible to conclude that the Ferms were profoundly self-deceived. Educational experiment in fact comprises one of the most powerful forms of environmental manipulation available to man. Especially is this so when education is defined not as an isolated classroom phenomenon but rather—as it was in the Living House at Stelton—as more or less coterminous with life. What is crucial is not the presence or absence of manipulation in some absolute sense, but its quality and degree. From this point of view, the Ferms emerge as a good deal less authoritarian than some of the gurus in mystically oriented social movements. Even with their presence Stelton remained far different from a closed-off, conformist community.

The conflict that developed at Stelton between political and cultural radicalism was no doubt unavoidable. The Ferms' personalities only brought it into sharper focus. Indeed, what are usually called "radical" ideas in education probably link much more naturally with political liberalism than they do with radicalism in that sphere. "Self-expression" as an aim has been historically connected with the rise of the middle class, though its more extreme advocates usually seek somehow to "drop out" of that class. Factory workers have generally been too busy struggling to survive and to advance their worldly condition to care much about goals of "inner" personal development. The Jewish immigrant workers, with their special traditions, furnished an unusual hope of effectively bridging this gap. But even in their case, and despite much initial enthusiasm, it could not finally be done.

Under different circumstances middle-class radicalism can be far more meaningful. Indeed, the hip revolt of the 1960's would prove it to be a more potent force than the older forms of worker-oriented political militance. The trouble with the cultural radicalism of the Ferms lay in part with their characteristically nineteenth-century emphasis upon self-reliant individualism rather than upon a warmer ideal of social brotherhood, and in part upon their insistence in linking radicalism too strongly with the specific realm of education, no matter how drastically redefined. The middle-

195. Elizabeth Ferm, *Freedom in Education*, pp. 23, 102, 129. She also used the word "license" approvingly, daringly calling it the necessary first step toward an ideal kind of order in the classroom. *Ibid.*, pp. 42–43. In fairness, it should also be noted that Alexis Ferm once wrote: "Freedom, not absolute freedom, but as much freedom as is possible . . ." *The Problem of Education*, p. 23.

class youth of the 1960's took the whole of their lives into their own hands, often rejecting even the most permissive classrooms that were concocted by adults. Shaping their own communal experiments, they were more in keeping with the deepest spirit of anarchism than early twentieth-century forerunners like the Ferms.

At Stelton the Ferms had created, in effect, a divisive counter-culture within a counter-culture. Each of these two counter-cultures, the school and the colony, was genuinely more radical than the other in certain respects, and yet more vulnerable in others to the accusation of being "soft" toward mainstream America. The situation was thus well made for mutual recrimination and contempt. If the school represented the "inner," or self-developmental, route toward liberation, and the colony represented the external or political and social route, the two did not successfully mingle or merge in this environment. Rather than reinforcing each other, as Harry Kelly and Joseph Cohen had originally intended, the school and colony remained curiously separate worlds.

Every year while the Ferms ran the school most of the older children would be withdrawn and placed elsewhere. As early as 1921 one local observer noted that "the opposition to a radical application of revolutionary ideas in education is chiefly from the most extreme 'revolutionists.' This paradoxical attitude . . . is based on a subconscious fear of the social system which the same individuals have determined to extirpate completely."[196] Even more tellingly, it became apparent that most political radicals simply did not care very much about educational questions or panaceas at all.[197] Though the school did continue until 1953, largely through the great devotion shown by a protégée of the Ferms, Anna Schwartz, it increasingly became a mere kindergarten, whose dwindling numbers were partly supplied by referrals of "problem" children from the state of New Jersey.[198] Most of the residents of the Stelton colony had long since withdrawn their own children from it.[199]

Decline and Disappearance

It remains to recount the later years of the Stelton colony. Prolonged factional controversy began to sap its strength during the early 1920's, the

196. Anonymous, "Fighting for Freedom at the Modern School," *Modern School*, VIII (October, 1921), 23. Alexis Ferm also pointed to this paradox in *Sketch*, p. 104.
197. See *Modern School*, I (September 1, 1914), 4; *Road to Freedom*, V (April, 1929), 2–3.
198. In the late 1940's the school was helped financially by a "Wall Street friend" of the Ferms, who also sent his three children to it.
199. *Sketch*, pp. 68–69.

very years when the Ferms were bringing new vitality to the school. Stormy arguments had always been bound into the style of the Ferrer movement, but they had taken place within a deep consensus. A newcomer who sat in the recently finished assembly room of the school during the heated debates at the annual convention of 1920 reported how impressive this combination of ardor and fundamental good will seemed to him at the time. "The crowded auditorium was vibrant with life. . . . The atmosphere was so electric, the proceedings so earnest, the spirit of unity so profound that I was soon saying to myself, 'here are workers who know what they want and are determined to get it through their own efforts. Surely this is not just another school. Only something worth while could evoke such enthusiasm.' "[200]

Harry Kelly credited the success of the colony to the high level of personal freedom, the respect for individual differences. But this implied an underlying measure of cooperation and trust. Too much individualism, taken alone, might lead only to epidemics of stealing and vandalism, which, surprisingly, were at times major problems at Stelton.[201] At its best the colony was characterized by a delicate balance between individual assertiveness and group spirit.

Much of the credit for the survival of the colony must be given to the striking blend of egalitarianism and shrewd leadership which marked the handling of affairs, even though anarchists do not like to talk about leadership. To begin with, efforts were made to erase customary lines of status. At certain times nearly everyone participated in manual labor.[202] The teaching staff of the school was deliberately merged with the custodial staff at the Living House, and for a while all the teachers took their terms as janitors, though this did not work out well in the long run. The abolition of status differences between teachers and children was also an ideal at Stelton, along with the avoidance of anything like an "institutionalized feeling" in the Living House. Though blatant cases of favoritism did arise in practice, the existence of these ideals—and the frequent efforts to realize them—had great importance in defining the atmosphere.

Stability would seem to be produced by a balance between leadership

200. Paul Scott, "Some Personal Reminiscences," *25th Anniv.*, p. 13.

201. *Sketch*, pp. 51–52; Alexis Ferm's report, September 1, 1941, p. 2, M.S.A.N.A. Papers. Some colonists apparently justified stealing from a belief that all property should ideally be shared, much as did Abbie Hoffman in the 1960's.

202. "During the summer [of 1920] a singer was digging ditches and building hencoops in the colony. . . . A journalist managed the co-operative store. Another journalist delivered milk. . . . The teachers in the school do chores that usually fall to the lot of the farmhand, and they do them willingly." Jacob Robbins, "Some Impressions of Stelton," *Modern School*, VII (November, 1920), 204–205.

and democratic equality, rather than by an extreme of either sort. This is precisely what, for a few years at least, the Stelton community must have enjoyed. Harry Kelly, especially, appears to have been a leader of unusual talents, superior to most of those who took command in other intentional communities of the day.[203] His down-to-earth awareness of the problems this role involved emerges in the most striking passage of his autobiography. One of the most "knotty problems" confronting those "who seek to build a new society," he said, concerns

> how to keep alive the enthusiasm of people who give material or moral support to a social project, and yet keep them from interfering with the individuals who perform the essential technical work or with the effectiveness of the work itself. It is a dual issue of a highly sensitive character. . . . We debated this issue endlessly. . . . But, while it took time and patience —which authoritarians seldom relish—in the end, it worked out fairly well. We felt . . . that it is a risky thing to destroy people's enthusiasm for a cause by depriving them of the right to have a say about methods to be employed, for it almost invariably follows that when a man is denied a voice in the operation of that in which he is especially interested, it is merely a matter of time before he loses interest in the thing itself and, when others have the same experience, the project disintegrates for lack of support.[204]

More consciously than the Ferms, Kelly here lapses into a vocabulary of manipulation. Indeed, it might be claimed that he was arguing for open discussion and debate solely for its psychological value—for the sense of participation, and therefore of loyalty, which such debate would provide. Kelly managed to inspire the Stelton colonists because he constantly made them each feel valuable and important.

At the same time Kelly's dislike of authoritarianism was genuine and deep; it kept him from putting on many airs. The existence of a certain strain of shrewd manipulativeness in his makeup should, therefore, hardly cause one to despair of the human race. Experimental communities as well as universities and nation-states require more than the crude forms of participatory democracy if they are to enjoy a continuous existence. And, as against that of the religious gurus to be encountered in later chapters, Kelly's style of leadership seems mild and benign. If anything, the Stelton colonists appear to have suffered from too pronounced a reliance upon town meetings, rather than the reverse. For it is remembered that many

203. Except perhaps Job Harriman of the Llano colony. Charles Pierce LeWarne's forthcoming study of intentional communities in Washington state, 1885–1915, reveals a generally very low caliber of leadership there.
204. Kelly's manuscript autobiography, p. 230.

important things remained forever undone because the interminable discussions about them wore everyone out without leading to clear-cut decisions.[205]

It was therefore a sad fact that in 1923 Harry Kelly decided to remove himself from the scene and return to New York to live. Moreover, his withdrawal occurred in the context of what could easily be interpreted as a secessionist scheme, though Kelly never wanted to admit that this was its meaning.

Early in 1923, Kelly began to discuss the possibility of establishing a summer camp at some new location near New York to be operated commercially as a source of additional income for the school at Stelton. Then he accidentally learned of the availability of a large property fronting on Lake Mohegan, about thirty miles due north of New York City. This property, once the Pawling estate, belonged to the Baron de Hirsch organization, which operated several farms in different parts of the world as pilot models for a Jewish "back-to-the-land" movement.[206] The enterprise of this kind at Mohegan had not proved successful, and the organization was in a mood to sell—especially to some other equally idealistic group. When Kelly learned of this, he began to dream of founding a whole new colony on the site. Mohegan had great advantages over Stelton. It was in a beautiful hilly, wooded area, with a two-thousand-foot frontage on the large lake. Roads, buildings, and landscaping were already completed. Commuting to the city, though more difficult than at Stelton, was not out of the question. In one great leap it would be possible to escape from the physical squalor of the New Jersey site, where the nonexistent roads, inadequate water supply, and general lack of beauty were becoming more wearisome each year.

Through some of his most persuasive talking, Kelly managed to buy the Mohegan property for a very reasonable sum.[207] From this time forward, although he continued to live mostly in New York, he poured his energies into creating the new colony at Mohegan. This venture was financed just as Stelton had been—by the resale of the land in smaller amounts to individual colonists. However, this time the purchasers had to agree to "certain fixed conditions," which were embodied in a written constitution. The effort obviously was to screen prospective buyers more adequately. As a group, the Mohegan colonists were noticeably more well-

205. There are hints that in some of his dealings Kelly may have become more authoritarian after leaving the Stelton colony. Joseph Cohen, too, is remembered to have been far more authoritarian at the Sunrise colony in the 1930's than he had ever been at Stelton. The size, diversity, and individualism of the Stelton population, and the fact that most property was not held in common, must have served as important intrinsic checks upon strong leadership.

206. Concerning Baron de Hirsch, see Brandes, *op. cit.,* p. 27.

207. He paid $60,000 for land which today is reputed to be worth $2 or $3 million.

to-do than those at Stelton, though they were also drawn from radical circles in New York. In 1925 the Mohegan colony even gained a Modern School of its own—for Kelly still very much wanted to link the two ideas of school and community. Finally, not long after this Kelly also created a second new colony, called Mount Airy, at Harmon (now part of Croton-on-Hudson), New York; however, it had no school and was much less elaborate.

Although Kelly wanted to think of the Mohegan and Mount Airy ventures as logical extensions of the Stelton idea (and although only a few families moved from Stelton to Mohegan), it is clear that they accompanied a growing disillusionment with Stelton on his part.[208] From then on Kelly's participation in affairs at Stelton greatly declined, and in 1927 ceased entirely.[209] In producing this shift in his attention, besides the physical beauty of Mohegan, it is not inconceivable that Kelly was also secretly jealous of the degree to which the Ferms had become personally dominant at Stelton following their arrival in 1920, although Kelly's relations with them appear to have remained outwardly cordial. Some of these same considerations may have affected the decision of Joseph J. Cohen also to withdraw from the Stelton colony in 1925 (though he returned there to live again for a time after 1939).[210] Since soon afterward the Ferms were temporarily driven from their position, in one way or another all the major personalities associated with the colony found themselves suddenly exiled from it at the end of its first decade of existence.

There are strong hints of prima donna-ism in all these departures, though open quarrels were at a minimum. In the short run, an atmosphere

208. "The school [at Stelton] has been and is far more successful than the colony but the latter has not been a failure by far and has in my judgment been well worth while. I lived there for eight years and know. There are holes in the road and the condition of the latter is a disgrace to a group of people claiming to be radicals. . . . The water system has not been solved satisfactorily although it has been done better than the roads. Comrade Koch solved the problem for himself by going away and working in capitalist society, I tried to solve mine by starting another community and providing for better roads at the start." Kelly to Abe Grossman, April 23, 1924, in possession of Nathan Marer.

209. "I have been engaged for several—or some—years now trying to organize colonies along the lines of Stelton. . . . I have not been to Stelton for three years as a very fundamental difference of opinion separates me from the people in charge of the school there but of course I have friends there and they know where I am." Harry Kelly to Carl Nold, September 27, 1930, Labadie Collection, University of Michigan. As late as 1926 Kelly had accepted a committee post at Stelton; see Isaac Lehrer to Joseph J. Cohen, January 10, 1926, Cohen Papers. References to Stelton in Kelly's autobiography cease with the founding of Mohegan colony in 1923.

210. Cohen said that "serious differences of opinion which arose concerning the school's methods, coupled with the demands of my duties as an editor in New York, induced me to withdraw." Cohen, In Quest of Heaven, p. 25.

of tolerance for individual self-assertion had strengthened the bonds of group cohesion by legitimizing open disagreements. But, in the longer run, so fragmented and "democratic" an undertaking could not continue to attract the loyalties of the several strong-minded figures who, between them, had given it so much stability.[211] The leadership lost its inner élan; perhaps Kelly, Cohen, and the Ferms all simply became weary of so much endless talk at meetings.

Still, both the Stelton school and colony were able to survive the Mohegan split-off and the withdrawal of all the early leaders.[212] Other quite different events proved to be even more important for the future of the colony. For already in the early 1920's, and to a much greater extent later on, the general atmosphere began to be affected by disputes which had their origin not in personal rivalries but in the logic of the world political situation. A more decided kind of factionalism took shape which put Kelly, Cohen, the Ferms, and the Dicks together in the same basic camp, regardless of the intricacies of their own personal relations. Further, it spread to Mohegan as well as Stelton, becoming if anything more bitter at the newer colony.

This factionalism was produced by the decision of some of the colonists to become Communists. The beginnings of a split along these lines may be glimpsed as early as the summer of 1920, when a visitor referred to Stelton as temporarily torn between two opposing camps, one composed of self-conscious "proletarians," who wanted to give full support to the Russian people and to establish a dictatorship of the proletariat in America, and the other of "intellectuals," among whom apparently were most of the colony leaders.[213]

This kind of polarization was entirely understandable in the political context of the day. The meaning of the Russian Revolution of 1917 was, of course, the central question in the minds of all deeply committed radi-

211. However, the self-restraint shown by all of them in their mutual dealings is, from another point of view, enormously impressive. All these people (except Kelly and the Dicks) remained outwardly on good terms with each other most of the time. They often attended reunion dinners long after their active participation had ceased. Indeed, of all those whose names figure prominently in the history of the school and colony, it is difficult to recall anyone whose departure occasioned an angry public break. All this reveals a very different atmosphere from the steel-edged polemics of the American Communists.

212. The school came to the verge of utter collapse in 1927–1928, until the sudden return of James and Nellie Dick from Mohegan put it on a strongly upward course once again.

213. Robbins, *op. cit.,* pp. 203–204. On the Communist-anarchist split among American radicals generally during the 1920's, see Kenneth Rexroth, *An Autobiographical Novel* (New York: New Directions, 1964), p. 207.

cals during the years that immediately followed it. For anarchists, a special problem existed in this respect. Hostile to all state authority, they nonetheless found themselves strongly tempted to honor and support the social revolution that had suddenly toppled the hated czars. Emma Goldman revealed both phases of this inner debate. Deported to Russia by the American government at the end of 1919, at first she threw her energies into active support of the Bolsheviks, despite her qualms about their authoritarian tendencies. Within two years she had become openly disillusioned and hostile.

Among the Stelton colonists, the attractions of the new regime in Russia also were strong. Here was the only society in the world controlled by men whose viewpoints were even remotely similar to their own. In the chaos of civil war and economic collapse, it was easy to excuse the harsh measures of the Soviet rulers. Further, one should recall that Lenin was no Stalin, and that even the early Stalin (down to the purge trials of 1936) by no means fully revealed himself as the Stalin to come. No one could foretell the future of the Soviet Union, which in the 1920's was still a place of lively and relatively diverse cultural and social ferment. So it was quite reasonable at this time for some erstwhile anarchists to disagree with Emma Goldman, swallow their previous dislike for political authority, and actively join the Communist cause.

No other political affiliation then seemed as forward-looking. To remain an anarchist in the 1920's was to run the risk of being branded as a diehard member of a hopelessly lost cause. Socialism, meanwhile, had moved in a timidly moderate direction, and it too was no longer a vigorously expanding force. Communism, despite its numerically tiny base in America, could claim affiliation with the most hopeful large-scale revolutionary movement anywhere on the world horizon.

Stelton and Mohegan colonists who turned toward Communism thus announced their continued primary commitment to the world political scene. With considerable justification they accused their neighbors who remained anarchists of having given up any claim to being part of an effective revolutionary movement, of having surrendered to defeatism. Some of Harry Kelly's statements in the early 1920's gave these accusations support. It must have struck the more militant colonists as rather remarkable when he frankly said, in the fall of 1921:

> We have never pretended that colonies such as the one evolved at Stelton will abolish capitalism or change the social system; the men and women there do, however, learn from actual daily life and experience how to raise

children into strong healthy men and women. . . . Modern life is pretty sordid for the mass of men and women . . . but it has to be lived if one wishes to do anything; if one is not to live a dull and futile existence, some joy must be extracted on the way and oases like the Ferrer Colony become more and more necessary to make life livable.[214]

In a speech he gave in New York shortly after the Mohegan colony was established, Kelly referred even more openly to the loss of heart in radical circles since the First World War, a mood which he clearly shared:

> Instead of the war being of short duration and bringing in its train a social revolution it lasted long enough to kill a very large part of the youth and revolutionary forces of the world and so impoverish the rest, excepting [in] this country, as to create the weariness and pessimism of the present time. The world is weary and sadly lacks the faith that animated it twenty-five years ago. I have what the psycho-analist [*sic*] calls a complex, a horror of being so fossilized as to hark back to the "dear old times" like the old fogies I formerly scoffed at. In spite of myself I must admit that as far as the naked eye can see there is an absence of that idealism that was prevalent before the war. Meetings were held and papers and pamphlets published with enthusiasm and sacrifice. Life had color and adventure whereas now it seems a round of quarrels and futilities.[215]

Truly there must have seemed only two alternatives to the people in these circles—either become a Communist or else admit that one was giving up hope.

Kelly admitted still another dimension of his disillusionment in a sentence of that same speech which he crossed out and decided not to deliver. In it he expressed fear over the psychological consequences of having made his own living from the radical movement—that is, over having become (from one point of view) just another suburban land speculator in the prosperous 1920's. It was not, of course, that he had literally profited very much from his new colony ventures; the point was that he keenly sensed how his chosen course of action was leading him back toward an accommodation with the habit patterns of the American mainstream. In the same vein, he experienced a great pang of sadness at witnessing the way in which the Mohegan colonists, by 1925 or so, had begun freely discussing how well their stocks were currently doing on the market.[216]

214. Kelly, "The Ferrer Colony," *Modern School,* VIII (October, 1921), 19.
215. Kelly's manuscript speech, "25th Anniversary Freie Arbeiter Stimme," ca. 1925, p. 2, in possession of Nathan Marer. As the *Freie Arbeiter Stimme* (the Yiddish anarchist newspaper in New York) had first been founded in 1890, this speech must have been given at the twenty-fifth anniversary of its revival after a period of lapse. For a less extreme statement of his mood, see *Sketch,* pp. 117–19.
216. Kelly's manuscript autobiography, p. 453.

The Communists adopted no less of a suburban manner of living than did many remaining anarchists during these years of economic boom, but their intense commitment to a global political ideology gave them an important form of protection against the ravages of self-doubt. Lacking such protection, those who clung instead to anarchism were apt to feel increasingly bereft. Men like Harry Kelly had a far greater degree of self-knowledge than men like Mike Gold. But self-knowledge may not necessarily offer comfort. Comfort, amid guilt over one's own growing good fortune, is far more likely to be provided by a rigid faith which is reassuring in its very harshness.

Perhaps the contrasts between these two rival outlooks as they collided at Stelton might be summed up in a single paradox: the Communists constantly preached solidarity but practiced the fomenting of divisive conflict; the anarchists preached individual initiative and self-reliance but practiced something much closer to brotherly love and community feeling. Therefore, because they refused to be sharp-edged in practice, the anarchists found themselves more vulnerable to the subtle external pressures which, in the American social context, can easily result in loss of one's distinctive identity.

At both Stelton and Mohegan, the school became a major center of contention between the two factions. In Communist eyes, the school was an unjustifiable diversion from the primary end of furthering the class struggle. Thus, though the Communists at Stelton by no means comprised the whole of the opposition to the Ferms, their politically motivated criticism added a further dimension to the controversy between aims of "self-expression" and social commitment. The Communists were among those who withdrew their own children from the Modern School at an early date and placed them in the public school even while they continued to live in the colony. Not being satisfied with this way of expressing their lack of confidence, the Communist faction, both at Stelton and at Mohegan, also tried to take over the respective schools, through the technique of packing the annual convention meetings. Since by the late 1920's a large proportion of the Stelton and Mohegan colonists had become Communists, the anarchist friends of the schools had to import a great many of their own sympathizers from New York for these occasions. At Stelton the noisy battle occurred year after year, but the Communists never gained control. At Mohegan, after a decade, the Communists along with a faction of religious conservatives did win out, but the school there collapsed completely a year or two later.

The struggle between Communists and anarchists lasted altogether for more than twenty years, with neither side winning a clear victory.[217] In this curiously protracted situation, it is remarkable to observe the extent to which communal bonds did survive. Particularly was this true at Stelton, where communitarian sentiment was far more pronounced than it ever became at Mohegan. It is notable, for instance, that the men of Stelton are recalled to have been far more deeply stirred by these factional loyalties than most of the women. This, plus the fact that so many of the men commuted to jobs in New York, put an unintentional brake upon factional strife. While the men were off at their work (and therefore powerless to prevent it), the women would fraternize socially despite their husbands' convictions. Further, the children continued to play at each others' houses freely throughout the colony, regardless of politics.[218] Many friendships continued for a while to cross party lines; Mike Gold, for instance, was nursed back to health after a serious illness by anarchist friends in the colony whom he could not publicly acknowledge.

The tone of the controversy, at least during its first decade, is probably well conveyed in a letter written by James H. Dick when he was principal of the school:

> Ours is a mixed crowd of Anarchists and Communists and it takes the school enthusiasts to steer them clear of high words in these strenuous times. Of course the Anarchists have their meetings and the Communists theirs, and so long as the twain never meet all is well with the school. The school Saturday evening [program for adults] is confined to lectures, concerts etc., and altho we have both Anarchists and Communists holding forth, there is no *definite* propaganda. These lectures generally bear on affairs in Russia, and altho the controversy following the lectures becomes somewhat heated it never—seldom becomes boisterous.[219]

It must be borne in mind that the colonists always thrived upon controversy as such, relishing "a good knock-down drag-out fight . . . and some of the colony meetings were humdingers." But, recalled Jo Ann Burbank, "no real, lasting animosity appeared to result . . . at least not to my rather puzzled eyes."[220] Aggressive contention was simply a shared value (as one understands it is in Israel today), in contrast to a culture where it is considered important to hold one's feelings in. In such a context, it could even be argued that the constant agitation over the threat of a "Communist

217. Mohegan factionalism was further complicated by the existence there of a third group who became militant Zionists.
218. This last was not true at Mohegan.
219. James H. Dick to Leonard D. Abbott, January 19, 1931, Dick Papers.
220. Jo Ann Burbank to the author, September 23, 1970.

takeover" created a rallying cry that enabled the school to survive with greater vigor.

Still, a definite worsening of the tone of conflict appears to have occurred at Stelton around the years 1931–1932. This was a period when the Communist party became extremely militant, in response to the nationwide depression, but in terms that were narrowly sectarian. A number of the colonists actually went to Russia in these years, to help answer an appeal for skilled labor there. But the more important local effect of this intensification of ideological commitment was the creation at Stelton, for the first time, of a uniformed cadre of Young Pioneers—Communist youths who marched around wearing white shirts and red neckties. This divisive display created a new feeling of bitterness, making it less easy than before to visit freely in other persons' homes. Mrs. Ossip Kenner, wife of the local Communist leader, began organizing aggressive welcoming parties for newcomers in the colony, seeking to win them for her faction. The anarchists never were able to sustain such tactics, and their resentment grew. There is some evidence that the more thoughtful children in the community became disgusted with their elders' factionalism on both sides.[221] One Communist remained on the school's board of directors. Yet in 1941 the Communist youth at Stelton were apparently creating deliberate disorder in the school building whenever they had the chance.

The split between the Communists and anarchists, and the subtler rivalries among some of the colony leaders and school principals, of course scarcely account for all the disagreements, large and small, which plagued the Stelton and Mohegan communities, just as they are apt to bother all face-to-face societies. The private letters that have survived from the 1920's, and also the pages of *Road to Freedom* (which was edited by Hippolyte Havel from Stelton until 1926, and thereafter by Havel and Kelly in New York City) echo with the overtones of further disputes whose outlines are only dimly perceptible.[222] The issue of permitting religious ob-

221. See, for instance, *The Stelton Outlook*, II (February, 1933), 3, 6, 8, a teenage publication in the colony, a copy of which is in M.S.A.N.A. Papers. However, it may represent only the feeling of the anarchist youth who remained loyal to the school. Also highly suggestive, though it appeared much earlier, is the article, "Our School, and Why Children Leave It," in another youthful publication, *The Stelton Appendix*, No. 2 (May 14, 1927), which complains in effect that the constant quarreling of the adults is leaving the children stranded.

222. The tone of such routine conflict is well captured, for instance, in Isaac Lehrer to Joseph J. Cohen, January 10, 1926, Cohen Papers, which describes what happens to be going on in the colony at the moment. Lehrer reports how one teacher at the school has had definite ideas about education which no one else on the staff (or among the children) will accept and now is threatening to resign. Meanwhile,

servances within the colony, for instance, long remained heated. By the time of the Second World War, a main problem had become the emergence of stridently pacifist and social-credit tendencies in the thinking of one man who had lived at Stelton for many years, which were interpreted as "fascist" leanings by others. This factional bitterness created a new rupture in the school staff. And one could name a large number of more temporary factional groupings, many of them quite short-lived.[223]

The coming of the Second World War presented new intellectual problems. People who had long forgotten to think of themselves as Jews became sharply reminded of their ethnic origins. Hitler encouraged the upwelling of patriotic emotions, as an international proletarian identity came to seem meaningless. Most of the colonists, whether anarchist or Communist, Jew or Gentile, were reunified in support of the war, but it was a unity which no longer set them apart very clearly from the rest of the American population.[224]

What is truly remarkable is how long the Stelton colony continued to survive, despite these sources of tension within it. The colony was dealt its final major blow not by internal discord but by external intervention of a kind which, at least for the remaining anarchists, was extremely ironic, since it came from the American military. During the defense boom period in 1941, the federal government began quietly buying a vast tract of farmland immediately adjacent to the property owned by the Stelton residents. On this land, in the weeks after Pearl Harbor, Camp Kilmer came into being. Within a short time seventy-five thousand young men were living in barracks in the fields where until then the Stelton children had freely romped in solitude.

Before this the Stelton colonists had never had to lock their doors at

---

another staff member who is far more conscientious is secretly filling the children's minds with religious propaganda and tolerating the presence of Christian missionaries in the colony! Still a third staff member was hired primarily to help clean the shop but has taken on too many airs and will not do the work. But is this kind of three-ring circus enormously different from the staff problems and gossip that constantly occur in most conventional organizations?

223. For instance, in 1921 the Group of Action of Ferrer Colony accused other colonists of losing their idealism and becoming profiteers, building ugly shacks and then renting them at exorbitant rates. *Action,* I (April, 1921), four-page printed issue in M.S.A.N.A. Papers. In 1926 a Work and Play Centre was established, representing a bold secession of some parents and children from the Modern School; see *Road to Freedom,* II (July 15, 1926), 3. Meanwhile, a related faction, known as the Road to Freedom Group of Stelton, had also sprung into existence; see *ibid.,* II (August 1, 1926), 4. This later became called the Kropotkin Group, and probably represented those in the colony who remained loyal to anarchism and friendly with Kelly.

224. Jo Ann Burbank to the author, September 23, 1970. As one of the very few pacifists at Stelton, she felt this change of mood keenly.

night. Now they discovered that near proximity to many thousands of soldiers produced an atmosphere of theft, vandalism, and (apparently) rape. Life immediately became unbearable to a large share of the often aging radicals who still resided there. As some moved out (occasionally going to Mohegan, but more often to milder climates in Florida or California), conditions seemed even less pleasant for the waning few who remained.[225] By the end of the war, the colony had been decimated. Most of its homes now belonged to black soldiers and their families, since the colonists had been the only persons living close to Camp Kilmer who were willing to rent or sell to those of any race. Today, except for Sally Axelrod and one or two other survivors, Stelton is a solidly black neighborhood.

It is true that the colonists were noticeably aging by the 1940's, quite apart from the sudden appearance of Camp Kilmer in their midst. It seems likely that the intrusion of the military merely speeded up a process of slow disintegration which would have occurred in any event. The sons and daughters of most of the colonists were already scattered in the larger world. The Modern School was not receiving the members of the new generation. The counter-culture, in other words, was not reproducing itself. Whether anarchist or Communist, its members were by now tacitly merging themselves into the suburban middle class in every respect except symbolic and nostalgic associations.

Seen from one perspective, the community had shown a remarkable staying power; from another, it had long existed as little more than a fossilized curiosity. It had survived a remarkable series of internal conflicts, but it lacked the ultimately essential capacity to recruit a steady stream of younger newcomers into its midst. The radicals of the 1960's would gain no inspiration from the totally unfamiliar names of Francisco Ferrer, Harry Kelly, and Elizabeth and Alexis Ferm.

During their own last years, the leading personalities of the earlier Stelton revealed a growing awareness of their evident failure. Harry Kelly retired to New Rochelle, where to his disgruntlement it was necessary for his new wife, a school librarian, to support him all through the depression. (Some friends tried to get him a post with the Tennessee Valley Authority, but his radical ties proved too potent a memory and he was regretfully refused a job.) When France fell to the Nazis Kelly confessed that he felt "like a babe in woods over-run with bears and armed only with a toy

225. The school survived without interruption, but only with much reduced numbers. Already bedridden, Elizabeth Ferm died in the shadow of Camp Kilmer in 1944. Alexis Ferm and Anna Schwartz quietly carried on the work; Alexis then retired in 1948.

pistol. . . . I feel at times like one who has been following a Mirage for forty or more years and wakes up at last disillusioned and unhappy."[226] Organizing sentimental reunion dinners, Kelly lingered on, gradually growing blind and feeble, until his death in 1953. Joseph Cohen died the same year after a long period of restless travel in Europe and Mexico—still a convinced opponent of Zionism but now an equally firm supporter of Adlai Stevenson. That year Leonard Abbott also died in New York; he too had difficulty holding a job in the depression, though he served for a time in the Federal Writers' Project in Washington, D.C. In the closing period of his life, Abbott revealed much disillusionment about the failure of his ideas and the general lack of progress toward ending war and poverty in the world. And finally, from his self-made dwelling in Fairhope, Alabama, where he had moved four years after his wife's death, Uncle Ferm also pondered the apparent futility of his struggle for libertarian education. But his regrets were of a different kind, for he wished that he had poured still more money and energy into the great effort. At least he enjoyed the satisfaction of proudly being able to recall, during the long years of an extreme old age, dozens of affectionate Stelton graduates individually by name. He died in 1971 when he was a hundred and one.

Back in 1916, Leonard Abbott had said, "Our school is a training-ground for a new world, for a society in which, as we hope, human beings will ultimately live their own lives in their own way, without coercion and without intolerance."[227] One must finally ask to what extent this aim of building an effective counter-culture ever became realized at Stelton. This question goes beyond the ultimate fate of the Stelton and Mohegan colonies. It concerns the extent to which the colonists or the schoolchildren had ever succeeded in extricating themselves from the values and habit patterns of the American mainstrean, even during the earlier and happier period of the colony's existence. By exploring this subject we may reveal something of the subtle processes whereby a fledgling cultural revolt is overwhelmed by the immensely powerful traditional society which surrounds it.

Especially relevant to such an appraisal are attitudes on the subject of economic success. The American dream of upward social mobility captured the minds of nearly all immigrants and native-born persons alike, especially during the early twentieth century, constantly pushing everyone toward a

226. Harry Kelly to Agnes Inglis, July 6, 1940, Labadie Collection. Of course many liberal democrats could easily have expressed themselves in identical terms at that particular moment in history.
227. *Modern School,* III (October, 1916), 106.

closer embrace of the established economic and political system. Effective resistance to this alluring vision was the *sine qua non* for any would-be counter-culture.

This is one reason why in the beginning the prognosis for the Ferrer movement might have been unusually favorable. Its members (except for some of the native-born leaders) were relatively poor; its resources were almost nil. Stelton, we saw, often struck middle-class outsiders as a wretched rural slum. The Ferms, moreover, positively loved a bare style of living. The attitude of the parents, who remained so greatly concerned about the teaching of the three R's, was far more ominous, but their strong sense of class consciousness held out at least some hope that they too might avoid falling into conventional thought patterns. In the work of the Ferrer Center, wrote Harry Kelly in 1912, "the taint of business and success" should "forever be absent—unless by success we mean the opening of new worlds to the vision of man."[228]

These were brave words. But a cynical observer might well have interpreted the actions of the Ferrer membership, even in the early history of the movement, quite differently. Deliberately leaving aside all questions of intellectual commitment, these colonists might be viewed as immigrant workers who were clever enough to purchase acre plots in the suburbs at a time when land values were still low and few garment workers could hope to escape from the slums.[229] Indeed, for many Stelton must have been primarily a pleasant place to spend a summer vacation. From this same perspective, the move onto the Mohegan site in the early 1920's was another important step upward in the achievement of suburban (or exurban) contentment. The summer-camp aspects of the Mohegan venture were still more prominent, and became increasingly so as time went on. The depression of the 1930's gave these particular immigrants a setback, like most other Americans. But by the 1940's, when the elderly colonists began selling their houses (whatever the motive) and moving in large numbers to Miami and Los Angeles, the group could well be described as having played the standard American life-improvement game, if anything a step ahead of most of their nonanarchist tenement neighbors on Manhattan.

That such an interpretation of the group's history is plausible does not mean, of course, that it is necessarily the most valid. For one thing, it ig-

228. Harry Kelly, "What Is a Modern School?" *Modern School,* No. 3 (undated issue, Winter, 1912–1913), p. 2.
229. "Most of the folks who had built little shacks to live in [at Stelton] were there because they could buy an acre for very little money. . . . I don't think any of them would have refused a big income & many of them had comparatively good income for workers." Alexis Ferm to the author, September 11, 1970.

nores entirely the role of the school. But quite a number of the colonists, especially women, remained where they were only to stay with lovers or relatives, and this somewhat diluted the purity of the counter-culture. On the other hand, there seems to have been a strong tendency to marry within the group, and thus preserve a sense of exclusiveness.

As these radicals grew more prosperous, verbal and emotional identification with the working class remained enormously strong. (In this respect Communists and anarchists still agreed.) Though one might live in an attractive house in beautiful surroundings and commute to Manhattan daily on the New York Central, it was taboo to admit openly that one had become middle class. Stories of the deliberate ostracism of a few colonists who violated this taboo reveal the great intensity of feeling which existed on the matter, beneath the surface. But style of living counts for more than such convictions in the long run.

The school, with its austere poverty, long remained a somewhat more effective focus for counter-cultural values. But evidence about its degree of success in this respect is confusing. The staff, during both the early years and the Ferms' regime, appear to have inculcated the children with a rather snobbish attitude toward the public schools. Such a prejudice could serve as a useful form of insulation, strengthening the sense of a barrier against the outside world. Yet it does not seem to have been strong enough to prevent a large share of the Modern School graduates from doing well academically later on. Such academic success, of course, was a major sign of weakness for the counter-culture; it indicated how rapidly the children could be swallowed up in a world of conventional praise and aspiration.

Equally important, there is no evidence that most Modern School graduates raised their own children according to libertarian principles, and there are some indications to the contrary. It is most unlikely, of course, that these parents proved to be peculiarly harsh. But it is probable, on the other hand, that they tended simply to melt into the large mass of fairly permissive parents in recent America. In this essential respect the school at Stelton failed to leave an unmistakable mark upon succeeding generations, comparable, say, to that which endured in Quaker circles over a very long period of time despite great changes in outward circumstances. And the major share of the new generation seems to have retreated into some version of political liberalism.[230]

---

230. Rina Garst said this about the many former Stelton families she knows. Charles Pierce LeWarne says much the same about the generation who were children at the Home anarchist colony. Jo Ann Burbank emerged from her Stelton years deeply loyal to their memory but with "one abiding emotion . . . a hatred of

There are a series of fascinating glimpses into the everyday life of the children which cast some doubt upon the effectiveness of counter-cultural values at any point, even within this tiny oasis. For instance, when Alexis Ferm wandered into the "middle" dorm room of the Living House on one November day in 1923, he found the boys and girls playing a game in which one boy was wearing a crown made of paper and all the rest had capes or cloaks with swords and were pretending to be kings, queens, lords, and princes. For anarchists who believed strongly in social equality, must this not have seemed like a forbidden game? Some years later, the children were reported eagerly playing cowboys and Indians. In 1945 one little boy at the school was playing a game of killing "Japs"; when reprimanded by a girl, who told him he should invent "good Japs" so that he wouldn't have to kill them, he replied that there were no "good Japs."[231] On this last occasion Alexis Ferm openly complained about how the school could not possibly overcome "the home, the disagreements of parents, the impact of the commercial world with its foolish fashions, the feeling of not wanting to be left out in the cold when the crowd is going one way and they happen to be going another."[232] But perhaps the most telling, and amusing, example of the seepage of the larger world into the lives of the Stelton children had already occurred in 1936, a year after the firm of Parker Brothers first introduced an extraordinarily popular new pastime to the American public. "A friend sent us a game called Monopoly, which the children have been playing," Alexis Ferm recorded. "It has to do with the acquision [sic] of land etc."[233]

Now, of course, these examples of spontaneous children's games at the Modern School can all be taken lightly if one so wishes. To play "kings and queens" might be highly conducive to egalitarian values if it led to an "unmasking" of pretense, which children are so often freely capable of doing. Cowboys and Indians can similarly dramatize the discomfort of being a victim of violence and oppression, if the roles are exchanged among the players regularly enough. Monopoly might be defended as an excellent practical introduction to the chancy hazards of the capitalist system. And of course actually to forbid any such game would deeply violate the libertarian ethic. Permissiveness, to be genuine, must include even the right to

---

fanaticism in any form or shape, good or bad"; moreover, she says she lost her faith in the perfectibility of man.

231. Alexis Ferm's report, December 2, 1923, p. 1; September 2, 1939, p. 4; 1945, p. 3, M.S.A.N.A. Papers.

232. *Ibid.*, p. 4.

233. Alexis Ferm's report, April 12, 1936, p. 2, M.S.A.N.A. Papers. According to Ferm, however, Monopoly was invented by a follower of Henry George and was intended to show the evils of land acquisition under capitalism.

act out roles which, when long continued, would destroy the counter-culture. On the other hand, when taken together, these episodes suggest something other than a completely un-American version of childhood. They seem to reveal a steady tendency for the values, the interests, and the pastimes of the great outside world to enter the Stelton Living House.

There is some opposing evidence, it is true. Many Modern School graduates recall, for instance, that the atmosphere at Stelton was so full of basic human trust (despite the factionalism) that the everyday behavior of ordinary Americans, and the alertness necessary to protect oneself against it, seemed frighteningly alien when they first left Stelton to live elsewhere. It is claimed that the boys never learned the four-letter words that are nearly universal. Perhaps most impressive was the refusal of the school, as the years passed, to update its image, raise its fees, and attract a more fashionable following. This kind of practical calculation was beyond the leaders' ken, even though it eventually resulted in the slow death of the whole endeavor. Many were the symptoms, therefore, of a persistent unworldliness of tone.

Fidelity to one's ideals in some areas of belief and practice can surprisingly coexist with a creeping conventionalism in others. Thus the record of Stelton emerges as mixed and inconclusive. But to have fought the outside world for so long to a kind of draw is in itself impressive in the American social context.

The poet Sherwood Trask declared: "Stelton . . . (chicken-coop that it was) had *the real thing*."[234] This was also Harry Kelly's judgment during the spring of 1921, when he disarmingly said:

> The colonists are often laughed at by smug defenders of our moribund society and denounced by those who consider themselves ultra-radicals for "deserting" the labor movement by moving to the country. We make no claim to saving the world; we are but trying to save our own "souls." . . . If we have not reached the promised land, we have at least stumbled into one of its by-paths, and that is something.[235]

In the context of what was by no means a "moribund society," but actually a tough, resilient and almost entirely heedless social order, the very existence of the Stelton alternative had indeed amounted to "something."

234. Sherwood Trask to Leonard D. Abbott, March 23, 1940, Abbott Papers.
235. Harry Kelly, "The Seventh Anniversary of the Stelton School," *Modern School*, VIII (Summer, 1921), 25–26.

CHAPTER THREE

Contemporary Anarchistic Communes

The differences between Stelton and present-day communes influenced by anarchist or libertarian ideas at first loom enormous. It is true that formal structure and organization were deliberately kept to a minimum at Stelton, and this aim has become even more central in many recent communal experiments. But Stelton and Home were the only two anarchist colonies in early twentieth-century America. Both enjoyed relatively long lives—in each case, about a decade of idealism and vigor, followed by a protracted period of slow decline. By contrast, anarchistic communes of the last few years have been far more numerous. They have also been less clearly tied to anarchism as a historical movement, and they show every sign of tending toward much shorter life spans.

An especially revealing difference is the heightening of the genuinely communal element in their pattern of living. The individualistic strain in earlier American anarchism, present among both the immigrants and the native-born at Stelton, appears to have been muted.[1] Anarchistic communes of the present share in the strongly stylized forms of thinking and living which characterize the "hip" movement. The uniformity of the tribe, more than the spontaneity of "doing your own thing," seemed to pervade the commune in New Mexico, here to be called Rockridge, which my wife and I visited twice during the summer of 1971.

1. For a more carefully qualified discussion of the issue of declining individualism in the recent counter-culture, see below, pp. 422–29. Rosabeth Moss Kanter, *Commitment and Community* (Cambridge, Massachusetts: Harvard University Press, 1972), p. 184, offers a different impression of contemporary anarchistic communes in this respect.

Would I have become aware of a similar patterning if I had been able to drop in at Stelton around the year 1920, or at Home still earlier? I greatly doubt it, because (despite the ethnic bond at Stelton) their populations were far more diverse, not only in age span, but in viewpoint and intent. At Home and Stelton lived many believers in diverse ideologies, including spiritualism, Theosophy, and Communism. There were outright diet and nature cranks, and people who remained only for the sake of their lovers. Individual stubbornness, assertiveness, and disruptive rambunctiousness appear to have been far more evident in these settings two generations ago than they are in the most nearly comparable ones today.

Oddly enough, one reason for the change may be a certain tendency toward "tolerance," or something akin to it, in radical circles. Personal differences are no longer proudly strutted forth as they once were. Despite all the talk about openness and honesty, it is now bad form to display one's rough edges with a "take it or leave it" attitude. Similarly, in the encounter movement, "genuine" display of emotion is inseparably linked with the assumption that everyone is deeply dissatisfied with himself and wants to change. In such an atmosphere real personal differences are sometimes concealed. Today, in a commune like Rockridge, one may be "into" astrology or not, "into" religion or not, but everyone enters the same basic flow of daily life. If ideologies were paraded more openly, they could lead to rigid, standoffish self-identifications, divisive in their impact.

Yet both the earlier anarchist communities had an amazing toughness, a capacity for longevity, perhaps because their members so often kept everyone else at arm's length. Now, though differences survive, they are apt to be subdued, low-key, defined as personal "tastes" or "interests" rather than as a total identity. To formally announce a philosophy, a universal regimen, to display oneself as an individual model for the future of mankind, is to appear pompous, self-important. Instead, the common desire to "groove," in a nonverbal quest for fellow feeling, takes over. But when the feeling declines, as eventually it must, there is less patience, less willingness to stay put in order to "see things through." Physical departure is often the only recourse if one does disagree in such a tolerant yet smothering environment. And so, in the long-range sense, the community suffers, even though its life has been far more intense during a brief period.[2]

Yet, granted all these important differences, there are fascinating ele-

2. The fact that land was subdivided among individuals at Stelton is doubtless relevant to its longevity as well, although in many socialist colonies of the same period land subdivision led to an immediate relapse into middle-class landowner attitudes among the colonists.

ments of repetition. Some of these have to do with the cycle of migration. Urban anarchism, for a time in the late 1960's, closely repeated the initial recourse to violence, the hatred of authority, and the strength of commitment to social revolution, which had characterized anarchism at the turn of the twentieth century. Yet what soon happened, both in the New York area and on the West Coast, was almost identical to what occurred in the Ferrer movement in 1915. A section of the urban radicals, tired of the city and the extreme politicization of their everyday life, yet wishing to demonstrate their anarchist philosophy, began to think of retreating to the countryside. Thus in 1967 some members of the New York group called the Motherfuckers moved to a newly founded Vermont commune, Cold Mountain Farm, in much the same spirit as the Ferrer group had gone to Stelton. Once again these radicals chose to put up with the charge of "retreatism" rather than endure the daily hassles of urban existence in an overwhelmingly hostile environment. To be sure, certain differences in the modern story that is about to unfold will seem obvious—above all, the elements of looseness and drift, the seemingly random quality of the further shifts of locale. But the underlying commitment to group experiment in rural surroundings partakes of the same mood that led to the founding of Stelton.

However loose the connecting threads in this narrative of the 1960's, the story was reconstructed for me, complete with copies of the significant books (handed to me in their dugout house), by the Rockridge couple to be called Frank and Leora. I am merely retelling their own account of the chain of events that had brought them to live, for a year and a half at the time of our visit, in a remote, comfortless wilderness.

New York

To begin with, the youth in the New York area who began calling themselves anarchists in the 1960's seldom had a direct connection with the older, still surviving anarchist movement. Yet they were often from radical backgrounds in a broader sense. Sondra,[3] who lived at Rockridge for a time in 1971, illustrates this. Her parents, New York Communists and Jewish immigrants, were the kind of people who might easily have lived at Stelton. And Sondra had read Emma Goldman with great reverence in her childhood. Yet it was necessary for her to rediscover a more intense and spontaneous version of radical commitment on her own after she grew

3. Except for the authors of printed materials that are quoted, the names used in Chapter Three are nearly all fictitious.

up. In this spirit she daringly joined the Motherfuckers as a teenager around 1965. When asked, Sondra said she had never heard of the Ferrer colony, or of such a classic American anarchist figure as Voltairine de Cleyre. Within a few blocks of her in New York City were the aging members of the Libertarian Book Club, who might well have provided a link with this past, furnishing her with lore and legends to inspire her. But this did not happen, and perhaps a girl like Sondra had no need of such a precise identification. (Historians prefer to think that everyone would somehow be better off with a highly accurate sense of history. But this is very much open to question.)

Growing up in New York in the 1960's, Sondra turned not to the circles that still faintly kept alive such names as Harry Kelly's but to a young anarchist group far more immediate and real, the Motherfuckers. Famous for their armed patrols to protect hippies against violence, the Motherfuckers were one of several new, grassroots anarchist movements on Manhattan; others included the New York Federation of Anarchists, and the East Side Anarchist Group, whose leading spokesman, Murray Bookchin, published an occasional magazine called *Anarchos,* starting in February, 1968. All these groups were at least loosely interrelated. All, let it be noted, were entirely distinct from both the Weathermen and the Yippies, who emerged somewhat later in time and who were eventually regarded by these people as less than genuine—mere showmen on flamboyant "ego trips." The founders of the New York Federation of Anarchists were already in their late twenties and early thirties. They were serious-minded and, even then, somewhat seasoned. Most had once been college students. A number of them, in the mid-sixties, decided to secede from conventional institutions and live together communally in a loft. This was well before the idea of communes had gained general currency. The group was already heavily into psychedelic drugs.

The articulate figure of Murray Bookchin appealed to these young radicals during their initial phase, which was not only urban but still quite intellectual. A former Marxist who had come under the influence of the German libertarian thinker Josef Weber (1900–1958), Bookchin was engaged in his own struggle to come to terms with the older anarchist tradition. Alan Hoffman and others were pulling him toward the new counterculture, though he continued to write in the abstract, polemical style which one associates with the Old Left. As Bookchin began teaching courses at the newly established Alternate University, he saw his role as that of someone trying to update contemporary anarchism, freeing it from too literal or slavish a dependence upon the classic thinkers of its own past.

Viewed from a broad historical perspective [he wrote], anarchism is a libidinal upsurge of the people, a stirring of the social unconscious that reaches back, under many different names, to the earliest struggles of humanity against domination and authority. Its commitment to doctrinal shibboleths is minimal. In its active concern with the issues of everyday life, anarchism has always been preoccupied with lifestyle, sexuality, community, women's liberation and human relationships.[4]

The arguments of the ecologists seemed to furnish anarchism with new ammunition, for they showed that no matter who was right in the old battle between libertarians and statists, economic decentralization simply must come about if the environment were not to be irretrievably ruined. Not only should anarchism display its flexibility by embracing the new cause of ecology; it should also free itself from the extreme anti-progressivism which Bookchin found in its traditional posture. Technology must not be shunned; rather it should be re-examined and somehow reshaped along "humanistic" lines. This would indeed mean "managing" the environment, and in that sense manipulating it, Bookchin conceded (presumably to the horror of an older-generation anarchist). But the style of this management would be more like steering a boat than playing a game of chess.[5]

The masthead of *Anarchos* stated that the magazine was published "by a group of people in New York City who seek to advance non-authoritarian approaches to revolutionary theory and practice. . . . Revolutionary theory must now look primarily to the future, rather than to the past, for inspiration and clarity. . . . A qualitatively new order of possibility faces our generation—the possibility of a free, nonrepressive, stateless and decentralized society based on face-to-face democracy, community, spontaneity, and a new, meaningful sense of human solidarity."

In this manifesto, the genuinely new note, as compared with the writings of the earlier radical generation, centered on the casual acceptance of left-wing Freudianism, evident in such phrases as "nonrepressive" and "spontaneity," and no doubt mediated by such thinkers as Herbert Marcuse. Yet, since the earlier anarchists had themselves believed in sexual freedom, even here the continuity may seem more striking than the contrast. There was a Whitmanesque as well as a Marcusean note to Bookchin's manifesto:

We believe that technology has now advanced to a point where the

4. Murray Bookchin, *Post-Scarcity Anarchism* (Berkeley: The Ramparts Press, 1971), p. 19. Though this volume mainly reprints his essays from 1965 to 1968, the quotation is from a new introduction.

5. Murray Bookchin, "Ecology and Revolutionary Thought," *Anarchos*, No. 1 (February, 1968), especially pp. 19–20. Cf. *ibid.*, No. 2 (Spring, 1968), 43–60.

burden of toil and material necessity could be removed from the shoulders of humanity, opening an era of unprecedented freedom in every aspect of life, a nonrepressive civilization and human condition in which man could fulfill all his potentialities as a rounded, universal being. . . . There can be no abstract liberation of society without the concrete liberation of life in all its intimate, everyday facets. Revolution . . . must culminate in the here and now with the dissolution of power as such—the power of the state over society, of centralized political entities over community, of the older generation over the younger, of bureaucracy over the individual, of parental authoritarianism over youthful spontaneity, of bourgeois routine over daily creativity, of sexual, racial, cultural, and national privilege over the unfettered development of human personality. . . . The revolutionist must not only fight for the revolution; he must *live* the revolution to the extent that is possible.[6]

Unlike the older anarchist tradition, Bookchin disavowed even the slightest tinge of elitism, announcing his faith in a spontaneous, simultaneous, and therefore utterly democratic rising of the workers and youth in this country. Yet, in contrast to this Spartacism on the subject of the revolution itself, Bookchin declared himself a sober realist on the matter of social structure in the long-range sense. Harry Kelly could never have so openly written, as Bookchin did, that

freedom has its forms. However personalized, individuated, or Dadaesque may be the attack upon prevailing institutions, a liberatory revolution always poses the question of what social forms will replace existing ones. At one point or another, men must deal with how they will manage the land and the factories from which they acquire the means of life.[7]

Yet, urging popular assemblies as the appropriate means for such day-to-day management of resources, he unwittingly returned to the very device which had been clung to for many wearisome years at Stelton.

There were certain contradictions in Bookchin's attempt to revitalize the anarchist tradition in the New York of the 1960's. Though claiming to free anarchism from its excessive burden of theorizing and ideological rigidity, he wrote as yet another theoretician, merely the latest in a long line. The basic idea of an anarchist society, he believed, could still be gleaned from the writings of William Morris and Peter Kropotkin. Bookchin's prose, even as he railed against "theory," was filled with the telltale citations of classical thinkers which marked him as, if anything, far more actively in tune with European ideological currents than people like Kelly,

6. *Anarchos,* No. 1 (February, 1968).
7. Murray Bookchin, "The Forms of Freedom," *Anarchos,* No. 2 (Spring, 1968), pp. 23, 31.

Cohen, or Voltairine de Cleyre had been a half century earlier.[8] Bookchin's influence on the younger people who eventually migrated to such places as New Mexico was thus strongly in the direction of intellectual continuity, despite his own fervent disclaimers to the contrary.

Another apparent contradiction in the mind of Bookchin was that while he urged radicals to leave the city and return to the land,[9] he remained personally wedded to the urban environment. After trying out life in Vermont for a while, he returned to New York, reaffirming the belief that counter-cultural styles would spread to the blue-collar workers.[10]

A second prominent figure in New York anarchist circles, the poet Alan Hoffman, had an entirely different personality. Bookchin was respected, but Hoffman was worshiped as a kind of saint (especially after his early death in a California car accident). Hoffman's manifesto of the rural commune movement differs from Bookchin's in its much more genuine contempt for intellectual abstraction:

> for us the future is in groups of people who establish more profoundly human relations wi each other & their environment / those who return to the land & to communal forms of living together / those who abandon ideologies so they can respond to ever-changing nature wiout pre-conceived notions / those who are flexible, who find ways where there were thought to be none / those who scavenge the endless waste of a decaying society for the raw materials of a new culture / those who find use for what is discarded—who gather, assemble or steal the elements of their life from the whole long history of human experience, & all that modern man has learned. . . . / what we dream & what we attempt must either be the beginning of a new ecological era or the last brave act of human life. . . .[11]

Alan Hoffman also liked to think of himself as a realist. Before his death he was willing openly to concede that most communes had not yet fulfilled their expectation. "Let there be thousands of communes," he urged, "so that a few survive."

The members of these New York anarchist groups in the mid-1960's have since scattered far and wide. Some never left the city. Others departed, mainly in 1967 and 1968, by a great variety of routes. Dispersing to New England, to California, to New Mexico, eventually to Oregon and

8. Bookchin even liked sometimes to use the pen name of Lewis Herber, perhaps in direct imitation of Louis Fraina (Lewis Corey).

9. *Ibid.*, p. 42.

10. See the review of his collected essays, *Post-Scarcity Anarchism*, by Todd Gitlin in *The Nation*, CCLIV (March 6, 1972), 309–11, which calls attention to Bookchin's unusual role as a serious anarchist theorist in America at present. However, see also above, p. 41, n. 64.

11. From an untitled, undated, unpaginated broadside, published by the San Francisco underground paper *Good Times*.

British Columbia, they merged with a thousand other shifting streams in the constant migratory motion of the counter-culture. Everywhere new groups were continually forming, bringing together people from diverse places. Eventually reaching extremely remote locations, some of the most determined survivors learned to separate themselves both from the counter-culture and the established society in every possible way, to put down their own roots in privacy and stay well hidden. Alan Hoffman and several others from the New York circle lived for a time in an unusually stable and successful commune in a distant part of California. Another of the Motherfuckers, who had a strong influence on many people in New York, played for a time the game of armed "self-defense," then retreated to New Mexico (not joining any commune). There he is said to have begun living in a totally self-sufficient fashion alone with a girl and two horses.

In this fashion the web of the counter-culture soon grew extremely complex. The single strand in it which reaches from New York to Vermont to New Mexico is merely the one which I happened to discover, almost at random.[12]

Vermont

Heeding the advice of people like Murray Bookchin and Alan Hoffman, some of the New York anarchists left the city in the early summer of 1967 and traveled to a far corner of Vermont to try to establish a rural community.[13] Those who did so, according to their own historian, deliberately retained the label "anarchist," as perhaps the only word all their number could agree upon. But they no longer identified it (if they ever had) with the tradition of politicized engagement in the classical sense. Both younger and older people from New York were in the group. The younger element were reportedly least political but at the same time most deeply hostile to all forms of coercive authority. The books they were reading at this time were those of Marcuse, Norman O. Brown, Wilhelm Reich, Frantz Fanon, Malcolm X, Che Guevara, and the *I Ching*.

We know all this because the story of that first Vermont summer has been told in a painfully honest narrative by one of the participants, Joyce

---

12. However, it turns out to be somewhat the same strand discovered by Robert Houriet, *Getting Back Together* (New York: Coward, McCann, and Geoghegan, 1971), pp. 6–24, 209–10.

13. Their saga exactly parallels that of Raymond Mungo; see Keith Melville, *Communes in the Counter Culture* (New York: William Morrow, 1972), pp. 81–82. It can be taken as a fairly common pattern around the year 1968.

Gardner.[14] Not only does it contain many echoes of the Ferrer colonists'
initial experiences at Stelton; just as inexorably it makes one think back to
the short-lived communitarian experiment at Fruitlands in 1844. The
young adventurers from the city seem to have known no more than Bron-
son Alcott about how to live practically in an unfamiliar setting. Within a
few weeks the initial period of vigor and communal spirit had begun to
wane; well before the winter snows sent the last diehards scurrying back
toward warmer shelter, the group had already begun to enter the disinte-
grative phases which at Home and Stelton only appeared after a decade of
existence.

The narrator of this tale, it should be kept in mind, is by all reports a
perfectionist; later on she would be severely dissatisfied with the quality of
human relationships at a California commune which other witnesses have
described as unusually inspiring in precisely this respect. Still, her account
makes it impossible to believe that Cold Mountain Farm was in any sense
a success during its brief life.

The setting was pleasant enough—an old farmhouse, lacking electricity
and too remote for easy automobile access, set in a secluded valley surrounded by an attractive rim of hills. But, to begin with, there was almost
no continuity of residents. People drifted in gradually during the early part
of the summer. Many soon drifted out again. A succession of accidents
further plagued them, and ignorance compounded their effects. The tractor
they bought and moved so laboriously into this isolated upland soon broke
down. The only man who knew how to fix it was delayed unavoidably in
the city. Meanwhile, the proper time for planting crops passed them by.
The early arrivals (knowing nothing about agriculture) had waited for
good weather before putting seeds in the ground, another reason for the
fatal delay.

Other details of their free life style caused them trouble. Many of them
took advantage of their hard-won isolation to work outdoors all day entirely bare. But in Vermont rumors of such a practice travel fast. Nearby
villagers, perhaps at first merely curious about the newcomers, hiked
through the forest to peer at them from behind trees. Returning to town,
they told others what they had seen. Soon afterward their neighbors, who
had at first been friendly (admiring their rural idealism), turned against
them. Though the colonists decided henceforth to wear clothes when outside the house, they had already become stigmatized as "hippies" and
could not remove the curse. In their own eyes, they had little in common

14. [Joyce Gardner] *Cold Mountain Farm: An Attempt at Community* (n.p.:
[1970?]).

with the "flower children," who were attracting far more attention that same summer at the opposite end of the continent. The Cold Mountain colonists were considerably older, much more their own masters (for instance in the use of drugs), and thought of themselves as descendants of the fifties beatniks rather than as part of the current generation. Politically, too, they were in a no-man's-land somewhere between the Old and New Left. But such fine distinctions were clearly beyond their neighbors' ken.

At the same time, the community's isolation became apparent in another sense. Some had come to it expecting to retain a close tie with anarchist friends in the city. A constant back-and-forth movement was imagined between New York and Vermont, giving everyone a sense of variety and outlet. But it turned out that the urban radicals did nothing to keep in touch with their departed comrades. In part this was caused by ill feeling; those who remained in New York accused the others (just as had their counterparts fifty-two years before) of copping out when they chose the tranquil countryside. One imagines this lack of communication also partly resulted from a life style in which letter writing, in a prompt and dependable fashion, had no usual place. In any event, the Cold Mountain colonists soon felt stranded and alone in a hostile local environment.[15]

The severest difficulties, nonetheless, came from within. Joyce Gardner had dreamed of the community as "a family of incestuous brothers and sisters," in which everyone would share everything and everyone, a place "where energies would flow among and between everyone, and all relationships would be voluntary," made up of people "whose love of life and of each other would give us an almost superhuman strength for survival."[16] In reality they were all too busy even to spend much time in lovemaking. Older attitudes about sex also remained noticeably in evidence. Of still more importance, as new arrivals kept coming it became the thing to start building one's own shelter, as an individual couple, entirely away from the farmhouse. When the whole population had lived in the farmhouse, there had briefly been a feeling of community, linked with the free sharing of goods. But now possessions became personal once more, and people started spending more time apart. The instability of the population caused all agreements about household tasks, such as cooking, to break down.

Some of the newer arrivals also had disruptive personalities. In one case, the self-imposed rule of the "open gate" (no one would ever be

15. For a thoughtful discussion of some of these problems, see Mark Kramer, "Folk Wisdom: City Cousins and Country Radicals," *The Phoenix* (Boston), II (December 8, 1970), pp. 3, 6.
16. Gardner, *op. cit.*, p. 14.

forced to leave) poisoned the group's atmosphere like a running sore. By midsummer "laziness and resignation had set in, very firmly." The few gardens that had been planted were no longer weeded. Then physical illness, in the form of a hepatitis epidemic, struck them down. It also placed them at the mercy of alien, unfriendly health officials and doctors. With each new day of autumn chill, the population of Cold Mountain dwindled, until, in falling snow, the last colonists fled. One of these, a staunch, hermit-like woman who had spent the entire summer doggedly building herself a stone house to live in, suddenly decided to buy a car and take off for Oregon.

"We didn't become NEW people—we just became physically healthy people," Joyce Gardner concluded. "We weren't ready yet to put the blade to our own skins and expose the raw, tender, inner flesh inside; to plant the seeds of the people we wished to become; to grow new and beautiful skins from the inside out; to rediscover our tribal consciousness, our human brotherhood, divested of all the lies and mannerisms and armoring which we carry with us from the time of childhood."[17]

In her view, there had been too great a diversity of aims in the Cold Mountain group. Some had thought of themselves primarily as communitarians; some as farmers or "back-to-the-soil 'green' revolutionaries"; still others as revolutionary guerrilla anarchists establishing a base in the hills; others again as "tao-anarchists," for whom farming and community were an integral part of the totality of a new life style; and some as just plain hermits who wanted to live in the woods. Though all these people came to exist side by side for a brief moment, there had been no shared vision.[18] This diversity makes Cold Mountain Farm sound more like Stelton, in a certain way, than like Rockridge. In the four years after 1967, a sifting process undoubtedly went on, leading to far greater patterning and uniformity. But at Cold Mountain there seemed to be missing even a minimal form of communal cement.

By the next summer, 1968, a few of the Cold Mountain people, including Joyce Gardner, were willing to begin all over again. This time they went to another location in Vermont, called Bryn Athyn. Some thirty persons were in the Bryn Athyn community; in age they ranged from the teens to over forty. A few of the older people had been in other intentional communities previously. Now the communal spirit flourished more strongly. A regime of task sharing on an entirely voluntary basis appears to have functioned smoothly a great deal of the time. That last great symbol of privacy,

17. *Ibid.*, p. 33.
18. *Ibid.*, p. 29.

the bathroom, succumbed to the ideals of openness and sharing. After initial hesitation, it became good form to use it in public, deliberately not closing the door. But the ideal of complete sexual freedom still did not work out well in practice.[19]

One of the youngest arrivals at Bryn Athyn was Leora, a dark-haired, soft-featured girl from Baltimore. At the Rockridge commune in 1970, Leora and her husband, Frank, were to become central figures. But it was in Vermont two years earlier that she fell under the influence, at one remove, of Murray Bookchin and the New York anarchists. Meanwhile, Frank had met many of the same people and imbibed similar ideas. Neither Leora nor Frank ever met Bookchin in person, however, and they did not even begin reading his essays until 1969, long after they had traveled to New Mexico. In the beginning, what worked upon Leora's mind was not any abstract theory but the experience of living in Bryn Athyn, in close company with many members of the New York circle.

Until the summer of 1968, Leora had led an unexceptional life. She was the daughter of middle-class German Jewish parents (though many of her girlhood friends were of Russian Jewish background). The family was not religious, but she went to a Reform synagogue largely for cultural reasons. Jewish identity was never important to her. Her grandparents had been born in this country, and for some reason her father had been raised as a Quaker. A college graduate in sociology, he went into the jewelry business, failed in it, and thereafter became an insurance salesman; Leora said he always remained unfulfilled in his work. As a teenager the girl became involved in the psychedelic movement ("let it flow—the earth will provide for you—don't hold on to things," she recalled as the essence of its meaning for her). But she spent three dutiful years working toward a degree at a local college of art.

Meanwhile, her older sister had already become radicalized and moved to Bryn Athyn. Visiting her there in the summer of 1968, Leora was immediately converted to the communal style of living. "I dropped out," she told me, "because I wanted to live in the country and raise my own things. I took a lot of drugs. I wanted to find a mate, too." But as yet she had not become religious.

At the end of the summer of 1968, most of the people then living at Bryn Athyn suddenly decided to move to New Mexico. (They were replaced by a new wave of arrivals, who kept Bryn Athyn alive until the end

---

19. *Ibid.*, pp. 52–53. Houriet's description of Bryn Athyn from this point of view (*op. cit.*, p. 12) is more optimistic, but it concerns a later period with almost entirely different people.

of 1969.) The original Bryn Athyn group, which had included quite a few armed Motherfuckers, was panicked by the appearance of FBI agents, looking for draft violators. Faced with this situation, the young radicals rather naïvely hoped that the Southwest would be vast enough to end all their fears of "busts" and harassment. Several of the girls now had babies, adding to their desire for security. (In a "bust," the children of unmarried mothers may easily be taken away from them.) So, in a caravan composed of all their ancient vehicles, the group took the long journey westward. Because Joyce Gardner had already moved to a community called the Sun Farm, at Placitas near Albuquerque, the others followed her there to try to begin still another new life.[20]

New Mexico

Communal living had already existed for nearly two years at Placitas when the people from Vermont arrived. Originally that community had been led by a single dominating figure, a graduate student in English at the University of New Mexico, whose energy, will, and knowhow kept the entire venture moving ahead with high hopes. But there were many rapid changes. In the summer of 1967, only a few months after the group had first established itself (buying some land but also squatting on some to which it had no title), a great share of the people left to visit San Francisco, as reports circulated of the wonderful new happenings in the Haight-Ashbury. At the same time, there was already a reverse flow of people leaving the West Coast for the simpler, slower-paced existence possible in New Mexico. In short, there was a great deal of coming and going.

The life style at Placitas was very unstructured, although (in contrast to Cold Mountain and Bryn Athyn) it was not formally anarchistic in philosophy. People worked only when they felt like it—which in this initial period usually meant only when the single leading figure was so moved. But, in one part of their settlement, two very striking geodesic domes were constructed, in which some chose to live. The domes also resulted from one man's energy; they were built by Steve Baer, an intense, self-absorbed person in his late twenties with an engineer's mentality somewhat after the style of Buckminster Fuller. (Baer has since tried to turn dome manufacture into a commercial business, marketing the improved

20. Some of the Motherfuckers who moved to New Mexico at first remained highly politicized and formed another commune elsewhere in the state which resembled an armed fortress. However, after six months they became converted to a nonviolent way of life. *Ibid.*, pp. 183–84. For the ex-Vermonters who stayed at the Sun Farm, depoliticization was even more rapid.

model which he calls a "zome." He now lives in Albuquerque and has cut his hair very short.)

As time went on, the inner feeling of community at Placitas became steadily weaker.[21] The ex-graduate student who had been the original dynamic spark eventually got tired of the whole undertaking, decided not to keep up the land payments, which he had personally been carrying, and left the area entirely. (When last heard from, he was a cook in a boy's camp in northern California.)[22] Steve Baer was not outgoing enough, not communal enough in temperament, to play the same role. By this time the Placitas colonists had also divided into two very distinct locations, separated from each other by a fairly long walk, and with surprisingly little mutual contact. Though the two groups are said to have remained on good terms, they developed rather separate atmospheres, and did not intermingle much. Lacking leadership, the colonists just drifted along, and as time went on many stole away. Someone in the art department at the University of New Mexico stepped in to maintain the land payments, and the open-gate policy remained—anyone was free to stay there. Later an unstable, authoritarian man for a time played a dominant role. A double murder in December, 1970, apparently not committed by an outsider, created a chilling effect. By 1971 the domes had become almost deserted, and the entire population was much reduced.

Nonetheless, Placitas had been an important way station in the migratory circuit, a funnel through which many people had passed. Some had come to it from Timothy Leary's retreat in Millbrook, New York; others directly from a commune in Manhattan. Still others had been graduate students at the University of New Mexico who dropped out. In the other direction, the present leading figure in the Lama Foundation lived for a time at Placitas, concluding from the experience that far more structure was needed. Rockridge, even more directly, was a "daughter colony" of Placitas.[23]

Rockridge was founded in the spring of 1970, when four couples at

21. This account comes not only from the people at Rockridge but from another witness who had lived at Placitas in the beginning. For a description of Placitas in 1970, see Richard Fairfield, *Communes, U.S.A.: A Personal Tour* (Baltimore: Penguin Books, 1972), pp. 164–85.

22. This seems to be a recurring pattern when communes have been founded through the largesse of a single well-off sponsor; it was also true later on at Bryn Athyn. Houriet, *op. cit.*, pp. 10–14, 23–24.

23. Of course one must not exaggerate the connectedness of the recent communal movement. As of 1970, New Mexico had at least thirty-two communal groups. Some of the most famous ones, such as the New Buffalo and the Hog Farm, had by 1971 become mere crash pads, their memberships turning over completely more than once.

Placitas (including Frank and Leora) decided to leave for a new location in a much more remote and inaccessible part of the state. The decision was prompted by the uncertainty of their land title where they were living, but more broadly it stemmed from a desire to prove their ability at pioneering under really severe conditions. They wanted to show themselves that they could create their own shelter, grow their food, in short, make a permanent, self-sufficient home, starting from scratch, with minimum help from tools or machinery. They also wanted to go on wearing their hair long (it was so meaningful a symbol that they habitually referred to people like themselves as "longhairs") and smoking dope with less fear of harassment. So they left Placitas in another caravan on May 18, 1970. Two other men who were supposed to come with them backed out at the last minute.

One might well regard these four couples as among the most seasoned and tested representatives of the counter-culture anywhere in America, and a commune like Rockridge as one of the ultimate proving grounds of the new way of life. These men and women—they were nearly all in their mid- or late twenties—had already been through a great deal. They had lived in other communes, often in more than one, and were in a position to learn from the mistakes they had seen. Two of the couples (Frank and Leora, Jake and Ellen) had lived together previously as a foursome in California, where Leora had gone for a while, and where she met Frank, then a college student on the verge of dropping out.[24] So some of the rough edges of human relations had already had a chance to be rubbed off. Moreover, these couples were all intensely dedicated and serious. Their commitment was long term. They had left the summer-only people of Cold Mountain Farm far behind. At Rockridge and a few places like it, one might hope to find, if anywhere, a present-day Stelton in the making. Indeed, in keeping with the mood of the recent counter-culture, one might hope for a much deeper sense of community than probably ever had prevailed among the more individualistic New Jersey anarchists.

Yet, physically and emotionally hardened as they now were, a certain innocence remained. Frank and Leora lost their rather substantial savings while living at Placitas, because they too trustingly lent the money to a friend who was helping the group obtain some necessary legal aid. The friend was never able to return it. Then, in seeking a site for their new

24. For a while Leora lived in a Berkeley commune and did political work for Eldridge Cleaver. Jake eventually returned to the university to complete his degree, solely that he would have proper credentials to serve as schoolteacher for the New Mexico commune in the future. He was nonetheless a good student. It was through him that I first learned about Rockridge and was given the privilege of visiting there.

community, they turned to a single real-estate agent, whom they paid a fee of $150 to locate appropriate land for them somewhere in the state, which they said they must obtain in time for the spring planting season. The agent told them that only one site of the right size and the appropriate characteristics existed anywhere in New Mexico, and that they would have to take it or leave it. The men, for some reason, had one brief chance to see the property before the decision was made, but the women had to accept it sight unseen. This was how the group obtained its present land. The chanciness of the whole affair—perhaps stemming from a dislike of the protracted personal contact with "straight" people which is necessary if one is to get one's own sense of real-estate values in a given area—is rather astonishing. The land was obligingly purchased by the well-to-do parents of one of the girls in the group.

And in smaller things mishaps continued. An old gas refrigerator was purchased, hauled in laboriously by truck, then carted the last half-mile where no roads go, only to expire completely within a few weeks. The histories of earlier communal groups are, of course, filled with similar episodes. But it is rather dispiriting to see them recurring, even among these seasoned people, in the present.[25]

The site is nonetheless reasonably secluded and beautiful. The scenery there is not spectacular, like that at the New Buffalo near Taos, but it is very enjoyable. The land in this entire region is carved into innumerable small ridges, usually no more than fifty feet high, divided from each other by intervening valleys which are perfectly flat. The commune is located astride one such ridge, on forty acres. The site commands the surrounding area in nearly every direction, creating the feeling of being on top of a castle. On the north side, brilliant red cliffs fall away sharply to the valley below, a portion of which is also included in the communal land. On the opposite side, huge boulders form a natural throne at the edge of the dropoff. From their protected heights can be seen every vehicle on the dirt roads which lead outward, through a complicated maze, toward civilization. It is seven miles to the nearest gas station, grocery store, and post office, fifty miles to the nearest supermarket and Frosty Freeze. Well over a hundred miles away is the nearest doctor, other than a general practitioner.

The area is not entirely uninhabited. Rainfall and winter snowfall are

25. Of course, the practical mistakes made by experimental communities are always very conspicuous; one would like to know whether the per capita rate of such errors is really so much lower among the backyard do-it-yourself population of suburbia. Many Americans buy their homes in astonishing haste. And the second contemporary community in New Mexico, to be discussed in Chapter Five, appears to have acted with great practical shrewdness most of the time.

enough to permit some forms of ranching and dry farming. The flatlands have been cleared and belong to large surrounding ranches; cattle run on them. Low-flying airplanes have sometimes deliberately buzzed the commune from overhead, reportedly seeking a glimpse of the girls working in the gardens bare-breasted. Gas wells abound in this area, and maintenance trucks pop in and out every few days; the utility company maintains the network of dirt roads in the region. But on the ridge itself the forest has been allowed to remain, and it adds much to the landscape. Piñon pines are taller than a man, and oaks grow much bigger yet. There are sagebrush and some blades of grass. Ravens fly by, flapping their wings. Dragonflies buzz continually in the air. It is a life-filled environment, more like mountains than desert, and oddly Californian in the way that it blends the feeling of both. But its winter temperatures, which can fall far below zero, are those of Mid-America. The soil is not very fertile, but, as Frank likes to insist, similar soil was used for subsistence farming several decades ago just a few miles away, so obviously it can be cultivated.

The boulders, the trees, and the juxtaposition of nearly level land with sudden dropoffs and vistas all create a pleasing mixture of regularity and surprise. By no means is it a tedious environment in which to spend a long period of time. Yet Jake confessed to me that they become so engrossed in their daily labors, and sometimes in their human relations, that they rarely take walks to explore the countryside. No one there seemed really to be "into" nature anywhere close to the degree of a Gary Snyder.[26] In this respect, the people at Rockridge are oddly similar to most nineteenth-century American farmers, talking vaguely of "the land," and not, like Thoreau, of precisely observed details which harbor mystical delights. One even imagines that to them Thoreau might seem a bit pretentious or contrived in his point of view, for they carry their anti-intellectualism, their preference for plainness, astonishingly far.

Winding upward into the property along a heavily rutted road, which rain makes nearly impassable, one reaches a clearing. A small sign tells hunters to stay away and drivers to park and walk in. Here sits an ancient school bus, its seats removed and half its roof cut away, used to carry tools and water to the several gardens scattered about the commune. In the summer, several visitors' cars may also be nearby, as well as the old Volvo which belongs to Jake. Hidden near this clearing is the one-room dugout house where Frank and Leora live. (Snug and attractive inside, it has been rebuilt with a sturdy roof after the first one fell in on them.) Above it, on

26. Or of the "dune hermits" (Chapter Six) or of Swami Paramananda (Chapter Four).

the ridge with the superb view, is a house where another of the four couples live—it was destroyed once already by fire but has now been rebuilt. Several summertime tents and tepees are scattered nearby, occupied by more recent arrivals.

A path leads on through the trees, up steep rocks, and eventually to a wooden fence with a gate. There one beholds a large purple-and-white silk banner, commanding in absurdly immense letters: "CLOSE THE GATE." It is one of the very few violations of the norm of plainness at Rockridge. Obeying the injunction, one enters a large enclosed garden. Along one side of it are several corrals for the animals, which range from rabbits and goats on up to a horse. Passing by this area and through another gate into a muddy barnyard, one reaches the focal point of communal life at Rockridge, the principal community building, which is called simply "the Barn." It is just a single room, and very primitive in construction, with an earth floor and a low roof that leaks badly in heavy rain. But it is large enough so that the whole population can easily gather in it. At one end are a sink, shelves for dishes and food supplies, and a table where all can sit for the evening meal. Elsewhere there are chairs and mattresses for lounging. A couple of hundred paperbacks line a segment of the wall. One side of the room has been constructed into the edge of the cliff. It is very dark, as there are few windows, and at night only one or two kerosene lanterns are lit. During the daytime, one often finds two or three women in the Barn, and some small children playing, while the men are off doing other tasks. Toward nightfall, but at no set time, the whole group gathers here. Grass is passed around, and sometimes wine. Drums are played, good vibes flow, and spirits rise. At Frank's instigation, the group joins hands and silently prays for a moment before the evening meal. After dinner there are more drums and perhaps a flute. At this time of day most people get very high.

As one leaves the barnyard area through another gate at the far end, the path resumes. Here on a gentle forested slope are more temporary dwellings, used mainly by the summer population. One of these is the canvas tepee in which Jake and Ellen still live while building their permanent house high on the ridge above it. It is sometimes a welcome refuge for the entire group, since it is fully waterproof. The whole commune can just barely fit inside it to eat a meal. A short distance beyond, to the west, comes the property line, and the wilderness abruptly resumes.

Another path takes off southward to one of the vegetable gardens and to the well, which was completed in mid-1971 and represents a major concession to modern technology. Before then, water had been hauled by permission from a neighboring ranch, but it was not of good quality, and the children were constantly sick. The new well gives them a pure product (its effect on their health was immediately noticeable), but it requires the operation of a noisy gasoline pump whenever water is needed. One girl who decided to leave the commune after spending several months there in 1971 declared (when we ran into her afterward) that the pump had utterly destroyed the tranquillity of the place as far as she was concerned. There is something uncanny about how an unpleasant technology has followed these people into the very bosom of their remote lair. For Frank would like, if he could, to do away with all motorized equipment, even scrapping the school bus in favor of horsepower, and yet he too must drink the water from a well that works only in this fashion. The pump can be turned off whenever they have no immediate need of water. But that in turn complicates their lives whenever they are thirsty.

This is the everyday landscape of Rockridge. Perhaps twice a month they will venture outside to shop for staples; someone will go more often to the nearest store and post office. Occasionally, for medical reasons or to make a special purchase, two or three people will travel together to Albuquerque. In midwinter the members may drive to visit relatives for a few weeks on the Pacific coast. Otherwise, all their time is spent together on these acres.

A striking fact about this group, as about many of the other "new" (i.e., "hip") people in New Mexico, is how many of its members come from well-off families. When I asked about this point, I was told (after a mental head count) that no more than half the people at Rockridge were from such backgrounds, but this in itself constitutes a conspicuously high proportion. We found this to be true, incidentally, everywhere we went in the state. A later neighbor of ours that summer, who lived in an old adobe without water or electricity in the village where we were then staying, was the daughter of wealthy, conservative parents in Albuquerque and had formerly been married to a Harvard instructor. The life such people are now undergoing is far too rough to conjure up memories of Marie Antoinette playing milkmaid, but I was many times forcibly reminded of the extent to which the really determined dropouts had previously led privileged lives. In this stratum there may well be the greatest need to prove that one can make it on one's own, especially in the classic tests of manhood. Moreover, the so-called dropout life style, as these people are leading it, requires some of the same qualities of long-range determination and achievement orientation which one expects to find especially well represented in the middle class. In one profound sense all the people at Rockridge are working to provide their own homes, and are unusual only in their collectivism and in their insistence upon doing everything themselves.

At present, however, their pride in self-sufficiency must suffer the severe blow of continuous dependence on the state. With only one exception (and it is involuntary), members of the commune are on welfare. They defend this by saying that it is fair to plunder a government as corrupt as America's.[27] Food stamps remain an absolutely vital source of sustenance. Although the gardens have flourished reasonably well, they do not sustain life most of the time. The last few days of the month, before welfare checks arrive, the group is apt to be reduced to eating large quantities of beans or similar staples, with almost no other food to break the monotony.

Most of the parents have apparently taken quite a sympathetic view toward what their offspring are doing. An exception is the father of one girl from Ohio, who will not even allow his wife to receive letters from her at their home. But several of the other parents have actually paid brief visits to Rockridge, and at the opposite extreme are the girl's parents who bought the land. A number of the parents seem to be liberal-minded; Frank's are Unitarians who live in a rather expensive Southern California coastal resort town; David's are atheists.

From day to day, the commune members do not let themselves be bothered by these glaring compromises in their quest for self-sufficiency. Instead, they are concerned with the practical questions of gardening, construction, and survival. But a seemingly unending series of matters come up, testing their willingness to go "all the way." The issue of how much machine technology to allow has remained a lively one. Frank would like to live almost entirely without it. David, another strong voice in the group's affairs, is mechanically inclined and tends to accept these aids more freely. Jake is in the middle, but leans toward David. The installation of the noisy well pump might make all such discussion seem pointless, but the differences in attitude remain. Frank would probably never have moved to put in a sink or a refrigerator, though he accepted them peacefully when David did so.

There can be no doubt about the seriousness of commitment among the four "core" families at Rockridge. Their alienation from much in the standard American culture, including the political system, clearly runs very deep. The gadgetry, waste, and pollution of the usual middle-class life style are constant topics of scornful conversation. When, several months after we

27. Both the situation and this way of defending it are widespread in the communes; see Houriet, *op. cit.*, p. 47.

left New Mexico, some of them came to our small California home, David especially made me feel uncomfortable because of his obvious disapproval of our standard amenities, which, through no malice, he was incapable of fully hiding. I felt placed in the odd role of a pope in the presence of Savonarola.

Along with this holier-than-thou rejection of physical comforts goes an apocalyptic view of the future of mankind. The outside world is seen as heading for disaster, and everything other than their own way of life is tacitly condemned as part of the established system. Such attitudes are, of course, scarcely surprising, but the outsider is never allowed to forget them; they are what he constantly rubs up against whenever he makes any effort to find rapport. In this very important sense, the group is indeed ideological —the world view is not allowed to retire to the background when human contacts are being made. Warm with each other, the members show a puritanical sternness toward the larger society.

They do claim to believe in pleasure. David, who sometimes likes to orate, declared to me: "We're dealing with the Form [i.e., the System] out there, which isn't working to make people happy. It has a family form, and a WASP Puritan work ethic form." Asked whether their own hard physical labors, which I had been witnessing, weren't merely a further instance of the same Puritan ethic, Frank refused to admit that this was the case. He claimed that the natural rhythm of the land imposed the work they were doing, and then spoke in Darwinian language about a "mere need for survival." David declared that work was only a temporary necessity as far as he was concerned—"as soon as I finish building my house I want to goof off" (just as a professor might say when writing a book). But Leora evidently felt David had not shown enough devotion to the idea of work, for she chimed in: "In *my* life, discipline is natural. Work is simply one's joy."

Commune members at Rockridge believe they are demonstrating a new way of life, even if they hide away most of the time from the prying world. They are quite willing to preach their message to others if the right occasion comes. When some of them were in California, early in 1972, they were glad to be able to speak to my history class. None of us was prepared for the result: a barrage of highly critical, sophisticated questions from an interested handful, and obvious boredom or revulsion from a majority of the students. The visitors' low-key voices and the crying baby they brought with them may have helped create this result. But they had desired very much to communicate with such an audience, and the painful fact was that they lacked the ability to do so. Until that afternoon I had not fully realized the gulf which separates these hard-core dropouts from the merely liberal college longhairs, and perhaps the 1970's from the 1960's.

The general serious-mindedness at Rockridge has made a voluntary policy as to labor fairly successful. People actually go out into the gardens enough of the time to get the basic tasks done. Yet the reasons for this are closely bound up with the controversial matter of leadership in the commune. Jake, David, and the others vehemently denied any suggestion on my part that Frank and Leora were playing the role of leaders. And if by leader is meant a position comparable to Harry Kelly's or to the Ferms' at Stelton, they are certainly right. But there are subtler forms of leadership. While staying at Rockridge, I observed Frank often setting the example for the performance of work. I also heard him checking with others as to where they were going and what they were planning to do that day. Nor did Frank hesitate to ask me to work on a specific task, if he happened to see me. Moreover, the one emotional blowup I saw during our first visit was brought about by this same tendency: a recently arrived young boy attacked Frank for having insinuated that his girl friend wasn't working hard enough.

In certain ways, Frank and Leora have set themselves apart from the rest of the group. They do not always choose to attend the common evening meal, sometimes dining separately. Leora has acquired definite ideas about religion and diet, and the others sometimes feel they have to resist her efforts to impose them upon everyone else. Leora has a certain definiteness of manner, and she does not hesitate to express her opinions openly. Frank, on the other hand, is far more the self-contained master of his emotions. His dogged, utterly faithful performance of tasks is in itself enough to put the lazy to shame. A wry,. inward-turning humor lightens his mien and makes him easy to be around. Small things reveal that he believes in precision and order far more than he'll let on. He might be described, then, as a "natural-born" leader of an unusually fine type. But Jake insists that David, not Frank, gets his way more often in decisions about policy. And of course anything truly important would go before an open meeting of the entire group.

Frank also serves as leader by occasionally initiating deliberate experiments. Anything along the lines of an encounter group he shuns. However, believing they were in "a rut" in their mutual relations, he once announced that he would sleep in turn with every girl in the commune, as part of an effort to unlimber their emotions and bring them all closer together. The report is that he went ahead and did this, while Leora endured it protestingly;

her own view of family structure is highly conventional. Frank's choice of an "experiment" was scarcely insignificant; whatever his conscious intentions, it established him as a universal patriarch. There is no report that anyone else, male or female, went through the same ritual, and in general the commune is remarkable for how distinctly it is divided into couples. (A single person of either sex would not feel at home at Rockridge, any more than at a suburban block party. And no one, apparently, is bisexual.)

Much more openly acknowledged is the dividing line between the four "core" families and everyone else. In a sense, the commune belongs to the eight people who originally settled it, and the others are guests. Newcomers are not allowed in freely. The group would be glad of an increase in the year-round population to as many as twenty or twenty-five, but above that they intend to forbid further growth. It was expected that twelve or fourteen might actually spend the winter there in 1971–1972. Meanwhile, the fact that the four couples have already remained for two years contributes greatly to the stability of Rockridge and to whatever chances it has for a long life. Others come and go, sometimes quite rapidly, but the eight remain. Actually, Frank confessed to me that he and Leora had been thinking about pulling out—perhaps because of their difficulties with some of the others. If they did leave, it would unquestionably be a major blow.

Of the twenty who lived at Rockridge in the early summer of 1971, only six had been at Placitas; the rest had come from elsewhere. Their backgrounds were diverse; some had been college students, some had been into hard drugs, and still others had been urban political radicals. Yet at dinner there could sometimes be a great feeling of immediate communality. When Frank asked us all to join hands and pray—for instance, that the influx of summer visitors not make us lose sight of our reason for being there—the moment was moving in its directness.

The sense of community was real, but several people spontaneously spoke to us about the problem they still had with a recurring feeling of loneliness and depression. All of them have retreated from life, in the sense that the complexity of existence in California or New York appears to them not merely undesirable but too frightening to be handled easily. They shy away from it. As David put the matter to me: "Mankind has too many eggs in one basket. That's why I can't live out there."

The people at Rockridge, especially the four leading families, appear to have a great inner need for simplicity. (In a broader sense, this may be true of most of the "new" people who have deliberately migrated to New Mexico. One frequently hears the local pace of life being favorably compared to that of the West Coast.) Whether this urge to protect themselves from too many conflicting external demands goes back deep into their life histories, I have no idea. Much of it may be a cultural insignia acquired since their arrival in the state. At any rate, the slow rhythm they admire has become deeply internalized; it even affects their speech. This is another reason why the Santa Cruz class found it so hard to connect with them. Yet they do not seem to be deeply introspective either, certainly not in a religious sense. (Only Frank and Leora are religious, and they are eclectically non-Christian.) It is just that they speak in a tentative drawl and often move rather deliberately. They are becoming what they would like to be, slow-paced and traditional.

Yet there is a positive, highly attractive side to their search for simplicity. In a humble spirit, the members of the four principal families are determined to practice continuing charity toward one another, in the imagined spirit of the early Christians. Aware of their individual differences, they are nonetheless strongly impelled to maintain this attitude of mutual acceptance on an unvarying basis, for they know that unless they succeed in doing this the communal ideal will have proved chimerical. The strain of keeping up such humility must at times be very great, and one could easily picture it becoming a highly artificial role. But, to their great credit, this does not visibly seem to happen. Perhaps their slow, simple rhythms are what enable them to avoid such a pitfall. In any event, they are making an extraordinarily earnest attempt to prove that diverse people can live together without an impossible accumulation of tension.

We were lucky in talking to two people who had either recently left the commune or were just about to do so. The same reason came through from both of them: it was too boring. You did your work stint, then got high in the evening, and that was that. There was nothing else. The four families felt no need for anything beyond this, aside from the shelf of paperbacks. One of the deserters, who was returning to Chicago, criticized the group for being too serious, for lacking any playful quality or sense of fun. They would have parties, but always just sit around and play the drums; sauna baths were a special treat, but hardly a novelty after a while. Group sex was evidently something they shrank from. Except for Frank's single experiment, and for the use of marijuana, there was little that was novel or colorful about their way of living. A large share of new arrivals, after several months of this routine, began to feel restless in the isolation. Stability was thus being gained at a price of discouraging quite a share of the potential new recruits from outside. My own feeling was that the group would probably disappear within the next two or three years, though Jake and Ellen (and perhaps others) had the temperament to remain as long as they possibly could.

The central criticism of the Rockridge life style, in my mind, was that it failed to transcend the customary division in industrial society between duty and pleasure—between periods of work and periods of "letting go." In this important sense, Rockridge no more than Stelton brought about a fundamental merger of the inner and the external routes toward liberation. Instead, if anything, the dividedness of the members' lives in this respect was greatly intensified, because there was so little choice either of occupations or of forms of inward exploration. Farm and then get high; that was all, over and over. This lack of choice was not simply imposed by the physical environment. It was basically the result of a strong cultural conformism. Life at Stelton had been diverse, many faceted, and lively. Life at Rockridge was unnecessarily monotonous. People did not take walks, either alone or in groups, because it just wasn't the thing to do. They did all smoke home-rolled cigarettes, because this *was* done. The women did not share in the heavy work outside, but stayed in the Barn most of the day, "because they just felt like it." There was little individual initiative, little imagination about many aspects of their daily routine. Quite a bit of time was spent simply standing or sitting around, waiting for someone else to show up with whom there had been a vague plan possibly to do something. Their dislike of mental activity was so great that they were apt to dismiss astrology as too wondrously and "heavily" intellectual—too much of a "head trip"! This lack of interest in experiment hampered their pursuit of pleasure along with everything else. They were basically a harmonious and unassuming group of people, and very likable. We seem to be back to the ancient platitude that goodness is often dull.

Finally, one may ask, in all this loosely linked chain of events leading from New York to Vermont to New Mexico, what really was the role of anarchist "ideology," of the writings of Murray Bookchin? Besides Frank and Leora, Jake and Ellen had read Bookchin since coming to Rockridge (a most flattering gesture, since they so seldom read). And Leora had placed his magazines, and Joyce Gardner's pamphlet, in my hands. But it is clear that, despite these formal fealties, someone like Bookchin plays very little role in their lives. Frank and Leora, who talk most about him, are also the persons most deeply opposed to technology at Rockridge; but Bookchin, it should be recalled, was himself far more willing to compromise on the subject. In a general way, too, we saw that Bookchin was still an intellectual, a writer of abstract rhetoric. Such a tone has now been entirely lost at Rockridge. Is this the final Americanization of anarchism as it retreats into the wilderness? Frank likes to define Rockridge as an "anarchist" community, holding on to that word. But it is doubtful if the others often think of it in such definite terms.

And yet this shift away from the verbal articulation of ideology can in turn be very deceptive. Beneath their avoidance of abstract language, the idealism that keeps them going reveals itself in their everyday choices. Theirs is a rural decentralist community, officially without leaders. This has always been the anarchist goal. If they were suddenly to read the classics of anarchist thought, they would feel an immediate rapport, a bond of kinship. Their understood point of view remains "political," in the sense that they are reacting against a social order and seeking consciously to create an alternative of their own. Their community is rooted neither in the psychiatric world view nor, apart perhaps from Leora and Frank, in that of religion. Neither self-development nor contact with cosmic beings gives fundamental meaning to their lives. Rather, it is the effort to demonstrate the practicality of communalism, and of freedom too as they understand it.

The end of formal ideology, in their case, meant no return to the American mainstream. Instead they had moved into the position of semi-outlaws, bound together by a revulsion against mass society and a vision of the good life which is still far closer to anarchism than to any other. It was not at all clear what would someday become of them.[28]

---

28. Houriet, *op. cit.*, pp. 205–206, argues that unstructured communes like Rockridge are giving way to structured communities, such as Ezra's in Chapter Five. But it seems more accurate to see them as existing in parallel fashion. For much more discussion of the fate of anarchism in the 1960's, see Chapter Six.

PART II / COMMUNITIES OF DISCIPLINE

Only for a genuine yogi, who has seen life as mere play, is it possible to play with satisfaction the game of life. To him the prizes are not blanks but the bliss of a free soul. We can play the game of life well only when we recognize that it is not everlasting, that joys and sorrows are in their very nature impermanent. The genuine yogi enjoys the game, plays it better than does one who clings to the enjoyments of life and finds to his despair that they elude his grasp at every moment.

    —SWAMI PRABHAVANANDA, *The Spiritual Heritage of India*
      (Garden City, New York: Doubleday, 1963), p. 278.

Seek, above all, for a game worth playing. Such is the advice of the oracle to modern man. Having found the game, play it with intensity—play as if your life and sanity depended on it. (They *do* depend on it.) . . . Though nothing means anything and all roads are marked "NO EXIT," yet move as if your movements had some purpose. If life does not seem to offer a game worth playing, then *invent one.* For it must be clear, even to the most clouded intelligence, that any game is better than no game.

    —ROBERT S. DEROPP, *The Master Game* (New York:
      Delacorte Press, 1968), pp. 11–12, adapting an argument
      from Pascal.

CHAPTER FOUR

Vedanta Monasteries

The "internal" path toward liberation from the claims of the everyday world has its own long history in America. If in the secular realm anarchism utters the most piercing cry of desire for escape from social bondage, a religious counterpart has always existed in the mystical tradition. Here too, when the urge is extreme, conventional obligations are regarded as alien impositions from which it is one's higher duty to flee. In the mystical realm of belief and practice there is again the potential of a counter-culture, a reordering of human life which will radically depart from the rhythms of the mainstream. The same need arises as with anarchism, to compare earlier American attempts to move in this direction with their current counterparts among youth.

The mystical form of withdrawal from society, like the anarchistic, immediately raises the question of authority in all its dimensions. Mystics reject both Biblical Christianity and empirical science, between them the historical arbiters of the cosmology of most Americans. Let there be no mistake. The refusal to accept either of these traditional paradigms, at least without drastic revision, is every shade as determined as the anarchist's quarrel with the authority of the state, though it proceeds much less conspicuously. Moreover, among mystics all the consequences of an eagerly embraced substitute authority, in the form of the guru or inspired teacher, become far more starkly visible. Anarchism has produced a number of moderate, self-effacing leaders, like Harry Kelly at Stelton and Frank at Rockridge, whose tendencies toward control remained checked by a membership keenly attuned to the reflexes of participatory democracy, as well as by their own scruples. In mystical circles there is no such check, save the residue of norms unconsciously carried over from one's early upbringing. Perhaps in no other American realm, outside that of crime syndicates and old-style city politics, can patterns of domination and submission become fixed with such a tenacious hold upon individuals. This characteristic, quite apart from the special attributes of the beliefs themselves, signals our arrival at a counter-culture of rather a different stripe, both in the past and present.

The intensity of the bond between leader and follower brings an unusual quality to the communal life style which mystical groups have created as an alternative to mundane American existence. There is also a more extreme withdrawal from the everyday focal points of industrial and indeed human life—the family, sex, property, ugliness, crowds. Naturally, many American mystics have made their compromises in each of these areas—for instance, in the decision to live in a city like Los Angeles. But the injunction, the tendency, is always to move as far away from them as possible.

On both these counts, mysticism (when pursued on a profounder level than mere Yoga exercises) furnishes the basis for a cultural radicalism potentially more thoroughgoing, more deeply uncongenial to the usual American temper, than a secular philosophy such as anarchism. In this respect appearances are deceiving. Unlike left-wing radicals, mystics operate quietly, in an aura of relative respectability. They draw no attention from the government, and they dress and behave in public much like other men and women. But the drummer they hear and obey is a very different one indeed.

The Vedanta Movement in America

Organizations such as the Vedanta Society are not normally discussed in the context of cultural radicalism or the formation of communities. Yet Vedanta, which catered to an interest in Eastern mysticism in this country several decades ago, almost immediately began reshaping the lives of its most wholehearted devotees on a communitarian basis. Shortly after 1900, in several locations on the East and West coasts, native Americans who had decided to spend the rest of their days as Hindu monks or nuns began living together in ashrams, or peace retreats, which later became full-fledged monasteries. A pattern of existence emerged which included renunciation of all personal property, the sharing of tasks required to maintain the household, and a broad willingness to discipline oneself by giving up egotistical assertions of the will. These ashrams were not intentional communities in the full sense, but the impulse behind them was similar to that found in many secular utopias: a desire to secede from the larger world and to make every moment lived in the new surroundings an expression of consciously adopted principles.[1] The urge toward ideal perfection, prominent in certain nineteenth-century experimental communities, never revealed itself more clearly in the twentieth century than in these unorthodox religious environments.

The Ramakrishna movement, which in America became known by its more philosophical name of Vedanta, began in the 1870's in Bengal.[2] A dozen or so young men, nearly all from well-educated upper-caste families which formed a Westernized status group called Bhadrolok (or "gentlemen"), became greatly influenced, one at a time, by the magnetic figure of Sri Ramakrishna, a nearby *sannyasin* or ascetic sage, himself from a Brahmin family, who had been raised in the priestly tradition. Though Ramakrishna stood for the nonintellectual virtues of inward ecstasy and devotion (some had thought him half mad), he was literate enough to have spent time as a young man studying Christianity, Mohammedanism, Buddhism, and Sufism in an eclectic spirit. Some of his disciples were far more intellectual in their backgrounds; typically they had been rationalistic and cosmopolitan-minded until they met Ramakrishna. At least two, including their eventual leader, Vivekananda, had been members of the Brahmo Samaj, a strongly Westernized reform society, whose liberal, humanely ethical spirit offers a parallel to American Unitarianism.

Why these well-educated young men, readers of Mill and Spencer, should have been inveigled, in such a steady succession, by a semiliterate, relatively conservative Hindu, a believer not in reason but in ecstatic contemplation, is by no means easy to discover. One can postulate a certain inner emptiness in the lives of this generation of Indian intellectuals, who found themselves divorced from the native culture around them, yet not accepted by the European overlords. Or is this phenomenon simply a recurrent

1. Vedanta monasteries have been more like intentional communities than Roman Catholic monasteries, if only because Vedanta is a faith almost always voluntarily chosen by adults after a period of deliberate seeking, rather than the kind of religion one is born into. This element of willful choice strongly colors the whole monastic experience.

2. An official history of the movement, nonetheless quite revealing, is Swami Gambhirananda, *History of the Ramakrishna Math and Mission* (Calcutta: Advaita Ashrama, 1957). Naturally it focuses on the movement in India. The best history of the American phase of the Vedanta movement is Carl Thomas Jackson, "The Swami in America: A History of the Ramakrishna Movement in the United States, 1893–1960" (unpublished Ph.D. dissertation, University of California, Los Angeles, 1964). Wendell Thomas, *Hinduism Invades America* (New York: Beacon Press, 1930), is oddly prejudiced, though it contains some useful survey data.

one throughout the modern world? As one reads about the disciples of Ramakrishna, one is oddly reminded of Ralph Waldo Emerson's conversion from the "pale negations" of Unitarianism into the enthusiastic state of mind known as transcendentalism, which indeed allied itself directly to Hindu and Buddhist thought. Still more cogently, one is reminded of well-off young Americans in the 1960's, again usually from liberal backgrounds, suddenly craving release into new and far less rational states of consciousness. Like many hip American youth of recent years, Ramakrishna's disciples abandoned their families and possessions (sometimes with great inward struggle) and went off to live collectively in extreme poverty, deliberately adopting the life style (including the improper clothing) of illiterate sages and beggars. Moreover, they endured much the same opprobrium from their unconvinced middle-class friends and relatives.[3]

But there the parallel, fascinating as it is, comes to an abrupt end, for only a few years after Ramakrishna's death in 1886 the movement, under the leadership of the bright attorney's son Vivekananda, began an extraordinarily rapid transformation. At the outset it had been a thoroughly charismatic, antinomian manifestation. A band of disciples renounced the world in devotion to a leader whose claim lay in his ability to enter extraordinary states of bliss. But within a few years the movement had decisively shifted in the direction of stable organization, dependable financial backing, and the regular performance of charitable good works, in short, respectability. This transformation amounts to a classically pure instance of the routinization of charisma. In less than a generation the Ramakrishna movement, on a much smaller scale, achieved nearly all that had required centuries in the case of the Roman Catholic Church.

It was a feat all the more remarkable in view of the absence in Hinduism of more than faint precedents in the direction of organized monasticism. Up till this time sages had simply wandered about the country or lived with a few informal disciples in the forest. There had been no buildings known as monasteries; these Vedanta imitated either from Buddhism, Jainism, or from the West. Even the formal bestowal of the title of "Swami" to characterize the holders of a certain rank within the Ramakrishna hierarchy was a total novelty, for hitherto the term "swami" had simply referred to any widely revered holy man who happened to be in the vicinity.

In much of its theology, the Ramakrishna movement was rather conservatively Hindu, emphasizing the loftiest and most universalistic interpretations of the classical scriptures (Vedas). But, in its grasp of practical

3. Swami Gambhirananda, *op. cit.,* pp. 47–55.

matters of organization, the Vedanta movement was strikingly Western almost from its inception and became increasingly so in the decades that followed. It had arisen, after all, in the most Westernized part of India, and a pre-British state of thinking was no longer possible among the native elite. In this sense, Americans never made contact with "pure" Hinduism when they became interested in this Asian movement. By the 1880's bettereducated Indians, rather like Theosophists, were already living in an ill-defined region located somewhere between (or beyond) the classic East and West.

This may be seen in the position taken by the Ramakrishna movement in the realm of politics and social reform. In India, its leaders began engaging extensively in "good works" (famine and flood relief, schools and orphanages). The idea for these organized charities was largely copied from the West, though there were again precedents in Buddhism and Jainism. Apart from the largesse of individual landlords and merchants, it was alien to the Hindu tradition. At the same time, the movement fostered a strong cultural nationalism. But such a nationalism, though elevating the Hindu cultural heritage, in turn amounted to an imitation of the nationalisms of European countries, all of which took pride in their own particular version of "civilization." Much of the motive for preaching a quite conservative brand of Hinduism was to lay claim to cultural parity with the West, that is, to play the West's own chauvinistic game on a worldwide stage and thereby confound the Western nations. In the process Indians would gain the same kind of patriotic self-pride as Englishmen, Frenchmen, or Americans, and thus become all the more like Westerners in the process.

Swami Vivekananda might be termed the St. Paul of the Ramakrishna movement, though he had (by every account) a far more delightful personality. His were the instincts of the organizer and speaker who knows just what to say on any given occasion, though he was also disarmingly good-humored and childlike. Most important, Vivekananda had the same impulse as Paul to free the Vedanta movement from its rather parochial (if already strongly Westernized) beginnings. In 1893 he internationalized the movement, traveling across the sea to the United States for the first time. He hoped to be able to present the message of Vedanta at the World Parliament of Religions, scheduled in conjunction with the Chicago World's Fair of that year. Lacking know-how or credentials, by sheer force of personality he managed to make himself a delegate and then went on to capture his audience with a masterful speech on the need for worldwide religious tolerance, a theme congenial to many liberal Christians in America. As newspapers carried the story of his address, Vivekananda briefly became a nationwide sensation. He remained in the United States for most of three years, and soon returned for another year, during which he visited California as well as the East Coast. While here he conceived the idea of establishing permanent Vedanta centers in some of the major American and European cities; other swamis sent from the new Ramakrishna monasteries in India were to take charge of them. New York and San Francisco became the earliest locales of such Vedanta organizations, soon followed by Boston and then, in 1923, by Los Angeles.

The Vedanta movement never attracted a mass American following. Federal religious census figures show only 340 members in 1906, a decline to 190 ten years later, and a slight rise to 200 in 1926. A renewed period of growth occurred in the 1930's, when several new centers were founded in such other cities as Portland, Seattle, and St. Louis. Total membership rose to 628 in 1936, to around 1,000 in 1960, and perhaps 1,200 today. The movement's tiny size is especially striking in comparison with another Westernized Hindu movement which began to be promoted in the United States after 1920, the Self-Realization Fellowship of All Religions (or Yogoda Sat-Sanga Society) of Swami Yogananda, a man who had no connection with the Ramakrishna Order in India. Yogananda, the son of an Indian businessman, emphasized techniques of salesmanship, promising highly practical personal benefits through Yoga exercises and unashamedly parading the occult and the miraculous.[4] The Ramakrishna movement may have been considerably Westernized, but it was far too elitist to indulge in these tactics. Therefore, relatively speaking, it lost out. Though Yogananda's eventual claim of 125,000 American followers is no doubt an exaggeration, his movement soon attracted members and money on a much larger scale than Vedanta ever succeeded in doing. In the late 1920's Swami Paramananda, representing Vedanta, would attract up to several hundred people on a major Sunday occasion at his Ananda Ashrama near Los Angeles, but Yogananda was then lecturing to crowds estimated at three to five thousand in a number of American cities.

Like anarchism, Vedanta was thus numerically tiny, appealing only to an unrepresentative handful of persons. It was an elite movement within its own realm. But, unlike anarchism, Vedanta made its appeal in a context of understood social propriety. The movement always recruited disproportionately from among the well-to-do, and it has invariably been housed in tasteful, sumptuous surroundings, in such neighborhoods as the Back

---

4. Paramahansa Yogananda's *Autobiography of a Yogi* (Los Angeles: Self-Realization Fellowship, 1959) displays the tone of his movement.

Bay, Pacific Heights, and the Hollywood hills.[5] The source of converts has been still more specific. A survey in 1930 indicated that more than three-quarters of the members were female, their average age was unusually high, and more than two-fifths were unmarried.[6] Here, then, is a striking instance of an urge toward the unfamiliar among affluent women evidently dissatisfied with the barren materialism of their everyday lives.

On the surface, the message which a newcomer first hears in Vedanta is one of harmless ecumenicism—the unity of all religions, the need for tolerance and brotherhood. Beneath these bland assertions, a listener at Vedanta services soon begins to uncover a message which has two apparently conflicting faces. The first side of it is deterministic, and therefore unpalatable to most Americans. Its focal points are the classic Hindu conceptions of karma, reincarnation, and renunciation of appetites and desires. If we really believe in reincarnation, why should we want to hold on to our present round of life, as if it were uniquely precious to us? Why should we shield ourselves from a lightning storm? Today why should we be afraid to be sent to Vietnam? The most that can happen to anyone is the end of his temporary physical vehicle. We must accept, accept. Rapid death might even speed our spiritual evolution. To American ears, this side of the Vedanta message must seem grim, depressing, and unreal, though irreproachably logical in terms of its own premises.

Yet this argument is shared with another, seemingly its opposite. There is also in Vedanta a far more optimistic theme, an emphasis on the need for willful inner self-improvement, similar to that in the mind-cure movement of American "metaphysical" Christianity. (This too has a certain basis in Hindu asceticism.) Vedanta sermons are thus apt to be confusing mixtures of these two approaches to the problem of how man is to deal with his unhappiness. Up to a point he is told he must simply submit to life as it comes; but then he is also told that, through meditation and inner purification, the mind can advance closer to union with God, thereby gaining inner peace. Like Marxism and Puritanism, Vedanta manages to balance a sense of preordained pattern with a call to freely chosen action.[7]

5. During his first visit to America in the mid-1890's, Vivekananda rebelled against always being held prisoner in these fashionable environments and for a time deliberately selected headquarters in a less desirable district of New York. But never again, from then forward, does one hear of such protest on the part of Vedanta swamis in an American city.

6. See data from questionnaire sent to all American Vedantists in 1930, with replies received from one-fifth of the total. Thomas, *op. cit.*, p. 117. Women overbalance men as members of most American churches, but not in anything like this proportion. However, the percentage of women in Vedanta appears to have declined somewhat since the Second World War.

7. The emphasis on active self-development often seems stronger. E.g., see *Mes-*

But what really has mattered for the most devoted membership, much more than anything in the way of theology, is the personal bond between guru and disciple.[8] Vedanta is sometimes familiarly said to follow "the guru system." The student or devotee wishes to be in the physical presence of the guru as much as possible. This is not merely for the spiritual instruction to be received, but for a further compelling reason: the guru, it is believed, literally absorbs the sins, or impurities, of the followers. To live near the guru is to remain immersed in a purifying spiritual "bath," which, from the guru's point of view, is a never-ending act of loving self-sacrifice. (If a guru is ill, it is sometimes said that he has absorbed too many poisons from those he is helping.) To receive these benefits from the guru, the devotee must willingly accept discipline, dedicating the entire remainder of his or her life to the guru's service.

These implications help explain the highly personal nature of the tie between guru and follower in the Vedanta movement. When a swami returns to India, there is often a great falling-away among those who had been especially attached to him. The new swami may be accepted only grudgingly or not at all. He must work all over again to attract a core of loyal disciples. The most extreme instance of this occurred in 1940, when, upon the death of Swami Paramananda, his entire following in Boston and Los Angeles refused to welcome a replacement and instead seceded from the Ramakrishna Order. Now, more than thirty years later, Paramananda's memory is still maintained supreme at the surviving secessionist centers in Cohasset, Massachusetts, and La Crescenta, California.

Probably few other American religious (or political) movements of the past century have been based so largely upon the notion of willing, steadfast obedience to *another person*.[9] Most Americans, unless they become addicted to some forms of psychiatry, are uninterested in the idea of placing their lives in the hands of a single superior figure. A great irony attaches itself to the process whereby this has often apparently been done in Vedanta. It is linked to the desire for purification. Anxiety over inner impurities was bequeathed to Westerners by the Christian tradition, in the

---

sage of the East: Vedanta Monthly (Boston and La Crescenta), XXII (June, 1933), 163; XXXV (January, 1946), 41–42; XLIV (January, 1955), 43–45. But, in the more fatalistic vein, see *ibid.*, XXVIII (January, 1939), 50–52, and XXXI (July, 1942), 175–85.

8. E.g., see Gayatri Devi, "Master and Disciple," *ibid.*, XXXI (January, 1942), 49–56.

9. Roman Catholic monasticism, by comparison, emphasizes loyalty to an organization, or to remote persons (dead saints, Italian popes), rather than to authority figures who are physically present.

form of the concept of sin. Sin and guilt form no part of the Hindu view of the world. Thus, paradoxically, the Christian culture of the nineteenth century may have led a few Americans to embrace the "guru system."[10] This culture gave them their hunger for purity even as they consciously sought to escape from its limiting confines into a much broader, more universal frame of reference.[11] Seen in these tacitly Christian terms, the guru may offer a steady source of strength against sinful backsliding. Forgiveness and purification come not just once (or, as in Catholicism, once a week), but, for the full-fledged member of the consecrated community gathered around the swami, on a daily, almost an hourly basis.

The initial appeal of Vedanta to a small number of well-to-do, predominantly female Americans has other sources, which link it more precisely to its time and place. In late nineteenth-century America and England, Indian culture and philosophy already possessed an exotic quality in the minds of a liberally inclined, cosmopolitan elite.[12] For a few persons within this elite, who often had reasonably good educations and who liked to think they had risen beyond the provincialism of their upbringings, the wisdom of the East might have a romantic attraction, and Vedanta might seem daringly adventurous. Indeed, in urbane circles of those years, it must have been almost as shocking as a flirtation with anarchism. It was bold to attend Swami Vivekananda's classes in New York, just as a few years later it was bold to offer support for Emma Goldman. (Though Vivekananda's name was for a time in nearly every American newspaper, only a few hundred people across the nation dared become dedicated followers of such an alien figure.) A tiny segment of the American social elite apparently relished precisely this kind of venturesomeness, though it was more conventional in its moral beliefs than the similar segment that turned toward anarchism or socialism.

10. Even if Freudians might insist that guilt is a human universal, it is surely striking that some cultures have given the concept great weight (including, historically, our own), while others, such as the Hindus and the ancient Greeks, have not. Guilt may therefore be as much of a problem in intellectual history as in psychiatry.

11. Talking with Gayatri Devi, present head of the La Crescenta–Cohasset group of Vedantists, I mentioned how forcibly the theme of inner guilt had revealed itself in conversations I had had with several Vedanta nuns. Her reply was to acknowledge that this was indeed so, and was the result of nothing within Hinduism, but of the Christian backgrounds of these women, which they could not completely transcend despite their new religious connection.

12. In this vein one prominent early American Vedantist declared: "As students in the past have gone to Paris to study art and to Germany to study music, so they will in time turn to India to acquire . . . the most efficient method of developing the religious consciousness." Sister Devamata, *Days in an Indian Monastery* (La Crescenta, Calif.: Ananda Ashrama, 1927), p. 326.

Moreover, Vedanta, no less than anarchism, might seem attractive to a liberal, rationalistic, "seeking" mind, unafraid of going against the customary grain. Such a mentality conspicuously revealed itself among a minority of free-thinking Americans and Englishmen in just those years. "Free thought" often led people into agnosticism and socialism, but it could also carry them into some version of transcendentalism. Just as a few persons who had become receptive to socialism then went on into the more dangerously extreme point of view called anarchism, so a handful from among the transcendentalist seekers might move on toward Vedanta. These people had often first been explorers of New Thought, Christian Science, Theosophy, or perhaps merely readers of Emerson and of Sir Edwin Arnold's best seller of 1879, *The Light of Asia,* which attractively popularized the life of the Buddha for an Anglo-American audience.

The adventurous, free-thinking liberal of those decades might easily look upon a commitment to an Eastern religious movement as a natural outgrowth of what had begun as a skeptical questioning of Christian theology.[13] Thus it was by no means unusual for agnostics such as Annie Besant suddenly to flip over into an embrace of Theosophy. Militant agnosticism does not seem to have figured in the backgrounds of a majority of Vedantists, but it did sometimes, as in the later case of Christopher Isherwood.[14]

On one level Vedanta could seem like a much more rational religion than Christianity, if one was still going to be religious at all. Compared to the awkward doctrines of the Trinity, the vicarious atonement, and a static afterlife in heaven or hell, the ideas of reincarnation, spiritual evolution, and a series of avatars (or saviours) born as great teachers in different societies, could seem far more reconcilable with a modern liberal awareness.[15] As with Darwinism itself, the grimmer deterministic implications of

13. E.g., see the suggestive though turgid phrasing in Sister Shivani [Mary Le Page], *An Apostle of Monism* (Calcutta: Ramakrishna Vedanta Math, 1947, pp. 28, 31.

14. Christopher Isherwood, *An Approach to Vedanta* (Hollywood: Vedanta Press, 1963), p. 12.

15. Thus John Spencer Clark, a staunch Christian in his young manhood around 1850 but afflicted by doubts during the Darwinian controversy, finally discovered Vedanta and "was profoundly impressed by the vastness, the rationality, the inspiring character of the philosophic and religious thought here presented. . . . My mind was taken entirely away from the consideration of the limited personal God of Christian theology, and led to the contemplation of a Divine Being, the Source and Sustainer of all things. . . . I found the Cosmic Universe presented, not as a fiatistically created Heavens and Earth of recent date, the outcome of will and caprice; rather as an infinite Cosmos of order and law, existing from all eternity, ever in process of evolution to some predestined purpose." *Message of the East,* V (February, 1916), 44.

karma and reincarnation could be neglected in favor of a teleological optimism. Moreover, Vedanta tended strongly to monism and to pantheism, though disagreements within the movement have centered upon subtle distinctions in just this area. With all respect to Claude Lévi-Strauss's argument for the deep human significance of the number two, monism has probably been more satisfying than dualism to the rationally inquiring mind of the last two centuries. Monism may of course be either materialistic or spiritual. It is perhaps as easy to move from one of these forms of monism to the other as it is to move from dualism to either one. The monistic implications of Vedanta also gave it the flavor of an adventurously "far-out" but distinctly liberal philosophy.

As if to improve upon this image, Vedanta, unlike Theosophy or the later Self-Realization Fellowship of Swami Yogananda, deliberately deemphasized the occult and the miraculous from the very beginning. Most American followers of Vedanta have thus adopted the rather interesting position that occult phenomena are indeed real, but that it is not helpful to dwell upon them mentally, much less to seek them out. In this, Vedantists behave rather like Episcopalians who are confronted with the issues of "enthusiasm" or divine healing in the lower reaches of Protestant Christianity. Vedanta probably lost any chance for mass-based support in America by its steadfast refusal to engage in faith healing, easy Yoga exercises, or formulas for increasing one's psychic powers. Its public avoidance of these areas, despite a general privately held belief in the occult among the membership, again marks it as a would-be inheritor of the liberal "free-thought" tradition in the nineteenth-century West.

But why were the early followers of Vedanta so disproportionately feminine, besides being well-to-do and cosmopolitan? One answer is relatively simple. Their husbands were too deeply absorbed in the tasks of earning a living to pay the same heed to exciting new doctrines. When swamis moved into fashionable neighborhoods, the women rather than the men would have the leisure to hear them and to begin reading the literature of the movement. Eventually, if their commitment became sufficiently intense, they might carry their husbands along with them; this sometimes happened. But there might also be greater indifference or outright resistance on the male side of the family.

Perhaps to many this will seem a sufficient explanation in itself; it is surely a large part of the story. But there is also the fact of the intensely personal attachment of so many of these women to the swami. This suggests that a more deeply psychological need may often have been at work. These years were marked, for the middle class in America and England, by a higher degree of concern for moral purity, and therefore a de-emphasis upon sex, than has probably existed in any other time or place. It was an age permeated by genteel reticence, by the standards of what was called "civilized morality."[16] There was then no mockery whatever attached to the concept of "purity," especially where women were concerned. The word itself was emblazoned high on the face of the new First Church of Christ, Scientist, in Boston.[17]

At the end of the nineteenth century, these strictures may well have been felt with special force by middle-class women (since men were partially absolved from guilt for their transgressions by the prevailing double standard). The emphasis in Vedanta upon purity may thus have offered a deeply reassuring anchorage to certain women whom their own culture had previously given a great anxiety in just this respect.[18] In the Hindu tradition, celibacy is associated with the most advanced state of consciousness.[19] One may choose to remain a "householder" (i.e., a married person with a family), but to cling to this role throughout the whole of one's life is to confess a certain degree of weakness, even if an understandable one. An admirable course of action for the male "householder" is to renounce his family in middle age, strip himself of all possessions, and adopt the existence of a wandering mendicant *sannyasin,* or spiritual seeker.

Even in India, on the other hand, there have long been distinct limits to a general embrace of celibate asceticism. Nearly all the wealthy parents of Ramakrishna's disciples, for instance, were bitterly opposed to their sons' adoption of a monastic life and sometimes went to great lengths to try to "rescue" and reclaim their offspring. For young Hindu men and girls, despite the classic ideal, monasticism is no more regarded as a desirable course of practical action than it is in the United States.[20]

16. Henry F. May, *The End of American Innocence* (New York: Alfred A. Knopf, 1959), especially pp. 3–117; Nathan Hale, Jr., *Freud and the Americans* (New York: Oxford University Press, 1971), pp. 24–46.

17. For the explicit elevation of the ideal of "purity" in Vedanta, see Swami Paramananda, *The Path of Devotion* (Boston: Vedanta Centre, 1907), pp. 27–37.

18. See David Riesman, "Some Informal Notes on American Churches and Sects," *Confluence,* IV (1955), 141.

19. "This subject [chastity] always stirred him [Vivekananda] deeply. Walking up and down the room, getting more and more excited, he would stop before some one, as if there were no one else in the room. 'Don't you see,' he would say eagerly, 'there is a reason why chastity is insisted on in all monastic orders? Spiritual gains are produced only where the vow of chastity is observed.' . . . He seemed to plead with us as if to beg us to act upon this teaching as something most precious. More, we could not be the disciples he required if we were not established in this." Sister Christine [Greenstidel], in Swami Chidatmananda, ed., *Reminiscences of Swami Vivekananda* (Calcutta: Advaita Ashrama, 1964), pp. 182–83.

20. I am indebted to Dilip Basu for these insights into Indian society.

Regardless of how typical the Vedanta movement was of Indian society, at the opening of the twentieth century "East" and "West" might meet enthusiastically on the basis of an unyielding commitment to moral purity.[21] Moreover, beyond this, the romantic figure of the guru supplied a concrete object for adoration entirely within the context of such a purity.[22] A close personal relationship became entirely legitimate without requiring the submission to male physical grossness which many American women, raised to enshrine purity in their minds, apparently found it difficult to accept even within the marriage bond.

Whatever the importance of all these considerations, as the twentieth century advanced American culture changed in certain respects, so that Vedanta attracted converts on a considerably different basis. The Jazz Age greatly reduced the number of middle-class Americans to whom Vedanta might appeal by its extreme emphasis upon purity. At the same time, as Americans increasingly lost interest in religion altogether, Vedanta no longer could seem deliciously bold. Christian opposition to Vedanta was very real during the first two or three decades of the movement, but it tended to die out in the atmosphere of bland, secularized ecumenicism which characterized mainstream America by the 1930's and 1940's. Even the magnetic personality of the swami did not go unchallenged, for Krishnamurti (a figure respected and listened to by many Vedantists) persistently attacked "the guru system" down through the years after his famous break with Theosophy in 1927.[23] With Krishnamurti urging Americans interested in spiritual advancement to do so entirely on their own, unaided by any guru, many Vedantists now had to reexamine their reasons for wanting to remain attached to a swami. On the other hand, the collapse of Katherine Tingley's wing of Theosophy noticeably swelled the ranks of Vedantists in California.

The survival and slight numerical increase of the Vedanta movement in recent decades may suggest a continued desire, in some fashion, for the guru's direct presence. But for many followers of these teachings, it may of course suggest nothing more than the persistent attractiveness of the

21. An American Vedantist who traveled to India around 1910 wrote approvingly: "The structure of Indian society makes for greater quietness of spirit, greater restraint in the relation between men and women. I have never lived in a country where the sex-consciousness was so little apparent, and this conduces to a simpler rhythmic expression of feeling." Devamata, *Days in an Indian Monastery*, p. 172. It hardly matters whether these observations are entirely accurate; they certainly represent her idealization.

22. One long-time Vedanta nun told me that in her opinion all truly "advanced souls" were physically beautiful.

23. See p. 416.

philosophy it presents, as an avenue toward peace of mind. The tensions and anxieties of industrial living have scarcely lessened since the turn of the twentieth century. Vedanta offers a promise of withdrawal from these everyday afflictions into a world of calmness and restored inner strength. At its best the movement creates an oasis of gentleness, beauty, and idealistic consecration. Its otherworldliness is far more genuine than that of many other religious organizations. And, despite the severity of certain aspects of its message, it has often called into being a sense of community founded upon love.

But Vedanta was not well equipped to benefit from the upsurge of interest in Eastern religion among the youth of the 1960's. Its tone was still too respectably middle-aged and upper-middle-class, too quiet and austere. To most people it now seemed altogether too unexciting. The movement drew a sprinkling of the young and the hip at its Sunday morning services,[24] but remained nonetheless distinctly to one side of the revived transcendental counter-culture of the decade.[25]

Vedanta and Community

From its beginnings in America, the Vedanta movement recurrently assumed a communitarian form. In the summer of 1895, when Vivekananda gathered a dozen of his most ardent new converts at Thousand Island Park on the St. Lawrence River, to give them prolonged spiritual instruction, the idea seemed automatically to occur to these women

> that they should live as a community, without servants, each doing a share of the work. Nearly all of them were unaccustomed to housework and found it uncongenial. The result was amusing; as time went on it threatened to become disastrous. Some of us who had just been reading the story of Brook Farm felt that we saw it re-enacted before our eyes. . . . One whose work was to cut the bread, groaned and all but wept whenever she attempted the task.[26]

After a few weeks the group surrendered to custom and hired a servant.

24. Also of middle-class blacks, attracted by its dignity, ecumenicism, and dark-skinned leadership.
25. Concerning an encounter between Timothy Leary and Vedanta, see p. 438. In India, though the movement became much larger than in the United States, it is also relatively static. Its charitable work in famines and floods is widely applauded, but its monasticism has so little appeal that the Ramakrishna Order admittedly has difficulty recruiting "sufficient material of high quality," causing "a real manpower shortage." See John Yale, *A Yankee and the Swamis* (Hollywood: Vedanta Press, 1961), p. 212; cf. also J. N. Farquhar, *Modern Religious Movements in India* (Delhi: Munshiram Manoharlal, 1967; 1st published 1915), p. 206.
26. Sister Christine [Greenstidel], in Swami Chidatmananda, *op. cit.*, pp. 176–77.

But what is so significant is not the failure but the impulse toward community. Among these neo-transcendentalists, such an urge had apparently been lying fallow, waiting to spring to life when the swami appeared in their midst.

A second instance of this impulse is even more striking. In 1909, shortly after the Vedanta Centre in Boston had been opened by the youthful Swami Paramananda, he was invited to live for the entire summer in the suburban home of a motherly admirer, Katherine F. Sherwood. For the next several years, Paramananda came annually to Miss Sherwood's residence and again there were striking innovations in the pattern of living. One of the half-dozen followers who began sharing the house in Milton wrote about those days:

> It was interesting to watch the gradual transformation of the house, through the Swami's subtle silent influence, from an acknowledged centre of social and intellectual activity to a quiet retreat hermitage, not unlike the woodland retreats of ancient India. . . . The rooms were crowded with pictures, ornaments, and old embroideries, collected during frequent journeying in Europe. The second summer everything of secondary artistic value was put away. . . . Entertainments were reduced to a minimum, and only those were invited to the house who were in sympathy with the new order of things.

But this was still only the beginning.

> The third summer all servants were given up, to create a freer atmosphere for meditation and study, and the members of the community family divided the labor of the household. . . . We swept and dusted, weeded and sewed; then when the morning's work and study were done, we played croquet or other games on the lawn. . . with lemonade under the trees. . . . The Swami's side was invariably victorious.[27]

In this small group, though women were dominant, there were members of both sexes.

Meanwhile, in other parts of the United States, three formally organized Vedanta communities had already come into being. Two were called ashrams, or peace retreats. One of these, Shanti Ashrama, was founded in 1900 on a 160-acre site on the slopes of Mount Hamilton, east of San Jose, California. Despite severe physical problems—the nearest water was six miles away, everyone had to live in tents, and the overbalance of women hampered the rough jobs—ardent groups came to Shanti Ashrama

---

27. Sister Devamata, *Swami Paramananda and His Work* (2 vols.; La Crescenta, Calif.: Ananda Ashrama, 1926–1941), I, 114–16. See also *Message of the East*, XXXVI (April, 1947), 120–21.

in the summertime for a number of years. There they would rise at 5 A.M., meditate three times each day, engage in an hour of reading and discussion, and sometimes push themselves to such extremes of austerity (for instance, self-imposed periods of isolation or silence) that the Swami had to intervene and establish limits.[28]

In 1907 the Vedanta Ashrama was created on a 375-acre estate in the Berkshires, at West Cornwall, Connecticut. Originally intended for summer retreats, in 1910 it became the year-round residence of Swami Abhedananda, one of the most forceful and commanding of the early swamis. He lived there until 1919, when he sold it and returned to India. Much of the site consisted of forested rolling hills, which were left untouched. Two cottages (former farmhouses), renamed Lotus and Peace, sheltered the permanent population. Agriculture was practiced, and it is reported that Swami Abhedananda sometimes worked in the field alongside his male and female devotees. One man, who led the life of the *sannyasin* in these rather severe surroundings, wrote in 1909: "I handle crowbars, picks, shovels, and the axe; draw wood down hill slopes through swamps, first making a road with branches of trees; upset the wagon, break the sleigh, repair all in turn, fix up the horse, eat three meals a day and sleep, making sure there is wood in the fire." Later, when more of a community had been established, work and leisure were blended as "hundreds" came "to learn yoga in the still woodland of Berkshire. They lived under tents, they lived like brothers and sisters—a life of peace and serenity without any care for high or low."[29] Rising at six o'clock to take a dip in the local brook, they would fast all morning, then pick vegetables in the garden at eleven and eat a breakfast-lunch at noon. Berrying, canning, preserving parties and picnics followed. On walks they would visit nearby Ramakrishna Rock.[30] The adoration of nature was an especially strong theme at this ashram. Animals were raised. "The place was kept in good repair without hired labour. Always there was hard work to be done, always some addition be-

28. The site had been donated by an American admirer of Swami Abhedananda, Minnie Book. When it opened it drew hostile newspaper publicity. Shanti Ashrama lapsed into a state of dormancy before the First World War. On it see Jackson, *op. cit.*, pp. 270–72; Swami Satyananda, *Abhedananda: The Messiah of Vedanta* (Calcutta: Sree Ramkrishna Sevayatan, 1967), pp. 96–97; *Vedanta Monthly Bulletin* (New York), I (April, 1905), 13. It long had a full-time caretaker, and there was hope at one point that a swami would live on the site permanently.

29. *Ibid.*, V (January, 1909), 100; Swami Satyananda, *op. cit.*, p. 116.

30. There was, however, no strictly defined schedule. *Vedanta Monthly Bulletin*, V (April, 1909), 127. Cf. *ibid.*, III (October, 1907), 129; III (November, 1907), 146; IV (April, 1908), 7; Swami Satyananda, *op. cit.*, pp. 108–110; Jackson, *op. cit.*, pp. 261–62; Shivani, *op. cit.*, pp. 179–80. It too attracted some hostile attention from local Christians; *ibid.*, pp. 179, 191.

ing made, some project under way, nothing ever finished. Season after season the works went on. . . . We learned our Yoga on our feet in that Lotus Cottage kitchen."[31]

Meanwhile, the first urban monastic community in the Vedanta movement had begun at San Francisco, starting around 1906, when ten young male devotees began living in the Hindu Temple which had just been built. During the day they took ordinary jobs, but otherwise they spent all their time in the Temple, attending its functions and practicing austerities, which included a vegetarian diet. A nunnery was later established nearby, but it failed for unknown reasons in 1912. The number of male monastics remained steady until 1913, when it too began to decline. A change of swamis brought an end to the experiment by 1915.[32]

Swami Trigunatita, who had fostered these San Francisco efforts, also was the moving force behind the only large-scale Vedanta colonization venture. It was begun at Concord, then a small town in a hot valley an hour east of the bay by newly-opened electric interurban. A highly efficient organizer from a wealthy Bengali family, Trigunatita appears to have been consciously inspired by the utopian tradition in Western thought; he was the only Vedanta swami (apart from Vivekananda) to declare himself a socialist. But his aim was also said to have been "practical"; he hoped a communal arrangement could help make the spiritual work economically self-sustaining. Under his plan, much of the land would be sold to individuals who would come there to live (exactly as at the anarchist Ferrer colony in New Jersey). Even this long ago a retirement angle was mentioned—older Vedantists were encouraged to think of this as a place for their last years. There would also be farming and home industries. The Vedanta Society would retain part of the land to be collectively farmed by the monastics. A total of two hundred acres were bought, and all but twenty-five resold to colonists. A few people made large financial contributions to the project. A building was put up as community headquarters and as living space for the workers. Development of the site continued for several years. A number of houses were actually built, Vedanta families moved into them, and orchards and crops were planted. The Swami came out to the colony once a week to give a religious class and oversee the management. As time went on, his dreams grew increasingly ambitious. He planned a temple, a library, an orphan home, an old-age home, and a hospital. But all this was cut short by the Swami's sudden death early in 1915.

31. *Ibid.,* p. 175.
32. Jackson, *op. cit.,* pp. 298–300.

(He was shot during a service at the San Francisco temple by a deranged ex-member of his monastic community.) It is revealing that, without his charismatic presence, not only did the plans for expansion cease, but the entire community withered away in a very short time.[33]

Of all the early swamis, only Trigunatita had any deliberate interest in communitarian aims. In the other instances, a communal pattern took shape which was strikingly similar to that of secular utopian movements, but from rather different motives. At Milton, for instance, the servants were banished, not because they violated an egalitarian conscience, but simply because they were outsiders—in an atmosphere of devout commitment their presence had become extremely uncomfortable. In fact, neither the swamis nor their American devotees were believers in social equality. They would openly defend the Hindu caste system in large measure; as believers in reincarnation, they thought it quite just that some souls should inhabit "lower" forms than others during the course of their common (but uneven) upward evolution. Much in the Vedantist life style, even in these communities, remained tacitly elitist as compared with the surrounding American population. Vedantists may often have felt pangs of guilt, but only in terms of their personal strivings toward purity. They did not feel guilty about the fact of their wealth, as did some left-wing reformers from well-off backgrounds.

Vedanta communities were exclusivist, not universalistic, emphasizing the desire to cut oneself off from all the distractions of the normal world. The great aim was to be physically close to the Swami, and to abandon everything else in one's life that might interfere with this. In important ways they were thus polar opposites of communities dedicated to an anarchistic philosophy.

These themes are best revealed in the history of a Vedanta monastic community about which there is unusually rich documentation, the one which formed under Swami Paramananda, first in Boston and then, after 1923, at La Crescenta, near Los Angeles.[34] Without any doubt, Paraman-

33. *Ibid.*, pp. 300–302; Dorothy F. Mercer in John Yale, ed., *What Vedanta Means to Me* (Hollywood: Vedanta Press; 1961), pp. 70–71.

34. Though the community still exists, my effort will be to describe it as it was before Paramananda's death in 1940. The memoirs of Sister Daya (Georgina Jones Walton) comprise the most revealing source; they were published under the title "From a Disciple's Notebook" in *Message of the East* from 1945 to 1954. The magazine itself is an important mine of information, despite its reticence. It was published from 1912 to 1964 (a complete set is in the Harvard College library). Devamata, *Paramananda*, is also reticent but helpful. The John Percival Jones Papers at the Huntington Library contain a few relevant materials.

anda was the most remarkable and influential personality (though not the leading intellect) among the swamis of the Vedanta movement who came to America in the early decades of the twentieth century. More lately, his memory has been downplayed by the present leadership of the Vedanta Society.[35] His life and career are well worth unearthing for what they show of the guru and his band of devotees in a classic form.

Paramananda resembled the other swamis in coming from a cultivated, highly Westernized Bengali family. He was the youngest son of eleven children, and his mother died when he was nine. He grew up on the family estate in East Bengal, which was surrounded by a moat to keep out intruders. Tutors entered the property to give him his schooling. He was a beautiful-looking boy, besides being the youngest, the product of a second marriage in his father's old age. Perhaps for all these reasons he appears to have been constantly loved and petted by everyone. In such an environment, he could grow up with a certain fearlessness, an open, sunny, childlike forthrightness which never left him. To an extraordinary degree, he seems never to have known insecurity. Possessed of a quick intelligence, he was unashamedly impatient with books and study, despite his father's respect for learning. He enjoyed being a dare-devil, climbing trees and jumping into water from heights. As a youth, a dream or vision led him in a religious direction, and he slipped away to the Ramakrishna monastery at Belur. There the older swamis at once became enormously devoted to him, struggling successfully to hold him there against his father's initial opposition. Paramananda seems from the first to have received unusual protection and encouragement. He received special privileges—for instance, Vivekananda invited him to become a swami much sooner than was usual. And, perhaps because he had always been so much loved and sought after, the astonishingly handsome youth began to display in a strong form the kind of magnetic personal force that marks the unhesitating guru.[36]

Paramananda's fearlessness was never better revealed than in his rapid conquest of the American environment, after his arrival in New York in December, 1906, when he was only about twenty-one. Initially sent to assist Swami Abhedananda there, he won over a large share of the membership and thereby created a divisive factionalism. Moving on to Boston, then virgin territory for the Vedanta Society, he soon had a flourishing congregation. In 1912 he was able to purchase a large house at 1 Queens-

35. E.g., see the highly unfair account in Dorothy F. Mercer, "Vedanta in California," *Pacific Spectator*, X (1956), 38–46. Paramananda's name is never mentioned in the publications of Swami Prabhavananda's center in Hollywood.

36. The facts of his early life are in Devamata, *Paramananda*, I, 21–72; the interpretation of them is very much my own.

berry Street, on the Fenway, both to hold public services and as the head-quarters of a fledgling monastic community.[37]

Paramananda himself commented upon how effortlessly he had adjusted to American life. One aspect of his emerging style is revealed in his recollection that "when I first came to this country I imagined that people expected me to talk philosophy, but I found out later that automobiles create a quicker point of contact. As soon as I learned to drive a motor car I had an unfailing topic of sympathetic conversation with everyone I met."[38] He at once began writing a steady stream of books in easy, colloquial English—books in which the philosophical was downplayed in favor of the psychological, the ethical, and the devotional.[39] Nonetheless, like some of his predecessors in the Vedanta movement, he was invited to speak before the Philosophical Club at Harvard, and he numbered at least two Harvard professors (one of Sanskrit, one of electrical engineering) in his regular following.

In all this successful activity, there was a peculiar combination of astute insight and childlike spontaneity. How one interpreted the Swami's role might well depend upon how one regarded the seeming candor of a passage like this, in an informal talk to those who were close to him:

> I do not want the work to grow in pomp and glory. This work cannot be carried on by advertising, but by lofty conduct. I cannot see how anything sensational or spectacular can be abiding. Whatever abides must be gentle, profound, silent like the dew-drop, fundamental. My method may not be materially profitable, but the standard I hold is whether it helps people. . . .
>
> We must never lose the spirit of humility and simplicity at the Ashrama. Money must never become a dominating factor in it. Simplicity has a tremendous power over people. If my efforts have had any appeal, it is wholly due to their simplicity. Those things which spring from the soul spontaneously, not with calculation, are undying.[40]

Clearly one could not take such statements as these literally. Urging simplicity, the Swami dressed with fashionable elegance and enjoyed owning and driving powerful, expensive automobiles. Claiming to be indifferent to the numbers of people he attracted, on other occasions he let slip how keenly aware he was of these figures.[41]

37. *Message of the East*, XXXVI (July, 1947), 181.
38. Quoted in Devamata, *Paramananda*, I, 302.
39. His easy eclecticism (Easter lilies on the altar, a high white collar he sometimes wore) dismayed more orthodox Hindus who observed him in Boston. For a highly negative allusion of this kind to Paramananda, see Cornelia Sorabji, "Hindu Swamis and Women of the West," *Nineteenth Century*, CXII (September, 1932), 372–73.
40. Quoted in Devamata, *Paramananda*, I, 265–66.
41. Cf. *Message of the East*, XLI (April, 1952), 117–18, with XXXVI (April,

Yet the Swami's childlike, spontaneous side was genuine. It revealed itself in making puns, in impulsively donning outlandish costumes, or in building and flying kites, sometimes day after day, either at Revere Beach or from the roof of their Back Bay domicile. In such an exuberant vein, the Swami could dash off a poem recording his great delight in an American confection:

> Ice is nice
> And cream is a dream.
> Ice cream
> Is a nice dream
> Of human life.[42]

And yet all this represented only one of the Swami's moods. He was usually earnest and thoughtful (though never downcast).

Compared, for instance, to Yogananda of the Self-Realization Fellowship, Paramananda was a rather aloof and dignified figure; he would not claim, for instance, to possess the power of healing by faith, nor would he teach Yoga exercises by correspondence. Thus, though his adaptation to America was graceful and rapid, it usually stopped short of embracing the techniques and appeals which would have given him a mass audience. However, he did participate in radio broadcasting for a time in the late 1920's, and earlier, for a brief period in 1921–1922, he had accepted invitations to address a large number of "Psychology Clubs," in the mind-cure tradition, which were faddishly springing up in the Middle West. There he spoke on such subjects as "The Conquest of Fear."[43] Though these episodes show that Paramananda could sometimes be tempted by the idea of gaining a wider following, his devotees were always successful in pulling him back into the quieter life that would give them a more exclusive claim on his attention.

He was radical enough to argue in October, 1933, almost like a leftist, that we should not hope for a return of material prosperity if it meant returning to "the selfsame trend of conditions which threw the world into its chaos," including scientific inventions and armaments. "I am rather inclined to believe," he said, "that in every country there will be produced certain types of human beings who will have the courage to liberate them-

---

1947), 115 (regarding the early days in Boston). Paramananda had once flatly said: "True greatness consists in the simple life." *Ibid.,* XII (February, 1923), 46.

42. Devamata, *Paramananda,* I, 87.

43. "It is gratifying," said Paramananda's magazine at that time, "to see how eagerly the psychology movement, which has swept the country and dotted it with clubs, links its eminently modern point of view with the age-ripened teaching of Vedanta." *Message of the East,* XI (March, 1922), 72. On this episode, see also Devamata, *Paramananda,* I, 260–62. Sister Daya also gave radio talks in the 1950's.

selves from the bonds of custom and habit. I want men who will show by their lives that they have something other than just a material background. . . . The destiny of man can be revolutionized through the individual."[44] Such words might well have been uttered by the Ferms at Stelton. Paramananda, it should be noted, was a man who could win the liking and respect of the austere, demanding Krishnamurti.[45] Altogether he was a perspicacious, complicated person. As with Vivekananda, his childlike "simplicity" was only one element in his make-up, and it is fascinating to observe the hold he acquired on several hundred American devotees, predominantly well-to-do and female, during the long span of years from 1906 to 1940.

In 1916 Paramananda visited California for the first time, and it immediately delighted him. In letters back to Boston, he repeatedly praised the climate, exclaimed over the newly invented cafeterias, and even mentioned the pleasure of being able to park his car all day in downtown Los Angeles for only ten cents.[46] He also found a strong interest in his message. An informal community of Theosophists, called Krotona, existed in the Hollywood hills.[47] Many who lived there were receptive to someone like himself. His success encouraged him to begin a series of transcontinental trips which frequently brought him back to Los Angeles. In 1923 he decided to buy property in Southern California to establish a new rural ashram, where he would be spared the cold, dirt, and relative confinement of Boston living. Through a fortunate connection, he learned of the availability of a 140-acre estate at La Crescenta, which, from nearly every point of view, was to prove ideal for his purposes. It combined great scenic beauty with seclusion and accessibility. Though only a forty-five minute drive from downtown Los Angeles, it was in a remote and spectacular world of its own.

Even today, despite smog and housing tracts which have encroached on the Ananda Ashrama from two sides, it is not impossible to imagine the appeal of this setting in the 1920's. The La Crescenta Valley, due north of Los Angeles but separated from it by the high range of Verdugo Hills, is unlike the neighboring and better-known San Fernando Valley. Far from being flat, the whole of it is tilted at a sharp angle, rising toward the five-thousand-foot peaks of the San Gabriel range which mark its north end.

44. Swami Paramananda, "The Need of the Hour," *Message of the East*, XXII (October, 1933), 225–27.
45. See Sister Daya to her mother, April 24, 1930, Jones Papers.
46. Devamata, *Paramananda*, I, 247.
47. See p. 253.

The Ananda Ashrama was located in a canyon where the sloping valley floor met these mountains. From it in the clear air of those years one could gaze upon the lights of the city and in daytime at a thin slice of the Pacific Ocean in the far distance. Closer at hand, one could spy automobiles crawling up the slope toward the Ashrama from several miles away.

Practically none of the Ashrama grounds were on level land. The community buildings were constructed on a series of slopes and terraces, often very attractively landscaped. The architecture, personally planned by the Swami (with some aid from "a well-known architect of Pasadena"), made it harmonious in its own time and place. Only the Temple exterior was at all ornate or Oriental, and the Swami complained that it had been finished in his absence in a way that violated his original instructions. The effort was to blend in with the California foothill landscape, not to impose upon it, and it was rather successful.

A highly disciplined community can accomplish wonders in the way of physical construction in a short time. The buildings at the Ashrama were all erected between 1923 and 1928, sometimes almost entirely by the male and female members of the group, only the electrical work and roofing being done by outsiders.[48] The disciplined atmosphere at the Ashrama also permitted a unified architectural motif to come into existence, utterly opposite from the jerry-built shacks at the Stelton anarchist colony.

One house was already on the property; enlarged, it became the Cloister, the nuns' residential area. A row of wood cabins to the east housed more of the women and the several male members of the household. In 1926 a large two-story guest house was built to accommodate a steady stream of less permanent residents. Later called the Community House, its ground floor could hold large-sized informal gatherings. Then, two years later, a hillside was leveled to make way for the Temple of the Universal Spirit, the final goal of the building program. When completed, the Temple was approached through a courtyard framed by covered walkways next to which were the Swami's own living quarters.

The Temple seated more than a hundred persons on rows of plain upright chairs. (When crowds were often much larger in the early years, many services were held outdoors.) Along the sides of the Temple interior were niches in which candles burned, representing each of the major religions of

48. "One member has spent days in an effort to secure materials at wholesale figures. . . . Two other members have left their places of employment to aid in the building and have put into the construction a true spirit of consecration. One gentleman made a donation sufficient to pay the wages of a carpenter for a short time. . . . And so the walls [of the Community House] are being raised in love." *Message of the East,* XIV (November, 1925), 216; cf. *ibid.,* XVII (February, 1928), 62.

the world, thus emphasizing the universalism of the Vedantist claim. A
large recessed chamber at the rear, opened during services, contained the
Temple shrine. A manual organ was eventually placed at the rear of the
Temple. Organists, singers, and musicians, when they performed, were thus
always out of sight directly behind the congregation. The Temple was rest-
fully dark inside. Incense was burned to purify the air.

One entered the Temple in silence. People often arrived early on Sunday
mornings, deliberately craving this atmosphere. No music played as they
came in, one by one, and seated themselves in the collective stillness. A
nun would light the candles at the rear of the speaker's platform. After
chimes were rung, the organ would begin, and there might be a vocal number, in the Western style. Except for this touch, the services were marked
by an unsentimental austerity and directness which could be deeply affecting. Aside from a few announcements and the bits of music and prayer at
beginning and end, they consisted of nothing but a long sermon delivered
by the Swami (when he was present, otherwise by one of his assistants).[49]
Special observances were made at a number of times throughout the year,
such as Christmas, Buddha's birthday, Ramakrishna's birthday, Vivekananda's birthday, and Easter sunrise. People drove to these services from as
far away as San Diego. Several times a year Paramananda personally
cooked and served a "Hindu dinner" for an assemblage of invited guests,
often more than a hundred people. These major occasions were high points
in the life of the community.

Behind the Ashrama buildings, the terrain rose even more rapidly. All
of it was canyon and mountain wilderness, covered with low chaparral,
yucca, buckwheat, "old man," and sage. Several steep side canyons
branched off to the rear. The immediate presence of nature was always a
highly important aspect of life at the Ashrama. Though not dogmatically,
the Swami practiced *ahimsa* (reverence for all living creatures).[50] There
was (and is) a special atmosphere of serenity on the grounds. The pines
make the air sweet as one climbs the steps toward the Temple. In the early
years, deer were frequently seen at close range. Warm sunshine, coastal
fog, and winter rains provided a pleasing climatic interplay. "Among these
hills," an ecstatic early visitor wrote, "the feeling of ideality increases, the
sense of the unknown expands and the veil which falls between the human

49. To an outsider these Vedanta services might "give an impression of flatness
and tameness. . . . It is rather innocent and not greatly different from local [Ameri-
can] forms of worship." Jules-Bois, "The New Religions of America," *The Forum*,
LXXVII (March, 1927), 421.

50. He would reluctantly kill rattlesnakes, but not mosquitoes. *Message of the
East*, XXXVI (January, 1947), 47; XXXIX (July, 1950), 181.

sense and the ultimate disclosure seems to grow more thin."[51] Another new arrival described her feeling of rapture as she climbed up the narrow path from the Community House one evening, glimpsing ahead of her the forms of "white-veiled Sisters leaving their cloisters and moving slowly and silently toward the great Temple. . . . The Sisters kept ahead—far ahead— and in the dusk, with the scent of so many flowers from trees and shrubs filling the night air, their fluttering white veils might have been so many fluttering white butterflies winging on, and beckoning the soul on and up . . . up higher!"[52]

Paramananda did not abandon his Boston Vedanta Centre. He moved most of the members of his resident monastic community to the West Coast and sold the Queensberry Street house, occupying a series of less spacious (though still very substantial) locations in the Back Bay thereafter. He continued to divide his time between Boston and La Crescenta, traveling incessantly between them by train. Indeed, between 1923 and his death in 1940, he seldom lingered in one of his two centers for longer than a few weeks before moving on to the other. A curious kind of "commuter" life thus developed for the Swami. At both ends of the continent a band of followers hungered insistently for his physical presence, grieving if he tarried too long away from them and demanding his return, yet he could satisfy only half of them at once. In a typical compromise, he would spend Christmas of each year at the Boston Centre and New Year's at La Crescenta. The Boston members felt, no doubt rightly, that Paramananda had transferred his first loyalty to the California undertaking. However, as if to balance matters, in 1929 he purchased a beautiful wooded and secluded twenty-acre site in Cohasset, Massachusetts, twenty miles southeast of Boston, for another ashram, which thereafter was used during summer seasons.

Swami Paramananda's frequent comings and goings created a continuous stir of excitement among his following. The rationale for such an exhausting schedule, from the point of view of the Vedanta movement, was a shortage of swamis available for the American branch of the work, and the desirability of covering a wider territory with those who were already here. (He also habitually visited smaller groups of admirers in Cincinnati and Louisville during his train trips.) But such constant disappearances and reappearances also had the undeniable effect of intensifying Paramananda's impact. Because his presence, so much desired, could never be taken for granted, each return became a newly electrifying experience for the faithful. As one devotee expressed it, "When Swami comes, people

51. Mildred Phillips, "The Hills of Vision," *ibid.,* XVI (October, 1927), 250.
52. Maud Keck, "Ananda-Ashrama: An Impression," *ibid.,* XX (May, 1931), 154.

seem to rise out of the ground and swarm over the Ashrama like ants about a lump of sugar."[53] And the days the Swami spent, every few weeks, staring peacefully at the desert and prairie countryside from his Pullman car, gave him his only real rest, his only respite from the intense emotional demands being placed on him by devotees gathered at the two ends of the continent. In this sense they were no extravagance.

The Swami and his following received two rude shocks in quick succession at the end of the year 1933. On November 23 of that year the Ananda Ashrama was very nearly destroyed by a raging brush fire, the bane of so many well-situated Southern California properties. It happened while the Swami was in Boston.[54] Then, a few weeks later the denuded hillsides began to wash away in an enormous flood, so powerful that it carried boulders, trees, and entire houses down the valley slope for distances of nearly a mile. At least one life of an Ashrama devotee was lost. The Swami, now in California, personally dug ditches to keep the main flow of water away from the buildings, and once again all were saved. Thereafter, however, something of the original beauty of the site was lost.

There are signs that in the last years of his life Paramananda's following began to slacken. Yogananda's Self-Realization Fellowship had come to Los Angeles in 1925. Within the Ramakrishna Order, after 1930 Paramananda faced the growing competition of Swami Prabhavananda, who opened a new Vedanta center in Hollywood which would eventually lure such notables as Aldous Huxley, Christopher Isherwood, and Gerald Heard into its growing congregation. In Boston, though Paramananda retained a core of deeply attached persons, he did not seem to be reaching many newcomers.[55] His larger California following tended more toward religious shoppers and seekers who ebbed and flowed, expressing initial enthusiasm but then suddenly vanishing. In the 1920's Paramananda had expanded his work to its full proportions. In the early 1930's, there are definite signs of a crisis which involved disloyalty and factional discord at the Ananda Ashrama—perhaps because of Prabhavananda's Hollywood activities, perhaps for an entirely different reason.[56] For some length of time, especially

53. *Ibid.*, XXXVIII (July, 1939), 192.
54. *Ibid.*, XXII (December, 1933), 302–303.
55. See *ibid.*, XXXII (July, 1943), 175.
56. See the letters by Paramananda to various individuals, 1929–1936, reprinted *ibid.*, XXXI (January, 1942), 33–41; XXXVIII (April, 1949), 124–25. See also *ibid.*, XXI (May, 1932), 129. Another oblique reference, *ibid.*, XXIII (March, 1934), 95, strongly implies that communication had ceased between the San Francisco and Hollywood Vedanta centers and La Crescenta. But there was an evident outward reconciliation by 1938, when Prabhavananda attended a moonlight festival service at the Ashrama and "spoke feeling-fully" to the audience. *Ibid.*, XXVII (April,

around 1932, Paramananda appears to have been in an uncharacteristically discouraged frame of mind, retreating from people altogether into nature and even saying things that suggested guilt-ridden moods.[57] But, as a firm believer in deliberate cheerfulness, he soon bounced back and rode out the crisis.

Though fewer outside groups sought him as a speaker than in the 1920's, he continued as actively as ever, making the last of several return trips to India in 1937, where he was received as a hero.[58] Suffering from increasing fatigue, he was struck down suddenly by a heart attack in June, 1940.

Ten Americans (nine women, one man) took full monastic vows under Paramananda. In addition, others lived in the community for long periods without taking vows or giving up their Christian names. Twenty-five people, I am told, was quite a typical total figure for the population living at the Ananda Ashrama; another one or two held on as caretakers at Boston. Among the monastics, very few seem to have dropped out, especially in comparison with the turnover in the Vedanta movement more recently. Most of the sisters who became devotees of Paramananda remained residents in the community for the rest of their lives, usually outliving the Swami by some years.[59]

Paramananda's first disciple, Sister Devamata, occupied the position of mother superior for the group. Originally named Laura Glenn, she was a descendant of Benjamin Franklin. The family was Episcopalian, her father an army officer. She graduated from Vassar and then went briefly to the Sorbonne to study, living also for a while in Italy. As a young woman she gradually became interested in Asian culture and ideas, reading Edwin Arnold's *The Light of Asia,* a translation of the *Bhagavad Gita,* and Max Müller's version of the *Upanishads.* A Swedenborgian minister, whom she and her mother and sister met on a chance encounter in a small Ohio town, spoke glowingly of Vivekananda's recent performance at the Parliament of Religions in Chicago, which he had attended. Back in New York, Laura Glenn went to hear him lecture and subsequently became a member of the

---

1938), 127–28. Paramananda also helped lay the cornerstone of the Hollywood temple building, and Prabhavananda attended Paramananda's funeral in 1940.

57. *Ibid.,* XXXI (January, 1942), 38–39.

58. Though there are hints of declining attendance at La Crescenta around 1936, and the magazine shifted from a monthly to a quarterly schedule in 1937, several hundred people would still visit the Ashrama on major festive occasions in the late 1930's. More than five hundred attended Paramananda's funeral services in 1940.

59. Sister Amala, last of his own disciples to remain alive and in good health, played the organ on Sundays at the Ananda Ashrama as late as 1970.

nascent Vedanta Society there. Thus in 1906 she was one of two devout Vedantists who went to the boat dock to meet Paramananda on his first arrival from India. Immediately in him she found a personal allegiance. Shortly afterwards, at his suggestion, she spent two years in India, living in the monasteries of the Ramakrishna Order (although the movement in India normally was restricted to males; this changed only in the 1950's).[60] Back in America, she became Paramananda's chief assistant, helping him found an unsuccessful center in Washington, D.C., and conducting services in Boston whenever he was absent.[61]

Devamata was small, dignified, and ever on the alert, constantly present on the scene. Toward the Swami she could be motherly, seeking to protect him from the demands of outsiders, cautioning him against overexpanding his commitments. Toward the younger members of the community, she could seem unremittingly severe.

> Though possessed of a tiny body [Sister Daya recalled], her will was adamant and was set on creating a perfect spiritual community. Unfailingly conscientious, she spared neither herself nor others. . . . One day the the disciple [Daya] was entrusted with the task of dusting the books in the lending library. They were valuable books, of peculiar interest to an aspirant, and the disciple took time to read a page here and a page there, neglecting the dusting in the meantime. The senior Sister [Devamata] appeared in the doorway and, standing quietly, took in the situation. "Are you serving yourself or the Lord?" she asked. "The true devotee has no other interest than the work which has been given to her to do. This does not seem to be true in your case."[62]

Devamata fought against allowing any tendency toward the "lazy" or the "vague" in meditation or in spiritual life. "We must keep to specific tasks," she said, or else "sooner or later, we grow sentimental and visionary. . . . We must guard ourselves very carefully lest we make our devotional life into an emotional life. It must not become in any way an indulgence." Devamata taught the students that such traits as a heavy step or a high-pitched voice "were evidence of *rajas* or feverish restlessness, in other words, of ego. . . . Students must watch for ego in their every thought,

60. Unlike some other Western women who traveled to India in this fashion, Devamata remained totally uninterested in politics, refusing to take part in the independence struggle. She favored some modifying of the caste system, but said that recent efforts to do away with it were "unwholesome." *Days in an Indian Monastery*, pp. 275, 301, 311.

61. On her life, see *Message of the East*, XXXII (January, 1943), 35–40, and L (January, 1961), 84–91; her memoirs, which appeared, *ibid.*, from 1950 to 1952; and Swami Chidatmananda, *op. cit.*, pp. 131–39.

62. *Message of the East*, XXXV (January, 1946), 38; see also *ibid.*, XXXVI (April, 1947), 112.

word and act as the zealous cat watches for the mouse." Tardiness at a public service was considered by Devamata a major offense.[63]

The other members of the community seem to have had less dominating personalities. Sister Daya (Georgina Jones Walton), who will later be described at some length, embodied an utterly serene austerity but lacked Devamata's hard-driving, restless bustle. Sister Satya Prana (a name that means "true heart") was from a cultivated family of Dutch descent. She was recalled as not speaking often and at times responding rather abruptly to others, yet always consistently devoted.[64] Sister Achala, a young woman from Indiana trained as a stenographer, joined the Swami's household in Boston in 1918. Although often in poor health, she became a mainstay in the practical running of the community, serving as secretary, shopper, cook, and general correspondent. It was she who recorded many of the Swami's talks. When happy or excited, she would cry easily, and she was a lover of cats. Sister Amala, who grew up in St. Louis, came into the community in 1919. The only one of Paramananda's disciples still living at the Ashrama in 1970, she told me that her mother had been generous about her decision to become a nun, raising no objection, though later she learned that her mother had suffered much because of it. "My mother and father were great people, holy people," she declared with pride. "They were free people, not bound to any dogma." Amala struck me, as she has others, as another extremely severe person.

Sister Vimala made music her specialty, combining it with weaving. Less is said of her than of the rest. Sister Seva (whose name means "service") occupied a unique place at the Ashrama because of her strenuous duties as beekeeper. Daya admired Seva's great rapport with animals of all kinds. She would speak coaxingly to a pet turtle taking a daily walk in the sun parlor of the Boston Centre. Later she would don heavy protective clothes to handle without fear the thousands of bees kept in the Ashrama hives. Lastly among the nuns, Sister Shanta, formerly from Louisville, joined the Swami's household in 1921, moved to the Ashrama, but returned to Boston permanently in 1928, serving as the general manager, treasurer, shopper and cook for the Vedanta Centre there until her death in 1950, with only a lay brother to help her. A steady, silent, self-sufficient person, she endured a long exile so as to have the privilege of unusually close contact with the Swami during his Boston stays.

63. *Ibid.,* XLI (July, 1952), 142–51, reprinting a talk given by Devamata before 1923; and *ibid.,* XXXVII (July, 1948), 180.

64. These impressions of other community members and descriptions of their group life come from Daya's memoirs and from other memorial articles in *Message of the East* and from an untitled manuscript by Daya, Jones Papers, Box 35.

These were the eight women who took monastic vows from the Swami.[65] Of them, only two appear ever to have traveled to India, despite their adoption in America of a largely Hindu life style. Collectively, their steadfastness is remarkable. Their fidelity to the Swami created a household which, after more than sixty years, is still in existence. Yet the Ashrama community was larger than they, containing quite a few people of both sexes who desired to become more or less permanent resident members, but in a lay status.

Most prominent among these was Katharine F. Sherwood, in whose home at Milton the nucleus of a communal life had first begun. For five years Miss Sherwood chose to close down her own house (except for infrequent visits) and live instead at the Boston Vedanta Centre. Like Devamata, she had an essentially motherly relationship to the Swami; indeed, Paramananda called her "Mai," or "mother." A cosmopolitan, hospitable New Englander, she retained perhaps too great an independence to want to take vows like the others, though she never married. She is described as enormously vital in body and mind, with a zest for life, a "keen and sparkling humor and a delightful way of reciting stories." In 1937 she finally decided to move to La Crescenta but did so in an unusual fashion, building a home of her own on the Ashrama grounds with the Swami's blessing.

A recurrent phenomenon in Paramananda's communities, both in Massachusetts and California, was the appearance of a succession of lay brothers who willingly lived at the Ashrama or the Centre, helped with the construction work, and generally functioned as handymen-retainers for the largely female population. A former Austrian peasant maintained the gardens at La Crescenta for many years. A slight man with a short, pointed beard, he had little formal education but a great love of information and philosophy. He had once been married and was smiling and good-humored. By contrast another lay brother was a gruff, taciturn bachelor who maintained the animals. The two men were often at odds. A third such man, the nephew of Sister Satya Prana, could build anything from a kitchen cupboard to a large handloom. Forever busy, he whistled every day while absorbed in his tasks. He demonstrated his independence by always leaving the Ashrama on weekends, never once attending a religious service there. Another older man who arrived later had a warm, sunny disposition, never showing irritation; he too worked constantly and was a great lover of chil-

65. Another monastic disciple, Sister Mangala, come to the Ashrama at its opening but left it fairly soon afterward to live with her mother. The one man who took vows also appears to have dropped out early.

dren. From time to time, several other men lived in the community. One of them, a Ukrainian, used to sing songs in Russian at many of the services in the late 1920's. Another was a Hindu student temporarily in the United States. At least one married couple lived on the Ashrama grounds, apparently practicing celibacy.

Long-term women residents who also took no vows performed a variety of functions. One elderly woman spent most of her time taking care of Sister Devamata in her last years. Another, a graduate of nursing at Johns Hopkins and a very forthright personality, often helped Sister Achala preparing the meals. Still another down-to-earth kitchen worker was remembered as someone who could be a bit bossy, though she labored tirelessly. A second trained nurse, with a deep Boston accent, spent much of her time away from the Ashrama on cases. A gentle, somewhat sentimental Polish woman lived at the Ashrama, as did another unmarried person described as idealistic but somewhat aloof. Yet another older woman who lived there was said to take life very seriously, meditating much and saying little. While the talk flew at the community table, on all subjects from motor cars to spiritual illumination, she would merely sit listening watchfully. A final staunch helper had an artistic bent, painting miniatures. Though shy and self-conscious, she was recalled as lovable underneath.

After 1926, the resident population further included several of Paramananda's younger relatives, whom he brought back from India. The most important of these was his niece, Gayatri Devi, then a young girl and now the head of the surviving organization. She is an extraordinarily winning person who has since gathered a number of devotees of her own, and these comprise the present-day monastic population. Other younger sisters and cousins came more briefly, singing Hindu songs on public occasions and adding a note of exuberance to Ashrama life as a result of what Daya called "their endearing, sometimes maddening, ways."

In still another category were a bevy of nearby nonresident friends and followers of the Swami, some of whom moved to the town of La Crescenta from the Boston area so that they might remain near him.[66] Because such families often spent long hours at the Ashrama, contributing their labor to its maintenance, children's voices were not unknown on the property.

The daily routine for the resident group began early. Paramananda himself generally rose before dawn. At the household shrine the Swami would conduct the morning worship, which always followed a simple form including prayers and at least one song. (It was not a meditation period.)

66. It is especially remarkable that they did so in view of the fact that the Swami continued to spend a large fraction of his time in Boston.

Two of these services were held at the shrine daily, in the morning and again in the evening. No one was permitted to be absent from either of them for trivial reasons; even an ill person, unless absolutely bedridden, was urged to attend. This expectation effectively prevented members of the community from casually accepting invitations to dinner or for overnight visits away from the Ashrama, although exceptions might be granted for special reasons.

During the day, community members usually saw little of the Swami. To be sure, each devotee had a regular weekly private interview with him. But for the most part he was either busy in his study, working on the monthly magazine and dictating letters, or else he was out in the larger world. Sometimes the community would be invited to share afternoon tea with him. Meanwhile, the sisters engaged in numerous tasks connected with maintaining the Ashrama or else in arts and crafts.

Meals, commonly vegetarian, were simple but tasteful. There would be general conversation, sometimes with questions and answers from the Swami. In the evenings, the Swami usually spent his time with the community, although one or two nights a week there would be a public class or service. Sometimes, especially in the early days in Boston, the Swami would read aloud to the group, or there might be "simple games" for relaxation. Again, some nights the Swami would lead them in group meditations, "which forever abide in remembrance, like . . . great music." These almost always ended "with holy songs—songs of India, in the Bengali—sung by the Swami, while interwoven with these were the ancient Sanskrit chants, deep, sonorous. . . . The Swami's voice was rich and round—a golden voice with a full sustained quality." Before the evening gathering ended, the Swami might reappear wearing "long black tights and athletic trunks," in order to perform Yoga exercises. After this he might give an informal bedtime talk, often a very serious exhortation.

Then each member would retire to her chamber, where she maintained a private shrine, "always kept fresh and clean, with holy pictures and favorite holy books, vigil light and incense holder. Before this altar a meditation was supposed to be held or a prayer said before the eyes were closed in slumber." The prayer ended with these words: "Humility, obedience, love, tolerance, peace, to these we consecrate our lives."

The private side of Ashrama life contained moments of relaxation and gaiety. During hot weather, both in Boston and California, the Swami would fill his car with as many sisters as it could possibly contain and they would all go to the nearest beach for a swim. Or he would take them on rides through the countryside. The Swami's love of kite flying was only one instance of his zestful impulsiveness. He had a tendency to throw himself into such other passing fads as "the Egyptian craze," which hit America around 1922, briefly garbing himself in sheik-like costumes within the privacy of the Centre. Or he might suddenly appear dressed as Hamlet or as a French chef.[67] The Swami deliberately insisted upon cheerfulness and good spirits. He once told the group, in a bedtime talk, that he would not allow "a depressed person" to stay near him; everyone must rise above such a tendency.

And yet these "merry" episodes, which so often were connected with the Swami's childlike impulses, must have amounted to brief lightning flashes in an otherwise somber sky. Arriving community members, according to Sister Daya, "were made to feel that boisterousness, familiarity, loud speech, vulgarity in any form, and all habits closely associated with a purely worldly viewpoint were not in keeping with the fragrant [*sic*] atmosphere of the Vedanta Centre." The tone must be one of sanctity, and this, "so the Swami taught, must always include gracious manners, reverence expressed for one's fellow beings, especially for those to whom respect is due."[68]

Moreover, a whole series of minor rules and practices were enforced, many of them designed to maintain an unusually high standard of cleanliness. Food must be prepared in a certain way, household tasks must be done just so, temple offerings must be prepared in an exact manner. Not only were shoes to be removed when entering any shrine (in the accustomed Hindu manner), but the shoes, placed on the floor, must never point toward the shrine. Nor must feet or legs be thrust conspicuously toward any object of deference, such as the teacher himself. When a member returned to the household after performing an errand in the outside world, the Swami would often require her to put on fresh clothes at once. He commanded that the sisters' rooms be kept immaculate. They were to sit in an upright posture at all times, not lounging about languidly.

The rationale for so much stress upon cleanliness was said to be the existence of *"Tanmatras,* or subtle elements of matter"; that is, in Western language, vibrations. A clean atmosphere was necessary in order to produce these good vibrations. The result was that "a newcomer to the Centre often had her ears assailed by the command, 'Wash your hands! You have

67. *Message of the East,* XXXV (April, 1946), 114; XXXVI (January, 1947), 44–46; XXXVIII (July, 1949), 185–86; Sister Daya to her mother, May 27, 1921, June 7, 1921, September 21, 1922, September 9, 1929, Jones Papers; Devamata, *Paramananda,* I, 305–307.
68. *Message of the East,* XXXVII (July, 1948), 175.

just touched the floor so you must not handle that book (or that food, or whatever it might be) till you have washed them.' At first this would be confusing and discouraging, sometimes irritating; but it was surprising how soon these ways became entirely normal and spontaneous."[69] Meticulousness was demanded in yet other respects: when cooking, no food must be wasted, not even a single grain of rice. Life at the Ashrama thus demanded the acceptance of a rigid discipline even in the most automatic daily actions.

And, if there were moments of unusual levity, these were balanced by others of collective inwardness. Labor Day of 1933, for instance, witnessed a four-hour period of silence at the Ashrama, after the sounding of a gong at nine o'clock. Some sixty-five people were on hand for the occasion, sitting outdoors facing the Swami, on chairs or on the ground. Again in 1936, April 28 was set aside by Paramananda as a day of silence and prayer. "At 3 P.M. the Swami began the non-speaking period with a beautiful Service. For the next three hours the entire Ashrama remained wrapped in quietude. At intervals only, the Swami broke the silence with practical instructions. At the close, all were invited to attend the household evening worship—a rare privilege, as ordinarily it is only for the resident members. Soon after, a feast was served and the day ended in friendly intercourse."[70]

There was, needless to say, a purely physical side to the community's existence. This involved first of all the frequent, intensive housecleanings which the Swami's standards of sanctity required, the preparation of meals and the marketings. (In Boston, weekly trips were made to the Italian section to buy vegetables, which were cheaper and better there, Daya or Seva piloting the Swami's huge automobile up the narrow streets.) Beyond this, crafts were as definite a part of the Ashrama life style as they would later become in hip communes. For a time the group owned a press and prepared the magazine itself; this was finally given up as too arduous. In La Crescenta, a whole array of "creative" projects burgeoned. When the Temple of the Universal Spirit opened, it was noted that one member had decorated the walls, another the woodwork; still another had installed the lighting fixtures; another had woven the curtain at the rear; and yet another had composed an anthem, which was sung at the first service. Vegetable gardens were immediately planted, and livestock at one time totaled nine goats, two cows, and a donkey. The community probably drank goats' milk for a while, but the animal population appears soon to have declined. An orchard, planted by the previous owner of the property,

69. *Ibid.*, pp. 176, 181–83; XXXVII (October, 1948), 248; XXXVIII (April, 1949), 116–22.
70. *Ibid.*, XXII (October, 1933), 254; XXV (May, 1936), 156.

bore peaches, apricots, pears, and walnuts. In the California setting, all this meant constant irrigation, the digging of compost pits, the clearing of underbrush and the building of stone retaining walls. In one brief period, nearly 150 young trees were planted, many by the Swami himself.

Some of this activity was stimulated by a fairly serious attempt to raise money and become more economically self-sufficient. (All the Vedanta swamis have depended upon gifts from the members of their congregations to survive.)[71] A major activity was incense making. "Under the Swami's guidance, sweet smelling herbs were gathered from the Ashrama hills. These were ground with various Indian spices and then moulded, much as they made the incense sticks in the Indian monasteries. These with hand-illumined book marks, pretty book covers, picture post cards with views of the Ashrama, are giving the Ashrama workers ample opportunity for artistic expression." In the 1930's weaving came into fashion. Bazaars were held, featuring honey from the abundant Ashrama beehives, knitted garments, brightly colored hand-woven scarves, copper and pewter bowls, butter and eggs, oranges and lemons, as well as incense and hand-illumined cards.[72] The prices for these articles as announced in the magazine were extremely high. (Perhaps it was believed that their products were worth a good sum because they had been made by consecrated labor and carried a high vibration. But in the depression decade they strikingly reveal the well-to-do social basis of the movement.) Much of this activity ground to a halt soon after the Swami's death in 1940. For this reason, one suspects that, like so much else in the Ashrama pattern of life, the arts and crafts existed largely because of the Swami's personal wish to have them. But by then the sisters were growing older too.

Although group living was a secondary consideration in the minds of the devotees, the Swami would speak of the community as a distinct ideal in its own right. To live in one, he said in a bedtime talk to the household, was "the greatest blessing, even though sometimes it may seem a discipline. We learn in a community to do things for one another."[73] As in all communal endeavors, Ashrama life required the constant sacrificing of individual impulses, which were regarded as unwholesome manifestations of

71. *Ibid.*, XII (December, 1923), 240, thus mentions "a love-offering to the Swami, —a surprise check enclosed in a charming silk case,—which was given to him in the name of many devoted followers." In 1928 an "Association of Friends" of the Swami was formed, "the dues of which will be elastic to suit the resources of the contributor." *Ibid.*, XVII (December, 1928), 320. The Swami seems never to have had to curtail his travels or other activities because of lack of funds.

72. *Ibid.*, XIV (February, 1925), 48; XXXIX (October, 1940), 256; XL (April, 1951), 116; Sister Daya to her mother, June 15, 1930, Jones Papers.

73. *Message of the East*, XXXVII (October, 1948), 251.

"ego." Thus, as Daya noted, "often deep inner desires to do some special form of service had to be put aside in order to care for the common welfare." Sister Lillian, the trained nurse, spent much of her time washing pots and pans. Daya herself complained that, whenever she thought she might be free for a few hours, either a picnic would suddenly be planned or visitors would arrive, and she would feel the need to fit in gracefully with the rhythm so as not to stand apart.[74] Sometimes the group ideal was stated more indulgently as that of "a spiritual family living together and evolving their specific gifts through divergent lines of art, industry, music, literary work and spiritual inspiration."[75] As in nearly all communities, a certain front had to be maintained. The Swami told them that "community spirit" required them to hide any internal differences from the gaze of outsiders. In much the same vein he exhorted the sisters: "Be careful, be courageous, be happy, be staunch. . . . We should be as fresh and fragrant as flowers, full of helpfulness and love. That is the spirit we must try to hold."[76]

There is no doubt that a remarkable solidarity of feeling was fostered at the Ashrama over the years; the very low dropout rate within the inner circle, especially when juxtaposed against the disappointingly fickle Sunday congregations, must have created a strong mood of group loyalty. So did collective sacrifice and endurance at moments of extreme hardship—during the fire and flood.[77]

And yet, while these things were true on one level, disruptive impulses could also reach the surface. Sister Daya's notebook for December 15, 1919, recorded, for instance, that it had been "an off day for most of the household. One was in tears, another was a bit temperish, and I was decidedly off color." That night the Swami had to teach them an especially beautiful mantram to help them surmount their feelings.[78] The immensely powerful bond between the Swami and each devotee operated not to rein-

74. Sister Daya to her mother, August 18, 1928, Jones Papers. This kind of pressure seems nearly identical at hip communes such as Rockridge.

75. *Message of the East*, XX (May, 1931), 159. "It is at once a wholesome, mutually helpful community and a family, bound by spiritual ties." *Ibid.*, XIII (June, 1924), 141.

76. *Ibid.*, XL (October, 1951), 239; XXXV (April, 1946), 120.

77. "I could write another volume about the women workers [during the fire]. Seva was a marvel of strength and fearlessness; Achala was full of efficiency and quick thoughtfulness; Gayatri was calm, brave and cheerful; Hilda was a real heroine, full of initiative and resourcefulness; Amala, Jessie and Alice showed the loveliest possible spirit of service, patience and endurance. The whole family was so gentle and loving with one another. I can never forget it. A new nobility and mellowness was born in every character." Devamata to the Swami, November 25, 1933, quoted *ibid.*, XXII (December, 1933), 309.

78. Quoted *ibid.*, XXXVI (October, 1947), 245.

force community sentiment, except insofar as it encouraged submission to the Swami's will. If anything it operated in a divisive way, to work against that very sense of solidarity. At bottom each follower wanted to maintain an exclusive link with the Swami even though this could never be openly admitted.[79]

Paramananda once frankly told his household: "You wound me when you talk against one another. Everyone here, those with few defects and those with many, are equally a part of me."[80] The constant danger, built into the very warp of an undertaking where all worshiped the same teacher, was mutual jealousy. How easy it was, Sister Daya wrote in her private notebook in 1920, for this community to slip down into a "mean struggle for favors, a comparing of benefits received [from the Swami]. We wound each other in a rivalry to serve."[81] Apparently these jealousies were sometimes widespread among the sisters. "There were few indeed of the community," Daya wrote, by no means excluding herself, "who had not at one time or another gone through this dark valley, who had not said: 'Why does Swami discipline that one' or 'Why does Swami not discipline this one?' "[82] In truth, the only sure remedy for such a source of discord was to lessen the intensity of the charismatic bond, but this was the last thing desired by any of the sisters.

In this highly difficult situation, Paramananda, for all his childlike enthusiasms, functioned as a skillful leader. He told the sisters that they must give up "egotism" in order to "remove all torment, all depression, all anger from your hearts." He urged them to regard any of the other members whom they saw "going through a struggle" not with criticism but with full sympathy and help. Meanwhile, rather than imposing standard rules upon everyone in a rigid way, he urged each devotee to formulate her own. "We should [each] have a schedule. . . . We should memorize verses, memorize them each day. If we fill our mind with thoughts like these there will be no room for anything lower."[83] Moreover, he commanded them, in extremely straightforward language, to be humble: "There are some people who have to teach. It is given to them to do. . . . But do not ever want to be a teacher! Never desire to assert your voice. . . . Criticize nothing; demand nothing; find fault with nothing. Those are not our concerns at all. We are just children, doing the way we are made to do; staying wherever

---

79. Note the same tendency in Ezra's group, Chapter Five.
80. *Message of the East*, XL (October, 1951), 243.
81. Quoted *ibid.*, XXXV (July, 1946), 170.
82. *Ibid.*, XXXVI (January, 1947), 52; cf. *ibid.*, XXXVII (October, 1948), 250.
83. Quoted *ibid.*, XXXVI (October, 1947), 246–47. There is an echo here of the Catholic use of the Rosary.

we are placed. We have nothing to complain of. If we have a complaining heart we suffer."[84]

Paramananda did not hesitate to crack the disciplinary whip. "The law of true discipleship is obedience," he was heard to tell the sisters. "If you receive an order from the Guru, obey it at once and question afterwards."[85] A sister tempted to nap on a rainy day was told by him that this was not permissible. When a sister failed to make her bed before afternoon, he reprimanded her, even though he knew she had been extremely busy. There must be, he said, "no carelessness in the spiritual life." Again, when someone inadvertently turned her back on him when leaving the room, he admonished her for failing to show the Hindu courtesy of never exiting in that fashion from a teacher.[86] He could use military metaphors in his exhortations, asking the sisters to stand guard over the shrines like brave soldiers, and saying the community "is not for the weakling." Yet hardly ever did he need to resort to open coercion, so great was his hold upon his following. Thus he could maintain, "I am a great believer in freedom. . . . There must be order and system but as much freedom as possible." At the same time he could effectively tighten his grip upon the members merely by declaring to them: "I must have workers that can endure. . . . The workers can sustain me or hinder me in the work. If they lack in discrimination or act unwisely they can undo, to some extent at least, what I am trying to do. . . . They must feel it a sacred trust to be members of a spiritual household." He summed up his disciplinary ideal and also the degree of control he had achieved over his terrain when he said: "I want workers who will do everything spontaneously and with fervor of spirit."[87] In practice, his techniques of control seldom involved open rebukes or condemnations of behavior. Sometimes he relied upon mimicry, for instance to correct casual shortcomings. "His mimicry, however, is so intermingled with loving-kindness that it does not wound," Devamata insisted. And, despite all the instances of apparent harshness which she openly recounted, Sister Daya asserted that Paramananda was "like an indulgent parent" and that his followers often took advantage of his propensities toward loving forgiveness.[88]

Doubtless the ratio of love to sternness in the Swami's makeup would

84. Stenographic transcript of talk to the community in 1920, quoted *ibid.*, XXXVII (October, 1948), 249; cf. *ibid.*, XXXVIII (July, 1949), 183.

85. *Ibid.*, XXXIV (July, 1945), 148.

86. *Ibid.*, XXXVIII (April, 1949), 115, 117; XLI (January, 1952), 46–47; XXXVII (July, 1948), 183.

87. Devamata, *Paramananda*, I, 328–31.

88. *Ibid.*, I, 319; *Message of the East*, XXXVIII (July, 1949), 183; XLI (January, 1952), 46.

vary somewhat as beheld by differently placed observers. Devamata and Daya, themselves scarcely easygoing in temper, took for granted his great aura of authority, considered it natural, and dwelt instead upon his capacity for kindness. But an outsider, weighing the Swami's words and actions, might have tended toward the view that he was a highly effective autocrat.[89] For his part, Paramananda liked to say rather disdainfully that Americans, unlike Indians, had no real capacity for discipline; in his view, the trouble with his followers was that they were too soft.[90] One hint of Paramananda's real role emerges from the fact that he would often have sudden whims about major projects to be started and completed within extremely short periods of time, which demanded long hours of special labor from a substantial work force. (For instance, an elaborate arrangement for a particular Sunday service, requiring much new physical construction.) And he would, in nearly every case, see the tasks completed prior to the deadline he had imposed, while his devotees marveled at the latest "miracle" of this kind. Also revealing of his authoritarianism was a practice, in the Boston days at least, of ending his talks to the members of the household by asking each of them separately in turn: "Is what I say true? You? You?"[91] And in Boston he would stand at the bay window of the Vedanta Centre in the late afternoon, looking into the street for any members of the household who might be returning from outside errands. "His solicitude for each and every one—like a mother's brooding love— seemed symbolized in that not infrequent vigil."[92] Such window pacing was bound to create anxiety in the mind of the follower, making her less likely to linger on her way home. But to say that the Swami promoted an atmosphere of fear would be to put the matter too strongly, for there is no doubt of his basically pleasant nature, or of his common sense.

Paramananda's firm leadership helped to sustain what may well have been the stablest, most long-lived communitarian venture founded during the twentieth century in the United States. Important in creating this longevity was the evident desire of the sisters, remarkable for its unchanging quality, to submit obediently to discipline, to go on playing the role of the unquestioning follower, over several decades of their lives. This did not prevent them from continuing to indulge in gossip and in personal comparisons, but it did prevent them from ever breaking the group asunder.

89. Daya revealingly admitted, while discussing his disciplinary policies, that Paramananda's sense of humor "was the sugar coating for many a bitter pill." *Ibid.,* p. 48.
90. *Ibid.,* XXXVII (April, 1948), 114–15.
91. *Ibid.,* XXXVII (July, 1948), 184.
92. *Ibid.,* XXXIV (April, 1945), 109.

The whole flavor of the Ananda Ashrama, aside from its Hinduism, may remind one strongly of some of the early religious communities in American history—especially, perhaps, of a group like the Shakers. It may be, therefore, that it has depended for its success upon a personality type no longer often produced. Even these women, in their youth, had commonly been liberal free thinkers, and there was something a shade artificial about the genteel ritualism at La Crescenta. But the bare existence of this Vedanta community over so long a period refutes the notion that such voluntary familial groups always break down rapidly. No one could pretend that for its deepest adherents it was any mere fad.

Though the monastic communities at La Crescenta and Cohasset still survive after more than sixty years, divorced since 1941 from the Ramakrishna Order of India, other Vedanta monastic communities have continued to be founded within the order, again with considerable stability despite very small numbers. The Vedanta group in San Francisco became more active in this direction once again during the 1950's, purchasing a rural ashram at Olema in Marin County. About fifteen monks and nuns live there or next door to the temple building in San Francisco. Still better known, and about equally large, are the Vedanta communities which have grown up under Swami Prabhavananda, Paramananda's younger contemporary, in Southern California. These are located at Hollywood, Santa Barbara, and Trabuco Canyon, near Laguna Beach.[93]

Noticeable among Prabhavananda's monastics is their desire to appear "ordinary," respectable, and noncontroversial. The men deliberately wear western dress rather than robes. They are apparently encouraged to cultivate a hearty manner with outsiders. They seem anxious to convince people that they are merely regular Southern Californians, rejecting pacifism and even denying being vegetarian. Any communitarian implication about their style of living is avoided, perhaps because it seems too "political." (At Trabuco, I was told, "We are not a community, we are simply a monastery," whereas at La Crescenta Gayatri Devi said the exact opposite, "We are not a monastery, we are a community, and want to think of ourselves as somewhat experimental.") Prabhavananda's monastics now emphasize their obedient tie to the Ramakrishna Order. Most of them travel to India sooner or later. Since the Ramakrishna movement there has long been highly organized and centralized, in certain respects Prabhavananda's

93. On the earlier history of Trabuco, see pp. 270–73.

monks and nuns increasingly resemble Roman Catholics. Ritualistic devotion to Sri Ramakrishna, rather than a quest for expansion of individual consciousness, appears to loom large in their lives.[94] In these ways, though the movement survives, it is becoming increasingly less interesting. To a degree, the "normality" may be a deliberate disguise, but such disguises have a tendency, over time, to become more and more the reality.

Encounters Between Swamis and American Seekers

> I am pure spirit—spirit through and through!
> He who would know me must be spirit too.
> Pure love am I and love I bring to birth;
> There's none can measure me with thoughts of earth.
> I am a light, a subtle fragrance! Lo—
> He who would hold me, he must let me go.
> —SISTER DAYA[95]

Here at the Ashram . . . the hills range with the vibrations of a released cosmos, sentient and articulate. Questions answered themselves unvoiced as the reverberations of some great bell returns the echo of its gong. Truth was self-revealing, swift and sure. . . . The memory of that visit is like the chastity of God. . . . Years passed before I found again far out upon the Mohave Desert such a day of suspended thought and life and experienced again this overwhelming realization.

—SISTER SHIVANI[96]

Descriptions of the Vedanta communities do not in themselves reveal all we would like to know about the lives of the devotees as individuals and the reasons for their conversion. The scattered accounts we possess of Vedantists' personal backgrounds remind us initially of the great diversity of external situations, even among well-to-do women, which have brought them to form such a commitment.[97] The note of personal crisis is explicitly struck quite often, but not always.[98] Parental patterns appear to have varied greatly as well. In at least two cases, there are now second-

94. A very full description of the life style at the present-day monasteries directed by Swami Prabhavananda is given in *Vedanta and the West* (Hollywood), No. 120 (July-August, 1956). Today, about 10 per cent of all the monastics in the Ramakrishna Order are Westerners.

95. *Message of the East*, XXI (December, 1932), 318.

96. Shivani, *op. cit.*, pp. 154–55.

97. A variety of autobiographical accounts by Vedantists are in John Yale, ed., *What Vedanta Means to Me*, and there is much scattered information of this kind in Swami Chidatmananda, *op. cit.*, and in Jackson, *op. cit.*

98. These crises, which so often appear in the biographies, should of course not be confused with mental illness. Persons of highly visible abnormality would not have been able to find acceptance in Vedanta. "In all who came close to him

generation Vedantists. No doubt any generalizations about a "seeker" mentality would fail to comprehend a fair proportion of these individuals.

And yet they were all attracted, in one way or another, to Vedanta, which as we have seen is a movement apparently carrying far more definite psychological overtones than, say, anarchism or socialism. Its teaching is hostile to the worldliness and permissive sexuality of the larger culture. It demands lifelong obedience and subordination of a highly unusual kind. Earlier several general explanations for adherence to Vedanta in the early years of the twentieth century were advanced. The challenge now is to link them to specific biographical detail.

A study of the lives of two women who became prominent in the movement will reveal some of the contrasts in background and temperament which could exist within it, while also showing how each of them in her own way developed the restless hunger for "truth" which characterizes the unorthodox seeker. Sister Daya was, after Devamata, Paramananda's chief American-born lieutenant. Sister Shivani, an ardent disciple of Swami Abhedananda during the days of the West Cornwall community, demonstrated the outermost limits of independence of mind within the ranks of the faithful. In the 1920's, these two women became acquainted with each other, but so different were they that little love was lost between them.

The story of Sister Daya's family and early life deserves careful attention, for it offers the fullest available account of the circumstances which led up to a conversion to Vedanta. It also opens a window on an intriguingly complex segment of American upper-class existence during the early decades of industrialization. One wonders how many families in the United States were at all like the remarkable Joneses.

Georgina Jones, the future Daya, was probably born in 1883, her father's youngest child, the issue of a second marriage when he was over fifty. Her father was John Percival Jones, United States Senator from Nevada for an uninterrupted thirty years ending in 1903. Jones, brought to America from England in his infancy, had taken part in the gold rush of 1849. Remaining in the West, he jumped into politics, gaining the Republican nomination for Lieutenant-Governor of California in 1867. When the ticket was defeated, he moved to Nevada as superintendent and part owner of silver mines in the Comstock Lode. This investment suddenly made him a millionaire. In a hotly contested election in the Nevada legislature, during which money was freely spent, Jones was sent to Washington. There he became closely

---

[Paramananda], he demanded normalcy. 'Don't let us have any queer ones,' he would say." *Message of the East*, XXXV (January, 1946), 39.

allied with Roscoe Conkling and dined often in the White House with Ulysses S. Grant. Jones said little on the Senate floor, but he was a man of commanding appearance, and he defended the silver interests of Nevada so energetically that he had scant trouble being re-elected, at least until the 1890's, when his notorious absenteeism from his "home" state began to be widely resented by his constituents. Years before, Jones had purchased a ranch which is the present site of Santa Monica, California, and there, in a mansion called Miramar overlooking the sea, he usually chose to live when not in Washington. At Miramar he gathered around him all the members of an extended family and presided over them (many months of the year by letter) like a kind of patriarch. Meanwhile, generosity and bad investments had lost him most of his fortune. Determined at any cost to rebuild it, he used his official influence in an unsuccessful effort to have the Los Angeles harbor built at Santa Monica (where his own real-estate holdings would rise in value) rather than at San Pedro. Thus, like many senators of the day, he drew no firm line between his family's interest and that of the public.[99] The unsuccessful harbor fight dragged on for years while Georgina was a teenager. The family fortune continued to ebb. The Senator's only son among his four children, Roy, drove himself toward nervous collapse in the effort to save its last remnants during the 1920's and 1930's. Bitterness and worry over declining finances must have been a constant theme in the Jones household during all the years when Georgina was growing up. Anxiety was compounded by loneliness—both for the wife and the daughters—during Jones's repeated absences three thousand miles away. Their world seemed to be in real danger of sinking. First in Theosophy and then in Vedanta, Georgina would find an absolutely steady rock.

For someone so agreeable to Conkling and Grant, Jones had certain views and interests which were surprisingly wide-ranging. For one thing, Jones proudly wrote poetry, even if it was only doggerel. For another, he could privately show genuine sympathy for the striking railroad workers

99. There is no good life of Senator Jones. I have read the abundant letters between all the members of his family in the two separate collections of Jones Papers, at the Huntington Library and in the Department of Special Collections, University of California Library, Los Angeles. (Unless UCLA is specifically mentioned in the note citations, they refer to the Huntington collection.) In addition, see David J. Rothman, *Politics and Power: The United States Senate, 1869–1901* (Cambridge, Massachusetts: Harvard University Press, 1966), pp. 28, 148, 153, 169, 211; [Myron Angel, ed.] *Thompson and West's History of Nevada, 1881* (Berkeley, California: Howell-North, 1958), pp. 92, 592; Gilbert Ostrander, *Nevada, the Great Rotten Borough, 1859–1964* (New York: Alfred A. Knopf, 1966), pp. 69–70, 104–105; Mary Ellen Glass, *Silver and Politics in Nevada, 1892–1902* (Reno: University of Nevada Press, 1969), pp. 17, 78–79, 117–18, 201; Wells Drury, *An Editor on the Comstock Lode* (New York: Farrar & Rinehart, 1936), pp. 270–71.

(and for the problems of the poor in general) in 1877.[100] Interestingly, he sent his wife a copy of Sir Edwin Arnold's *The Light of Asia,* the fictional treatment of Buddhism, urging her especially to read it.[101] Jones also had moods when he suddenly withdrew from crowds and social obligations, insisting upon solitude.[102] His religious position was unusual for an American politician; he was an agnostic. (Here his Nevada constituency no doubt gave him a special degree of freedom.)

In his second wife, Georgina Sullivan, Jones had found a highly cultivated, cosmopolitan, liberal-minded woman. The daughter of a federal official in San Francisco, she had studied in France and acquired all the tastes that usually went with good breeding—active interests in music, theater, literature, and art, the enjoyment of travel to the major cities of the world; and, most of all, a keen awareness when anything was gaudy, vulgar, or overdone. (Thus she liked to stay in small, quiet, elegant hotels.) An acquaintance, seeing her face at the close of her life, exclaimed, "She looks like a cross between a medieval saint and the Queen of England."[103] Highly practical in her own way—she was always urging her husband to retire from the Senate and devote himself entirely to business—she was also the kind of woman who would earnestly read the novels of Meredith, personally give French lessons to her children, and really pay attention to the operas they saw. Later she knowledgeably conducted two of her daughters (including Georgina) on a year's tour of Europe. Altogether she was a humane and clear-headed woman, equally an agnostic with her husband in religious matters, and capable of remarking in an aside, "for what can be better than love and beauty?"[104] She was an active supporter of woman suffrage and was the author, in March, 1899, of a deeply felt poem criticizing the American role in suppressing the Philippine insurrection.[105]

Into this family Georgina was born. When she was an infant, an illness nearly claimed her life; it took her several months to recover.[106] Later she became a self-contained, imaginative child. Her mother would often find her "dreaming or composing. At such times she would say, 'Please don't

100. John Percival Jones to his wife, July 24, 1877, Jones Papers.
101. Jones to his wife, February, 23, 1880.
102. Jones to his wife, September, 15, 1879.
103. *Message of the East,* XLIV (October, 1955), 212.
104. Georgina Sullivan Jones to her husband, February, 4, 1892, Jones Papers, UCLA.
105. Georgina Sullivan Jones, "The White Man's Burden," Jones Papers, Box 35. She had also been opposed to jingoism at the time of the Chilean naval incident of 1892.
106. Georgina Sullivan Jones to her husband, October, 19, October, 21, 1883.

disturb me. I am writing poetry.' "[107] This self-sufficiency may have signaled that underneath she was already lonely, despite the large family around her, perhaps as a result of her elderly father's long absences. She relished her books of fairy tales, clung to them, refused to throw them away.[108] Still later she became, by every indication, an extremely dutiful child, grinding out formal letters daily to her father even when she had little to say. From her mother she was learning an articulate command over matters both social and intellectual, and she was imbibing a rather profound sense of distance from the common people.[109] For certain periods she was sent off to boarding schools.[110] The whole family traveled constantly, often separately. Across the miles, when she was about fourteen, she revealed to the distant Senator her bitter disappointment in learning that he would remain away from them that summer.[111] Though a great many of Georgina's youthful letters were happy-sounding, full of excitement over daily incidents and activities, this kind of ache, compounded of moves, separations, and never-ending fear of declining fortune, must have lain in the back of her mind. On top of all else, at least twice she nearly lost her mother owing to illness.[112] Openly she would mention her loneliness when her mother and both sisters were absent; she would then bring a friend home from boarding school every weekend for company. She also developed a strong aversion to discord; it is clear that for some reason she had a special loathing for rivalries and fights.[113] Underneath a good deal of surface gaiety, she had to look about rather deliberately for "interests"—tennis tournaments, society dances, and, later on, singing lessons. There is no mention of boy friends in her letters as a young woman. On the other hand she was already listening keenly to stories about reincarnation.[114]

107. *Message of the East*, XLIV (October, 1955), 224; see also the anecdote on p. 207.
108. *Ibid.*, XXI (February, 1932), 49–50.
109. See Georgina Jones to her father, February 4, 1896, Jones Papers, also her letters to her father during 1892, and her mother to her father, January 28, 1892, January 30, 1892, Jones Papers, UCLA.
110. Georgina's home and her older sister Marion are described by her classmate at the Marlborough School in Los Angeles, Lucy Sprague Mitchell, *Two Lives* (New York: Simon and Schuster, 1953), pp. 112–14, who said that in the Miramar mansion "lived so many relatives that it was hard for me to keep track of them . . . four families besides her own, ranging over three generations . . . [a] complex family, with their casual and independent ways."
111. Georgina Jones to her father, [July 17, 1900], Jones Papers.
112. Her mother to her father, February 23, 1892, Jones Papers, UCLA; Georgina Jones to her mother, December 19, 1901, Jones Papers.
113. See Georgina Jones to her sister Marion, n.d.
114. *Message of the East*, XLIV (January, 1955), 35–36.

Though she had been a diligent student at school, she did not go to college. Instead she spent the year 1899–1900 living in Europe with her mother, an experience which made her homesick. In 1902 she moved to New York, still with her mother, and began working in a college settlement house on Rivington Street, an interlude which she described with rather matter-of-fact detachment.[115] As she stayed on in New York, her friends increasingly became musicians and artists. One unknown young man, whom she helped support and often invited to dinner, was Pablo Casals.[116] In 1908 she wrote a comic opera in collaboration with an Englishman. It was a project she took very seriously, and its rejection must have greatly disappointed her.[117] She also tried to sell poetry to the magazines.

During the summer of 1904, when she was in her early twenties, an illness affected her right kidney which made her a semi-invalid for the next sixteen years. Though there were many days during this long siege when she felt quite well, she also had to endure seemingly unending bouts of pain.[118] At one point she was operated upon unsuccessfully, and the operation nearly took her life.[119] Finally, in 1920, shortly after her conversion to Vedanta, she consulted a doctor in Los Angeles who appears to have treated her with something like radiation therapy. Immediately thereafter the kidney began to return to normal. From that time forward she enjoyed ordinary strength and good health.[120] Since the cure came so soon after her new life in Vedanta had begun, it was natural for her to think that Swami Paramananda's spiritual influence had something to do with it. But her letters show that the malady was by no means psychosomatic, and that a purely physical cure was affected by someone entirely outside the Vedanta movement.[121]

115. Georgina Jones to her father, November 7, 1902, Jones Papers.
116. See Georgina Jones to her sister Marion, March 23, 1902, January 11, 1904.
117. See Georgina Jones to her mother, July 29, 1908, June 7, 1909.
118. "When pain comes," she wrote afterward, "if instead of shrinking from it, throw open all the gates of our body as though we welcomed it; if we cease opposing it with tense nerves and contracted muscles we shall find that it becomes more friendly." *Message of the East,* XII (February, 1923), 37.
119. *Ibid.,* XXXVIII (October, 1949), 242–43. See also Georgina Jones to her mother, September 28, 1904; to her father, January 9, 1905, November 9, 1912; to her mother, October 12, 1917; and her mother to her father, July 11, 1910, December 9, 1910, December 20, 1910, and February 17, 1911, Jones Papers. As late as June, 1904, she was taking long horseback rides through the Santa Monica Mountains, but in September she had to spend four weeks in a hospital. In 1917 she still sometimes had to spend afternoons resting.
120. Sister Daya to her mother, September 5, 1920, May 27, 1921, April 9, 1922, September 22, 1930.
121. I have heard some scholars informally explain adherence to movements such as Vedanta in terms of physical health problems, the suggestion being that an ill person might turn to a swami in desperation, just as he or she might turn to an unortho-

Long before this, just after a second trip to Europe and a particularly severe phase in her illness, she married Robert Walton, an aspiring young lawyer from Michigan. Soon they moved to California to live. They remained together for about five years before peacefully separating. He shared her own growing interest in Eastern philosophy, and indeed they may have met in Theosophical circles. After their marriage came to an end, they remained on friendly terms. Her letters reveal nothing about why the union did not last.

What mattered most to her by this time was her rapidly deepening commitment to Theosophy. She had long been receptive to the occult; a teenage letter to her sister casually mentions a horoscope that she had constructed, and by 1904 she was a firm believer in reincarnation.[122] But these interests only began to dominate her life, paradoxically, after her marriage. In 1912, as a newlywed still living in New York, she was playing an active role in the Theosophical Society, hearing Claude Bragdon lecture, and gaining a private interview with the head of the Bahai movement. At the same time, she became noticeably more democratic, a shade less genteel, in her attitude toward other people.[123] In all this one may perhaps detect the influence of the musical and artistic circles in which she was then moving. She had entered a milieu several degrees more conservative than Mabel Dodge Luhan's, but not entirely unlike it or unconnected with it. Political crusades also engaged her attention at times. Unable to march in a suffragette parade because of her illness, she cheered it militantly in her imagination. But what claimed her most was the unworldly point of view, which added a distinctly new note to her letters after 1912. Five years later, all her news and gossip was of Theosophical people, though they still often had artistic or musical connections.

In 1917 she went to live at Krotona, the Theosophical community then located in the Hollywood hills. Life at Krotona had a distinctly communitarian flavor, though people made their own living arrangements. A continual round of lectures, plays, concerts, and forums brought everyone together, as did the high-pitched atmosphere of occult mysteries, vegetarian diets, and personal chatter.[124]

---

dox medical expert. Superficially the illness of Sister Daya might seem to bear out such an interpretation of her conversion. Yet I do not find this explanation convincing as more than an occasional added factor in these life histories. Profound spiritual and intellectual crises, such as Daya was to experience, cannot so neatly be reduced to a purely physical cause.

122. Georgina Jones to her sister Marion, n.d.; to her mother, January 11, 1904.
123. See Georgina Jones Walton to her father, November 9, 1912.
124. The name was borrowed from the Pythagorean community in ancient Italy. For a vivid portrait of the Krotona community in Hollywood, see the novel by Jane

At this time, still very much aware of her family's perpetually declining fortunes, Georgina expressed the belief that in the present period of general world upheaval it was necessary for each individual to learn to survive with minimal dependence upon the larger society.[125] The rather worldly tone of her letters as a girl and young woman had now utterly vanished. She voiced a new dislike for large cities.[126] By contrast, she enjoyed visiting the peaceful Ojai Valley, where she went on milk diets, sunbathed in the nude, and slept outdoors every night on a flat roof.[127] The one-time composer of a comic opera had now turned to nature—and to the pursuit of cosmic consciousness. This basic change in her makeup had been completed well before her first meeting with Swami Paramananda.

At Krotona she fell in with a Burmese girl, later to marry a premier of that country, named Elizabeth Paw Tun. So close were the two of them that the gossipy community called them the "Siamese twins." Lady Paw Tun had already met Swami Paramananda in San Francisco and Cleveland, and in 1919, when it was announced that the Swami was coming to Los Angeles on a speaking tour, she invited Georgina to go with her to his first lecture. For some reason Georgina did not, but Lady Paw Tun came back so impressed that she urged her to return with her the next night. Georgina did so, and this first encounter immediately kindled her deepest interest in the Swami as a person. At the close, the two women went up to have a long talk with him.

Each day thereafter they went to the lectures, and Georgina grew ever more enthusiastic. A dinner was soon arranged where she could meet the Swami in a more intimate fashion; shortly afterward, Georgina invited him to a second dinner.

As she described these occasions many years later, writing in the third person, "her spiritual need was very great and her heart was crying out, crying out, for genuine guidance. . . . She looked forward to the meeting with an eagerness she herself could hardly understand. The few days of waiting seemed endless." At the first dinner, when Paramananda entered the room, "his very presence [was] like a light, conveying the strength and beauty and peace for which her whole being longed." Breathlessly she

---

Levington Comfort, *From These Beginnings* (New York: E. P. Dutton, 1938). See also Alice A. Bailey, *The Unfinished Autobiography* (New York: Lucis Trust, 1951), p. 154, and Georgina Jones Walton to her mother, October 12, 1917, [January 6, 1919], Jones Papers. There would, for instance, be evening debates between spokesmen for Theosophy and psychoanalysis.

125. Georgina Jones Walton to her mother, March 30, 1917, Jones Papers.

126. Georgina Jones Walton to her mother, March 23, 1917, and n.d., ca. 1918.

127. Georgina Jones Walton to her mother, November 22, 1918; *Message of the East,* XVIII (April, 1929), 96–97.

rushed over to him before the others could enter the room, in order to be able to ask him the question which had long been in her mind: " 'Swami, tell me, how does the supreme Vision come?' He looked at her with a certain tender compassion and replied, 'It comes gradually, just like the sunrise.' " A few days later, at the second dinner, the Swami thrilled her by telling some of the intimate details of his life as a young *sannyasin* in India which she had assumed he would be far more reticent about revealing.[128]

Meanwhile, in the house in the hills which she shared with Elizabeth Paw Tun, Georgina Jones Walton began days of restless inner debate, often uttered aloud to her friend, about the relative merits of Theosophy and Vedanta as systems of belief. "And day by day," recalled her housemate, "I saw the great change come into her life. I heard her try to resolve all the problems of her outer life and finally her decision to renounce her present life. . . . Those were precious days to me: when I saw her soul laid bare; when she reached the point that—although it would cause personal suffering which would have to be faced—deep in her soul she knew that she wanted to dedicate the remainder of her life to Vedanta by being a disciple of Swamiji."[129] At this time, she was in her late thirties, the Swami slightly younger.

Though Georgina went through this distinct period of internal hesitation, less than three months passed between her first meeting with Paramananda and her arrival in Boston to join his household at the Vedanta Centre on Queensberry Street. In her mind it was still to be a trial of a year's duration. After that year had passed she went out to Krotona briefly to clear up all her remaining personal affairs and then immediately returned to Boston. Three years later, on a return visit to Los Angeles at the Swami's behest, her own contacts led to the discovery of the La Crescenta property for the future Ananda Ashrama. Meanwhile, the Swami had given her the name of Daya, which means "compassion."[130]

"Meeting one's true teacher," she wrote afterward, "is like beholding a sunrise: it is overwhelming, absolute, not to be denied. It comes with the authenticity of pure beauty, of truth, of love unsullied by the things of this world. There is an element of great destiny in it; for one knows it could not have been otherwise—that it was ordained somehow, somewhere, deep in the beginning of things." Looking at Paramananda, she would be filled "with a strange sense of wonderment. He was different from

128. *Ibid.,* XXXIV (April, 1945), 101–02. For Elizabeth Paw Tun's account of the same episodes, see *ibid.,* L (July, 1961), 145–50.
129. *Ibid.,* XXXIV (April, 1945), 101, 107.
130. In accord with the sound of the long "a" in Sanskrit, it was always pronounced "Doya."

all that she had hitherto seen or known."[131] Was there then nothing in her previous life that might have suggested the possibility of her forming such an intense attachment? Her husband, by all indications, had never played anything like this role for her. Once, indeed, a Buddhist monk who spoke at the Theosophical Society in New York greatly impressed her, and she described him at the time in language not unlike her later writing about Paramananda.[132] This incident, and her close friendship with Elizabeth Paw Tun, revealed how strongly she was attracted to Asian men and women as people. Still, these are slender straws for an explanation. Her conversion to Paramananda as a personal guru was a sudden, spectacular event, scarcely to be anticipated, except in terms of her long-time interest in Eastern ideas.

It was an event which greatly changed the pattern of her life (for even at Krotona she had rented a comfortable house where she could enjoy full privacy). Always used to servants, she would now be asked to share in the menial tasks of maintaining the Vedanta Centre. The first time she was requested to wash the Swami's automobile, in her ignorance she did not even know the chamois was supposed to be moistened. And, when she was told to cook a meal, the results were so poor that the Swami decided she must henceforth be excused from that particular task (instead, she earned the title of champion dishwasher).[133] Her tall figure was now enclosed in a dark blue habit; in later years, she wore a white one, indistinguishable from that of a Catholic nun. Thus humbled and made conspicuous, she was vulnerable in an entirely new way in her everyday contacts. As she remembered how it was, "one had merely to state that one was a follower of a Swami to have a cold silence descend upon a company, or worse still, to invite the unwholesome curiosity of the seekers after the mysterious or forbidden."[134] In the early years, strange rumors even circulated among outsiders about midnight orgies at La Crescenta. Well did Georgina know what she was getting into, in terms of these hostile stereotypes.[135] Hers was in many respects a course of great bravery.

Her mother's first reaction, on learning she had gone off to live with the Swami in Boston, was to rush to her side with two return tickets, clearly aiming to bring her away, in the belief that her daughter had lost her senses. But Daya was unshakable, while all the time protesting her

131. *Ibid.*, XXXIV (April, 1945), 106; XXXV (July, 1946), 165.
132. Georgina Jones Walton to her mother, n.d., Jones Papers.
133. Gayatri Devi, "Sister Daya: An Intimate Picture," *Message of the East*, XLIV (October, 1955), 226; *ibid.*, XXXIV (April, 1945), 110–11.
134. *Ibid.*, XXXVI (October, 1947), 240.
135. See Sister Daya to her mother, September 5, 1920, Jones Papers.

deep, unchanging love for her mother.[136] For about two years after her departure for Boston, Daya's relations with her mother remained difficult. But the family tie proved extraordinarily strong. Her mother visited her at the Boston Centre and met the Swami, at first hesitatingly, then with increasing enthusiasm. By the end of 1922 she was actively promoting the Swami's books in Los Angeles. In later years she visited the Ananda Ashrama frequently, and so did many other of Georgina's relatives.[137]

As early as 1920, Sister Daya could confidently affirm that she was experiencing a supreme inward satisfaction.[138] For the remaining thirty-six years of her life, Daya followed the new course she had chosen with unremitting steadfastness. Once having found her anchor, she never detached herself from it again. This did not mean that she experienced no further difficulties. In her memoirs, she frankly admits how deeply she was at first affected by the problem of jealousy within the household. There are also hints of a certain spiritual pride on her part, which the Swami sought to counter. (Thus she handed him an elaborate horoscope which had been done of her, seeking his opinion of it, and he deliberately paid it no attention.) In a great variety of ways, Paramananda tested her at the beginning. Though he clearly regarded her as an extraordinary find, allowing her to conduct services in his absence and otherwise revealing his high esteem for her, he also made sure that she tasted the humility of her situation. He did not have to be at all harsh in his discipline, for even a rather mild reprimand from him might make her burst into tears, so anxious was she to please him.[139]

Such a regime eventually produced a personality of a type rarely seen in twentieth-century America. In it were mingled the dignity and humility, the vigilance and serenity which in her milieu were taken to be the marks of a genuine saint. She was remembered as "magnetic and regal," a woman of vitality, "by nature free and sociable, gay, with a sparkling sense of humor, a dreamer, a poet, and aesthete, but primarily a devotee, intense in her love of God, Guru, people, animals and all."[140] My own recollection of her, when I was occasionally taken as a young boy to her services, was of the deeply hypnotic quality with which she would intone the customary

136. Sister Daya to her mother, n.d. [1919].

137. A long series of letters from Daya to her mother, in the Jones Papers, records her difficult transition to a new relationship between them. See also Sister Daya to her mother, August 18, 1928, Jones Papers, and *Message of the East*, XXXVI (October, 1947), 241.

138. Sister Daya to her mother, March 9, 1920, Jones Papers.

139. *Message of the East*, XXXV (April, 1946), 109.

140. Anonymous memorial article *ibid.*, XLIV (July, 1955), 192; cf. Gayatri Devi's description of her *ibid.*, XLIV, (October, 1955), 227.

chanted phrase, "peace . . . peace . . . peace," at the closing moment. The measured pauses, the stillness and the authority created an overpowering impression.

Physically tall, full-faced, with high color in her cheeks, she hid her golden hair in long braids beneath her nun's habit. Though extroverted on the surface, her deeper love was for silence and isolation; she felt ill at ease among noisy, unrestrained children. Her love of nature was profound. A nearby caterpillar could distract her from earnest conversation. As a mature woman, arriving on the beach, "she would run to meet the high waves, or spend hours gathering sea shells of many shapes or hues, or pile up multiferous rocks in the trunk of her car and bring them home with the utmost care as if they were her many children. On those occasions she would live in timelessness and often return home late for her scheduled assignment, somewhat rushed and conscience stricken."[141] The Ashrama constantly felt her presence on many levels. She would stick "silly fortunes" into walnut shells or write verses on eucalyptus leaves for place cards at a dinner. Outside this world into which she had retreated, she fared less well. Reviving her earlier ambition as a playwright, she authored a musical based on Edwin Arnold's *The Light of Asia;* it played on Broadway for several weeks in 1928 but was not a success.[142]

A humanitarian in her sympathies, she did not give up political convictions. Passionately longing to help "unfortunates," she preached openly against racism and was an ardent supporter of Gandhi. As early as 1930 she believed in boycotting Mussolini's Italy, and she remained a staunch advocate of both the League and the United Nations. In her own way she was consistently opposed to the militant nationalism of the modern age, a liberal idealist even though she chose to focus most of her energy in another direction.[143]

That direction, the heart of her message, was the "eternal" one of the nearness of the Divine. Her sermons rang eloquent with the mystic's apprehension of the unity lying behind all particulars, and of man's natural inward quest toward it:

141. *Ibid.,* pp. 228–29.

142. See the hostile review of it by Brooks Atkinson in the *New York Times,* October 10, 1928.

143. *Message of the East,* XXXVI (October, 1947), 226; Sister Daya to her mother, August 18, 1928, April 24, 1930, June 15, 1930, October 15, 1933, Jones Papers. In 1933 she actively backed a scheme for world government put forward by such figures as Einstein, Tagore, and Salvador de Madariaga. Sister Daya to Frederick MacMonnies, February 16, 1933, Jones Papers.

The first glint of true vision comes as we begin to sense that in us and through us flows the same river of life that is moving in and through every created thing; that there is nothing outside of that life; and that we are, each one of us, a fractional expression of that infinite beauty and being pouring out into manifestation at every moment of time, at every point in space.

When this realization stirs the heart, it becomes a sort of ecstasy in the blood. . . . In every atom of the body is locked the secret that all men would know. Therefore, who should find it quicker than each man in himself, if he will but plunge into his own depths and strike out into that shoreless sea, in which there can be no drowning or death; only endless existence.[144]

Yet it has ever been hard for mystics to avoid combining this impersonal, universal message with a dependence upon intermediaries who are, like Paramananda, recognizably human. Daya would never have admitted that her choice to live to the hilt the role of disciple in any way beclouded her larger, more ultimate goal of God realization. In her mind, the two loyalties fused into one. Only from a psychological perspective, which to her represented an alien belief system, does her willing subordination to another human being come to seem the most remarkable fact of her existence.

The explicit evidence of her self-imposed bondage is nonetheless striking, to say the least. Proudly she confessed her belief in Guru Bhakti, "pure and selfless devotion to the Guru." By means of this yoga, she explained, "the Guru himself becomes the path which ultimately leads the disciple direct to the heart of God. Any lesser relationship misses the mark and becomes merely academic or personal in the ordinary sense of the word." The teacher is "the dispeller of darkness, as the word itself indicates—*Gu* meaning darkness and *ru* the dispelling of it." The true disciple "lays all that he has and is, even to life itself, at the feet of the *Guru*. Is not one little life a very small thing to give in exchange for God-knowledge?" She even went so far as to speak of an "unbroken guru line" in India, almost like a continuous ordained priesthood, and linked this conception with the seemingly unrelated idea of respect for one's parents. Doubt must be fought as an enemy. "If the mind and the heart of the taught are blocked by distrust of the teacher or untrueness toward him in any form," she admonished herself in the early days in Boston, "the quickening impulse cannot flow and the purpose of the relationship is defeated."[145]

Seemingly beyond question, Daya was in love with Paramananda. In

144. *Message of the East,* XL (January, 1951), 42–43.
145. *Ibid.,* IX (October, 1920), 185–86, 189–90; XXXIV (April, 1945), 106–07; XXXV (July, 1946), 168.

Boston she experienced cycles of elation and anxiety which are the classic symptoms of this state of mind.[146] She felt sustained by the Swami and leaned upon him emotionally. She could hardly bear his frequent departures. His physical form was very important to her. His hand, placed lightly on her for a moment, seemed instantly to heal her.[147] In a crowd, her eyes would remain riveted upon him, heedless of all distractions. When Paramananda once gave her a little box of cough drops, she preserved each one and still had them twenty-seven years later. Long after the Swami's death, thinking herself unobserved, she would lay her head upon the rug where Paramananda had often prayed.[148]

Her situation was thus a highly unusual one, especially when so long sustained. But for her the Swami clearly symbolized an utter purity. Purity had always been a major concern for her, as someone inclined toward perfectionism. As a young girl she had abhorred and perhaps feared anything too rough or vulgar; she had strong desires for neatness, cleanness, and order.[149] Small mistakes would sometimes fill her with inordinate remorse, producing an intense wish to begin over again with a clean slate.[150]

These themes were originally linked with a great need to show dutiful affection to her parents. Her devotion to her mother was especially strong, reflecting itself in ardent poems and dreams which continued even long after she had found the Swami.[151] Her father she also explicitly idealized, although there is a hint that it cost her more effort.[152] On the surface, her parents seem to have been remarkably different from her. They were worldly agnostics. Her mother could write that "belief or *faith* . . . is one of the gifts the fairies who presided at my birth denied me. . . . With me *seeing* is believing, & I might sometimes doubt my own senses if *reason* disapproved."[153] Yet her daughter insisted that "the essence of religion" seemed to be in her parents' atmosphere, "exemplified in their persons.

146. *Ibid.,* XXXVIII (October, 1949), 244–45; XL (October, 1951), 235–36; XXXV (April, 1946), 109–10.
147. *Ibid.,* XLI (April, 1952), 113; XXXV (July, 1946), 173; XXXIV (April, 1945), 105; XXXVIII (October, 1949), 243.
148. *Ibid.,* XLIV (October, 1955), 224, 246; XXXIX (April, 1950), 110–11.
149. See Georgina Jones to her father, August 4, 1895, and to her mother, May 22, 1896, Jones Papers.
150. See *Message of the East,* XXXIV (April, 1945), 101–02.
151. Her annual birthday poems to her mother are in the Jones Papers. See also Sister Daya to her mother, April 29, 1930, June 15, 1930.
152. "My father, too; I don't exclude him. He was magnanimous to a fault. I never heard him say a hateful or a horrid thing against anybody." *Message of the East,* XLIX (July, 1955), 213–14, quoting an autobiographical sermon shortly before her death.
153. Georgina Sullivan Jones to her husband, February 2, 1892, Jones Papers, UCLA.

They did not go to church. . . . But all through my life the exquisiteness, the power to follow an ideal irrespective of personal consequences, the thought for others that was not a compulsion of duty . . . the tender touch, the spirit that knew no hatred, constituted for me a kind of spiritual fragrance that hovered over both my father and mother."[154] The Senator's keen political realism, his close relations with Roscoe Conkling, his manipulations in the harbor fight do not entirely rule out the daughter's picture of the man. His letters testify to his great family devotion. But his practical life was of a style which may indeed have required a willful effort if someone were to elevate him onto so great a pedestal of purity. He died in 1912, the very year in which Georgina became a noticeably more ardent Theosophist. She may have spent the rest of her life seeking (and then, in her mind, discovering) a totally unclouded exemplifier of purity. This is by no means to suggest the overly crude idea that Paramananda was a father figure in her later years. Their ages must have precluded that. But a strong tie of this kind need not be defined in so literal a way.

Kenneth Keniston has suggested that the kind of person who is extremely dutiful and "overconforming" becomes prey to movements on the radical right.[155] Here is a striking case to the contrary. Sister Daya remained, as we have seen, a political liberal, a resolute opponent of fascist totalitarianism. A scheme which presents left-wing and right-wing tendencies as mirror images of each other in psychological terms is too simple to include her. In her instance, political liberalism was part of her own family heritage, strongly in the person of her mother, and even to a degree in that of her father. Thus her continued liberal idealism was yet another aspect of her fidelity to both of them, her desire for dutiful conformity to their principles. Her strong dutifulness, not her actual beliefs, forms a meaningful polarity with the anti-authoritarianism of many anarchistic rebels.

Regardless of this effort to find a precise psychological pattern in her life choices, the impact of her family situation in a broader context remains profound. The Joneses were a new kind of family in late nineteenth-century America. Without railroads and steamships their form of national and international globetrotting would have been impossible, as indeed would have been a husband's career three thousand miles away from home. An industrial technology had created opportunities for the wealthy which might foster a severe sense of dislocation for the children who were ex-

154. *Message of the East*, XLIX (July, 1955), 207–08.
155. Kenneth Keniston, *The Uncommitted* (New York: Harcourt, Brace and World, 1965), p. 471.

posed to them. Eventually she would retreat from the cosmopolitan, advanced society which had given her this kind of existence. In nature, only less than in Paramananda, she would find the security which upper-class American life in that generation had denied her.[156] If in some respects she appears to fit the model of the overconformer, she seems equally to illustrate the need of certain people to develop an inner strength as a buffer against the deprivations of modern life when it is lived close to the centers of power. For her, such strength became so intermingled with a new locus of dependency as to make it impossible to separate them.

The life of Sister Shivani, born Mary Hebard, offers a remarkable contrast to Sister Daya's.[157] If Daya fulfilled the role of the submissive devotee at its most extreme, Shivani revealed how Vedanta belief might curiously combine with the rugged pioneering individualism traditional in America. In Shivani's case one may also find direct continuity from the age of religious ferment in the "burnt-over district" of upstate New York and embrace of the Vedanta movement much later.

Shivani was a few years older than Daya. Her family, originally Welsh on one side, owned and operated a Rochester newspaper, the *Post-Express*. Her parents were nominally Methodists and Republicans. But her mother was not deeply religious, while her father and her grandmother were both intellectual rebels, influenced by the strong flow of radical ideas which had passed through the region in the early nineteenth century. For a time, she, her sister, and her brother all revolted against conventional values, thereby carrying on a family tradition. Her sister became an ardent socialist, and remained close to Mary, but the brother eventually went into the insurance business. A cousin became a Theosophist, and her daughter a Christian Scientist.

Their finances were wavering and uncertain; on a much smaller scale they paralleled the Joneses' declining circumstances. (But is declining social status relevant in explaining third-generation radicalism? Perhaps only if it leads to an intensification of family loyalties, which in this case would reinforce the tendency toward radical beliefs. In this sense Shivani's and

156. Of course this does not dispose of the fact that she alone from her immediate background chose Vedanta. It is for this reason that psychological inquiry, however limited in its results, becomes relevant.

157. The two main sources for Shivani's life are a book which may be regarded as her spiritual autobiography, *An Apostle of Monism* (which, though turgid and confusing, essentially rings true), and an extensive interview with her eldest son, Kali Le Page, at Pearblossom, California, in December, 1971. I am very grateful to my colleague Dilip Basu and to Professor B. K. Bagchi of the University of Michigan for bringing Shivani to my attention.

Daya's lives may have run parallel.) When Mary Hebard was fifteen or sixteen, a severe loss of income occurred, forcing the girl to learn an occupation. At first she worked on the family newspaper as a typesetter. Shortly afterward, in 1895 when her parents separated, she and her father moved to New York City. She got a job with a typeface company and continued learning every phase of the printing trade. In her work she was not very fast but extremely accurate.

Meanwhile, she became a Unitarian and an aggressive feminist. There was an extraordinary, restless dynamism about her. Red-headed, physically slight, she exuded vitality and seriousness of purpose. Her mouth was firm and decided; her eyes gazed directly ahead through rimless glasses. In some photographs, she revealed that she could smile warmly too.

Eleven years later, in 1906, the promise of a better position caused her to return to Rochester briefly. This new encounter with the more provincial surroundings of her childhood seems to have provoked a spiritual crisis:

> To whatever ideology I turned there was friction and opposition [among her Rochester relatives]. I had read a great deal of Emerson and Thomas Paine, Walt Whitman and some of the Greek philosophers; and following in the footsteps of my father who was known in Rochester as a rebel and iconoclast I found myself a ship without a sail, alone in one of the most outstanding centres of conservative education and culture. I turned to Theosophy as much to defy the relatives as to find some anchorage and tenets that would give me a contactual and working thesis. I soon found the teachings held nothing for me and the Unitarian Society . . . could at this period of my life give nothing. It was a dark unhappy year within my forming mind. I knew not what I wanted nor how to seek it. I experimented with Spiritualism, threw over Theosophy and then in despair gave up my position and returned to New York City, drawn by what force I knew not.[158]

There, in 1907, an Englishman visiting the Theosophical Lodge one evening "was kind enough to realize my mind was in a dangerous tangle, going in circles and getting nowhere," and suggested she visit the swamis at the Vedanta Society. The next day, for the first time, she went there. She had no immediate conversion experience. Instead for several months she continued to attend Vedanta lectures occasionally, not making any closer personal contact with the swamis.

In New York at that time the stern, imposing Swami Abhedananda was in charge of the society; the youthful Paramananda had arrived from India as his assistant just a few months before. It was Paramananda whom

158. Shivani, *op. cit.,* p. 147.

Mary Hebard first heard speak on Sundays. In complete contrast to Georgina Jones Walton some twelve years later, he utterly failed to excite her. Instead, as soon as Abhedananda returned from a trip to London, she realized that in him she had found her own true spiritual teacher. "And from then on," as she later described it, "my crazy mind was in good hands."[159]

Rapidly she now began to go through some of the same emotional states that Georgina would eventually experience. A personal interview with Abhedananda she termed "an hour in which I seemed to be in the presence of some omniscient, omnipresent Being." Intent upon becoming a loyal disciple, she exaggerated the import of very small personal lapses and guiltily regarded herself as a "difficult" person.[160] Soon she was begging to be allowed to stay at the Vedanta Ashrama in Connecticut. A first visit to West Cornwall during the Christmas holiday of 1908 lifted her to a state of rapture. "For the first time in my 29 years I knew what it was to be clothed in an honesty so honest neither explanation nor analysis were needed to relate one's self to one's companions or to one's environment."[161] Immediately she began to dream of living permanently at the ashram. For some reason, perhaps because she was still such a newcomer to the movement, Abhedananda would not at first allow her to do so. Instead she remained in New York, editing the *Vedanta Monthly Bulletin*. After dutifully following these instructions for some months, she again went impulsively to West Cornwall and insisted that she be allowed to remain forever. She had now sold all her possessions and cut her ties with the outside world. Even her friends in the movement clearly believed she was rushing into these decisions in too headstrong a fashion.[162] This time the Swami let her stay four months, whereupon she willingly returned to New York to take over the publications department.

Swami Abhedananda gave his students a choice between Jnanin yoga (the way of intellect) and Bakhti (the way of devotion). Unlike Daya, she chose the former. "None so hard upon the *Jnanin* as the *Jnanin* himself," she wrote. "One refused initiation several times lest he should put upon the Master loads he felt were not the Master's to assume. . . . They may have been wilful, these *Jnanins,* and stubborn, too prideful at times perhaps, but they were no weaklings, accepting poverty, hardship and responsibility. They wrapped themselves within a strange and lonely security,

159. *Ibid.*, p. 150.
160. *Ibid.*, p. 173.
161. *Ibid.*, p. 154.
162. *Ibid.*, pp. 171–72.

wearing down the days, not knowing how to yield the guardianship of an utter surrender."[163] In her view, the followers of Bakhti were chained to an excessively narrow and literal Hindu ritual. Such a one was Sister Devamata, whom Shivani had to encounter in New York just as Daya would in Boston a decade later. Shivani recalled how Devamata once entered the Swami's room, which she had just been cleaning, and insisted on rearranging Abhedananda's chair so that his back would not be turned to the photograph of Sri Ramakrishna. "But the sun will be in his eyes and he cannot see his visitor," the more practical Shivani protested. "Well, put it this way," Devamata replied shortly, moving the chair again. "Is God only on the altar?" Shivani persisted. "I supposed He was everywhere." But Devamata remained adamant. Characteristically, Shivani waited for her departure and then restored the chair to her own preferred position.[164] Such routine defiance would have been inconceivable to Daya.

Interestingly Shivani's intense commitment to the Swami and the ashram caused no great, permanent change in her pattern of living. Unlike Daya, she had reached no new plateau of stability. While at West Cornwall she met a young man five years older than herself. Thomas Le Page, the eldest boy among thirteen children of a fairly prosperous Guernsey cattle farmer, had migrated to America as a young man and had similarly been seeking new beliefs among the lecturers of the New York circuit. By this time he was deeply devoted to Abhedananda and had become chief builder and caretaker on the ashram property.[165] The Swami had given him the spiritual name of Haridas. Less than a year after her four-month visit at West Cornwall, Mary Hebard (now already Sister Shivani) married Haridas. This, she recalled, was quite a surprise to many of the Vedantists in New York, "so insistent has been the legend 'Vedantists do not marry.' " But, she said by way of explanation, "the West is not monastic minded. The Dharma of the Western peoples is 'wife and child.' "[166]

In quick succession Shivani and Haridas had five children. She now obtained an excellent position as proofreader for Princeton University Press. For several years she lived in Princeton, while her husband spent long periods at West Cornwall helping maintain the ashram for the Swami. She still dreamt of the ashram, but saw that her "householder" life with several children would not permit her return there.[167]

Another abrupt change came in 1916, when she and the entire family

163. *Ibid.*, p. 65.
164. *Ibid.*, pp. 66–67.
165. See *Vedanta Monthly Bulletin*, IV (April, 1908), 7.
166. Shivani, *op. cit.*, p. 182.
167. *Ibid.*, pp. 191–93.

moved to Los Angeles, there to join Shivani's free-thinking father. Now husband and wife were steadily united, but at the seeming expense of Swami Abhedananda, who visited them occasionally during his lecture tours but otherwise lost firsthand contact with both these fervent disciples.

The changes, which seem shockingly casual from someone like Daya's point of view, were not over. In 1920, tired of "city living" (for Los Angeles already had more than half a million people), Shivani persuaded her husband to move to rural Tujunga, a few miles west of La Crescenta, where they proceeded to build an eleven-room house with their own hands. By this time Shivani was in her early forties, and if anything growing in energy and determination.

For this was not all. Attending at Grauman's new Egyptian theater a Hollywood preview of *Covered Wagon,* a silent movie with a Western theme, Shivani suddenly conceived the desire to become a true pioneer. Learning that desert homestead land was still available in the Antelope Valley across the mountains from San Bernardino, she visited the area on a camping trip and decided to stay. Haridas was at first reluctant to give up everything they had so recently established, but, as always, allowed himself to be convinced.

Before smog and development, the Antelope Valley was a beautiful section of the California desert. The land slopes gently away to the north. Buttes and mesas create varied long-range vistas, and scattered Joshua trees give the landscape another element of irregularity. Behind, to the south, mountains rise abruptly, usually snow-covered in winter. The elevation is enough to take the edge off summer heat. There has always been insufficient water for large-scale farming.

When the Le Page family arrived in September, 1923, only a sprinkling of other people, mainly homesteaders like themselves, inhabited the vicinity. Some had been members of the Llano colony, a long-lived socialist community which had existed here for over a decade and had moved off to Louisiana only the year before. Others were bachelor veterans of the First World War, living in crude cabins on their minuscule pensions. Many of them in their isolation became alcoholics. Women did not often care for life in the Antelope Valley. There were almost no paved roads. For the first twenty-five years of their stay, the Le Pages did without electricity. But Shivani thrived on all these challenges. She raised her family of three sons and two daughters successfully on the 280 acres they had obtained. To a large degree, theirs was a subsistence economy, supplemented by odd jobs —hence very similar to that of the recent rural communes, except for the prideful lack of dependence on government welfare programs (other than the Homestead Act itself).

In this demanding, highly practical life she had chosen, Shivani forgot neither Abhedananda nor the ashram concept. Always keenly interested in the history of American communitarian experiments, the Oneida colony in particular, she dreamed of establishing a new one on this land. With this in mind, she named the property "Abhedananda Acres." On a press she had brought with her, she and her son printed a prospectus for a proposed Vedanta community. Though not dated, it was issued about the year 1933, and began as follows:

ABHEDANANDA ACRES: A RETREAT FOR SAVANTS
The Plan
A life-lease in an acre-site awaits, upon request, every representative Swami of the Vedanta Teaching, irrespective of Order and organization. . . . The idea is that all accommodations established here are established for the use of the Swami from the Center donating the funds for his cabin and furnishings. The Swami may come at any and all times to pursue his writing, independent research, or to conduct some special intensified training he may wish to give a student or student-group.[168]

At Abhedananda Acres, the prospectus went on, "the Swami may always have a Retreat in America where unhampered by activities and restraint he can rest," "an Ashram where he can meet his brothers and peers." Perhaps the Swamis might want to hold summer schools. In any event, "Abhedananda Acres offers a Retreat, as did the Academes of old, for all earnest Savants west and east." Here was the idea of the esoteric school, a theme still prominent in the thinking of some present-day mystical communities.[169] The plan also seems clearly to have been a response to certain lines of division then existing among the American swamis. But of course it was absurd to suppose that Shivani could serve as a mediator, or indeed that any swami would relish coming to an ashram named for someone else. It was sheer wishful thinking to imagine the swamis all pitching their tents on her remote, windswept land, learning to like each other better as they gulped down quantities of her famously good food. The realms of Vedanta and of American pioneering did not that easily mix.

Still, Abhedananda Acres did have an embryonic communitarian flavor. In the 1920's, no fewer than thirteen people lived on this land much of the time. Some were relatives with no religious connection, but until 1926 Sister

168. In possession of her son, Kali Le Page.
169. Including the New Mexico group to be described in Chapter Five.

Bhavani, another of Abhedananda's disciples, lived with them at the Swami's request. Another Vedantist from Santa Barbara asked Shivani if he could build a cabin on the property, and she gladly gave permission. A number of others came on long visits.

B. K. Bagchi, once a Swami himself and a close friend of the Le Pages, has described Abhedananda Acres in their prime. Listening to the "chug-chug" of the gasoline engine pumping water from their hard-dug well, he realized that here one did not find the passive resignation of an Indian hermitage. There had been a definite union with the spirit of "American science." Yet, from the Indian point of view, this household contained a pleasing absence of luxuries. "There was a heating stove, simple furniture and a good-sized family library of philosophical and religious books with a sprinkling of scientific literature. Gathered wood was the fuel, kerosene was used for the lamps and heated and wrapped iron bricks were used for keeping warm in bed in sub-freezing wintry nights."[170]

Shivani did not like to recognize any contradiction between Vedanta philosophy and American activism. One of her complaints against Para-mananda was that he was too spiritually indrawn, too contemplative. Shivani set aside no time for formal meditation. As a Jnanin, she believed that a constant discussion of ideas, along with the consecrated performance of everyday household tasks, might take its place. The members of this family (three of the children had been given Hindu names) grew up with a constant verbal diet of Eastern philosophy. At the same time, they were all expected to be "practical." "It was fascinating to watch the boys take apart and put together old automobiles," Bagchi reminisced. "They would drive proud miles in their home-repaired cars to the nearest store. . . . At table or under the balmy evening sky they would listen to or join in discussion, the subjects ranging from politics through science and internationalism to *Nirvikalpa Samadhi*."[171] How well one performed one's everyday physical tasks, Shivani firmly believed, had much to do with the rate of one's spiritual evolution.

Toward nearly everyone and everything Shivani remained fiercely independent. Krishnamurti she thought a pitiable victim of Annie Besant. Aldous Huxley, who was a neighbor of theirs on the desert for a time in the mid-1940's, she considered a superficial novice in the realm of spiritual ideas. Paramananda was too dreamily mystical, and Prabhavananda too much wrapped up in social life among the wealthy of Santa Barbara. In the early years, she and her family would occasionally go to La Crescenta

170. Basu Kumar Bagchi, introduction to Shivani, *op. cit.*, pp. 4–5.
171. *Ibid.*, p. 5.

for services, where Daya (it seemed) always regarded them with a peculiar aloofness. Later Shivani also spent some time at Miramont, a Meher Baba retreat center on the Sulphur Mountain Road near Ojai. But for the most part she held aloof from all groups and organizations, now that Abhedananda had long since returned to India. The one other exception was the Democratic party, which she campaigned for vigorously and consistently. Often she would write two or three letters a day to newspapers and magazines on subjects that aroused her.

As she grew older, she began to lose her headstrong quality, taking life more as it came. After her husband's death she sold some of her acres and spent her last years traveling by jet all over the world and loving it. By this time she had gradually given up all her communitarian dreams.

Her son Kali thinks that her family tradition, with its mixture of physical pioneering and free thought, in fact set the tone of her actions more than did her formal commitment to the Vedanta movement. Unlike most Vedantists, Shivani was never puritanical. Unhesitatingly and without condescension she made friends with ex-prostitutes. She is remembered as a "natural-born flirt," someone who in this fashion could "butter up" any man, including her own husband, and draw him out. Despite her often highflown style of writing, in person she was a very down-to-earth woman, an excellent practical budgeter with a sharply developed sense of humor. Nor did it occur to her to put Vedantists and non-Vedantists in different categories of friendship. No vegetarian, in the 1920's she even made her own moonshine. A distinct memory is of her husband (who also loved good liquor and tobacco) with Swami Abhedananda, during a California visit before his return to India, both happily under the influence.

Of the five children whom Shivani raised on Vedantist principles in the isolation of Abhedananda Acres, only the two daughters remained faithful as adults to her world view. Kali, the oldest son, was actually sent to India when he was in his mid-teens to study under Abhedananda, remaining there several years, but he has since become an active Episcopalian and thinks back to his mother with loving detachment. Even while he was in India, he confessed, he had never been entirely convinced by the theory of reincarnation. In the three male children, the practical, pioneering side of their youth seems to have retained dominance. Kali Le Page, still living in the Antelope Valley, now defends the controversial new jetport just being added to the local landscape. Several generations of rebellion seem to have disappeared with scarcely a ripple into the American mainstream.

Whether Shivani's conversion to Vedanta and her devotion to Abhedananda are to be interpreted in psychological or in cultural terms, they simply did not have the meaning in her life that these experiences had for a woman like Sister Daya. In the Vedanta movement, Shivani was the clear exception. Still, it is important that it could just barely contain her.

The Limitations of the Monastic Impulse

Unorthodox monasticism, sparked by the impulse toward perfectionism among a continuing minority, has created a few unusually stable communitarian environments in twentieth-century America. The strength of commitment among Paramananda's followers at La Crescenta was, by all indications, steadier and more enduring than that of the anarchists at Stelton, New Jersey, though they too had been relatively successful. But what does such an achievement really amount to?

Communities of this kind, if they are to succeed, first of all require a heavy sacrifice of intellectual and personal venturesomeness. Loyalty, obedience, and devotion make bonds which can easily endure for a lifetime. But, for better or worse, only a few Americans have been willing to accept such great limitations upon their own freedom to think, act, and maneuver. Even within Vedanta persons like Shivani would appear, willing impulsively to pull up stakes and honor their swami from distant locations where they were very much their own masters.

Restlessness of this sort could lead to the rapid downfall of a monastic venture, if the followers were more intellectually assertive or if the guru was plagued by self-doubts foreign to a Paramananda. These hazards are illustrated by the fate of Trabuco College, a pacifist meditation community established in 1942 in the hills behind Laguna Beach, fifty miles southeast of Los Angeles.[172] Trabuco was founded by the Englishman Gerald Heard, who, with his friend Aldous Huxley, had migrated to Southern California in 1938. Heard was an intense, self-absorbed, but magnetic figure, who had developed deep religious convictions along mystical lines and had begun thinking of creating a community which would train a "new race" of spiritual leaders, neo-Brahmins as he called them, to lead mankind away from the destruction threatened by the oncoming Second World War. Heard had originally moved in intellectually respectable circles in London, and he always tried to speak in the language of science as well as of devotion, even when he became increasingly interested in psychic phenomena and, ulti-

172. The story of Trabuco has emerged from interviews with nine active participants named in the Acknowledgments. The prospectus of the community is in the Gerald Heard Papers, Department of Special Collections, UCLA Library. These papers are, however, primarily useful for other aspects of Heard's life in California.

mately, flying saucers. He was a prolific author and forceful speaker who communicated a tone of urgency and of moral and intellectual certainty which attracted a small but ardent personal following. He argued for a vitalistic, teleological cosmic evolution which promised the arrival of a New Age out of the ashes of the present global crisis, if only its spiritual guides could be trained in time to assume command.[173] This was to be the pacifist's meaningful form of service in a war-torn world. Essentially his own philosopher, Heard remained aloof from all established religious organizations. However, upon their arrival from England he and Huxley had both been greatly impressed by Swami Prabhavananda of the Vedanta Center in Hollywood, and for some years Heard was invited by the Swami to speak to his congregation one Sunday morning each month.[174]

A large legacy and other contributions enabled Heard to build Trabuco College from scratch along substantial lines in the months just after Pearl Harbor. Huxley helped write its prospectus, though he never lived there. Felix Greene, later well known in the context of political radicalism, played an indispensable role in supervising the construction. Graceful brick buildings, in a subdued Mediterranean style, were equipped to house thirty people, though the actual number in the community was nearly always far less than that. The property was isolated in beautiful rolling hills, far from any neighbors.

Despite these handsome facilities, the spirit of the undertaking was rigorously ascetic. Austerities included a near-total absence of heat and (for wartime reasons) of electricity. More than this, it was understood that no physical pleasures were supposed to be enjoyed by the residents, even eating. Meals were deliberately sparse and colorless, beyond mere vegetarianism. To prove her zeal, one woman ate mud. Even nature worship was discouraged as a distraction from pursuit of the Divine. In a remarkable round windowless building called the Oratory, whose interior was always kept completely dark, the members spent three hour-long periods of silent meditation daily. Aside from this, everyone was free to create his or her own regime. The only further rule on which Heard absolutely insisted was celibacy, even for any husbands and wives who might visit Trabuco together. (Most of the residents of both sexes were unmarried.) Heard's homoerotic inclinations, which he had never fully accepted in himself, gave him a strong revulsion against sex of any kind. So Trabuco was to be a

173. See especially Gerald Heard, *The Third Morality* (London: Cassell and Co., 1937); *Pain, Sex, and Time* (New York: Harper & Brothers, 1939); and *Man the Master* (New York: Harper & Brothers, 1941).

174. The Vedanta Society naturally liked to claim Heard as an adherent, but I am told that he rarely attended services unless he was the speaker.

genuine experiment in monasticism in a mid-twentieth-century California setting.

Heard soon ran into the problem that some of his most ardent followers were women. Unlike Paramananda, who could live gracefully in this situation while practicing celibacy for a lifetime, Heard found it an enormous strain to play the role of spiritual teacher to the sex whose very presence he could sometimes hardly bear. Still he held on for a time after the war, hoping to receive an influx of conscientious objectors and pacifistically inclined veterans searching for this kind of spiritual training. A handful of such young men did appear. Occasionally as individuals they had important mystical experiences while at Trabuco, but nearly always they drifted away again after some months. Discouraged, Heard closed the community in 1947 and returned to Los Angeles to live. In 1949 he donated the entire property to the Vedanta Society.

The atmosphere at Trabuco had not been conducive to long-term commitments. Heard proved unable to handle the role of guru smoothly or with full assurance. Ever since boyhood he had lacked something crucial in terms of self-acceptance. Now he seemed inwardly torn, wanting to function as teacher and spiritual counselor, yet shrinking continually from the human contact and direct assertion of authority which would have made it possible. He was only intermittently at ease with people. There was an aloof shyness in his make-up, a tendency to retreat into isolation, which suggested that he was fundamentally ill suited to group living. His own emotional conflicts also lay too near the surface, creating a tone of tension. Suppression of feelings was general in this community; in contrast to Stelton, disagreements were never openly talked about. As a result, public quarrels were at a minimum, but the everyday mood was one of mutual isolation and somber indrawing. Life at Trabuco became a form of solitary confinement. One man even retreated to his room, where he spent his time cutting out paper dolls. In the real meaning of the term, a community had not been created.

In a larger sense, Heard and most of the others at Trabuco lacked temperaments suited to lifelong stability in one group setting. Though they were pacifists and some were deeply committed to a regime of inner perfection, they were worldlier and more cosmopolitan than the nuns at La Crescenta. To a degree they were intellectuals, infected with the restlessness of their age, even as they sought to flee from it into a realm of inner peace. Yearning for quiet self-development, their minds could not stay put. They could never agree upon a regime of daily living which satisfied them in all its details, and Heard refused to impose one upon them. The resulting form-lessness was hard to take, even if it stemmed in part from their own in-decision. The craving for discipline was intense but it was never satisfied. In the end the people drifted off into a variety of personal solutions. Mo-nasticism itself became an issue. A prominent member of the community, a long-time friend of Heard's, suddenly announced that he wished to get married. Heard was dismayed and heartbroken. When the marriage was performed by a minister on the community's board of trustees, the crisis brought the undertaking close to collapse then and there. Meanwhile, Heard also shrank from the perfectionist extremism of several other residents, such as the woman who ate mud. To his British instincts, there was some-thing too wild and uncontrolled about these efforts to rush headlong into purification and bliss.[175]

The instance of Trabuco reveals the fragility of monasticism as a com-munitarian alternative in twentieth-century America. A handful of people had gathered on a California hilltop, to meditate rather than kill while the world was in flames. But pacifism, unlike anarchism, did not seem to fur-nish enough ideological content to hold them together, and nothing else filled the breech. This negative case may imply that the role of the guru is in-deed all-important in secessionist communities oriented toward discipline. Unless there is strong, unhesitating leadership, such as the Vedanta swamis often provided, American individualist antinomianism soon begins to tear things asunder.

But in a larger perspective, all monastic or ascetic communities, no matter how enduring, pay a severe price in psychological terms for their success. In part this involves the individual burden of a relentless, willful striving for self-mastery. Also it concerns the effects of prolonged with-drawal from so much that is in everyday life, a retreat which is here far more pronounced than in anarchist or socialist communities. These issues, equally with guru worship, get at the heart of what the monastic impulse represents.

Individuals attracted to the pursuit of a sustained inner quest often are marked by a pronounced dissatisfaction with themselves. Otherwise why embark on a lifelong course of self-development, which becomes ideolog-ically objectified as "soul advancement" in cosmic evolution? A higher self, an ideal self, is defined so that it may be contrasted with an existing lesser or mundane self. All the striving is for the purpose of realizing the higher

175. For all his own sense of urgency, Heard liked to retain such customs at Trabuco as afternoon tea.

and eliminating the unwanted characteristics of the lower. Self-dividedness is at the root of the driving demand for inner purification.[176]

This internal struggle fosters an attitude of unending self-analysis, a restless tension during which one yearns for a state of peace or final respite. At an extreme, it may take the form of an explicit desire to achieve sainthood. In conversation with me, a present-day Vedantist monk openly affirmed that sainthood was the goal of their efforts, and it seems likely that the more extreme personalities who were at Trabuco in Gerald Heard's day had a similar intent. For her part, Sister Daya said that "every human being should try to resemble the saint, the real saint, who does everything that he does as an offering to the highest Divinity that he is capable of apprehending, with no care for what his effort will bring him in the way of censure or praise from the outside world." She saw this as the only alternative to egotism and self-centeredness.[177]

In contrast to the anarchist spirit, which at its best called for the open expression of all dimensions of one's being in a mood of shared self-acceptance, the monastic spirit is one of perpetual inner struggle, of learning to repress and control one's own unwanted parts. It is hard not to conclude that it is based on some element of self-distrust, perhaps verging at times on self-hatred. To quote Daya again: "There has to be heroism, something flaming that causes one to wipe out the self as if it did not exist, to smother the word of self-pity that rises to the lips, in order that wisdom, beauty, rapture may issue forth. In this way life becomes incandescent, blissful, yet full of peace."[178] Translated, her imagery becomes one of burning away the grosser desires, a wrestling with inner devils that almost suggests self-immolation. The mystic's torment of this kind has a long tradition, espe-

---

176. In the nineteenth century, the Christian perfectionist John Humphrey Noyes (founder of the Oneida community) had said very strikingly in this vein: "Here we may see the nature of true *repentance*. . . . It may be, at the beginning, a conviction of individual sins—a sorrow for personal deeds done; but in the end it becomes an abhorrence of the devil, and of self as spiritually identified with the devil. The spirit of God . . . begins to insinuate itself between the individual and the evil spirit which envelops him. The effect of this infusion is to turn the eye of his conscience on his spiritual state, and to produce self-loathing. That part of the man which receives and sympathizes with the spirit of God, imbibes God's hatred of sin, and thus begins to hate that other part which is in union with the devil, as God hates the devil.—Instead of looking at his works, the man literally 'hates his own *life*,' as being 'part and parcel' of that poisonous spirit which is the fountain of universal sin." John Humphrey Noyes, *The Berean: A Manual for the Help of Those Who Seek the Faith of the Primitive Church* (Putney, Vermont: The Spiritual Magazine, 1847), p. 120.

177. *Message of the East*, XLIV (October, 1955), 210–12.

178. *Ibid.*, XXXII (April, 1943), 105. Cf. also *ibid.*, XXXV (April, 1946), 91.

cially in the West, where Christianity has bequeathed a strongly dualistic conception of human nature. But too often in our own day the people who have embarked upon a strenuous path of self-development appear only to have tied themselves up in complicated knots, or, if like Daya they have found respite, it is inside a frame of belief which can have little appeal to persons who are more internally at ease to begin with.

This is certainly not to criticize all forms of introspection or to cast aspersions upon deeply satisfying forms of subjective experience. But one may distinguish between the kind of inner life which involves a playful, intermittent immersion in such experience (in the form of fantasies, day-dreams, poetic visions, or moments of ecstasy) as against the kind which emphasizes constant self-analysis, guilty probing of one's motives, and the never-ceasing attempt to change oneself into another person, someone more "advanced" or "harmonious." This latter form of inward preoccupation can stem from a continuing fear of life, rather than from a desire to embrace it. Willful self-improvement of this sort is an artificial substitute—like the recent encounter groups—for the direct flow of human involvement. It is a symptom of an unhappy, troubled spirit rather than a remedy for the malaise.

Among other things, it leads to a degree of self-absorption which in a broader context may appear highly unrealistic. During the depression of the 1930's, the Vedantists of La Crescenta ignored the widespread physical suffering of the nation more imperturbably than Herbert Hoover. On one rare occasion when Swami Paramananda referred to these matters, he said that it was a superficial answer to give food and clothes to the needy, because hunger and lack would merely return to each person later on unless they experienced some change in consciousness.[179] It is easy for those who are spiritually oriented to assume a fatalistic posture toward the happenings in the material world, even while they implore their followers toward willful effort in the private realm of "soul advancement."

Once only did a follower of Paramananda openly come to terms with the issue of retreat from the ordinary problems of the world. "Retreat . . . is neither rout nor flight," wrote Maud Keck.

> There is nothing precipitate about it. A man retreats because he refuses to be stampeded. An army under fire retreats in order to rest its men, re-align its forces, renew its courage for a fresh attack. We were an army of men and women . . . [who had lived through] the most disastrous war in

179. *Ibid.,* XXII (October, 1933), 230. Of course Daya's politically liberal response to the world situation in the 1930's must also be recalled.

history, and . . . its subsequent depair, depression and disillusion. Sometimes we thought that even now we were trembling on the brink of a cycle so overwhelming in its possibilities that suns, moons, and planets might be the only undiscovered countries left! We had not lost our courage altogether, but our nerves were frayed, our minds disquieted, our souls dismayed.[180]

It was more an apologia than a positive manifesto.

In his own way, Gerald Heard was deeply concerned about the world crisis. He conceived of meditation and spiritual training in part as answers to Hitler and Stalin. But can the expansion of consciousness ever be more than a frail reed in the age of the nation-state? The anarchists of Stelton, though they had entered into another version of rural retreat, believed (with only one or two exceptions) in a more down-to-earth answer to Nazism. Again, it may be that retreat has since become more justifiable; in a global situation of push-button war and relatively little moral difference among the superpowers, fatalism may seem like quite a sensible response. It can, after all, induce a decision to lead one's life at full pitch, just as easily as to one of renunication. But, when fatalism is applied indiscriminately to every occurrence lying outside the realm of the self, it is an attitude which still invites careful questioning.

Gerald Heard, for one, was keenly sensitive to this issue. In a Vedanta talk titled "Is Mysticism Escapism?" he articulated the logic of withdrawal with unusually forthright bravado. Escapism, he said, means only

to leave a position which has become impossible. . . . To escape is therefore a neutral term. It may be a wrong thing to do, or a right. "When they persecute you in one city flee into another," is an instruction which spread the Christian church. The man who leaves the ship to attempt to swim on shore with a rope, is escaping, but for the sake of the rest on the wrecked ship—and he is risking his life. Our motive therefore decides whether escape is good or bad.

He went on to point out that "most of those who charge others with escapism" believe in some kind of a political utopia.

Now Utopianism can be called escapism, for it is a wish to live in the future, not in the present, and it certainly is as vague as "otherworldliness" because biologically and meteorologically we know it is impossible for any race of animals to achieve a permanent home, let alone a "heaven on earth," on this planet. As far as hard-fisted certainty is concerned there is then nothing to choose between the two futures which idealists put in front of themselves—neither can be proved to be manifestly evident.

Finally, he insisted that in mysticism lay the only effective path to social

180. Maud Keck, "The Beauty of Retreat," *ibid.,* XXVI (December, 1937), 275.

change. The mystic, when placed beside the ordinary man who is "economically obsessed," is "a realist and a daring man of action."[181]

This was brave talk (though it dealt only with left-wing radicalism, avoiding the challenge of the political center). But when war actually broke out in Europe in 1939, Heard went into a profound depression, repeatedly expressing the fear that a new, prolonged Dark Age for mankind was at hand. So deeply did his gloom persist that when he arrived with friends at Yosemite he did not even bother to get out of his car and take the short walk with them to see the falls. And, when news came of the defeat of France, he spent twelve hours of anguished prayer alone upstairs in his friend Allan Hunter's Hollywood church. Despair was a very human reaction to that moment in time (the anarchist Harry Kelly also expressed it). But what matters is that, when the cards were on the table, the "real" world influenced Gerald Heard far more than he was able to influence it. Moreover, it may be doubted whether mystics such as Paramananda and Heard ever made much real effort to combine the inner and the external approaches to liberation, even to the degree that was attempted by anarchists at Stelton and Rockridge.

Can the whole ideology of "spiritual striving" be vaporized by the pin prick of external reality when, for an instant, it is extraordinarily compelling? In this respect, Swami Paramananda conceivably offers the most extreme indication of the effect of world events upon the mind of a consistent believer in the supremacy of the spiritual life. For it so happened that his premature death by heart attack came immediately after he had heard the same news of the fall of France.

> At about a quarter to four in the afternoon, he left the house at 420 Beacon Street, Boston, Massachusetts, and with two companions started for Cohasset driving his own car. Those who saw him off at the town house will long remember the picture. Swami came down the broad stairs in a playful mood, half dancing and singing a Bengali song, "O, love everyone! Love all, that your mind may be free of stain!" . . .
>
> On the way, he was rather indrawn and thoughtful which was often the Swami's mood. As he neared the Ashrama, he listened over the radio to the news of the surrender of France. He became very grave and turning to his companion said, "You see, although these French generals were outwardly quiet as they accepted defeat, in their hearts they were saying, 'Someday we shall avenge this wrong,' thus sowing the seed of the next war in their minds. They do not understand each other; they need someone to come and teach them understanding; and someone will come." After this remark,

181. In Christopher Isherwood, ed., *Vedanta for the Western World* (Hollywood: Marcel Rodd Co., 1945), pp. 30–32.

the Swami remained very quiet until he reached the Ashrama. His mood changed as he listened to the songbirds and twice he said, "Listen to the birds! How they sing!"[182]

Minutes later, shortly after he began to walk on the Cohasset Ashrama grounds, the fifty-six-year-old Swami succumbed. No connection, of course, can ever be proved between these events. But he had chosen one of the gloomiest days of the twentieth century for his passing.

There might be something awe-inspiring about a saintly individual so out of touch with the ebb and flow of worldly affairs as to be genuinely ignorant, or uncaring, about such news as a major Nazi victory. But the point is that these spiritual leaders, from what we know of them, were not so unaffected. They were, by all indications, no better off at these moments than the mass of ordinary men huddled beside their radios. Meanwhile the political leaders, everywhere in the world, were having the last word. The advanced souls and the unadvanced share the same physical fate in the mushroom cloud of modern war, just as they have alike been unable to dispel that other brownish cloud which has increasingly enveloped La Crescenta, Trabuco, and the rest of Southern California, robbing the region of much of its beauty.

Despite its universal, eternal claim, the monastic tradition appears to have little hold over the conditions that seem important to most men in a postindustrial society. It provides an alternative which is not likely to be widely chosen in circumstances less desperate than the collapse of a Roman Empire. And at bottom it often seems to be related to rather special psychological needs.

But now it must be seen whether the counter-culture of the 1960's, reworking certain of these themes, has achieved something more relevant and exciting.

---

182. *Message of the East,* XXIX (July, 1940), 154–55. Paramananda was a forthright pacifist. Early in 1939 he had spoken unequivocally against war. *Ibid.,* XXVIII (April, 1939), 131–46.

CHAPTER FIVE

New Mexico, 1971:
Inside a "New Age" Social Order

"Earlier groups failed because they didn't integrate the inner with the external. Here we're deliberately combining them, in a total new formula for life." So speaks Ezra, the leader of a community of about thirty people who have been together for several years on an isolated ranch in the New Mexico desert. Let him continue: "Western civilization isn't simply dying. It's dead. We are probing into its ruins to take whatever is useful for the building of the new civilization to replace it. This new civilization will be planetary. The whole earth will be our home. We are no longer Americans, or Westerners, even though as individuals we were once raised in that tradition. We will build a series of centers in various parts of the world to demonstrate the new way of life. This ranch is merely our first training-ground."

These pronouncements gain weight when one learns what the group has already achieved in line with its master plan for helping usher in the New Age. A visitor is astonished at first by all the signs of flourishing stability he encounters, from buildings and workshops to gardens and animal pens. Indeed, he may feel that he has wandered into an entirely new social order, where every detail is the deliberate product of fresh thinking. While he is still marveling at the totality of it, he receives a new surprise: on top of everything else, this is a theater group, which spends a good share of its time rehearsing classic and original plays, and touring the United States performing them. The group's aura of energy, planning, and pride in diverse accomplishments begins to seem overwhelming. Here if anywhere, one imagines, the New Age may actually be in process of creation, guided by this cadre of dropouts who have turned themselves into Renaissance men.

Like all first impressions, this one begins to seem somewhat naïve after a period of prolonged contact, yet it is never wholly superseded. Instead, as one gets to know this community better, one gains a sense of the multiple levels on which its members live. The inner dimension of their work reveals itself alongside the outer. An ideology unfolds. Powerful psychological currents also become revealed. Some of these, such as the evidences of an emotional dependency lying beneath the apparent confidence, can seem rather distressing. Grotesque exaggerations of the old civilization also begin to shine through the trappings of the new. Yet, in the end, one finds oneself repeating the strangely cold and guarded word which had seemed appropriate at the beginning: "impressive." This community is impressive in the strength of the bonds that hold its people together, in their determination to let nothing prevent their collective arrival in the New Age.

The External Tour

This part of New Mexico is bleak and windswept. It is unendingly very cold or very hot. The empty desert slope presents a dazzling sameness to the eye, broken only by barren hills to the west. Scattered sagebrush grows to shoulder height. The dirt entrance road is jagged with rocks.

A giant blue canvas dome rises over the landscape. Next to it are a cluster of low-lying buildings. The whole complex, set off so far from anything else, seems emphatically divorced from the existing human realm. Yet it also seems carelessly exposed. It sits on a slight rise, making it more vulnerable to dusty winds. The nearby hills are too stark to offer a sense of comfort; instead they seal the mood of harshness. Altogether the locale is precisely where a flying saucer would choose to land and survey the terrain before making itself known to men.

Instead, huddled on these 11 acres in the midst of the 165 which the group owns, one finds a complicated nest of human activity. The several structures, some new, some old, all suggest important, variegated functions. A garden struggles against the drought. Barely audible sounds of barnyard animals come from another quarter. Here and there one sees piles of salvaged lumber and bricks. Half-dug trenches are filled with tumbleweeds. There is mess but no random litter. The entire scene conveys the sense that much has been done, much is still in the process of completion. Meantime, everything is glazed by the hostile sun and wind.

When one first arrives and shuts off the engine, there is apt to be silence, no immediate sign of life. The stillness makes the scene even more unreal. But then someone appears out of the empty air and takes the visitor into the maze of buildings, usually to meet Ezra, the man who will charmingly and keenly take his measure. With proper credentials and a display of interest, a tour of the property may easily follow. As it unfolds, the members of the community are gradually encountered, often in groups of twos and threes, scattered about in various parts of the honeycomb. All of them, wherever they are, are busily engrossed in tasks. The few words these people exchange with each other are about business at hand.

Entering one end of a large adobe unit, the visitor is told that he is in the woodshop, where dining and patio tables, benches, and small round seats are made for sale. To construct a large table requires fifteen or twenty hours of labor. Scrap lumber is used, mainly pine. The tables then sell for sixty dollars. These New Age products, created according to the principle of using technology to enhance life rather than to destroy it, are made almost entirely out of the debris of the old civilization.

"Would you like to buy a table?" one of the young woodworkers, who has had little else to say, now eagerly asks the visitor. The dirt floor of the dim chamber is thick with sawdust chips. Electric power tools are in evidence. It is explained that everything depends upon the use to which such technology is put. Whatever is really necessary from the existing civilization may be freely borrowed. Many everyday things turn out not to be necessary, but the woodworking machinery is vital to the result. The community's diesel-operated electric generator runs only for a few hours a day, in the early afternoon and late evening, so that resources will not be wasted as they are in the old order.

At the opposite end of the building is a large pottery, where in equally dim light several girls work on their productions, rapidly moving about, again with a minimum of talk. One young man busily makes candles nearby. A large kiln stands outside. It too requires electric power, so its use has to be scheduled carefully. A showroom at the front displays the finished products.

All the crafts are the individual enterprises of the members, who are expected to work four hours a day on one of them. (If more than four consecutive hours are spent in any one pursuit, it is explained, the attention wanders.) One girl is learning to keep bees. Some persons have recently received orders to make props for a movie being shot in the area. Adobe bricks are also sold to others in the neighborhood. Can the members truly support themselves in this fashion? Everyone pays into the community the sum of $46 each month for room and board. The community also receives 10 percent of everything a member earns from sale of his products, or from that person's outside income in general. A three-week bazaar held to stimulate sales in the summer of 1971 brought in over $3,400. The previous year a three-day show earned only about $600. This seems encouraging. But the amount still falls far short of a satisfactory income for every individual. So recourse is had to regular contributions from parents and from welfare. A few people take temporary jobs in town. The community, for its part, survives quite well on the monthly levies it assesses.

Tools and machinery are paid for and owned individually, with the exception of a few items which are of wide service, such as garden hoses and nozzles. The basic economic rule is thus individual ownership of the actual means of production—but of nothing else, aside from one's clothing and a residue of personal possessions. This combination of land communism and private enterprise suggests the thinking of Henry George, but his name is never mentioned and he is probably not a conscious source of inspiration. One girl who has extra money lends it informally at a low rate of interest to others who need to buy tools.

A much smaller room in the same adobe unit is devoted to the study of ecology, another of the group's main concerns. Subcommittees are devoted to projects covering its various aspects; these often meet here. Maps, scientific books, and sheets of drawing paper lie scattered across its built-in desks, suggesting work underway. On the wall is a large chart with the periodic table of the elements. Besides being a successful craftsman, each member is seriously expected to become an expert in science. Another four hours of time daily is supposed to be spent in this endeavor, and everyone has been assigned one acre of the surrounding desert for close personal observation from this point of view. However, in practice the work in ecology tends to become concentrated in short periods leading up to public conferences and demonstrations.

The large adobe unit also contains a middle section with an open courtyard in its center. Along one side are doors and windows marking small individual dwelling units. (One realizes at once that, though the group consists of young people of both sexes, they do not live openly in pairs, contrary to the situation in most contemporary communes.) Doors left ajar onto these dark, narrow cubicles reveal glimpses of dirty clothing and other disarray on the earth floor inside them. Not much of one's life could center here, apart from sleeping. They are unheated, despite outside winter temperatures that may fall below zero. According to report, kerosene lanterns keep the indoor temperature slightly above freezing.

Another large building complex lying behind a row of parked cars is called the Theater, although its functions are actually as diverse as those in the adobe. While the adobe was built from scratch by the community, this plaster structure is much older; it once housed the stables of the former ranch. The group's first major task after arriving here early in 1969 was to remodel it, adding on a final side so as to give it a completely enclosed courtyard. This became the original outdoor theater, in which plays were held until the finishing of the dome two years later. Rows of backless wooden benches, weathered and Spartan, fill its space, seating an invisible audience of about seventy. A few raised beach umbrellas stand forlornly at scattered intervals to offer protection from the sun. But the mood of this courtyard remains harsh. In one corner of it a welding unit has been set up.

Up and down two of its sides are more individual dwelling units. Some of these were fashioned from the former enclosures for horses; the large Dutch doors strongly suggest that animals, rather than men and women, still belong inside them. Along both upper walls of the courtyard, just below the roof line, inscriptions have been boldly painted. One learns that they spell out the relationships between the intellectual and emotional elements believed to be needed for work in the theater.

A number of other varied-purpose rooms lead off this courtyard into the corners of the building. One of these is the "art studio," containing table space upon which projects may be laid out, along with a small but discerning library of art books. Next to it is a much longer, emptier room with a wooden floor, now the general library. One end of it is entirely bare except for a disconnected potbelly stove, the ceiling above it scorched by a former fire. A single naked light bulb hangs down in the center of the room. At the other end are several low bookshelves, made of boards sitting loosely on concrete blocks. These are dwarfed by the vast surrounding space. In a corner a richly covered mattress and a few cushions are spread out for readers. A few handsome Oriental rugs cover the floor at this end only. The entire space seems sealed off and unreal. The dense heat produced by its unopened windows makes one anxious to move outside again.

Still another good-sized room, bearing far more signs of life, houses the "Destination Transport Company," familiarly known as D.T.C.[1] Here all the vehicles are repaired. The group collectively owns a Microbus, which is available for rent by individuals when not being used on group business. Privately owned cars and trucks—about half the members have them—are worked on for much less than would be charged outside. Though car ownership is theoretically discouraged as ecologically wasteful, this conces-

1. The group abounds in catchy, intriguing formal titles of this kind for its many subdivisions and phases of operations. Unfortunately, I cannot include most of them in this account, for they might too easily reveal the community's overall identity.

sion is made to its partial survival. In one way or another, members usually go into town at least once a week. The Laundromat there is a necessity, for such facilities are oddly lacking on the ranch despite its other concessions to technological self-sufficiency.

Opening off the D.T.C. is a "press room," containing a typewriter, stacks of plays which have been printed on the mimeograph, and all the trappings for publicity releases. A few old copies of the *New York Times* and local newspapers lie scattered about. This room, like the library, has the air of a place only seldom in use.

In the opposite corner of the building are several more darkish, crowded chambers. One is the prop room, which also contains many other general supplies on its tall shelves. When the ranch is overcrowded, newcomers sometimes have to be assigned sleeping space on its floor. But everyone must pass through it to reach the only shower and washbasin facilities, lying immediately behind. These are cluttered and dank, the basins foul-looking with brownish discoloration from the mineral content in the water. Still another larger room is filled with costumes and other theatrical paraphernalia, including some ancient treadle-operated sewing machines. Beyond it is a two-room apartment where live the only married couple among the ordinary membership.

At the rear of this whole complex, one steps out into a small garden plot, also beholding one of the four crude outhouses that lie scattered about the property. But attention is immediately fixed on the fifty-foot canvas dome rising into the air only a few yards away. Stepping inside its rounded vault, one enters yet another world. The interior floor is bare dirt on which a few old rugs have been laid for comfort, since the actors always perform barefoot. Looking upward, one gazes at the intricate pattern of two-by-four wood supports for the canvas, rising steadily to the top. Circular metal pieces at all the junction points add grace and strength to the design. The intersecting beams form a never-ending series of pentagons. The canvas is grommeted to the wood, a necessity in these suddenly rising winds.

Theater forms yet another major segment of expected daily activity for everyone here. Again, in practice the pace accelerates when drama festivals are about to be held. Sometimes the rehearsals go on till past midnight. The dome, barely completed before the festival of August, 1971, is an enormous source of group pride, a constantly visible testimonial to their capacity to carry an arduous project through to completion. Sewing the huge sheets of canvas to exact proportions, measuring each wood support precisely, and hauling heavy materials into position high in the air occupied a large share of the membership for many months. Now, when they stand

inside, they marvel at the acoustics which their labor miraculously produced. From the center sounds ricochet off the canvas to create startling
illusions of intimacy and closeness.

To the rear of the dome, hidden from casual visitors, lies a vast junk
heap. Closer inspection reveals that it, like everything else, is highly organized. Piles of scrap lumber have been arranged by size. Old flush toilets
and washbasins squat uselessly on the open ground. This area is called the
"materials yard."

At the rear of it stands a school bus, gleaming in bright new yellow
paint. It is used by the group on its cross-country drama tours. An official-
looking destination sign above its windshield spells out the single word
ACTIVITY. This must mystify passersby on its travels, since the bus has no
other markings. One cannot help pausing to compare this vehicle with the
famous bus which carried Ken Kesey's Merry Pranksters along a hundred
Main Streets.[2] The contrast shows at once how widely the image of this
community differs from that of the standard counter-culture. For this bus
has none of the decrepit, flamboyant air of a hippie vehicle; instead, it is almost conspicuously neat and unassuming. Yet that one word ACTIVITY displays a quiet sense of self-importance, suggesting an inner purpose of some
semi-secret kind.

In front of the materials yard stands a one-room adobe. Ezra used to
share it with his wife, Eva, but now it is called "Eva's house." It has a
pleasant little walled garden, violating the purely utilitarian spirit of everything else here. Before the group purchased this land, it was a radio shack.
Inside it is tastefully furnished in a style suggesting casually forsaken
wealth. The mattress lies directly on the floor. A window, tactfully placed
on the side away from the materials yard, gives an expansive view of untouched desert.

Eva's position in the community, the visitor might soon learn if he
lingered, has not changed in the slightest despite her separation from her
husband. She is the manager, responsible for the practical functioning of
the operation in all its phases. Thus she stands at the top of a hierarchy
in a formal chain of command. Below her are a series of departments, each
with its own assignments. One person is in charge of all the construction
and drainage projects, another of the kitchen, and yet others of crafts,
theater operations, the gardens, animals, finances for the individual enterprises, ecology and utilities, and the running of vehicles (D.T.C.). Every
week all these department heads meet with Eva to review each phase of

2. See Tom Wolfe, *The Electric Kool-Aid Acid Test* (New York: Bantam Books,
1969).

their activities and to establish priorities for the immediate future. This Monday-night meeting, as it is called, usually starts very late and often goes on until nearly daybreak. Eva turns out to be the daughter of a Boston financier.

On the slope below Eva's house stretches the main area of gardens, occupying about half an acre. It is fenced to keep out jackrabbits. At the far end is a small greenhouse, covered by an old sheet of thin plastic in great disarray. The gardens are divided into numbered subplots, with narrow paths running in between them. Two faucets stand at central locations, from which great lengths of hose loop outward. In the midday heat the garden is apt to be deserted. But every morning and evening community members will steal time from other obligations to look after their assigned area of plantings. Each subplot is shared by three or four people, a scheme which offers leeway if someone's labor is needed elsewhere more urgently.

In 1971, thanks to an unusual drought, the garden looked less healthy than it had the previous year. In some areas corn, tomatoes, cabbages and peas were achieving full height, but in others the early plantings were stunted and dying. Thus the garden can be a source of strain and anguish. The desire to succeed in it is keen, for it is the obvious bastion of an ecological self-sufficiency that is much hoped for. Yet, as in so many other experimental communities, none of the members came with previous experience in agriculture.

This did not prevent Ezra and Eva from rapidly promulgating a definite theory about how best to proceed, one which they term "bio-dynamic gardening." It was apparently borrowed from Anthroposophy.[3] The main principle of bio-dynamic gardening is that "life supports life." Therefore seeds of many kinds are supposed to be planted close together. Straight rows are designed for tractors, they point out, and therefore appropriate only to the commercial agriculture of the old civilization. The close clustering of a variety of different species, in an interlocking swirl, is supposed to allow plants to help each other to grow.

Bio-dynamic gardening has other corollaries, each of which is mercilessly insisted upon in instructions given to newcomers. Watering is done on a rigid schedule, partly to enable the two hoses to be shared, partly out of anxiety that the well might run dry, though it never has. In an extreme version of the idea that frequent, shallow waterings are a waste, each

3. See Ehrenfried Pfeiffer, *Bio-Dynamic Farming and Gardening* (New York: Anthroposophic Press, 1943). Anthroposophy is yet another movement in the general Theosophical tradition.

subplot is allowed to be deeply moistened only once a week, even in a season of no rain, once the young plants have appeared above the soil. To counter fears that this policy does not give the plants enough water, it is pointed out that one plot, near the top of the garden, has been doing conspicuously better than the others, though the people assigned to it swear they have watered it no oftener, only giving it unusual care in such other ways as mulching and harvesting. (Frequent "harvesting," i.e., pruning, of young plants is believed to increase their capacity to keep on growing; for the same reason, all leaves that are dead or poorly formed are diligently removed, so that the plant will not waste its strength giving them support.) Straw is spread around the plants to help keep the soil from drying out in the long intervals between waterings. The only chemical fertilizer is derived from the men's urine, which collects in buckets and, after standing for three days (so that the extraneous chemicals pass into the atmosphere), becomes almost pure ammonia, which is dumped into the compost pit. The group is proud of these ingenious efforts at recycling. But, despite so many intricately controlled practices, well over half the plants were withering away before they reached maturity. Also scattered about the property are many young fruit trees, which are watered on an even less frequent schedule; it is too soon to know how they will fare.

Near the garden lies the rubble of a former ranch house that burned down. A small amount of new adobe construction was once begun here, but it has been abandoned. The area is a great eyesore. Invisible beneath it are two large underground rooms, formerly cellars; in one of them, a woman in the group lives with her two very young children. The other is intended for a future library.

At the rear of the property a substantial population of animals is kept. Like the garden, this is conceived as a deliberate training exercise, though it occupies only a few of the members' time. There are two horses and a number of goats, sheep, pigs, and chickens. Eggs, though regularly gathered, are not enough for the group's needs. One of the pigs was slaughtered for a solstice feast—the spirit of the group is far from vegetarian. Elsewhere, behind chicken wire, live a flock of ducks and geese; they seem healthy but ill at ease on the parched terrain. Eventually the group would like to do much more with animals; it has even dreamed of running cattle.

Behind the pens, the generator suddenly begins to roar, indicating that the afternoon period of electric power is now under way. The sound drones out all over the landscape and is deafening at this close range. A windmill is quietly turning, too; it drives a subsidiary pump which gives water to the animals. Nearby are located several of the ecology experiments, aimed at demonstrating alternative sources of energy in the hope that someday the community (and the world) can live independently of fossil fuels.

One important building has yet to be entered, a small, yellow wooden house which stands by itself near the barnyard, obviously one of the former outbuildings of the original ranch. Now it provides still another major focus of daily activity.

Entering it, one arrives at once in the middle of a crowded, narrow dining room, with scarcely room to squeeze past the benches. A long table, accommodating the whole population, has been formed out of several smaller ones. In the early afternoon its surface is nearly bare, except for flies hovering near bowls of sugar and powdered milk. Two members are cleaning up and starting advance preparations for the evening meal. Kerosene lanterns are spread along the tabletop, even though electric fixtures hang from the ceiling. (The generator is not run during the dinner hour.)

On the right-hand wall of the dining room two descending columns of words have been painted, spaced like this:

Civilization	Biosphere
Individual	School
Groups	Psychology
Soil	Organisms
Atoms	Crystals
Hylé	Heat

Upon questioning, one learns that hylé is primary cosmic substance. On the left wall at the far end of the room one's eye catches the following:

THE LAW OF OCTAVES
Higher Value
–Shock–
Completion
Detachment
Insight
Picking up the Pieces
–Shock–
Realization of Personal Difficulty
Apply to Yourself
Value

Still elsewhere one reads: "Only the truth can save us. What is the truth."

Beside this seven scientific formulas descend in a ladder; the first is $E=mc^2$. On the end wall above a doorway, "The Inexhaustibility of Phenomena," and across from it three handsomely stylized deer.

A doorway leads to a tiny alcove, which is called the Conscious Cook's Room. Indeed it contains a large shelf of cookbooks, in a wall full of battered paperbacks whose titles range from *The Wonderful Wizard of Oz* to Ruth Benedict's *Patterns of Culture*. Yet, as in the other room called the "library," one senses that these books are seldom read; only the cooking manuals see daily service. The room serves for still more committee meetings, though it is barely large enough to hold a table, sofa, and one or two chairs. An old wall telephone reveals the group's willingness to maintain ready contact with the outside world.

Another door leads into the kitchen, which is on two levels, having recently been enlarged. At the far end of it are two huge ranges, ancient but sturdy, which devour bottled gas. There is a large work table, and everywhere the shelves are lined with battered utensils. The dishes are commonly cracked or chipped, a great hodgepodge of sub-Goodwill castoffs. The whole room has a reasonably clean, well-kept air. Kitchen tasks, like everything else, are regularly scheduled. A different person, male or female, cooks each night, a second person is assigned to afternoon clean-up duty, generally assisting the cook, and two more perform the late-evening clean-up. For breakfast and lunch, everyone is on his own, and all are expected to wash their own dishes. The fare at these two meals is rather Spartan: eggs, coffee, bran flakes and powdered milk in the morning; for lunch, only the chancy contents of one of the refrigerators which holds leftovers, invariably rice or vegetables or bread from dinner the night before. Everyone is entitled to eat one orange per day. Those who want more fruit must pay extra for each item.

Dinner is thus the main meal. No one misses it, not only from hunger but because it is the most serious daily occasion. People who have had to go outside on business always manage to get back before the dinner gong, which usually sounds around eight o'clock.

The cooking for the dinner is also taken very seriously. It is regarded as a deliberate attempt to fashion the cuisine suitable for the New Age. The cook is supposed to begin consciously meditating about the meal the night before. Every dinner must have a theme. Sometimes it is a place, sometimes a mood or a feeling, around which the entire meal is planned. Table decorations are hastily assembled to illustrate it. But at the same time the cook works within the limits of rules which are every bit as arbitrary as those for the garden. One such rule, established after long experience, is that the meal itself cannot be thrown together intuitionally, but must follow printed recipes. Hence the need for all the cookbooks. Moreover, the basic marketing for the whole week is done in town on Mondays. The meat and vegetables are kept in the cook's refrigerator, which members are not allowed to rifle. Each day the cook must work with what is actually on hand. Still another rule restricts the meat for the main dish to those kinds which sell for no more than 58 cents a pound, the going price of hamburger at the nearest Safeway. Ground beef, chicken, cheap chuck roast, and more rarely fish or liver are the mainstays. There is also a green fresh vegetable, which must be bought since the gardens still produce so poorly, a salad (to which the garden does contribute at least a symbolic amount), and a filling starch dish, usually rice or potatoes. Often the cook will bake bread or cookies, and there may be a cake or pudding for dessert. Big pots of coffee and tea are made; several flavorful kinds of the latter are purchased in bulk. In hot weather it is a special treat when the cook decides to make iced tea, lemonade, or fruit punch; this always disappears halfway through the meal.

Every Sunday evening the group has a special meal known as a feast. At these occasions beer or wine is invariably served, though in such small quantities as to be merely ceremonial. It is drunk to the accompaniment of a long series of toasts. Four times a year, at each equinox and solstice, a special midnight feast is held, even more elaborate, though it follows the same basic pattern.

This small building also contains a bathroom with the only flush toilet on the property, which women are allowed to use, though it is much too foul to be inviting. To guard against disease, the bane of so many less-organized communes, all dishes are rinsed in Clorox each time. A similar rule is that one must always lower the toilet lid after using the outhouse, to keep the flies away from the excrement. Sickness still occurs, one is told, but it follows an oddly uniform pattern. Within the first month after arrival, nearly everyone is briefly laid low by diarrhea, as if it were an initiation through which they must inevitably pass. After that, except among the small children, there is almost no ill health. Waste disposal is performed with careful efficiency. Outside the crowded pantry which adjoins the kitchen, a series of barrels stand close together, marked "glass," "cans," and "paper." The persons on clean-up, afternoon and evening, must burn the combustible trash while standing alertly by the fire to keep it from getting out of hand. Garbage is divided into the kinds the pigs do and do not eat; the latter is taken to the compost pile in the garden. Waste water from the kitchen flows by gravity through an open trench to the duck enclosure. The smallest details of daily life are thus marked by forethought. In this connection, the word "commune" is never heard around here, except as an unfavorable epithet, for it implies the disorder and lack of conscious planning and effort which this community strongly rejects.

A rapid tour of the property reveals certain other intriguing clues as to the kind of life being led here. In their manner and physical appearance, the members fit into neither of the common categories "hip" or "straight." The men's hair is usually cut quite short; only one or two wear beards. Despite the heat, no one goes half naked (as in other New Mexico communes), and in fact long sleeves seem to be the rule. Only a couple of the girls habitually go barefoot. Yet Levi's and ancient work shirts, sometimes falling apart and nearly always deeply caked with grime, are the uniform of most of the men and some of the women. On the street in town, it would be impossible readily to place such people—they are dirty and unkempt, unlike their gleaming bus, but they are not exactly hip. Perhaps they most resemble a team of surveyors or engineers accustomed to working in an area remote from civilization. It is this aspect of their style which makes one's mind turn involuntarily to science-fiction images of men from another realm.

Something else one notices immediately on this ranch. The members, wherever they are or whatever they may be doing, will suddenly break forth into cries that sound like chants, addressed to no one in particular. Often these are uttered at the top of their lungs. They can occur when several people have gathered, or, even more commonly, during the isolated performance of a task. Only while filling their plates at the Sunday-evening feast does everyone chant together. Yet, though chanting is an individual act, it is strongly stylized, always following the same pattern. A few prolonged vowel sounds are invariably uttered, and always sung in a minor key: "Ooooooooooh—laaaaaaaaa—eeeeeeeeee—laaaaaaaaaa—ooooooo-oooooh!" But the particular syllables appear to be randomly chosen by the person rather than coming in a set order. No one else pays any attention to such a chant when it occurs. It is evidently regarded as an utterly natural form of periodic inner release.

Journal of a Five Weeks' Stay

Many kinds of tours of these eleven acres are possible, because the group's policy is to treat each stranger individually in accord with his perceived vibration. Those who are hostile will almost literally be pushed out at once. Innocently admiring hippies will be shown around with apparent good will which masks secret contempt. A Texas tourist will be courted for the sale of craft products. Foreign visitors are for some reason given the best treatment, no matter if they are hip. Even Canadians are often invited to stay for dinner or (a far rarer privilege) for overnight.

My own tour was for five weeks. Why I was permitted to stay with the group and to write about it with no conditions attached, other than its anonymity, long puzzled me, for it did not seem that my vibrations (as an academic outsider and in many ways a cool skeptic) could be so very good. Partly I think it stemmed from a tendency, as in Vedanta, to treat anyone who displays interest in them as a potential convert. Ezra also revealed a transparent pride in having the group written up in a scholarly book, though he shuns publicity in the mass media. Beyond this, one side of his mind approves of the ideal of scientific objectivity, which he had absorbed in an earlier phase of his life. "Fair, honest, objective" were the words he used repeatedly to describe his understanding of the kind of account I should be writing, though he assumed it would contain some of my personal responses as well. These were words which I welcomed, because I felt they represented my own aims exactly. But as time passed I became increasingly less sure that these phrases held a common meaning for both of us.

Toward the end of my stay, Ezra volunteered two more reasons as to why my presence was being allowed. First, I had come with a definite *purpose*. I had corresponded with them for many months, maintaining contact, and then I had physically shown up. Will, purpose, and the carrying of tasks through to completion are values given the highest respect by this group. Secondly, the summer of 1971 was a time when the group could afford to be unusually open to outsiders. It was throwing its weight into a series of public, external activities—a bazaar for the sale of crafts, an ecology conference, and a new three-week festival of plays. Later on, the group might require greater seclusion. It is interesting in this connection, however, that Ezra seemed to conceal nothing in the way of his behavior. Most of the time he appeared too pleased with himself, and too involved with the group, to regulate his words or actions, though he could indeed turn on a deliberately engaging manner to casual visitors.

Ezra's domination of the group is open and for the most part undisguised. To the uninitiated who arrive here, his influence can seem almost unbearably pervasive. One soon realizes that every small practice which makes up this complicated rhythm of daily life carries the stamp of his considered approval, and that the major outlines are wholly the product of his mind. This entire social order is the tangible enactment of his own vision. To it he addresses an attention which is immediate and constant. Though he rarely takes part in routine labor, he wanders about the property frequently, choosing what and whom to see. As he passes by, everyone's inner attention automatically turns toward him, though tasks are still being performed. Living here, one quickly falls into the pattern of unconsciously wishing for his approval in everything one does. This is a community where the physical presence of a leader plays the same role that it evidently did among the Vedanta nuns in Boston and La Crescenta.

Nor is this all. Suddenly, it might be anywhere, Ezra will explode into wrath, usually directed at one person. Calmly in control of himself one minute, in the next he will be shouting the most hurtful words conceivable in a furious assault upon the ego of some trapped individual. During these rages he will accuse the person of harboring deliberately destructive motives, often involving the way in which a task has been performed. He will seize upon what appear to be innocent failures to follow precise instructions and transform them into calculated acts of sabotage. The recipients of this intense abuse have seldom if ever done anything which might seem to merit it. But the verbal attack rolls over them for many minutes, while they are expected to return no more than mild, rational explanations. These merely feed the fuel of his invective. He reiterates his accusations until no possible response is left. Then, all at once, his tirade comes to an end, and everyone continues as if nothing had happened.

As will later appear, a definite rationale for these outbursts exists; they are called "confrontations" and are given a meaning as part of a deliberate regime of inner self-development. Thus they can be said to form yet one more element in the many-faceted pattern of living which has been adopted on the ranch. But their immediate effect is awesome and chilling. The spectacle of these unrestrained scenes impels some newcomers to leave precipitately, planning never to return. And for those who decide to remain, Ezra's spell grows all the deeper as the result of these seemingly gratuitous moments of emotional reckoning.

So total is Ezra's authority that I realized my presence in the community was entirely dependent upon his continued good will. Soon I heard stories, some of them recent and highly specific, about persons who had been told without warning to get off the property immediately. Moreover, twice during my stay I heard him threaten members with expulsion if they did not perform particular acts of penitence. One night at the dinner table Ezra reprimanded me briefly for not performing enough physical labor. (It was, everything considered, a just complaint.) The effect of all this was to give me a tinge of uncertainty and fear. While Ezra was there—he was absent during the last ten days of my stay—I never lost the feeling of being watched, tested, and judged. But in this I was surely an equal with everybody else. I shared in a general ethos of psychological domination and submission, the only difference being that I openly admitted the existence of this situation to myself. Because I was keenly conscious of the authoritarian dimension to this community's way of life, while everyone else seemed to repress this awareness, I remained much more the observer than the participant. I frankly think that if I had tried to extend my sojourn with the group for a much longer period of time, my mental reservations would have become increasingly evident, and one day I would have been told to leave.[4]

My relations with the rank-and-file were as good as could have been expected, given the brief period of mutual contact and the undisguised nature of my purpose. The style of the community fosters impersonal, work-oriented contacts between people, especially in the early stages of one's stay. On the day-to-day level of communication, the general absence of explicit warmth or expressiveness made it easy for me superficially to merge with the others. It was rather like being a newcomer in a highly technical organization, where what matters most is one's greenness in the relevant skills—in this case, building construction, cooking, bio-dynamic gardening, carpentry, acting, and the construction of solar-energy devices. Beyond this practical level, those members who tended to be somewhat warmer and more relaxed appeared to display these qualities freely with me, while those who were either silently standoffish or crudely authoritarian in their general bearing treated me according to form. In other words, I do not honestly think that I was much of a factor.

During the five weeks, I interviewed everyone individually at least once, usually without a notebook, asking them a few basic questions about their backgrounds and life histories and then encouraging them to expand as freely as they wanted about "why they were there." Naturally they did not reveal all the important things about themselves, but they seemed mostly to be very honest and helpful as far as they went. (I wrote these interviews down the moment they were over.) Several persons really opened up to me, but, as an anthropologist friend had warned me would happen in advance, they tended to be among the most marginal members of the group.

Throughout my stay I kept a copious journal, writing down events as

4. Ezra's response to me was strikingly similar in many ways to that of the leader of the religious group studied by John Lofland, *Doomsday Cult* (Englewood Cliffs, New Jersey: Prentice-Hall, 1966).

soon as I could do so in privacy, often several times a day. I trained my memory (quite successfully, I felt) to retain exact phrases and details in the interim. These journal notes form the basis for this entire chapter, including its direct quotations, though some of the latter, especially from Ezra and Eva, were openly recorded in shorthand at the time.

Dinner is the high point of every day. Any unlucky person who has been standing outside the little yellow building hungrily waiting is asked to go the rounds of the property beating the heavy triangle chime that announces it. Magically people converge into the cramped dining room. It is the one time when everyone is together. Still, they arrive separately, from their scattered locations, and it is only inside that one has the sense of a crowd. A few have dressed up a bit, because Ezra recently reprimanded someone for wearing a "dirty undershirt" (by which he meant a white T-shirt). An exact number of places have been set, with large serving dishes filling the center between the row of lighted kerosene lanterns. Plates are at every place. You take your own from your permanently assigned seat and walk with it up and down the table, heaping it with food. Squeezing past the others rather awkwardly, you return to your seat and begin eating at once, as is the custom.

Soon all have served themselves and are seated in the tight space. Now you perceive the most striking characteristic of the dinners here—an almost total silence. The sounds are the mechanical ones of thirty people eating, broken only by: "Please pass the water," "Salt, please," and "Liquid milk." As in Vedanta before the service begins, the quality of a group silence maintained in this fashion is impressive. If asked, people will say that there is no rule of silence at dinner. But if chatter breaks out and goes on too long, it will be reprimanded by one of the older members. After some minutes, the cook may fetch a dessert, which if sumptuous will bring forth a brief "Ah!" from many in the group, but the quiet, busy eating continues. Cups are continually passed along the table for coffee and tea, which are served by those sitting near either end.

Only Ezra breaks the silence. The tempo is his to set. He will often start by throwing out a brief, stereotyped question, addressed to no one in particular: "Any speeches?" "Any encounters or adventures?" "Any confessions?" "Any songs?" After a pause individuals will respond voluntarily to his chosen question of the evening. An uncanny rhythm becomes established. Though particular "speeches" may lead to a lively interchange afterward, there are never any interruptions; two people never talk at once. Sometimes there are short periods of general silence between the speeches, which increase the "heaviness" of the atmosphere. The scene has some of the artificiality of theater about it, yet it often brings forth extremes of personal emotion. Certain people weep as they briefly confess their innermost feelings. Or there can be contagious bursts of laughter, which sweep the entire table like a forest blaze, only to die down again just as rapidly. At times these collective reactions, highly stylized and yet deeply genuine, make the entire group seem to merge into a single organic entity, now breathing, now laughing, now remaining silently alert. This, one realizes, is the kind of fusion that can occur when a body of people live together month by month, in some cases for several years. It is all the more powerful when one ponders the mutual isolation in which these same people appear to remain during the long hours of the day away from the dinner table, and the lack of gossip or casual sociability at almost any time. Freed from these distractions, the group spirit grows in a less visible form, which is ultimately more intense. The dinner table is an occasion when it may—though it does not always—come fully forth.

And yet, on another level, one comes back to Ezra, who seems forever to be pulling the strings. Hardly at all does one person from the rank-and-file speak directly to another. Remarks pass through Ezra, and he responds to each (unless, in his mind, it is too greatly off the track to merit comment). Ezra recognizes people; sometimes hands are even raised. This is how the tempo is controlled. It is almost like a classroom, though far more powerful emotionally. As the discussion plays its course, Ezra takes it over with increasing openness. He finds generally applicable lessons in what people have chanced to say; he makes these explicit. He loves to talk, and the group is spellbound, seemingly no matter how long he chooses to go on. It may be for an hour or an hour and a half. The spirit of his discourse is like what one imagines a Puritan sermon to have been: often abstract for long periods, yet coming down vividly into the lives of individuals from time to time, better to rivet their attention; and, through it all, unfathomable rhetorical self-assurance. To this mixture are added real flashes of intellectual genius, along with other evidences of an overreaching quality. Toward the end, he shows the ability of all good teachers to pull together everything that has been said, rolling it into a solid ball of convenient size, and handing it to each person with a final verbal gesture.

When Ezra is done, he signals the fact by rising immediately from his seat and taking his dishes out to the kitchen. Everyone else remains motionless and silent. A moment later Ezra returns and slides inconspicuously into a chair in the corner, where he sits in near darkness, joining the silence of the group. The period of stillness may then last for quite some time, a quarter of an hour if the evening has been especially profound. It is called, in the technical vocabulary of the group, the "eating" period—when one is to "eat" what has been built up by way of collective psychic force, drawing in the energy rather than letting it be dispersed and wasted. One does not close one's eyes; it is not an inward meditation. Instead one looks straight ahead with reasonable attention, yet not focusing on any single object too exclusively. There is a great feeling of dedication and rapport. I too would share in this; my sense of merger with the group was then apt to be at its peak.

Finally, someone (usually a long-established member) dares break the silence by rising, as quietly as possible, and taking his utensils to the kitchen. Still, there is no rush to leave. Gradually, one by one, people get up. Someone may make an announcement, for instance of a theater rehearsal in a few minutes, though these are deliberately kept to a minimum. One or two private conversations may now occur in low tones, arranging committee meetings or firming up engagements for work on projects. The screen door bangs as individuals leave, often to make themselves ready for theater or to work late into the night on their crafts. In another ten minutes the room will be deserted except for the two members of the clean-up crew and perhaps one or two hangers-on.

Though this is their pattern, no two dinners are ever exactly alike. Sometimes in place of profundity there is practical pep talk, again dominated by Ezra, on such topics as how best to sell theater tickets (by dividing potential customers into sociological types and dealing with them on that basis). Or Ezra will call for actors to recite their lines from one of the plays, which makes for a much briefer session. Another variant comes each Thursday night, when Ezra gives a formal lecture, still seated at the table, which is open to outsiders for a small fee (one or two older women from a nearby town usually come out to hear it). When I was there, a five-week series on Buddhism was beginning. Their tone often tended to be schematic and dry, almost too academic. But without fail everyone would bring out a notebook and dutifully record his words.

The Sunday-night "feasts" provide another variation. Ezra and the others enter the dining room chanting and continue to chant while they help themselves to the food. Once all are seated, for a few moments there is the usual silence. Then the toasts begin. It is very bad form to drink any of one's beer or wine privately, outside the structure of the toasts. Instead, at every toast one is expected to raise one's glass and touch it to each of the neighboring glasses within reach. There is no letup in this; it is done seriously and elaborately each time, until the final "bottoms up." In-

dividuals are encouraged to propose toasts, but all of them must be fun-
neled through the toastmaster, Jacob, who sits at the far end of the table.
Thus someone says, "Mr. Toastmaster, I propose a toast." Jacob recognizes
him. The toast is said out loud. Then Jacob repeats it, to give it sanction.
If it strikes a general chord of response, many other voices may also repeat
it, as glasses are touched. There is a rule against toasts addressed to particular individuals within the group, even the cook of the night's meal.

The toasts are expected to be light in character; they have nothing to
do with the group's inner philosophical beliefs. For instance, the beer itself
or the brewery may be toasted. (One such toast, addressed to Adolph
Coors, revealed the group's political unconcern, since Coors is a well-
known promoter of right-wing causes.) On the Fourth of July, which happened to fall on Sunday, toasts were made to various founding fathers; one
girl was asked to read part of the Declaration of Independence; and a single
firecracker was set off outdoors at the end, with everyone happily looking
on. There were no gestures of anti-American alienation. In keeping with
this deliberate mood of Sunday-evening lightness, there is no discussion
after the meal; after a brief period of silence, people leave one by one.
Afternoon tea, incidentally, is another Sunday ritual; usually held at four
o'clock, with homemade cookies, it is the closest equivalent to an ordinary
social hour which the group is ever allowed to experience. Since work on
projects is not otherwise suspended on Sundays, the tea and the evening
feast serve as the only tokens of weekly letup in the severity of the community schedule.

A few of the weekday dinner discussions in the period of my stay stand
out with special force. One of these took off from the cook's theme of the
day, which was the "West Village." Ezra began by asking if there were
"any reminiscences." One by one people came forth with stories about their
own past experiences in the Village. (It was characteristic of the literalness
with which they take Ezra's cues that, when anyone's mind wandered accidentally over to the East Village, he was quickly called to order, unless
the purpose was a direct comparison with the West. Thus a certain dutifulness underlay even the apparently innocent nostalgia.) It turned out that a
large share of the group had spent some time in the Village and knew the
scene there intimately. Lively anecdotes emerged about particular characters, hotels, and restaurants. Wonderful gusts of laughter broke forth at
appropriate times. But then Ezra began to intrude more and more, as if
determined to switch the light mood over into a heavy one. He suddenly
lashed out at certain persons in strong terms, accusing them of "lying" and
of "suppressing" their real feelings in all this storytelling—even though,

one should recall, it was he who had first encouraged them to open up. He said the Village had a deeper meaning for them than they would acknowledge, as a symbol of emancipation from their parents. Ezra's tone became ever more intense, until it succeeded in killing the happy nostalgia. He bore down on several individuals, demanding that they come clean with what they had been previously "suppressing." Two of the young men confessed, with actual sobs, that the Village had stood for the kind of rupture with their middle-class parents that they had been incapable of making during their teenage years. This admission of personal inward battle, and an inability to break free, produced a profound wave of emotion at the table. These two stood revealed in sharp contrast to the larger number whose reminiscences showed that they had easily entered a pronounced bohemian phase early in their lives, even if they had later grown beyond it. Between these confessions and Ezra's harping accusations that some people were "lying" about what they really felt, the entire table was now gripped by a mood of high-pitched inner agitation.

Then Ezra began to lecture forcefully about the West Village as the one-time cultural capital of the United States. He said that it was calculatedly destroyed by economic interests, who tore enough of the old buildings down to kill its flavor. Much was convincing in his historical recapitulation, though parts of it sounded too conspiratorial. The West Village, he went on, had been *the* center of everything that was vital in the United States. This was demonstrable because, first of all, everyone inside New York looked up to it as the place where one could get away from the humdrum and the routine, experiencing art and theater and cultural innovation; while, secondly, everyone of any creative aspiration who lived outside New York looked to that city as a whole in the same manner. Its only failing as a cultural climate, Ezra noted, was in its lack of scientific resonance. Our own community, he said, using a phrase he repeated with great emphasis, is to be a community of "actors and scientists." Thus it is more balanced intellectually than the Village had ever been. What came through very strongly in all this was Ezra's identification with the older bohemian tradition in America—and thus, interestingly enough, with freedom in that classic sense.

A few nights later the discussion topic was fear of the hydrogen bomb and the destruction of civilization. Here was a theme which could produce a heavy mood without much forcing by Ezra. As a way of preparing for the forthcoming ecology conference, Geiger counters had been purchased and were passed around to everyone at the table so that we could hear the tick of the gamma rays (from background radiation) over the earphones.

It made the dangers seem very real. After this, encouraged by Ezra, nearly everyone present described the effect the bomb had made on their imaginations. Many in the group had been young children during the mid-1950's, when fear of nuclear war was at its peak. They recalled, in a variety of ways, the great impact of this atmosphere on their lives and thoughts. Several had even experienced recurring dreams of atomic attack. Champ, who was the most authoritarian troublemaker in the rank-and-file, stood out in this discussion for admitting to an extreme attitude of alienation. Let the bomb fall, he said in describing his innermost feelings; he didn't care, in fact he almost liked the idea.

But Ezra's line of approach—and of course again he came to the fore as the conversation went on—was of a contrary kind. His point was that we *can* survive through intelligence. Shrewdness is the correct response to any overwhelming situation. This is our real intuition, he insisted, despite all the fear and despair in these unearthed memories. And we should follow it, never allowing ourselves to become fatalistic (for this is at bottom a suicidal impulse). In fact, Ezra reminisced, during the height of the Cuban missile crisis of 1962, his own response had been actually to board a plane and leave the United States for a neutral location. The builders of the New Age must always carry on somewhere in the world. In a way, this is their supreme moment. They must flee temporarily in order to be ready to help direct the construction of the new civilization among the survivors.

But, for the others, the sudden sharing of hitherto secret fears remained uppermost. An impromptu show of hands revealed that nearly everyone expected the bomb actually to be dropped someday. The next morning several people, including Eva, remarked that they had been unable to sleep after so depressing an evening. I too was pulled in by the mood and began to feel, by the end, that my classroom teaching of this topic had been much too complacent in the past. It was Ezra, I felt, who tended to reduce the question too easily to the mundane level of survival mechanics. His position was understandable enough in terms of his commitment to the New Age. But it could not set the tone of response inside his own rank-and-file, which remained at the level of my own primitive awe and despair. Perhaps for this reason, Ezra bore down heavily on no one during the course of the evening; instead, the mood remained that of "considering" the issues thoughtfully together.

At a dinner some days later we witnessed the opposite extreme. An accident had occurred that afternoon owing to a faulty tire repair by a member in charge of D.T.C. Driving down the desert highway in her convertible at fifty-five miles per hour just afterward, the girl had lost her wheel, careening to the side of the road. The man responsible—here we shall call him T.—had not tightened the bolts carefully enough. Ezra commanded that the tire be brought in and placed on the dinner table as a centerpiece, where all could see it. Then he accused T. of trying to kill the girl; he said T. secretly hated both this girl and one other whom he named; indeed, he implied that T. disliked all women. (The girl quietly joined in these accusations.) Then Ezra attacked T. in terms of his upper-class New England background—a theme to which he also returned on other evenings in various connections. The girl whose car had been "sabotaged" was a Catholic; the other girl he disliked was a Jew. Do Protestant New Englanders really fix tires for Catholics or Jews? he insinuated.

What followed was, from an outsider's standpoint, truly remarkable. T. tearfully *accepted* the idea of his deliberate intent, without the slightest sign of contrary resistance. Ezra then kept hammering further: T., what do you *really feel* at this moment? But T. kept intellectualizing in his submissive vein. He began talking about his hatred of the school and university system he'd been through. While living here he would periodically forget this hatred, and with it his conscious purpose of self-transformation within the group, and then he would become murderous in an unconscious way. This argument was somewhat hard to follow. All through it, despite his sobs, he actually maintained a verbally resourceful, stiff-upper-lip manner of self-criticism, which suggested the Boy Scout code of an upper-class good guy. Thus it seemed right to me at the time that, as Ezra kept saying, T. was still being evasive, keeping his vulnerable self out of reach, even while formally admitting such a monstrous kind of guilt. For instance, T. attacked his own Anglo-Saxon family tradition but did so in a curiously literary vein: "William Blake was the only good Englishman who ever lived." His own family, he declaimed with great feeling, was rotten beneath the façade of its social pretension, because illegitimate children were sprinkled throughout its past (what an old-fashioned proof of rottenness, I thought). Again Ezra said that T. must break through all this and express what he really felt, or else it would remain bottled up and come out in these murderous ways. Do something right now, Ezra shouted.

So T. took one of the glass water jugs from the dining table, raised it deliberately, and threw it against a wall, shattering it to pieces. But this again, I realized even while it was happening, constituted a formal, stylized act of obedience to Ezra's command, a controlled response rather than a real release of emotion. The thought also passed through my mind that T.'s control was a great source of strength in him, and Ezra was thrusting his surgical scalpel very far toward the center of his being.

In the world outside this community, such an episode would of course have been handled far differently. T. would have been accused of mere carelessness. But the guilt would have festered much longer despite the kindlier initial treatment. Ezra's approach, though it involved his authoritarian style at its most extreme, did have the virtue of bringing every possible feeling squarely into the open. The girl, for instance, volunteered that T. always reminded her of her father, who, she said, was also trying to kill her. Once these thoughts were all lying on the table, a much quickened process of healing could take place. Finally, Ezra asked T. to fetch his William Blake and read some of his favorite poems to the group. This was a kind of absolution, a signal that the matter had been ended and that he was being taken back into the group. But Ezra also imposed a penalty: T. must give the girl his total income for a one-year period and take her income in return. The alternative was expulsion. Early the next morning, when I happened to spend an hour with him, T. was completely his usual self.

A Thursday-night "class" given by Ezra, on the Buddhist approach to meditation, brought forth another dinner-table scene of still a different kind. It was a surprise initially to be told that many here were "deeply" into meditation of any sort. No specific time of day is set aside for it, and everyone's schedule is crowded with other responsibilities. But I was told that one usually meditated in the midst of the performance of one's external tasks. What sort of meditation could this really be, I wondered? It could not mean the traditional retreat into isolation still in vogue, for example, at the Lama Foundation. Now the dinner talk promised to clear up the mystery.

As Ezra began describing in detail each of the first four stages of consciousness which a young monk should achieve, it became evident that the group was actually trying to practice meditation while Ezra continued to speak. This seemed astonishing, for I linked the idea of meditation to long, uninterrupted silence, preferably in solitude. Yet here were people asking questions, verbally describing their blocks and difficulties, in short carrying on a conversation, while they simultaneously claimed to be reaching the second or third level of inward awareness. Did all this reveal an incredible superficiality and self-deception? Or was the group tuned to such an achievement through long practice?

While I was inwardly debating these matters, the verbal interchange finally stopped. For another forty-five minutes the group sat at the table without speaking. Many people now began to breathe heavily. Surprising things began to happen. Several of the girls started to cry out. These cries grew ever more distinct and insistent. "Out, out!" a couple of them started saying, over and over. I realized this must be the casting out of devils from within. In their own language, it was an act of affirmation against negative internal resistance or "denial," so that the energy created by this very self-division would reach a high peak (such energy was termed by Ezra "third force"). Inward conflict was being deliberately used as a device for personal transformation, as if self-hatred offered the key to self-transcendence and growth.

This way of proceeding made me think back to another dinner session, shortly after my arrival, when in response to Ezra's initial question, "Any confessions?" about half a dozen members of the group had one by one volunteered statements about themselves which were both desperately sincere and yet, somehow, extremely stereotyped in format. Each of them described in concrete detail unwanted aspects of their personalities, which they invariably labeled in the third person or called by their own given names. The confessions always culminated in the affirmation that such-and-such an "I" should no longer exist. The "decrees" of partial self-destruction uttered on that former evening were now being translated into the so-called "meditation" of this one.

I saw the inner consistency of what they were doing on these occasions, yet I also had a much simpler reaction on another plane. Tonight, I noted, only women seemed to be involved in the open outpouring of emotion. And, as several of them continued to cry, "Out, out!" while breathing with the rising involuntary rhythm that one associates with sexual climax, I began to think I was eavesdropping on pure and simple hysteria of a kind which might even suggest Salem in 1692. The tension produced by their isolation on the desert, and by the unremitting discipline under which they labored, was finding an avenue of release.

But in their own view all this clearly meant the reaching of a desired crescendo in their "inner work," in which, it was now evident, most of them were constantly engaged. Meanwhile, even at this point Ezra continued to test them. Hearing a girl begin to wrestle with herself out loud, he would suddenly call to her: *"Who* are you, so-and-so?" (addressing her by name). She was not expected to reply. But her power of concentration was being honed. Or, more directly, Ezra would call upon a girl in trouble to "get past the negativity" that was blocking her—to triumph over her devil within.

Meditation for these people, I concluded, was clearly not the "real" thing. Yet, whatever it was, it was something very familiar to them, deeply consistent with their own beliefs and philosophy. How true to form that it should be practiced at what amounted to a forced pace, athletically, in the spirit of one more work project, one more goal to be achieved, like the construction of a new building. Ezra's lecture on the subject this evening had revealed, when one stopped to think of it, an utterly mechanical view of differing states of consciousness. You were always supposed to be able to know which exact stage you were on at any given moment. Everything had a label, like a mountain path which had been re-engineered for freeway motorists. Was I correct, then, in my hunch that the real signpost pointed to hysteria, and predominantly of a female variety? The sounds I heard during that forty-five-minute period seemed deeper and more pitiful than any merely intellectual interpretation of them could account for.

When Ezra departed during the last ten days of my stay for an engineering education conference in the Midwest, I had a chance to see what the dinners would be like without him. (This change was complicated, it is true, by the simultaneous arrival of several summer-only visitors and other newcomers to the community.) With Ezra gone, the difference in mood was very marked—and it left me with mixed feelings. At times the atmosphere now suddenly resembled that of a summer camp. On one or two evenings the whole table became animated by everyday conversation between individuals. People began turning up late, and the kerosene lanterns would not be properly lit. All the emotional heaviness was gone. We gulped down our food, went through a brief, perfunctory period of silence afterward (once, not even that) and then left. Had I arrived here during that particular week, I would have gained no idea of the community's real vibrations.

Finally, after several days of this, an open discussion took place on the group's state of mind since Ezra's departure. It was led by a deeply committed young man who often seemed hyperserious and standoffish. He pointed to mass instances of people being late or not showing up for meetings, in addition to the problems at dinner. Several persons admitted they were "fleeing," as they put it, not facing up to the realities of deadlines. Some confessed they felt "scattered," and T. gave another of his stylized confessions of sins. Would they be equal to the heavy responsibilities that lay just ahead—the ecology conference and the drama festival? The young man who had initiated the discussion solemnly announced that they would indeed have entered the New Age if they completed all their summer tasks on schedule.

A day or two later Eva, who had once missed dinner entirely because her (inner) "clock" was "wrong," spent hours at two meetings in public self-analysis of her great crime. At several dinners, core members of the group would now reprimand newcomers for talking too freely, or for becoming too silly when proposing toasts. Only once during Ezra's absence did the group at dinner achieve anything like the high, intense mood which was so frequent when he was there. This was during a discussion of the treatment visitors should have been receiving at the crafts bazaar. Confessions of extreme inner hostility both to the straight middle class and to hippies (on the part of different individuals) made the level of talk seem real and important. An unstated consensus emerged to the effect that visitors ought to be treated better—as if this were an unpleasant, inevitable duty. Consciously surfacing their animosities toward members of the larger society, and trying to deal with them, they succeeded in evoking a profound dialogue without Ezra's guidance, and their pleasure at this was quite undisguised. Eva and one or two others even commented freely on their need to learn to reduce their dependency on one individual. Yet the general trend during this unusual period remained that of floundering and marking time. Dinner had become a routine get-together rather than an awesome challenge.

One aspect of the more usual scene at the dinner table deserves emphasis. The evenings I have described were special in one important respect: a single prevailing mood dominated them throughout. More often it was notable how rapidly the group could change its tone from moment to moment during the same after-dinner hour. T., the same T. of the tearful confessions, might get us into stitches in describing the oddities of that day's visitors to the bazaar ("he looked like he was wearing dark glasses, only he wasn't"). Next, Gypsy, who was in charge of the bazaar's finances, might be accused angrily by Ezra of "sabotaging" it because she was not including orders for future delivery in her sales figures. A moment later, as the total income for the day was announced by the persevering Gypsy, the mood would switch again to one of simple applause for their mutual success. In these rapid shifts between humor, heaviness, and matter-of-fact group solidarity, there are hints of an extreme suggestibility. When these instant reorientations effortlessly occurred, the group seemed most clearly to fuse into a single pulsating person, an organism which could instantly alter its colors. In all this, Ezra was of course constantly signaling the shifts of tempo. But the group was something more than his mechanical instrument, a chameleon on which he might blow. At the very least, it required all his skill and force of personality to steer its course.

Physical construction under the hot sun. The need is to build a roof, my first assigned task. Everyone who arrives in the community is given a definite trial of this kind, often in connection with making ready one's own living quarters. Mine were privileged and luxurious by the normal standards of the group, for I had been placed in the future library, in the basement of the burned-out ranch house. One reached it by walking down a sharp incline of cement steps into the ground. Below, one stood in a thick-walled chamber of perhaps ten by twenty feet. This was to be my "territory." One's "territory" is highly important, the first thing one must establish in the community, Ezra told me, referring to the writings of Robert Ardrey.

Despite their spaciousness, these quarters somewhat disappointed me when Ezra first led me to them. I like to feel I can merge with the open air and landscape. Being asked to build the previously unfinished roof over this cellar and then live below it, I could not help but think of someone who is constructing his own tomb. Place only for one small skylight was being left in the center. Yet to complete this living space according to instruction was my definite assignment; I knew I would be watched to see how it was progressing. So I fell to work.

The heavy crossbeams (*vigas*) for the roof had already been laid in place, and adobe walls were completed up to the new roof line. About a third of the roof itself had also been laid on, using grooved lumber which interlocked to reduce the chance of leaks during cloudbursts. I found out that this initial portion had been done some time before by a perfectionist, since departed from the group, who had taken nearly a month to complete that much. Yet I was blithely told by Malcolm, the young man who was to supervise me, that the rest of the roof could be done in about a day and a half.

Frustration in all its petty varieties is built into the work projects of this community. In fact, one suspects that it is deliberately fostered as a further inner test. Frustration begins with the need for elementary tools, such as a hammer and saw. Since tools are owned by individuals, their loan is grudgingly granted. One has either to beg or to go hungry. Next come nails. The only abundant ones are a shade too small, but nails are bought in bulk on infrequent trips to Albuquerque. Then there is the question of the wood. All of it is salvaged scrap lumber. The remaining supply of grooved boards proved so warped by exposure that repeated effort was unable to make the grooves fit. Ungrooved wood, though available, was also warped, causing the edges to be slightly curved. This in turn made for small, uneven cracks between the boards as they were laid next to each other. Such a roof would do poorly in rain.

The chain of command was consulted. It led through Malcolm, who wanted to take no responsibility (especially in the beginning, he begrudged every moment spent on instruction, since it took him away from his profitable adobe-brick making), to Eva as manager and ultimately of course to

Ezra. (Champ, who was nominally in charge of building and construction throughout the property, took so little interest in the project—except once to order me to perform a certain operation in a way I knew to be unnecessarily inefficient—that he is best forgotten.) Finally Ezra himself came over briefly to inspect. The word was pronounced: finish the roof the best you can with the wood you have. And he showed me some fairly wide cracks in the boards that had been used for the roof of the new adobe building.

Somehow this response disappointed me, although I am not in general a perfectionist. It seemed to imply that beneath all the great pride in building a new civilization by do-it-yourself methods lay a certain willingness to accept third-rateness in technique. But I realized that standards of this kind can be rather evasive, especially as it was said that the whole ranch was regarded only as a training ground, and that it would shortly be sold, since the group was planning to leave the country soon for overseas. In this complicated situation, blind obedience seemed by far the most appropriate response. The laying of the roof was finished, using the ungrooved wood that was easier to work with, in exactly a day and a half.

Then came a pause of several days, owing to a real or imaginary crisis in tarpaper. On hand was a single roll of decent roof material, far too little for the area to be covered, plus two longer rolls of what some people referred to as an inferior grade, but which really proved to be thin undercoating material, used for the final roof only by extremely poor Chicanos in the area and then in several layers. Again, what should our standards be? Eva took pride in her penuriousness about purchasing any materials. Malcolm was not sure she would authorize such an outlay. Yet it was understood that the roof must be covered with tarpaper.

In the end, Eva did say yes. A girl was asked to make the purchase while she was in town on other errands. She returned with two rolls of good tarpaper, but of the wrong color. It was readily decided to create a two-tone roof, even though, nearly at ground level above the basement, it would be unusually conspicuous. Meanwhile, after being laid out, even these two new rolls proved not quite adequate. Fortunately, a fragment of another roll, in the first color, turned up.

The next day I learned how to build the right kind of fire (sheltered by adobe bricks at just the proper distance) which would cause an ancient bucket of tar, congealed for many months, to melt once again, and yet which would not make the bucket itself catch fire—a tendency it often displayed. Malcolm and I worked together on the tarring (using old rags wrapped around a stick to spread the tar). It required close coordination between the two of us, as the nailing had to be done while the tar remained hot. When the long day was over, we spontaneously shook hands; the task had broken down barriers between us.

Still, there was no door at the bottom of the steps where one entered the underground room. Nor was there any frame for one. The frame posed all the complex problems of joining wood and cement, especially since the latter was worn and uneven at some of the most vital places. Now other tools must be found, such as a tape measure. By this time I had adopted a policy of simply taking from the wood shop what I absolutely needed, if it was in evidence—always returning it promptly when finished. This greatly speeded things up. Two-by-twelves which were alleged to be in the materials yard turned out when measured to be two-by-eights. Still, Malcolm reluctantly said a frame might be built from them. I devised a little wooden landing, flush with the bottom cement step, with a removable top piece which would make it easy to empty out the accumulated mud and water after a rain. It was my own design, and made me feel a bit proud. Unfortunately, I strongly suspected that it was too small to do much good in a real cloudburst. But of these doubts I prudently decided to say nothing, since no easy alternative appeared. Rain water was bound to flow in great quantities down an open staircase leading to a basement. From this standpoint, it was foolish to locate a library there, especially since the present library seemed admirable and the group was moving soon anyway. But to question stated goals in this fashion simply was not done. Pure obedience again seemed the only road of escape from such mental confusion.

The building of the door proved to be a far more agreeable task. Malcolm showed me the basic techniques necessary at every stage—planing, use of the power-operated joiner, and gluing of the sections with the aid of clamps. Beyond this, I was on my own to make it a work of art if I could. One side I scrub-planed with pleasing results. The other side I hand-chiseled with the smallest gouge in the woodshop, following the contours to create an intricate rolling effect. This took many hours of work. I had never done anything like this before and greatly warmed to it. All sorts of people passing through the woodshop, some of whom seldom spoke to me otherwise, complimented me on its emerging appearance. Frustrations continued; the gouge kept disappearing when I would return after an absence, hindering rapid completion. But this could not take away from the clean, honest feel of the pine wood itself.

Meanwhile, I interrupted these occupations from time to time to help clear rubble from the ruins of the old ranch house, and to work with someone else removing accumulated dirt from the bottom of a deep cistern. This last task never got finished; a tendency toward half-completed projects was lamented by the members in their moods of self-criticism.

The permanent members of the community were overwhelmingly engrossed in a variety of physical projects. Even so, their desire for work constantly outstripped their actual performance. Again and again in casual conversations one heard the same refrain: how am I possibly going to have time to do everything that I simply must do? I've got to work harder, schedule more carefully, stay up later to finish things. This recurring state of mind reflected genuine self-discipline, although Ezra, by assigning tasks and establishing deadlines and by his frequent unannounced inspections, was in another sense calling the entire tune of their output.

How can so much energy be commanded for projects in a community like this? The do-it-yourself tradition remains extremely powerful in American folk culture, and this New Age group no doubt capitalizes upon it. In this respect several of the individuals on the ranch reminded me strongly of other people I had known long ago in standard American life. But the psychological and philosophical undertones of the labor in New Mexico went far deeper. These people believed they were being cosmically tested. Their own opinion of themselves, and Ezra's opinion of them, became the constant bench marks of such testing. Thus the fact that everything they were doing would be rendered meaningless in literal terms by their forthcoming sale of the property made no difference. To roll a stone endlessly up a mountain may amount to a surprisingly acceptable form of self-improvement.

Themes of self-punishment and self-correction dominate the attitude of the New Mexico group toward its physical labors, just as they do in its dinnertime explorations. "We've made an important discovery," one is told. "If it seems as though we're floundering and not getting our tasks done, even though we've been throwing all our energy into the work, what always unblocks things is to add *another* major task, with its own deadline, on top of the others. Then suddenly the whole of it gets done, and done well."

Laboring night and day as if possessed, often far into the early morning, these people might almost be called the Do-It-Yourself Stakhanovites. Of course Ezra pins no medals on them; indeed he often mercilessly criticizes their results. But he gives them the conviction that everything they do is absolutely vital, both in terms of their inner growth and the achievement of a new direction for mankind. To be a pioneer in the building of the Aquarian Age is every bit as powerful an incentive as to perform a similiar role in the creation of Communism.

Acting class for beginners is held each Wednesday in the dome at 6:30 P.M. It is led by Eva, who is a slender, girlish woman in her late twenties with the face of a storybook princess and a deep staccato voice. In everything she is demanding, relentless, and mercilessly quick; this is no exception. She pushes everyone to an utmost limit. A universal will to perfection is casually assumed. Every so often she allows herself a warm flash of human feeling, and then she is suddenly very likable.

Eight of us appear exactly on time, barefoot. We are the recent arrivals in the group, who must learn from scratch.

The first exercise consists merely of running around the dome for several minutes as a warmup. The object is to become unlimbered and breathless. When this is accomplished, we assume standing positions and begin the "molding" exercise. It is an extremely hard one to perform for any length of time. We must simultaneously rotate our hips, our shoulders, our head, the small muscles of the face, and extend our arms and rotate our wrists and fingers. Everything must be kept going at once; if Eva notices one movement missing, she calls you on it. She freely admits that it is difficult. It is actually designed to be contrary to the natural conditioning of one's body. It might be called a method of fighting the body, imposing conscious will upon it. "If you get tired and your arms want to fall or your neck begins to crack, *don't stop,*" Eva calls out to us while we endure our pain. "Don't stop, but *work through* your tiredness." All the good of the exercise will be lost, she says, if we halt even for a moment, and we will have to begin again at the beginning. "Even if you feel sick, *don't stop*. Many people feel sick when they do this at first." Again, as in all the physical labor, there is a desire to push everyone to the breaking point, a glorying in the mere fact of arduous effort. At the same time, in the special philosophical vocabulary of the community,[5] the aim of this exercise is to "warm up" the several bodily "centers" which are believed to be basic to man's nature. And by performing all these movements simultaneously one is also developing one's capacity for attention—attention to every aspect of one's personal existence.

We continue the "molding" exercise for an agonizing length of time until Eva announces that we can stop.

It is followed by a far more pleasant one which aims at the release of what is called "conscious energy." This is described as the highest level of energy, above both the automatic and the mind-directed forms. Energy of this kind comes directly from one's "moving center," bypassing the brain.

5. Explained at more length on p. 342.

Start with your right arm, and—very simple—let *it* do whatever it wants to. Impose nothing on it. To make sure that you don't direct it, occupy the mind simultaneously with a routine but absorbing exercise, such as counting to a hundred by sixes and then back down again. Meanwhile, your arm should be deciding what it wants to do, and doing it. Gradually you extend this self-direction from your arm to the whole body. It is actually fun— like being playfully possessed by a spirit. I get deeply into it, more so (I think) than many of the others. I am truly watching myself walk, fling parts of me in various directions, and twist and untwist my fingers without any sense of control.

All too soon this ends, and we switch to our vocal practice. We start with the vowels. The object is to bring forward one's voice from deep down in the stomach rather than from high up in the throat. This is called finding one's "natural voice." Standing near the edge of the dome, addressing the canvas so as to be able to hear ourselves distinctly, we call out "aaaaaaaaaa-eeeeeeeee—oooooooooo—uuuuuuuuuu," for several minutes at a time. The dome resounds with our noise. Without being told, we fall into a tonic unison, varied only by a few harmonious subdominant chords. Not understanding why, we find ourselves in the vocal mood of a minor key. It is exactly like the "chants" that we hear the older members of the community breaking into as they work or move about.

Then we move to the consonants, shouting them in a certain order, repeating each group several times:

"Rah-gah-kah-wah-yah!"
"Muh-nuh-duh-tuh!"
"Juh-chuh-shuh-x-c-z!"
"Fuh-vuh-muh-buh-puh!"

And back through these combinations again and again. By this time our voices are indeed limbered up, fuller and richer than they were at the beginning. Eva tells us that we should be practicing all these things out loud for at least an hour a day on our own.

We move on to the major exercise which finishes each week's acting class: exploring one of the "octaves of the emotions."[6] These exercises are original to this group; they appeared to Ezra in a moment of inspiration. Briefly, the theory underlying them is this: that in man, each major emotion is actually composed of a series of component emotions, in a necessary sequence like the musical scale. Starting with the third of the eight "notes" on this scale, one may either descend into an increasingly negative chain, or

6. Again, the relation of this concept to the inner philosophy of the group will be made clearer later, p. 341.

one may rise (by a combination of shock and conscious effort) in a positive one. The emotion of anger illustrates this. The first "note" in the octave of anger is "apprehension." The second is "confusion." Then comes the crucial turning point, with the descent into negativity: "overwhelming self-pity." This is followed in sequence by "resentment," "envy," "contempt," "righteous indignation," "fury," and, finally, "coldness." Reaching that last note, one must work one's way backward down to the third note, and replace it by the positive one, "courage," meaning the kind which enables one to remain steadfast within confusion; then "peace," "brotherhood," "compassion," "wrath" [*sic*], and, finally "goodness."

The exercise, which requires well over half an hour, consists of saying each of these words out loud in turn, repeating them until the leader signals movement onward to the next "note." As one says the words, one is supposed to feel them as deeply as one can and express them through bodily gestures in any way that seems genuine and appropriate.

This whole approach, in all its elaborateness, struck me as extremely artificial. At various times we would be asked if we could divine, from our own intuition, what the next "note" on the scale might be. Usually people were not able to guess correctly. In this instance, at least, the spirit that moved Ezra seemed to be in touch with nothing self-evidently universal. Instead it smacked of arbitrary fiat.

Starting the third week of the class, Jacob (one of the most mature and respected members of the group) came in to give us instruction in physical gestures. We were taught an elaborate series of bodily movements based upon three principles—speed, direction, and weight. (Thus a given gesture might be fast, straight, and light; its opposite would then be slow, curved, and heavy; but other gestures were constructed for each of the possible combinations.) Only one movement was said to exist for each set of attributes. It became fairly easy to learn them all and to switch, as we were told to do with increasing rapidity, from one to another. Again, much about this seemed arbitrary. But the group's theater is strongly built upon such stylized gestures, and in finished form they often give the acting a certain power.

The acting class, like the nightly dinners, ends with the "eating" exercise—a period of silence in which we are supposed individually to "consume" the energy we have been building up together. After it, not long before the dinner gong, people quietly steal out of the dome one by one, and the class is over.

I was understandably excluded from the numerous play rehearsals devoted to bits and scenes. But I was allowed to attend those which offered a run-through of an entire play, provided I entered the dome not a second later than they began.

Rehearsals began with what was called a "warmup" period. During these sessions, which might go on for twenty minutes or more before the acting started, an unaware visitor to the property (or a wanderer on the dirt road nearby) would come away with the strangest impression imaginable of what might be going on out here in the desert. For the warmups were a vastly speeded up and intensified version of the exercises used in the acting classes. Each in his own manner, all the players ran and "molded" and practiced their voices and emotions and just plain shouted, producing an incredible cacophony of unorganized yowls and grunts and bellows, interspersed with occasional outpourings of lines of text.

In the normal course of things, the warmup period would end with the clashing of cymbals, and then Ezra (in yellow pajamalike theater garb, with silk cap) would give the signal to begin the play. But if he felt that all was not developing as it should, and more preliminary work was needed, Ezra might instead interrupt the players for a special kind of "confrontation." Such "confrontations" were apparently regarded as a means for further unlimbering the emotions.

One of the most awesome scenes of my entire stay was the "confrontation" that preceded and followed a rehearsal of their Shakespeare play, by far the weakest play of the five they were performing that summer. Ezra began it by asking one of the girls to answer as fully and openly as possible the question "Who do you hate?" She was to go around the entire group in this fashion, expressing these feelings toward each person. She was never to intellectualize or "associate," but confine herself to a direct display of emotion throughout. The girl did this at great length, in a style which was itself a dramatic performance, yet deeply genuine. The connections she made with each person, in her recital of hatreds, seemed to ring wholly true. She announced her feeling that most of the others were barely able to tolerate her, that she was always being made to play the role of a "little girl" instead of an adult. She said that she always felt Eva could do her some nameless but sinister harm. Most impressive of all, she spoke her mind directly to Ezra, saying she hated him because she wasn't sure there even was such a thing as the inner life or the esoteric—and if there was, she didn't understand it—and therefore she didn't know whether she belonged here at all. As still another symptom of her genuineness, she made two exceptions: one girl whom she didn't hate, and one boy whom she said she loved, though from afar. Though it was all so extremely direct, the recital was also beautifully composed and articulated on the spot. Indeed, it had to be voiced almost at the top of her lungs, because throughout it the other members of the company continued their warmup exercises, though more quietly, as a kind of chorus.

Then, more briefly, a second girl was asked to describe who it was that she cowered before. Her performance was halted before it had gone on very long.

The cymbals did finally sound, and the acting began. The whole play was performed without a break, requiring nearly three hours.

After this, Ezra immediately launched into his criticisms of it. He bore down on Champ. Why, Ezra asked over and over again, was his performance so poor? Then Ezra directed him to go through the same routine of confrontation that the two girls had followed earlier. But the spirit of it turned out to be very different. Champ, true to his usual personality, did not so much express his inner anguish as take the opportunity to say snide things about others in the group, often in the manner of high-handed corrections. Indeed, as Ezra pointed out, he was bullying them. Yet he was clever about it, continually hitting the mark in his hostile appraisals, and even made Ezra smile or laugh at some of the things he said. Clearly he enjoyed the chance to perform in this way, as the girls had not. Fearlessly he unveiled his belief that it was Ezra who was continually blocking him, keeping him from expressing himself. (Ezra turned this aside by briefly remarking that he was only one out of twenty-five people; it was far too smooth and easy a response.) For Champ, unlike the girls, the confrontation had been no supreme challenge, but merely another way of gaining general attention.

Ezra now asked them to go through a central scene with Champ once again.

The rehearsal had begun at 8:30 in the morning; it ended at around 3:00 in the afternoon. During the whole of it, no one was expected to leave; I saw no one do so even to use the outhouse. Total, unbroken attention was demanded. Like so much else here, it amounted to a kind of endurance test. Back alone in my basement quarters, I found myself so deeply under the spell of the confrontations I had just witnessed that I could hardly raise my hand to write. For several hours I continued to feel washed out, drained, unable to function (yet knowing that, from their point of view, to go on functioning was precisely the point).

Drama, like physical labor, I realized, was less important for itself than as a further instrument of self-development. This was strongly implicit even in the content of the beginning acting class. At the rehearsals,

Ezra sometimes did talk about the need to "feel" the inner reality of the parts that were being played, and he was capable of giving individual actors important insights into their roles. But the overall emphasis was far less in this direction than one might have expected. Too often Ezra satisfied himself with reiterating stock phrases such as the need to keep in mind the "through line of action." Feeling was being neglected in favor of theater as an exhibition of mere collective energy and strength. Theater is not life, Ezra once told them explicitly; it is something that stands apart from life. It might be fair to translate this: Theater is an exercise, still another act of will.

Nonetheless, there were major ambiguities in this group's idea of theater. On the one hand, the posters that announced the season were prominently headed, "Theater of Individuality." And the theme of all five plays, Ezra emphasized a number of times, was individual transformation, a theme which merged general dramatic interest with the inner life of the group. Yet in another sense individuality was the least of the group's aims. They liked to stress their belief in ensemble acting and their disdain of the "star" system, an attitude they underlined by refusing to print the names of the actors on any of the programs. And Ezra liked to declare that Western drama had gone wrong with Euripides, a point of view which seemed totally alien to the notion of portraying individuality, at least on the level of the mundane human emotions. But perhaps for this group individuality meant something else—something abstract, colorless, defined as "essence" rather than as personality in the ordinary sense.

What kind of theater results from such an approach? One of the newest and least satisfied members of the group, a sophisticated girl who had acted for some time in a company in Boston, had a low view of the dramatic product. The emphasis on stylized gestures she saw as merely an overused crutch. The group was not throwing itself into drama as she understood it. Its enormous energy and will to succeed were not connecting with anything real.

In my own estimate, as a typically casual playgoer, the group's productions varied greatly from one to another. When it performed Shakespeare, the result was a sheer fiasco, often no better than a high-school performance. The playwright was over their heads; none of the actors recited their lines as if they had any real sense of their meaning. Several of them rushed through their speeches athletically, as if they were competing in the manufacture of adobe bricks. The solemn person who played the lead had fallen into the enormously irritating rut of uttering his words in a monotonous singsong, all on the same level.

Their original play (apparently written by Ezra) could not be judged in the spirit of the others. It was basically a dance drama, and on this plane I found it quite impressive. The text was uneven. There were moments of brilliance, but many more where it seemed to trail off into an unsatisfying vagueness of intent.

The two Greek plays were, I thought, considerably better. Some of the prominent parts were played with too little resonance of feeling. But many of the other roles were quite powerfully done, and several members of the group who had seemed rather bland and quiet outside the theater came to life in a fashion that was remarkable. Even here, the great flaw of their inability to express varied feeling, to communicate the emotional savor of their lines, revealed itself far too often.

The central problem, of course, is that they are trying to do theater along with everything else. They are not living it (and their roles) throughout their waking hours. Indeed, complaints were heard that hardly any notice would be given for important rehearsals, such as would allow the actors to study their parts carefully in advance. The fact that each actor often had roles in five plays simultaneously compounded the difficulty. The members rehearse all these demanding assignments at odd intervals in the midst of other kinds of backbreaking labor, and in a context of unremitting self-analysis. This is precisely their aim—to be universal men, to be both "actors and scientists," to do everything at once. But their theater raises the same question of standards as does the construction of doors and roofs, and just as visibly. Most of the members did not join the community (as will be seen) because it was a theater group. Some of those assigned the most prominent roles had hardly ever attended plays until they arrived here. All this means that some degree of failure is easy to understand.

In theater, as in every other aspect of the group's life, Ezra's special role must be given its due. Each play has its own nominal "director," but at all the rehearsals Ezra continuously plays the real role of director. His own background, as will be seen, is primarily in fields far removed from theater, though he claims that he was once asked to be a drama teacher by an unofficial company at Oxford, while he was staying in England. Yet in the present setting he receives unquestioned authority in this as in everything else.

I could observe one unfortunate tendency in his criticism, which was consistent with his personality in general. This was a habit of bearing down in a seemingly arbitrary manner on one particular member of the cast on a given day, raking him or her over the coals to an extreme, while leaving other members, who to my eyes and ears had been even more mediocre, entirely alone. In fact it often seemed that he chose relatively minor parts to single out in this fashion, rather than addressing himself to the principals of a given play. In some cases these principal roles were being taken by long-established members of the group; they may also have been sacrosanct simply because to speak one's mind about them might have made the whole effort appear hopeless. For whatever reasons, certain people were being allowed to continue with transparent faults that were never adequately pointed out or challenged, unless this was done in private, while others were being called on the carpet mercilessly. Still, the overall effect of Ezra's interventions seemed far less remarkable in the theater than it did in the other affairs of the community, for stage directors are a notoriously high-handed lot. Judged by this yardstick, oddly enough, he could sometimes appear too mild as well as too uneven in his choice of targets.

The ecology conference was held at the ranch just after my departure. Fervent effort to prepare for it went on during my stay. It was conceived as a major test of the group's skill at entering this field on a par with the attempts in crafts and drama.

This conference was a public event, but it soon became evident that its main purpose was as a hurdle for the members, rather than to reach out to the world with a message. Elaborate preparations were being made for an occasion designed to attract no more than twenty to thirty weekend guests—that is, a number no larger than the group itself. Nor did it seem to matter very much who these people were; instead of going to great lengths to try to attract opinion leaders, they were willing to sign up whoever might be interested and would pay the fee. In the end, the participants appear to have been a haphazard assortment of concerned radicals and liberals; some of them did come from as far away as Colorado.

The conference divided its focus between presenting basic information about the worldwide environment and the dangers facing it, and publicizing the ranch itself as a model of what an ecologically sound community might be like. Somewhat more emphasis was placed on the latter theme.

To prepare for the conference, the members of the community were divided into four committees, each of which sought to develop prepared speeches, maps, charts, and in some cases actual demonstration projects. The committees dealt respectively with the food chain, recycling, the monitoring of environmental hazards, and alternative sources of energy. Each committee had been given a series of specific mandates by Ezra some months before, and in the weeks prior to the conference their chairmen would call frequent meetings to apportion assignments and find out how each person was progressing. Thus it was all very bureaucratic, a complicated structure of a temporary kind superimposed upon all the other normal roles which everybody was also continuing to fulfill. Twice in the weeks preceding the conference, entire evenings were devoted to reports by each of the committees, in the spirit of a dress rehearsal.

These deadlines imposed a great sense of pressure; in the days immediately preceding them, many would drop their normal tasks and go scouting across the countryside gathering relevant information. These forays sometimes led them to libraries, including the distant one at a state university, where in the span of a few hours they would try to become familiar with the scientific literature. An important part of the challenge was to be able to locate the most trustworthy information about the environment, proceeding from scratch and usually without much previous training. A deliberate kind of populism underlay this approach. At a time when many scientific experts are in the pay of established governments or business corporations, the men and women of the New Age are told they must succeed in becoming their own experts, lifting themselves up by their bootstraps so as to be able to reach conclusions about environmental hazards, unaffected by the tugs of vested interest. Confidence in the results to be achieved by these do-it-yourself techniques was an unwritten law of faith. Ezra's harshest words during the evening dress rehearsals were reserved for those who (in his view) were depending too much on establishment sources of information and not doing their own digging in a critically independent spirit. Yet, at the same time, scientific monographs in university libraries (for instance, the ten-volume report on world sources of energy published over a decade ago by the United Nations) were assumed to have high standing as references, and various state offices were approached for data concerning fuel consumption in the region.

These problems, to be sure, greatly affect anyone who seeks to learn about ecology in this day and age. But the approach to information gathering in this community seemed hasty and inconsistent in the extreme. One member of the energy committee tried to milk local sources of information on unusual wind or solar-power installations in the area; I went with him for the day. First he sought out two personal contacts (neither of whom had any special knowledge of the subject); then, on the strength of a rumor which one of them cheerfully handed us, we set out on a fifty-mile goose chase to run down a hippie who was thought to have built a water-power mill. It turned out that he had only been thinking of doing it in the future and had meanwhile moved away. Other members turned up much apparently solid scientific information. But the amateurishness of the whole undertaking remained painfully evident.

These problems were compounded by a further marked tendency of the group, to avoid ecology-minded "liberals" like the plague. Thus, at a distance from the community no greater than the libraries that were being consulted, there happened to exist an organization which for some months previous had devoted all its time to developing ecological information geared to the local environment, in the spirit of a conservation-minded legislative lobby. When I suggested that we might call on this group to find out what materials they had already assembled, it was clear that this idea came as an alien threat to the mind of my committee mate. He would have to phone back to the ranch to check with our chairman before he could do anything like this. And he did not really want to make the phone call, at least on this subject. Behind this reluctance lay some unnamed but very powerful fear. Would Ezra severely criticize anyone who made use of the data furnished by "liberal" political action groups? But why so, if state offices were also being consulted for data? My sense of a self-imposed isolation was heightened when one of the outside contacts we met, a highly intelligent craftsman in the area, began delicately needling us for our ostrichlike posture out on the ranch; our committee had never heard of the most widely publicized recent work going on in our exact field of interest, work which this craftsman (himself a complete layman in ecology) could cite from the tip of his tongue.

Still, if the preparation for the conference is regarded purely as a beginners' exercise, in a small way it moved the members closer to their goal of being a community of "actors and scientists." The "food chain" committee in particular struggled bravely to get together an illustrated lecture on the phosphorus and nitrogen cycles, and the product in rehearsal was one from which I (as a scientific ne'er-do-well) could gain some genuine instruction. The performance of the monitoring committee continually drew Ezra's wrath, but its goal of setting up a continuing monitoring station to check the level of hazards offered by radiation, pesticides, and air pollution, to furnish a yardstick against official government counts, was a meaningful one, and the daily readings of its instruments (however few and primitive) suggested an important job being squarely tackled. The energy committee concentrated, in the end, on pilot demonstrations designed to show what ingenuity might accomplish. A wind generator was located on another ranch a few miles away, purchased for fifty dollars, removed from a sixty-foot tower (a project which involved enormous labor for several days), brought back, and mounted on a telephone pole. In a good breeze it was rated for three thousand watts. By the time of the conference it was furnishing enough power to brighten the light bulbs all over the property. Its eye-catching physical appearance, high up beside the existing windmill like a model airplane with a large, out-of-scale propeller constantly turning, was in itself a kind of coup for the group's prestige. A solar distillery produced enough water directly from the air to fill a teapot which could sit proudly before the assembled guests. The attempt to build a solar heat concentrator, capable of focusing so much heat on a single point that it would weld metal, was less successful. But the achievements produced a reasonably decent show.

Ezra's attitude toward ecology (when he stopped blazing forth at the inadequacies of the members' presentations) was, I thought, an eminently reasonable one. It was hopeless, he believed, to argue on economic grounds that existing energy sources or commercial agriculture might be replaced by new, less harmful practices. Financial considerations were all in favor of the existing order, and one might just as well frankly concede this. Instead, the argument must proceed on the plane of fundamental morality. It was wrong to pollute the earth if any life-enhancing alternatives existed, even if one had to lower one's standard of living in order to adopt them. The issue was clear: either the present American style of living, with all its destructive by-products, or else a new, less affluent pattern, appropriate to the New Age, in which cities would no longer exist and the entire population would live in small, self-supporting communities like this ranch. The world must be convinced that the only viable future lies in this latter direction. But, if it will not be moved, then sooner or later it will be physically destroyed, and communities such as this one will offer a solution to the bewildered surviving remnant of mankind. In this New Age group, ecology is pursued in a way that mingles soberly rational argument with apocalyptic vision.

Ecology, crafts, theater, construction projects, gardening, and cuisine—these are the principal external areas which combine into a total pattern of living on the ranch. What is the effect of trying to be a universal man, equally skilled in such diverse fields, in the 1970's? An effort at objective evaluation must stand aside from the group's own vacillating self-appraisals, which veer from moods of enormous pride and self-confidence to those of extreme self-accusation. My own judgment is that in every department the group has achieved results which are rather middling in quality. The crafts (in the woodshop, for instance) are good enough to appeal readily to tourists seeking distinctive patio furniture for their homes in Westwood or Palo Alto. They are not good enough to merit the praise of specialist craftsmen in the neighborhood. The group's accomplishments in each of the other areas are roughly on this same level. Except for one or two of its dramatic productions, the group does nothing that is shamefully terrible; nothing, on the other hand, is as yet incontestably outstanding.

One wonders, of course, whether four years (or a much shorter time, in the case of a majority of the members) is a long enough period in which to become a universal man or woman. The group is convinced, for instance, that its theater is continuing markedly to improve, and members will readily admit how far they still have to go in mastering their craft enterprises and in learning to think ecologically. Considering how few people here had any previous training to speak of either in drama or science, the middling result they have so far achieved in both is nothing to deprecate. They see themselves as at the beginning of a long process of development, as a group and as individuals. It may be too early to say, on the basis of this still nascent experiment, the kind of thing that so many academics long to say—that to try to be universal, to try to fulfill several roles equally well, must inevitably result in mediocrity in an age of specialization.

Money is peculiarly important in the daily lives of these people, both on the managerial level and among the rank-and-file. Not big money, usually, but oddly small amounts. The complicated division of labors and accounts between the group, organized as a cooperative joint venture, and each individual, as an entrepreneur-craftsman and as a consumer of special services, produces a continual stream of petty cash transactions. Often these are for sums under a dollar. They are always concluded immediately. Thus, if a table is sold, the 10 percent commission owed the community is usually transferred within minutes. Or, if someone "rents" someone else's car for a trip to town, he pays the owner just as soon as he returns. Everyone always seems to have plenty of change for these small debts tucked away in his dirty jeans, because there is astonishingly little delay on that account. Sometimes quarters and nickels are being passed around so fast as to resemble a never-ending game of Monopoly. Or, in language far more congenial to this group, the trickle of cash is like a constant mopping-up operation to prevent karma from forming at its source.

On broader levels, too, people here are anxious about money. (Of course so are most others in our society, but it is striking that this concern continues in a group of this kind.) In some cases the worry stems from the fact that individuals have invested heavily, perhaps several hundred dollars, in the tools and supplies necessary for their craft enterprises. They want to recover these investments and not see them disappear irrevocably. Thus they are pulled toward the tightness of attitude which afflicts a great many small businessmen. In fact, monetary concerns of one kind or another regularly alternated with profounder themes as after-dinner discussion topics. One night Ezra offered an explicit justification for this: money is a form of energy, like sex. In monetary encounters, as in physical ones, it is extremely necessary to reach an instant understanding agreeable to both sides. Honesty consists in the flash of mutual acceptance which accompanies each and every "deal." Otherwise the karmic implications spring up. This might be seen as a good insight. But on some evenings Ezra's pep talks, for instance about selling theater tickets, verged dangerously near the vocabulary of old-time "success" oratory.

To gain perspective, one should recall that the group deliberately rejects the affluent living standard of the present middle class; in this respect its attitudes are at one with those of hippie dropouts. The group aims always to live very simply. The only luxury that is envisioned is periodic worldwide travel. The ideology of "success" displays itself on small-scale, immediate levels of self-sustenance. For us, said Eva, money is just one of the many elements needed for practical survival.

Nonetheless Eva, the Boston financier's daughter, is openly proud of each penny she saves. A distinct penuriousness (not to be confused with asceticism) underlies her rejection of the idea of a middle-class living standard. She is boastful, as well she might be, of how much further money goes on this ranch than in the usual American family. As she put it to me: "With twenty-five or thirty people we can operate on a basic budget of $15,000 a year—which normally a family of three will spend and not feel they are particularly well-off. What others get out of $10 or even $100, we realize from $1." Exact figures aside, this result of planned community living is indeed impressive.

She went on to tell an interesting story that reveals a certain shrewd flexibility in the group's handling of money. It seems that the original monthly fee to members for room and board was much steeper than the present one—$75, plus $500 a year. But many individuals found it impossible to keep up their contributions at this level, and as a result the actual income fell disastrously. So about a year and a half ago the decision was made to lower the monthly amount to $42, along with the new 10 percent commissions, but really to collect it. (It was raised thereafter to $46.)

But, whenever specific sums are due, one glimpses Eva's saving side most clearly. When she approaches you for a monthly payment, she fastens upon you like a cat and will not let go until the check is in her hand. It occurred to me, during the moments when I saw her operate in this fashion, that her upbringing must have left her with a basic need for security. But she explains her attitude in quite different language: "Money is one of the most interesting ways of approaching someone. I know more about another person through this kind of exchange than almost any other way. You can tell their attitude about a lot of things, by whether they give you money, and how rapidly they give it to you."

On major transactions such as the purchase of land, Eva is a shrewd, tough businesswoman. Clearly, with her at the helm, the group has nothing to fear from basic financial mismanagement. And, while the affairs of the community may seem overorganized from this point of view, the grave dangers which can stem from a contrary policy are being vigilantly avoided.

Ezra has conceived this pattern of living as a totality. Its combination of elements is implicitly assumed to be all-sufficient, providing the necessary ingredients for a well-rounded existence. Yet there is one glaring omission from the recipe. Children are not taken into account. Even a brief stay on the ranch reveals how brusquely they are shunted aside.

Several children do physically exist here, and that is what makes their irrelevance to this version of the New Age so apparent. No special provision has been given to the role of mother—or, for that matter, of father. Women, regardless of their young offspring, are expected to be as busily engrossed in their many daily projects as anyone else. The result is that the toddlers wander continually about, alone and unattended. Frequently dirty and bare-bottomed, as a time-saving way of dealing with their diarrhea, they cry pitifully for an attention they seldom receive.

It is curious and disquieting that their needs have been given no regular place in the planning of the group, which in other respects is so formidably complete. Here is one of the most noticeable contrasts between this structured, disciplined group and a hip commune of the standard sort, where children are usually loved and looked after by everybody in a perpetual rhythm of respectful affection. But on this ranch absorption in a life of tasks is so complete as to lead to comparative child neglect.[7] One concludes that these people are so driven by their anxiety to succeed in all the

---

7. Two of the mothers were obviously doing everything they could, within the limits of their daily routine, to give their children loving, heedful care. But their style in this respect conspicuously clashed with the general norms of the group.

tests of their daily existence that any external distraction, even that of their own young, is simply not to be allowed.

In this respect, Ezra's community carries a distinct overtone of the earlier tradition of monasticism. Yet on the surface its members are young and "normal"; sexual activity is not forbidden them, and at least one of the infants was conceived on this ranch. Unlike some Vedantists, Ezra would certainly not want to abolish sex if he could. But children find just as small a place in his scheme of things. Only once did I observe him interact with one of them. It was during the Sunday-afternoon teaparty, the curious once-a-week social interlude in the schedule. For some reason he decided to amuse one of the toddlers directly. He did so by bellowing forth his accustomed chants while extending his fingers and smiling a big smile. The child was not terrified; he smiled back steadily. But the encounter was a curious one. Not for an instant had Ezra slid out of his usual role of powerful domination. And the force with which he briefly projected himself onto the child showed no real ability to shift gears for the occasion.

Life here means work, performed with constant, unremitting attention. When people speak, it is briskly, urgently, about the practical jobs they are doing. They race against schedules and quotas. Though they are also a theater company, they resemble no group of flamboyant, spontaneous bohemians. Instead they shun any outward flair to the point of being almost colorless. The one great sin, the *faux pas* never to be publicly committed, is to stand around in a pose of unashamed leisure. In hip language, there is no provision for ever becoming "spaced out." Even sexual affection, such as hand holding, is displayed only in brief, almost furtive snatches.

There is a kind of social life, especially among some of the women, which flickers spasmodically in the dining room and kitchen area late at night. While the clean-up crew works to restore order, people drift in to make popcorn and sometimes to chat idly or kid around a bit. There can be a lapse into routine feminine chatter, though in my hearing it never became truly gossipy. Only some of the warmer individuals engage in this, and they are not usually those who stand near the center of the group.

But these moments of letdown (and the sexual pairings which will later be mentioned) can occur only at the margins of the group's round of living. From morning to night, only work is encouraged, and individual isolation in work. Warmth of the ordinary human kind is regarded as a break in the manufacture of energy, a subversive lapse into the "automatic" behavior and "false personality" of the outside world. Ideally, every waking moment is to be devoted to the willed pursuit of heightened consciousness, and consciousness is defined not as escape from the mundane, but as the merciless application of one's full attention to it in labor.

This also means that there can be no romantic urge directed toward nature, for, like sociability, it would be a wasteful form of diversion. The external environment is implicitly viewed as something hostile, a source of resistance to be continually overcome. Nature offers a test of one's hardihood and resolution. Thus the members boast that they came to this part of New Mexico because if they could survive here they could do it anywhere. Beyond this, nature is seen as a source of energy, to be tapped and exploited—more rationally, to be sure, than is now being done by governments and corporations, but with much the same cool calculation. "One thing about us," Eva remarked to me, "there certainly aren't any sentimentalists here." I had to agree. Only a few of the newcomers (and one exception among the longer-established women) showed the open relish for natural beauty and direct contact with the earth and sky which so strongly mark the hip scene. Instead, the whole point of being here is to strain against obstacles—in nature, in one's fellow man, in oneself—and thereby generate the energy which can transform one's will into a sharpened, dependable instrument for a "higher" purpose.

It is time to leave these concrete memories and impressions, and explore the group's background and philosophy in a more systematic fashion.

History and Intellectual Sources

The group was formed early in 1967 in a small town just a few miles from its present location. Ezra and Eva had moved there from the East, and in its art-colony atmosphere they began to attract a cluster of younger people around them. In the beginning there were only about a half dozen in the group.

Later that year it moved in its entirety to San Francisco. This was in the wake of the Haight-Ashbury summer. Important things were happening on the West Coast, and it seemed the place to be. After its relocation, the group began living communally for the first time. It also began its theater productions, initially one-act plays. To gain self-support, it started running a restaurant. In San Francisco a lot more people were attracted to the group. But after a while there was also a feeling of letdown and loss of force. The atmosphere seemed too distracting; people were being pulled off into irrelevant directions. So after nearly a year, in the fall of 1968, the community again picked up stakes and moved, this time to New York.

There it lived in an old house in Brooklyn and rented a studio on Fifth Avenue, commuting by subway. It put on its first full-length production. Still more people joined. But in the end it stayed there only two months. The idea of getting away from the city, buying land, and founding a "real" community now came to the fore. A couple of advance agents were sent back to New Mexico and began looking at property. Meanwhile, most of the group went on to Houston for six weeks, early in 1969, where they performed Molière with discouraging results. By then the land was ready for them, and the community moved onto it in March, 1969.

The acreage used to be a fancy horse ranch. But, because the main house had just burned down, it was available at a bargain price—165 acres, containing a good well, for $40,000. The group lost some of its members during the course of all these upheavals, but it gained others and now numbered nearly thirty persons. Ezra and Eva were the guiding forces in all its travels, and the land was purchased in Eva's name, ostensibly for mere convenience.

The group performed its first cycle of plays in New Mexico in late October and November of 1969. As always, the completion of such a major task was deemed more important than any external hindrances. One day, when they were doing Shakespeare, it snowed in the outdoor court-yard and only three people were in the audience. Yet they kept speaking their lines to the end.

In the summer of 1970, while they were working full speed to com-plete the large adobe building, they deliberately held another drama festi-val at the same time, during which full-length plays were put on three times a day, morning, noon and night, for three solid weeks. Asked why they had done this, they replied, "We knew that if we could act *and* build the building, carrying it all through to completion at the same time, we would have equaled or surpassed what any other group of our size has ever done. It was a very important test for us."

On one level, at least, the history of this group appears to define itself as a series of ever-widening acts of will. It is a saga of bold deeds. For four years, down to the time of my visit in 1971, these had been piled on top of one another in an escalating crescendo. Now the biggest step of all had been announced—the purchase of nearly thirteen hundred acres over-seas, in a beautiful river valley, where they would use all their training to produce an ecological experiment of enormous magnitude and at the same time begin to fulfill their mission on a planetary scale.[8]

8. The sudden changes in these plans, which came late in 1971, and their effects upon the group, are described on pp. 402–406.

But the group also possesses a history of another, quieter kind. It is one that requires careful, detailed probing. From what sources came the ideas that underlay their efforts, first in Ezra's mind and then with increasing awareness in the minds of his followers?

One of the things that intrigued me about this particular community when I first learned of it was its seemingly favorable attitude toward intellect. From every indication, here was a group which did not share the pervasively anti-intellectual mood of the contemporary scene. Instead, it appeared to take ideas and "thinkers" very seriously, absorbing them, combining them, wrestling with them. What other present-day group would trouble to send me a specific reading list long in advance, urging me to master it before my arrival?

This reading list contained the following titles:

Stanislavsky on the Art of the Stage (New York: Hill and Wang, 1961).

Lewis Mumford, *Technics and Civilization* (New York: Harcourt Brace and World, Harvest edition, 1965; originally published 1934).

R. Buckminster Fuller, *Operating Manual Spaceship Earth* (New York: Clarion Books, 1969).

W. R. Bion, *Experiences in Groups* (New York: Basic Books, 1961; earlier published in London).

Upon my arrival, Ezra told me that a fifth book should be added:

Robert Ardrey, *The Territorial Imperative* (New York: Atheneum, 1966).

However, I soon learned that, though each of these titles was indeed important, I had not been given the names of certain other books which actually played a deeper role in shaping the group's world view:

J. G. Bennett, *The Dramatic Universe* (4 vols.; London: Hodder and Stoughton, 1952–1966).

P. D. Ouspensky, *In Search of the Miraculous* (New York: Harcourt, Brace and World, 1949).

Maurice Nicoll, *Psychological Commentaries on the Teaching of G. I. Gurdjieff and P. D. Ouspensky* (5 vols.; London: Vincent Stuart, 1952).

More generally, the other major writings by and about Gurdjieff.

Idries Shah, *The Sufis* (Garden City, New York: Doubleday, 1964).
Idries Shah, *Tales of the Dervishes* (New York: E. P. Dutton, 1967).
Idries Shah, *The Way of the Sufi* (New York: E. P. Dutton, 1969).

Comparing these books against the actual pattern of thinking and living in the community, it seems clear that Stanislavsky plays much the least role. His emphasis on the need for inner attention and concentration on the part of the actor is certainly congenial to the group's philosophy of willful effort. His idea that each play has an inner meaning and a "through action" does get an explicit echo in Ezra's approach to drama. Finally, his belief that the acting group should function as an interchangeable ensemble, without the imbalances of a star system, is being carried into practice.

But the people here probably think that their theater owes much more to Stanislavsky than is really the case. The Russian director had called for total immersion of the actor in the life of the theater and particularly in his role of the moment. He would have been appalled at the dividedness in the daily lives of these performers; from this standpoint he wouldn't have called them true actors at all. Moreover, the heavy reliance of their theater upon standardized gestures might well have impressed him as the sort of dependence upon automatic or mechanical action which he explicitly associated with the work of hacks. Though he advocated a kind of internal warmup before each performance, the style of group warmup indulged in here would have been alien to his notion of deep immersion in character; it would seem too hectic and collective, above all much too forced. Stanislavsky's central concern, feeling for the inner nuances of each part, is actually the precise weakness of this group's theater.

A minor suggestion of Stanislavsky's, thrown out hypothetically at one point, nonetheless is related to the kind of confrontation in which the group sometimes indulges during its warmups: "Suppose I give you, Miss X, the following problem: come into this room and pick a quarrel with every one of us who are sitting here. But, remember, the quarrel you are to pick with me must in no way be like the quarrel you will pick with A, B, C and so on."[9] This exercise, carried out literally, created the awesome scene at the play rehearsal I attended. Yet Ezra's basic notion of the confrontation clearly comes from elsewhere.

The ideas of Lewis Mumford and Buckminster Fuller have penetrated more genuinely. (Fuller has visited with the members of the community at least once.) The concept of a life-enhancing technology, which underlies the craft enterprises, originates in Mumford's book, where there is a single unelaborated reference to a "biotechnic" phase of civilization to come in the distant future, replacing the present "neotechnic" one, in which Mumford elsewhere places most of his hopes.[10] Fuller enunciates the concept

9. *Stanislavsky on the Art of the Stage* (New York: Hill and Wang, 1961), p. 239.
10. Lewis Mumford, *Technics and Civilization* (New York: Harcourt, Brace and World, Harvest edition, 1965), p. 353.

of "synergy," to the effect that a collective whole is more than the sum of its parts.[11] This idea has been given some importance in the thinking of the New Mexico community. It is taken to mean that a group can achieve a far higher output of energy than the same number of people could produce on their own; in this sense it is similar to the better-known idea of the "multiplier effect," though it can also be interpreted in a vitalistic fashion.

Both Mumford and Fuller have a strongly evolutionary perspective. Both of them accept technology, though Fuller's embrace of it is more wholehearted. Neither of them wants us to return to a primitive past. Both men are optimistic about the future of mankind, despite their apprehension of great evils in the present time. (Fuller's optimism is wildly Saint-Simonian; Mumford's, far more reasoned and tentative.) Both writers place emphasis on energy conversion as the basis for life, and the special need to utilize new sources of energy—especially from the sun and the wind—in order to stop using up irreplaceable fossil-fuel deposits and end pollution. Philosophically, both believe in a unified teleological universe and accuse man in the recent past of having gotten seriously out of step with natural harmonies. In economic terms, both authors define wealth as the state of life sustainment, not as the arbitrary hoarding of supplies.

The community has accepted Mumford's chronology of the history of civilization, his divisions of it into "eotechnic," "paleotechnic," "neotechnic," and "biotechnic" phases, each with its own characteristic forms of invention and use of materials. The community believes that its own approach to tools and resources is, however, "polytechnic," in that it takes what is still useful from all previous periods. Mumford himself had asserted that all new civilizations are the product of such syncretism, incorporating various fragments from the old which are found still to be relevant. "Consciously to assimilate the machine is one means of reducing its omnipotence," writes Mumford, in a spirit profoundly congenial to these planners of a new social order.[12]

More basically, the community has adopted Mumford's vague but crucial distinction between life-enhancing and life-destroying values. "And what does *this* mean?" Eva once frankly wondered out loud in my hearing. "Nobody knows. All we can do is feel our way according to the vibrations each thing has." Here Mumford offers little help, for, although

11. Buckminster Fuller, *Operating Manual for Spaceship Earth* (New York: Clarion Books, 1969), p. 71. The same term appears in the writings of J. G. Bennett, described below. I have heard that it originated among certain anthropologists of the 1930's, but have not been able to trace its earlier history more exactly.

12. Mumford, *op. cit.,* pp. 107–08, 344.

this distinction is essential to his entire argument, he tends to treat it either as self-evident or as a matter requiring careful definition in the future.

The more reasonable parts of Mumford's arguments tend to be shunted aside in the community's use of his ideas. Mumford, writing in 1934 (but in a manner that remains surprisingly up-to-date), had an outlook which stemmed from the Fabian socialist tradition, extended by a Freudian humanism and sharpened by a depression-born sense of the crisis of capitalism. He retained an ultimate faith in democracy and a vision of the good life which stresses leisure and the playful uses of the imagination. To him, the New Mexico community might well embody the never-ceasing work orientation, the grim self-denial, which he associates with the "paleotechnic" era of nineteenth-century industrialism. In this central respect, his own outlook is more modern than the community's.

As for democracy, Fuller's attitude of open contempt is much more in keeping with the mood of this group.[13] The breathless, all-encompassing self-confidence of Fuller creates a tone which the group finds very congenial. There is no room for idle reflection in Fuller's definition of "thinking"; all is rational calculation based upon literal, absolute "facts."[14] His dualism, or psycho-physical parallelism (as it used to be called at the turn of the century), to the effect that thought follows the same intrinsic pattern as the external universe, is again congenial to the attempted conjunction of "outer" and "inner," exoteric and esoteric, which the community takes from other sources. His hostility to intellectual specialization, his insistence upon viewing life processes and the universe as an inseparable whole, is of course also on the group's wave length.

One might still wonder how Fuller's unshakable optimism fits in with the apocalyptic vision of the death of Western civilization harbored by this community. In its own way, the community is indeed convinced that man is in the process of evolving onto a higher stage. Yet Fuller's astoundingly complacent résumés of recent history must seem as superficial to the members as they do to me.[15] His vision of utopia, moreover, unthinkingly incorporates far more existing and expanded technology, far more affluence and worldwide centralization, than can mesh with the vision of Ezra and his followers. Here Mumford strikes a more accurate note, with his friendliness toward regionalism, decentralization, and local economic self-sufficiency. But neither writer goes far enough in these directions to match the community's conception of the future, which instead resembles the classical

13. Fuller, *op. cit.*, p. 85.
14. *Ibid.*, p. 67.
15. *Ibid.*, pp. 95–96, 104.

anarchist one of an unending series of small rural communes, trading only for a few specialized essentials. True, the "planetary" quality of the new civilization is also emphasized by the community, and this coincides with the anti-nationalist, worldwide perspectives of both Mumford and Fuller.[16] But the "one future world" of this community's imagination has been far more drastically reorganized in the direction of small, independent groups. In economic and technological terms, its thinking is more primitivistic, less comfort-oriented, than either Fuller's or Mumford's, though it is far less extreme in these directions than the genuine "hip" communes.

Robert Ardrey seemingly introduces quite a different, almost a contrary note. The idea of territoriality, the existence of irreducible self-seeking elements in human nature, has a strong appeal for Ezra. Man's need for concrete territory is reconciled with a "planetary" perspective by emphasizing an extreme decentralization. But this is a weak argument. Enlightenment optimism about man's reasonableness (producing the necessary worldwide peace in such a situation) clashes with the social Darwinian pessimism underlying Ardrey's concept of territoriality. All one can say is that both strains are independently pronounced in Ezra's thinking.

The external side of the community's blueprint depends on none of these thinkers in too literal a way. It is in constructing a complicated social pattern of its own, and simultaneously prophesying it as the basis for the entire future of the human race, that the group has in fact been most original. The official reading list turns out to have been somewhat misleading, even though it helped elucidate many particulars. One ends up sensing that any number of other social philosophers might have been placed on it, with only incidental effects upon the practical result. The recommended books mainly show the rather uneven yet intense way in which Ezra consciously seizes upon certain authors and ideas.

The final book I was told to read in advance, W. R. Bion's *Experiences in Groups,* raises considerations of another order. Eva told me that in the early period of the group's existence "we simply couldn't have survived without Bion's book. It made us conscious of all the patterns we were falling into, and this knowledge of what was happening to us gave us the insight into ourselves which kept us going." The absence of such a guide was the reason, she clearly meant to suggest, for the failure of so many other intentional communities.

16. Mumford once speaks (*op. cit.,* p. 142) of "the essential planetary basis of technology itself." Fuller's contempt for nationalism is pervasive, and he looks forward to physical interbreeding to end racial distinctions and create a uniform, superior human stock (*op. cit.,* p. 127).

Alone among all these authors (except perhaps Mumford), Bion is highly regarded in academic circles. Bion was placed in charge of a psychiatric rehabilitation unit in the British army during the Second World War. This kindled his interest in group dynamics, and he made it his special research concern in a variety of settings during the years that followed. His own intellectual perspective is psychoanalytic, but with a strong underlay of the no-nonsense and let's-help-people-to-get-on-with-the-job which is characteristically British. Like Stanislavsky, Mumford, and Fuller, he believes that people must become conscious of their problems in order to deal with them effectively. At the same time he revealingly declares: "If group therapy is to succeed it appears necessary that he [the psychiatrist] should have the outlook, and the sort of intuitive sympathetic flair, of the good unit commander."[17]

The method which Bion evolved for dealing with his unit in wartime was to keep the men busy from morning to night in a variety of ways, overwhelming them with all sorts of group activities from physical training to crafts, and then bringing them together in a daily meeting where they could briefly try to become spectators of themselves, standing outside their routine and looking at the whole of it. There is more than a hint of the life style of the New Mexico community here, with the nightly dinner forming the opportunity for detached self-observation.

Bion's assumption throughout is that a work-oriented group, efficiently engaged in some specific, productive task, is the normal, wholesome ideal. Thus, unlike many other researchers in the field of small groups, he is interested in the study of social interaction not as its own end, but only for the practical purpose of learning to identify the patterns that crop up in work groups and interfere with their productivity.

Bion identifies three such basic patterns, which continually operate to deflect work groups away from their true purposes and pull them onto a more primitive and instinctual level. These are: (1) fight-flight; (2) pairing; (3) dependency. The first consists of the diversion of the group's energy into one or the other of two complementary channels: reaching outward in hostility toward some external enemy, or else fleeing into self-protective isolation. The second pattern is for the group to break down internally into pairs of individuals, often though not always along sexual lines, the energy given to these paired relationships replacing the energy that had previously gone into identification with the goals of the group. Finally, a third alternative consists of escape into total emotional subservience to a single leader, who (for some uncanny reason) is often the

17. W. R. Bion, *Experiences in Groups* (New York: Basic Books, 1961), p. 22.

most nearly psychotic member of the group, commonly with paranoiac tendencies. "A group structure in which one member is a god, either established or discredited, has a very limited usefulness."[18]

"Evasion and denial" of work-oriented responsibilities may thus take any of these forms, all of which exist as constant dangers. But Bion is optimistic; he believes (and Ezra underlined this passage in his copy) that the work-oriented group "triumphs in the long run."[19] "Organization and structure" are its weapons in the struggle against the upsurge of the more primitive emotional patterns. The sophisticated group learns to suppress the impulses of its members which are associated with these three types of energy-deflection. By becoming conscious of the hazards it overcomes them. Moreover, it interprets its mission as one of gradual development toward given goals rather than believing unrealistically (as do groups subverted by these other patterns) in their "full equipment by instinct" for whatever they have to do. Beyond this, the successful work-oriented group brings to the surface capacities in individuals which otherwise remain only potential. "The group, therefore, is more than the aggregate of individuals, because an individual in a group is more than an individual in isolation."[20] To Ezra, this last passage must have seemed a remarkable echo of the concept of "synergy."

No doubt for many such reasons, Bion's little book came to seem the most appropriate manual for group living in this community. Ezra had first encountered it several years earlier, when it was assigned to him in a course at an Ivy League business school he was attending. It may very well have played the key role in keeping the group together with which Eva credits it. But if one looks at the actual community in New Mexico from Bion's own perspective, the "victory" Eva implies the group has won may seem oddly illusory, despite the members' compelling fixation upon work. First of all, the intention later to move overseas could easily be interpreted as an instance of the pattern of flight, no matter how it is dressed up in the more positive vocabulary of planetary planning and adventure. Second and more serious, the group's continuing dependency upon Ezra, a theme that recurs in every aspect of its daily life, would seem to illustrate the kind of deflective force which Bion was most concerned to unmask. Of course other groups, whose morale has been sustained by other bibles, have revealed the

---

18. *Ibid.,* p. 56; cf. p. 79. The same kind of warning is made in another book on Ezra's shelf, Robert S. DeRopp, *The Master Game: Pathways to Higher Consciousness Beyond the Drug Experience* (New York: Delacorte Press, 1968), pp. 175, 207.

19. Bion, *op. cit.,* p. 136.

20. *Ibid.,* p. 90.

same propensity to be found wanting in terms of the very scriptures they endorse.

The philosophy of the New Mexico community on the deepest level really begins with the books which Ezra left off his advance reading list. All of them center in two philosophical traditions having to do with the mystical and the occult: that of Gurdjieff, and the centuries-old movement within Islam known as Sufism. Ultimately, the two chains fuse into one, for Gurdjieff is believed to have been greatly influenced by Sufi teachings during his youthful wanderings through the Near East. Coming to these writings, one realizes that here finally is the esoteric heartland of the group's beliefs, a region not disclosed to casual visitors on the ranch, though painted "enneagrams" on the walls of the dining room would inform anyone already initiated that Gurdjieff's ideas had an important role here.

Gurdjieff was one of the spiritual leaders to appear on the margins of the Western world (Ramakrishna was another) offering an alternative "truth" precisely at the moment when Christianity was losing its intellectual grip at the end of the nineteenth century. As we saw in discussing Vedanta, some men and women of that day, unable any longer to accept the orthodoxy of their upbringing, restlessly hungered for the certainty of a new cosmology which could replace it. The main direction of Western thought was away from such certainties altogether, but the mechanistic implications of physical science repelled a number of people who desperately wanted to go on believing in an organic, vital, teleological principle at the center of reality. Romanticism had conditioned them to demand this, as it had also legitimized the posture of intense inward seriousness in a search for truth. Why, at the beginning of the twentieth century, certain people felt that the basic coherence of the universe would be shattered if they were denied an organic prime mover with whose purposes they could identify, while others glided cheerfully on into pragmatism and jazz, their sense of coherence in the world blithely unaffected, remains a most fascinating question, especially if one assumes the intrinsic superiority of neither choice. In the Vedanta movement, the lure of the Swami and the high incidence of women followers pointed to a rather concrete psychological explanation. But the appeal of the Gurdjieff movement, which came to America at a slightly later moment in time, cannot be accounted for quite so specifically, though it has many resemblances.

Gurdjieff was a Greek of fairly simple origins who grew up in the Russian Caucasus, early developed an interest in the supernatural, and claimed to have traveled to a number of wisdom schools in Iran, Turkestan,

Tibet, and elsewhere. Around 1912 he appeared in Moscow and began collecting a band of disciples, recruited mainly from among the lesser intelligentsia, promising to teach them inner truths about man's nature and the meaning of the cosmos. The need for willful, arduous effort to attain self-development, the need for total submission to the will of the teacher, and the need most of all to set oneself in deliberate opposition to the normal emotional currents of everyday life, including warm ties with other people, were the most striking aspects of Gurdjieff's message. Beyond this, he unveiled a cosmology which agreed with the earlier movement of Theosophy in its main outlines, though it was noticeably more elitist in character. (Thus reincarnation and the existence of the "astral body," which Theosophy had posited as basic to all mankind, were both denied by Gurdjieff save to a small number of exceptionally "advanced" individuals; they were held out as the plums to be received after many years of tortuous inner growth.)[21] In sum, it might be fair to characterize Gurdjieff as a later, more austere and intellectually complicated version of Madame Blavatsky, though Gurdjieff demanded from his followers an arduous course of self-punishment peculiarly of his own devising.

By 1916 Gurdjieff had established groups of loyal followers in both Moscow and Petrograd, traveling constantly between them. (This makes one think, inevitably, of Swami Paramananda's twin centers and his incessant travels. Again one notes the effect of frequent arrivals and departures in intensifying the emotional sway of a guru over his disciples.) When the Revolution came, Gurdjieff, who was fanatically anti-Bolshevik, fled to south Russia (where dissensions first notably began to appear in his circle), then to Istanbul, Berlin, and finally to France. Near Fontainebleau his reconstituted following enabled him in 1922 to purchase a château where he could direct a "school" and community in complete accord with his own ideas. He remained headquartered on this property thereafter, initially attracting great attention as the leader of his band of "forest philosophers," until his death in 1949. In 1924 he toured America, explicitly for the purpose of money raising.

The daily regime at Gurdjieff's "school," as it existed in the mid-1920's, again bears strong resemblances to the life style of the New Mexico group. All day long each individual labored at the particular task which Gurdjieff

21. The most revealing and dependable account of Gurdjieff in his Moscow period and of his entire system of ideas is P. D. Ouspensky, *In Search of the Miraculous* (New York: Harcourt, Brace and World, 1949). Though Gurdjieff sometimes railed against Theosophy, his frequent allusions to it as something familiar to his followers revealed that he was recruiting in the same pasture. E.g., see pp. 32, 37, 66, 227, 286.

assigned him, breaking work only for meals and for gymnastics or dancing in the evening. In an exact parallel, special meals called "feasts" were held weekly.[22] However, there was less of a deliberate fragmenting of tasks to create variety during the day, and at the château Sunday was a complete day of rest. Gurdjieff personally supervised every detail. He would goad people on, freely criticize them, and help "contribute a feeling of furious, senseless activity to the whole proceedings."[23] Heavy physical labor was intrinsic to the daily round. Projects under way included crushing rocks for a new road and clearing an area of woodland by removing entire acres of trees, as well as the routine chores of gardening, weeding, cooking, and housekeeping.

Gurdjieff was a despot whose rule makes Ezra's in New Mexico seem quite mild by comparison. Yet in all sorts of details it was of the same basic style. Work was expected to be performed at the maximum level of output that an individual, straining himself, could achieve. Such work was never re-warded with praise. But, if there was any tendency toward slacking off, the person was judged unfit to be in the community. Work was to be done more and more rapidly as individuals developed skill and familiarity with it. But it was always understood that the only point of working faster was to be able to take on heavier and heavier workloads as time went on. Gurdjieff, like Ezra, would fall into periodic rages against his leading subordinates. These rages were more than merely spontaneous; they were conceived as tests of the individual's ability to deal in a conscious rather than an automatic fashion with the abrasive qualities in others. But their effect was to intensify the mood of anxiety, the tinge of outright fear which continually infused the community. Everyone was slavishly obedient to Gurdjieff, suppressing their own feelings whenever they bore the brunt of Gurdjieff's attacks.

After Gurdjieff's death, those who took over the movement, both in Eu-rope and America, appear to have increased the tempo of authoritarian con-trol, until it assumed the proportions of a psychic reign of terror. At the same time, as so often happens in these circumstances, with their master gone they lapsed into a slavishly literal, dulling orthodoxy, prescribing meaning-less repetitive activities.[24] The movement was also apt to repel outsiders (for instance of the younger generation) because it seemed, from their point of view, too intellectual in tone. It was this peculiarly lifeless, stag-

22. An unusually vivid, believable source concerning life at the château is Fritz Peters, *Boyhood with Gurdjieff* (New York: E. P .Dutton, 1964).
23. *Ibid.*, p. 67.
24. See Rafael Lefort, *The Teachers of Gurdjieff* (London: Victor Gollancz, 1966), pp. 7, 11–12, 39–40, 94.

nant, yet terrifying movement which briefly drew Ezra into its midst in New York during the mid-1960's, just before he developed the desire to form his own community in New Mexico.

Ezra likes to hint that his group represents only the latest fulfillment of a grand plan that has been initiated elsewhere. All through the ages, at least since Plato, he announces, there have been special "schools" which have gathered small groups of followers around them. This is clearly designed to be such a "school," though he sometimes speaks as if it has yet to prove itself in these terms. He does not discourage the impression that he has been "sent" from some place "higher up" to create such an undertaking. But when I asked him whether he was speaking of esoteric centers in touch with the Masters, in the manner of Theosophy or the Rosicrucians, he disavowed any direct supernatural contact and said that the teachers of these schools had always been ordinary human beings, though of a greatly advanced inner development. This answer, which leaves the door more than slightly ajar for the occult if one listens carefully to it, is consistent with Gurdjieff's handling of similar questions in Moscow around 1915.

But the relations of this community to the Gurdjieff movement are more complicated than this. Though Ezra refers unusually often to Gurdjieff in the course of his afterdinner discussions, he clearly regards him as but one source of authority among many. Moreover, Ezra quarreled with his teacher in the Gurdjieff movement and in effect broke with it. An orthodox Gurdjieff group exists nearby in New Mexico and, I am told, distrusts Ezra's community, believing that it has wandered too far from the true paths. (In an odd coincidence, this other group very nearly bought the same ranch property just before it was purchased by Eva in 1969.) "No, this is definitely not to be thought of as a 'Gurdjieff group,'" Eva declared in response to my question.

Still, it might properly be called neo-Gurdjieffian.[25] When I asked Ezra for the history of the community, his immediate, considered response was: "In one sense it began forty thousand years ago. In another it began in 1912. In still another, it started in 1966." The intermediate date is of course when Gurdjieff began proclaiming his message. And its inner spirit is deeply pervaded by the Gurdjieffian view of man's nature.

The starting point for Gurdjieff is revulsion and disgust with ordinary

25. It is somewhat curious that Ezra pays little open homage to the recent book by Robert S. DeRopp, *The Master Game,* even though he owns a copy. An outsider seeking an explanation of the point of view which dominates Ezra's community could in fact do no better than to give DeRopp a careful reading, for he offers a viewpoint deeply in harmony with the neo-Gurdjieffian perspective of this group in nearly every detail, and his is by far the most attractively credible presentation of it.

life, including one's own. "Life taken by itself without any added explanation," writes Maurice Nicoll, a leading British exponent of Gurdjieff's ideas,
"is largely meaningless, 'a tale told by an idiot,' a history of crime and
bloodshed and frustration."[26] The normal, everyday man is asleep, a walking automaton or somnambulist. He is in prison but does not know it.
Nothing that he does is willed; everything is merely automatic reaction.
"This machine of Personality to which each person is attached works mechanically. You put a penny in the slot and everything goes by routine."[27]
The Gurdjieff teaching is designed for people who feel estranged in this
way from themselves, that is, who feel self-alienated. It feeds upon a deeper,
more thoroughgoing sense of alienation than Marx had conceived of, because it is defined as the product of no particular set of external circumstances (such as might be changed through collective revolution) but instead as the universal, given condition of man. One's emerging revolt
against this condition is not directed outward toward exploiters whom one
can easily locate and rise against, but is instead focused within, upon the
self that continues "automatically" to stir sugar in one's cup of coffee and
dream about having an affair with a woman. One may temporarily forget
an exploiter, but there is no escape from this inward enemy, which goes on
forever reminding one of its existence as every detail of habitual daily action unfolds.

Only a few exceptional people begin to realize that their lives up till
now have been completely mechanical. (Here the elitism of the esoteric,
as opposed to the Marxian, version of the attainment of "consciousness"
shows itself.) For these few there is hope. Man "can undergo a definite and
pre-arranged transformation in himself . . . a real evolution or rebirth, if
he knows and understands gradually what he has to do."[28] In this process,
mechanical man dies, and conscious man is born.

But, to accomplish this, the individual "must find a Teacher and a
Teaching—that is, a Teaching that is not arbitrary, invented by ordinary
people, but one that comes from those who have awakened and left behind
them instructions to those in prison in the sleep of life, who wish to get out,
to awaken."[29] Once a teacher has been found, the way is still extremely
arduous. One is constantly tested from the beginning and given unending
labor to perform. This must go on for many years; indeed, it may be life-

26. Nicoll, *Psychological Commentaries on the Teaching of G. I. Gurdjieff and
P. D. Ouspensky* (5 vols. London: Vincent Stuart, 1952), II, 398.
27. *Ibid.,* II, 415.
28. *Ibid.,* II, 399.
29. *Ibid.*

long. But Gurdjieff hints that, though sacrifice is necessary for a very long time, it is not required forever. Eventually one may reach a state where everything comes without strain, where one becomes a kind of superman, a "law unto himself"—a Gurdjieff.[30] Meanwhile, no energy must be wasted. There must be no idle daydreaming. The struggle against one's lesser self must be unremitting, and the obedience to the leader unquestioning. Above all, one must never object to instructions, even if one dislikes them intensely.[31]

This struggle toward self-transformation is defined, in the vocabulary of the movement, as the Work. The Work is inherently opposed to life. Life is continually pulling us back into it, toward the level of sleepwalking. In particular, when we "identify" with other personalities—with friends, wives, neighbors, lovers—we are dragged down by them and tempted to forget the Work. Even after many years, we may find it possible to live in the Work only for a small portion of each day, because it runs so squarely against our ordinary nature, which has been conditioned to go on functioning otherwise. But in the energy generated by this very conflict lies the source of strength for the developing inner will. "All Work-force is derived by going against yourself, by going against your natural mechanical reaction at the moment."[32]

Shock and abrasion are the main sources of the energy needed for internal development. Harsh, unpleasant encounters with others generate the resistance which provides inner power and capacity for awareness. They are the essence of human relations within the Work, as opposed to the enervating warmth of human relations within life. "When you have your own way," Nicoll goes so far as to assert, "when things go smoothly, you are not going against yourself, and you are not conscious."[33] Thus, as one of the members of the New Mexico community expressed it in my hearing, without abrasion and a degree of enmity there can be no true "being-contact" with another person. Everything else, including superficial pleasantry, is sheer waste of time.

The very act of breathing, said Gurdjieff, provides an initial shock to all mankind on a continuing basis. But for the person who has decided to embark on the Work, there is a First Conscious Shock which he will soon receive. This is also referred to as the act of self-remembering. It involves a sudden sense of separation from oneself in which one becomes aware of

30. Ouspensky, *op. cit.*, p. 33.
31. Nicoll, *op. cit.*, II, 735–36.
32. *Ibid.*, II, 720.
33. *Ibid.*, II, 412.

one's own mechanicalness. It is "just as if an actor on the stage who had become completely absorbed in the role he was playing suddenly remembered that he was merely acting the role and that he was really somebody else and not the part he was playing. This would mean that he would wake up."[34] (How ironic is Nicoll's image, in view of the efforts of the New Mexico community in theater. Stanislavsky had repeatedly insisted that this very act of losing one's identity with the role was fatal to the success of a player.) Self-remembering, or extreme detachment, is to be sought after as frequently as possible, but at times it may come as a distinct experience of an almost mystical order. Ouspensky describes how forcefully this peculiar mental state once hit him in Petrograd, where for a long period he moved through streets in which everyone around him had literally seemed to become a sleepwalker.[35] Thus through untold effort and practice those in the Work can learn to wrench themselves ever more completely away from life.

True evolution is not a part of nature; it is against nature. The ordinary circumstances of daily existence, including nocturnal sleep, conspire to deplete us of energy; they drain our vitality away from us. Through self-remembering, we willfully counter these influences. On a grander level, the entire universe "is a vast distilling machine, to extract the finer from the coarser. . . . What is individual evolution, in the esoteric sense? Seeing by long inner work, and then choosing the *finer,* and eventually willing and ultimately living the *finer.*"[36] But there is little or no cosmic pull to which we can attach ourselves in search of a free boost; in this respect the Gurdjieff teaching is far less optimistic than the American "mind-cure" tradition exemplified by Christian Science and New Thought. (Vedanta, as we saw, falls somewhere in between.)

Ouspensky once commented upon how those in the Gurdjieff group appeared to their ordinary friends after they had been engrossed in the Work for some length of time. In the view of these friends, "we had begun to change for the worse. They found us less interesting than we had been before; they told us we were becoming colorless, as though we were fading, were losing our former spontaneity, our former responsiveness to everything, that we were becoming 'machines,' were ceasing to think originally, were ceasing to feel, that we were merely repeating like parrots what we had heard from G."[37] Seen from an external perspective, that is, from someone who is in life rather than in the Work, these are symptoms which

34. *Ibid.,* II, 737.
35. Ouspensky, *op. cit.,* p. 120.
36. Nicoll, *op. cit.,* II, 431; his italics.
37. Ouspensky, *op. cit.,* p. 245.

also appear among some of the most loyal and "advanced" members of the New Mexico community. Though, perhaps happily, many of them still have a long way to go in these directions, one senses that it is this "colorless," mutually isolated pattern of existence which they are consciously trying to move toward. In Gurdjieff's system of thinking, personality is opposed to essence. To develop one's essence in the Work, personality is deliberately to be weakened.[38] In particular, Gurdjieff said on one occasion, inwardly advanced people never have a need to laugh.[39] If all this sounds inhuman, from Gurdjieff's perspective this is precisely the point. And if it appears life denying, again this is what is explicitly intended. For it is life, no more, no less, that one is seeking to be saved from. If one does not hate life—including one's own life—the whole system becomes meaningless or abhorrent. It is a system founded upon an initial desire for self-destruction, which it then ruthlessly cultivates and intensifies. Conceived as an effort to free man from mechanicalness, it transforms him (if it is wholly successful) into a chillingly detached automaton, at the beck and call of higher Masters.

Again, I do not mean to imply that the present group in New Mexico offers this picture as its complete face, or that it is largely composed of would-be suicides. The great psychological variation among people there will become apparent when they are described as individuals. But something like this is the direction that Ezra is defining for them as growth, and he himself openly says that shock and abrasion are the necessary basis for human relations. The isolated, austere, quasi-monastic atmosphere on these acres is the product of this philosophy. No one comes there (to stay for any length of time) who is in search of love—unless it be the highly special form of it that attaches to the magnetic, in this case highly masculine figure of a single leader.

The student of Gurdjieff further gains an esoteric understanding of the universe. He learns a mystical version of chemistry, according to which "hydrogen" exists in various numerical weights and densities, each being absorbed by a different level of animal life. He learns that there are forty-eight different "Rays of Creation," each emanating influences which affect mankind. (The sun is superior to the earth, but the earth is superior to the moon; the influence of the moon on our behavior is most to be resisted.) He learns of two basic laws, the Law of Three and the Law of Seven, also called the Law of Octaves, which then become combined in the figure of the enneagram. ("It is useless simply to take it [the enneagram] as a dia-

38. Nicoll, *op. cit.*, II, 401.
39. Ouspensky, *op. cit.*, pp. 236–37.

gram. It is a living thing and all life depends on it.")[40] The student learns that he must discard ordinary notions of causality; the future as well as the past may influence the present. He learns that in each human being there are four centers—intellectual, emotional, instinctive, and moving. "They are four kinds of intelligence or conductors of meaning." Each of them is related to particular chemical elements.[41] He learns that there are precise numbers and labels to be attached to nearly everything, including each state of mind or consciousness. Mastering this terminology, he feels he has been given a complete, totally satisfying key to all areas of existence. The system has become his only source of information, even though it is so complicated that it may still contain what appear to be baffling mysteries and unsolved problems (just as these always exist in the fields of natural science).

How seriously, one may wonder, do Ezra and his followers take this "informational" aspect of the Gurdjieff teaching, as distinct from its view of human psychology? Certainly on one level they claim to be keenly interested in physical science of the usual sort, especially in relation to their study of ecology. The chemistry lectures prepared for the ecology conference had none of this esoteric content. And, in a series of four afterdinner talks during Ezra's absence, one member explained the functioning of DNA and RNA to the group in a manner entirely reminiscent of a college course. Ezra, whose own background was in engineering, never speaks of the mystical "hydrogen 12, 24, 48, 96, 192," which figure so largely in Gurdjieff's account of the universe.

And yet—listening to Ezra talk, one realizes that his mind has established no clear cut-off point between the "respectably scientific" and the miraculous. The four centers within the human psyche are constantly referred to and taken literally. Even more revealingly, Ezra enthusiastically embraces the writings of another British disciple of Gurdjieff named J. G. Bennett. Bennett, originally a mathematician, became disillusioned with the human situation during the First World War and thereupon began a search for a complete, totally meaningful system (the phrases are his own) in which he could have confidence. At first he confined his studies to natural science, but around 1921 he met Gurdjieff and Ouspensky and was converted to their basic outlook. Eventually he founded the Institute for the Comparative Study of History, Philosophy, and the Sciences, located at

40. Nicoll, op. cit., II, 385.
41. Ibid., II, 393–94. Sometimes Gurdjieff gave an independent role to a fifth, the sex center.

Coombe Springs, Kingston-upon-Thames. There he still presides over a small band of followers, some of whom hold British or American academic degrees. "Seminars" are regularly given; in 1966 they attracted 114 people. A journal called *Systematics,* imitating the style and format of a university-based scholarly publication, was begun by the institute in 1963 and Ezra's file of it shows that it is still in existence. It combines lengthy disquisitions, in a style which I am unable to distinguish from much academic writing in philosophy, with recent reports on the fate of Atlantis.

Over the years Bennett gradually gathered steam for the production of a "complete" philosophy, eventually published in four volumes under the title *The Dramatic Universe.* This tome, more than any other, has become the Bible for the community in New Mexico. Numerous phrases which Ezra uses in his conversations can be traced back to it. This does not mean that all the members of the community have read Bennett, but the more deeply involved "core" people in the group appear to have made the attempt. Ezra and Eva met Bennett personally some time ago, and when the group went to England briefly at the end of 1971, it spent a week at Coombe Springs.

I cannot claim to have mastered Bennett's four volumes. But the last of them, which constitutes a survey and interpretation of world history, drew my interest. In it, Bennett reviews the whole sweep of recorded events with a brevity and sureness which far surpass Arnold J. Toynbee's. Where Toynbee might take several pages to deal with the rise and fall of an empire, Bennett finds two or three sentences sufficient.

More important than Bennett's handling of details is the overall conception he presents of historical chronology and of the nature of influences upon events. Following Gurdjieff, he rejects the orthodox view that only the past may affect the present; so also may the future. The ordinary notion of time is thus dissolved. At first sight, this idea might seem to intensify rather than to reduce the degree of determinism in history. But in fact for Bennett its role is severely minimized. Instead he emphasizes the chanciness of the outcome. History is a gnostic struggle between the forces of good and evil. One is sometimes led to infer that the good will win out in the long run, but matters might conceivably go another way. Thus a large place is reserved for the cumulative impact of individual human will and consciousness. Teleology exists, but it limps and falters. In this curiously mixed situation, the role of small groups of "advanced" individuals, dedicated to furthering the cosmic plan, may prove crucial.

These groups have already existed for many thousands of years. "We shall use the term Hidden Directorate to designate those who are aware of the purposes pursued in the evolution of mankind and know the action that has to be taken." The role of this Directorate is compared to the producer's (in America, the director's) role in a drama.

> Its task is to help mankind to develop both individually and socially to the point at which man can assume responsibility for his destiny and the fulfillment of his mission on the earth. The Hidden Directorate is presumed to have developed out of the group of Guides and Initiates who took charge of the diffusion [of culture] from the Four Centres [where Bennett believes human culture originated, during a period of profound inner "withdrawal," roughly from 10,000 to 8,500 years ago]. These in their turn were the descendants of those who established these centres at the beginning of the Great Cycle that started 12,500 years ago and of which about one half has now been completed.
>
> If we postulate the reality of the Great Work, we must allow that it is directed by Intelligences whose time-scale is measured in thousands if not tens of thousands of years. We are to assume, then, that the Hidden Directorate can see ahead and make plans that will take a long time to mature; but we are not to assume that they are supernatural beings able to interfere with the operation of natural laws. This does not mean that they have no powers beyond those of ordinary people. . . . They probably use higher forms of energy than are known to man.[42]

On the same page Bennett inserts a footnote which provides a highly interesting revelation of the extent to which he is aware how his beliefs may be received by outsiders:

> Terms like 'Inner Circle of Humanity' (P. D. Ouspensky, *In Search of the Miraculous,* p. 310), 'Mystery Centres' (Rudolf Steiner), 'The Hierarchy' (Alice Bailey),[43] 'The Masters' (H. P. Blavatsky, *Secret Doctrine*) have been misunderstood and misused. This is almost tragic as nearly all serious students of History and of the Origin of Religions have come to regard such notions with suspicion and usually have come to disregard them entirely as the equivalent of space fiction. This makes it more hazardous than it should be, to put forward an interpretation of history that postulates the work of Hidden Guides.

Be this as it may, such "hazards" have not lessened Ezra's enthusiasm for Bennett as an authoritative philosopher.

A further detail in Bennett's cosmology may have helped stimulate this enthusiasm. Like Buckminster Fuller, Bennett embraces the concept of "synergy," which he defines as "structural cooperation" and inserts into history as "a stage of integration in which the parts of a whole surrender

42. J. G. Bennett, *The Dramatic Universe* (4 vols.; London: Hodder and Stoughton, 1952–1966), IV, 325.
43. See p. 42.

some of their independent existence, in order to participate in a higher gradation of being." In more mundane language, this is an era of collective effort. The Synergic Epoch, according to Bennett, quietly began around the years 1844–1851, initially unobserved by nearly everyone. It will continue for the next two to three thousand years. Among its symptoms were the revolutions of 1848, the appearance of Darwinian evolutionary theory, the theory of relativity and the rejection of absolutism as a philosophical concept, and the growing belief in large-scale organization, which has accompanied an intellectual emphasis on man's collective destiny. The Bahai and Vedanta movements are singled out as important synergic symptoms, reflecting the ecumenicism of this New Age. But so also are the writings of Kierkegaard and Karl Marx (with only the briefest pause to deplore Marx's seeming materialism); and so are the Impressionist painters and the rise of spiritualism.[44] Modern life assumes the aspect of a vast synergic symphony, gaining in force. In this worldwide tendency there is nonetheless a special place reserved for groups like the one in New Mexico. "Synergy implies not only co-working within each level of history, but also an interpenetration of different values," such as economics, science, society, religion, and the vegetative areas of activity.[45] So Ezra's undertaking might well have appeared as a direct answer to Bennett's most profound hopes.

The Synergic Epoch also marks a decline in the role of the Hidden Directorate in human affairs, for it means that man is ever more actively taking charge of his own destiny. Still, there are extraordinary dangers lurking in the present time span, and once in a while Bennett expresses the belief that the human situation is today running out of control.[46] In these moods, the element of extreme chanciness returns. But more often, as he views recent events, Bennett slips instead into an oddly complacent note. The risk of war, he argues, has decreased greatly in the fifteen years between 1951 and 1966. To explain this, the higher powers are again invoked. Peace has been maintained owing to the "intervention by the Hidden Directorate aided by Demiurgic Intelligences. The destiny of mankind did not require a Third World War and so, in spite of human foolishness, total war has been averted."[47] And yet elsewhere Bennett will again

44. Bennett, *op. cit.,* IV, 386–91.
45. *Ibid.,* IV, 399.
46. *Ibid.,* IV, 404.
47. *Ibid.,* IV, 402. Bennett's political views are obscure. He blames both sides for the Cold War, but also cites with seeming approval a 1945 statement by Jan Christiaan Smuts to the effect that European supremacy was the best hope of the world at least for the next century. *Ibid.,* IV, 401 and n. Politics in the ordinary sense simply does not matter for Bennett.

blithely affirm that the universe is "dramatic" precisely because it is *not* predestined, because there is "hope and hazard" in the process of its unfolding.[48] Despite a lifetime spent developing an all-embracing system of thought in which he could believe, Bennett was content to remain far less than consistent in his rendition of some of its most central details. Like many astrologers, Bennett used the idea of "destiny" whenever it pleased him and the idea of "will" (and hazard) whenever it in turn seemed more inviting. On balance, there is far less "will" in Bennett than in, for example, William James, and yet he clearly thought that an emphasis upon it was his most distinctive philosophical contribution.

Bennett is the "house philosopher" of the New Mexico group. But just how seriously do they take all of his statements? He seems to be regarded with a kind of undifferentiated awe, as if from far below. Did the Synergic Epoch really begin in 1844? I asked Eva. And, if so, how does this square with Ezra's statement that the New Age is only coming into being right now? Her answer was that she had simply not thought much about these minor details. (And who indeed but an academic historian would be so greatly interested in a single century, when the cosmic time scale is measured in such broad strokes?) Yet Eva is the most openly "ideological" in her style of conversation of all the members of the community, except for Ezra himself. For many of the others, Bennett's formulations probably remain only vaguely apprehended, and some newcomers clearly know nothing of this dimension of the group's beliefs.

The final major source of influence upon Ezra's thinking is Sufism. Sufism, though an ancient tradition within Islam, also turns out to be an organized international movement of the same vintage as Vedanta and Gurdjieff's. It was brought to America in the fall of 1910 by Pir-o-Murshid Inayat Khan, of Baroda, India, who toured here for two years much as did Vivekananda. By 1930, eight Sufi centers had been established in the United States, controlled by Americans who, again like Vedantists, often had assumed Asian names and titles.[49]

To my mind, Sufism lacks the resonance of Buddhism, Hinduism, or Taoism. It appears to harbor a series of numerological and symbolic mysteries on the same level as the enneagrams and esoteric chemistry of Gurdjieff, and therefore suffers in a similar way from misplaced concreteness. On the ethical side, however, Sufi tales possess some of the wit and whimsy

48. *Ibid.*, IV, 435.
49. Wendell Thomas, *Hinduism Invades America* (New York: Beacon Press, 1930), p. 226.

one associates with Zen, though they can also descend to the plane of an Aesop.

These collected tales are the Sufi literature which the members of the community have taken most fully to heart. Many persons at the dinner table are able to recite several of these brief, pungent stories from memory, as happened one evening during Ezra's absence. At that same dinner, a lengthy reading from Idries Shah's major descriptive work on the Sufi tradition occurred. It is a very dry book. Yet in discussion afterward there was much collective straining after profound inner meanings in what had been presented. I felt that everyone was doing this because they knew they were supposed to be found there. During the conversation two group members with high status (one of them Eva) frankly admitted that, in one sense at least, they thought the book was somewhat tedious and hard to connect with. As they put it, one part of them remained skeptical or thought it was lifeless, while another part of them was absorbing it. (Not even these two, with Ezra out of earshot, could dare simply say that it was dull and leave it at that.)

One comes back to the fact that Gurdjieff was taught by the Sufis. According to one recent book by a disillusioned follower of Gurdjieff, many passages of which are underlined in Ezra's copy, Gurdjieff's "orthodox" disciples are off the track and it is the Sufi groups which have the true message for mankind.[50] Here probably lies the reason that the group has turned in this direction.

Much of the time Ezra's vocabulary straddles the delicate borderline between the psychological and the openly esoteric. One might even hear him hold forth for several days at a stretch without becoming distinctly aware of his cosmology. He openly dislikes the word "spiritual," perhaps the favorite adjective among earlier mystical groups in America. To him it connotes a closet atmosphere of unreal divorce from the everyday world. He is intensely proud of the way in which this community joins the "inner" (a word he does freely use) with the "outer," the way it puts ideas into practice in a visible, tangible display. The realms of physical achievement and socio-economic planning loom large in his imagination.

Yet for Ezra the "inner" does unmistakably connect with the world view of J. G. Bennett. On an ultimate level, the group he has nurtured is yet another in the long line of those that have emerged ever since the days of spiritualism, Theosophy, and Vedanta. There has been no real break. The novelty of this would-be "new civilization" lies elsewhere, in the realm

50. Lefort, *op. cit.,* especially last chapter.

of its complicated external life style. Though somewhat disguised and re-interpreted for an age dominated by Freud and encounter groups, his version of "self-development" is in the older tradition of willful outreach toward cosmic consciousness. Thus it still bears all the burdens of an emphasis upon the guilt-ridden rejection of an unwanted "lower" self. The Vedanta nuns and Ezra's youthful band turn out to be struggling against the same inner demons. A measure of sexual freedom has been added to the current recipe for withdrawal from the world with these ends in view. But this is only a variation on a time-honored theme.

During my weeks in the community, I received many conflicting impressions of its general intellectual caliber. Some of these variations will become clearer when individuals are discussed. Yet there is also a fairly pervasive tone.

First, let there be no mistake. Some of the younger members of this group not only were fully capable of getting A's in their courses in reputable universities, but actually had done so on a regular basis. Moreover, they have what they consider to be a lively curiosity about ideas. They are, as will be seen, often from highly advantaged backgrounds and have been reading books on their own since childhood. They are now thoroughly anti-academic in their perspective (though they never made me feel directly uncomfortable because of this bias). Their own explanation of themselves is that they found their college courses narrow and stifling, sometimes with the exception of a single unorthodox professor, who was very often in the process of being fired. Talking with them casually, one begins to think of them as a very bright group of dropouts, exactly the kind of people who would have become leaders in the established order if the times had not been peculiarly out of joint. How natural, then, to find them here, training instead to become the leaders of the New Age. This is certainly a view of them which gives them pleasure when it is expressed, and there is a considerable measure of truth in it.

Despite what has been said about their colorless tone, in some contexts the group can seem incredibly lively, energetic, "on top of things," and "with-it." "We're really just a bunch of rascals," one of the girls suddenly declared to me in an ebullient mood. Tearing across the desert in the Microbus, accomplishing half a dozen errands at once, picking up people and leaving them off, even an occasional hitch-hiker, making a last-minute swerve for an ice cream, it was almost possible to believe her statement. This image of the group, as sharp, fast-reacting, and keenly alive, is never altogether wrong, if applied to certain levels of their daily existence. Their sharpness takes the characteristically American form—instant readiness for anything, pride in being able to do several things at the same time, and in being able to sound out the practical realities of any unfamiliar situation. It is pride in know-how—in being able to manipulate the world with ease and relish, and thereby to accomplish just about any mission that is handed them. This aspect of the group's mental life was revealed at its highest pitch one evening early in my stay when four members who had gone overseas to find land to buy returned to New Mexico and presented a full account of their month abroad. Their sense of pace in the telling of their adventures, the way they left out nothing that seemed significant while never allowing matters to drag, their conscious savoring of highly amusing details, the well-honed memory for particulars which these in turn disclosed, and their ability mercilessly to sum up the personalities of those they had encountered—all bespoke an exceptional collective talent, as well as a gleeful awareness of the coup they had apparently pulled off.

The intelligence of the group, especially of its more prominent members, shines precisely in practical, manipulative contexts and situations of this kind, where skill and deft perceptiveness connect directly with the group-oriented projects at hand, whether going to town or going overseas. The members demonstrate the calculative nimbleness of the untheoretical man of action whose ultimate loyalties have already been firmly established. That is why it may be accurate to picture some of these same personalities as potential business executives or government planners of a superior order, if circumstances were different.

Conversely, the intellectual caliber of the group is lowest in areas having to do with quiet reflection or speculation. Here they are dominated by the assortment of ideas upon which Ezra has placed his official sanction. They have totally surrendered their independence of mind in this respect, though the eclecticism of their "reading list" gives the illusion of a more open universe. They do not discuss ultimate questions freely in the manner of a really good college class. They reach for definitions and phrases that have already been handed to them. They become literal whenever these speculative regions of the mind are called upon to be exercised. Unlike many other bright dropouts of the new generation, they display a willingness to accept and to parrot rote answers.

Great manipulative shrewdness, great worldly wisdom on some everyday levels thus combine with an extraordinarily cheerful and thoroughgoing surrender of intellectual independence on a broader one. At some unnamed point their verve disappears, merging into dutiful commitment. In these key zones they are untouchable, as if suddenly placed behind a solid wall of glass.

As I took the final "inner tour" of the community, reading the philosophical texts which are their authorities and listening to Ezra's words with the growing realization that he too was ultimately in their grip, I began involuntarily to sink into a mood of disappointment. The initial "reading list" had promised the kind of variety which connotes a much greater degree of intellectual liveliness than was actually proving to thrive here. The vision of the universe which dominated their inner realm seemed to me a dank chamber, far more airtight than the underground tomb which I had finished building as my living quarters. And in it lived the demons of self-hatred, which were defined as "negative emotions," "resistance," and "false personality." Inside the closed box within which they speculated, the people here were flagellating the "grosser" parts of their own beings as if they were Penitentes. It is perhaps a meaningful accident that Ezra consistently mispronounces the name of Gurdjieff, to make it rhyme with "grief."

I felt that I had found the true source of the underlying severity of tone in this community and the inner isolation of its people, which all the busy work on projects and theater could not conceal. And all I could do was wonder, once more, why it is that some people must go through the whole of their lives engaged in self-struggle, never being satisfied with themselves as they are, while others radiate an automatic, happy self-acceptance. From the group's point of view, the former were "advanced" souls, the few who had chosen to wake up out of the "sleep" of normal human life. But from my own they were pathetically self-enclosed, locked into a pointless struggle with their own emotions which gave every sign of being never-ending, and in which many years of self-observation and self-combat were likely to produce someone worse off than when he or she began. This did not mean that such tortured individuals would be entirely without strength; indeed, they might be razor-sharp in some particular directions and impress a casual visitor with their confidence, know-how, and apparent *joie de vivre*. Dissatisfaction with oneself does not always cripple one's entire being, and few of these people were cripples in any obvious sense. But it is a doubtful basis on which to build a life.

Individuals

Who are these people of the New Age? After five weeks' acquaintance, I can hardly pretend to write about them like an Erik Erikson. It was not even possible to subject them to standard tests such as the T.A.T. But in the course of my interviews with each of them, and beyond this in my daily association with them all, I gained some knowledge of their past histories, the circumstances under which they entered the group, and their present states of mind. Many substantive details as well as all names have been freely changed in the sketches that follow, in order to protect their anonymity. The individuals are presented in the order of their length of stay with the group and include only those persons actually living on the ranch as of July, 1971. The present tense is used to refer to that date.[51]

EVA.   Hers is an old New England family living in the suburbs of Boston. The parents had no artistic interests. She went to an exclusive girls' school and then to a well-known college for girls, where she received a B.A. Painting was then her one serious pursuit. Soon after graduation, on an impulse, she decided to travel around the world. (Her family had always been globetrotters, so readily approved.) She met Ezra in India, which he happened to be visiting. Before this meeting she had been exposed neither to Gurdjieff nor to the theater. Indeed, she had never been philosophically or religiously inclined. Thus she went through a complete change, with no idea that her life would take this sudden turn. She went to see Ezra a second time in Vietnam, then married him. In New York, where they lived at first, she had her initial exposure to a somewhat bohemian style of life. A small group began to gather around them, even then. A year or two later they moved to New Mexico for the first time. She has been married to Ezra for six years. Though she no longer lives with him, she still submits to him on many levels. In part this may be a necessary survival technique. When he lashes out at her angrily in an open confrontation (of which there are many), she ducks under the wave by instantly confessing to a greater degree of error and inadequacy than he has accused her of. Meanwhile, she has become close to someone else. But this change has not in the least affected her total absorption in the movement. And, despite her drift away from Ezra, she retains a highly special status of authority within the group.

AL.   Though temporarily living away from the group in the early summer of 1971, he rejoined it later and must be mentioned. Al had been an electronics technician from upper New England. He had never gone to college but had become a Harvard Square bohemian before he encountered Ezra in 1963. He came west with Ezra and Eva when they first traveled to New Mexico in 1966. Though he separated from the group for a long period thereafter, it was with the understanding that he was actually pursuing their work in another environment. His return, just before the 1971 drama festival, gave the group another strong and utterly faithful presence.

CLOVIS.   Her father is a cost analyst for a university-connected research institute on the West Coast. Though he is completely rationalistic in outlook,

51. To learn which of these people remained in the group as of February, 1972, after several major tests of their loyalty, see pp. 402–404.

Clovis's mother was a spiritualist medium and clairvoyant. Thus the girl grew up steeped in the occultist scene, attending Spiritualist Sunday school. Yet the family life style was entirely respectable. Starting in her sophomore year of high school, she entered a period of profound disillusionment and inner despair. Whatever she took up she would rapidly lose interest in. Her family wanted her to go to Radcliffe, but she was in no state of mind to attend college at all and never did. On the other hand, she says she took hardly any drugs. After high school she moved to a bohemian neighborhood in San Francisco and began studying modern dance, working at it twelve to fourteen hours a day. She was already interested in theater. Now she also began to rediscover some of the mystic philosophers, including Gurdjieff, whom she had let lie fallow since childhood. In August, 1967, she found herself living next door to Ezra, who struck up a conversation with her. From the very beginning she knew "this was it." The group offered her a complete pattern of life far richer, she says, than any other she had known. "It was a total life-philosophy and vibration thing, right from the start." She denied that she had ever been the type to get into "groups" before then. Her family have mixed feelings about her involvement.

Clovis is an earthy, feminine girl with long black hair and deep-set eyes which like to establish contacts with people that undercut the formal level of relations. She and several other of the girls here seem to be personally attracted to Ezra. Yet her talk seldom strays from the literal duties, projects, and obligations of external life on the ranch. She is always anxious to follow instructions dutifully and minutely and to perform well in each small task.

LAURA.   Though the externals of her life parallel Clovis's, her personality is far different. She also grew up in a Western town; her father is a purchasing agent for a prominent business firm. Her brother once played the role of a kind of guru–philosopher figure in her life, though she says this had no direct connection with her later commitment to the group. Very early she developed a strong, positive interest in the dance; she majored in it at a state university (earning a B.F.A. degree), and then went to San Francisco to continue her study. There, late in 1967, she happened to hear of Ezra's circle and approached it thinking it was just another theater or dance group in which she might be interested.

Like Clovis, she took to it immediately and stayed in it. Yet she says she had not been unhappy or drifting before; nor had she read any philosophy to speak of. She recalls no "deep" interests outside the dance. She was already confident about her career as a dancer and believed she could have done perfectly well in it on her own. She was not "searching" for a group, to the best of her own knowledge. Yet she walked into this group one day and it "clicked." She went with it to New York. Then, however, she left it for nearly a year, thinking that she ought to get more perspective on it, since she had rushed into it so unhesitatingly. Also at that time she had certain doubts about the quality of effort inside it. But, when the group came back to New Mexico, early in 1969, she rejoined it. She says she is now committed without reservations. She has an infant daughter.

Laura is a sunny, happy person—self-confident and "well adjusted" in every way that is casually apparent. She is not at all heavy or openly troubled with anxieties. One feels that she would fit in well anywhere, an "ordinary" good-natured kid. She is warm, open, and friendly, extremely easy to be with. Yet she has the supreme talent of knowing how to blend in unobtrusively with those here who do have problems. Surprisingly, she is now paired with Champ, the most obviously authoritarian member of the group. There is a side to her which connects with dare-deviltry; this may explain why.

MONA.   She grew up in New York. Her father is an independent film producer in the suburbs and her mother, a piano teacher, was once a Communist. The family was Jewish but not very religious. She too became a dancer and choreographer, eventually in ballet. Though she enjoyed the dance, she felt that the life that usually goes with it is an empty one, lacking in meaning. She was living in San Francisco four years ago when she heard of Ezra through a friend and met his group. He was giving lectures on certain epochs in the history of philosophy, and this attracted her. She stayed with the group for two years but then left and returned to New York and lived on her own for nearly two years, working as a waitress and having a long love affair with a Greek. She suddenly returned to the group four months ago. Acting, as distinct from dancing, is still new to her.

She believes in the cosmic philosophy behind the group, but her personal style is not at all intellectual. Instead she radiates a throaty, self-contained sensuousness. She is also very alienated and "with-it" in her attitudes, deeply estranged from conventional society. She doesn't accept the idea of marriage or the nuclear family and feels she fits in well here, where they are not expected. In explaining her presence here she continually stressed the meaninglessness of life on the outside. There "everything is set up for you." You have to fit into a mold. She says she can't relate to these fixed structures. She returned to the group because she found this alternative empty and unbearable. A quiet, rather withdrawn person, she may well be subject to fits of depression. Yet she also has an inner strength. Because of her inarticulateness and shy reserve, I did not get to know her at all well.

HERB.   He is in his mid-twenties, like the others so far discussed. He is small, dark, and wiry; he remains silent most of the time, but has an underlying warmth that once in a while shows itself. He was raised in San Francisco in a Jewish family. His father has done many things and is apparently not too well off. Despite somewhat more artistic interests in his youth, he has recently become an investment counselor. Herb went to college for his freshman year in 1963 but then dropped out. Thereafter for several years he was deeply into the drug scene in the Fillmore and the Haight-Ashbury. He discovered the group when it was running the restaurant at the end of 1967.

Herb is probably the most obvious psychological "problem case" in the group. He freely confesses that he felt completely torn apart before he came into it. He remains strongly affected by a protracted, inwardly searing break with his own past. Even after all this time in the community he doesn't feel at the center of it; he retains an anxiety which makes him think he has to work harder and accomplish more all the time in order to measure up to general standards. Recently, however, he has begun to take a definite pride in his acting (in certain character roles he can be extremely good). He is paired with Melinda and the father of her new-born baby.

After having nearly been destroyed by intense inner turmoil, Herb has become a slavish, literal, unimaginative "follower"—on a level far more obvious than for most of the others. He undergoes great agonies trying to make a minor personal decision on a matter which hasn't been spelled out for him by superiors in advance. He likes to boast about the "intelligence" of the whole group, and is proud to be associated with it in these terms, yet he has none of the quickness displayed by quite a few of the others. He once confessed that when he tries to meditate he finds himself engulfed by a primitive terror. But, beneath his silent, busy, dutiful façade, he is also capable, in off-guard moments, of a deeply reverential outreach toward the qualities and atmospheres he respects, such as those of the nearby Indian tribes.

JACOB. In his late twenties, he is a very strong, intelligent, able, thoughtful person. He conveys this strength while not being at all casually outgoing. But, when he chooses to open up, he is both warm and articulate. Altogether, he is perhaps the most impressive rank-and-file member of the group.

His background is Jewish from New York, and not well off; his father was a cab driver. Still, all his friends went to college. He chose to go to Israel instead and spent a year in a kibbutz. Returning to New York, undecided between college, Israel, or what, he found himself drifting in a new direction—toward mind-expanding drugs. This was back in 1961, long before they had become widely fashionable. He spent the next six years in that scene, though he also studied sculpture and a bit of theater, briefly tried homesteading in Alaska, and lived with a girl for a long period. He was in San Francisco in October, 1967, and had just decided to get a "straight" job and think out what he really wanted to do, when Ezra's restaurant opened around the corner from where he was then living. His conversion was instantaneous, as he recalled it. He has never left the group since, nor would he admit to any doubts about it.

The group, he says, helps him to feel that he's continually moving toward a better understanding of cosmic purpose and of his own reason for being. Inside it, he retains a constant sense of self-exploration, but he does so quietly, rather contemplatively, without any reliance on jargon. He had earlier reached a complete feeling of dead end in the drug scene (heightened by his involvement in a bust); now he feels he is renewed, freed from the sense of pointless circularity. What emerges from his entire narrative, however, is the basic steadiness, the inner balance which he retained throughout his adventures. (Thus he never went into "hard" drugs, despite the length of time he spent in that milieu.) His life has represented a series of positive moves, of which he has always remained the master. Yet no one seems more loyally committed to the present group. A thoroughly attractive, even somewhat inspiring person.

GENE. He is another highly respected member of the group, with an informal status probably only below that of Ezra and Eva. His background, unlike that of most of the others, was entirely in science. He grew up in a university town, where his father was an engineer. He attended the local university, planning to work for a Ph.D. in mathematics or physics. After one year of graduate study, however, he dropped out and went to work for a while as a computer programmer. He recalls having gone through a distinct period of internal dissatisfaction and drift at this point, lasting about a year. He felt far too isolated from other people, unable to take part in normal social relationships. This feeling intensified after his marriage soon collapsed. Though major scenes of political confrontation occurred on his campus, he moved through them uninvolved, absorbed instead in his private intellectual world, yet increasingly haunted by the notion that there must be something more to life than he was experiencing. He had read almost no philosophy; it was the purely personal sense of crisis, in his recollection, that was catalytic in bringing about a change.

His sister suggested that he seek out a local Gurdjieff group, which it cost him $200 a month to attend. He took to Gurdjieff's ideas—the contention that man was normally asleep seemed especially relevant to him—but did not care for the particular group. At this point someone where he worked told him about Ezra. After he met Ezra's entourage, again the ideas first drew him in more than the people. He joined the community in San Francisco in May, 1968, and stayed with it thereafter, quickly assuming his position of informal leadership and responsibility. Now he plays leading roles in the group's dramatic productions, although he had hardly ever so much as gone to see a play before he met them. He says that he sees no conflict between his scientific knowledge and the group's inner cosmology.

He remains very much the cool, detached rationalist, courteous and reasonably outgoing, but always somewhat distant. Others admire him for his boundless work capacity and his unmatched know-how about tools and machines. He states that one part of his mind wants constantly to be doing things while another part wonders whether they are worth the bother. But the visible picture he presents is one of tireless, extraordinarily competent dedication. He is methodical rather than dynamic, yet with a playful humor about his intellectual calculations which dilutes the heaviness of his bearing. Though not unpleasantly pushy, he is a severe judge of other persons' efforts. Above all he is steady, calm, even-tempered, an extremely strong human being whose sense of inner crisis was of a very special kind. He is now paired with Eva.

JACKEEN.   She met the group when she was only sixteen, working for a large bookstore in Manhattan. She had spent an unhappy childhood, in Queens, Brooklyn, and other nearby locations. Her father is a lithographer and union organizer, her mother a policewoman. Both are Irish Catholics, and they had separated from each other. The girl had a strong wish to escape from home and from high school—to college or anywhere else. She had always wanted to be an actress, going to theater classes in the summer while her friends were at the beach. She transformed herself into a precocious intellectual, studied the theater of cruelty, surrounded herself with a wall of avant-garde paperbacks. She also blew her mind with LSD for a while and had lengthy periods of depression, during which she would withdraw behind closed blinds and think about suicide. But she acted in a Brooklyn company that has since gone on to become famous.

Having coffee one day across the street from her bookstore, she ran into Ezra. Initially his group interested her solely because of its theater; she tried out for one of its early performances. She had never heard of Gurdjieff or Ouspensky till she met the group, and she was not consciously looking for something to join at the time. But the group attracted her with its atmosphere of "really working," instead of just sitting around and talking; also, she said, she was lured by a "certain quality" she sensed in the people. She began to grow more interested in its ideas too, coming to Ezra's Thursday-night lectures. Meanwhile, she finished high school and started taking night classes at the New School. For a certain period she almost lost touch with Ezra's group; she had a strong urge to travel to Peru. In the end, she felt she should stay with her father until she was eighteen, which she did. For a while she lived with Mona in an apartment; later she met Laura while she was in New York on her own. She and Laura finally decided to fly out to New Mexico to join the group on September 15, 1969, and did so.

She has returned twice to New York for visits since, but is sure that this group is now her life. She had to change her acting style drastically, but has come to believe that theater outside this group is exploitative and meaningless, lacking any conception of the whole human being. Perhaps explaining her attachment to Ezra, she said she had a great weakness for "intellectual types." At first she regretted not having gone to college, but she no longer cares.

Although she is outgoing on a certain level, she is not easy really to get to know. The group (and Ezra) have clearly given her a new kind of strength. She seems to have walked safely past the abyss, though in the process something that was valuable in her may have been subdued.

MELINDA. Twenty years old, plump, with long golden hair, always barefoot in ankle-length dresses; the most hippie-looking girl on the ranch. She is from an old Philadelphia family, her grandfather a Ph.D., her mother an expert in ancient languages. Her stepfather (whom she is not close to) was once involved in theater, though he is now in business. Four years ago, they all moved to Texas. Melinda went to a fancy boarding school in Vermont and was all set to go to Bard College and be an English teacher when she encountered Ezra's group during its brief stay in Houston early in 1969. Until that time she had been extremely academic in her orientation, though the Romantics —she mentioned William Blake and Ralph Waldo Emerson—had appealed to her most strongly. She had definitely not been interested in psychology or self-development, though she had liked drama to a point. Nor had she been interested in groups. Hippie communes repelled her by their lack of discipline, their feeling of aimlessness and waste.

She came to New Mexico for two weeks to try to figure the group out, and then simply stayed. For her it also seemed to click immediately. At first, in Houston, she had had reservations about the low quality of their theater, but these vanished in New Mexico, when it seemed greatly to improve. To her, life on the ranch means freedom, yet also total system, and theater has come to seem the least important part of it. It means much to her to be doing something immediate about ecology rather than merely talking it. She consciously wishes to spend her life helping to found a new civilization. The disciplined, work-oriented quality of this life appeals to her strongly, as does the stability of the group in contrast to the transient atmosphere in most communes. In comparison, she feels that college simply wouldn't have offered her a real test, that she would have sailed through it easily, without learning much that was important from it.

Thus she presents the picture of a satiated young girl from a highly advantaged background for whom the more conventional challenges had no appeal. In many ways she reveals that she is highly pleased with herself; whether this masks uncertainties that she omits from her accounting I cannot tell. Her choice of the undemanding Herb as a partner may be revealing from this point of view. She has a deliberate, considered manner of speaking which suggests a tinge of egotistical (and self-protective) false front. At times, despite her free use of four-letter words, one thinks she is still being the overly sweet and self-conscious hostess of a child's tea party. One is always so aware that *she* chooses when to speak.

CHAMP. He stands out easily from the others, a living expression of Texas-style masculinity, handsome, tough, belligerent, and aloof, utterly aware of his power over other people and relishing every moment of it down to each bodily and vocal gesture. A dare-devil show-off (shouting at other drivers as he cuts sharply in front of them), loving to dominate, blowing up frequently, he can get away with putting others down harshly. He is authoritarian through and through; even his occasional warm smile is merely another extension of his desire to captivate and hold attention, to be looked at. It is small wonder that he is disliked by some of the other men.

At the same time, he takes the inner ideology of the group with great seriousness. In answer to my question during the interview, which he insisted on holding in public, he said that he had joined the group in order "to explore all the potentialities of living in a dramatic universe, to consciously participate in the creation of the new planetary civilization." It was an official speech, culled from the phrases of J. G. Bennett.

He is the son of a psychiatrist from a medium-sized Texas city, with two sisters. He flunked out of three colleges, including the state university. He says that his family are glad that he is living in this community (could it be that he was always a problem to them?). He has lived all over the country, including Berkeley. His years of wandering he prefers to keep in obscurity, though he had some extreme adventures and was in jail at least once. He was in Houston when Ezra's group came there early in 1969. He had become "a rock song writer and recording artist" (these, again, are his own carefully chosen words). He was living in a loft at a rock concert hall when the group arrived nearby and he was told something about them. Then and there, before meeting them, he remembers saying, "I'll probably join them," even though he had not been looking for a group. Yet he had been reading Gurdjieff on his own for some time previously. Why? "Because somebody showed me a book of his with his picture on the cover. The picture drew me in." Clovis offered him a part in their local production. He refused at first but finally agreed. Two or three days later he decided to join the group. He says that theater is still the aspect of the life that pulls him the most strongly.

Like most bullies, Champ is thin-skinned under the surface. He will openly weep at the dinner table, recalling moments and longings in his life which he would prefer at other times to forget. Yet he usually retains great control. His degree of self-intoxication and his consciously held belief that abrasive put-downs are the only meaningful form of contact with other human beings make him the most controversial person in the entire community.

STAN. He is from a middle-class Jewish family in what he calls "split-level Queens." His parents came from Poland; in the McCarthy period they were threatened with deportation because his father was a Communist, his mother a socialist. In Stan's eyes, his parents nonetheless compromised their idealism by their growing acceptance of material comfort and conventional standards of success. All the children in their circle were headed for the professions. Stan went to an Ivy League college on a scholarship. After a year he became very dissatisfied, but stuck it out, majored in philosophy, and received a B.A. (*cum laude*) in 1968. He is now very down on academic education, though he also thinks he's moved beyond his initial state of blind rebellion against it. His interests developed in the direction of mysticism, Buddhism, and consciousness expansion. After college, returning to New York, he was a social worker, a copy editor for *Time-Life,* then a cab driver, and finally an unemployed cab driver—thus ever circling downward. He read Ouspensky, but his main trip was into LSD. After several months of frequent drug experiences, he began moving away from them, and his last occasion with LSD seemed to mark a dead end for him in that direction. He also tried other techniques, such as fasting—"everything down to holding my breath." He joined encounter groups, which gave him some preparation for life here.

Unlike many of the others, he says he was consciously looking for a group just like this one, and had even made a definite decision to seek one out a week before he heard of it. He learned of its existence when he phoned the bookstore in Manhattan where Jackeen worked, and she answered the call. His inquiry about a book by Ouspensky sparked her interest, and she mentioned that she was about to leave for New Mexico. So he also came out, in October, 1969, and has never departed since. He had no previous interest in theater, and merely put up with it when he first arrived. Even now, what especially attracts him is the challenge of woodworking, though like everyone else he stresses the totality of the life pattern.

An intense, heavy idealism characterizes Stan, a deep scorn for everything that is sham or soft or fancy. He is usually taciturn and can play the role of the gruff authoritarian, speaking out only to scold the failings of others or to make sure they have mastered the minute points of the daily routine. Yet when he opens up he is surprisingly articulate, on top of things in a broad way, and thoughtful. Though much hardened, he remains contemplative. There is not much obvious kindness or warmth in him, though it can appear rarely; it is as if these qualities had been burned out by so much intense, lonely seeking. He told me he had "tried sex" as a means of consciousness expansion too, as if it were something one uses entirely as a tool for internal growth. (Yet he is presently paired with Gypsy.) There is a strongly ascetic temper in him; he scorns the comforts and pleasures his parents seem to symbolize. (His mother regards his life as idiotic, seeing the movement as a utopian socialist colony like those of the 1840's, and declaring it will never work.) Stan is clearly a perfectionist. Thus he says he alternates between thinking this is a highly efficient, well-organized group of extremely talented people and thinking it is instead composed of people who *never* do a job right or finish anything they start. He is deeply intolerant of frailties in himself and in others.

Stan exemplifies the typical dropout pattern that has been identified by Kenneth Keniston. He seeks to live through his parents' ideals, while blaming them for having fallen short, for selling out. Though his commitment is strong, he has a refreshing ability still to look at life from a larger "outside" standpoint. But he usually masks this in silence and hard labor.

NORA. In her early twenties, she is an earnest, plain girl who takes no pride in her personal appearance. Her family came to America on the *Mayflower;* she is descended from a well-known hero of the Revolution. She was raised in a college town in western Massachusetts, where her father owns a chain of stores and plays the stock market. The oldest of four children, she fell into the role of a "brainy" girl and teacher's pet, which put her in conflict with her unintellectual sisters; however, she does not recall her childhood as a time of extreme isolation. She then had two distinct circles of friends, one social and one intellectual; it was the dividedness of this situation which disturbed her. She now regards the New England tradition as something she must purge from herself in order to achieve her own identity. A trip she took to Europe the summer before college opened her eyes; after it, she was unable to tolerate the social scene which surrounded her. Then, a year later, her mother died, forcing her to confront family relationships more closely. Deciding to strike out on her own a bit, she chose not to attend a small college but rather a large Ivy League university in a city some distance from home, where she looked forward to a greater degree of intellectual and social variety. But the actual scene at this university sharply disappointed her. It turned out to be socially stifling and was rigidly divided along ethnic lines. Though the catalog was indeed jammed with courses, most of them turned out to be hollow; only very rarely was a teacher stimulating. Deeply alienated but still holding to intellectual values, she changed her major several times, eventually creating an individual one in western and Oriental psychology. At the university, she found the same dividedness that had marked her childhood; the students she knew were intellectual on weekdays, meaninglessly drunk or stoned on weekends. Oriental philosophy began attracting her more strongly; she considered transferring to another university which offered better instruction in it. She also became interested in Gurdjieff's ideas. She went to a few lectures given by the orthodox Gurdjieff group in that city, but found the people staid and upper-middle-class and the presentation of ideas too formalistic. She began definitely looking for a group to join; for a while she considered joining an artist colony in Seattle. Yet she also confesses, somewhat incongruously, to a strong bent toward economics, mathematics, and even the natural sciences; had she stayed in the establishment world, she feels she might well have gone into money management, a talent she doubtless picked up from her father.

At the university she had gotten to know Isaac Hull (below) and learned of Ezra's group through him. Though she lacked only one year of finishing her B.A., in the summer of 1969 she decided, after writing a preliminary letter, to fly out to New Mexico. Nora thinks that the ranch offers a far richer environment than any she's experienced before, that there is more chance for personal growth here. "You can get a *real* education here. I could never be a potter out there, for instance." Initially, she admits, she had to get used to certain things about the community—the diversity of backgrounds, the unsparing personal confrontations and combats. But "freedom" is the word she now uses to describe this environment, and she means it in a collectivized, not an individual sense (such as Melinda, for instance, would still retain). The totality of the life style engages her; she has, for instance, no special interest in theater, and had no contact with it before her arrival.

Nora is a level-headed girl, often silent and seemingly in the background. She is still very much the intellectual, quietly going her own way. She remains on an even keel (despite a few hints of hysterical tendencies buried underneath) and with a broader sense of perspective than most group members retain; thus she was almost the only one to show real curiosity (and comprehension) about the nature and total scope of my book. I believe that she is somewhat disliked by some of the others for her seeming air of superiority. She is paired with David (below) who also attended the same university but whom she only met out here.

ISAAC HULL (this is his choice of pseudonym; my own instinct would have been for a name like TERENCE). Isaac combines great strengths and weaknesses more intricately than anyone else here. On the surface he strikes one as a highly intelligent, verbally imaginative "good guy," dedicatedly placing his resources at the disposal of the common aim, like the leader of an Explorer Scout troupe or the star pupil in a college literature class. He is in his mid-twenties, sturdy-looking, with a round, well-bred face.

The son of a cultivated English mother and a New England father who became a middle-level government bureaucrat and later a businessman, Isaac grew up deeply subservient to the service- and culture-oriented idealism (and the class traditionalism) of the Anglo-American aristocracy. Like Nora, he now perceives these attachments as an enemy to be constantly fought within himself. The family seems to have been a remarkably close one, though his older brother has now grown distant. He has never really rebelled from it even to the extent of becoming visibly hip. On the ranch, no matter how dirty he gets, he always looks somehow as if he were at a private Eastern summer camp.

At the same large Ivy League university which Nora attended, he majored in English. Like Nora he became disillusioned, dropping out for three semesters. He heard of Ezra's group initially when it was in New York, and sporadically attended the lectures Ezra was giving. He says that he was not strongly affected by the contact at the time. Nora, who preceded him to the ranch, wrote of it in terms which again drew him toward it. Deciding first to finish his degree, for which he lacked only a semester, he flew out on January 1, 1970, and has remained ever since.

Why is he here? Like Champ, Isaac replied with a deliberately composed statement. He would like, he said, to become "a sailing master," that is, some-one who works with nature, man, and technology all at once and is equally skilled in each realm. The choice of a nautical image was deliberate, for he is strongly attracted to the sea, and looks ahead eagerly to the day when the group will build a boat which is to become a floating "center" to promote the plane-tary work. Again he said his aim was "to dance with life." Certain exceptional people have done this; he identifies with them. His ambition runs very strong; already he openly talks about the time when he will lead a group of his own. The cosmic purpose of these groups is highly meaningful to him; he has read Gurdjieff, Ouspensky, Maurice Nicoll, and J. G. Bennett with great diligence. Thus universal goals merge with the personal ones of attaining skill and grace, the qualities of a leader. He freely compares his conversion to the aims of the group with that undergone by the disciples of Jesus.

Though he takes himself this seriously, he also declares that he doesn't like too much "heaviness." And in fact he often enjoys playing the deliberate role of the clown. His mind is quick with hilarious imitations, staccato verbal byplay, the use of tongue and voice to mimic someone or sum up something in a single sound. In these moods, he conveys an enormous zest for the variety of life. The hearty raconteur, the savorer of such sights as that of a well-preserved 1933 Austin in the neighborhood, modify and humanize the overgrown Boy Scout. Still, even in these lighter moments, there is a touch of something like pompousness or overcultivated preciseness in him. He has an overwhelming need to display elocution-school enunciation and an equally careful choice of words.

All these sides of him recede during scenes of self-chastisement, sometimes provoked by dinner-table "confrontations" where Ezra is often the aggressor. Then he appears suddenly tormented—by his own past, by the unwanted parts of himself, by the awareness of failure in certain tasks he has been assigned.

I ended up thinking of him as a strong person. Only in intellectual terms has he surrendered to the group's ideology; thus he preserves all the resources inherited from his upbringing, even while consciously trying to disavow them. Underneath, he is an old-fashioned patriot adventurer. The image of the war-rior appeals to him positively as something to emulate—so removed is he from anything verging on left-wing humanism. He grew up being stirred by boys' books about naval heroes in the Revolutionary War and about Civil War bat-tles; now he would add the figure of the Hopi tribal warrior to the list. One of his favorite movies is the Disney production of *20,000 Leagues Under the Sea*. Born a generation or two earlier, he would have been as gung-ho as either of the two Roosevelts. All these instincts have merely been transferred to the task of building a new civilization. Establishment America has lost one of its most ready-prepared sons. I suspect, incidentally, that he is the only one on the ranch who usually sleeps alone.

GYPSY. A woman of thirty-six who looks much younger; casual, hearty, sensuous, direct. The daughter of a nuclear physicist, she went for one year to an obscure college in Pennsylvania. Having to get married, she left and moved to California. For several years she and her husband managed a cattle ranch in a remote part of Big Sur. Finally she couldn't stand the isolation any more and left. Later she came to New Mexico and lived with a man who was heavily into Zen. But she wasn't at all metaphysically inclined, and her indifference toward it contributed to their breakup. Along the way she has had four or five children; two of the smallest are with her at the ranch.

She first heard of the group during its earliest days in New Mexico. She began reading Gurdjieff and Ouspensky just to try to figure them out and was pulled into the philosophy, despite all her earlier resistance to Zen. At the same time, she was attracted to the group by its rejection of the nuclear family pattern; her own experiences had made her feel that she was not cut out for the standard life it implied. She had not been looking deliberately for a group to join, though she was very wise in the hip scene. She had no previous interest in theater. According to her own admission, she had felt rather at the end of things before coming here, but remained too fond of life ever to think seriously about suicide. She joined the group at the beginning of 1970 and remained continuously with it thereafter. She confesses that she isn't at all sure the community will last forever, but, then, she asks, what will? At the very least, it seems a comfortable landing place. She couldn't relate to real hippie communes, she says, because they have no respect for privacy, such as she claims she finds here. She is paired physically with Stan, though she is keenly aware that he is much younger.

She is a reasonably strong person, a hard worker. One of the best things about the group's plays are the costumes, which are entirely the product of her imagination. What is really striking is her attitude toward her children, which many conventionally-minded persons would wrongly interpret as complete indifference. Reacting strongly against her own mother, she believes that any parental influence on children is harmful, that they must grow up in total freedom. She practices this philosophy to a degree which would have puzzled and disturbed Alexis and Elizabeth Ferm. Though they are mere toddlers, her little boy and girl are left to fend for themselves hour after hour while the mother absorbs herself in the never-ending routine of projects.[52] Yet, for at least a few moments a day, she will play with them affectionately. A memorable scene of this kind, entirely in character, was that of Gypsy running toward

---

52. As we saw earlier, this is generally true on the ranch, but only Gypsy practices it as a deliberate matter of principle.

them outdoors near the woodshop, calling to one of them with real love in her voice, "Hey, little squirt! Let me bite your ass!"

MALCOLM. A slender boy of about twenty, whose hearty, deliberate manner compensates for a certain frailness. His father is a physicist in a nearby state, and his mother is a freelance writer; other members of the family have been connected with theater in the past. He went to a local prep school, where he began to develop such an extreme reaction against being pushed academically that it still pains him even to read a book. He tried being a student at two campuses of the University of California; at one, he lasted six weeks, at the other, two weeks. Then he tried the drug scene, but found it similarly meaningless and unsatisfying. An ordinary urban life on his own, which he pursued for a time while doing construction labor, proved equally futile. More and more he came simply to feel that "there's no place for me out there," either in the culture or the counter-culture.

He heard of Ezra's group, oddly enough, through his mother, who had written a feature article on it for a local "liberal" magazine. The dramatic productions, several of which he saw, sparked his interest. He came here to live in May, 1970. He likes to ponder the matter of commitment far more openly than do most of the others; it is clear that he has often considered leaving, and that the "official" cosmology has a relatively loose hold on him. But, in personal terms, this has become a final refuge, the only place with which he can presently connect. The ideas of service, of detached self-observation, and of "making a mark on history" all appeal to him positively. But he is still desperately searching for personal clues.

And yet, if he is unsure about his relationship to the group, it may be, oddly enough, because he craves an even more rigorous personal testing than it can satisfy. Burning within him is a desire to submit his mind and body to an unending discipline, to subdue both of them, as if he must constantly prove to himself their utter subjugation to his will. This goes far beyond the long hours of labor that are normally expected, and which he regularly extends. One hot afternoon I saw him running at top speed down the dirt road, several miles from the ranch; afterward he explained that it was a "self-imposed task." He is deliberately trying to turn himself into a tool, a sharpened instrument—perhaps to fulfill the cosmic purposes of the group, perhaps to answer an undefinable impulse within his own being. Openly he fears that this self-chastisement may grow so extreme as to cause his literal, physical destruction. Meanwhile, on another level, he continues to indulge in pleasant, thoughtful conversation marked by an engaging modesty and a down-to-earth irony of tone.

JOHN and JERI. They are the only married couple on the ranch, aside from Ezra and Eva.[53] In a curious but very noticeable way, their personalities (especially hers) fail to mesh with the surroundings. Their living quarters are a kind of middle-class enclave; her dresses would be appropriate for a young

---

53. Several marriages have broken up when one partner insisted on staying in the group and the other felt compelled to leave it.

faculty wife; while her solicitous, conventional style of child rearing stands at a polar extreme from Gypsy's. Desperately this family tries to fit in; one wonders why.

John grew up in a small Midwestern city, the son of a salesman, while she is the daughter of a realtor in a similar town in Wyoming. They met in California (after an earlier childhood acquaintance); he was then doing graduate work in architecture and city planning. She had graduated from a private college in Colorado (majoring in French), he from a Southwestern state university, though he had also spent two years at Haverford. He is in his late thirties and about ten years older than she. While at Taliessen with Frank Lloyd Wright in the 1950's, he had read Gurdjieff. In 1963 he took peyote and feels this experience basically changed his life; before this he had been an agnostic. For six years, he says, he stayed high, meanwhile worrying increasingly about the H-bomb and finally letting his hair grow long. (It is now short again, though he wears a well-trimmed beard.) At the same time, he explains much of his life as a quest for self-toughening; an only child, he thinks he never had to face real hostility. He seemed to maintain a good relation with his mother; she visited the ranch later in the summer, plunged wholeheartedly into the routines, and identified herself with the community in an exaggeratedly defensive manner.

In New Mexico, where John successfully found a good job in pleasant surroundings, he began going to the Thursday-night lectures Ezra was giving during the group's earliest days of existence. When the group bought the ranch and returned to the state early in 1969, he again came to the meetings. Meanwhile he had left his orthodox job and tried to organize an idealistic business venture which somehow would combine the aims of log cutting and "consciousness expansion." In it he lost large sums of money. The couple moved to the ranch in September, 1970.

He approaches the group very much in the spirit that "this will be good for me," rather than because it is what he likes. He openly says that it is very difficult to live on the ranch, though he emphasizes its increasing rewards. He confesses that he has hardly any "friends" among the others, and that it is hard to take the constant isolation, mutual watchfulness, and severe criticism and confrontation; all his instincts, and Jeri's, are for a much warmer, more trusting environment. "None of us would probably choose to live with each other," he remarks. His recent trip overseas, with three others to buy land for the group, gave him a new sense of relatedness. Still, it is remarkable how apparently unaware he remains of the degree to which his conscious commitment fights against his whole earlier temperament.

As for her, when asked why she was here, her immediate reaction was to blurt out: "I get so depressed." (With life here, did she really mean?) Then she gave what sounded like too carefully composed an answer: "I don't think I could ever operate out there in the old civilization, with my false personality [the phrase taken from Gurdjieff] and all." How does one square these words with her enormous, unconcealed pleasure at attending the tenth reunion of her high school class in Wyoming, to which she flew even though they could scarcely afford it? And with her open announcement that her main regret, while visiting with her classmates, was that she had been too aloof from them, had not established enough close relationships, in those days? The conclusion seems obvious: she is desperately *trying* to feel alienated in order to please her husband and the rest of the group, while, left to her own devices, she would instantly be the pillar of conventional society in her village. She is making a very brave sacrifice.

DAVID. One day in the summer of 1970 a quiet, methodical, cautious boy of twenty-three was wandering through a nearby town in New Mexico, saw the posters advertising the drama productions on the ranch, became curious, drove out to it, and has never left except for a brief trip home at Christmas. Had he not made this discovery, his own impression of his alternative future is to have gone into a fancy business of some "creative" kind and to have married an "arty" wife.

Still, one wonders if this could really have been in store for him. He was raised in Kansas City, in a well-to-do business family which was rather liberal and cosmopolitan (for instance, interested in psychoanalysis and encounter groups). The father was in investment management. They traveled a great deal. During his childhood, David was strongly absorbed in his own interests. Though somewhat lonely, he had a small circle of friends who were interested in such topics as philosophy, and he says he was quite capable of playing the standard social game as well. Until his junior year in college his main interest was in the natural sciences. The university he attended was the same large Eastern one which Isaac and Nora had also passed through, though he did not know them. Like them, he was deeply disappointed by it, eventually staying in it only because of one unusual professor who let him do anything he wanted.

Around his junior year he went through a distinct change. He felt that he was observing the collapse of American society. He participated in a sit-in over housing conditions in a nearby black ghetto, becoming keenly aware of its hopelessness. He went to Aspen, Colorado, for a summer and formed the idea of leading a group of people who would retreat into the mountains to pursue a regime of photography study mixed with self-development. Back at the university he switched to an individually defined major in communications, including photography, art, and linguistics. As a senior he began living in a large urban commune near the campus, spending most of his time in it, observing the group and himself while also taking drugs. Then he went to the Boston area for a few months to study photography under a man who had a small group living around him in an old house. At that time he first became acquainted with Gurdjieff's ideas and also with Zen. But, after a short while there, he felt he had reached another dead end, that there was no further challenge for him in photography. Perhaps with some egotism, he believed he was already as good as his teacher. For a while he taught his own class in nonverbal communication through photography; the group would go off to the mountains for two days without speaking, communicating only through their Polaroid pictures. David also paid a visit to a Gurdjieff commune in New York State; he says he was well liked and had permission to return whenever he wished. Three units short of a master's degree in communications, he returned home at the beginning of the summer of 1970, decided to sell all his possessions and travel west again to see more of the region. (In his mind lingered the idea of settling in the Gurdjieff commune afterward.) It was on this trip that he made his present connection. What especially attracted him to Ezra's group was the fact that it conceived of itself as undertaking a work for the ages, the building of a whole new civilization.

Despite his intelligent articulateness and varied experiences, there is a deadened quality to David's mind, a slavishness of which he is entirely unaware. His own opinion of himself is extremely high. To an unusual degree even in this circle, he holds himself apart, moving silently across the landscape with the aloof bearing of someone who believes he is rather profound. Yet he is really the kind of person who plods dutifully along the expected paths. More than Nora, for instance (with whom he is physically paired here), he is completely caught up in the ideology of the group, incapable of exercising any independent imagination on a topic where the line has been laid down. His movements, bodily and verbal, are noticeably slow, geared to doing each thing step by step. There is no ebullience, no emotional lightning, in his makeup. His acting is crippled by lack of inner feeling for the parts he is playing. It is rather odd that in this group, which so much emphasizes self-critical awareness, David's pride has apparently never been challenged.

FRIEDA. A hearty, deep-voiced, masculine woman of thirty-three, who wears her blue work shirts with a bare midriff above her Levi's. She says she had no feeling of family while she was growing up, and has found this for the first time on the ranch. Her parents were "groovy," but just young kids themselves, moving all over while her father worked at a series of low-grade engineering jobs. Though they were not at all religious, she remembers being very upset (so angry, in fact, that she would physically smash things) because of a feeling that religion was not true and that there was no point to life on this planet. Deeply skeptical, she kept hungering for something she could really believe in. She went to a junior college in California for two years, intending to become a nurse. Then she became a dancer, a chorus girl in night spots; she also had a little experience in theater. This period of her life contained many extreme adventures which she prefers to pass over. She was married twice, each time very briefly. For a long while she had been studying the occult; her reading of Gurdjieff, Ouspensky, and Nicoll dates from five years before she entered the group. She is the only member of the group with a keen enthusiasm for diet and health foods.

Feelings of meaninglessness kept periodically assailing her. Her pattern was to find a new interest, throw herself into it with intense energy and enthusiasm, then after a while get bored with it and enter a new phase of depression. Thus in show business she began with the aim of earning a lot of money fast in order to do whatever she wanted. But, when she succeeded, she realized that she couldn't really think of any important way of spending it. Again, she would try drugs but gain no real satisfaction from them. Once she went to Yucatan (in company with Georgia, below), to take up farming there, for she has a keen interest in the land and in the outdoors. Deliberately she gave away all her possessions, even selling her car when she arrived, in order to prove to herself that she could get along on nothing. Soon she had everything she needed for her new life, given her by the Indians—land, mules, a dwelling. Still, after a year of this adventure she got bored once more. She and four other women (Georgia and Harriet among them) went to Montana and again farmed together, aiming at total self-sufficiency. No men were in this group, as she tells it, because they simply couldn't find any who were strong enough to do the things they wanted to do! Later she and Georgia went to Canada briefly and tried homesteading there. She had impulses just to walk off alone into the wilderness. Before this, at other times, she had thought of suicide. Meanwhile Harriet had discovered Ezra's group, and so they came down here and entered it in October, 1970. She believes her "flight pattern" is now over, though partly because the group itself is so frequently on the move. Further adventures overseas, as promised by the group, answer her desperate inner need for rapid change.

"Totally committed!" These are her words about her response to the community. She says that when she arrived last October her knees buckled and she cried, so powerful was the immediate feeling of connection. For the first time in her life, she has lost her great pang of loneliness. She has a boy friend now, too, a long-time member of the group. She emphasizes her continuing need to feel entirely independent of the outside system, which she equates with "death." In her, the drive for economic self-sustenance connects with some deep psychological root. At the same time, Ezra has become her missing father. She says that when he bears down on her in his critical moods, she feels good inside— the result is an instant release of energy. Outwardly she is a warm, appealing, though very intense person.

GEORGIA. She is in her mid-thirties, very masculine, low-voiced, and hearty. She openly admits to being gay. Her father was a welder and custodian in a West Coast suburb. She went to business college, thereafter working as a secretary for many years. She had no previous involvement with theater. Her interest in Gurdjieff dates back five years, though her conversation is never at all heavily philosophical. Instead, her visible enthusiasm is for the land and all the tasks connected with a loving and self-sufficient relationship to it. Indeed, she says she can't stand the very idea of being indoors. One day she walked out of her office and gave way to her homesteader impulses, in company with Frieda and some others. Though she doesn't expand much on the subject, her commitment to this group appears rather deep.

She is probably the pleasantest, most cheerful person in the community. Her easy sense of humor melts whatever it touches, spreading relaxation and naturalness. She is extraordinarily easy to be with. She gives every sign of being completely at peace with herself.

At this point, or somewhere near it, a definite break occurs. Those who have thus far been described form what is often called by Ezra the "core group" of the community, those who have spent enough time in it to prove themselves and to be approved. They have passed through a kind of apprenticeship, which normally lasts for about a year. At its conclusion they agreed to be bound by five "inner rules" of conduct, which (with one exception) have not been revealed to me. They have also been accepted as partners in the external business venture. The remaining individuals, more recently arrived, are still in the initial period of trial.

LENNIE.   He is the most typically hip person on the ranch, with long hair and beard and a soft Southern drawl. He is extremely warm, outgoing, helpful, with a reassuring combination of idealism and practical strength. He grew up in a large Texas city, where his father is a self-made businessman. At one point the father actually threatened to have Lennie committed as insane for his radical ideas. Lennie had been a great disappointment to his family, dropping out of school after the tenth grade and traveling all over the world on his own, going heavily into drugs (except heroin), in short, daring to be a super-hippie. For self-support he eventually became a journeyman machinist. He remains close to a younger brother, for whom he is a kind of hero figure.

Following a marriage that lasted two years, he decided to come to New Mexico to look the whole scene over, in search of "a place" he could identify with. He felt at a dead end and rather desperate. Through Melinda's sister in Houston he learned of Ezra's community. He arrived around June, 1970, and says he felt connected with it after three or four days.

Unlike most of the others, he remained indecisive about his new attachment and began a series of comings and goings. He first remained only a month and a half, then fled back to his old life in Texas, believing he could not measure up to the self-imposed work load and constant sense of responsibility. But the community remained in his mind, and in December he returned again for nine days. This time his reasons for leaving were the cold weather and his concern for his dog, to whom he was enormously devoted and who was crippled and needed care. But now he continued to pay his monthly rent even though absent, as a sign of his commitment to return. After another five months he did come back, and spoke to me during our interview as if he had made a permanent decision. He said that the idea of cosmic evolution, of being part of the future, appealed to him strongly, although he had done no previous reading in the group's philosophical sources and had no prior interest in theater. However, in late July, 1971, he deserted the group once again. There was a clash between his open, spontaneous, extremely hip personality and the far more austere tone of life on this ranch. I suspect that every time he left he did so blaming himself for his "inadequacies."

HARRIET.   A very plain, quiet woman in her mid-thirties, raised in the Midwest, though she lived for several years in Los Angeles, where she worked as a laboratory technician. Her personal problem, which she freely describes, is an inability to feel herself connected with anything or anybody she's with, a sense of removal from life (and therefore of loneliness) which has drawn her to groups to see if they offer a way out. She discovered Ezra's in the summer of 1970 when she came to see one of their plays. She began coming to the Thursday-night lectures, then started working here four hours a day after her regular job. She joined the community full time in April, 1971, and (when talked to in June) still regarded herself as in a three-month trial period, after which she was not at all sure that she would stay.

Though the group has somewhat assuaged her sense of loneliness, it has also denied her the privacy she is used to having. She has begun to dream of having her own property again, and of being connected with a group merely as a part-time supplement. The idea of self-development attracts her but makes her fearful, because when she looks deeply into herself she doesn't like what she sees—confusion and lonely inability to relate to others. She is simple and honest to the point of homeliness. Clearly the inner ideology of the community means nothing to her, and theater is basically beyond her capacity.

MARK and MIRIAM.   Though not married, they lived together for years in New York City. He formerly ran an employment service for engineers, earning a very comfortable income; they are in their thirties. She had met Ezra in New York years ago, and in April, 1971, they came out to join the community. At the end of June they left abruptly, apparently because, when they were asked to make a long-term commitment to stay, they refused. I suspect, without any proof, that she found herself unhappy in these surroundings.

Both of them are unusually warm, outgoing people; as with Lennie, these traits clashed with the cooler, more silent and reserved pattern of most of the others. Their romantic love of nature again made them conspicuous here. And she, especially, found it hard to adjust to the long hours of physical labor.

They decided to go traveling together in Europe.

LISA.   About eighteen; not very hip; alternates between fairly warm moods and others of rather self-satisfied (or insecure) standoffishness. Her father is a publisher in Europe, her stepfather an anthropologist. She heard of Ezra's group through Malcolm, whom she had known at prep school. In May of her freshman year, 1971, she dropped out of a well-known avant-garde girls' college in New England to come to this ranch instead. (The previous summer she had visited here for two months.) She says she likes the community because she feels what she does counts, makes a difference, whereas at college (incidentally, a very small one) she felt lost in an anonymous environment. Self-development strongly interests her. She did not know about the cosmic purpose of the group until very recently, and she is not sure she entirely accepts it. What matters, she said, is not the permanency of the group, but its immediacy. The demonstration *now* of a new way of life is enough. She had not been strongly interested in drama before this. It seemed to me, during the weeks of my stay, that she was visibly slipping deeper into the ethos and style of the group, and might end up staying with it for a long while.

BRENDA.   She is in her mid- or late twenties and grew up in Boston and

New York, the offspring of an international Jewish family; her father is now in business in London. She is an actress. Warm, quick, realistic in the best New York style, she retains much more objective awareness of what this community is like than anyone else and has many major criticisms of it. She came here in June, 1971, after a marriage broke up, invited by Jacob, whom she had known for years. Only her tie to Jacob holds her here, and even so she will probably leave within a matter of weeks.

CELESTE.   An attractive, very feminine girl of nineteen, from Virginia. She has already been married and divorced and made the drug scene. Recently, after she arrived in New Mexico in a state of personal crisis, an older friend suggested the community as something to try out. She is critical of the way children are treated here, of the absence of music, and of the general lack of warmth in the atmosphere. Again, one perceives her inclinations leaning much closer to the standard hip ethos than to this peculiar one, so perhaps she will not be a long-term adherent.

TANYA.   In her early twenties, from a Midwestern city, she arrived in mid-July, 1971, hoping to stay permanently. Totally "out of it," and desperately trying to fit in, she lived her first weeks in the community in a constant state of near-hysteria.

BETTY JO and FRANK.   These are a young married couple from Texas, with two small children; she arrived just before the end of my stay, in mid-July, 1971, and he followed soon after. She had gone to a state university, but her strength is of the practical, down-to-earth sort; she has an inbuilt sense of pulling one's oar and is a very hard worker. She heard of the group because her sister was formerly a member of it. Though she had only been here for a three-day visit once before, she and her husband have arrived with permanent intentions, expecting soon to be part of the advance party traveling overseas.

One wonders how many other people have belonged to the group since its inception in 1966–1967. Some idea of the turnover may be gained from these facts: that in the summer of 1970, a year before my visit, the group reached a size of thirty-four persons, the largest it has ever been to date; "then we upped the vibration rate," as Ezra put it, "and some couldn't take it and fell away." Two years earlier, in New York City, the group numbered roughly twenty persons, of whom the majority clearly have vanished. Going back still further in time, when the group moved from its original location in a New Mexico town to San Francisco late in 1967, it numbered Ezra, Eva, and three others, none of whom are still with the group. Altogether, then, the number of persons who had dropped out before the summer of 1971 is probably greater than the number of members who are recorded here. Still, in comparison with most of the new communities, the continuity seems highly impressive; six people had actually stayed with the group all the way from San Francisco in 1967–1968, through three subsequent changes of location.[54] I was told that the present overbalance of women in the community is quite new, and that in the past men if anything have outnumbered the women.

The Strength of the Fledgling Culture

The conversion histories of these individuals, as they have been recounted, appear strikingly to reinforce the conclusions reached by John Lofland in his study of a West Coast millennial group during the early 1960's, although Ezra's recruits are clearly of a much higher intellectual caliber.[55] Just as in that other case, people who had known each other beforehand tended to convert in small clusters. Situational "accidents" appear to loom larger than "deep" predispositions in accounting for decisions to join, though they often combine. Affective bonds, most of all to the leader's charisma, are revealed as the underlying germ carriers of what then becomes an ideological commitment. A high level of alienation and personal tension, a sense of being at loose ends during a turning point in one's life, were often present at the time of these conversions, though not (so far as I could tell) in all of them. However, in an age when so many Americans, of every level of intelligence and disposition, tend to view themselves as plagued by "problems," and as moving through a life cycle marked by endless inner "turning points," it becomes difficult to make meaningful use of these concepts. Even more than Lofland, I would stress the variety of personalities that can be attracted to a group of this kind, and the great number of circumstances that can surround their entry into it.

These biographies reinforce the conclusion that what matters is not so much the individuals' past histories, or the precise manner of their induction into the group, as the content (and internal potency) of the regime into which they have now entered. The community is worth studying because it is a functioning reality of such apparently high tensile strength— a nascent would-be culture, or, in the group's own more grandiose language, a "new civilization." Whatever these people were before, the important fact is that they have been "taken over" by something which imposes its norms upon them in a strikingly uniform fashion.

54. However, see p. 402, where it is shown that some of these longest-time members left the group at the end of 1971.

55. Lofland, *op. cit.,* pp. 57–62. Unfortunately only in a few cases could I ascertain, within the context of a polite interview, whether individuals had lacked any strong affective ties prior to entering the group, a point which Lofland emphasizes.

I have mentioned more than once the "alien," self-contained quality of the life that flourishes on the ranch. To a remarkable extent, neither the patterns of the traditional outside culture nor of the standard counterculture count for much in shaping the group's everyday behavior. No matter how the term cultural radicalism may ultimately be defined, this surely is its concrete signature. One realizes that for these people everything in the world beyond has retreated into the relatively unreal. The casual breaking-forth into chants at any time of day, the lack of concern for child rearing, and the robotlike attention to task performance all reveal how automatically the members take their cues from Ezra and from each other, rather than from any other source. In a fundamental sense, this is a "strange" environment. I would feel this most strongly late at night, returning to the scene after a walk by myself in the nearby desert. Approaching this nest of furious activity after an interlude in the surrounding stillness, I always became gripped by the illusion that I was coming back to the planet Mars. The steady roar of the diesel generator mingled with the unrestrained chants and shouts of a theater warmup invisibly under way in the dimly illuminated dome, creating an eerie total effect. A population was unconcernedly following its own laws.

There is perhaps no real difference between what has usually been called a "social movement" and a new culture or subculture in the process of birth. At least this is true if the movement harbors a distinctive cosmology and conception of human nature and at the same time inducts people into a new mode of living. The dream of Elizabeth and Alexis Ferm at Stelton, that a new generation would one day overcome the ordinary processes of socialization, appears to be fulfilling itself to a striking degree on the New Mexico ranch, even if their ideology has deep roots in the past.[56] But it is happening not in a climate of spontaneous freedom but in one of enormous inner discipline which shapes the people into a new uniform mold. The power of a social movement such as early Christianity must also have been precisely of this nature—to draw its members into radically distinct patterns of thinking and behavior which after a time begin to push their former selves back into the limbo of a stale, half-remembered dream.

The standard manner of chanting, the routine of toasting after the

56. Here, as with anarchism, a certain trouble arises from a tendency to confuse two distinct senses of the word "new." Radical intellectual traditions, such as anarchism and mysticism, are anything but new, and the psychological patterns associated with adherence to a social movement likewise seem recurrent. But such movements are always "new," sociologically speaking, in the very fact of their rupture from the mainstream society and culture of the moment. See p. 62.

weekly feasts, the "eating" periods of silence, and other similar details reveal the living achievement of new collective forms and the suppression of
any behavior which would be inconsistent with them. As one might expect,
special patterns of vocabulary have developed within the group, going
beyond the jargon of the official intellectual sources. The words that are
very much "in" during casual conversation include: confrontation, negative, energy, planetary, karma, vibration, inner, vectors, fucking, fucked
up, shit,[57] project, completion, check with, zap. Other words are noticeable
by their absence: spiritual; God; commune (to refer to themselves); man,
you know, and most other hip phrases; society.

Each individual learns quickly to imitate all these details, and this in
turn sets severe limits upon further novelty or change. Innovation is discouraged when it appears to go contrary to the group's aims. Thus one
evening, when a new girl who had been assigned the job of cook produced
abundant bottles of beer for dinner, even though it wasn't Sunday, one of
the more severe senior members of the community took her publicly to
task, accusing her of trying to buy favor in this fashion because she was
inwardly fearful of her cooking skill. In this way people who wander too
far are brought into line.

The commitment to shared norms is the constant, unifying reality on
the ranch, joining people who have great personal problems with others
who, by every external indication, are strong and reasonably happy. Despite the theme of self-alienation which so often rears itself, psychological
theories alone seem inadequate as explanations for the presence of this
diverse collection of individuals. It is the sociological fact of mutual commitment which is the strongest common denominator of the people here.
Among them one can detect no single deep-seated personal pattern more
powerful than the routines and the cue signals of the nascent culture itself.
Though the total effect (in daylight, at least) is less that of a new civilization than of a strikingly distinct subculture, on a par with those of tourna-
ment bridge players, jazz musicians, or railroad enthusiasts, the very fact
that it constantly involves the whole of daily life gives it a powerful impact.[58]

57. The larger society furnishes a great many four-letter words, but only these
have been unconsciously selected for intensive use here. The others I heard very
rarely.
58. The terms "culture" and "subculture" are almost impossible to differentiate
clearly in a context such as this one. I have employed them without intending to be
overly precise, in the belief that readers will accept the one which seems more appropriate after pondering the whole of the evidence. My point is to emphasize the link
between what have often been called "social movements" and the *attempt* (which

The relative water-tightness of this fledgling culture is shown in the style of the group's relations with the outside world. The group's attitude toward the "old civilization" is one of severe detachment, though this is masked by strange collective shifts of attitude, which occur sometimes every few weeks, between moods of uncompromising inner withdrawal and those of deliberate external outreach.[59] According to a nice bit of community folklore, so extreme did the atmosphere of withdrawal become in February of 1971 that for six weeks each inquisitive car coming up the road turned around immediately and went back, sensing the force-filled barrier of alien vibrations. At the opposite pole, on the first night of the drama festival group members were eagerly scanning the horizon for every possible approaching vehicle, seeking as it were to "pull" it in toward them. And it is also a regular practice after each play to serve coffee to the audience, the actors returning (no longer in costume) to share in the sociability. But when, as at such times, the mood of standoffish rigor is broken, it is always with calculation. The efforts which are made to bridge the chasm often unintentionally reveal its true depth and extent.

According to Ezra, the outside world is to be *used*. It is an important source of "data," and therefore to be approached with constant alertness. This image of data gathering runs parallel to his conception of the group as poking among the ruins of the dying civilization in order to snatch whatever is genuinely of service to the new. If this perspective were maintained without fail, it would mean that every relationship with an outsider must be a manipulative one. One is taking something from that person which is of value to the growth and welfare of the group; one is milking the outside world. And in fact this kind of vocabulary is often used, sometimes very explicitly, in recounting particular episodes of contact that have occurred. Ezra and Eva both strongly evince this manipulative shrewdness, this skill at always knowing how to reach for an advantage. Their sense of "we" and "they" is razor-sharp, with the boundary being drawn at the edge of the ranch. All the members of the group echo these attitudes more or less consistently, depending upon their degree of inner commitment to the group. Indeed, this point of view is what measures one's full participation. There is no room, in theory, for halfway commitment. Every trip beyond the border of the ranch, except perhaps for an occasional visit with rela-

---

can achieve any degree of success or failure historically) to create a new collectively shared way of life.

59. "The cessation of the inner octave tends to recur repeatedly and demands from the leader of the community much watchfulness and insight, for his task is to apply the needed shock that will restart the inner octave." DeRopp, *op. cit.*, p. 210.

tives, must be on group business of some kind; there is no allowable conception of personal affairs (or curiosity).

Just prior to the drama festival, members were told that they were expected to spend one day a week traveling outside (often in pairs) to canvass for ticket sales. This meant going to public events, such as nearby rodeos and horse races, soliciting on sidewalks and in hotel lobbies, and possibly going from door to door in certain towns within striking distance. Under this kind of pressure, many persons developed an unremitting "hardsell" style. When the Microbus was stopped at an intersection for a traffic light, flyers would be handed out the window to pedestrians passing in the crosswalk—and these people would be individually greeted, despite the necessary brevity of the encounter. No moment, no occasion must be wasted. This behavior was all the more striking because it ran counter to the shyness and inner hesitation about approaching strangers which most group members freely admitted they retain underneath. Against their own inclinations, they were willingly transforming themselves into the obedient agents of blatant organizational promotion. "How many flyers did you hand out today?" became the test of loyalty, one which everyone freely accepted.

The manipulative view of outsiders which I have been describing is, of course, extremely common among organizations of all kinds; some version of it is functional to their survival or success, whether they are businesses, universities, or social clubs. But one meets it in the extreme, on the level of overt speech and behavior, in ideological movements and alienated communities such as this one. What does this parallel suggest? The special quality of alienated social movements does not lie in the mere fact of their reliance upon these manipulative techniques. Rather, it concerns the manner in which they are expressed. Such movements might be said to be characterized by a peculiar intensity in their relations with outsiders, which is the result of an altogether less secure, more vulnerable situation. They are vulnerable because, lacking cultural acceptance and the dignity and prestige which go along with it, they can be much more easily struck down —by indifference as well as by overt hostility. Edginess and insecurity are built into the very nature of the relationship between an "undignified" social group and the outside world.

When compared with the promotional campaigns of established bodies, the whole endeavor can take on a rather sad air of unreality. Despite every effort at aggressive salesmanship, only about twenty people were in the audience on the opening night of the drama festival for a reasonably good performance of a Greek play, and many of them were old friends of the

community. (The crafts bazaar, it is true, did far better in luring customers.) The frequent disparity between the efforts at contact and their
practical results places a still higher demand upon unquestioning inner
loyalty in making the attempt. Even more obviously than for the vendors
of Black Panther newspapers, salesmanship for the members of this community remains primarily another form of inner test.

Thus one found a curious mixture of calculated outreach with lapses
which revealed its forced quality. During the bazaar the Microbus made
two trips a day to visit the hotels of a nearby town, seeking to lure tourists
to visit the ranch. Characteristically, in terms of the penurious attitude so
often displayed, visitors were to be charged $1.50 simply to make the tour.
The first morning of the bazaar the person assigned as driver of the bus
made the run unshaven and in his usual filthy work attire. (Since he is not
hip-looking in appearance, he thus resembled an old-fashioned lower-class
hobo.) Also, as he realized afterward, there had been no visible identification on the bus; it looked like any ordinary private vehicle. The hope of
attracting well-heeled tourists in this way revealed how unused the members were to planning in terms of worldly wisdom.

The group usually lived in an atmosphere strongly insulated from world
events. One girl did perversely subscribe to the daily edition of the *New
York Times,* but Ezra is said to have once told her that he never wanted
to see issues of it lying around the dining room. Ezra's position about
politics is that, as a protective shield, the community must avoid any kind
of involvement. (Here the parallel with the Vedanta movement is exact.)
This is not just a pose, for he was capable of offhandedly commenting: "I
don't care if the Black Panthers and the FBI are *all* shot." Yet, as individuals, spokesmen for outside interests are not always abruptly turned away.
A Catholic priest was invited one evening to have dinner with the group
and show his slides of remote Mexican villages. He was treated with every
outward cordiality, even though at one point he boldly expressed his hope
that the group believed in a supreme being.

Whether or not its tone exactly resembles that of a monastery, the
community demands that the individual "give up" the world in a very
profound sense. This reality underlies all questions of tactics. "I'm here
because out there is *death,*" Frieda said to me during our interview. As one
stays within the group and observes small revelations of unconscious attitudes, one sees that the members curtain themselves off from the world
even more deeply than they like to admit. The ranch is their only home,
and their life on it the only reality. They have to force themselves to go
outside, to talk to strangers, to gather "data" from the old civilization. No

wonder, then, that efforts at public relations are often so strained and exaggerated in quality. These efforts are accepted as necessary medicine, to be taken for their own good and for the service of the undertaking. But their true hunger is for isolation and apartness.

This view of the outside world has an interesting parallel in what the members now think about their own earlier lives. The norms of this new culture demand that they reject their previous patterns of existence, their former selves, to a very marked degree. (This is true quite regardless of whatever psychological syndrome they brought with them; as we have seen, these appeared to vary considerably.) Their inner struggle becomes centered in this rejection, in the effort to become a new person in the immediate present.

At dinner one night Ezra launched specifically into this area, putting forward the concept of "time lines." (I later discovered he had taken it from Nicoll.) "Time lines" are what ordinary people in the world are caught up in—particular goals, particular social or psychological roles, which bind us to a given future. Usually we have not one but several of them operating in our lives concurrently. They make our behavior conditioned, predictable. Entering this community, one sunders them all, stands apart from them and confronts one's true self. There are no time lines here on the ranch, Ezra emphasized. (When he said this, I realized that in their minds the community's own elaborate future goals are seen on an entirely different plane.) The discussion brought forth many recollections of specific time lines which had been given up. In one case it was toward becoming a film star; in another it led in the direction of suicide. Now one's aim must be to gain conscious mastery over these former time lines, Ezra continued. Don't go on blocking or repressing them or fleeing from them. Instead get to the point where you can *use* your own past life (as one aspect of the outside world). Be at the center of all these vectors, pulling the strings, turning them into a series of advantages. This was more complicated—and in its own way more affirmative—than a purely monastic response. But a powerful conception of total divorce lay at the bottom of it, no matter how greatly one stressed the need later to transcend a reaction of flight. In this firm notion of separation from the world and from one's own past lies the basis for building a new culture or "civilization," the source of strength to withstand the continuing bombardment of memories representing an earlier socialization.

According to one informant, this group had not begun with such a definite feeling of apartness from the old civilization in America. In its first phase, back at the time of the Haight-Ashbury summer in 1967, the dominating idea was merely to create a subculture of a certain kind which might help America to get back on its proper course. But thereafter, as America's stance worsened, developing increasingly in the wrong directions, the conviction grew that the total cultural situation had become hopeless and that a whole new civilization would have to replace it. From this it followed that the group would have to deal directly with the "planetary" mind, and go into either literal or psychological exile to undertake its work. If this shift in attitudes did take place, it reveals a remarkably precise parallel at the radical end of the spectrum to the growing sense of hopelessness over American foreign policy experienced in the liberal sector of the population during 1968 and 1969.

My informant developed this point further. America, as they saw it, had originally been destined as a unique land where a new way of living would be experimentally pioneered and worked out; it was the chosen vehicle for the entire planet in these terms. But then America went off course—"began spreading its poison around the world." And this made total separation from the American mainstream the only viable response.

These ideas seem to echo, at one remove, much of the standard mythology about America's peculiar role in the world, the belief in Manifest Destiny which has continued to thrive in a remarkable way within the New Left, shaping its own recent sense of betrayal. The community in New Mexico by no means deserves to be called a left-wing group, for it is genuinely quite oblivious of politics. But, if this story of its evolution can be trusted, it too is the product of very recent and specific changes in the American political atmosphere. Alienation appears at least sometimes to be spawned by the larger culture in a concrete, traceable way.

Now they refuse to attach themselves to any definite place. Eva once declared at the dinner table that she always had the feeling she could pack up and leave permanently for somewhere else with the group tomorrow morning. In mid-1971 they were planning to move soon to the new location abroad. Their feeling that America had recently gone off course in a mad world, and of the need for a new elite, uncommitted to the old order, reminded me strongly of certain fringe-type organizations which existed in the 1930's, such as Mankind United, Technocracy, and the I Am movement.[60] At that time the outside threats of fascism and communism triggered these extreme responses among small bands of people. Now, one realizes, the policies of our own government, and the tendencies broadly

60. See pp. 41–43.

at work in our national life, seem to have driven some individuals in a similar direction.

Of course there has also been pervasive talk of a New Age within the hip minority in recent years. But Ezra's community is rightly proud of its distinctive posture. Though it moved to San Francisco during the magnetic season of 1967, with a desire to be close to where "it was happening," it emerged from the experience claiming mainly to have learned a whole variety of mistakes to be avoided. These mistakes, Ezra told me, centered in lack of organization and, even more, in the indiscriminate invitation to participate, preventing any control over admission to the movement. (Behind these comments I nonetheless sensed a serious underlying identification with the original goal of cultural revolution.) Now the group maintains no definite contacts with hip groups in its own area, excepting the Lama Foundation, where it presented one of its original plays a couple of years ago. Along with the term "commune," the concept of the "counterculture" is pointedly rejected as well, with the assertion that it is merely another part of the standard culture, engaged in an unconscious, uncomprehending reaction to the actions of the mainstream. Only this group, and a few similar groups like Bennett's scattered throughout the world, are believed to stand outside this pattern of automatic action and reaction, consciously willing their own future.

The group is also proud of its toughness and cohesion. Long-time members boasted of the extent to which it has apparently succeeded in reducing the amount of openly displayed internal friction during the course of its history. (In making this generalization, Ezra's own displays of temper, which are not unambiguously spontaneous, are excepted; they certainly do not appear to have declined, as far as one can judge.) But in the early days of the group, Eva recalls, there was an atmosphere of frequent, loud conflicts, some of them tending toward violence, though it might be expressed in one's behavior toward a particular fellow actor on the stage, or in dance gestures. Even in the summer of 1970, an anthropology student who visited the community noted far more flare-ups and "confrontations" than she did a year later. Eva dates the change to the period after the 1970 drama festival and before the fall tour that took them to the East and South. She feels that the group gained a basic self-confidence at that point which made it easier for its members to shed mutual suspicions and work peacefully together. Thus in mid-1970 the drama festival had brought forth all sorts of "incredible" conflicts; that of 1971 went smoothly, by and large, despite discouragingly poor attendance. To my eyes and ears in the summer of 1971, the degree of open discord (not involving Ezra) was remarkably small. And an overwhelming share of it involved one person, Champ, who was always telling off everyone else.[61]

In Ezra's own mind, the potential for growing harmony is not an accidental characteristic of this group. He claims that the policy toward admissions is very selective. Like Swami Paramananda, he insists that no one who is "badly adjusted" to life in some deeply neurotic sense would be let in. Such people, if accepted, would deceive themselves by believing they were saying yes to genuine insights when actually they were giving rein to their dammed-up impulses. The kind of person who is accepted into this community, on the other hand, should be able to deal with his or her personal traumas or hangups within the span of an initial year or two. Thereafter he should be capable of consciously making use of his own past, along with the rest of the external world, without either surrendering to private impulses or side-stepping them in an extreme asceticism.

One doubts whether in fact the selectivity has been so careful as is claimed. Initial contact with the group, as revealed in these life histories, often took a highly casual form. Certain of the members do continue to have intense personal problems. Some of them—and this is simply a speculation—may be unconsciously reliving an earlier experience with a powerful parent, as they willingly subject themselves to what amounts to a highly authoritarian regime. Still, they are all (except possibly Champ) stable in the everyday sense of the word. A person who lived too much in his own world while here could not throw himself wholeheartedly into the many group projects and would undoubtedly be asked to leave. And the belief in selectivity may in its way be just as potent a source of self-discipline as its reality.

Defection from the group is extremely difficult, not just because so many of the members have a strong inbuilt desire to believe all its promises, but because of the variety and the constant succession of moves, changes, and deadlines which are built into its pattern. There is always this play to rehearse for, this craft order to get done, this week's crucial stage in the planting season in the garden. When one feels inadequate or defeated in one realm, something else equally urgent grasps one's attention, demanding to be accomplished. There is the transcontinental drama tour, the European tour after that, and eventually the move to an overseas location. One gets swept up in all these concrete plans and goals. To abandon anything

---

61. However, early in 1971 a dissident member pulled a knife on Ezra one evening. He was instantly disarmed and the sheriff was called in to take him away to jail, where he was charged with trespassing.

is to leave the group in the lurch, especially when one is playing a part on a literal stage. The impulse is always to carry through. And no sooner is a task halfway over than a new, more grandiose one is announced, and personal responsibilities in it are quickly assigned. There is never any convenient point to leave, and one's doubts dissolve, or are shoved to the background, as one grabs onto the next assignment.[62] Like Bion's psychopathic army patients, these men and women regularly forget themselves when they are given something to do. Unlike the situation in that other group, nothing appears to be made-up work, even when they diligently plant fruit trees a few weeks before "permanently" leaving the ranch.

And yet is this truly a community? Though its norms are so visible and so strongly imbued, from another point of view it might be argued that it comprises no more than twenty or thirty individual disciples of Ezra who happen to be in physical proximity with each other. Each person here is told always to travel in his own psychic "territory." The group's ideology discourages personal warmth. Several people in the preceding biographies who were naturally of a more outgoing temperament did not fit in well in this setting. The intense pursuit of "self-development" fosters a tendency toward isolation, despite all the committees and projects, which may even remind one of the atmosphere at Gerald Heard's Trabuco College. As in some earlier monastic movements, one confronts the paradox that an unusual degree of self-contained collective stability accompanies a pattern of interaction among individuals which follows highly artificial, repressive rules. Perhaps hip communes may rise and fall so fast, by contrast, because their members hold back so little from free mutual engagement.

Finally, is sex regarded here so very differently from the way it is in the monastic tradition? Pairing, one recalls, was viewed by Bion as a danger in the life of work groups. Pairing in this community is deliberately de-emphasized. Indeed, I was surprised finally to learn how many people had actually entered into definite relationships, because there is so little surface indication of their existence. Sex and love are tolerated, but one senses that that is all. They lead a more or less underground life. At the dinner discussion, Ezra even warned one of the young men that sexual exploits such as he was apparently engaging in were inconsistent with full devotion to his current acting roles! (Meanwhile, Ezra has no hesitation about openly showing affection to several of the girls.) There is much compro-

62. Again this point confirms Lofland's findings. Ezra's group has used group migration and geographic dispersion on occasion, which Lofland pointed to as devices for maintaining a high level of morale. *Op. cit.,* pp. 248–53. However, the travel and dispersal of late 1971 reached a point which clearly became counter-productive in these terms; see p. 402.

mise and contradiction in all of this, but the overall tone is certainly not one of license.

Communities of discipline in the current generation have the same peculiar strength as those of earlier times, if they are led by a strong, self-confident guru. But it is a strength gained at the price of the ordinary forms of intimacy between people. Such communities do not flourish in response to an onrush of brotherly feeling. Rather they feed upon a recurrent impulse toward discipleship in a context of austerity. Then and now, they are the product of the shrewdness and imagination of their leading figures. Only a leader immune from self-doubt can create the cultural norms, and the climate of obedience to them, which offer any hope of long-term survival.

Ezra

> We all hope he's a teacher
> We fear that he's a lecher
> How can we gain satori,
> Not just adorn his glory?
> These questions shake our minds. . . .
> It used to be so easy. . . .
> If you wanted to learn
> You went to a university . . .
> Or off to India by air or sea
> Took up art or science
> Philosophy or seance
> But we're the sophisticated
> Aquarian generation
> And all the past we've hated
> Prayed for the new creation!
> Who is there to teach us?
> Who is there to reach us?
> Ezra at least's a candidate,
> He's better than the State,
> Before we lynch or leave him
> We'll try to believe him.[63]

The creation of a reasonably watertight new cultural style is Ezra's doing. The others all look to him constantly for their cues, for the subtle signals which tell them what to do and what not to do. His chanting rhythms they imitate with their own voices, his instructions they seek to

63. From one of the group's original plays, probably written by Ezra himself. Nora and one or two others would spontaneously sing out these passages while washing dishes late at night.

apply in the theater, his time table they follow for planetary outreach. His words, uttered privately or openly on any subject, carry incalculably more weight than anyone else's. All trails lead back to Ezra.

His eyes are the great magnets. They stare directly into yours, fixing them with total attention and understanding. Or else they deliberately, purposefully resist your look (though fully conscious of it), gazing reflectively ahead into space, declaring, "Now is the time for each of us to be centered in ourselves, doing our appointed work." Lighted by the kerosene lanterns at the dinner table, they are the glazed eyes of a fanatic. Greeting you in daylight, perhaps after an absence, they are the eyes of a cordial, smiling emissary. In a dream which I had shortly after leaving the ranch, his eyes were totally immobile, impassive, closed to outside suggestion. You immediately scan his eyes whenever he appears, even at a great distance, seeking to read their expression of the moment.

Ezra's hands next attract attention. They are big, out of scale. They rest powerfully in front of him as he speaks after dinner; in the garden they wield a hoe assuredly, with careful measure, to show all of us how the tasks are best done.

He has a large mouth. His voice is rich, deep, full of masculine energy, always the instrument of his purpose, even when he shouts in rage. It carries far as he strides around the property, chanting early in the morning: "Skol—laaaa-la-skol!" When he is being courteous and friendly in conversation, it is an almost Southern drawl, still hearty and commanding even at this subdued level. There is the wistfulness of a prematurely wise little boy in it at times, yet it conveys a tenacious awareness of his rightness, of the fact that he will always come out on top. He makes his point. The words roll on, expand, become garrulous, as the eyes and the smile remain the same. Then his voice will cease and his eyes will suddenly abandon everyone, as he moves to get up or to walk away; he has determined the fixed end of his own outpouring. His listeners stir, pondering the message they have been given, relating it to what has been said before. Everything seems significant. When, very rarely, he cracks a joke, certain members of the community will repeat it among themselves for hours or days; it has uplifted them.

Ezra is a tall, broadly built man of forty-two, with a neatly trimmed beard in 1970, beardless in 1971. His dark hair is conventionally short and parted. He wears gray or green work pants and shirts, with a kerchief around his neck on public occasions. Superficially he looks like a construction foreman or farmer; he often carelessly leaves his fly a quarter open. In this attire he is perpetually ready to let suddenly arriving dignitaries know he is no hippie. Several years ago, in San Francisco and New York, one guesses that he was more bohemian.

An inward button clicks, any time, anywhere, and he is the open tyrant. The voice barks at maximum. Hatred flows, reaching for the psychological weapons which lie closest to the victim's vitals. "You're lying!" "You're trying to sabotage the whole bazaar," the play, the project. Talking before everyone else to a girl he may be sleeping with: "You cunt! You're nothing but a fucking, lying cunt!" To another girl at dinner: "You want to commit suicide? Well, let me tell you, there are a thousand different ways of doing it." And to the whole group, at the end of a theater rehearsal: "You're only giving yourself ninety percent. You've got a ninety-percent mentality, all of you! You come in late, you never finish anything! You're just a fucking bunch of soft, lazy Americans! If you don't shape up, I'm going to burn the whole place down at the end of the summer and start all over again with a group of people who aren't Americans." The lighting in the theater happens to be what he is so strenuously objecting to. After five or ten minutes of this monologue, he returns to the matter at hand. He calls the lamps they are using "storm lanterns." Someone else casually refers to them as "Coleman lanterns." He takes that up immediately. "They're *storm* lanterns," he shouts, reiterating the term. He cannot bear to be corrected about any detail.

Then the internal button, shining red for anger, just as suddenly cuts off. He is "himself" again. He smiles as if nothing has happened. Perhaps a moment later he puts his arm around one of the girls and they walk out together.

I wonder how the group can take these scenes, which may occur two or three times a day (though in certain weeks they may not happen at all), without wanting to flee from them utterly, if for no other reason than their ultimate tedium. But, with the rest of his nature, he is constantly pulling every person toward him, promising them his approval (which, coming in small snatches, attains an enormously high value), assuring them, beyond any doubt, that there is meaning in him, in them, in their tasks, in the universe.

There are other reasons why these blowups create far less unrest in the community than one might think. The recent craze for encounter groups has conditioned people to accept anger as a legitimate form of testing. Ezra himself observes that this fad makes things easier for him. But he will privately admit that what he does has nothing in common with the procedure in an encounter group. For one thing, except for Champ's outbursts (which to a degree deliberately imitate Ezra's), these scenes almost invariably involve Ezra with some one other member of the community, rather than two rank-and-file members with each other. For another, one realizes that their aim is not to give both parties the release of bringing their emotions fully out into the open, but quite the opposite: to teach the "victim" self-control. He or she is not to respond in kind, but to stand there and calmly take it. The confrontations, Ezra also told me, are designed only for the core membership of the group, never for newcomers. They are indeed like Gurdjieff's rages at his château in the 1920's.

A further reason why the confrontations are passively accepted by the others has to do with the five "inner rules" which the core members agree to follow. One of these, the only one Ezra would reveal to me, is that "each man or woman travels in his own territory." The meaning of this is that when one witnesses an event such as a confrontation one is not supposed to think about its literal content and the personalities of the people involved, but rather to find some lesson in it applicable to oneself. In this way, it becomes wrong for people to begin sympathizing with each other or start banding together, even mentally. This rule (and by implication the four other rules) contributes powerfully to the atmosphere of individual isolation which prevails on these acres. Each person is locked in a lonely self-struggle, with Ezra as the only external arbiter. Why do people come up and "check with" Ezra for a moment whenever they are uncertain about how to proceed in their tasks? Answering this question, which he had posed himself, Ezra denied that it was to receive specific instructions, for he claims to be uninterested in such detailed matters. "It is for a vibration check, to compare the level of our vibrations." And he insisted that at certain moments his own vibrations might be lower than those of the other person. (Though not usually, one was led to infer.)

Finally, John Lofland has argued that erratically authoritarian behavior by a leader enhances that person's claim to have unusual powers, to be privy to special knowledge. It thus intensifies the submission and respect of the followers.[64] After watching Ezra in action, and the humble

64. Lofland, *op. cit.*, p. 216. Note the following passage concerning an episode in the Vedanta movement: "It often happened that even while the disciple was being reproached by Maharaj, he would feel a strange undercurrent of joy. The indifference of Maharaj was the only thing we could not have borne; but the Maharaj was never indifferent. The harsher his words, the more intensely we felt his interest in our welfare. . . . Sometimes, a disciple would be reproved for quite insignificant reasons, or on grounds that seemed to him utterly unjust. But, as time passed, he would realize that there had been certain tendencies and karmas stored in his subconscious mind, and that Maharaj had seen them and was working to annihilate them before they could appear and become harmful. Thus, at the cost of a little unpleasantness, the disciple would be spared years of painful struggle and self-

and subdued responses to his outbursts, I am prepared to believe that this is profoundly true. Whether one may conclude, as Lofland does, that for this reason an authoritarian style is always appropriate in social movements, is another, less easily resolved question. The record of anarchist communities gave us some reason to hope that this need not always be so.[65]

How does Ezra view his own role? It seemed to me that he is keenly aware of all its psychological dimensions but justifies them in terms of the cosmic ideology he has embraced. His self-identification with the historical chain of planetary Guides, of teachers in wisdom schools, has already become evident. But he does not always like to appear so grandiose. I heard him say: "Some people specialize in raising chickens, some people in creating new civilizations. Both tasks are equally necessary, and it would be wrong to say that one is 'higher' than the other, only different." But this sudden declaration, uttered informally at noontime and sparked by a dialogue I was having with him, rang of a rather too inventive modesty.

The question that kept burning in my mind throughout my stay, and about which I never entirely satisfied myself, was whether Ezra's outbursts were as controlled and deliberate as the other aspects of his daily behavior. Were they always indeed a series of "tests," designed for the inner growth of specific individuals? Or did they represent a recurring facet of his own personality? In this and in other ways, was the community obligingly furnishing a series of animate stage props to feed his own drive for power? "How can we gain satori,/Not just adorn his glory?"

There should be a pause at this point to explore Ezra's own life history in depth. Unfortunately, this is possible only to a limited degree. He chose to reveal no more than bits and snatches of his past, often at the dinner table, and what I have learned from others by no means fills in all the gaps.

He was born in a small town of five thousand in the Southwest, his father a sometime salesman of books. His mother was petite, dynamic, Southern, highly concerned with moral values, deeply religious. His father was more balanced, stable, matter-of-fact, and came from the North. A sharp contrast between the parents created a fertile polarity. Ezra was re-

---

discipline." Swami Prabhavananda, *Brahmananda: The Eternal Companion* (Hollywood: Vedanta Press, 1947), p. 69. Such a passage could be transferred almost verbatim to the relations between Ezra and his followers.

65. However, in the specific context of the mystical tradition, one recalls that Gerald Heard's refusal to play such an authoritarian role may have had much to do with the failure of his Trabuco College; see p. 272.

membered in the town as an unusual boy, but the reverse of a success: a "black sheep," compared unfavorably with his brothers and sisters.

Then, grown big, he became restless and moved out into the world, aimlessly at first. Too footloose to stay at one college for long, he drifted in and out of several (in the late 1940's, before this pattern had become widely fashionable). He picked fruit, worked on a railroad, and for a while became a labor organizer. Then he completed the course at a well-known mining school. Despite his earlier drifting, he became a success, a "crackerjack" engineer, though lacking the mind of a pure scientist. He was made manager of a third of a large uranium plant, run by a well-known super-corporation; this meant that he was in the second or third echelon of its management. Stimulated by this achievement, after several years he went back East to attend the full two-year course at one of the nation's most prestigious business schools.

This experience changed him, further developing his ambitious dreams. He became very political; the world was now his horizon. To a close friend he poured out his fantasy of one day becoming President of the United States. In New York he obtained a job with a private corporation developing proposals for American aid projects overseas. On his own, he traveled impulsively to far places. For a while he helped run a private humanitarian project in South Vietnam.

Meanwhile, he went through two marriages and began his third, with Eva, the worshipful but dynamic, grasping young girl he first met in India. With one former wife he had a child, but this was why the marriage ended, for he couldn't stand the idea of being tied down by children. He was too change-oriented, too much concerned with his own plans and his own freedom. But everywhere women found themselves dazzled by his magnetism.

He has also written at least two novels and translated poetry. He is good at languages; he has the kind of mind that can immerse itself in something rapidly, assimilate its essentials, and then move on freely to something else. His novels, when his friends read them, did not seem up to the level of his brilliant conversation. They were good enough, though, for publishers to send him personal letters of rejection. He also wrote a book, never published, on the subject of power—in all its dimensions, but most of all on personal power. This topic clearly held a deep fascination for him. But he was also continually pulled by his own restlessness, his desire for new places.

More than in his wives, he confided in a succession of male friends. With them he formed deep ties, but often seemed to fall out with them eventually. In New York, he began an intensive study of Gurdjieff, whose writings he first encountered when he was eighteen. But he soon got ideas which went beyond the orthodox teachings he received. He developed the yen to put these ideas into practice. On another level, he became entranced by the possibilities of the theater. People began to visit with him in the evening, attracted by his wide knowledge and his vision of the future. He fell into the role of their informal teacher, liked it, and started dreaming with them of a community. A total system of living emerged in his mind. As an engineer, he had always shone in systems analysis. Now he had only to fill the system with people, live with it, and watch it beginning to work.

In company with a long-time friend, now a business partner, he came to New Mexico, ostensibly to start a venture in metals in which they would both prosper. But as soon as they arrived he quarreled with the friend, the business deal fell through, and instead, in the small town where he was staying, the nucleus of a group began to congeal around him. He openly became its guru. The group infiltrated an existing local theater company, creating stir and dissension because of its already tightly bound, peculiar ways. It antagonized many people because its members believed in provoking deliberate "confrontations" with strangers everywhere, in stores and other public places. (Only later did Ezra learn a craftier diplomacy in dealing with the outside world.) Thoroughly ostracized, and also lured by the reports of the New Age coming from the Haight-Ashbury, he moved the group to San Francisco. From then forward, his steady craving for new scenes was to be fortified by an entourage traveling with him.

"Are you happy?" the wife of his former business partner abruptly asked him, paying a rare visit to the ranch during the bazaar. The question seemed to floor him, leaving him speechless, at least as she recalled it. Normally so articulate, with an answer to everything, he could not respond to this simple thrust. In her mind, his hesitation signaled a great loneliness. He had broken with everything and everyone in his past. He no longer had friends in the ordinary sense (or in the uncommon sense that he used to have them). He had traded them all to become king of a small mountain.

But he might well have been floored by her question for an entirely different reason. Happiness is not the aim of life, say Gurdjieff, Ouspensky, Nicoll, and Bennett; it is internal growth, increase of energy and consciousness. He might have paused wondering what he could possibly say to such an irrelevant question. And as for friends, to move away from them, to move away from life, was to move ever further in the direction of the cosmic Work. It was one of his great burdens in the Work that, as a teacher, all his relationships must now be based on some degree of domination. He had always for some reason possessed an extraordinary magnetism. All he had now done was to put this automatic gift, which he could not help having, to use. Indeed it had undoubtedly been given to him for such an eventual purpose.

Until he left New York in 1966, there had been no reason to imagine that he was anything other than a highly talented, rising man in the world. Only his dynamism and magnetism, and perhaps his restlessness, his inability to settle down in one location for long periods, set him apart. Except for the further fact that he had read and responded to Gurdjieff.

While I was staying on the ranch, I once tried to write down a "balanced view" of his personality, one that would account for every aspect of the behavior I had seen him display. Six such discrete elements occurred to me:

1. The planner-organizer. In this role he is the man who always knows everything that is going to happen and how it should be handled. Practical know-how, several stages in advance of everyone else, merges with absolutely unshakable vision and will. Everyone receives the supreme confidence that the group is doing the right thing, that they ought to continue, that a majestic array of plans will always continue to be unveiled and will just as surely be fulfilled. Ezra is the bestower of external challenges, the judge of how well they are being met, the instructor, persuader, and field lieutenant.

2. The father-lover-confessor. Here is Ezra with his arms around the young girls, or listening intensely and understandingly as the boys tell him their problems. In this guise he is warm, enveloping, respectful. One gesture, one all-knowing response causes the person to catch fire in renewed loyalty and dedication.

3. The guru in the strict sense. Here he is colder, more literal and matter-of-fact in style, more intelligent than would befit a saint, more like a scientist or pseudo-academic. But here he also runs away a bit too soon from his precision, going off in the direction of garrulous expansiveness; in his conversations there is just a bit too much naked eagerness to be the authority on anything and everything.

4. The dominating anecdotalist, more casual and relaxed, like the store-owner philosopher or the shop foreman with a few moments to kill. In this mood he can make jokes, offer running commentary, give strikingly true pronouncements about people and events. At such moments he is the kind of person one might well meet at certain levels of a business firm, or in a factory: the down-to-earth summer-upper who implies, "We know what the score is, and isn't it amusing, friends?" This is half camaraderie,

half self-assertion of a rather routine kind. But, even when he is in this role, you are expected to agree with him, though he may expect you to chew the bone he hands you a bit first.

5. The bully. This is when the inner button has clicked on, and the ugliness occurs.

6. The gracious emissary, the completely adequate, charming host, shepherding everyone, no matter if a deaf, elderly lady from Texas, on a careful tour of the property.

In all these roles, excepting only the last, one finds domination at the core of it, taking one form or another, disguised or open.

The signposts leading into Ezra's mind are many, and some of them appear to conflict.

One of the plainest, continually reappearing in his conversations, is a frank elitism. The mass of men, he says freely, have "a herd mind." There are three kinds of people, historically: those who operate on worldly knowledge alone, the masses; those who follow rules, whether in a religious movement or in Communism, and who can be called fanatics; and thirdly, the tiny minority who compose an elite culture, geared to intensive self-development. The elite does not impose rules on anybody else, but it consists of people who transcend the ordinary regulations freely in order to experiment with what is truly applicable to their own needs. One can't be eligible immediately for the elite culture. First one must go through the rule-following phase, whether in scientific or religious terms. His own community, he clearly believes, is engaged in forming an elite, meanwhile masking itself (for instance, as a "theater group") for self-protective purposes. All new civilizations, Ezra says in a mood that connects with Spengler as well as with Bennett, are consciously created by a leader and a small group who surround him in a "school." Cultural change is always of this kind, he believes; even tribal societies evolved from small groups clustered around their magicians. Athens and England, his favorite examples, were governed by small minorities.

Yet even higher than the elite group stands the fully conscious individual. The men in Plato's cave symbolize the group but the sun represents individuality. Psycho-kinetic groups (a term taken from Bennett) lead toward the evolution of psycho-kinetic man, that is, the man who works continually to improve his own psyche rather than trying directly to change the external conditions of mass existence. A magic minority of psycho-kinetic individuals could create a great civilization, as temporarily happened both in Athens and England. But so far psycho-kinetic man has never succeeded in dominating on a planetary basis. Meanwhile, individuality is not really required or expected of ordinary people. It is only for the elite. Thus the elected leaders in a nation have no genuine authority, for they represent nothing more than the operation of the blind political forces of the moment.

In his negative assessment of the present political and intellectual leadership of Western society, Ezra also finds scope for a seemingly contradictory populism. The clash between this and his elitism produces a curious ambivalence toward the East Coast, Harvard, and English culture. On the one hand, he repeatedly attacks certain members of the group who are from such backgrounds for their "snobbishness," becoming highly emotional. On the other hand, he boasts (whether truly or not) that he was invited to stay on and teach at the famous Ivy League university whose business school he attended. And, at least for my benefit, he sometimes launches into very laudatory talk about the spirit of scholarship at such universities as Harvard and Oxford, reserving his scorn for places like the University of California, which have wrongly attempted a "mass education" that can never possibly succeed. The older private institutions, in his view, have retained a realistically low view of human nature; they are doing valuable work, and should at all costs keep their independence from other forces in the society. Many contradictions run through these various attitudes, not least of which is the fact that he, a plain Southwesterner, married a well-to-do New Englander whom he now continually "confronts" with the accusation that she is a snob.

Less emotional in tone, yet no less strongly argued, is his conviction that the whole course of Western civilization, at least since the Reformation, has been fundamentally wrong, and that he has personally seceded from Western culture. He applies this point of view to everything from music to mathematics. (Conventional music, he argues, drugs the mind, reducing one's degree of awareness.) Thus in his own thinking, the community he has created is entirely non-Western, despite the fact that its visible face is so largely scientific and even technological.

Science indeed poses a difficulty for him. In one breath he will appear to attack the Western scientific tradition for its narrowness and externalism, in the next he will seem to embrace it, defining it as an elite occupation which the Western masses themselves have never truly comprehended. One evening he seriously claimed that American culture was hostile to science and especially to the habit of precise measurement. I thought I could hear Benjamin Franklin stirring just a bit beneath the sod. Western notions of causality (that C follows B follows A) he will criticize in the spirit of the meta-historian J. G. Bennett. But again he will say that reason is necessary and useful, at least in its place, and that everyone here must study logic and scientific method. Trained minds, in this sense, are what he wants to produce, certainly not minds that bask in a continual ecstatic "high." Becoming more precise about what he means, he will say that Western culture has made science and money into its central preoccupations. The new civilization will retain science and technology, but only among a number of other "vectors" which form its configuration of values. Science will be retained as a tool at the service of life, but it will no longer call the tune. This position, while entirely defensible (and even, to my mind, rather attractive), by no means reconciles all the extreme statements about science, pro and con, which he made within my hearing.

On more concrete matters of history and politics, which he does still talk about from time to time, Ezra reveals a greater degree of seeming idiosyncrasy, though no less fervency of conviction. Many of his statements in this realm have an arbitrary, disconnected quality. Thus he once volunteered a curious list of organizations which, like his own group, are helping to create the new culture: Esalen; the Institute for Advanced Study; the Lawrence Radiation Laboratory; and the Center for the Study of Democratic Institutions. Another day, however, he sharply distinguished Esalen from his own community, claiming that it was seeking through pretentious means to adjust people to their present lives, like all psychoanalysis. Again, he will suddenly say that he thinks J. Edgar Hoover and Ronald Reagan have "a point," to use his phrase, about the danger of Communist infiltration in the New Left. There is a definite anti-Communist undertone in his thinking, though he is respectably anti-fascist as well. "The gutter elite, the *fascisti,* would close us down immediately if they ever came to power in America," he said to me. And he made the comparison with Socrates' fate in Athens. But, in another context, he claimed that Franklin Roosevelt had really surrendered to all the large corporations just before the outbreak of the Second World War. Altogether I had the distinct impression, despite Ezra's apocalyptic vision of the rottenness and doom of the old culture, that the wisps of concrete political conviction which he had carried over into this phase of his life were moderately conservative in many instances, more congenial to a straight than to a hip view of what was going on. The white-controlled nations of the British Commonwealth figure strongly in his planetary vision of the future, and with no seeming awareness of the reactionary racial implications in this perspective. A man with a partly Southern background, Ezra says nothing that would reveal so much as a casual sympathy for the civil rights movement. No blacks are in his group, and their absence never seems to be commented upon. It is clear, from many angles, that his is not a left-wing group by any definition. Yet it would not be at all fair to call it a right-wing group either. At bottom, it is truly nonpolitical. Ezra explicitly pictures us as living in Rome around zero A.D., beginning an underground work which may not bear widely visible fruit for several centuries. Beside this conception of one's place in history, ordinary political implications rapidly fade.

A deeper symptom than politics of the malady of Western civilization, as he conceives it, is the nuclear family structure. Here his attitude is entirely clear-cut. The triadic form of mother-father-child leads to self-destruction. The character of Oedipus is interpreted as a liberated one from his point of view—he is a person who has seen through all these conventional limitations and has freed himself from their tyranny. Revolt against one's own parents is assumed to be the normal course in life, and it should be accomplished without lingering guilt. As against the Western family structure, Ezra refers with rather wistful enthusiasm to the polygamy of Islam. (Could his strong pull toward Sufism have this as a further basis?) In such a notion there is, incidentally, more than a hint of male dominance. With the recent spread of talk about women's liberation, the women in the community have begun holding weekly meetings of their own. But the content of these meetings, as reported to me, would scarcely go against the philosophy appropriate to a rather well-educated harem. The La Crescenta branch of the Vedanta movement is now far more genuinely woman-oriented than this community, all of whose members exist under the spell of a single male leader, highly alive to his own powers.

Behind all these particular convictions and prejudices, there lies a mind which is strongly absolutistic, characteristically satisfied with schematic classifications. It is thus, like J. G. Bennett's own mind, a survival from the nineteenth century, yet, far more than Bennett's, it can disguise itself in a seemingly up-to-date and supple posture. But, when it connects with a word like "truth," its genuine dimensions are revealed. "Truth" is not a word which Ezra ever regards playfully or ironically, in the way that has now become widely general. Instead it is taken with deadly earnestness. "You can't disagree with any truth," Ezra declaimed during my longest interview with him. "Truth cannot contradict itself. In Western life people are always disagreeing. But we are only seeing small parts of the elephant. If there is disagreement then there is not an understanding of the truth." Again, when parts of the Declaration of Independence were read after dinner on the Fourth of July, Ezra commented that neither "property" nor "pursuit of happiness" was an adequate third term to follow "life" and "liberty." And he proposed that "truth" should have been inserted there instead. He often puts forward an entirely closed view of the nature of science: "We already have all the facts, and all we need do is apply them properly."

Truth is organized, fixed, final. It became clear during the course of my stay that Ezra takes seriously all the various charts and enneagrams which have been painted on the wall of the dining room. He expects the members of the group to learn them by heart and to refer any questions they may have to them. Behind this attitude lies the assumption that any entity contains a finite number of interrelated elements. It is an assumption common both to Gurdjieff and to the more old-fashioned aspect of the Western scientific tradition. Revolting, at least in part, against Western science, Ezra seems to have landed somehow among the philosophers of the 1850's and 1860's, who still give him his basic intellectual cues.

He reminds me of this earlier epoch also in his willingness to settle rapidly for easy definitions. "What is life?" he asked rhetorically one night during a session preparing for the ecology conference. Only briefly did he pretend to let the group fumble for an answer before he announced triumphantly: "The *cell* is life." This was the profound truth that the audience was expected dutifully to write down in its notebooks. Yet at other times, as when introducing the topic of Buddhism in his Thursday-night lectures, he also knew how to retreat into the driest, most noncommittal form of academicism (telling everyone that it was "important" to study Buddhism, but taking no overt stand on its truth), though even here his rendition of the subject was highly schematic, brimming with overprecision.

Far more powerful than his solemnly literal truth telling is Ezra's critical cutting edge, vividly ridiculing its targets, both personal and in the realm of ideas. Equally impressive is his facility at reaching for concrete examples, often taken directly from the lives and problems of individuals who are present. But still more relevant to explaining his intellectual force is the tone of utter conviction in which he says everything. It is a tone which makes contradiction impossible, no matter whether he is bullying or being thoroughly engaging. With this constant tone of voice and the glazed directness of his eyes he welds submission and belief. Still, at the dinner table one or two of the more skeptical members would occasionally challenge him up to a certain point, or merely say with reluctance that they were unable to follow his direction. To them he replied that they were using their "intellects" too much at the expense of the other "centers" that form their makeup, or that they were "blocking" or "resisting" him mentally. Any suggestion that is not on his own wave length is put down as evidence of such "resistance," and the person is made to feel that he should get his own mind in better order fast. Or, if an independent thought is ventured, one that does not play into his hands, he may simply ignore it and rapidly pass on. Thus he never loses control of a conversation, whether during the height of an open confrontation, or in the most innocuous moment of a Sunday-afternoon teaparty. This constant air of command is essential to his leadership. The tone of unshakable conviction causes the inconsistencies, the exaggerations, the merely garrulous meanderings to which he sometimes falls victim to be forgotten, to become blurred in the single, uniform, ongoing impression of intellectual and personal power.

The classic textbook version of the ideologue emphasizes an extreme rigidity, an inability to adapt pragmatically, like middle-of-the-road leaders, to circumstances. But Ezra's style is more adroit than this model would allow. There are strong hints that when his abstract ideas clash directly with urgent necessity, the latter wins out. A small example of this was the decision, which he personally issued, to abandon the weekly watering schedule (over which such great fuss had been made) when it appeared that most of the plants might really die during the prolonged drought. But the same tendency can be observed in the shrewd business sense underlying the group's deals for land. One foot remains solidly planted on the ground while all the ideas spin.

In another important respect, Ezra does conform to one's expectation of such a figure. This is in his hyper-seriousness and general (though not total) lack of humor. At a theater rehearsal he once pondered out loud why it was that he chose to spend all his time working with such a small number of people, when, in his own words, he could be lecturing to hundreds or thousands. He said it was because this group is to form the leaders of other similar groups in the future; because it is the special elite, the nucleus. The closest he ever came to a joke at the group's own expense was once in an afterdinner discussion, when he casually predicted that at some future time their effort would probably become institutionalized and fossilized like everything else. Many immediately broke into a hearty, knowing laughter. But such an episode is brief and rare. Far more revealing and true to form is the sense of threat which he and the others earnestly display at the idea that the universe, at bottom, may be nothing more than a cosmic joke. Whenever this notion manages to appear (and why it ever does so is another interesting question), it is treated as something terrible, to be immediately disposed of, preferably by an intense gust of ridicule. Here, one gathers, is an intellectual enemy of peculiar importance.

Underlying all his flexibility, his considerable agility of mind and temperament, there is a terrible hardness. His elitism springs from a genuinely low view of human nature. Enmity and hazard are for him the basic conditions of life. Every so often Ezra uses the word "loving" in a sneering, contemptuous way, just as he also uses the word "democracy." Unclean people, he says, clean each other through their mutual abrasion—one hand scouring the other, while both remain nothing more than ordinary hands. It is a fundamentally grim view of life. "Even one day is a terribly long time for anyone to waste." The new social order comes to seem like the last outpost of Massachusetts Bay.

At times Ezra can be genuinely brilliant. Once he gave an incidental discourse on American history which I, as a teacher in the field, felt to be a pithier, more powerful treatment of the subject of nineteenth-century "pioneering" than I would probably have given myself, even if it exaggerated to make its point. There were *no* pioneers in the romantic sense of our schoolbooks, Ezra stated flatly. "Pioneering" is a nostalgic myth superimposed upon the past. Instead, America at that time was already advanced technologically as compared with most other regions of the world. Large areas of the West were settled after the railroad and canal had arrived, making matters relatively easy. The so-called pioneers were actually a highly advanced, acquisitive, skillful people who were also closely tied in to the private-property system and a network of business interests. George Washington had been a land surveyor and speculator. The whole process was a vast real-estate grab, undertaken by an energetic, shrewd, exploitative, and very nearly industrialized people who knew full well what they were doing. That this account was somewhat crudely Beardian cannot, of course, be denied. But the point is that for five minutes Ezra lectured on the broad sweep of earlier American history in a way that made every sentence neatly and provocatively hit its target. I was greatly impressed.

He does not sustain this brilliance; his conversation all too often lapses into arbitrariness, confusion, and obscurity. After about three weeks I found myself beginning to get bored. I began to get tired of having to look forward to an hour, or an hour and a half, of nightly conversation, sitting motionless at the closely packed dinner table. The sound of his self-assured voice had become so deeply familiar, such an inevitable, recurring fact of life, that it destroyed my initial fascination, which had been very real. I also knew that no one else present felt the way I did.

Ultimately I came to realize that neither the group's commitment nor my own growing detachment were the product of Ezra's ideas, his mind in the narrow sense. His hold over the members was a total, personal hold.

The common denominator of their biographies was no earlier intellectual or psychological tendency, but the brute fact of this hold, which in most cases had taken effect with astonishing rapidity after an initial encounter. Similarly, my growing aversion was based not upon a peculiar reaction to the belief system (for Christianity is scarcely more credible on its face than J. G. Bennett), but upon seeing what Ezra did to other people. Again and again at the dinner table I would observe him creating opposition from nothing, by means of enormously exaggerating the ambiguity of what someone else had innocently said, and making this the basis for a personal accusation of "lying," "resisting," "blocking," being "negative" or "stupid." Though confrontations could always be excused as necessary private "tests" for the person involved, in purely human terms they added up to one person taking unfair advantage of another, rubbing his or her nose in the subservience that had already been freely coughed up. I realized that there was no clear way to tell where ideology left off and nose rubbing began, since Gurdjieff's beliefs gave a leader with such propensities free scope. But I could not enjoy the sight of such techniques in practice, even if they had been disguised in a Christian ideology of love for one's neighbor. The members are conditioned to accept Ezra's view that there is never such a thing as an "honest mistake." Every personal error, real or invented, must be an occasion for deep inward soul searching and correction. Guilt, abasement, and self-hatred may indeed offer the ruggedest timber for the building of a new civilization. But it is not pleasant to behold the man actually wielding the axe.

On top of everything else, Ezra can be astonishingly open about his awareness of the effect he is creating. At dinner he once said it was "amusing" to see everyone here working sixteen or seventeen hours a day and feeling guilty, anxious, and depressed at the same time. The lesson he drew from it was that they had a fixation with the idea of failure. But to me he appeared to be gloating about the success of his psychological handiwork.

How can the committed members of the group see Ezra so differently from the way I see him? The constant response is one of admiration shading into awe. When he tells them he might burn the ranch down and throw them all out into the world, their reaction is to pledge themselves to work harder and harder. Only occasionally, with Eva and one or two other longtime members of the community, is there open discussion of the fact of their dependency upon him. The common pattern among people on the ranch is to speak of Ezra only rarely, and then always in connection with some matter-of-fact item of business. I think this amounts to a continual repression within their minds of the fact of his domination. It is something that they simply prefer not to think about on too broad a level. This interpretation is strengthened by their tendency either to be evasive (actually changing the subject without realizing it) or to deny the extent of his influence, when the matter of his role is forced upon their attention. One of the men began telling me what an overwhelming intellect Ezra had, and briefly commented that it did have the effect of making the rest of them too passive. But he followed this with a kind of set statement, copied from Ezra himself, to the effect that "I (Ezra) am not the teacher, you are all the teachers," an oddly transparent discrepancy in view of the fact that Ezra freely describes himself, on most occasions, as their "teacher." Another of the men, who opened up to me very fully, declared that the discipline here was not external or imposed; he insisted that I would miss the innermost reality of the undertaking if I didn't see it as a collective phenomenon, the result of the interplay of each individual's vibrations and external efforts. Casual visitors will even be given an account of how the group operates "democratically," which avoids mentioning Ezra entirely.

Beyond this level of reinterpretation, the members evidently have a need to avoid dwelling upon Ezra's role in their lives. And this in itself is interesting. Present-day American culture does not place a high value upon abject obedience. In this respect, Swami Paramananda's nuns had been much more oblivious of outside norms and therefore more forthright in acknowledging the reality of their personal subjection, which they openly gloried in. Perhaps the difference is due to the fact that the nuns were entirely women, and women with the more readily submissive self-conception of an older generation.

The Old in the New

In sociological terms—the way in which it combines diverse elements into a pattern of living—the group is quite distinctive and rather original. But, from the standpoint of intellectual history, or in terms of the psychology of its leader-follower relationships, the continuities between it and earlier tendencies in American cultural radicalism (and, for that matter, the mainstream) seem highly pronounced. How one deals with this paradox will determine one's final estimate of this community. The case for novelty has already been made, in the description of life style and emerging collective norms.

"Gurdjieff defined man as a 'cosmic apparatus for the transformation of energy.' "[66] Fascination with energy sources is no mere product of the

66. J. G. Bennett, *Energies: Material, Vital, Cosmic* (Kingston-upon-Thames: Coombe Springs Press, 1964), p. iii.

present modish concern for ecological harmonies. Belief in using the will to increase one's personal store of energy lies at the very core of what has been called "the mind-cure" tradition in American popular thought. It is a tradition which goes back for at least a century. And, as such figures as Gurdjieff, Nicoll, and Bennett remind us, it is really an international tradition. Somewhat similar quests for "self-development" along these lines were occurring both in Moscow and Los Angeles around the year 1915. In a milder, non-authoritarian way, the New Thought movement paralleled the early Gurdjieff groups in seeking to tap the ever-normal reservoirs of cosmic strength. Through all such groups, whether broadly democratic or esoterically elitist, runs the following theme: that unenlightened man is weak, "asleep," drained of vitality; that men (or some "advanced" men and women) can willfully transform themselves into powerful, dynamic, and, yes, successful individuals, able to manipulate their surroundings, because they learn to unlock the cosmic reservoir and bathe themselves in its infinite vitality. Later, in the 1930's, such derivative but extreme movements as the I Am and Mankind United dwelt even more nakedly upon energy, power, and manipulation as their obsessive central concerns.

On this level the aim of the contemporary group in New Mexico is indeed hoary with age. In one sense it links directly with the positive-thinking tradition popularized by Norman Vincent Peale. ("You're being negative" is a favorite term of reproach on the New Mexico ranch.) The existence of exercises to promote mental concentration, relaxation, and subjugation of the body to the mind's will further reveals such a tie.

The tradition of self-development through will power has had to face an increasingly strong rival during the last half century, in the version of Freudianism which argues that head-on willful attack upon "problems" is self-defeating and hopeless, and that a fully liberated expression of one's impulses and "instincts" alone provides the real breakthrough. A battle has raged, in psychoanalytical circles and elsewhere, between the upholders of ego and conscious self-direction and believers in unleashing the primitive and the unconscious, weakening the ego if need be, as in the taking of LSD. To be sure, rank-and-file seekers after cosmic energy do not always pay heed to this distinction. They may indiscriminately pursue Yoga, drugs, and fasting (which is partly willful, partly a short-circuit of the will). But, if one studies the rhetoric of self-development, one finds that much of it divides itself logically into these two approaches.

The community in New Mexico reminds us that this long-term battle between them is still raging, perhaps linked in some way with the split between anarchism and discipline, spontaneity and structure. The spokesmen for the New Age are still taking sides on the matter, and on this ranch the attitude is an uncommonly extreme one. The coming civilization, it appears, will have its Arminians as well as its Antinomians. If Ezra's group is any indication, there is no danger that salvation will be offered on too easy a set of terms. Therein, perhaps, lies the distinction between the widely popular versions of mind cure, such as those of New Thought and Peale, and the "underground" or esoteric versions of Gurdjieff, the I Am, and Ezra's undertaking. Here anxiety and fear are much greater and lie much closer to the surface, as compared to the input of bland optimism in the ultimate outcome.

Seen in these terms, this particular New Age group has many of the same signs of strength as did the earlier ones. It may have the strength, that is, to survive, among very small numbers of people, for at least several decades. And this capacity places it in altogether another category from the communes of the hip counter-culture, whose life expectancy seems measured in a very few summer and winter seasons.

Beneath a few surface trappings, the style of the shrewd, self-confident guru does not appear greatly to change from one generation to the next. In this sense, Paramananda and Ezra are almost interchangeable in their mastery of a clear-cut role. They are fascinating not as spokesmen for a particular time and place, but as representatives of a remarkably persistent strain in the long-term history of cultural radicalism. The urge to gather a band of admiring disciples, to regulate their lives in every respect, and to confirm one's hold over them by giving them an extraordinary mission which requires them to break their ties with the outside world seemingly has a perennial quality. A similar but milder urge drove the Ferms to create a school at Stelton which would build a wall between the children and the materialistic values of American society.

The record of counter-cultural movements seems to suggest that, even in the United States, the most heavily authoritarian and intensely charismatic of these social movements possess the greatest internal élan. Though the number of people they can hope to attract is severely limited, those who do join acquire a loyalty not easily broken in the course of a lifetime. In contrast to the relatively faddish commitment of millions of youth to a new life style in a decade like the 1960's, the far smaller numbers who attach themselves to a leader and a system of beliefs in this more intense fashion— whether in 1910 or in 1970—are more likely to remain where they are, unyielding until death. Intellectually, the mystical and occult tradition appears to be a peculiar home of such movements, though they are certainly not unknown in the political realm.[67]

67. For further discussion of this point, see p. 462.

Ezra's group distinguishes itself from earlier mystical movements by an insistence upon rapid-fire visible applications of its accumulated internal power. Here the inner and the external are more truly blended, though the inner has been much redefined in the process. Unlike the I Am movement around 1938, it does not waste its energy gathering in the Shrine Auditorium to "blast" Franklin D. Roosevelt by mental decrees. Instead, it raises tomatoes and performs Greek plays. Also, whatever their limitations in ultimate independence of mind, it gathers an altogether more lively and intelligent kind of person, as it could do at a moment in history when dropping out appealed to some of the most hard-driving and talented youth of both sexes. The community carries a tone of genuine adventure and robust physical pioneering which purely "spiritual" enterprises based on the same inner philosophy sadly lack. Never before have the memory of nineteenth-century frontiersmanship, the philosophy of rural decentralism, and the tradition of willful self-development been so interestingly combined. But, if it has to be done by a guru of the authoritarian stripe, once again—as with Vedanta—is it worth the price? Only a desperate assessment of the American and global future permits the members to keep on reaffirming that it is so. Perhaps most of us who come upon such a scene from the outside will find its cost in terms of lifelong inner subjugation an unbearable one to pay.

Then, too, there is the further paradox that this group so strikingly emphasizes the time-honored values of diligence, hard work, and never-ending drive toward achievement. Even more than the Ferms had done at Stelton, it offers an exaggerated repetition of precisely the qualities that "made America great" from the beginning. Its ethos therefore stands opposed to what is no doubt the most appealing ideal of the broader counter-culture in recent years, the desire to expand rather than contract the generally available supply of human warmth and fellow feeling, to invoke the emotions that lead to a realization of brotherhood and sisterhood, the melting of barriers. Genuinely to work in that direction, whatever the odds, may seem more rewarding than to spend a lifetime deliberately inducing abrasive shocks in the effort to steel one's nerves. The followers of Gurdjieff, even more than those of Vedanta, may well be intensifying their own inner difficulties rather than moving away from them. And, in the social order they produce, the worst psychological failings of conventional industrial civilization may actually be magnified and given freer reign. At the very least, this version of the New Age will resemble the old one far more than its crew of midwives likes to believe.

Seven Months Later

During the last three months of 1971, Ezra's group went through a series of highly traumatic experiences, involving several sudden changes of plan. It faced the anxiety of having to perform well on short notice in an unfamiliar part of the world and then the frustration of being abruptly recalled to the United States, where members were suddenly told that their long-term overseas adventure was to be canceled and that they must return to the bleak New Mexico environment which they had imagined themselves to be abandoning. All in all, one could not have devised a series of circumstances better designed to test the loyalties of each member.

Early in the fall the group began a drama tour on the East Coast as scheduled, playing to several university audiences in the Boston area. Though their reception was reasonably good at several campuses, in Cambridge they felt themselves snubbed. Previous arrangements were not honored, and the last-minute audiences they secured were very small. The group appears to have reacted to the experience of a cold reception at Harvard in a particularly extreme fashion. The remainder of its Eastern tour was instantly canceled and the decision made to travel to England instead. Ezra wrote to me from there, stating somewhat mystifyingly: "Psychic situation in U.S. such that we are now in London. . . ."

The group spent three weeks in England. Besides visiting the seventy-five-year-old J. G. Bennett, the group presented its plays during a two-week run in London. Initial reviews were discouraging, and again morale sank disastrously. In the midst of this Ezra decided to fly by himself to India, on only a moment's notice, but he ordered the group to complete its scheduled run and to get "good reviews" before it finished. Individuals were told they should then travel all over the world on assignments to study particular topics relevant to future projects; for instance, one person was to go to Bali. But Ezra himself would not be on hand for the dispersal. The group was to reunite on the land it had purchased on still another continent, where its future home was to be.

Three people—Mona, Brenda, and Gypsy—had already deserted the group before it flew to England. Now, after Ezra suddenly abandoned them, leaving them with all these demanding and complicated instructions, a major internal crisis developed. Toward the end of their stay in London, the strain upon their loyalty, in unfamiliar surroundings and with uncertain financial arrangements, was too great for a minority of the members. At least four persons—Champ, Jacob, Melinda, and Herb—seceded from the group at this time. Moreover, they did so more or less in a body.

The others still did as they had been told. An advance party of several members was already on the site of their new overseas headquarters, having gone there from New Mexico earlier in the fall. Others actually departed from London for such locations as Bali. But then the new bombshell broke. The group would not leave the United States after all. The "psychic situation" had changed entirely once again. Instead, everyone was asked to assemble post-haste in an old house temporarily rented in Los Angeles. After spending a few weeks there, the members were to put on a West Coast drama tour and then return to the New Mexico property for the indefinite future (though with time out for a visit to Alaska during the coming summer).

By this time, in one way or another, several other persons had defected, including Frieda, Georgia, and Harriet. Another member, Lisa, was not with the group, but was expected to rejoin it after it returned to New Mexico. Betty Jo was still attached, but the decision had broken up her marriage, for her husband, Frank, who had been with her for a time in New Mexico during the summer of 1971, sorrowfully exited from the house in Los Angeles, refusing to take further part in the group's affairs.

Altogether, roughly a third of the group as it had existed in July and August of 1971 was shaken loose by this rapid sequence of events. The defecting third included many of the most talented, stable, and forceful members, although it also included Champ, the perennial troublemaker, and Herb, whom I had pegged as unusually docile in his style of obedience.

When I learned the names of those who were gone, and those who had stayed, I realized that I could never have predicted them on the basis of my visit during the previous summer. *Ex post facto,* I could easily think why each of them might well have reached such a decision: Georgia and Frieda were looking forward to life overseas with special keenness and had openly confessed that it was a major factor in their desire to stay with the group; Melinda really believed in a romantic style of freedom and in that sense had never properly fit in with things; Herb, owing to his very lack of initiative, might well stick with Melinda if forced to make such a choice; Mona had been unusually reticent with me in New Mexico, and with hindsight this might suggest the existence of doubts; Brenda's skepticism had been open and constant. Only Gypsy, Jacob, and Champ were the really big surprises, though all of them were strong, forceful personalities, and perhaps it could be expected that they would assert themselves at some time if pressed too far.

But it is all too easy, of course, to speculate in this fashion after the fact. There were many surprises, when all is said, not only among those who departed but among those who remained. For instance, the previously off-again, on-again Lennie not only had returned and was still with the group, but he had cut his hair short and shaved off his beard. And Celeste, who confessed to no deep commitment in the summer of 1971, was enthusiastically on hand in Los Angeles. Longevity of previous commitment certainly furnished no clue, since Mona and Laura had joined almost together, back in the old days in San Francisco, and yet Mona alone decided to leave. (And Laura had been paired with Champ, who did leave.) Moreover, one should recall that a number of those who remained faithful during this particular six-month period had experimented with departure from the group at some previous time. Indeed, the one prediction I was tempted to make after surveying the missing names in February, 1972, was that at least one or two of them would trickle back into the group at some time in the future.

The really striking fact was that roughly two-thirds of the group had been willing to stay with it through such an extreme series of trials and disappointments. To sit down with them at their regular evening dinner in Los Angeles, on Lincoln's Birthday, 1972, observing no important changes in their style of thinking, speaking, or behaving, was a most remarkable experience. To balance the missing faces there were three new members, and one recalled how the group had gone through similar "purges" at earlier periods in the history of its migrations ever since 1967. The toughness and cohesiveness of its central core seemed now utterly beyond challenge. Several of the strongest and stablest members remained—Gene, Laura, and Eva, to name only three. As I spent nearly eight consecutive hours with them that day in Los Angeles, it seemed to me that in only two cases might there have been a distinct deterioration of personality since I had left them.[68] This was balanced by a contrary impression that several of them were much warmer and more outgoing and relaxed than they had been when in New Mexico.[69] Beyond all these signs, the simple fact stared out of the overwhelming continuity of form, style, and action. Twenty places were set for dinner that night, not counting my own, and the evening proceeded exactly as it might have the summer before in every possible respect.[70]

68. In both instances, these persons seemed to have grown a tougher protective shell, making them appear to an outsider as less responsive, less flexible, more like living automata.

69. In part, of course, this may have been a result of the fact that I was now an "old" or "returning" acquaintance. Some of them were doubtless proud to be displaying themselves to me, their historian, knowing that I would note who was still in the group.

70. The only important novelty was their willingness to hire a paid outside baby-sitter during certain hours of the day.

The level of the group's theatrical efforts did seem to be slipping, if one could judge from a single rehearsal. Two of the better actors, and the girl responsible for the outstanding costumes, were among those who had left the group. One of their original plays had now been rewritten substantially for future productions, but in a way that struck me as notably worse than the earlier version. The changes seemed to be the result of too much tinkering with the previous play in an intellectual vacuum, rather than of fresh contact with an audience mind. Less and less was being said to the world outside.

I had other highly subjective impressions during my brief return to the group. In the first minutes of conversation with Ezra, when he was earnestly explaining to me the reasons for their decision to return permanently to the United States, I was hit (as never quite before) with the feeling that in some simple sense he might not be entirely rational. It was a response that took me quite by surprise, as we stood together on the cement driveway. Rapidly he was pouring out the following sequence of thoughts, as if they formed a logical argument: The world situation had totally changed in the last few months, first, through the devaluation of the dollar and secondly by the emergence of India as a world power in the course of its war against Pakistan (which occurred at the very time when he, Ezra, had been in India). Therefore the group could safely return to the American fold, even though, as Ezra himself went on right away to admit, the Nixon administration had not supported India in the war. It was clear, from things said at dinner that evening, that Ezra believed a fundamental turning point had occurred, one which allowed the group again to work within the American system, indeed to consider itself intensely patriotic, though the "planetary" ideal was not altogether forgotten.

That evening during Ezra's usual lengthy discussion-oration, I was more aware than I had been in New Mexico of vagueness and confusion and tedium, though I still saw flashes of uncanny accuracy and forceful technique on his part.

There was, to be sure, a likely rationale for many of the group's recent changes of plan. The decision to abandon the East Coast tour and go to England was doubtless the result of a somewhat paranoid (but in a way quite understandable) overreaction to the generally "cool" environment of Harvard. The decision to give up the overseas migration had an even more practical basis. The New Mexico property, it turned out, had never actually been sold, though two buyers in succession had placed options on it, keeping their hopes high for a time. Lacking money from this sale, the group may well have been unable to carry through with the deal for the land it had acquired abroad. At this point, the devaluation of the dollar (mentioned by Ezra in his account of the "psychic situation") may have figured on a purely mundane level, for it would have increased the cost of such property to an American buyer. It seems probable, therefore, that Ezra directed the group to return to New Mexico only because there was no other economically sensible alternative. And, if all this is true, then at bottom Ezra is still of highly sound mind. In a way, one can even see the functionality of creating stories about changes in the worldwide "psychic situation" to cover such an impasse. Without them, the group's impotence before ordinary small-scale economic difficulties would be too nakedly revealed, and the resulting demystification would be too severe.

On another level, the group's renunciation of its more extreme posture of alienation from American society appears once again interestingly to parallel much wider changes in the American climate. If the group veered in a more uncompromisingly radical direction around 1968-1969, that was a season when militancy and polarization had reached a peak. Now, at the end of 1971, its decision to continue living inside the United States came in a time of decreasing violence and social tension, marked by a new willingness in many sectors to resume working within the system.

One does not usually dream of a day's events on the same night that they have occurred. But that night in Los Angeles I dreamed I was walking along a city street with several members of the group, and suddenly I surprised myself by opening up to them very apologetically, almost sobbing. I told them how close I had come to wanting to join with them and how sorry I was that it just could not be. The striking thing about this dream was its revelation of how deeply I had been pulled toward them on an interior emotional plane, although I had always wanted to think of myself as a detached observer. The tone of the dream ran strongly counter to all my moment-by-moment reflections of the day preceding. Consciously I had been tempted toward harsh summary judgments of the kind which I had tried so hard to avoid while in New Mexico. On an unconscious level, I was unburdening (and perhaps freeing) myself of lingering emotional obligations. There is a certain justice in recording the dream alongside these other, far colder final impressions.[71]

71. As of May, 1973, the group remained in existence.

And then there was the immensity of the crowd. God, how can you capture the feeling of being with 400,000 people and everyone being stoned on something? Were we pilgrims or lemmings? Was this really the beginning of a new civilization or the symptom of a dying one? Were we establishing a liberated zone or entering a detention camp? . . . Heh, there certainly are a lot of questions that come to mind.

—Abbie Hoffman, *Woodstock Nation*
(New York: Random House, 1969), p. 92.

CHAPTER SIX

The Trend of American Cultural Radicalism

What then is strange and what is familiar about the surge toward cultural radicalism in the 1960's? The signs of strangeness were visible everywhere on the surface.[1] Suddenly around 1965-1967 a new way of living revealed itself on many American streets and in the national parks. It flaunted a defiance of basic conventions, brazen in its seeming casualness. Public exhibition was indeed bound up in it; boldness helped confirm a new identity. Youths whose parents often had plenty of money, who could speak complicatedly if they wanted to, chose to use four-letter words, wear rags, and walk barefoot in the broken glass of Massachusetts Avenue. Wildly painted figures danced unannounced into classrooms during final exams, releasing balloons. A boy from Maine advertised his bodily liberation by having the word BARE stamped on his Volkswagen's license plates. It was not unknown for young faculty members to go off and live in trees.

The racial and sexual hangups of centuries' standing seemed to melt overnight. Blacks and whites held hands openly in the lines outside art theaters. On a California commune, a girl and man made love during her labor pains, a few minutes before she gave birth to their son; then she ceremonially ate her own placenta. The underground press cheered an

1. Thus Theodore Roszak defined a counter-culture as "a culture so radically disaffiliated from the mainstream assumptions of our society that it scarcely looks to many as a culture at all, but takes on the alarming appearance of a barbaric intrusion." *The Making of a Counter Culture* (Garden City, N.Y.: Anchor Books, 1969), p. 42. Roszak's discussion of change and continuity is very offhand. The best treatment of the problem which I have seen is Michael Lerner, "Anarchism and the American Counter-Culture," *Government and Opposition,* V (Autumn, 1970), 430–55, though it dwells disproportionately on the question of violence.

honest Boston boy who reportedly took his girl to watch him having group sex with several gay friends before spending the rest of the night with her. In the same city visitors were told, with what exaggeration we'll never know, that "they were doing it on the sidewalk" along Charles Street during the invasion of flower children in 1968. By 1970 it was possible to walk into a movie theater in quite a few parts of America and watch attractive couples perform the act of love in explicit close-up from start to finish. Crowds were drawn to a film which good-humoredly celebrated incest. By comparison, the vaguely sensuous pastoralism of J. William Lloyd's 1902 fantasy might seem only a remote premonition.

On a deeper level than these deeds and postures, the 1960's was an exciting season in which to be alive. During a brief, exhilarating moment, everything seemed possible—as it had for notable minorities in the 1840's and again from about 1912 to 1917. By contrast, the growing predictability of the 1970's is surely not an unmixed blessing. Today many Americans, groping for a sense of where they have now arrived, are seeking to understand the most recent counter-culture, recognizing it as a major landmark. Even though it has so clearly peaked, failing to carry the bulk of American youth with it in any extreme sense, an episode of this kind stays ingrained in the memory. Like the great depression, it will long form a staple of boastful or uneasy reminiscence.

To weigh such a spectacular near-contemporary phenomenon against the record of the past requires unusual care. But an avenue into such comparisons was suggested at the beginning of the book. If cultural radicalism is tied to a number of characteristic areas of intellectual and emotional engagement,[2] then one may inquire into the novelty of the ideals, mood, and behavior of recent radicals in each of these concrete respects. There are also certain broader questions about continuity which can be posed, involving the relations between radicals and the mainstream, the sources of recruitment into radical ranks, the staying power of counter-cultural efforts such as intentional communities, and, finally, the general manner in which radically inclined people have viewed the prospects for the future of mankind, themselves included.

One major formal difficulty is sometimes said to stand in the way of a comparison of this kind. The earlier radical world appears more usually to have comprised a series of specific social movements, i.e., organizations one could join. When an individual announced that he was an anarchist, a socialist, a Theosophist or a Vedantist, the words had a very definite

2. See p. 56.

meaning. The new counter-culture seems to be far more amorphous, defined by shared values and ways of living rather than by card-carrying memberships.[3]

Yet this contrast can be exaggerated. The radicalism of previous generations often took a generalized form. Emerson had called it "the party of the Future," recognizing that in his own day it was already broader than any particular check list of reform societies could reveal. Again, the bohemianism of Greenwich Village in the period before the First World War had all the markings of a counter-cultural upthrust; it signaled a generalized revolt against social conventions. The "youth revolt" of the 1920's was even more inchoate. Finally, the Beat movement of the 1950's, though far smaller in numbers, again involved like-minded individuals who informally shared a common temper.

From the other end, the 1960's witnessed a new array of concrete organizations, among them Ezra's group in New Mexico. Though there was indeed a shift toward greater diffuseness, which in itself was one of the most interesting symptoms of change, it was hardly so clear-cut or all-pervasive as to render historical comparison meaningless. The diversity of the counter-culture from this point of view indeed makes it necessary to go beyond the close study of particular intentional communities, suggestive as this has been, into a wider survey of the contemporary scene. But there are a multitude of landmarks, intellectual and organizational, both in the past and present. The problem is rather one of finding a way through this tangled forest.

The first major area of concern among cultural radicals in my earlier accounting was religious belief. Here recent patterns may seem especially bewildering, yet there are very striking continuities.

Among radicals who are religious believers, the rejection of the older, established church organizations has remained constant (aside from a curious small-scale movement within the Catholic priesthood). Instead, loyalty is transferred to specific new faiths which assume the character of social movements, or else there is an endorsement of a vaguely ecumenical or syncretistic attitude, to the effect that "truth" may be abstracted from all great philosophical traditions. The 1960's spawned a dazzling new array of concrete religious movements, among them the Hare Krishna and the Children of God, thereby revealing that the process of cult formation continues along lines that have been familiar at least since the Swedenborgian

3. The distinction between "general" and "specific" social movements in this sense has been developed by Barry McLaughlin in an unpublished paper.

and spiritualist upthrusts of the 1840's. And all such movements remain rooted in interpretations either of the Bible or of Eastern wisdom, as has always been the case. In the earlier instance of Vedanta, we saw that such specific movements could themselves use the appeal of syncretism as a tactic, advertising universality while actually putting forward a definite faith demanding homage to its own gurus and prophets. Much the same situation prevailed in Ezra's group, where a seemingly eclectic reading list masked the pervasive tie to Gurdjieff and to Ezra himself. Thus even the strategies appear to have changed little.

It is true that a small number of movements have embodied a seemingly more genuine eclecticism. In the 1940's, Gerald Heard's Trabuco College had been in the vanguard of such a trend. The most striking recent attempt of this kind has been made by the Lama Foundation, near Taos, New Mexico. Its tone appears to be somewhat less charismatic, and it is beset by fewer personal handicaps. At least officially, everyone at Lama is free to pursue "truth" on his own.[4] But there are reports that even here the leadership is more overbearing and the search for truth more patterned than one might at first think. In any event Lama and other communes where people are "into" mysticism without being more precise about it have not carried the day. In a sense they concretize the initial stage of the radical life cycle, when one is still a "seeker." But it may be suspected that those who seek will continue to find, ultimately undergoing a definite form of the conversion experience.

A stronger trend in far-out religious circles appears to be one of more openly embracing a psychological as distinct from a spiritual vocabulary of self-development. The psychiatric world view has certainly gained in force in the last several decades, and it has made incursions into the religious realm.[5] The rank-and-file seeker of this generation discusses his or her personal "problems" more freely and candidly, in the expectation that this is the agreed social norm. Yet it is interesting that the flurry of organizations which appeared in the 1960's devoted wholly to self-exploration without religious overtones, such as the encounter groups, Synanon, and Esalen Institute, resulted in rather few full-fledged communal movements. True, there were group marriage experiments, such as Harrad West, but they were individually small and lacking in long-range tenacity. Only Synanon, among such ventures, seemed able to supply the firm cement needed to

4. On Lama, see Robert Houriet, *Getting Back Together* (New York: Coward, McCann and Geoghegan, 1971), pp. 361–70; Richard Fairfield, *Communes U.S.A.: A Personal Tour* (Baltimore: Penguin Books, 1972), pp. 113–30.
5. See pp. 15–16 and 446–47, concerning its failure to win out decisively.

create a durable undertaking. Moreover, the psychiatric world view, like ecumenicism, could often be used as a ploy to attract people to organizations which actually held to the older cosmic philosophy at their core. Again Ezra's community offers a prime example. And this in turn had not been unknown some decades ago, when Vedanta sermons dealt heavily in such topics as "the conquest of fear." Self-development and positive thinking, as the historians Donald Meyer and Richard Weiss remind us, are long-lived traditions which have often been associated with the desire to tap infinite reservoirs of power. The 1960's saw not a creation of these themes, but their widening amid a final divorce from the dream of economic success.

Ultimately what seems most remarkable about the religious scene of the 1960's is the survival of a wholly conventional style of enthusiasm, apart from any form of deeper self-exploration. The Hare Krishna, the Children of God, and the Brotherhood of the Spirit in Massachusetts are far larger than Lama or Ezra's group,[6] and the Jesus freaks might well be able to shout down the believers in Eastern wisdom, if both groups were placed side by side. The desire for old-fashioned 'salvation," basically unchanged since the Great Awakening of the 1740's, competes vigorously even now with the post-Freudian quest for self-discovery. So long as such a yearning familiarly reasserts itself even among the most recent generation of ex-drug users, this highly traditional impetus toward one form of religious radicalism will keep on replenishing itself. But it presents discouragingly little novelty.

On its secular and left-wing face, the radical mood has noticeably de-emphasized militant atheism. The fervent outcry against belief in God, so blatant in anarchist literature of the turn of the century, may be seen as the dated product of the Darwinian controversy. In this respect secular radicalism has taken its tone from the larger culture, both then and now, more than it would be willing to admit. It does not seem terribly relevant in the hydrogen age to spend one's breath denouncing the cosmology of ministers and priests, men who in any event have let it be known that they are no longer sure what they hold to. Expressions of pronounced disbelief can still surface at moments of Papal dispensation, but on the whole they are subdued by earlier standards. The pervasive climate of tolerance and relativism, the assumption that the individual should quietly make up his mind after private deliberation, has here invaded what were once the radical fastnesses of lecture-platform debate. While the religious believers in the counter-culture are vocal and militant, the unbelievers keep quiet.

6. For descriptions of them, see Houriet, *op. cit.*, pp. 331–61.

This dampened mood reflects a growth in sophistication in many sectors of the radical movement. Too much water has passed under the bridge to permit, for instance, a real looking backward to the example of unthinking devotion displayed by nineteenth-century communal groups such as the Amish and Mennonites.[7] The modern search for personal meaning and identity allows no such easy route of escape. Change can subtly intrude on this level even while time-worn forms of religious enthusiasm endure side by side.

Response to authority forms a second major area of radical engagement. Here the attitude has always been dual-edged. Established institutional forms, whether nations or churches, are vehemently rejected, but the charismatic substitute of either a guru or a rebel leader is embraced with surprising frequency. The ideal of "liberation," tied into this transfer of allegiance, has remained constant; perhaps it lies close to the very core of the radical stance.

Radical attitudes toward authority have shown few signs of softening over time. On its negative face, the argument has always begun by insisting upon the right of individuals to withdraw their support from the existing system. "I shall never be satisfied," wrote an anarchist in 1886, "till somebody heads a movement which shall agitate a protest resting solidly in the original root-springs of every species of authority." In personal terms, this meant an assertion of the right "to be let alone—to be allowed to ignore or practically to abolish the State" in one's daily life.[8]

Such a posture becomes conspicuous whenever it enters the political sphere, for the reason that government is actually expected to exercise coercive control over the lives of all of us in the modern world. (Though mystics were similiarly antagonistic toward the authority of Christian churches, the accepted American tradition of voluntarism in religious matters made their outcry seem far less controversial.) The reality of political coercion, however attenuated it may have been in the United States, roused anarchists of earlier decades to the same taut pitch of intransigence which

7. "The Amish and Mennonites have purchased their stability at a price. Their beliefs are fixed. Their communities are closed or nearly closed. They do not seek converts or willingly accept them. Their lives pass on a simple, humble level, for them richly satisfying but not necessarily so for others. One admires them for the same reason that Tolstoy admired the Russian peasants. . . . But their communities can hardly provide a blueprint for intellectually more adventurous spirits who are not prepared to confine themselves within a framework of fixed beliefs." Robert S. DeRopp, *The Master Game* (New York: Delacorte Press, 1968), p. 211.

8. *Liberty,* August 21, 1886, p. 4; Victor Yarros, *Anarchism: Its Aims and Methods* (Boston: Benjamin R. Tucker, 1887), pp. 17–18.

burst upon America in the late 1960's. Thus Paul Goodman daringly wrote in 1942: "The touchstone is this: *to advocate a large number of precisely those acts and words for which persons are thrown into jail.*"[9]

The roots of civil disobedience as a minor but tenacious undercurrent in American life go back to the early nineteenth century.[10] A tradition of tax refusal runs all the way from Henry Thoreau to Benjamin Tucker, Ammon Hennacy, and a somewhat larger group of Americans during the Vietnam War. Avoidance of military service, even at the cost of going to prison, was preached by a few nineteenth-century radicals and became noticeable in 1917 and 1942, though far more conspicuous in the 1960's.

For this reason, the political dimension of the recent counter-culture offers the least evidence of novelty. Domestic opposition to war—always more widespread than outright refusal to bear arms—has been an old American tradition. The public was deeply divided over the merits of the American Revolution, the War of 1812, the Mexican War, and the Civil War. Only the Spanish-American War and the two world wars had constituted rather peculiar exceptions—a partial one in the case of 1917-1918. The protest against Vietnam, which was not merely radical in inspiration, marked the return to what had once been a usual state of affairs. Within this widely based protest, a new upsurge of anarchist sentiment made itself known. But the anti-war movement did not long remain swayed by this mood. A president of only rather ordinary intellectual grasp, launching a policy of typical pragmatic compromise, was easily able to defuse the situation. The strength of resurgent loyalty to the American political system, on the left as well as the right, was striking. To declare oneself forthrightly against the word "patriotism" in all its meanings was to leave one almost as lonely in the 1970's as in 1900. Meanwhile, on a different level, the radical tradition had proved that it was briefly capable, during a moment of general stress, of recapturing the full-scale mood of revolt against authority which had always been its heritage.

In the context of such determined resistance, the less provocative tactic of internal secession was also being put forward long ago. "The problem would be very simple," suggested a writer for the *Firebrand* in 1896, "if the Anarchists possessed enough resources among them to enable them to

9. Paul Goodman, "A Suggestion for a Libertarian Program," *Why?,* I (April, 1942), 8; his italics. Later Goodman came to take a much more philosophical position on these matters.

10. See Laurence Veysey, *Law and Resistance: American Attitudes Toward Authority* (New York: Harper Torchbooks, 1970); Edward H. Madden, *Civil Disobedience and Moral Law in Nineteenth-Century American Philosophy* (Seattle: University of Washington Press, 1968).

be independent of the commercial system for all general purposes."[11] The notion of a counter-culture, or of alternative institutions paralleling the larger society, was alive even then, though as we saw when discussing J. William Lloyd, it ebbed temporarily in the period between the Civil War and the early twentieth century.

If radicals have consistently opposed established authority, they have also been peculiarly receptive to the surrogate forms of it offered by unorthodox leaders. This willingness to find substitutes has appeared within both the secular and religious sides of the tradition. But among mystics the hunger for glamorous and often highly authoritarian way-showers was always especially pronounced.[12] Indeed, the whole fascination with the occult world of powerful superhuman agencies may be interpreted in these terms. "Advanced" beings in the Himalayas or on flying saucers form the most fantastic answers to these all too familiar cravings.

We saw, in comparing the appeal of Ezra with that of such past figures as Swami Paramananda, that the young appear to obtain as much satisfaction from basking in the physical presence of a dynamic guru as did certain of their forebears. Nor do such leaders seem any less sure of their own roles. This aspect of the life of a social movement may indeed be the most perennial. A teacher such as Krishnamurti long ago discovered, when he tried deliberately to renounce the title of spiritual avatar which Theosophists had foisted upon him,[13] that his followers merely declared this to be exactly what a genuinely great soul would do, and from the 1930's to the 1970's they continued to cluster around him whenever he spoke, lining their bookshelves with verbatim transcripts of all his utterances. And of course Krishnamurti continued to speak. (Even the Meher Baba finally renounced his long vow of silence when he could stand it no longer.)

Certain superficial signs do exist of a somewhat greater sophistication on this subject today even among religiously inclined radicals. World experiences during the course of the twentieth century have made most Amer-

---

11. *Firebrand,* May 31, 1896, p. 1.
12. Only rarely was this openly admitted, but see Will Levington Comfort, *Letters: The Mystic Road* (Los Angeles: Comfort Book Room, 1921), II, 190–91. A common practice was to admit that this was indeed a factor explaining their friends' adherence to rival movements, but to insist that it had nothing to do with their own motivation.
13. "I do not want followers, *and I mean this.* The moment you follow someone you cease to follow Truth. . . . You can form other organizations and expect someone else. With that I am not concerned, nor with creating new cages, new decorations for those cages." Krishnamurti, *Dissolution of the Order of the Star,* quoted in Carlo Suares, *Krishnamurti* (Paris: Les Editions Adyar, 1933), pp. 136, 139. For a humane description of Krishnamurti just before the break, see "A New 'Messiah' in Tennis Flannels," *Literary Digest,* XCIX (June 26, 1926), 37–42.

icans somewhat more alert to the dangers of naked authoritarianism. In radical circles it is now inconceivable that children would be required to wear uniforms or be strapped in their beds at night to prevent masturbation, as occurred at the Raja Yoga school during Katherine Tingley's long Theosophical reign at Point Loma. In present-day movements such as Ezra's, we saw that there is a greater effort to disguise the source of authority, to erect a democratic stage set, than ever occurred in Vedanta, where the swamis were discussed reverentially with visitors from the first moment. Nonetheless, when one ponders some of the larger movements in the counter-culture, it is the continuity, the failure to learn lessons from the past, which is far more striking. In America, some people of all ages still display an overpowering need for a fixed anchorage. Ezra's followers revealed the mechanics of the self-deception which remains so easily possible on this score.

Secular radicals, both then and now, have had a somewhat better record in this respect. Anarchists were always more alert to this phase of the problem of authority than were mystics. Their religious skepticism often carried over into the human realm. Though it is true that their ranks were temporarily decimated by the claims of Lenin and Stalin, anarchists who did not thus desert could be proud of their relative immunity to leader worship. In the 1960's, even Bakunin and Kropotkin tended to be taken more lightly, as people who called themselves anarchists turned to the here and now rather than to the past.[14] Communes now often tried boldly to function without leaders, and though the effort (as at Rockridge) produced its own façades and exaggerations, even to make the attempt was to operate in a different universe. The idea of the leaderless group, no matter how impossible of complete fulfillment, was at any rate genuinely refreshing, an instance of counter-cultural novelty at its most experimental and stimulating.

On a broader plane of ideas, decentralization was always the anarchist's answer to the problem of political as well as economic authority. This traditional remedy was revived in the 1960's. If the idea of decentralization suggested an enormous array of practical problems, these had been anticipated—and dealt with as imaginatively as possible—in anarchist literature of the past.[15] On the other hand, anarchists had never properly confronted the issue that in a society without institutions or formal leaders, collective public opinion would become a far worse tyrant than Tocqueville had ever foreseen.[16]

14. See Chapter Three.
15. E.g., see Charles Storm, "Decentralization," *Why?*, IV (July-August, 1945), 2–3, 8.
16. It was this strong patterning of behavior and expectations which disturbed me

The problem of authority, as such groups as the anarchists faced it, has still another major dimension. Besides institutional authority in the larger society, which is rejected, and the personal authority of inspired leaders, which is viewed with increasing skepticism on the secular left, there is the matter of the attitude toward intellectual authority on the most basic level. Here one discovers an important shift in the thinking of nonreligious radicals during the last few years.

Nineteenth-century anarchist writers generally assumed that reason and science were on their side in the attack against all existing institutions. Victor Yarros wrote characteristically in this vein in 1887: "Sickly sentimentalism and ferocious savagery are alike foreign to Anarchism, which is simply and objectively the Science of Society and the text-book of Justice." The anarchists of that day took pride in their ability to convince others on purely rational grounds. Socialists would become anarchists, Benjamin Tucker affirmed, "if they were consistent, logical thinkers; if they were what the French call consequent men,—their reasoning faculties would long since have driven them to one extreme or the other."[17] In the spirit of positivism these men relished the clash of formal debate.[18] Their minds were attuned to the intellectual style which involves raising and answering a whole host of concrete "objections": without government, what would land tenure be like, how could people mail letters and travel on highways, what would be done about education and public health? Behind all these parries and replies one senses the clockwork brain of Enlightenment man still at work, constantly absorbed in the process of calculation. The vocabulary of natural rights and (voluntary) social contract was readily invoked.[19] Again, these radicals believed strongly in a natural uni-

---

at Rockridge. A leading figure in the Home colony innocently declared: "Under freedom—Anarchy—an enlightened public opinion will take the place of laws and jails. . . . If any restraint will be needed, in ostracism will be found a sufficient punishment. No man likes to be shunned by his neighbors. Indeed, so strong is the love of approbation that only under the strain of severe necessity does any man ever do aught that incurs the displeasure of his fellows." Jay Fox in *The Demonstrator*, February 20, 1907, p. 2. Even more ominously, James F. Morton, Jr., also of Home, argued that it would be impossible to shirk physical labor under anarchism because no one could conceal his idleness forever. "Not to work would be a crime inviting the vengeance of the mob!" Editorial, *ibid.*, November 21, 1906, p. 4. See also George Woodcock, *Anarchism* (Cleveland: Meridian Books, 1962), p. 207; James J. Martin, *Men Against the State* (De Kalb, Illinois: Adrian Allen Associates, 1953), p. 84.

17. Yarros, *op. cit.*, p. 7; Benjamin Tucker, *State Socialism and Anarchism: How Far They Agree and Wherein They Differ* (Alpine, Michigan: Charles W. Berman, n.d.), p. [2].

18. See Martin, *op. cit.*, p. 205.

19. E.g., see Ezra H. Heywood in *Lucifer*, November 7, 1890, p. 3; cf. Martin, *op. cit.*, pp. 244–45.

versal harmony—the same harmony in which early nineteenth-century college presidents had placed their faith—and this serene confidence in reason allowed them to argue that all laws and institutions were superfluous.[20] It is striking, to say the least, that a movement which often condoned violence and defended nudism and free love was at the same time so deeply bound up in the seemingly antithetical universe of natural law and appeal to reason. But it was a contradiction shared up to a point by many other perfectionists of the time; anarchists merely went the furthest route in both directions.

Only rarely did radical writers at the end of the nineteenth century invoke a lyrical mood. William Thurston Brown did once affirm that to create the new society was "to feel the thrill of a summons to heroic character. A holier religion than this cannot be. The voice that calls us is the voice of life."[21] Beneath its pompous phrasing, such occasional rhetoric does claim kinship with the resurgent romanticism of the 1960's. But in those years a full-scale appeal to the irrational was very rare; it occurred least of all when discussing matters of sex, diet, and health. J. William Lloyd may seem unusually modern from this point of view, but one must recall that he concluded his second novel with a major formal debate of just the kind that would have seemed most fitting to his reason-bound readers. Similar debates enlivened countless evenings at Stelton. Indeed, the decline in community feeling there may have occurred when these verbal contests began to seem too predictable in the local setting.

Among the interwar anarchists, and more spiritedly among the literary rebels who joined the movement in the 1940's, the basic tone of rational disputation continued to prevail. By contrast the model of man in anarchist thought most recently has been not so much Freudian as Reichian or Jungian. The early Marx introduced by Fromm and Marcuse helped make the transition smooth and painless. Only in some sectors of the political New Left was there adamant refusal to operate tactically on the basis of this altered view of human nature.[22]

This shift away from the standards of calculating reason paralleled a much wider movement of the same kind in American thought during the

20. See "Keynotes for a Free Society," *Free Society,* April 17, 1898, p. 7. One prominent anarchist, Victor Yarros, tried for several years to reconcile anarchism with the thinking of Herbert Spencer. Martin, *op. cit.,* pp. 232–37.

21. William Thurston Brown, "The Springs and Possibilities of Character," *Free Society,* X (May 31, 1903), 3.

22. Political radicals who in the early 1970's still talked of forming alliances between students and factory workers appeared to define themselves as members of this waning minority.

course of the twentieth century. It was small wonder, then, that academic social scientists, who were now among the last serious defenders of the rationalistic world view common in the nineteenth century, often became deeply hostile to the counter-culture, branding it a new "dark age." Joining science and reason to a defense of institutions, unlike the earlier anarchists, such men found themselves in the position of beleaguered conservatives on all counts. Meanwhile, as another result of this shift, anarchists might discover that they had more in common with humanistic believers in inner "self-development" than ever before. The strength of this new bridge between social and psychological versions of radicalism can be exaggerated. But its creation is one of the most notable changes of the last decade.

Pacifism and its extreme alternative, willingness to engage in violence, makes up another running issue in radical ranks. Here to begin with there is an unusual difficulty with the evidence. Published anarchist rhetoric yields little on this topic, despite its emotional urgency at many times during the course of the movement, because of the taboo against washing such controversial linen in public.[23] It is interesting to find Vedanta similarly reticent on the subject of pacifism, apparently because of the great dislike of speaking out on any political matter.

But the lacunae matter less than how the problem is conceptualized historically. Violence and pacifism are issues, far more than authority, which spring to life with startling vividness at particular seasons determined by the flow of events in the larger society. Pacifism comes to the fore during a war, or when the threat of war is great. Radical violence is at least in part a response to the violence of the mainstream—during industrial labor "wars" or again when an armed conflict overseas makes the idea of rebellion at home seem more appropriate or at least forgivable. Indeed, in certain situations, such as the one presented by Nazi Germany, nearly everyone short of a convinced pacifist views a resort to arms, even to kill a leader, with admiration. The judgments of liberals and conservatives in these matters tend in practice to be relative, varying with the appraisals

---

23. See Chapter Two. However, in 1887 Victor Yarros declared: "Gunpowder shook the thrones; dynamite paralyzes majorities." *Op. cit.*, p. 20. The problem of violence has confused some interpreters of the anarchist movement. Michael Lerner, *op. cit.*, pp. 431–37, does not see how torn and divided the earlier anarchists were on this question, e.g., often moving away from violence around 1915. On the other hand, William O. Reichert, "Toward a New Understanding of Anarchism," *Western Political Quarterly*, XX (December, 1967), 856–65, tries wrongly to insist that violence had never been important in the American anarchist tradition. See Martin, *op. cit.*, pp. 253–55. Lerner is right in emphasizing the ambivalent pull of the 1960's counter-culture toward love and toward violence.

given to particular political regimes. A subtle double standard also usually affects these judgments, whereby violence between nations is more easily condoned than violence within a single nation, as if it were somehow more "natural" to kill a foreigner. Anarchists and some socialists, around the turn of the century and again very recently, have applied a negative judgment to American society of the kind which American liberals themselves render to Nazism or to the Union of South Africa.[24] Without granting the validity of this particular parallel, one must accept the fact that all such judgments tend to ebb and flow historically, preventing the easy detection of a long-term trend.

Given the record of warfare in the modern world, it is certainly not true that radicals have been more willing to resort to violence than other people. Instead, what has been unusual is the extent to which they have agonized over such a tactic within their own ranks. Even in the domestic context, radicals have been far more sparing in their actual use of violence than the leaders of major crime syndicates. Here lies a recurrent myth which needs to be put to rest.

Both at the end of the nineteenth century and in Chicago in 1968, a few men and women in America have deliberately courted a marytr's death. (Self-immolation, a new twist on the same theme, reflects the penetration of Asian attitudes and techniques into this realm.) But to chart such incidents is to try to predict the central patterns of world history.

Pacifism, on the other hand, is a very modern idea, at least when it is divorced from a religious context. (It had been pioneered by certain Anabaptists and of course by Quakers and Hindus.) Perhaps only with its arrival in a wholly humanistic frame of reference did violence become an important issue in the minds of secular radicals, for now there was a contrary argument that all life should be held sacred. Though opposition to particular wars has had a long tradition in America, nonreligious conscientious objection is almost wholly a phenomenon of the present century, and its growing acceptability appears to be the product of the immediate situation in the 1960's. Though even now its numerical significance must not be exaggerated, it has made a certain novel impact upon popular consciousness. Within radical ranks, its significance is that it helps to bring mystics (who believe in the sacredness of life because it is divine) closer to humanists of a secular outlook. But much tension continues to threaten such a fragile alliance, based as it is only upon the existence of a common militaristic enemy.

24. E.g., see Henry Addis, *Roosevelt, Czolgosz and Anarchy* (Chicago: Free Society, [ca. 1901]), which, p. 7, defends Czolgosz.

The twin concepts of individualism and community jointly form a focal point in radical thought which poses some of the most baffling problems for historical interpretation. In some combination these goals centrally define the nature of the desired alternative form of society. The changes that have occurred in their meaning for radicals during the last several decades are peculiarly complicated, even though the basic impulse toward forming intentional communities has been so long sustained.

The simultaneous intensification of individual consciousness and communal spirit is a theme at least as old as Rousseau. Radicals from that day forward have generally wanted to develop both these aspects of life until they are expressed at a pitch incomprehensible to the ordinary run of men, for whom the conventional structures of the family and the nation-state provide an unquestioned meaning.

Fused with these twin desires, and complicating them further, is a democratic rhetoric more thoroughgoing than that of most spokesmen for liberalism, and yet, as Michael Wreszin has noted, it collides with a curious elitism which views with contempt the hopelessly unenlightened mass of mankind. This parallel issue of democracy and elitism should be untangled first. Anarchists have been among the earliest promoters of full racial and sexual equality.[25] But they have also (as in the case of Harry Kelly) been prone to give up any real contact with the working class in despair. Again, though professing belief in total democracy, they have revealed an equally pronounced cynicism about the effects of majority rule.[26] Indeed, they seem often to have conceived of themselves as a kind of counter-elite. Emma Goldman called the masses "inert and indolent, crude, lame, pernicious in their demands and influence."[27] "The intelligent and influential few are the sole *active* factors in reform. . . . The masses will not be practically enlisted in the reform movement," echoed Victor Yarros, who thought that the revolution would occur through a minority coup d'état.[28] Henry Addis referred admiringly to "the Thinkers, Philosophers, Humani-

25. For an interesting example of radical egalitarianism on the race question, see *The Demonstrator*, September 5, 1906, pp. 4–5. For the women's rights argument in brief form, see Emma Goldman, *What I Believe* (New York: Mother Earth Publishing Association, 1908), p. 13.

26. "If the real sentiment of the majority was crystallized into legal regulation as would be consistent with majority rule, the intelligent would have nothing worth living for." *The Egoist* (San Francisco), May, 1890, p. 4.

27. Emma Goldman, *Anarchism and Other Essays* (New York: Mother Earth Publishing Association, 1911), p. 84, quoted in Michael Wreszin, "Albert Jay Nock and the Anarchist Elitist Tradition in America," *American Quarterly*, XXI (Summer, 1969), 166–67.

28. Yarros, *op. cit.*, pp. 24–25.

tarians, the men to whom we owe the progress of society."[29] Thus only in limited respects should anarchism (and perhaps certain other left-wing persuasions) be historically termed "leveling" movements. The older anarchism was very different from populism; it stood at least implicitly for rule by the intelligent. This was yet another aspect of its faith in reason. It shared with many academic and literary intellectuals, though perhaps more crudely, the assumption that if businessmen were removed from power and persons with enlightened, scientific views were substituted, the world would be significantly better. Racial and sexual prejudice simply were not compatible with these enlightened standards. And if most American factory workers still went on hungering after a life of beer, possessions, and prejudice, they were to be scorned. Anarchists, like many liberal academics, have often secretly imagined themselves to be superior to the run of mankind.[30]

On the "inner" or mystical side of the radical tradition, elitism was much franker and the rejection of representative democracy more open. Both Gerald Heard at Trabuco and Ezra in New Mexico wanted avowedly to train the leaders of a new civilization—the guides for a "new race" which would transform mankind from above. Operating in the American social context, such men shunned a vocabulary that might sound fascistic; their attitudes were not "right wing" in any definite sense, and they harbored no secret admiration for Hitler. But the tradition of a spiritual hierarchy, a "lodge" or a "Hidden Directorate," inherited from Theosophy in the nineteenth century, prevented them from having any real respect for the "unillumined" mass of mankind. To create the New Age demanded discipline, obedience, and control. The undisciplined horde of hippies might also believe in the New Age, but they were worse than useless until they accepted the need for direction.

The counter-culture of the 1960's did not wholly do away with this half-secret issue. But, especially among left-wing radicals, it softened and muted it. Anarchists of the new generation found themselves able more easily to blend in with the young populists and egalitarian democrats who had just led the liberal crusade for civil rights. Major changes in American society had made possible a marked decline in radical standoffishness. America in 1900 presented a relatively well-marked social order. There-

29. Addis, *op. cit.*, p. 10. C. L. James identified anarchists with "the literary and scientific class." *Origins of Anarchism* (Chicago: A. Isaak, 1902), p. 16.

30. A point strongly emphasized by Judith Shklar, *After Utopia: The Decline of Political Faith* (Princeton, New Jersey: Princeton University Press, 1957), pp. 101–102, 107. Cf. Woodcock, *op. cit.*, p. 34.

after norms of informality and casualness in ordinary human relations gained greater sway in most sectors of the culture, even if these often concealed very important surviving prejudices. The less rationalistic view of human nature which now widely prevailed also made it easier to identify with both the sufferings and the casual pleasures of others. Earlier radicals had posed as would-be intellectuals in an unintellectual society. In the 1960's radicals joined nearly everyone else, except professors, in openly coming over onto the side of anti-intellectualism. Thereby disappeared a crucial element of previous counter-elitist pretension. For all these reasons, it was much easier for a college graduate (or someone laboriously self-taught) to be a populist in the 1960's than it had been in the 1890's. The image genuinely fitted better, even though rebuffs on the blue-collar front gave reminder of a major distance still to be traveled.

Meanwhile, the elitism of the religious mystics remained essentially unaffected. A conception of hierarchy, and of secret knowledge available only to a qualified few, appears to be too intrinsically bound up in this style of belief to permit its erosion. In this important respect, mysticism stood still while the rest of the society altered. In consequence, from this point of view, the distance between secular and religious radicals has recently been increasing. Though the members of the counter-culture in the 1960's may have appeared to dress alike and use the same verbal expressions, they were in fact deeply divided between those who now embraced democracy more believably than middle-class radicals had ever done before, and those who instead became caught up in the special insights of a given spiritual teaching.[31] Though even the latter put on fewer airs than the competitive occultists who gathered at such places as Krotona around 1915, their self-assurance stood out conspicuously in a generation so geared to a mood of open-handedly accepting the idea of general human worth.

All this had to do primarily with the radicals' posture in facing the existing social scene. Equally important was the quality of human relationship which they sought to promote in their own version of the future. In this respect as well, wider changes in thinking in America were to have important effects.

This brings us back directly to the issue of individualism and community. In a formal sense, utopian writings of several decades ago were promoting the mixed demand for a heightened expression of both which one could find in the pages of Rousseau. "Liberty" and "Comradeship" were

31. From this point of view the Jesus freaks, with their emphasis on the universality of salvation, deserve to be called relatively democratic.

the dual mottoes at J. William Lloyd's Vale Sunrise.[32] Superficially they seem to accord with the familiar twin aspirations of the 1960's toward "doing your own thing" and collective fusion.

But this apparent continuity masks very important changes that have occurred in the content of both ideals. A glance back at the radical literature of the late nineteenth century will make this clear. The present-day reader of anarchist pamphlets written seventy or eighty years ago is likely to be jarred by the image of individualism which they contain. The ideal is severely isolationist in its haughty demand for the right to retire from social obligations, and it is primly rationalist in its conception of the differences between one man and another. Especially among the native American writers of this persuasion, individualism has all the ruggedness—if not quite the lustiness—of the same quality in the mainstream. "But let no man take us off our feet; let the officious help of none prevent us from exercising our faculties and unfolding ourselves in accordance with our own law," argued the free thinker William Denton.[33]

Radical individualism of this stripe, it is true, varied significantly from the version of individualism which then dominated American popular thought. Writers such as Denton stressed the naturalness of variety, and therefore of nonconformity, in the constitution of the universe. This was in contrast to the usual emphasis on moral consensus in nineteenth-century oratory. Again, mainstream promoters of economic laissez-faire eulogized competition, which implied some form of mutual engagement between men, whereas Denton's individuals each operated in a self-contained vacuum. But the underlying conception of the sharply developed rational individual will reflected the general spirit of the age. Individuals were discrete units. The idea that their minds might actually merge for a long period of time was inconceivable, except perhaps for husband and wife. Among radicals, the great emphasis was upon freeing oneself from the constraints of dogmas, organized movements, and social conventions. "Creeds and parties fetter me and bar my way. I must get rid of them, and can do so only by heeding my own reason." So said another Boston free thinker in 1882.[34] J. William Lloyd's anarchist utopia, two decades later, is to a large degree still laid out along these lines. The inhabitants of Vale Sunrise were "as pleased with

32. J. William Lloyd, *The Dwellers in Vale Sunrise* (Westwood, Massachusetts: The Ariel Press, 1904), pp. 21–22.
33. William Denton, *Be Thyself: A Discourse* (Wellesley, Massachusetts: Denton Publishing Co., 1882), pp. 28–29.
34. W. S. Bell, *Liberty and Morality* (Boston: by the author, 1882), p. 11.

difference as people in the world are with conformity." Their houses were built in strikingly dissimilar styles, and no two people dressed alike. The residents spent much of their time busily absorbed in a hundred varying pursuits.[35] Privacy, the wish to be let alone, is regarded as a natural, central human craving in all the individualist anarchist literature of this period.

To be sure, the theme of communal fraternity also received some degree of attention. (As one might expect, those who called themselves communal anarchists gave it greater emphasis and scope.) But, from a later standpoint, this side of the equation seems oddly underdeveloped. The conception of "comradeship," though present, had a far less organic flavor than it did in the much earlier writings of Rousseau. At Stelton the Ferms tried to teach children, above all, to be self-reliant, dependent upon no one. In 1915 the anarchist Theodore Schroeder promoted an ideal of "liberty though impersonal service," extolling self-sacrifice in socially valuable tasks for the benefit of the common good. But it was a concept which deliberately sought to avoid close human contacts in practice. "Being without binding special friendships, you will yet be the friend of all; without doing personal charity to any, you will cheerfully devote your whole life to the impersonal service of all; while looking with . . . emotional indifference . . . [upon everyone], you can ignore the fellowship-claim of the infantile pharisee and yet extend your fellowship to him."[36] In such a labored pronouncement one senses the stiffness toward run-of-the-mill human beings which had kept anarchists of that day from being genuine democrats. This impersonal ideal of human relations would run squarely against the grain of the 1960's counter-culture, even if it had a certain echo in the Israeli kibbutzim.

Both the concepts of individual expression and of collectivity had been greatly transformed by the 1960's. These changes in turn could seem very hard to pin down. Some older observers saw in them only an abandonment of individualism—a new conformism among the far-out. Others misread them in an opposite direction. Carl Zigrosser of the Ferrer movement, when I talked to him as an elderly man in 1971, said that in his day the idea of self-expression had always been balanced by a sense of relation to the whole, whereas today's youth seemed entirely self-preoccupied. The very contradiction in these judgments suggests that instead of either of them being true, something rather different had occurred. The post-Freud-

35. Lloyd, *op. cit.,* pp. 16, 137–40, 174. This is not to deny that elsewhere there are inconsistent hints of a much more patterned existence; see Chapter One.
36. Theodore Schroeder, *Liberty Through Impersonal Service* (Riverside, Connecticut: by the author, 1915), p. 14.

ian view of man had again intervened, not clearly tipping the scales either toward individuality or the collective, but infusing each ideal with a new meaning that was uncomfortable even for most radicals of the previous generation.

Thanks to the writings of men like Herbert Marcuse and Norman O. Brown, as well as to more general changes in popular attitude, both concepts were now highly charged with sexual content. An individual fulfilled himself through "relationships" (on every level) with others. The very idea of the relationship, in this "deep" sense, was almost entirely foreign to the worlds of individual and communal anarchism—and for that matter to the world of socialism—as of 1900. It began to appear soon thereafter (as yet without the label) among Greenwich Village radicals, whose reading of Freud made them newly sensitive to this side of Walt Whitman's poetry. In a sense, the avant-garde of the twentieth century was recapturing the sensitivity toward passion of early nineteenth-century romantics, including many of the European anarchists, whose message had meantime lain dormant in the climate of late-nineteenth-century Anglo-American rationalism. But the new avant-garde was also pushing this sensitivity far more openly toward the sexual realm.

An extreme organicism, going far beyond any previous limits, came to fruition in the radical dream of community during the 1960's. The vision focused on a constant, spontaneous merger of individuals into a loving group. In its purest form, no one was to be held special; anyone could join, and all divisive memories would be dissolved in a total bodily and psychic fusion.[37] Though probably never achieved in practice, the ideal was so strikingly novel that it could only bring forth a sense of wonder. In part it was the product of the new sensual awareness; it also served as the logical culmination of egalitarian humanist thinking. Seemingly it suggested a will to blot out individuality, although the same people continued to speak at other times in a vocabulary of individual experiment, development, and growth.[38]

37. See pp. 187, 188.
38. From a Freudian perspective, such a desire for fusion could easily be seen, of course, as a wish to return to the mother's womb. For a striking instance of this, see Kenneth Keniston, *The Uncommitted* (New York: Harcourt, Brace, and World, 1965), p. 52. In terms of intellectual sources, the concept has sometimes been traced to Robert Heinlein's popular novel, *Strangers in a Strange Land* (New York: Putnam, 1961), although this does not explain why it caught on so widely. Robert Jay Lifton has speculated that radical youth have internalized fears of nuclear world destruction, transforming them into wishes for self-obliteration. See Lerner, *op. cit.,* p. 439. From such a viewpoint, loss of self (in ecstasy) may pleasurably anticipate, and thereby forestall, the horrifyingly predicted loss of self in a global holocaust. In

In the first chapter it was suggested that intensification and loss of self actually form a closely intertwined polarity in the imagination. At some point a desire to "expand" one's consciousness may finally merge with a wish for self-obliteration. Mystics had always talked in these ambiguous terms, and to a degree communitarian humanists were now sharing their language. The ego loss in the LSD experience vividly dramatized this possibility, as a half-ecstatic, half-frightening intimation of a "reality" far beyond, and yet inseparable from, individual consciousness.

Meanwhile, some younger followers of the mystical tradition were becoming more self-consciously communal in their thinking. Americans of this persuasion had previously seen spiritual growth as their primary aim, merely forming communities, as they saw it, for practical reasons. The mystical side of the counter-culture remained divided on this point. The pattern of living at the Lama Foundation retained far more aids to privacy and aloneness than were usual elsewhere. But others, such as Ezra, moved toward openly experimenting with the dynamics of group relations, even though their ultimate goal was still one of self-development.

The total fusion of sensually and inwardly aware individuals into a group was, of course, only the most astonishing of the new recipes for revitalizing the concepts of individualism and community. Other radicals embraced the less extreme concept of "synergy," the idea that the whole is more than the sum of its parts, and therefore that a group may accomplish more together than as separated individuals.[39] "Synergy" carried organicist overtones, but of a far less sweeping kind; it was compatible with specialization, task allotment, and indeed the entire trappings of conventional socialism.

All these trends reflected a marked decline in the individualism of the older kind. To someone like myself observing life at Rockridge, the round of daily existence seemed not only uncomfortably patterned but monotonously unvaried as well. My generation will doubtless never feel really at home in these free-flowing, slow-motion environments. The idea of the self has been so greatly altered, in its movement away from the reasoning, discrete mind toward something like a pulsing nexus of sensation and emotion, that to the person who remains outside the new ethos it appears simply to wither away and disappear.

Ezra's group there was evidence that childhood fears of the bomb were indeed strong, but still younger radicals (passing through childhood mainly in the recent years of détente) do not seem to be so profoundly affected on this level. On this subject see also Robert Liebert, *Radical and Militant Youth* (New York: Praeger, 1971), pp. 234–40.

39. See p. 329.

But in fact self and community are both still emphasized in the new counter-culture, even if it is too old-fashioned to speak of a "balance" between them. Moreover, the self is still sometimes being "tested" in ways that would have made sense long ago. The pride in pioneering, in "self-sufficiency," paradoxically remains strong at Rockridge, and achievement orientation even more strikingly dominates Ezra's group, as we abundantly saw. On quite another level, the flagrant narcissism of the counter-culture, which revealed itself in long hair, body painting, and the entire ethos of public physical display, was one of its most pervasive characteristics. It is far too simple to say that individualism is dead. Especially in the structured intentional communities, it sometimes survives in its rather familiar forms. More often it has been translated into the nonrational realm of sex and "personality," which the defenders of reason too readily assume means nonexistence.[40]

In this key area, when all is said, the changes seem more profound than the continuities. The bare survival of the polarity is probably less important than all these shifts that have occurred in its meaning, despite the continued suggestiveness of many pages in Rousseau.

If the penetration of Freudian ideas greatly affected radical conceptions of individualism and community, the radical response to sexual questions turns out, on closer inspection, to have many distinct ebbs and flows.

Drastic practices in the area of sex and the family have an age-old history in secessionist communities, beginning in America with the Shakers, the Mormons, and Oneida. Mystics have always tended toward celibacy, and anarchists have preached "free love," practicing it at the Long Island settlement Modern Times in the 1850's. Yet in the nineteenth century these matters seem usually to have been treated in a strangely cold spirit. The pairings of couples at Oneida were carried out with what now seems an absurd diplomatic formality, involving the use of intermediaries. In that period, only Walt Whitman spoke with a different voice.

The tone of most anarchists who spoke on sex around 1900 was still noticeably rationalistic, even if it was daringly bold in its own day. For Benjamin Tucker, freedom in love had to be proclaimed in a gingerly fashion:

> Even in so delicate a matter as that of the relations of the sexes the

40. Academics are here handicapped in forming judgments. They stand at an opposite pole from the counter-culture, not just because it is their own historically transmitted role to defend reason, but because they have been taught to view every form of open display as in the height of poor taste, since to them it connotes the life style of the *nouveaux riches*.

Anarchists do not shrink from the application of their principle. They acknowledge and defend the right of any man or woman, or any men and women, to love each other for as long or as short a time as they can, will, or may. To them legal marriage and legal divorce are equal absurdities. They look forward to a time when every individual, whether man or woman, shall be self-supporting, and when each shall have an independent home of his or her own, whether it be a separate house or rooms in a house with others; when the love relations between these independent individuals shall be as varied as are individual inclinations and attractions; and when the children born of these relations shall belong exclusively to the mothers until old enough to belong to themselves.[41]

If one reads all the clauses in Tucker's statement carefully, the door has indeed been opened to the full range of sexual experiments that have been practiced or dreamed about in America during the last ten years. Group sex, bisexuality even, can be squeezed out of these formal phrases, along with such living arrangements as Harrad West.[42] But abstract intellectual anticipation is one thing, freedom from inhibition quite another. The older anarchists might often spurn marriage as a legal rite, and some of the men would "play the field." But a rather conventional notion of "the couple" underlay most of this boldness. Tucker himself lived with one woman faithfully for thirty years, though Harry Kelly and Emma Goldman, among others, made the kind of switches that have more recently become common among Americans.

Even when people did go further, it was with much inner conflict. Hutchins Hapgood captured the flavor of sexual relations among some of the more determined anarchists in Chicago during the first years of the twentieth century:

The unnatural idealism of the group made it obligatory on the part of the male not only to tolerate but to encourage the occasional impulse of the wife or sweetheart toward some other man; or, on the part of the woman, a more than tolerant willingness to have her man follow out a brief impulse with some other woman. This is called varietism, and was supposed to be hygienic and stimulating to the imagination. No doubt it was, but the time always came when human nature couldn't stand it and when one or the other broke down and separation, sorrow, and disappointment followed. And yet these libertarian ideas, associated with a principled reaction against what was felt to be a system of slavery, gave to this way of living a certain pathetic dignity. Certainly, in comparison with the unbridled outburst of sexual looseness which took place among all classes after the World War,

41. Tucker, *op. cit.,* p. [10].
42. Houriet, *op. cit.,* pp. 235–76; Fairfield, *op. cit.,* pp. 292–304.

there was something almost academic in the sex conduct of these Chicago groups.[43]

Again in this account one notes that the long-standing couple is the assumed norm, and everything else is regarded as exceptional.

In practice the issue of sex divided the older anarchist movement. Just as many anarchists were strident atheists while a minority flirted with mysticism and the occult, so one gains an impression of a faction who resolutely practiced free love, and of others who shrank back. A definite streak of the puritanical is discernible in these circles, though it never dominates; it clashes (loudly at the Home colony around 1911) with the movement's official willingness to condone experimentation. A worldly visitor to Home complained that no tobacco was to be found anywhere in the community.[44] Nudism was most often praised as "scientific" and "healthful" rather than as voluptuously exciting in the spirit of Whitman or J. William Lloyd.[45] The whole issue of sexual and bodily freedom was internally disruptive. Anarchists should not form colonies, one writer warned, because "if the colony is based on economic or political unorthodoxy it will be destroyed by the sexual radicals. That is to say, the economic and political radicals who are not also sexual radicals will not permit freedom of speech and life in sexual matters, and so disruption ensues."[46] His words became sadly prophetic at Home a few years later.

By the early teens a romantic ideal of bodily liberation had filtered more widely into radical consciousness. Primness distinctly declined. But the new attitude still remained sharply set apart from the growing permissiveness of mainstream America. Its symbol, and to an important degree its instigator, was the dancer Isadora Duncan, who embraced radical causes and evoked a lyrical primitivism on the stage, but also (most significantly) detested jazz rhythms.[47] The Duncan mood was ethereal, trans-

43. Hutchins Hapgood, *A Victorian in the Modern World* (New York: Harcourt, Brace, 1939), p. 202.
44. For an abstemious view of alcohol, see C. L. James, *Anarchy* (Eau Claire, Wisconsin: by the author, 1886), p. 27. The figures of Harry Kemp and Upton Sinclair also illustrate this contrast.
45. E.g., in this vein see "Clothes," *Firebrand*, April 12, 1896, p. 4; Jonathan Mayo Crane, "The Evolution of Modesty," *Lucifer*, February 11, 1904, pp. 41–43, 46–47. Such healthy-mindedness was entirely consistent, of course, with the desire to spread accurate knowledge of the physiology of sex, a matter in which all anarchists were willing pioneers. E.g., see P. Smith, "Plain Talks About the Sexual Organs," *Firebrand*, October 11, 1896, pp. 3–4, and succeeding issues.
46. E. C. Walker, "Should Radicals Colonize?" *Free Society*, X (May 15, 1904), p. 1. Walker had earlier been a great advocate of colonization.
47. Because she so strongly disliked "low" sensuousness, Isadora Duncan was also a Negrophobe. *My Life* (New York: Boni and Liveright, 1927), pp. 195, 318, 324, 342. Alexis Ferm also opposed jazz; see p. 150.

cendental, and relatively genteel. Though it suggested sensual pleasure, usually narcissistic, its view of ecstasy was heavily stylized. It was oriented toward an upper-middle-class avant-garde rather than to the quite different physical abandon of the common man. It was pre-Freudian in that it identified the human form with beauty rather than directly with physical pleasure. Pretending to accept nudity, this attitude still covered the body with a protective film of noble nineteenth-century adjectives. Jazz rhythms were desperately resisted because they threatened to pull away this final veil.[48] In a sense, the last important defender of this view of the body may have been Norman O. Brown, whose own vision of ecstasy remained wrapped in a neo-transcendental halo of lyrical images.

For a time the Isadora Duncan mood caught on at the Stelton anarchist colony. When she toured New York in the winter of 1914–1915, some of the children in the Ferrer school went to see her dance at least eight times, and she was praised at length in the pages of *Modern School* magazine. A photograph of four young Stelton girls wearing white robes was labeled "A Quartet of Isadora Duncans." In 1916 one of the young immigrant girls at the colony, Rose Freeman, wrote a long prose poem in this vein, entitled "To My Body":

> I could expose my body freely, defiantly . . . Were I not desirous of cherishing it for the sacred few! . . . I can neither stifle my spirit nor force it into the iron vise of repression! No! nor sit secluded and meek while a devastating and terrible virginity saps my creative springs and shrivels my veins with drouth, for I am tameless and pagan! Oh body of mine, more vital, more pure, more aesthetic than sculpture, Hellenic marble.[49]

This was pre-jazz liberation at its most extreme, though even here the body was not entirely freed from the highly conventional imagery of the frozen statue. No doubt more widely acceptable was the linking of nudity with revolt against authority in the context of economic struggle. The immigrant poet Adolf Wolff, a frequenter of the Ferrer Center in New York, declaimed at this time:

> We who have but rags to wear,
> Let us go out on strike
> And face the robber-master class
> In all our naked might.

* * *

48. This posture is also exemplified in the character Hermione in D. H. Lawrence's *Women in Love* and in the Robinson Jeffers poem "Emilia," *Californians* (New York: Macmillan, 1916), pp. 10–21.

49. *Modern School*, III (January, 1917), 145–46. The poem went on into separate verses about her breasts, vagina, etc.

> Let us arise and from our bodies tear
> The fetid uniform that brands us slaves.
> In countless masses let us rally forth
> And through each pore of our free body shout
> Our right to life, to liberty, and joy.[50]

Undress as a form of social protest thus long precedes Abbie Hoffman in the American radical imagination.[51] During the teens, modesty yielded important ground to defiant delight. But it was an oddly transitory phenomenon among radicals, one which seemed to fade thereafter along with Isadora Duncan's memory.

The new wave of permissiveness in the avant-garde, interestingly enough, had made itself felt briefly among a few American mystics. Around 1915 Will Levington Comfort approvingly watched the youngsters in his circle shed their clothes in the country air. But, as might be expected, he and other believers in cosmic philosophy soon drew back. Nudity was wrong because "the human body is associated with [spiritual] darkness." Though, like Gerald Heard, Comfort claimed to disbelieve in the extremes of ascetic mortification, he ended up sanctioning intercourse only for the procreation of children.[52] Meanwhile, at Katherine Tingley's Raja Yoga school, the girls found their existence unbearable in the 1920's, with skirts maintained at prewar length, no bobbing of hair, no ballroom dances (for Mrs. Tingley believed that even a waltz was too sensuous), and rigorous chaperoning at parties. Few of the adults at Point Loma, including Mrs. Tingley, bore children themselves. In the 1930's the I Am movement was similarly extreme on the side of repression.[53]

There matters long stood, both for anarchists and for mystics. During the 1950's, in West Coast Zen circles, a first important premonition of change occurred.[54] But the survival there of tendencies toward passivity

50. Adolf Wolff, *Songs, Sighs and Curses* (Ridgefield, New Jersey: The Globe, 1913), p. 69.

51. For another clear instance of this, involving an incident in the C.O. camps of the Second World War, see *Retort*, I (December, 1942), 59–60.

52. Will Levington Comfort, *Child and Country* (New York: George H. Doran, 1915), pp. 140–41; Comfort, *Letters*, II, 147–48, 153–54, 162–63. One of his following, Malya Rudhyar, spoke more permissively of a form of "conscious love" (not merely animal or instinctual) between two people which had the function of creating spiritual "wholeness in each participant." Unidentified clipping from *Hamsa* magazine, ca. 1933. Even in such a formulation, the carnal is carefully translated into an aseptic realm of inner self-developmcent, rather than being rejoiced in as an independent route to liberation.

53. Emmet A. Greenwalt, *The Point Loma Community in California, 1897–1942: A Theosophical Experiment* (Berkeley: University of California Press, 1955), pp. 62–63, 96, 100, 193; Gerald B. Bryan, *Psychic Dictatorship in America* (Burbank, California: The New Era Press, 1940), pp. 179–86.

54. See Roszak, *op. cit.*, pp. 129, 135.

and exclusive homosexuality, long an undercurrent in American mysticism, make the Beat movement no more than transitional in these terms. The full celebration of orgasm in a mystical context began only among the youth of the 1960's, where it sprang from a fresh and far more wide-open sensual radicalism. It seems likely that the new permissiveness took its cue more from the liberal mainstream of the society than from these intermittent foreshadowings in the earlier radical tradition. Still, it was important that American radical thought had not always been linked with puritanical associations.

On one level, what then happened in the 1960's is well known. So dramatic was the outward eruption of sexual liberation that it rightly lays claim to be considered, alongside the related ideal of organic fusion, as the strongest element of "newness" in the counter-culture. One of its young spokesmen recognized that the sudden willingness to grasp this kind of freedom had upset many Marxists of a slightly older generation:

> Today America, or at least a section of the American population, is going through a moral crisis . . . in a way which is often as baffling and disturbing to old-line socialists as it is to arch-reactionaries. This moral crisis is the search for the free and meaningful, and involves among many other things a sexual revolution. This sexual revolution is especially pervasive among the "beats," the younger radicals, the university fringe element, and the younger civil rights workers, but is not restricted to these groups and has extended into large groupings which are non-ideological and non-political, and promises as its influence grows to give a shattering blow to rotten Judeo-Christian morality with its sexual shame, guilt, and its personality-destroying repressions.[55]

On closer inspection, the new wave turns out to have many distinct eddies, resistances, and degrees of depth. For instance, while some of the newer mystical groups moved to come to terms with it, others notably stood aside. Organizations such as Vedanta firmly held their ground. New Age communities of the structured and more rationalist kind, like Ezra's, took a middle path; not advocating celibacy, they nonetheless warned their members against excessive "energy depletion," or diversion of attention, through too much sexual activity. The climate of the 1960's had pushed them away from the abstemious injunctions of men like Heard and Comfort, but an undertow of reservation remained.[56]

Within the more enthusiastic sectors of the counter-culture, endorse-

55. Stan Iverson, "Sex and Anarcho-Socialism," *Appeal to Reason* (Seattle), II (March, 1966), 2–3.

56. Such prominent movements of the 1960's as Hare Krishna, the Brotherhood of the Spirit, and the Lama Foundation all still sought to discourage sex in varying degrees.

ment of free sex still had to face the psychological shock of actual experiment. To stop daydreaming and start acting was only a beginning. The account of a six-person "marriage" witnessed by Robert Houriet at Harrad West leaves no feeling of ultimate breakthrough about it; it reads strangely like Hapgood's recollections of the early Chicago anarchists. The people there slept with each other according to a time table, and desertions were frequent. This kind of "revolution" is undoubtedly real, for it finally dissolves the structure of the couple, but it produces, if not a single Thermidor, then certainly a series of discouraging morning-afters.[57] Sex remains a problem for the radically inclined, just as it did a hundred years ago, even if on a new level.

It is also hard to evaluate the broader attack on the conventional structure of the nuclear family which became such a conspicuous element in radical discourse toward the end of the 1960's. The demand for an extreme form of women's liberation came in a society where women had for a long time been free of the worst forms of male domination. Spokesmen for the movement oscillated between calls for complete equality and for new forms of special treatment for their sex. The hip lived together freely without marriage, and this was more casually accepted than ever before, but it is likely that only a few people really moved away from the structure of a twosome even now—and this was what basically counted. In most communes, pairing into twos, and indeed sex roles themselves, remained sharply defined. Illegitimate childen still faced poignant encounters with their prejudiced grandparents. Group sex had all the earmarks of a marginal fad. The movement to reshape the family produced some highly interesting talk, just as Emma Goldman had done in her own generation, but it showed signs of remaining stalled on that level.

The maximization of consciousness is a long-lived theme in radical thought which gained wider currency during the decade of the 1960's. Though the term has always had its own meaning in the Marxist tradition, in early twentieth-century America its use was more pronounced among the mystically inclined. The word "consciousness" was one of the standard hallmarks of writers in the mind-cure or "metaphysical" vein, for instance in the New Thought movement. It must be understood that in these circles

57. Keith Melville, *Communes in the Counter Culture* (New York: William Morrow, 1972), pp. 165, 188, comments on how frequently the sexual pattern in communes has slipped back into serial monogamy. Though some people in the 1960's clearly were living more far-out lives in this realm than had been dreamed of by the early twentieth-century anarchists, the general quantitative pattern in the counter-culture was probably little different from their practice.

the term had a special import, entirely apart from its everyday usage, or from that given it by Marxists or Freudians. Consciousness referred to the mental state achieved by the individual who progressively tapped the cosmic reservoirs of energy, wisdom, and insight. Thus it had an elitist overtone; advanced souls were those who had evolved, over the course of many incarnations, to a "higher" consciousness. Sometimes the phrase "super-consciousness" was introduced to refer to this ultimate zone of attainment. By contrast, the "subconscious," when it was recognized at all, was spurned as the abode of the unwanted lower self. This distinctive view of the human mind was the one accepted both by Vedantists and by the followers of Gurdjieff, though neither of them happened to give the word itself the overbearing emphasis which it received in a number of similar movements.

"Consciousness" could imply both a state of great inner clarity and the God intoxication of mystical ecstasy. Ideally, the two possibilities mingled as one. The word "truth," as it was freely used in these circles, carried this combined overtone. It was something one deliberately focused on, fought one's way toward in meditation, and seized joyously when it was re-vealed. Neither truth nor consciousness was conceived of as coldly intel-lectual. The analyzing intellect was held at arm's length. Though "higher" than the carnal realm, it was always a potential enemy, for its critical reach might poke holes in the truths which it was always one's first duty to seek out. Thus the mystical tradition was never as unreservedly pro-intellectual as the anarchistic one had been in earlier decades. Reason, science, and Darwin had to be dealt with gingerly, their findings carefully enmeshed in the context of higher realities. (On the other hand, mystics never allowed themselves to fall into the Fundamentalist trap of rejecting modern science. Several of their religious organizations even used the word in their titles.)

Consciousness transcended the normal intellectual sphere. Thus even when it promised mental clarity, it did so more in terms of a feeling of "arrival" than of logic. Clarity resulted from high vibrations, another word which has seen decades of use in this spiritual context. Thus clarity and ecstasy could easily be regarded as complementary inner rewards. The concrete images they then conjured up were ones of great purity and in-tensity—flashing white lights, visions of illuminated figures approaching, dressed entirely in white, who conveyed the majesty of fully realized cosmic power and compassion. Contact with these forms, in a dazzling and awe-some inner experience, was the final fruit of meditation. On a lesser plane one read the "auras" of the ordinary human beings around one. These auras were believed to be visible psychic manifestations, colors and lights which hovered above the heads of everyone at all times, constantly displaying the quality of the vibrations given off by that person. Only advanced souls could read auras, and the jealousies provoked by the claim to be able to do so simmered unendingly wherever Theosophists gathered.

From all this it will be seen that both clarity and ecstasy had a strongly stylized meaning in mystical circles during the early decades of the twentieth century. The counter-culture of the 1960's retained many of the key terms, such as consciousness, vibration, and the major astrological symbols, but the concrete imagery of realization shifted. Gone was the infatuation with purity and whiteness. Thanks no doubt to the properties of LSD, the new visions more often seemed to come in Technicolor. They were still dazzling indeed, but they were more richly varied and unpredictable.

This brings us to the subject of drugs in relation to the expansion of consciousness. It must be pointed out that drugs served a multitude of functions in the recent counter-culture, and that only the psychedelics were clearly linked with the cultivation of these states of inner awareness. Separately, at a later point, the broader implications of the drug scene will be discussed.

The use of drugs as an alleged short cut to profound insight came as a sudden shock wave in mystical circles. During the 1950's Aldous Huxley and Gerald Heard had experimented with mescalin and LSD, but these pioneers of the previous generation drew back at what they saw happening more widely to their brainchild in the early 1960's.[58] Meanwhile, other established figures, such as Alan Watts, wholeheartedly endorsed the new mind-expanding drugs and the entire hip movement as it emerged. The ex-academics Timothy Leary and Richard Alpert combined drugs and meditation in a new cult of an extreme kind which flourished for a few years in a communitarian setting at Millbrook, New York. Drugs became an in-

---

58. The interest of Heard and Huxley in drugs had grown out of an earlier absorption they shared in extrasensory perception and psychic phenomena. In this sense, like the entire spiritualist movement, they had always been peculiarly prone to run after short cuts. Gerald Heard recommended the general use of LSD under certain conditions in *The Five Ages of Man* (New York: Julian Press, 1963), pp. 192, 237–39. Timothy Leary wrote to him: "I have read THE FIVE AGES four times, and with each reading I grow in delight and admiration." Leary evidently regarded Heard with great respect. Timothy Leary to Gerald Heard, January 11, 1964, Gerald Heard Papers, University of California Library, Department of Special Collections, Los Angeles. In the early 1960's Leary and Aldous Huxley were on a friendly, first-name basis, though by 1963 Huxley had developed reservations about Leary's degree of enthusiasm for drugs. See Grover Smith, ed., *Letters of Aldous Huxley* (London: Chatto & Windus, 1969), pp. 778–80, 799, 802–805, 824–25, 845, 863–64, 881, 909, 929, 945, 947, 953–55. Huxley drew back from endorsement of the drug scene more emphatically than Heard, but neither of them was really at ease with the emerging hip movement.

tensely divisive issue within the mystical fraternity, creating the sense of an extraordinary generation gap.

Yet some astonishing efforts were made to bridge the chasm. The older mystics viewed the resurgence of interest in consciousness expansion among the very young with scarcely concealed hopes. A movement that had long been rather static now suddenly promised to sweep the land. It seemed an enormous pity that only the issue of drugs stood in the way of a generational laying-on of hands. At least one incredible scene is then reported to have occurred. Around 1962 Timothy Leary was invited to pay a long visit to the Ananda Ashrama at La Crescenta, California, which had always been a community of unusually genteel spiritual aspirants of the traditional kind.[59] It is claimed by an indirect informant that Leary persuaded some of the residents briefly to experiment with LSD.[60] But Leary's attempt at diplomacy was unsuccessful. Several years later the Ananda Ashrama bore only negative signs of the encounter. A fervent, almost total opposition to drugs was manifest there.

If, despite Alan Watts, there was little give from the older side, as time went on there seemed to be signs of flexibility from the younger. The ex-drug-user became an increasingly common figure among the more serious youthful seekers after consciousness expansion. As the older generation stood fast, the question began to become controversial within the youth scene. Psychedelics in particular seemed to ebb from use in the early 1970's; perhaps they had been only another passing fad. In these changes lay a basis for a possible rapprochement. And yet the prognostication for this was by no means favorable. The whole hip style, which included the important matter of sex, still stood in the way. It appeared likely that the rejuvenation of the mystical tradition in America would proceed without benefit of much direct contact between its adherents of different age levels. History often plays this kind of trick upon committed believers.

Meanwhile, the word "consciousness" had gained a new and wider fashionability. Partly as a result of the mystical revival, partly owing to its rediscovery among Marxists, the term became freely used in many sectors of the radical world. "Consciousness raising" became a major goal, for instance, in women's liberation. Applied in so many diverse ways, the word might lose its suggestiveness and force. Yet it still seemed to conjure up a mixture of the attainment of clarity and emotional exhilaration. Momentary ecstasy was now more widely sought, in sex, drugs, and communal

59. See Chapter Four.
60. The fact of Leary's visit, at least, is confirmed in *Message of the East*, LII (Spring, 1963), 28.

fusion, as well as in the older mystical context. Yet clarity remained the emphasis of Marxists, crusaders for women's rights, and also of such occultist sects as Scientologists and the followers of Gurdjieff. At any rate, few radicals now stood aside from the vocabulary of consciousness expansion altogether.

It is not so easy to trace changes in radical attitudes toward acquiring material possessions and maintaining fixed abodes. At first glance there would seem to be a definite shift in the direction of a more extreme renunciation. The earlier conception of a natural or simpler life, as explored at length in the first chapter, usually paused short of a complete rejection of civilized technology. The anarchist Victor Yarros could speak approvingly of industrial civilization, and C. L. James admired the inventive skill of an Edison. Henry Addis stated that a simpler mode of life "would not be a return to savagery by any means. In fact, it would be getting away from the barbarism, or tinsel-stracism and pomp that still prevail in our present-day society."[61] Even in the writings of J. William Lloyd, the stress was more upon a rational selection of what to retain for the future, less upon the embrace of a severely simple tribal past. One also recalls the judgment of Alexis Ferm, to the effect that most of the Stelton colonists would gladly have embraced the trappings of material success had they possessed the means to do so.

But among many radicals self-sufficiency was a strong desire even in those earlier decades.[62] And there was always a lyrical, romantic side to the craving for a simple life style, in contrast to the rationalistic discussion of such topics as individualism and sex. An anarchist of 1912 explained his decision to refuse an ordinary job by saying: "To live each day with no care for the morrow; to glory in the beauty of the sun and the stars; to be free of all restraint that I may live and love—all this . . . is impossible in modern society. Therefore, I cast myself out . . . I refuse to sacrifice my life . . . that parasites may live in sensual comfort and wealth. I, in turn, have become the parasite that I may live as becomes the man. It matters not at whose expense."[63]

By the 1930's at least a few Americans were actually leading the uncluttered lives, closely tuned to nature, which Walt Whitman and J. William Lloyd had much earlier dreamed about. In the deserted sand-dune country

61. Yarros, *op. cit.*, p. 11; James, *Anarchy*, p. 29; Henry Addis, "Savagery and Anarchism," *Discontent*, March 14, 1900, p. 2. Cf. Houriet, *op. cit.*, pp. 214–19.
62. See Charles Pierce LeWarne's forthcoming study of colonies in Washington state.
63. Saxe, "To the Outcast," *Mother Earth*, VI (February, 1912), 384.

near Oceano, in central California, an informal community sprang into existence, centered around the Celtic poetess and mystic Ella Young. As she described the life there, it evoked a mood which some people sought to recapture in the late 1960's:

> Every hermit had an oasis all to himself. It was his territory. He needed to be about two miles away from his nearest neighbour. His little tent or cave-like shack must be securely hidden: it must not affront any eye, even his own. He must feel that he discovered it, stumbled upon it by accident so to speak, when he returned from a foray. . . . The hermits, nurtured by Providence, could meditate on eternity, write verses, or in beneficent mood ray out blessings to the Universe. There was Hugo Seelig, the poet, who knew at what hour the evening primrose opened and in what place one might surprise the first blue gillia; there was George Blaise who went about long-haired and bearded, clad in suntan and a loin-cloth, George the Evangelist who had attained health and salvation in the Dunes and longed to spread the gospel of it to others: meat-eaters, dwellers in cities, their hide-shod feet ignorant of sand and sea-wave; there was Arthur the Navigator who had wonderful tales of the sea and could carve dragons in a stone, and construct galleons full-rigged with the aid of cord, some oil-soaked paper, and a piece of driftwood.[64]

Only the great sense of privacy, and the apparent de-emphasis of sex, make one realize that all this belonged to an earlier time.

The simple life was not always so closely tied to nature worship; it could also be more rationalistic. A "decentralist code," as published by Mildred J. Loomis of the relatively conventional School for Living, began with the affirmation: "I will content myself with a minimum of things conducive to a clean, comfortable and efficient abode. I will live on the land. . . . I will grow my own, use it up, build it myself, make it do, wear it out. I will hold only as much land as I can use."[65] Similar attitudes prevailed among many of the Stelton residents, even if they compromised by commuting. Gerald Heard, like Alexis Ferm, always lived in Spartan fashion, and he was occasionally interested in ecology.

Talk has grown more thoroughgoing in this direction lately, but Robert Houriet noted the ubiquitous presence of hi-fis in remote rural communes, and one remembers how Rockridge, despite its lack of electricity, decided that a noisy well pump was a necessity. Still more confusingly, a minor but distinct strain of technological optimism also found a niche in the counter-

---

64. Ella Young, *Flowering Dusk: Things Remembered Accurately and Inaccurately* (New York: Longmans, Green, 1945), p. 236. The dune hermits were sufficiently "together" to publish *The Dunes Magazine* for several years in the 1930's.
65. *A Way Out* (Brookville, Ohio), XXI (1965), 22. The code had been written much earlier.

culture, centered in the figure of Buckminster Fuller. Within the economic sphere, a rational style of decision making was still explicitly practiced, both at Rockridge and on Ezra's ranch. Here, again in contrast to questions of sex, much more of the flavor of nineteenth-century utilitarianism was actually retained. Anti-rationalism, at least on many of the most determined communes, did not cut quite this deep. And, though a pattern of frequent wandering from place to place was one of the most striking aspects of the counter-culture, it was partly modeled on the tradition of the hobo in earlier American life. Moreover, it did not eclipse a renewed enthusiasm for fixed communities.

Yet the breadth and intensity of nature worship seemed unmistakably to increase. Unadulterated foods had never enjoyed such a large vogue. Physical remoteness from civilization was probably never before pursued on so wide a scale; certainly it had not been a deliberate goal of most earlier radicals in the same sense. And, despite the compromises and contradictions that remained, not least of them the secretly nostalgic trips back to the city often made by those who had firmly chosen to leave it, the vision of simplicity had gained an unprecedented hold on the imagination. In it lay much of the strength of the new secessionist impulse, and therefore the possibility of a radical movement that could endure. A radicalism that centered in the rejection of frills and comforts would always cut unmistakably against the standard American grain. Out of a long-term strand in radical thinking had emerged a theme of unequaled potential in preserving for the movement a clear-cut sense of identity. The ideas of simplification and nonattachment to things could provide a shelter for people beyond the reach of all the homogenizing influences which threaten to strip modern life of individual choice. To choose little or nothing is indeed an extreme response to such an issue. Monotony, as we saw, was a very real danger at Rockridge, despite the promise of closely shared relationships with a handful of others. But the possessionless way of life was the most impressive and potentially creative aspect of the radical life style, for it could conceivably lead in a number of striking directions. A clean slate may be a help toward genuine cultural innovation, since it creates a vacuum which must be filled in some new way. Thus, though renunciation is scarcely a novel theme among cultural radicals, the more serious pursuit of it now gives contemporary radicalism much of its tone and fascination.

Lastly, we come to an elusive but revealing area of radical concern, involving attitudes toward the intake both of ideas and of tangible substances such as food and drugs.[66] In the first chapter I suggested that a peculiar mixture of squeamishness and enthusiasm in these respects, operating in parallel fashion at the levels of mind and body, may form an important part of the radical style historically. Obviously, the great element of novelty in this connection is the widespread embrace of drugs.

Drugs must be seen in this larger spectrum. Their own literal past history in America is unimportant, for their meaning is relative to their use in a given cultural context.[67] It is this context that has recently changed. What counts is when marijuana smoking, or the taking of LSD, is suddenly turned into a near ideology. This happened, for instance, when leaflets advocating the former were passed out in the dark in Berkeley movie theaters during the mid-1960's. At such a moment, drugs have become placed on a par with diet regimes as major instruments of self-development.[68] A somewhat similar cultural transformation in the role of alcohol had occurred long ago. Among Greenwich Village bohemians, and in the 1920's for the mystic Will Levington Comfort (who was also a novelist), alcohol had very nearly attained the status of a deliberate, formal agency for liberation. Writers then often believed that drink unleashed their inner creativity in a rapid, effective way. Drugs do form an important element of novelty in the counter-culture, but only as a partial substitute for other substances which previously played a like role.

Even further into the past, the nineteenth century had been a great age for experimenting with foods as well as with philosophies. Fruitlands briefly set the pace in both respects, and further examples are legion. Only uncooked foods were allowed at the Joyful community near Bakersfield, California, during the 1880's.[69] Diet fads, though partly related to a concern with health, have long flourished among physically lusty radicals, whether they were anarchists, socialists, or mystics.[70]

Radical concern over personal intake has always displayed two faces

66. The final category in my original list, having to do with optimism and desperation, is so historically revealing that it will be considered separately toward the close of this chapter.

67. Thus it matters little that one anarchist knew how to get heroin in New York during the First World War (Hapgood, *op. cit.*, p. 427), or that a few students at the University of Chicago smoked marijuana in the mid-1930's (James Weber Linn, *Winds Over the Campus* [Indianapolis: Bobbs-Merrill Co., 1936]).

68. This change is related to Kenneth Keniston's distinction between "seekers" (occasional users) and "heads" (regular, frequent users). See "Heads and Seekers: Drugs on Campus, Counter-Cultures and American Society," *American Scholar,* XXXVIII (Winter, 1969), 100–104.

69. Robert V. Hine, *California's Utopian Colonies* (San Marino, California: Huntington Library, 1953), pp. 140–42.

70. See pp. 57, 60, 128.

—negative and affirmative. On the former side, groups have sometimes appeared which focus upon a "conspiracy" of doctors, food processors, or fluoridators, who are believed to be deliberately promoting bodily impurity.[71] Parallel protest has sprung up about "agents" scheming to take over the human mind.[72] Though these extreme outcries of fear have seldom had any direct connection with the kinds of movements surveyed in this book, their existence indicates a potentially deep strain of concern over matters of purity and impurity not entirely unrelated to the mystic's affirmative quest for purity of soul, the nature lover's demand for purity of environment, and the quest among many radical "seekers" for purity of belief. All these forms variously illustrate the perfectionist tendency in American thought, already notable in the mid-nineteenth century, when John Humphrey Noyes announced his conviction that all men might become free from blemish. If pronounced fears of impurity, believed to be foisted upon innocent victims by outsiders, become articulated, then the term paranoia leaps into our minds; but it is a word to be used sparingly. For instance, though the recent ecology movement is linked intellectually with this same perfectionist theme, it is also founded on an argument so rational that even most businessmen have accepted it in theory.

The drug culture of the past decade can be understood as a newly important affirmative enthusiasm in this highly traditional matter of the intake of substances.[73] This means that one of the most logical comparisons is with the history of dietary experimentation. Seen in this light, some of the mystery which surrounds drug use is dissolved. Drugs are the latest in

71. "There is a supreme, pervading influence in this country which is seeking to destroy us, body and soul. How can our good, honest doctors, of which there are many, be so oblivious to these forces of disintegration? . . . How are we going to overcome this alien, infiltrated chemico-medical combine, which has taken control of the American medical system? It has the press, movies, radio . . . sewed up tight. Sitting in at its banquet of death and disease are the great industrial and commercial giants, which direct the strategy and control the medical trust." The Health Committee, *Fight On!* (New York: by the Committee, 1947), unpaginated. See also the publications of the National Health Federation.

72. E.g., see Arizonans for Mental Freedom, *Mental Health Alert* (mimeographed, May 31, 1963), p. 4, Social Documents Collection, University of Iowa. Not all this literature is explicitly right wing in political content; liberals tend too readily to compress all categories of anti-scientific protest into a single mold.

73. Here of course I am referring to drug use in the context of a radical life style. Heroin use among many "straight" city dwellers of various backgrounds and the widespread faddish use of drugs in urban and suburban high schools (which goes far beyond the limits of the radical movement) obviously are major topics which lie outside the scope of my concern. But the very fact that drugs were by no means necessarily linked to radicalism in America during the 1960's suggests again that their place in the radical outlook needs to be considered in careful and proportionate terms, and in the context of a wide-ranging discussion of the various aspects of radical belief and practice.

a long series of tangible aids toward bodily and mental liberation. They promise, like alcohol and like the mud eating which occurred both at Stelton and Trabuco, a "short cut" to a different state of being. Yet there is also an important difference. Early dietary fads had been closely linked with the quest for purity and perfection. Drug taking amounts more exclusively to a search for immediate sensation which has become its own end. One does not expect instantaneous results from a diet. In the resort to drugs, long-range-goal orientation of the perfectionist kind has nearly disappeared. (To be sure, in the use of LSD there was an expectation of gradually increasing insights over the course of a series of "trips.") It is in this sense, more than in their physiological effects, that drugs indeed represent a new willingness to abandon reason.

Thus, if drugs represent a gain when compared with the edgy and possibly paranoid concern among some older radicals for purity of intake, they also beckon into a mental realm of such total forgetfulness as to threaten any form of continuity. This again is not a new but a very old danger. In American society, it has often been remarked, alcohol has tended to be consumed compulsively, at a high rate of speed, for the sole purpose of rapidly gaining oblivion. This traditional mainstream tendency may play a surprisingly large role in the recent attitude of youth toward drugs. For this reason, the prominence given to drugs in some segments of the counter-culture is a matter of genuine concern, whatever the historical parallels with earlier substances may be. It might almost be regarded as a subtle form of co-optation.

Closely connected with drugs, a wider fascination has developed within some radical circles over the whole range of phenomena associated with madness. The plea of R. D. Laing that we enter sympathetically into the schizophrenic state of mind has been widely listened to. Symptoms of personal disorganization have been perversely celebrated. In these tendencies, if pursued with any consistency, it is hard to discern anything other than an impulse toward some form of suicide. There is a difference between the traditional goal of ecstasy, which found expression at the Woodstock festival of 1969, and this other desire to push ever further away from the ordinary light of day. Orgies always come to an end, but habits and obsessions merely lead one into the uni-dimensional world of a William Burroughs.

In this respect, the survival of such well-demarcated intellectual traditions as anarchism, socialism, and mysticism played an important role in keeping the counter-culture on a more even keel. They were a sobering influence in what otherwise might have been a rudderless plunge into oblivion. As in the nineteenth century, philosophies continued to mingle with physical substances in the radical imagination. The balance suddenly veered in the latter direction, but there was enough diversity of available intake to prevent general self-destruction.

This rapid survey of various key dimensions in radical thinking has left us with a mingled and highly complicated impression of its changes and continuities during the course of the twentieth century. The counter-culture of the 1960's clearly did not spring fullblown from nothing, yet the popular impression of its "strangeness" was by no means entirely ill founded.

Continuity appears most noticeable in the realm of the major intellectual traditions, among them anarchism and mysticism, which have affected the new counter-culture, and in the general mood of anti-hypocritical idealism which underlies them. It is also unmistakable at the political level, in the determined rejection of established forms of authority and the willing embrace of charismatic substitutes. But there is novelty—if also a kind of return to early nineteenth-century Romanticism—in the post-Freudian view of human nature which has gained wide credence. The democratic impulse has become more genuine, and sexual and bodily liberation have reappeared after a lapse and become more open. For almost the first time in an American environment, racial prejudice has been convincingly overcome, though the counter-culture has remained very largely a white movement. The position of women and the sanctity of the nuclear family have been argued about on a fundamental plane as never quite before. The long-standing themes of decentralization and simplicity have gained new prominence. A truly striking vision of the organic fusion of human beings into small groups has entered the imagination, lending a new kind of impulse to many communal undertakings. Reason survives in the realm of economic calculation, at least among the most resolute communitarians, but withers in the newer forms of consciousness expansion. The posture of a counter-intelligentsia is dropped in a democratic embrace of personal emotional validity wherever it is to be found (though mystics still hold aloof). In some circles, drugs and narcissistic exoticism threaten to sabotage any meaningful forward movement.

The radical scene in the United States would appear to have grown more rather than less divided and complex during the last ten years, as compared with earlier decades. Among recent observers, both Theodore Roszak and Keith Melville have argued for the existence of a developing rapport between left-wing radicals and their nonpolitical counterparts, such as religious mystics.[74] But, though we observed a few particular symptoms

74. Roszak, *op. cit.*, pp. 64–66; Melville, *op. cit.*, pp. 53–74. Rosabeth Moss

of this in our survey of ideas, on the whole it does not seem to be a convincing generalization. Programatically, only the Yippies and a few other anarchist groups tried to straddle this line. Meanwhile, certain issues, among them drugs and other nonreligious forms of personal privatism, have newly complicated the scene. Though a distinct generational bond did exist among diverse radical youth in the 1960's, beneath its surface lay both new and time-worn sources of friction and fragmentation.

At a much earlier point, I referred to the existence of three competing world views relevant to the universe of radical thought—the political, the religious, and the psychiatric.[75] The nature of man is defined very differently according to each of them. Both the political and the religious frames of reference were already on the scene, of course, long before 1900, and were exemplified in this study by anarchism and mysticism. The last few decades have seen the rise of a major rival, the psychiatric, which conceives of man as immersed in "problems," "conflicts," and "relationships," sometimes to the exclusion of any role as a political or social actor or as a cosmic being with an eternal destiny.

It is common to regard the diffusion of Freudian ideas as the central intellectual tendency in twentieth-century America, and therefore to expect that the growth of the psychiatric world view would have profound consequences for the evolution of radical thought along with everything else. If cultural radicalism is pursued in the realm of high theory, at the level of Herbert Marcuse and Norman O. Brown, as has recently been done with some skill by Richard King, then Freud, Jung, and Reich indeed stand at the center of all that has gone on.[76] But the limitation of such a pure version of intellectual history is that it chooses to dwell on the most verbally stimulating aspects of a movement rather than confront the whole of it in social terms. The psychiatric mode of self-conception indeed could sometimes appear to melt away the two older perspectives; we saw, for instance, how Ezra's night-time table talk often straddled the border between the rhetoric of personal self-development and that of contact with cosmic forces.

But a closer look, both at that one community and at the larger countercultural scene, reveals that during the 1960's radicals of these three cogni-

Kanter, *Commitment and Community* (Cambridge, Massachusetts: Harvard University Press, 1972), pp. 3–8, sees a clear movement over time from religious to socioeconomic to psychosocial motives in founding communities, though she admits that "there are many groups today growing out of all three traditions."

75. See pp. 15–16.

76. Richard King, *The Party of Eros: Radical Social Thought and the Realm of Freedom* (Chapel Hill: University of North Carolina Press, 1972).

tive persuasions continued to coexist somewhat uneasily side by side. It was now widely believed that all barriers between honest human beings should immediately be dissolved. But the very process of dissolution was defined quite differently, depending upon the identity of the advocate. Cosmologies did not disappear even in a climate where formal ideology was often regarded as a relic of outmoded intellectualism. A conscious dream of merging all avenues to liberation had indeed come into existence, but it did not magically erase predispositions that were sometimes centuries old. We observed, for instance, that, despite a more psychological vocabulary, at bottom the world view of Ezra's group remained religious, with the Gurdjieffian J. G. Bennett as its semi-official theologian. Within the fashionable ambience of categorical erosion, the old categories still lingered. On this basic level, the remarkable aspect of the counter-culture was not its religious eclecticism, as King would argue, but instead the survival of surprisingly definite, often time-worn versions of salvation.[77] These included everything from Christian Fundamentalism to Hinduism, Buddhism, astrology, and the occultist version of cosmic evolutionism. All these ideologies went back at least into the nineteenth century, and most of them were far more ancient. Moreover, they remained genuinely religious, if religion be defined as belief in man's ability to contact vital forces lying outside the ordinary human realm.

The psychiatric world view now claimed its own adherents, but if anything they remained an unusually sophisticated elite within the countercultural world. One was more apt to find them in universities than in communes. Indeed, one might go further and suggest that they were often politically more liberal than radical, and that this aspect of the counterculture stood in the greatest danger of melting away into the recreational patterns of suburbia. To be sure, such generalizations are never adequate, and I have already emphasized the importance of the sexual side of communal experimentation in settings genuinely removed from such taint. But in any event the psychiatric perspective clearly deserved to be regarded as no more than a third, independent force in the radical world, incapable of converting large numbers of youth who remained steadfast either to a political or to a religious view of the human condition. Members of Hare Krishna or of Students for a Democratic Society would find themselves equally bored or repelled if suddenly placed in a T-group.

On the political side, both anarchism and socialism have remained recognizably alive as traditions informing the vision of the good society. This is the case even though at Rockridge we saw how tenuous the connections

77. *Ibid.*, p. 194.

between formal philosophy and the pattern of living had become. But a tradition of this kind does not depend upon a literal poring over the texts of Bakunin and Kropotkin. George Woodcock has shrewdly assessed the situation in these terms:

> In general, the basic ideas of anarchism, like those of traditional socialism and pacifism, have come down to the New Radicals (that generation of voluntary semi-literates) not through direct reading, but in a kind of mental nutrient broth of remnants of the old ideologies which pervades the air of certain settings in New York, the Bay Area, Los Angeles, Vancouver, and Montreal. But the key tenets that have been on anarchist lips for generations are there: the rejection of the state, the abandonment of the comfortable in favor of the good life, direct action, decentralization, the primacy of the functional group, participation.[78]

The conclusion that various traditions survive, and do not easily become absorbed into others even during the course of an upheaval like that of the 1960's, is bound to seem disappointingly undramatic. Our minds are often geared to expect a final resolution in the competition among ideas, just as we may think that a physical war without victory is somehow unnatural. Yet historically these moments of resolution, even in a relative sense, turn out to be extremely rare. When I tune in to the counter-culture on the intellectual plane, I hear a number of conflicting voices, and as the years pass the cries which express the most traditional viewpoints of all, the several varieties of religion, if anything seem to grow stronger in proportion to the others. All too often the young, instead of engaging in cultural innovation in the realm of ideas, independently rediscover much the same array of dissonant and competing "truths" as had beguiled their elders.

But radicalism is more than a problem in intellectual history; it is a living movement of human beings, struggling to survive and expand their influence against the pressures of a far more powerful social order. From this point of view, the divisions of outlook within the radical world are less important than the conditions prevailing along the boundary line which runs between the entire counter-culture and the external world. The pattern of relations between radicals and other Americans during the course of the twentieth century needs to be closely examined if we are to gain any sense of radical achievements and prospects.

Like almost any group seeking to survive and gain favorable attention, radicals have sought both to raise barriers against threatening outsiders and

78. George Woodcock, "Anarchism Revisited," *Commentary*, XLVI (August, 1968), 56.

to move outward from behind them to win converts and sustenance. This duality bears uncanny resemblance to the posture of a university president or corporation head, engaged in the normal task of guarding and maximizing his institution's image, power, and resources. In this partial but important sense, an ongoing radical movement is simply another concrete, established interest, peculiar only in the disparity between its strength and its pretensions.[79] The need to prevent oneself from being swallowed up in the incomparably more potent outside culture, and yet to avoid the kind of isolation that would prevent any desirable impact, may explain why radicals have always been so ambivalent about their own "Americanness."[80]

In this dual-edged effort, only a few strategies are perennially open. Direct confrontation with authority is one, familiar from the days of Emma Goldman to those of Mario Savio. Open conflict can indisputably prove, to oneself and to everyone else, that there is a lively radical cutting edge. But where the society is nearly impervious to assault, this tactic diverts energy into a hopeless struggle, a blind battling against vastly superior forces. Only when the confrontation is nonviolent, and then only when the issue happens to draw sympathy from liberals, can such resistance temporarily produce positive results. A second alternative is to wage an ordinary campaign of propaganda. But this can easily become all too ordinary, as audiences fail to listen. (Radical education programs, as at Stelton, may be viewed as a more intensive variant version of this strategy.) Thirdly, there is the demonstration project, such as an intentional community, which appears to provide an attractive middle course. But here the danger of inconspicuous fade-away is again acute. These strategies for getting necessary attention have changed little. All of them, including platform debate, recurred with a flourish during the 1960's.

The history of American cultural radicalism suggests several major lines of inquiry from this point of view. How much overt or subtle persecution have radical groups faced at different times? To what extent has persecu-

79. A newly founded business or university, while struggling to survive, makes no claim to possess a message that can "save" the entire society. For more discussion of this comparison as it involved the public relations of Ezra's group, see p. 374.

80. Thus, concerning dress, radicals have always been torn between the desire to express themselves in an openly unconventional fashion and the opposing desire (apparent in the photograph of Mike Gold with necktie and sport coat used by International Publishers on the dust jacket of his anthology) to melt inconspicuously into the crowd. On this point see also Joseph A. Labadie in *The Demonstrator*, September 14, 1904, p. 2. The basic physical symbols of unconventionality have had a long continuity in America. In its *Triennial Record*, p. 16, Yale alumni boasted that *"grinds* are totally foreign to the whole history and nature of the class of '90. We never had any, either of the *whiskered* or the *long-haired* kind." (Italics in original.)

tion prevented them from gaining more influence, or simply from leading their lives in peace? What is the significance of the quieter but perhaps more insidious penetration of mainstream attitudes and values into various radical circles? Should one conclude that because Ezra's group believes so strongly in hard work, energy, and achievement it is not really radical at all, or, on the contrary, that it is all the more formidable as a radical movement? Are radical groups steadily being swallowed up in the mainstream, as many political historians used to think? Does the counter-culture of the 1960's represent a widening or a narrowing of the distance between radicals and other people? Are there notable shifts in the social backgrounds of persons who become radical? Has there been an important change in the survival rate of intentional communities? Do the children of radicals remain radical during the course of their lives? Finally, in the largest sense, how greatly has the posture of radicals toward the surrounding world changed during recent decades? In all these respects one wants to know the trend.

The question of overt persecution, seemingly so straightforward, actually involves the whole spectrum of American attitudes toward unconventional groups and individuals. In this respect, the long-range record of American society has been highly mixed. The experiences of Stelton and of the current communes mirror this unevenness. Seasons of governmental harassment and interference by vigilantes have alternated with longer periods of relative indifference. The mainstream dons both conservative and liberal masks, leading observers of diverse persuasions either to speak of tolerance for anarchic individualism as the classic American norm or else to point to a grass-roots demand for moral conformity as the truly persistent theme.

If one seeks out the sources for these contrasting impressions in the evidence of the nineteenth century, the same inconsistency is revealed. The Mormons were hounded from one location to another for practicing polygamy, while the Oneidans, despite their "complex" marriages, lived for years facing nothing more dangerous than lawsuits, often well-liked by their neighbors. As individuals, hermits and recluses might occasionally be stoned by neighborhood boys, but they were frequently left in peace by adults for their natural lives.[81] George F. Parsons probably expressed a widespread ambivalence toward followers of causes more radical than Reconstruction when he said of them in 1868:

> Often wrong, and when they are wrong, as obstinate as when they are
> right; often misled, and then misleading others; often enthusiastic to the

81. Richardson Wright, *American Wags and Eccentrics: From Colonial Times to the Civil War* (New York: Ungar, 1965), pp. 210, 233. This is a frustratingly poor book on a highly important subject.

verge of fanaticism, and then exercising a similar influence upon their surroundings, but in the main truth-seekers and expounders, light-seekers and diffusers, liberty-seekers and bestowers. After all said, these are the world's original men, bereft of whose energies and lacking whose onward struggle, our earth would be but a dull and stagnant planet.[82]

In moments of panic Americans could easily slide over from this distant and bemused toleration to an attitude of alarm, with results that are well known. Overt repression has always remained a significant element in the situation which radicals face, creating physical danger and, perhaps worse, lingering psychological handicaps. On many occasions fears of harassment have created tensions which made it harder for radical groups to thrive normally, and they have also doubtless increased the level of bickering among rival radical factions, though such jealousies are liable to occur when a movement is in a period of decline, for whatever reasons. The level of persecution for politically oriented groups, such as anarchists, has always been relatively high.[83] Interference with sexual unorthodoxy, originally pronounced, has greatly declined in recent years. Cultural radicals, so long as they are willing to avoid politically sensitive topics, have a greater chance to remain unmolested than they did in the nineteenth century, though the fate of the Oz commune in northern Pennsylvania reminds us of what is still easily possible outside the larger cities.[84] In New Mexico, violence against hippies subsided only after certain communes began arming themselves in retaliation.

If one grants the reality and importance of physical repression in the history of American radicalism, the greater threat has come instead from less tangible forms of pressure which are continually being exerted by a tough, self-confident civilization. In an enormous variety of ways, large and small, the standard culture draws radicals (and their children) back toward it. The war games which the young boys at Stelton spontaneously played in the 1940's return vividly to mind. The most omnipresent danger confronting radicals in America, unlike the situation in Czarist Russia or France during the Resistance, has been that of getting lost in the crowd.

82. George F. Parsons, "What Is Bohemianism?" *Overland Monthly,* I (1868), 430.
83. James Weinstein, *The Decline of American Socialism, 1912–1925* (New York: Vintage Books, 1967), has argued that American radicalism was all but destroyed by deliberate governmental repression around the time of the First World War. But an important deflecting force in that period would seem to have been the newly founded Soviet Union. See also William Preston, Jr., *Aliens and Dissenters: Federal Suppression of Radicals, 1903–1933* (Cambridge, Mass.: Harvard University Press, 1963). On the other hand, Kanter, *op. cit.,* pp. 102–103, stresses the positive function of persecution in helping to maintain group cohesion.
84. Houriet, *op. cit.,* pp. xxi–xxxii. Cf. Martin, *op. cit.,* pp. 122–24, 165–66.

The level of radical activity in Southern California, an anarchist revealingly complained in 1927,

> is not as it should theoretically be, there is a disadvantage in the beauty around Los Angeles. On arriving here one is immediately attracted by this beauty, by the out door life, by hiking, machine driving and numerous other attractions. The result of this is that many comrades who were active back home become inactive here. Instead of going [to] a meeting one goes . . . machine driving to the beaches in summer and to the canyons in winter and the movement is greatly suffering by it.[85]

If that same landscape could also furnish a backdrop where mystical movements flourished, such groups had their own problems in retaining a clear-cut identity, despite the fact that for several centuries the society had judged them harmless.

In America the danger of submergence in the larger society has always been peculiarly strong. The tug of the mainstream current, on a variety of levels, is very great. The most urgent need, year in and year out, is to retain a sufficiently distinctive posture to make an impact. And yet, as we have seen, the strategies which radicals can pursue in order to retain their identity and win attention for their point of view are severely limited.

Who does listen to the radical message? Who is likely to be converted to some version of it? In the audience for radicalism, no matter how slender it often is, lies the main basis for radical morale. Over time the condition of this potential audience can markedly alter. The novelty of the 1960's was no doubt very great from this point of view. Undreamed-of new sources for the eliciting of radical commitment suddenly opened up. These became the mainstay of hope for a significant rise in radical influence. Yet with hindsight it could be seen that the altered climate, though important, had distinct limits.

The changes in audience had little to do with social class. In these terms American radicalism was always multi-faceted, appealing to minor fractions of the well-off upper-middle class, sometimes to the lower-middle class,[86]

---

85. Joseph Spivak, "A Coast to Coast Observation," *Road to Freedom*, IV (September, 1927), 7. Kanter, *op. cit.*, p. 171, claims that it is now much harder to maintain firm boundaries between communes and the outside world than it was earlier, due to improved communications. But this minimizes the psychic, as distinct from the geographical, factor in isolation. In one recent urban commune in San Francisco, located near the heart of the city, it is reported that most of the members remained inside their building for weeks at a time. Rather, the case seems to be that at all periods in America physical escape has been so easy, and alternative possibilities so alluring, as to offer great temptations to desert, unless unusually strong countervailing forces are at work.

86. Some mystical movements have apparently been lower-middle class. LeWarne's forthcoming study of intentional communities in western Washington, 1885–1915,

and again to the most disadvantaged groups (who once joined the I.W.W. and now may admire the Black Panthers). Cultural radicalism has always been largely a middle-class phenomenon. It remained so in the 1960's. Though many examples were indeed found of hippies from all walks of life, they came in disproportionate numbers from middle-class, professional families.[87] Cultural radicalism may in fact be closely connected with affluence. Families in the early stages of an economic rise have never been notable for their indulgence of individual whims. This very fact may actually hold out some measure of long-term promise. The gradual drift in America is toward social and economic arrival, even if income distribution remains static. Though arrival will continue to mean different things in Houston and in San Francisco, the general trend, however slow-moving, would seem to be toward the social conditions which produce a letting-go from bourgeois constraints.

But social upheavals have a way of bursting out far more suddenly than may be accounted for in these terms. The counter-culture of the 1960's, though it by no means flattened out the American social landscape, was clearly such an upheaval. Thus the continuities in social class which it displayed were rightly given rather little notice.[88] It was seen first and foremost as a widespread revolt among youth.

Youth indeed strikingly dominated the radical life of the decade. It is true that the novelty of this phenomenon was sometimes exaggerated. Antecedents of generational rebellion had been present in the "flaming youth" of the 1920's, the Beat movement of the 1950's, and, to a degree, the still earlier bohemianism of Greenwich Village.[89] But the older anarchist, socialist, and mystical movements had been dominated by adults. Even in the 1930's, the young had been auxiliary to the main thrust of the radical movement, which centered in trade unions and other organizations primarily composed of the mature. The change was especially stark in

---

shows that those who entered the half-dozen experiments were from mixed working-class and middle-class backgrounds; some of them were poor, but few were absolutely destitute. Many members appear to have been single men just in the prime of life, or parents in their middle years with adolescent or slightly younger children. A minority were European born, but even they had spent time elsewhere in the United States before arriving.

87. For the evidence of this in California, see p. 72; in New Mexico, p. 196.

88. See, however, Melville, *op. cit.,* pp. 85, 90, and the head-on confrontation of the issue by Murray Bookchin, *Post-Scarcity Anarchism* (Berkeley: Ramparts Press, 1971), p. 26.

89. Thus it is possible to discern patterns of distinctively youthful rebellion running backward continuously in time. See David Matza, "Subterranean Traditions of Youth," *Annals of the American Academy of Political and Social Science,* CCC-XXXVIII (1961), 102–18.

movements oriented toward mysticism. These used to appeal very largely to well-to-do women, often in middle life. Now they attract the young of both sexes. Nothing revealed more sharply than this the reality of the new generational thrust.

But to call the counter-culture a universal "youth revolt" is far too simple. Only some youth, though a strikingly high number, participated. (George Wallace had also been disproportionately supported by younger voters in 1968.) Moreover, there were important variations in the degree of participation. Those who remained students generally held back from the sweeping embrace of cultural radicalism evident among nonstudents. To stay in a university however halfheartedly meant an acceptance of longer-range goals at the expense of immediate expressive gratification. Even the more left-wing students, though for a time deeply affected by certain radical symbols and ideals, actually occupied a position of compromise in terms of their basic values. (So, at a more moderate point along the spectrum, did many of their professors.) Given a further shift in the political climate, the students would easily retreat to working within the established system.[90] Here there is a hint that student demonstrations, shocking as they often seemed to the older people in their vicinity, were the product of a less deeply alienated outlook than the one expressing itself in quiet withdrawal to rural America.

90. At Berkeley, both students and nonstudent "street people" were drawn heavily from an almost identical spectrum of the middle class. But nonstudents had decidedly less conventional values, especially concerning immediate gratification, and also tended to be more estranged from their parents. William A. Watts and David Whittaker, "Profile of a Nonconformist Youth Culture: A Study of the Berkeley Non-Students," *Sociology of Education,* XLI (1968), 178–200; David Whittaker and William A. Watts, "Personality Characteristics of a Nonconformist Youth Subculture: A Study of the Berkeley Non-Student," *Journal of Social Issues,* XXV (1969), 65–89. These differences are confirmed in Herbert J. Cross, Rainer M. Doost, and James J. Tracy, "A Study of Values Among Hippies," *Proceedings of the Annual Convention of the American Psychological Association,* V (1970), 449–51. An unpublished study still in progress, by Larry Nucci, further reinforces these findings in comparing (with depth interviews and T.A.T. scores) seventy dropouts living in the Santa Cruz mountains with an equal number of Santa Cruz students. Nucci finds that the main distinguishing traits in the backgrounds of the dropouts are an early conflict with parental authority and equally early teen-age experiments with sex and drugs. By contrast, the students are surprisingly often still virgins, have never used drugs so heavily, and get along much better with their parents (though dropouts often return to superficially good relations with them after an initial breakaway). The Santa Cruz students thus seem similar to the activist liberals studied by Kenneth Keniston in his wrongly titled book *Young Radicals.* Of course it is natural that academics should have directed much of their study toward students, who were both more accessible and more congenial. But this seems to have deflected their vision away from the greater extremism of the dropouts. National polls show in any event that less than 15 per cent of undergraduates defined their position as within the New Left, both in 1969 and 1970.

If students belonged only partially to the new radical movement, ob-servers also noted sharp-edged differences within the ranks of the "street people." Some of the dropouts were engaged in a serious philosophical quest for meaning and identity. Mixed in among them were "heads" and "freaks," the drug-crazed equivalents of earlier alcoholics on Skid Row. Worshipers of Satanism and violence could also be found. In still another direction, each neighborhood of this kind contained weekend or "protean" hippies, who imitated the external fashions without sharing deeply in the beliefs.[91] And what are we to make of the daring youth in such locales as Iowa City or Helena, Montana, who caused neighborhood talk by letting their hair fall slightly below their ears? Though the idea of a single counter-culture no doubt survives such observations, the movement clearly amounted to far less than the uniform rebellion of an entire generation of American youth.

These qualifications make it somewhat easier to embark upon com-parisons between the youthful radicalism of the 1960's and earlier episodes of generational revolt in the American past. The bohemianism of Green-wich Village and of the Beat movement offers the most beguiling parallel, though these episodes had claimed far smaller numbers of young people. Both were revolts involving life style, and the Beats had directly anticipated the hippies in physical appearance. In a sense, the counter-culture of the 1960's displayed a tone halfway between them—less optimistically ex-uberant than that of the Village in its famous days around 1915, but less passive and morose than North Beach or Venice West.[92]

The parallel with the "flaming youth" of the 1920's stems from a very different and far more superficial kind of similarity. Prior to the counter-culture, only the 1920's had offered the spectacle of anything like a mass movement among the young, claiming a distinctive generational identity and pointedly severing their ties with the more conservative morality of their elders. But the comparison is only skin deep. As John Robert Howard has observed, "The deviant youth of the 1920's simply lived out what many 'squares' of the time considered the exciting life—the life of the 'swinger.' Theirs was a kind of deviance which largely accepted society's definitions

91. E.g., see John Robert Howard, "The Flowering of the Hippie Movement," *Annals of the American Academy of Political and Social Science,* CCCLXXXII (1969), 43–55.

92. The best source on the Beat movement remains Lawrence Lipton, *The Holy Barbarians* (New York: Messner, 1957). See also Francis J. Rigney and L. Douglas Smith, *The Real Bohemia* (New York: Basic Books, 1961). Roszak, *op. cit.,* assumes a great continuity from the Beat movement; Howard, *op. cit.,* stresses this even more after a summer of observation in the Haight-Ashbury.

of the bad and the beautiful."[93] The few deeply alienated Americans of the 1920's were found neither in Greenwich Village nor in Paris, but hidden away in the mystical movements of their day. And if the counter-culture of the 1960's sought joy in life, substituting drugs for alcohol, it did so in a world framed by gloom to a degree unknown even after Versailles.[94] Again, the deeply psychological view of man noticeable among some recent youth would have puzzled and disturbed even the most ardent Freudians of the earlier decade. Organic fusion in the life of a group was then undreamed of. The pleasures one sought were assertively masculine (even among flappers), and neither gentle nor narcissistic. The 1920's indeed witnessed a genuine sexual revolution, at least affecting middle-class girls.[95] But, in theory at any rate, the outlook of the 1960's cut far deeper into the core of culturally inherited sexual roles, and it also remained far more of a controversial minority phenomenon.

Even in comparison with the Beats, the hip counter-culture seems notably different. The bohemians of the 1950's were indrawn rather than outgoing or exhibitionist; they also had far less of an affirmative social vision. There are many degrees of privatism. Even the apolitical youth of the 1960's had far more social awareness, far more sense of mission, than their scattered predecessors of the pre-Kennedy years. The Beats had kept a culturally radical tradition alive during a season of low ebb, but their main direct function was to revitalize Asian mysticism, for the first time making it seem no longer a monopoly of elderly women.

Without the earlier radical tradition in America, the counter-culture of the 1960's could not have blossomed as it did. There were too many resemblances to previous bohemian episodes, often specifically involving youth, for one to discount the effects of half-conscious memory on the event. But these clues, like the growth of affluence and parental permissiveness, still do not seem adequately to account for its sudden burst. It was in

93. *Ibid.,* p. 53.
94. "It is true that to many of us our Bohemianism was a part of what we considered our Liberalism. We attended our own 'wild parties' and we were inclined to consider sex freedom as by no means the least important of the various freedoms we believed in. Yet in all of these things we did, nevertheless, genuinely believe, and we believed in them with hope. We were not . . . 'alienated,' at least not from man and the universe, though we thought ourselves thoroughly alienated from the United States of Coolidge and Hoover." Joseph Wood Krutch, *More Lives Than One* (New York: William Sloane Associates, 1962), p. 178.
95. Premarital virginity among middle-class American women appears to have declined with striking rapidity after about 1915. See Lewis M. Terman, *Psychological Factors in Marital Happiness* (New York: McGraw-Hill, 1938), p. 321.

part, as Theodore Roszak has suggested, more like a children's crusade in the Middle Ages.

This further comparison, however, suggests some of the movement's limitations. If the youth culture of the 1960's contained a dramatic numerical mass, there was a faddish quality about it as well. The central role of a musical style suggested this, for what is more notoriously liable to change rapidly with the passage of time? Though it would be quite wrong to underestimate the widespread depth of commitment to a new way of living, it was also clear that a large sector of rebellious or exhibitionist youth could easily be lured from one Pied Piper to another, whether in music or in meditation, during the course of a few years. More than this, the temptation to accept reasonably satisfying jobs on the terms offered by the essentially unyielding mainstream of the society remained strong in the end. The disadvantage of youth as the basis for a radical movement is that they can suddenly choose to "grow up" with minimal loss of face. When the society reveals that after all it has learned next to nothing, the mood shifts, however uneasily, to one of morning after.

Though it is too early to judge the staying power of the recent youth culture in general terms, the communal movement affords one concrete test of its stability as against the record of earlier radical efforts. First of all, it is necessary to know something about the longevity of the nineteenth-century communitarian experiments. Julia Elizabeth Williams, who once tabulated 236 earlier communities from this point of view, found that 25 percent of them failed during the first year, and 45 percent disappeared within five years.[96] From this it may be seen that the hardihood of the older ventures is easily exaggerated if one dwells only upon a handful of famous examples. Yet the figures also suggest a considerably greater rate of survival than obtained among the more than two thousand communes reportedly founded in the United States during the second half of the 1960's.[97] Though here statistics are lacking, nothing like 55 percent of them may be assumed to have survived for so long as five years. In this comparison, one again encounters the contrast between the more rational, goal-oriented outlook of radicals a century ago, as contrasted with the impulsive,

96. Julia Elizabeth Williams, "An Analytical Tabulation of the North American Utopian Communities by Type, Longevity, and Location" (unpublished master's thesis, University of South Dakota, 1939), pp. 15–16. A more discriminating tabulation by Kanter, *op cit.*, pp. 244–48, confirms this statistical impression.

97. Houriet, *op. cit.*, p. xiii, repeats the figure of 2,000 from a *New York Times* survey in 1970, also noting that a Berkeley sociologist, Benjamin Zablocki, has claimed 3,000. Melville, *op. cit.*, p. 23, more modestly says "at least a thousand." Since there is no firm criterion for what constitutes a *bona fide* commune, all these figures must be regarded as no more than informed guesses.

spontaneous urge toward experimental living in the present. Moreover, if one trusts these estimates, one realizes that the gain in sheer numbers is not as impressive as has often been assumed. If the recent communes total roughly ten times the number of communities founded in the nineteenth century, the American population has increased more than ninefold since 1850. (Of course this ignores the fact that the recent communal movement blossomed all at once, whereas the older communities were founded over a span of several decades.) It is also likely that the average membership in recent communes has been smaller.

These statistical yardsticks are too crude and incomplete to bear much weight. They may be supplemented by impressions that are more subjective. For instance, a small number of highly structured communities appear like occasional landmarks within the recent surge of informal commune-founding. They include Twin Oaks, the Lama Foundation, and Ezra's group, as well as larger social movements such as the Hare Krishna and the Children of God. From one point of view, it may be these which are most meaningfully compared with their earlier counterparts. They strike the observer as easily possessing more stamina than hip communes like the New Buffalo, the Hog Farm, or Drop City. Clearly they represent a continuation of the social movement in its classic form. Their existence proves that even within the radicalism of the 1960's older impulses toward concreteness, organization, and strong ideological commitment still survived. Some of these movements might well prove to be as long-lived as certain of the more successful nineteenth-century groups. But, to confuse the issue, they also seem little hardier than the early twentieth-century anarchist colonies at Home and Stelton, which were largely unstructured.

On what, then, does longevity depend? Structure, while not an absolutely necessary condition, does seem to promote a greater chance for survival. Of course at an opposite extreme it may occasionally be too rigid, cumbersome, or Byzantine. But this was more likely to be a difficulty in the early nineteenth century, an age of constitution worship (New Harmony, Indiana, went through five such formal documents in the span of a single year). There is now far less interest in amateur political science of this kind. Structure can still be elaborately minute, as at Twin Oaks and in Ezra's community, but it is underlain by a somewhat greater degree of pragmatic realism.

Very interestingly, the structured communities of both the nineteenth and twentieth centuries have commonly been intensely charismatic as well. This paradox has been too little appreciated, because Max Weber's typology of authority leads us to think of structure and charisma as distinct alternatives. Yet in fact an elaborately bureaucratic internal structure appears to go hand in hand with the magnetic sway of an authoritarian leader in creating some of the toughest and stablest counter-cultural environments. (Reflecting on this point, one soon realizes that this was also true of the Christian Science movement, and indeed of the Soviet Union under Lenin and Stalin.) In our own survey, Ezra's community offered the most striking case of this flourishing combination; seldom have formally established subgroupings and committees, dividing each individual into a multiplicity of roles, been so finely elaborated in a group of no more than thirty people, yet the whole was welded together by a subservience to Ezra's will. Vedanta was only somewhat less marked in this respect. In international terms, its organization rapidly became quite elaborate, and in India it was dominated by an increasingly conservative formal hierarchy of elderly swamis, though at the same time each swami retained a charismatic individual following. When charisma is routinized, as happened so strikingly in the Vedanta movement, rather than fading out, it can remain alive in a stable synthesis with structure to produce these remarkable results.

Of the two ingredients, structure and charisma, one is tempted from these examples to say that charisma is somewhat more crucial. Lifetime commitment on the part of the adherents, highly dedicated and unswerving, has appeared to stem most often from willing submission to the discipline of a guru, teacher, or revolutionary leader. Personal bonds of this kind seem stronger in practice than abstractly intellectual ones; indeed, the world of political machines and crime syndicates reminds us of how unyielding these ties between individuals can become when they are accompanied by no ideology whatever. And yet it is the ideology which defines a given group as "radical." In radical movements, when this personal commitment occurs in a communal setting, the group becomes most effectively sealed off from the alien influences of the outside world. The members have been taken over by the microcosm in every aspect of daily living and thinking. They are impervious to external suggestion. Rarely do they read literature from beyond the movement, and they find it hard to speak to outsiders except as potential converts. Wives commonly separate from their husbands, or children from their parents, when they join. Both Vedanta and Ezra's group tend strongly toward this pattern, as do the Children of God. And when to this personal basis for commitment is added the stabilizing regularity of a well-defined structure, there is an unequaled chance for long-term survival. The ability to make large numbers of new converts, however, will still depend to a very large degree on the circumstances prevailing in the outside world. If the established social order was ever genuinely tending toward collapse, one or more of these movements, like Christianity, might become the basis for a widespread new cultural pattern. Ezra expects that in the hydrogen age this will really happen. But historically so far in America, movements of this kind have shown only the relative toughness that enables them to endure, with increasing ossification, for several decades, in some cases (especially among the religious bodies of this type) for over a century.

But what of the seeming alternative to this basis for strength offered by such anarchist communities as Home and Stelton? To be sure, they each lasted for no more than a generation, and the bonds between their residents were too loose to permit them to be called unified counter-cultures in quite the same sense. The winds of the outside world blew more directly upon them, leading their children commonly to make peace once again with the cultural mainstream.

Still, even their degree of success was somewhat remarkable, and it depended neither upon charisma (in any extreme sense) nor upon formal structure. The examples of Stelton and Home—and indeed of Utopia and Modern Times in the nineteenth century—suggest that an anarchist outlook may actually be peculiarly suitable for a communal group of the relatively unstructured, low-key variety which wishes to endure. Most socialist communities, for instance, tended to sink back more rapidly into the American mainstream, sometimes literally turning themselves into real-estate promotions within a few years.[98] Anarchism, moreover, was always really intended to function on a small numerical scale of this kind. In quiet, inconspicuous settings anarchism may yet prove to be a fertile source of reasonably durable communitarian commitment. From this point of view, the experience of Stelton may well be the most relevant historical model for current efforts. And its success resulted from a recipe entirely unlike the one advanced by Rosabeth Moss Kanter in her recent pioneering study of communal undertakings, *Commitment and Community,* making it appear that she has undervalued the anarchist tradition.

One caveat must be entered even here. Both Stelton and Rockridge were greatly aided by a mild but definite degree of leadership. (This is an uncomfortable subject for anarchists, but it must be faced.) Harry Kelly, Joseph Cohen, and the Ferms at Stelton, Frank and perhaps two of the other men at Rockridge, contributed enormously to the "good vibrations" of these

98. See LeWarne's forthcoming study of several such colonies in Washington state. However, the Llano colony, founded by Job Harriman, endured equally long with a socialist philosophy. On it see *Gateway to Freedom* (Leesville, Lousiana: Llano Co-Operative Colony, 1924); also Hine, *op. cit.*

undertakings.[99] Such leadership, of course, is clearly of a different kind, or at least of a different degree, from that found in the charismatic communities of discipline. However, it seems to have been an important factor. And it is a slender reed. The tightrope between too much and too little control must be walked unendingly by the man or woman who plays this role. As the years pass, the key individuals are increasingly tempted to give up the effort, especially when, as is almost inevitable, they face factional discord. In nonradical settings, for instance the major political parties, such skillful leaders often keep going because of the practical incentives of prestige and power, though even here the party chairmanship is usually a rotating office as a result of its built-in headaches. In counter-cultural groups, the leaders must be impelled by idealism alone.

The prognosis for the truly formless hip communes of the present day, which lack charisma, structure, or mild but effective low-key leadership, is the most bleak of all. But one wonders how typical—or how seriously intended—is the very desire for longevity in such settings, though it was plainly present at Rockridge. In the recent counter-culture, the future tends to be screened over by the mind in favor of concentration upon the immediate flow of experience. (Even at Rockridge, house building was slow, broken by many hours spent in conversation or in getting high.) Then again, hip culture is marked by a constant stream of individual comings and goings. Indeed, one may speculate that the contemporary interest in communes stemmed more from the new urge toward organic fusion of individuals than it did from any sympathy with the planning-oriented rationale of earlier intentional communities. Plans are still projected, especially in rural settings, but they are usually made dutifully rather than with real zest. The nineteenth-century utopias seem very remote and relatively uninteresting to today's youth. Aside from the small number of classic social movements which have sprung into existence in the counter-culture, the communes appear to be founded on a basis which makes the very question of permanence seem old-fashioned and beside the point.

These conclusions, finally, suggest something further about anarchism and mysticism as traditions relevant to the forming of secessionist communities. The most revealing typology of these communities, in the past and present, turns out in the end to be sociological rather than one which divides them neatly along philosophical lines. To review the situation

99. Home does not seem to have enjoyed such happy leadership, and it did not last quite so long. Both the nineteenth-century anarchist communities Utopia and Modern Times lasted roughly as long as Home before slipping into conventionality, and Josiah Warren (founder of both) was criticized as an insufficiently forceful leader. Martin, *op. cit.,* p. 83.

briefly, first one finds a relatively small number of highly structured and formal undertakings, which are also often intensely charismatic (and which have been referred to as falling within the domain of classic social movements). These appear to change their character rather little from one generation to another. Second, one identifies the fairly long-lived communities which have been loose and unstructured but which have benefited from another kind of effective leadership. These are even more infrequent at any time. Third, and last, there is the great mass of communities which have been founded with none of these advantages; they have been most susceptible to generational changes of mood and tone (ranging from hyper-constitutionalism in the nineteenth century to hyper-immediacy in the present), and they typically disintegrate in short order.

Mysticism turns out historically to have been very often, though not always, identified with the first of these three sociological types of communal ventures. This pattern of belief is indeed congenial to an authoritarian form of leadership, though other intellectual traditions might in theory serve equally well.[100] In just about the same way, anarchism proves to be loosely related to the second type. Thus both mysticism and anarchism have been somewhat associated with unusually durable communitarian efforts, at least in twentieth-century America.

But this sociological typology makes clear the very different basis, and also the different extent, of the success in each case. Stelton was an extremely rare phenomenon. Mystical charismatic movements have been much more common and also hardier and more secure. If one dislikes authoritarianism, the contrast is quite discouraging. In any event, to this extent it seems likely that the "inner" and the "external" paths to liberation will remain distinct from each other in the future, because of their close association with such sharply dissimilar patterns of group interaction. (Or if they occasionally appear to combine, as in Ezra's group, it is, as we saw, only on the basis of a harshly unromantic definition of the inner life, imposed by an overbearing discipline.) The broad contrast in atmospheres between Rockridge and Ezra's ranch at any rate seems as pronounced as that be-

---

100. It used to be thought that religious belief of some kind was definitely related to the longevity of communal experiments, for instance those of the nineteenth century. But Williams, *op. cit.*, found it to be no more than a slight factor. In view of this, any form of religion might be regarded as a handily available source of disciplinary commitment in our culture, though today one can imagine the same style of subservient commitment attaching itself to a leader in the purely psychiatric (and perhaps the political) mode. Indeed, one realizes that Charles Manson was such an example, requiring no clear-cut system of beliefs to exert his extraordinary hold upon his following. Instead, he is reported as having made love to the members of his entourage an extraordinary number of times per day.

tween Stelton and Vedanta, though, especially in the realm of ecological thinking and practice, they also carry evidences of a common generational identity. In sociological terms as well as in world views, rival forms appear to march down from the past into the present side by side. And if there has been change, particularly in the secular and non-authoritarian realm, it is of a sort which casts doubt upon the ability of another Stelton to emerge from the recent communal scene. But of course there still may be time, and with it some reason to hope, either at Rockridge or in Oregon, Vermont, or somewhere else.

The problem of radical influence and staying power is a very broad one, with dimensions that go far beyond the ability of communal groups to survive. A subtler battle has long been fought in the realm of attitudes and beliefs. On a general plane, as we have already briefly noted, the mainstream has posed a series of insidious threats by invading radical minds with some of its own characteristic ways of looking at things. From this point of view, radicals have had good reason to be concerned about the purity of their intellectual intake.

For instance, a tradition of moral idealism has long been powerful in America, even if from a radical point of view it fatally compromises itself with nationalistic and materialistic ends. This tradition has sent its tentacles into every corner of the would-be rebel's consciousness. Anarchists of the late nineteenth century recognized this foe and greeted it with open battle.[101] Perhaps it was relatively easy to disengage from an enemy which was then so unsubtle and high-flown. But Victorian rhetoric faded after Woodrow Wilson, and by the 1960's "idealism" had become a good word in most sectors of the radical movement. Thereby a major formal boundary between the radical and liberal traditions had become erased. Even in the earlier period, anarchists did not firmly dissociate themselves from the "good" episodes in American history, notably those involving Thomas Jefferson and the abolitionists. Partly this was a tactic to win friends, but it also cut deeper.[102]

101. "As Danton loved peace, but not the peace of slavery, so I love justice, but not the justice of moralism and idealism." Victor Yarros in *Liberty*, quoted in *Egoism*, I (May, 1890), 7. Cf. *ibid.*, I (August, 1890), 2.

102. E.g., see Voltairine de Cleyre, "Anarchism and American Traditions," in Veysey, *op. cit.*, pp. 144–58. The recent industrial period of American history was the main target, just as for the Populists. For a strongly negative view of American history, resembling that of many radicals in the 1960's, see C. L. James, *Anarchy*, p. 24n. In their reconstruction of history, anarchists reached for past precedents and congenial ideas from outside their own movement wherever, in Europe or America, they could find them. Vedantists were even more resourceful at this use of the past on three continents.

Meanwhile, religious mystics (who were then so often from well-to-do backgrounds) met their own demon in the form of conventional gentility. They never really did it battle, and it persisted to haunt them long after the genteel tradition had faded from most of the rest of American life.[103] This refusal to distinguish themselves from an existing social class (except when they wore white monastic robes) made it hard to believe, unless one knew them well, that they were in any sense radical at all.

The mainstream offered another, still greater threat. The radical tradition, particularly on its secular side, always had trouble in defining its position with respect to such widely accepted values as hard work, achievement, pioneering, and pragmatic experiment. Individualist anarchists of the late nineteenth century had trouble clearly distinguishing their message from that of the extreme advocates of economic laissez-faire, though differences certainly existed.[104] Much later on, notions of adventurous, strain-filled enterprise kept on recurring in a wide variety of radical contexts. Communist youth of the 1930's styled themselves the "Young Pioneers." The persistent theme of energy accumulation was similarly revealing in these terms. Even mystics, whose focus on contemplation served to set them apart in this respect, sometimes spoke proudly of their endeavors as "hard work."[105]

Most curious of all are the relations between anarchism (including much of the recent counter-culture) and the central American tradition of pragmatism. In 1886 C. L. James was so modern as to relate anarchist ideas to the concept of relativism, as part of an attack upon idealist metaphysics. The truth of "the systems of ethics or metaphysics . . . depends on the point of view from which they are regarded. . . . Practical experience," not abstract morality, gives us "a sound philosophy of life." Governments, not their critics, are thus "dogmatical."[106] Though it was much more common for anarchists then to argue in the positivistic language of

103. A Vedanta audience would be genuinely shocked if anyone appeared in the temple wearing old clothes during a service. *Message of the East*, XXX (January, 1941), 56–57, describing a much earlier incident, but without apologetic comment.
104. In 1886, William Graham Sumner came to hear Benjamin Tucker give a lecture and debated with him in the question period. (Sumner of course was hostile to anarchism, though a believer in laissez-faire.) Sumner contended that the principle of economic interest existed in nature, while Tucker said it was the artificial result of monopoly. In economics, anarchists down-played the idea of competition altogether, emphasizing the peaceful coexistence of individuals instead. Tucker also did not like the idea of accumulating profits, the hoarding of resources over long periods of time. See also above, p. 425.
105. Lucis Trust, *The Arcane School* (New York: by the Trust, n.d.), p. [3]. Will Levington Comfort once declared, "The business of man is to produce something." *Child and Country*, p. 340.
106. James, *Anarchy*, pp. 30–31.

social science, the more famous example of William James reminds us that there was not always a firm distinction between these two perspectives, and radicals could occasionally follow the route that led toward an attack upon intellectual formalism.

In a broader way, as time went on, anarchists and other founders of intentional communities could claim that they were pursuing the hallowed American technique of practical experiment. If radicals of the turn of the century usually claimed an intellectually elite status, currents of anti-intellectual down-to-earthness were alive even then, especially among those with plain backgrounds. Even for the "intellectuals," the act of plunging so seriously into the realm of progressive education, as in the Ferrer movement, inevitably pulled them some distance into the arena of pragmatic discourse.

In the counter-culture of the 1960's, the deep response of American youth to the practical activism often associated with the frontier period of American history became especially striking. Though the tie was partly sentimental (despite its reversal of the usual heroic roles assigned to cowboys and Indians), it was also a good deal more than that. The idea of the simple life, especially as lived in the wilderness, took much of its tone from this effort to recapture an earlier reality. To do without labor-saving devices became an important test of manhood among many long-haired farmers and mechanics. As we saw at Rockridge and at Ezra's ranch, urban youth often now deliberately travel to remote settings in part to "prove" themselves in what is indeed a time-honored fashion—on the level of basic physical competency. They want, of course, to live an intimately collective life, and a sensually more attuned life than that of their straight neighbors. But, in such an environment, long hair and pot smoking can easily become almost the only important emblems of continued radical identity. For this very reason, it may seem urgent to cling to these symbols.[107] From this perspective, the counter-culture of the 1960's was at least as shot through with contradictions as all the earlier phases of American radicalism.

And yet if these values of practical pioneering made America prosper, could they not do the same for a radical tradition which retains them but combines them with other, highly unconventional ideals? This was the promise that lay behind the recent effort to break down certain customary roles and barriers between individuals. American culture had always thrown up a high barricade between the masculine sphere of tough realism

107. This was what I sensed at Rockridge; however, see below, n. 127.

and the feminine sphere of soft emotion. The new pioneering would be radical if it succeeded in dissolving these distinctions. But the widespread tendency for sex roles to remain conventionally defined inside the rural communes suggested failure in this crucial respect.

In a larger sense, the harsh necessities of communal existence force people who may have dreamed of timelessness to move back part way into a more conventional dimension of thinking. Crops, by their nature, require future calculation. To spend one's time cultivating them is to defer gratification. Work schedules must be arranged, whether they are called that or not. At Rockridge, the hip farmers dealt with the grinding realities of subsistence during the day, not unlike factory workers, then relaxed at night. The new rhetoric of spontaneous flow does not conceal the persistence of the customary division of life into separate spheres of duty and pleasure. When, in the urban hip scene, duty is reduced to the minimal chores involved in cadging and ripping off, the sense of being lost or adrift seems only to increase. Still another alternative, which has become fairly common around Santa Cruz, is to work at temporary jobs (for instance, in construction) about six months of the year and live on the savings the other half. Yet this merely extends the day-night alternation, producing a series of wrenching shocks all its own.

Nowhere in these several patterns is there a hint of breakthrough into a permanently satisfying regime of wholeness and integration, shared by all alike. Meanwhile, Ezra's group on the desert, despite its great pride in creating an intricate new formula for balanced living, was grotesquely dominated by the tough, achievement-oriented values of mainstream America.

In all these ways, the larger society has continued to deny its rebels the chance to gain more than a precarious degree of independence from it. During recent decades, several of the most important changes in radical tone have been the result primarily of changes in the mainstream rather than of a self-generating evolution in radical thought. Thus the decline of atheism has paralleled the increased privatization of religious attitudes in America generally. As Christianity widely evaporated, Asian mysticism also came to seem less eccentric. And the growing fashion of a humanistic quest for inner self-development (no longer closely linked with the theme of economic success seeking), which appeared in a liberal segment of the mainstream, encouraged similar tendencies in the radical world. The partial melting of the social class structure during the course of the twentieth century, the growing code of casual informality at most levels of the society, allowed radicals to become less standoffish and more genuinely democratic. A change of attitudes toward racial and sexual equality made radicals sound somewhat more like other people when they spoke on these matters.[108] The long decline of the older style of economic individualism in America permitted radicals to move more markedly in the same direction. This may also be observed about the rise of sexual permissiveness and the growing acceptance of the sanctity of life revealed until very recently in opinion polls about capital punishment. In all these respects, radicals may be said to have received a "free ride" from the society that surrounded them. This "free ride," somewhat ironically, may be at least as important as the contrary buffetings of persecution and indifference.

Except for the Freudian vogue, these external effects have acted mainly to encourage tendencies already present in the nineteenth-century radical imagination. And all these trends must be balanced against the many striking internal continuities which earlier were shown to have survived in radical thought. Yet, at least in a quantitative sense, the ups and downs in the history of American radicalism have closely followed trends in the larger society, indeed in the world situation. Except perhaps when the rapid inflow of European immigrants affected the scene in the late nineteenth century, radical strength has appeared to ebb and flow as a result of temporary changes in the general American political and social climate. The subtle receptiveness of "advanced" progressives around 1912–1913, of Franklin D. Roosevelt in the 1930's, and of John F. Kennedy in the early 1960's toward "new" ideas, or more lately styles of living, undoubtedly gave encouraging signals to radicals. The appearance of these figures with far wider audiences who were "getting away with it" makes still more pronounced changes briefly seem possible. The Russian revolution, which altered the world climate in the same respect, also created hopes that could linger for several decades. Negatively, the rise of a Hitler, or more recently of American saber rattling, can easily spark the growth of a militant and determined radical response. Both the positive lure and the negative frustration were keenly present during the 1960's. Perhaps their combined impact explains the scope and intensity of the radical upsurge during those particular years.

The flow of influence in the other direction, from the radicals toward the Roosevelts and Kennedys, is far less easy to trace with assurance. Even the

108. I do not mean to imply that the American mainstream has moved decisively toward belief in racial or sexual equality, or toward humanitarian values more generally. Indeed, in the 1970's it appears again to have reached a standstill in these basic respects. But from the 1930's to the 1960's there was a clear pattern of movement *part* of the way in these directions.

liberals of *The New Republic* seldom were able to bend a President's ear.[109] Only a Kissinger, not a Tugwell or a Schlesinger, could hope to go much farther, and he likewise found that there were limits. As for socialists, anarchists, and mystics, to speak of them in this context is ludicrous. On a broader level, changing American attitudes toward democratic equality—as far as they have gone—appear to result more from the revelation of concentration-camp horrors and from scientific education launched by the Boas school of anthropologists than from concrete pressure on the far left. Ruth Benedict, not Emma Goldman, was the opponent of discrimination who reached a really wide audience.[110] Anarchism and most forms of socialism have remained forever tainted with the stigmas of "alien" origin and crankishness. While the counter-culture made it harder to argue that these "diseased cells" came directly from overseas, the underlying sense of their strangeness persisted.[111] To survive and periodically revive under these conditions, with a certain degree of inner creativity, has been the main radical achievement.

Meanwhile, however, radicalism, like the surrounding world, has undergone a fundamental change of mood, broader than any of the particular elements in its complexion which have thus far been set forth. Along with the rest of mankind in the developed world, radicals during the course of the twentieth century have become far less certain of the fact of progress. Especially since the Second World War, a more grimly serious perception of the future has come to possess all thinking people. Hitler revealed how suddenly the modern ship of state might veer in a frightening direction. Stalin showed how easily ancient forms of despotism could be revived and expanded in the name of radical ideology. The United States, hitherto an exaggerated symbol of moral idealism, put on a more openly callous face as it maneuvered among these threats. Meanwhile, the mathematical argument for the ever-growing likelihood of hydrogen war remained unanswerable, despite all the reassuring talk about balance of power and détente. (As a constantly widening numerical sample of diverse individuals, in a

109. See Charles Forcey, *The Crossroads of Liberalism* (New York: Oxford University Press, 1961).

110. For her influence on George Jackson, for example, see *Soledad Brother: The Prison Letters of George Jackson* (New York: Bantam Books, 1970), p. 226.

111. Theodore Roszak, *op. cit.*, p. 51, overstated the case for change on the mystical side when he said: "Theosophists and fundamentalists, spiritualists and flat-earthers, occultists and satanists . . . it is nothing new that there should exist anti-rationalist elements in our midst. What *is* new is that a radical rejection of science and technological values should appear so close to the center of our society, rather than on the negligible margins." By 1973 it was possible to see that the "center" had survived, basically unaffected, the ecology movement notwithstanding.

variety of countries, came to possess temporary power to push the button, the odds that one of them would really do so were bound to increase over the decades and centuries.) Was Vietnam the last phase of the Cold War, or was it an equivalent to the Balkan situation in 1912? No one could be entirely sure. When a young adult chose to flee civilization and survive with Ezra in 1968, only half a decade after the world had almost destroyed itself in the Cuban missile crisis, the choice could be defended in purely reasonable terms. By comparison it might seem purely quixotic when Georgina Jones Walton answered the call from Swami Paramananda. The occasional evenings of mirthful gaiety at Vedanta Centre could not be recaptured even at Trabuco in the mid-1940's.

Radicals, like the rest of us, were fast losing their earlier innocence. It was now an age seemingly made for apocalyptic thinking. But the apocalypse was approaching under no one's control; it bore little resemblance to the classic dream of an advancing revolution or a New Age. (Only die-hard leftists like Murray Bookchin still lived in a dream world of expectations for converting the masses.) So in another sense it was a period when radicals wearily wrote themselves new and less confident time tables.[112] By contrast, when the Ferrer Modern School was founded, immediate hopes were high for the human race. "Socialism is advancing with a steady pace; the agnostic conception of the universe has all but become general; divorce is only frowned on by the most reactionary"—this could be the easy boast of 1907.[113] American radicals of that day were future-oriented, not nostalgic. Unlike the English Romantics of the early nineteenth century, they seldom longed to go backward in time. When J. William Lloyd briefly conjured up a vision of "tribalism," a more modern definition of the good life had won out by the closing scenes of the novel.[114]

---

112. "In the long view, communes have not yet created a new relationship with the land: & we may need a thousand yrs of accumulated experience before we know the spirit-of-place which animates this continent." Alan Hoffman's untitled broadside, San Francisco, ca. 1968. Ezra similarly spoke of being engaged in a work which might require several hundred or a thousand years. Even in the 1930's, Max Heindel's Rosicrucian group had calculated, on the basis of astrology, that the New Age would not arrive until the year 2654.

113. Leon Partridge, "Is Radicalism Effective?" *Lucifer*, June 6, 1907, pp. 94–95. To be sure, anarchists had to contend with the fact that their own movement was already declining, but the larger scene gave them reason to remain optimistic.

114. The tone of the new civilization to be founded in Uganda at the end of the Populist Ignatius Donnelly's *Caesar's Column* (Chicago: F. J. Schulte, 1890) is as modern as the motor-car manufacture at the end of Lloyd's *The Dwellers in Vale Sunrise*. The clash between Lloyd's primitivistic fantasies and his socialistic ending showed that a sexually based and perhaps rather timeless image could not then be easily integrated with the future-oriented social blueprint highly characteristic of its decade. By the 1960's pessimism could erase the problem within radical thought.

As long as the world appears to be moving in one's own direction, there is little call to flee geographically or to look backward toward the past. Isolated half-pessimists there indeed were in 1900, but they did not set the tone of the earlier movement.[115] To put this another way, alienation may sometimes have run as deep, but it was more readily replaced, among a far larger proportion of the earlier dropouts, by confident forms of newly adopted commitment. Radicals later on either embraced causes in the eerily total style of Communism, the Children of God, and a number of the mystical religious movements, or else they found it less easily possible to connect decisively with anything at all. Twentieth-century gloom has made the distinction between uneasy floating and the wholehearted embrace of a clear-cut solution grow somewhat more sharp-edged.

Even among very young people, the hope has become increasingly the one of merely "holding on."[116] The apparent ebullience of the counter-culture, the exuberant defiance of the rock music, the body-painting and public flaunting of sex, cannot disguise this very deep and important change. Much of the highly prized "spontaneity" actually stemmed from a joyless awareness of what can and cannot be squeezed out of a momentary situation, an almost Benthamite calculation of what is now possible but may be gone tomorrow. The desire to hold on to childhood pleasures as one moves into adult life partakes of this quality. The young are afraid that everything may be taken away from them. The fascists may take over; why not get high, go naked, and make love under the open sky in the time left before the deluge? The loss of faith in the long-range future perhaps explains another striking characteristic of the recent counter-culture, the previously unknown willingness to let one's body stay physically dirty for long periods.[117] Washing is a form of planning, a way of making oneself ready for future occasions. In a world which is believed to have no future, it becomes senseless. Going dirty reduces the need for devoting time to up-

115. Voltairine de Cleyre was one. But few secular radicals would then have agreed with James Armstrong, Jr., that "it is only when we turn from the sorrow and vanity of all human existence to the contemplation of the beauty of the unconscious world that life becomes at all tolerable through our partial forgetfulness of it." "The Suppression of the Sexual Impulse," *Lucifer*, December 8, 1904, p. 211. The deepest statements of alienation in that day (e.g., those of Luhan and Comfort, to be quoted shortly) came, interestingly enough, from a handful of the more avant-garde religious mystics.

116. There is evidence that the suicide rate for Americans under thirty increased dramatically during the 1960's, while that for old people (perhaps thanks to Medicare) fell off. *New York Times*, April 3, 1972.

117. Except for hoboes, this phenomenon was new among radicals in the 1960's. Even at Stelton, where visitors complained of dirt, it had usually taken the form of litter.

keep and makes one's life far more flexible. The mind is freed for immediate experience.[118]

The entire shift toward unreason, which may be partly a move from long-term calculations to shorter-term ones, is deeply conditioned by the the decline in hope for the future of the human race. In a situation of no dependable tomorrows, both the momentary and the cocoonlike escape routes seem attractive. Slightly different people end up at Rockridge or with Ezra. The mainstream American, who easily dismisses the threat of world destruction from his mind, finds these patterns of escape foolish and incomprehensible. But historically the calculated postponement of gratification has been closely joined to a basic sense of optimism. Reason, in its everyday meaning of amassing a stake for one's family, withers when confronted by the existence of nuclear stockpiles. The escape route of the mainstream is to avoid thinking about these weapons and the fallible men who control them. Only as that method of escape is taken do radical fears about Vietnam acquire the reassuring label of paranoia. Only then do radicals' decisions to revel in their version of the good life seem quixotic.

As one enters the world of the counter-culture, one is repeatedly made to realize how very seriously its members take the possibility of apocalypse. As the theme of impending doom (nuclear and ecological) recurs in one form or another in countless conversations, among radicals who otherwise display very different temperaments, one wonders whether such an assumption about the future is not at the very center of the radical outlook today. In a sense, everything else follows from this, or, if one is in the mainstream, from its denial. The kind of future one believes in determines how one responds to every suggestion concerning work, family, and pleasure. Radicals are now those who reveal in all the details of their lives that they take seriously the possibility of general disaster. This is what now profoundly continues to separate them from the majority of Americans. The majority retains its conventional faith in the likelihood of living out its life span essentially undisturbed. To be sure, this faith has been somewhat dimmed in a world grown more hazardous. But the ability of most Americans to go on acting upon optimistic premises must not be underestimated. It may well be sufficient in its momentum to keep America a "great" nation for at

118. At bottom, personal cleanliness appears to be nothing more than a cultural variable, though deeply ingrained within particular cultures. Theodora Kroeber noted that the wild California Indian Ishi was naturally very neat and tidy in his habits, but that Mojave tribesmen in the same state failed to take any such pains. Theodora Kroeber, *Ishi in Two Worlds* (Berkeley: University of California Press, 1961), p. 222. From this perspective, unconcern with dirt might be an important indication of a genuine impulse toward "cultural revolution."

least another century. And, during this uncertain span of time, the contrast between these very different perceptions of the future will serve to prevent any real rapprochement between radicals and the mainstream. The credibility of doom, among its other effects, now hinders co-optation.

The desire to do one's thing now, while it can still be done, gives the present counter-culture its noticeable monotony of tone. In the opening years of the twentieth century, "spontaneity" had been contrasted with "formalism"; it was a weapon in a hopeful campaign to free men from unthinking bondage to philosophical or social custom. The Ferms at Stelton could believe in a large degree of spontaneity because it trained an individually self-reliant character. In the present day, the "spontaneous" action often turns out to be the same greedily enjoyed pleasure which everyone around us is similarly taking.

Though sex and drugs may be more imaginative forms of pleasure than lawn mowing or ice fishing, they can pall sooner. Repeated LSD trips often make an individual draw back, feeling that there is no further insight to be obtained in that fashion. On a sorrier level, it is not unknown for "heads," after years of drifting in street life, suddenly to decide to join the Navy. Ultimately, even on Ken Kesey's bus, there are only the same things to do over and over again.[119] Finally the trip has to come to an end. The foul taste of satiation and self-disgust, which dominates a film like Andy Warhol's *Trash,* replaces the innocent ecstasy of the first "flower children." Naturally such a change is never complete, and it is wrong to let these isolated symbols stand too readily for the whole. From many points of view, the counter-culture of the 1960's was always far fresher than the wearily predictable political radicalism of the 1930's. But the tendency was to move toward a bored, played-out feeling, and this cast a shadow over all the fervent efforts of youth in the last ten years to reach for and claim a new measure of human liberation. Self-expression, like revolution, is only fun when it appears that the whole trend of history may be with you. In this sense, Walt Whitman and the Greenwich Village bohemians basked in a climate which has vanished beyond recall.

Though it is a bit soon for an assessment, the literary record of the recent counter-culture appears to reflect this half-deadened mood. Extreme alienation can of course inspire profound art, but the hip scene has produced no Dostoyevsky or Céline. Instead we have Raymond Mungo, whose *Total Loss Farm* is whining, obvious, and flat, ominously reveling in the

119. Tom Wolfe, *The Electric Kool-Aid Acid Test* (New York: Bantam Books, 1969).

minutiae of mainstream culture (radio station call letters, Ford heaters, and the like). Or we have William J. Craddock's *Be Not Content,* marked by a psychological honesty that is more appealing, but still a piece of mere reportage.[120] The novels of Ken Kesey engagingly pursue well-marked literary traditions (such as the exposure of authoritarianism in psychiatry and the evocation of a pristine natural environment in Oregon). But they convey little of the outrageousness of his La Honda escapades. Richard Brautigan, though both honest and intermittently funny, too often slips into aimless reportorial empiricism, even in his poems.[121] The poetry of Gary Snyder seems disappointingly matter-of-fact and derivative, when set along-side earlier writers in the Whitman vein. Again, a comic-book format suggests compulsive parody of the mainstream, not the forging of a deeply original insight. Thus *The Whole Earth* catalogs offered momentary enter-tainment, on a level with *Popular Science Monthly* or dime-store puzzle books. In the hydrogen age it is hard to strike the true note of frivolity, but one wonders why radical literature so rarely avoids the twin pitfalls of surrogate consumerism and whimper. The best writing on the counter-culture has been by outside journalists like Robert Houriet, Rasa Gustaitis, and especially Tom Wolfe.[122]

It may be objected that novels and poetry are forms which the counter-culture has itself made obsolete. But a life of being rather than of creating may end up as one of pointless drift. The quality of alienation in such a life may prove merely banal.

Of course rock music, rather than literature, embodied the driving spirit of the counter-culture. In this realm, to be sure, there was much more evidence of liveliness and engagement. Many of the best moments of the new scene were centered in musical experience. But here too often lurked sadness and desperation, sometimes openly, more often masked as frenzy. Rock musicians, like their jazz predecessors, actually formed a subculture marked by the deepest forms of loneliness and self-alienation. (Films such as *Don't Look Back* and *200 Motels* keenly conveyed this mood.) The

120. Raymond Mungo, *Total Loss Farm: A Year in the Life* (New York: E. P. Dutton, 1970); William J. Craddock, *Be Not Content: A Subterranean Journal* (Garden City, New York: Doubleday, 1970). Despite all his self-promotion, I like Abbie Hoffman better than these authors.

121. Richard Brautigan, *The Pill Versus the Springhill Mine Disaster* (San Francisco: Four Seasons Foundation, 1968); Richard Brautigan, *A Confederate General from Big Sur* (New York: Grove Press, 1964).

122. Rasa Gustaitis, *Turning On* (New York: Macmillan, 1969); Wolfe, *op. cit.* Houriet's outsider role gives *Getting Back Together* its observational cutting edge, despite his own self-conscious efforts to move away from it.

rhythmic beat promised instant liberation, but the lyrics and the backstage behavior of rock artists more often suggested an outcry from the depths of a tormented inner paralysis.

If the recent radicals have often struggled unsuccessfully against the currents of gloom and meaninglessness in their own time, there is perhaps another sobering lesson in the completed life cycle of the older rebel generation. For some of these people, especially certain of the religious mystics, the initial pain of alienation, the urgency of the desire to secede from existing society, had been as deep as among any dropouts of the present day. Mabel Dodge Luhan, melodramatic though she may have been, uttered a classic cry of this kind in recalling her move to Taos, New Mexico, after the First World War:

> I could leave the world I had been so false in, where I had always been trying to play a part and always feeling unrelated, . . . a dying world with no one appearing who would save it, a decadent, unhappy world, where the bright, hot, rainbow flashes of corruption were the only light high spots. Oh, I thought, to leave it, to leave it all, the whole world of it and not to be alone. To be with someone real at last, alive at last, unendingly true and untarnished.[123]

The young Will Levington Comfort viewed his fellow Detroiters across a yawning chasm of distance, which demanded a desperate effort to find some mode of contact:

> For a long time we only saw dimly the faces opposite in the long seat [of the streetcar], riding sideways. Vaguely they belonged to the same city. Then we saw them critically, as less than ourselves. Then we touched the Light and we began to fancy the ape and the tiger and the fox looking out at us. With more light we understood grimly that we could see the ape and the tiger and the fox with familiarity, because we were incorporate of these passions. Then came the day of still more Light and our great discovery, for behind the ape and the tiger and the fox we suddenly saw the Comrade, the Lover, the Player, the Workman Unashamed. No pessimism after that, but remember that the verity of our hope came only after the full realization of the horror of our plight.[124]

Such passages are highly moving, if one knows anything of the call toward inner secession. Growing up in Buffalo or Detroit, one recognizes first of all that one is not like the others; it is necessary to confront the

---

123. Mabel Dodge Luhan, *Edge of Taos Desert* (New York: Harcourt, Brace, 1937), p. 222.

124. Comfort, *Letters*, II, 219–20. A passage remarkably similar to this last one, down to the same image of the streetcar passengers, was written by the anarchist Voltairine de Cleyre; Veysey, *op. cit.*, pp. 142–43.

supreme fact of one's aloneness. Gradually, as a young man or woman, one discovers a few others who share a similarly estranged outlook. Now there is a flood of enthusiasm, which very often takes the form of joining a community. Taos and Krotona provide landing places, and one is temporarily caught up in the stimulation. Along with this comes a commitment to certain affirmative beliefs. Convictions form, about the way to live, the ideal society, the true nature of the universe.

But then the everyday tone of community life begins to harden. Leaders seem overbearing, companions gossipy and shallow. Too often one's hunger for an answering warmth goes unfulfilled. The sense of aloneness returns. The group had provided no more than a respite. If one is lucky, one emerges from it with a few deep friends. But these too tend to scatter over time, moving off in different directions. Except perhaps for one's own family, one is again left searching and adrift.

Eventually, often after more than one trial, the sense fades of a possible substitute community life to replace the unwanted life of the mass civilization. In their middle years, the members of this generation retire as individuals into a stance just noticeably outside the American mainstream. Perhaps they locate where they have one or two old friends. Thereafter, invisible among their neighbors, they drive Buicks up the hills of Laguna Beach or run art galleries only a few miles from the new communes on the New Mexico desert, with which of course they have no contact. Wherever they live, they keep their distance from all the main scenes of human activity, old or new. Wisps of their own youthful nonconformist radicalism mingle with standoffish comments about "hippies" in their conversation. Depending upon inconspicuousness and deeply ingrained psychic isolation for the preservation of their identity, they neither merge with nor in any effective way challenge the larger social order. (In this they are rather like academics.) The survivors of the older anarchist movement often live in a similar vacuum, though as individuals they seem more fulfilled and life-affirming than the ordinary run of senior citizens.

And what of the children of American radicals? As early as 1903 complaints echoed in the anarchist press of the failure of their own offspring to meet their expectations.[125] Ever since, these children have often slipped back into more conventional beliefs and styles of living. It was noted that the progeny of Stelton often became liberal Democrats.[126] At Home, they

125. *Free Society*, X (September 27, 1903), 2; *The Demonstrator*, September 4, 1907, p. 3.
126. Yet observers of the 1960's noted a counter-movement toward radicalism among youth who had been raised in permissively liberal homes. Both types of movement suggest that liberalism may have a symbiotic relationship to radicalism.

were soon enthusiastically playing baseball. In America it seems little easier for radicals to hold on to their children than it is for any other parents.

It is far too soon, of course, to know whether the newest rebels will go through a similar series of stages during their life span. The New England communes have lately revealed a noticeable de-emphasis of earlier counter-cultural symbolism. Exhibitionism has vanished, and there is more desire for a quiet integration with other, straight Americans who have decided to retire to the countryside. Quite a number of hip youth in these environments have cut their hair and begun dressing rather like everyone else.[127] Ken Kesey's recent life in Oregon carries the same overtones.

The fate of the pre–Civil War radicals as they grew older suggests an even more ominous pattern of willing return to the mainstream. As George Fredrickson has shown, most of the abolitionists and other extreme opponents of American social institutions in that day became suddenly absorbed in the patriotic consensus of the Civil War; nor did the postwar atmosphere of corrupt materialism reawaken their radical activism. A new tide of events could rapidly overturn convictions seemingly implanted on a very deep level in their minds.[128] The death of that radical generation was sudden and clear-cut.

American radicalism would always seem to be markedly episodic, even if, as we have seen, there is surprising continuity between the episodes. Though major seasons of radical upthrust never quite repeat themselves in the same way, it is far from clear that a sustained radical movement (on a noticeably bigger scale than in the 1870's or 1920's, for instance) has now begun.

And what, then, is the intrinsic value of cultural radicalism as a response to a world which is rushing in some other direction? At its best, what it offers is the possibility of a short season of rare exhilaration, a "magic moment" of suspension from the ordinary claims of time and society. A distinct experience of transcendence, which perhaps lay closer to the surface of the human mind in earlier centuries and in non-Western

127. Houriet, *op. cit.*, pp. 194–95, 396–97. In the same vein see Mark Kramer, "Communes: Delicate Collision," *The Phoenix* (Boston), III (September 14, 1971), 16.

128. George M. Fredrickson, *The Inner Civil War: Northern Intellectuals and the Crisis of the Union* (New York: Harper & Row, 1965), pp. 113–50, 166–80, 188–89, 196–98; cf. Martin, *op. cit.*, pp. 82, 97–100. This widespread susceptibility to change should cast doubt upon deeply psychoanalytic interpretations of the abolitionists.

places, bursts through the usual limits of consciousness. Or there may be a vaguer, more widely distributed feeling of shared well-being.

We should not inquire too closely as to how these brief states of liberation, individual or collective, may be defined, or what range of occasions may cause them to appear even in our modern life. The first months at Brook Farm seem to have produced such an unusual rapture; so may the first few summers at Stelton. As individuals Vedantists and other followers of mysticism have unslakingly sought this moment of joyous union, though rarely being able to move more than part way toward it. LSD gave it, or a counterfeit version, to many more people. At the Woodstock festival of 1969, as in the Kentucky camp meetings for a few months around 1800, participants emerged with the glad news of its presence on their lips.

If it is an illusion, it is at least a recurring one, reaching out to men and women of widely scattered times, places, and philosophies. As such it gains validity in the same way as the reappearance of a comet, though it is more unpredictable and mysterious. To some it takes the form of individual union with the Divine, to others (as a conscious ideal only recently) a merger of the self with those in an immediate human circle.

Whether measured in hours or in months, it is brief.[129] There must be a return to earth. The mystic eats his meal, the members of an intentional community begin to bicker and quarrel. But perhaps it has been given to most human beings to know the taste of such a temporary transcendence during the few seconds of orgasm. The living but intermittent link between an individual and something vital beyond him can thus be interpreted democratically. For a small number of persons in many centuries, there has been a seemingly richer intimation, though rarely long maintained.

"Communitas," writes the anthropologist Victor Turner, is an extraordinary mental state in which the normal bonds of relationship between men in a society are broken, and a flow of direct mutual sustainment intervenes. Suddenly there is wonder, surprise, ecstasy. But Turner cautions:

> Spontaneous communitas is a phase, a moment, not a permanent condition. The moment a digging stick is set in the earth, a colt broken in, a pack of wolves defended against, or a human enemy set by his heels, we have the germs of a social structure. . . . This is not to say that spontaneous communitas is merely "nature." Spontaneous communitas is

129. We can never stay continuously in the state of *samadhi,* Swami Prabhavananda advised. "One returns to normal consciousness when one is in contact with what we may call the outer world consciousness, but the illumination which one experienced in the transcendental state never again leaves one." *The Spiritual Heritage of India* (Garden City, New York: Doubleday, 1963), p. 110.

nature in dialogue with structure, married to it as a woman is married to a man. Together they make up one stream of life, the one affluent supplying power, the other alluvial fertility.[130]

If, as Turner argues, a mixture of communitas and structure provides the best formula for human life, then even the most seemingly ill-fated efforts to achieve communitas in twentieth-century America must be applauded for helping to correct a flagrant imbalance. The exploration of many blind alleys in this search must be forgiven, nor will it matter that all groups and organizations may be confidently predicted to lapse into ossification once a moment of communitas has been gained. All that matters is that there should be a constant succession of these moves toward revitalization.

Yet there is a further complicating factor. By itself this recipe ignores what has been one of the most omnipresent and disturbing ingredients in radical movements—personal magnetism. The matter should be squarely faced. Hero worship, not passion itself or the impulse toward passionate fellow feeling, is the truly unfortunate element in the legacy of romanticism. Repeatedly in communal settings, old and new, it rears its head. Charisma, in its extreme forms, intensifies enslavement rather than bringing about liberation. The radicals of the 1960's saw structure as their enemy. In this they were by no means wholly wrong. And we saw how easily structure could combine with charisma to produce counter-cultural movements of unusual toughness. But what is this worth if it creates environments so permeated by a slavish style of obedience as to repel all who believe in escape from bondage?[131] The historical record shows that charisma is the persistent enemy of human freedom.[132] The propensity among recent radicals to continue running after "inspired" leaders in the time-honored way is profoundly discouraging. Even in the academic world, the revival of an intense humanism during the past few years has been accompanied by a shameless emphasis upon the teacher as guru or prophet. It is no doubt

130. Victor W. Turner, *The Ritual Process: Structure and Anti-Structure* (Chicago: Aldine Publishing Co., 1969), p. 140.

131. Even Rosabeth Moss Kanter, who is far more receptive than I to the anti-individualist arguments of recent commentators like Philip Slater, admits that the longer-lived disciplinary communities can often create a suffocating environment in these terms. *Op. cit.*, pp. 116–17, 129, 211–12, 231–34.

132. I am here using the term charisma in its more specific meaning of authority derived from personal magnetism, in which the leader claims direct (usually divine) inspiration. Edward Shils, in "Charisma, Order, and Status," *American Sociological Review*, XXX (April 1965), 199–213, so extends the concept of charisma as to make it very nearly equal legitimacy, enabling him to claim that charisma is a necessary element in every social order. But the more usual, restricted meaning of charisma is far more empirically helpful and germane to the study of secessionist groups and social movements.

highly unfair to invoke the specter of fascism in pointing to the dangers involved in such a redefinition of role. But the examples of an authoritarian tendency within the mystical tradition, both past and present, which we have explored would seem to furnish compelling testimony of their own. One ends up being exceedingly grateful to the anarchistic tradition for having so long provided a partial corrective.

The radical movement has far too seldom succeeded in capturing even brief moments of communitas—fellow feeling that transcends social structure—without resorting to these perilous intervening diversions. Isolated examples, such as the Woodstock festival and perhaps the commune at Rockridge, seem to show that it can be done. But these episodes have failed to set the tone of the movement as a whole. The remedy is far from easy. It is truly taxing to maintain an attitude of skepticism toward would-be prophets as well as toward the leadership of the mainstream. Moreover, this skepticism must be combined with the idealistic faith which will permit dropping one's guard toward ordinary fellow men on occasions when the genuine promise of communitas is in the air. This situation, rather than the detailed mechanics of alternative economic or political systems, is the most urgent problem which radicals should confront.

In the United States, unlike many other countries, radicalism is of little present value in helping the external forms of the social order to become more just or humane. The mainstream is simply too numerous, too powerful, and too self-assured in its pursuit of the time-honored goals of accumulation and prestige. Of course we can go on working within the system, no matter how heavy the odds, to try to change the tone of American life and to avoid world disaster. The main value of radicalism, on the other hand, is indeed "cultural" rather than political. It lies in encouraging us, at the same time, to regain some degree of contact with mankind's long-buried capacity for ecstasy and unguarded sharing. But during these all too rare moments when we arrive back in the Garden of Eden, we must remain keenly alert to the many-headed serpent named charisma which resides there, luring us to linger on his own terms.

Even then there are the frequent bad trips (with or without drugs), the rip-offs, the "down" moments. Perhaps to avoid or minimize them, traditional societies have turned orgies into rituals, placing these episodes of communitas into a definite rhythmic context. Such safety is gained at the cost of the spontaneity which recent American radicals have so highly prized. But the growing series of disappointments in present-day efforts to achieve a collective renewal suggest that it may be worth re-examining this balance sheet. Periodic flights into heightened awareness and fellow-feeling, made under more protective auspices than at Woodstock, might better balance the inner and external dimensions of modern life, instead of falsely promising to merge them in a never-ending fashion. (For in this respect it seems unlikely that we can ever hope fully to escape from our long-term cultural heritage.) The promotion of rituals always used to be the province of religion. But a new basis for this kind of periodic occasion would have to be worked out in the present, for religions invariably prove to demand of their followers an unacceptable excess baggage of charismatic and ideological commitment. Then, too, religions are always somewhat divisive. The momentary breakdown of interpersonal boundaries, roles, and identities must be recognized as fully its own end.

Let us hope that collective experiments along these lines will go forward, despite an apparently waxing climate of satisfaction with the prosaic aspects of our existence. History teaches pessimism, to be sure, but cultural innovators have always operated with a less than perfect sense of what history allows. The future mental life of our society must surely involve more, on the one hand, than snowmobiles and boardwalk entertainments, or, on the other, unending struggles to fight the personal devils who refuse to give us peace of mind. Similarly, the solutions must transcend sex shows and authoritarian social movements. If we continually repeat ourselves, we have only ourselves to blame.

INDEX

Index